A SECRET HISTORY
OF THE **IRA**
Second Edition

Ed Moloney

PENGUIN BOOKS

PENGUIN BOOKS

Published by the Penguin Group
Penguin Books Ltd, 80 Strand, London WC2R 0RL, England
Penguin Group (USA) Inc., 375 Hudson Street, New York, New York 10014, USA
Penguin Group (Canada), 90 Eglinton Avenue East, Suite 700, Toronto, Ontario, Canada M4P 2Y3
(a division of Pearson Penguin Canada Inc.)
Penguin Ireland, 25 St Stephen's Green, Dublin 2, Ireland
(a division of Penguin Books Ltd)
Penguin Group (Australia), 250 Camberwell Road, Camberwell, Victoria 3124, Australia
(a division of Pearson Australia Group Pty Ltd)
Penguin Books India Pvt Ltd, 11 Community Centre,
Panchsheel Park, New Delhi – 110 017, India
Penguin Group (NZ), 67 Apollo Drive, Rosedale, North Shore 0632, New Zealand
(a division of Pearson New Zealand Ltd)
Penguin Books (South Africa) (Pty) Ltd, 24 Sturdee Avenue, Rosebank,
Johannesburg 2196, South Africa

Penguin Books Ltd, Registered Offices: 80 Strand, London WC2R 0RL, England

www.penguin.com

First published in the United States of America by W.W. Norton and Company Ltd 2002
First published in Great Britain by Allen Lane The Penguin Press 2002
Published in Penguin Books 2003
Second edition published in Penguin Books 2007

011

Copyright © Ed Moloney, 2002, 2007
All rights reserved

The moral right of the author has been asserted.

Map on page 135 courtesy of Bob E. Hall, Center for Earth and Environmental Science, Indiana
University–Purdue University, Indianapolis. Maps on pages 36, 76, 94, 351 reprinted from
Provisional Irish Republicans by Robert W. White. Copyright 1993 by Robert W. White. Reproduced
with permission of Greenwood Publishing Group, Inc., Westport, Conn.

Printed and bound in Great Britain by Clays Ltd, Elcograf S.p.A.

978-0-141-02876-7

www.greenpenguin.co.uk

This book is dedicated to
all the people who lost their lives
in the Northern Ireland Troubles.

CONTENTS

LIST OF MAPS

History, Stephen said, is a nightmare
from which I am trying to awake.
—James Joyce, *Ulysses*

Preface to the second edition

It is to the enormous credit of Penguin Books and my editor there, Simon Winder, that I have been given the opportunity to update *A Secret History of the IRA*. The first edition ended just after the IRA's first act of decommissioning in the autumn of 2001, following the September 11 attacks in the United States and the arrest of IRA personnel in Colombia a month beforehand. This edition brings the story to what I would argue is the definitive end of the Provisional IRA as an instrument of armed and revolutionary resistance to British policy in Ireland. With that event, I believe, it is now also possible to say that the Troubles have ended.

The ending was signaled in two ways. First, by the IRA statement in July 2005 that formally announced that its armed struggle against Britain was over; and secondly by the completion of the decommissioning process the following September. Doubtless the IRA retained some weaponry to protect its leadership and key members against rivals and enemies but the destruction of its Libyan-supplied arsenal robbed the IRA of the capacity to wage war. Not only that but the act itself was replete with symbolic meaning, indicating a wish to eschew armed struggle in favour of political methods from thereon. The event was unprecedented in the history of Ireland's struggle for independence.

This point came after five long and often turbulent years which saw the downfall of the Ulster Unionist leader, David Trimble, and his replacement as unionism's leader by his party's long-time loyalist critic and rival, Ian Paisley, leader of the Democratic Unionists and permanent Moderator of the Free Presbyterian Church. Nationalist politics were refashioned in an equally radical way with the IRA's political partner, Sinn Fein, replacing the SDLP as the dominant party and Gerry Adams displacing John Hume as nationalism's leader.

With that, the moderate center-ground of Northern Irish politics—in as much as it had ever existed—disappeared and potential executive power was transferred, as one acerbic critic put it, into the hands of a theocrat and an autocrat who might or might not agree to exercise it in the best interests of all the people of Northern Ireland.

That this state of affairs was brought about by the handling of IRA decommissioning is beyond dispute. It is a central thesis of the second edition of this book that the IRA could have decommissioned all its weapons much sooner, but chose instead to prevaricate and thereby to inject an even more virulent strain of sectarianism into Northern Irish politics. In such a way were Trimble and the SDLP destabilized and Sinn Fein catapulted to political and electoral success. It is surely no coincidence that once the process of destroying Trimble and sidelining the SDLP was completed, all the IRA's objections to final decommissioning suddenly vanished.

The plaudits that came the way of the British prime minister, Tony Blair, and his Irish counterpart, Bertie Ahern, in the wake of the IRA finally completing the decommissioning process are understandable. The two leaders had worked for years for this day to dawn, but any credit that they are due should, however, be balanced by the knowledge that it was they who facilitated this Sinn Fein strategy and it is they, ultimately, who bear responsibility for this triumph of the extremes in Northern Ireland.

At the time of writing, the DUP and Sinn Fein were still squabbling about the one issue remaining in the way of their sharing government: Sinn Fein's acceptance of the policing and criminal justice system. It remains to be seen whether their differences, which concern the practicalities rather than the principle of the matter, can be overcome but of a number of things there can be little doubt. One is that the Provisional IRA's war is over for good. Another is that the politics of Northern Ireland have been changed forever and in a way no one could have predicted. Whether this will be for good or ill is a verdict only the passage of time can deliver, but the democratic record of Northern Ireland's new potential political leadership gives little cause for optimism.

Penguin's decision to publish the second edition of this book has enabled me to tell that tortuous if significant tale in two new chapters—Nineteen and Twenty—as well as in an Epilogue which takes the story up to the Assembly election of March 2007. I have also been able to correct some errors and compensate for some omissions in the first edition and add new information about the betrayal of the gun-running ship the *Eksund* and the attitudes of different Army Council members, including Gerry Adams and Martin McGuinness, towards it. Fresh information has come to light about Adams's IRA career after his release from Long Kesh in 1977 and that section of the first edition had been amended accordingly. The sad death of former Fianna Fail taoiseach Charles Haughey in June 2006 also releases me from the pledge of confidentiality I gave him while researching the first edition. Haughey played a crucial and often undervalued part in the genesis and evolution of the peace process and I believe that without him the birth of the peace process would have been much more difficult. At this point I should put on record that Haughey, who was in the early stages of the illness that claimed his life when we first spoke, did not search me out but rather was a reluctant and often grudging source. "The stage," he once grumbled in the face of my persistence, "is already overcrowded with people attempting to claim credit." It was I who deduced that he had played such an important role and it was I who sought him out. Only after numerous and lengthy visits to Kinsealy was I able to persuade him to tell his part in the story. I am now very happy to be able to acknowledge all this.

One key part of his story, and in its own way an extremely valuable historical document, is the letter of May 1987 written to Haughey by Father Alec Reid, seeking a secret dialogue between him and Gerry Adams and setting out the terms for an IRA cessation that Adams would find acceptable. I was able to read and fully transcribe this letter in Kinsealy. It is compelling and extraordinary evidence that, many years before the Irish public and the bulk of IRA members and leaders learned of the peace process, the Sinn Fein president was seeking to end the IRA's war on terms little different from those implicit in the Good Friday Agreement. I am now able to reproduce this in full along with other documents pertaining to the early part of the peace process.

Father Reid himself has also started to acknowledge that the peace process began much earlier than any of the participants were previously prepared to admit. In a BBC Radio Four interview in November 2006 with Olivia O'Leary, the Redemptorist priest conceded that he began his discussions with Gerry Adams not long after the abduction and killing of a UDR soldier in South Armagh, an event that took place in the autumn of 1982 and was described in detail in the first edition of this book.[1] This is a welcome and overdue sign that the information permafrost surrounding the peace process is beginning to melt. It is of exceptional historical importance that those who were involved in the IRA during this time also begin to put their accounts and memories on record. History should not always be written by the victors.

By the time the second edition of *A Secret History of the IRA* is available on the bookstands, Gerry Adams's prediction that there will be a united Ireland by 2016, the centenary of the Easter Rising, will be only nine years away. We will not have to wait long to discover whether that statement was the product of irrational exuberance, political expediency or an accurate assessment of constitutional possibilities.

Ed Moloney
New York
December 2006

Preface to the first edition

There were never any strategic considerations at stake, like those in the Middle East, for example, nor did the killing ever approach the carnage or savagery of the Balkans or Rwanda. There were no oil fields or gold mines to be captured, or any ideology to be overthrown or vindicated. But the Troubles in Northern Ireland had one quality that marked the violence there as special, and that was the sheer length of the conflict—that and the fact that no one could really see an end to it.

By the time of the first IRA cease-fire of 1994, the Troubles had lasted for a quarter of a century, so long that the violence had become an almost permanent feature of the world's political landscape. Other conflicts would erupt, climax, and then fade away, their names soon forgotten, but the bombing and shooting in Belfast, Derry, and South Armagh seemed to last forever.

The Troubles were at or near the bottom of the list of significant global conflicts, a low-intensity war that occasionally exploded into spectacular bursts of violence but more often was characterized by a killing or two a week, deaths that by the end had become so routine that they scarcely merited a headline outside of Ireland. But the violence devastated a whole society, scarring two generations of Irish people, the baby boomers who came of age when the Troubles began in the late 1960s and their children, who grew up knowing only instability and bloodshed.

More than 3,700 people were killed in the violence, an average of just over two a week for the thirty years that the conflict lasted. Almost as many people died within a couple of hours in lower Manhattan on September 11, 2001, but to conclude therefore that the Troubles were a petty affair would be a mistake. Had a similar conflict consumed the United States, the equivalent death toll would have been over 600,000; in Britain, 150,000. Nearly

1 in every 50 of Northern Ireland's 1.5 million people, some 30,000, were injured in the violence. The comparable figure in the United States would be 5 million; in Britain, just over 1 million. Very few people in Northern Ireland did not personally know someone who had been killed in the Troubles, and many knew several. There are many definitions of a civil war, but that is surely one of the most compelling.

Thousands were caught up in the Troubles in a more intimate fashion, becoming members of groups like the IRA and, on the loyalist side, the Ulster Defence Association and the Ulster Volunteer Force, for whom they killed, wounded, maimed, bombed, robbed, and went to jail or early graves. Putting a figure to such numbers is by definition difficult, for these were not organizations that kept detailed personnel records. But Martin McGuinness, who has held virtually all the senior ranks in the IRA, once told the author that he reckoned 10,000 people had been through the ranks of the IRA over the years—and who could know better?—while at the height of its power the UDA could, given an hour or two of notice, put 20,000 men on the streets of Belfast. In all the important ways the Troubles pervaded Northern Ireland.

The conflict was not confined to the geographical boundaries of the state. It regularly spilled over into the Irish Republic, injecting an unwelcome instability into the body politic there and warping the institutions of the young state almost beyond repair, the media and the legal system in particular. Its effects were also felt farther afield, wherever the Irish diaspora had scattered its unfortunate people—in the United States, Australia, and Canada—and the violence was repeatedly exported to Britain, where scores lost their lives over the years in bombings and shootings, mostly carried out by the IRA.

The Troubles were, above all else, the latest and the most protracted phase in an Anglo-Irish conflict that had properly begun some four hundred years earlier, with the Tudor wars and plantations of the sixteenth century, although there had been resistance of some sort to the English presence ever since the Normans invaded in the twelfth century. Ireland was Britain's first colony and one of its last. Resistance to occupation went through alternating phases of violence and politics, and each stage in the conflict brought Ireland a little nearer to complete separation from Britain. The culmination of all this was the Treaty of 1921, a settlement that paved the way for twenty-six of Ireland's thirty-two counties first to govern themselves and then, in 1949, to declare themselves a republic while the remnant of the island in the North remained British.

Had the architects of the 1921 settlement set out to create an inherently unstable entity, they could scarcely have done better than to design Northern Ireland in the way they did. The state contained within its boundaries the seeds of its own devastation. Packed into its narrow confines were two troubled communities. One was the uneasy majority, the Protestants whose ancestors had planted or colonized native lands so as to make Ireland a safer place for Britain. But they paid a terrible price for their service to the motherland. They and their forebears lived in constant fear of retribution from the substantial minority of Irish Catholics in their midst, the native Gaels they had supplanted and whose land they had taken, while they came to distrust the British almost as much as they feared the Irish. The Protestants knew nothing but insecurity and learned to reject anything else as a distortion of the natural order.

Trapped in a state not of their choosing, the Catholics were bitter, resentful, and full of foreboding. Abandoned by their Southern co-religionists after 1921, confronted by arrogant, superior-seeming rulers, and subjected to intermittent salvos of pogrom-like violence, they knew they could look only to themselves for protection, and trust only their own. Each community feared and distrusted the other, and in such circumstances it would have been odd had bigotry and discrimination not shaped the politics of Northern Ireland or had this not, in the end, been the cause of a tremendous conflagration.

Thirty years after they exploded, the Troubles have ended in what is arguably a most definitive fashion, an ending that marks not merely the closing of a war but rather the conclusion of the historic conflict between Ireland and Britain.

They have ended with the leadership of the Provisional IRA accepting Britain's neutrality in Northern Ireland. No longer do its leaders preach that London is a colonial, occupying power, usurping the right of the Irish people to decide their own future. Instead, the republicans have accepted a political process whose foundation stone is the principle of consent, an acknowledgment that unionists cannot be forced into a united Ireland against their wishes. In their turn, unionists, with varying degrees of commitment and enthusiasm, have accepted that Northern Ireland must become a warmer and more welcoming place for Catholics. In a sense the two communities have struck a bargain—the Catholics agreed to abandon the goal of Irish unity in return for a secure place within the state, while the Protestants consented to behave toward their neighbors in a more civilized way.

None of this would have been possible without the proactive cooperation of the Provisional IRA leadership. Indeed it is the central thesis of this book—and its principal revelation—that it was that organization's dominating figure, Gerry Adams, who launched, shaped, nurtured, and eventually guided the peace process to a successful conclusion. Many excellent accounts have been given, in written and televised form, about the peace process; without singling any out for mention, it would be fair to say that they have all dwelt mostly on the negotiations and high-level talks that characterized the latter stages of the process. None have examined, or been able satisfactorily to explain, the events that took place much earlier within the IRA and Sinn Fein which made all this possible, or to tell how they happened.

This book attempts to redress that deficiency, tries to delve deep within the belly of the beast—or as deep as any outsider can go—to expose the entrails for examination. The conclusion is unavoidable. The Irish peace process was not a spontaneous phenomenon, tossed around by forces outside its control, nor was it forced upon its architects by the fortunes of war. The process was a little like a precooked dinner whose basic menu had largely been decided long before most of the diners knew the meal was planned, even if the table settings, the guest list, the size and shape of the crockery, cutlery, and condiments, and so on were not. The peace process was, in other words, an exercise in management toward an already decided outcome, as much as it was anything else. There were many delays and threats to the event, but at the end there was little doubt that people would sit down to eat, and eat well.

After twenty years of reporting on, writing about, mixing with, and observing the IRA at close quarters, I had come to a number of conclusions about the Belfast-based leadership that came to power in the 1970s. Principal among these was that the people guiding the organization were longsighted, bright, talented, dedicated, determined, pragmatic, cunning, and all too often duplicitous. They were also utterly ruthless in their mission, which above all else was to survive and prosper, and were devoted to their leader and inspiration, Gerry Adams. The idea that he or the people around him would allow any but one of their own to control and direct their journey was so absurd that it was not even worthy of consideration. The facts about the peace process revealed in this book substantiate that assumption.

A Secret History of the IRA is as much about Gerry Adams as about the organization he dominated for so long. He is, indisputably, one of the largest figures in Ireland's long and sad history, a revolutionary leader who deservedly ranks alongside those competing founders of Irish independence Michael Collins and Eamon de Valera, and a man whose qualities, both negative and positive, are fit to be measured alongside theirs. Collins, de Valera, and Adams all left indelible marks on the Ireland of their day, but whereas the veterans of the 1916 Rising and the subsequent Anglo-Irish war could allow much of their story to be told while they were still alive, Adams has not been able to. In December 1998 the Nobel Peace Prize was awarded jointly to David Trimble and John Hume, the leaders respectively of Ulster unionism and the Social Democratic and Labour Party (SDLP), for their contribution to the success of the peace process. Standing alongside them, sharing in the glory, should have been Gerry Adams and—arguably— Father Alec Reid, who between them kick-started and sustained the process. But while others have collected plaudits and the glittering prizes, Adams has been forced to stay silent, biting his lip lest by accepting the praise of the establishment he undermine the peace process in the eyes of his supporters. The truth was withheld to sustain the project, a fact to which Adams's own less than enlightening autobiography pays painful testament. This book is also an attempt to rectify that, although not many of his friends will thank me for it.

I do not claim this work to be an exhaustive account of this extraordinary period in Irish history. Many blank spaces remain to be filled in, but perhaps now that task will look a little less onerous. The job of a correspondent, after all, is to inform and increase understanding. If this book has helped make the Irish peace process more intelligible to the outside world, then surely that can only be for the good.

Ed Moloney
New York
February 2002

Acknowledgments

This book has taken about four years to research and write, mostly in secret. I have little doubt that, had it been more widely known that I was involved in this enterprise, the research would have been made much more difficult to conduct, perhaps impossible, and the book would probably have been stillborn. I must, therefore, first of all thank those people who knew what I was doing but kept silent, and, equally, I must apologize to others I was obliged to mislead or behave evasively toward. This was done not out of any malice or lack of trust but in the knowledge that to ask a person to carry someone else's secret is often to ask them to shoulder the most onerous of burdens.

Officially, the leaders of the Provisional republican movement did not cooperate in the research for this book, nor was their cooperation sought. They had made it abundantly clear to me, and to other journalists, on several occasions in the past that they had no interest in talking about, much less in assisting anyone in writing a book on, the genesis of the peace process. Having completed the research on this period, I can understand why. This work, however, is about more than the peace process. It is also a history of the Provisional IRA and as such reflects some twenty years of reporting the organization in *Hibernia, Magill,* the *Irish Times,* and the *Sunday Tribune.* For much of that time I kept notes of conversations and exchanges with many of the IRA's current leaders, and these have proved to be an invaluable aid in this undertaking, not least in illuminating the explanation for the peace process which was deemed fit for public and internal IRA consumption. Those among them unhappy to see this book appear can at least console themselves with the knowledge that I have not betrayed their confidence after all these years.

Many republicans, past and present members of both the IRA and Sinn Fein, were, however, happy to speak to me, and it is no exaggeration to say that without the information and insights they gave me, this book would have been impossible to write. They all know who they are. They spoke to me in the greatest secrecy, and I pledged never to compromise them. For that reason they must be nameless here, but nevertheless I must acknowledge the debt I owe them. A number of past and present officials in, and members of, the British and Irish governments added hugely to this story, and their contribution was likewise invaluable. Tom King and Peter Brooke were both generous with their time and information, but others asked to stay unnamed and I must respect their wish. So did members of the British army, community workers, and clerical figures of both faiths in Northern Ireland who also helped me enormously. I thank them all. The day may arrive, perhaps, when such people will be able to speak freely and openly about the part they played in the historic events chronicled in this book. But I fear that day is still a long way off.

Thankfully there are some to whom I can express gratitude by name. Many of my former colleagues at the *Sunday Tribune* offices in Dublin gave support and encouragement to me both before publication and afterwards. To them and to Seamus Dooley of the NUJ, I express my gratitude. In particular I would like to thank the paper's former news editor, Helen Callanan, whose decision to seek a more fulfilling life at the Bar has been a great loss to Irish journalism, who urged me to persevere at an early and critical stage, while Harry McGee, also of the *Tribune,* was generous with advice and morale-boosting comments. Dr. Anthony McIntyre gave me access to a number of embargoed IRA interviews he conducted for his doctoral thesis, which filled important gaps in the early history of the Provisionals. Frank Millar read the early drafts in London, and his positive response encouraged me to seek a larger publisher. Patrick Farrelly, Kate O'Callaghan, Sandy Boyer, and Terry Golway, all in New York, gave me encouragement, also at an early stage when it might have been easier to choose another path. Bob White and Kevin Mickey, both of Indiana University, helped obtain some beautiful maps, and while all the Irish photographers whose work is featured in the book were enormously helpful, I must thank Kelvin Boyes for going that extra mile. It is said that no book on the Troubles is complete without an acknowledgment of the part played in its production by the staff and management of the Linen Hall Library in Belfast. This book is no exception. In particular I owe much to the generous assistance of Yvonne Murphy and her staff in the library's priceless political collection. Joan McKiernan worked hard and long to compile a most comprehensive index, and for that I thank her.

I have been extremely fortunate to have been published by two most distinguished houses—Penguin, in the UK and Canada, and W. W. Norton, in the United States. I would like to single out Simon Winder at Penguin in London for particular thanks. He was the first to recognize the importance of this book, and his support for it has been wholehearted. He is lucky to have such an impressive team to draw upon, and I would like to thank Ruth Killick, Rosie Glaisher, Jennifer Todd, Mark Scholes, Pippa Wright, Louise Wilder, Clare Needham, and Andrew Stephenson for their sterling work. My gratitude also to Cynthia Good at Penguin (Canada) and to my editor in Toronto, Michael Schellenberg. At W. W. Norton in New York, I am indebted to Bob Weil and Jason Baskin, who had the unenviable, day-to-day chore of dealing with the author. Fate and geography decreed that the daunting task of editing this book would fall to Bob Weil, and I wish to pay him a special tribute. His efforts, characterized by patience and good humor, transformed a passable work into something to which I am pleased to attach my name. His is a unique talent. W. W. Norton also provided an enormously impressive team and to each of them—to Otto Sonntag, Nancy Palmquist, Rene Schwartz, Andrew Marasia, Louise Brockett, and Dan Deitch—I give my thanks. To my agent, Jonathan Williams, in Dublin, must also go a special appreciation for tirelessly and so successfully generating interest in the book. It goes without saying that without him, none of this would have been possible.

Finally, I must thank members of my family who helped and encouraged me. My sister, Michelle, and her husband, Tom Bray—not to mention young Lawrence and Liam—were generous with their hospitality during my trips to England, while, as always, Joan and Ciaran were the lights in my life.

A
SECRET
HISTORY
OF THE
IRA

Prologue

There was only one thought in Gabriel Cleary's mind, and it chilled him. As he checked the firing unit linked to the twelve explosive charges placed beneath the *Eksund*'s waterline, the signs of sabotage were unmistakable. With a growing sense of horror the IRA's director of engineering realized that the most ambitious gunrunning plot ever in the IRA's long war with Britain had been betrayed.

Cleary's fears had been growing ever since the *Eksund* had left the Libyan capital, Tripoli, some two weeks earlier, as he later told an IRA inquiry in messages smuggled from a French prison.[1] The Panamanian-registered vessel had been loaded with some 150 tons of modern, sophisticated weaponry at Tripoli dockside by sailors from Colonel Qaddafi's small naval service on October 13 and 14, 1987. Although that part of the operation had gone smoothly, Cleary was uneasy. This was the fifth trip since August 1985, but the four earlier cargoes, amounting in total to another 150 tons of weapons and explosives, had been safely and secretly transferred to IRA boats from a Libyan vessel off Malta, well out at sea and far from the sight of hostile, prying eyes.

This operation had to be handled differently. The *Eksund*'s cargo was as large as the four other shipments put together. The sheer size and bulk of weaponry involved meant that the loading process would be lengthy, and that made an operation at sea simply out of the question. With the CIA and other Western intelligence agencies taking an ever-greater interest in Libyan affairs, the chances of being spotted by satellite surveillance were too great. The *Eksund*'s manifest was breathtaking: 1,000 Romanian-made AK-47 automatic rifles, a million rounds of ammunition, 430 grenades, 12 rocket-propelled grenade launchers with ample supplies of grenades and rockets, 12 heavy Russian DHSK machine guns, over 50 SAM-7 ground-to-air missiles capable of downing British army helicopters, 2,000 electric detonators and 4,700 fuses, 106 millimeter cannons, general-purpose machine guns, anti-tank missile launchers, flame throwers, and two tons of the powerful Czech-made explosive Semtex. With a cargo like that to load there was no option; the work had to be done in Tripoli itself.

The Libyan harbor was a dangerous place for IRA men on a mission to smuggle weapons. The Tripoli docks were regularly jammed with ships unloading consumer goods, as a result of a massive oil-financed consumer boom; the bustling labor force was a mixture of Arabs drawn from nearly every country in North Africa and European expatriates lured by the high salaries offered in this former Italian colony.

Although the nearby British embassy was closed, emptied of its staff following a major diplomatic row with Qaddafi, everyone, IRA and Libyans alike, assumed that the British had left their spies behind. Some could easily be mingling with the crowds down at the harbor or at the nearby souk where traders bought and sold gold and silver and exchanged gossip.

The Libyans took precautions. The *Eksund* was loaded at nighttime to reduce the chances of being spotted, and the boat was moored in the military section of the dockside for added security. But even so, Cleary was glad when the *Eksund* finally weighed anchor.

Within hours of setting sail, however, the IRA commander's doubts returned. A plane flew directly over the *Eksund*, and Cleary suspected it was an RAF spotter aircraft. Every day of the voyage thereafter a similar aircraft would perform the same maneuver. There seemed little doubt that someone was keeping a very close eye on the *Eksund*'s progress. Off Gibraltar the plane swooped down so low that the pilot was visible. Cleary grew more and more nervous.

As the *Eksund* passed the Brittany coast and veered left for Ireland, the boat ran into a different sort of trouble. The fifty-year-old vessel, which had shipped grain most of her life, had endured a difficult journey out to Malta. At one stage the vessel had to dock in England for engine repairs, and at another point the steering failed.

The steering problem struck again on October 27. The crew tried to make repairs but with no success, and the *Eksund* drifted closer and closer to the French coast. The next day Cleary realized the mission was doomed and took the fateful decision to scuttle the ship and sink its precious freight before it ran aground. His orders had been precise: on no account must the British learn of the IRA's arms-smuggling operation; the very outcome of the war depended on secrecy being preserved.

As he assembled the crew on the top deck to prepare the inflatable dinghy that would take them ashore, Cleary started the process of triggering the timing device that would set off the bombs and slowly sink the *Eksund*. This was the job Cleary had been chosen for.

The colorful Dublin businessman Adrian Hopkins, who had found and purchased the *Eksund*, captained the vessel as he had the two other ships used by the IRA to facilitate the Libyan venture. The IRA had provided two sailors to assist him, James Coll and James Doherty, both of them County Donegal trawlermen. Hopkins's friend and sometime business partner Henry Cairns, the man suspected of having introduced Hopkins to the IRA, was along for the ride.

Cleary had spent most of his adult life in the Provisional IRA and had become one of the organization's most skilled bomb-makers. From the Tallaght area of Dublin, a vast sprawling working-class housing estate on the southwest edge of the city, he rose in the IRA engineering department, that part of the IRA which had the job of manufacturing homemade explosives and devising the organization's impressive range of improvised and homemade weaponry. Although well known to the Irish Special Branch, he had managed to avoid imprisonment. Only once had the authorities come near to pinning him, and that was eight years earlier, in 1977, when he beat a charge of making bombs in Kildare. By the time he was appointed to oversee the *Eksund* voyage, Cleary had advanced to the top of the IRA's military elite and was in charge of its vital engineering department. He was a natural choice to head the *Eksund* operation.

The *Eksund*'s ballast tanks had already been filled with water in preparation for scuttling. Cleary had crafted Semtex bombs that were just large enough to make holes in the vessel's skin but not so large that the noise of the explosions would attract attention. French forensic experts later calculated that the *Eksund* would have sunk within seconds.

The IRA man had chosen a hole known as Deep Hurd in which to scuttle the *Eksund*. The plan was to sink the vessel and then head in the dinghy for the Brittany coast, after which the crew would catch a ferry back to Ireland without the authorities' ever knowing about the IRA's audacious plan. That was when he discovered that a traitor had wrecked his plan.

A cursory glance at the bomb mechanism told Cleary that the plan would have to be scrapped; the firing unit for the explosives had been sabotaged, its wiring damaged beyond repair. The device, known as a timing power unit (TPU), was simple to operate and safe enough for a child to use, but it was just as easy to put out of commission. Whoever had neutralized Cleary's bombs would not have needed much training.

Cleary never got as far as even connecting the device. Instead the realization of treachery forced a number of thoughts to flash through his head, as he later told IRA colleagues. The British must have known about their plans all along, and soon the media would know as well. But the question that brought a cold sweat to his brow concerned the identity of the traitor. There was certainly a collaborator on board, but was there another one, someone back in Ireland who had betrayed the *Eksund* and its precious cargo?

Cleary knew that the TPU must have been tampered with after the *Eksund* had left Tripoli harbor and not before. The IRA man had made up the mechanism himself before sailing and had linked it to detonators fixed into slabs of Semtex not long after leaving the dock. The TPU had been in perfect working order. He had double-checked to make sure.

There was no time to repair the timing unit. The spotter plane had again flown overhead, and in the distance the crew could see motor launches speeding toward them. The net was obviously closing. Cleary watched the scene with a sense of grim satisfaction; his instincts had been right.

Within minutes the *Eksund* was surrounded and boarded by armed French customs men. Within hours a shocked and disbelieving public in Ireland and Britain would hear the news of the failure of this extraordinary smuggling venture. A few weeks later and the full scope of the IRA's operations would be made public; everyone would know that the organization now had some 150 tons of explosives and modern weaponry, delivered earlier and safely stored away in secret dumps throughout Ireland. But the greatest secret of them all, that the *Eksund* had been betrayed, was to remain sealed.

THE STORY OF the IRA's long relationship with the Libyan regime of Colonel Qaddafi is one of the most extraordinary and colorful tales to come out of the Irish "Troubles," and the history of their partnership is almost as old as the events that brought both into existence. Now for the first time the story of the links between the oil-rich Arab country and one of Western Europe's bloodiest conflicts can be told in full.

Both came into being in the summer of 1969. In Ireland the events that spawned the Provisional IRA began in August that year in the small streets that crouched beneath the towers of the Catholic Clonard Monastery in West Belfast, not far from where its future leader Gerry Adams had been born and raised some twenty years earlier.

In Tripoli, a few weeks after those violent events but some 1,500 miles away, Muammar Qaddafi, a young Libyan army officer only a few years older than Adams, led a group of soldiers to power in a bloodless coup that ended centuries of colonial rule in this large North African country. Neither man knew it at the time, but fate and a shared hatred of the British were to throw them together within a few short years.

By the summer of 1969 Northern Ireland had been simmering for months as Protestant resentment at a hugely successful civil rights campaign by Catholics, fueled by years of political and economic discrimination, threatened to spill onto the streets in violence. In August the cauldron boiled over, and the death and destruction began.

It was not long before the trouble spread to Belfast, the scene for over a hundred years of often vicious and regular anti-Catholic violence. The IRA had always been there to protect its communities, but in 1969 the IRA, by this stage a small, select, and secret body that was a shadow of the army that had fought the British to a standstill in 1921, stood by almost powerless to stop the shootings and burning.

By 1969 the IRA had come under the control of a group of orthodox pro-Moscow intellectuals and activists who had spent years patiently steering the organization away from the hallowed goal of driving the British out of Ireland in favor of a campaign to reform and modernize the Northern Ireland state.

In a process that uncannily echoes modern developments, the IRA of that day was slowly putting away the gun in favor of political methods, just as Gerry Adams was to do many years later. The ambition of the IRA's then leaders in Northern Ireland was to replace national struggle with class struggle; they had no time for Belfast's narrow sectarianism, no sympathy for armed struggle, no need for guns.

So when mobs of pro-British loyalists surged into the streets around Clonard, the local IRA had virtually no weapons with which to beat them off. An entire row of houses known as Bombay Street was burned to the ground, and a young boy was shot dead. When the IRA split acrimoniously later that year, the Belfast men who led the breakaway Provisional IRA swore they would never leave their streets defenseless again. For their icon they chose the phoenix, the mythical firebird rising in vengeance from the ashes of Bombay Street.

Within a few years those Belfast founders of the Provisional IRA, soon to be dubbed the Provos, were to turn to that small group of Libyan army officers and their leader, Colonel Muammar Qaddafi, for supplies of the guns and explosives they needed not just to defend their own streets but to use against the British army and Royal Ulster Constabulary in a twenty-five-year campaign of violence.

Libya had a history of colonial rule that surpassed Ireland's. It had been first seized as far back as the earliest days of the Roman Empire, which had cultivated the country's fertile coastal strip to feed Rome's growing population, and had been occupied by outsiders more or less continuously ever since. In the twentieth century Libya was ruled first by the Turks and then by Mussolini's Italy, whose grip on the country was maintained with brutal, bloody force. After the Second World War and Italy's capitulation, the allies agreed to grant Libya independence, and it was ruled by the Idris family, which led one of the country's largest and oldest tribal clans. But real power lay in the hands of the British, Americans, and French, who divided the country into spheres of influence and maintained large military bases to protect their political and economic interests in the region, especially vast oil fields that had been discovered deep in the southern desert. Oil wealth enriched the Idris family and the Western oil corporations, but little of the windfall made its way down to the ordinary population. Resentment at Libya's festering poverty and the revolutionary gospel of Arab nationalism then sweeping North Africa and the Middle East inspired Qaddafi and his army colleagues to overthrow the Idris family and expel the Western powers.

Qaddafi and the leaders of the Provisional IRA were natural allies. Both blamed colonialism for their country's miserable histories, and both believed that their occupiers must be ejected from their countries, by force if necessary. One of the first acts of the Qaddafi government was to order the British, Americans, and French to close their bases and leave. It would not be long before the new Libyan leader turned to the IRA as a way of doing one of Libya's former rulers, Britain, even more harm.

In the wake of the split in the IRA, events in Ireland moved inexorably to conflict. In 1970 the Provisionals began organizing for war and within two years had launched a shooting and bombing offensive against the British army and the Northern Ireland state. As the conflict intensified, the need for modern weaponry grew.

It was, curiously, the Breton nationalist movement in France that was responsible for putting the Provisionals and the Libyans in touch with each other. In early 1972 a meeting was held between the Bretons and the Provisionals, one of a regular series of contacts with like-minded revolutionary groups opened up by the Sinn Fein president Ruairi O Bradaigh, who was particularly keen on finding common cause with some of Europe's small and often exotic nationalist movements, such as those of the Basques, Corsicans, and Bretons. The contacts increased political cooperation and mutual understanding, but they also facilitated the mutual acquisition of weaponry and military expertise. During the 1972 meeting the Bretons suggested that it might be worth the IRA's while to get in touch with Qaddafi's government in Tripoli, a regime that had let it be known that it was ready and able to assist revolutionary movements willing to foment trouble for the old imperial powers that had once ruled the Arab Middle East. That duly happened, and in August of that year the contact was formalized when two members of the IRA's ruling body, the seven-person Army Council, Joe Cahill and Quartermaster General Denis McInerney, flew out to Warsaw to meet agents from the Libyan Intelligence Service (LIS) in the offices of the Libyan trade mission to Poland. The IRA men knew they were plowing a fertile field as two months earlier Qaddafi, eager to cause trouble for Britain, had publicly thrown his weight behind the Provisional IRA.

The Libyan leader had chosen his own state radio service to tell the world of the new alliance. "At present," he said in an address broadcast in June of that year, "we support the revolutionaries of Ireland who oppose Britain and are motivated by Nationalism and religion. The Libyan Arab Republic has stood by the revolutionaries of Ireland, their aims and their support for the revolutionaries of Ireland."[2]

The Libyans agreed to supply money and weapons to the IRA, as long as a suitably secure smuggling route, or "line," as the IRA called it, could be devised. The Libyans also offered to give the IRA semi-ambassadorial status in Tripoli. The IRA leadership readily agreed and set about selecting an envoy to send to the Libyan capital, where his task would be to liaise with Libyan intelligence and help set up the arms routes.

The man chosen to represent the IRA was, at the time, not a member of the organization but a strong sympathizer. A schoolteacher from the Border town of Ballybay in County Monaghan, he had already spent a year teaching English to Libyans and was back in Ireland on vacation when he was approached by a member of the IRA's Army Council.

The Army Council member, a veteran activist from Coalisland, County Tyrone, won the teacher over and, using his background in teaching English language as a cover, this time supposedly tutoring the sons and daughters of the Libyan army officer cadre at the prestigious Tripoli College, the IRA's newly recruited emissary flew out to the Libyan capital.

The man, known to his Libyan handlers as Mister Eddie, found himself housed in a splendid Italianate villa in the middle of Tripoli's embassy district. Ambassadors from other European countries would soon be aware that they had an intriguing new neighbor. The Libyans, it appeared, wanted the world to know all about Colonel Qaddafi's new friends.

Mister Eddie was put on a generous weekly wage and found that his villa had been sumptuously furnished. No luxury was spared; the crockery, stamped with King Idris's crest, had come from the former royal palace. Every week he would meet with officers from the LIS to discuss the IRA's needs and drink tea from an ornate china service.[3]

What the IRA got out of its first fling with Colonel Qaddafi is a matter of dispute. What appears certain is that in the three years of that IRA-Libyan liaison over $3.5 million ($10 million in current prices) was funneled via City of London banks to the IRA's coffers, an invaluable supplement to the IRA's income at a time when its campaign was at its height and its most expensive.

At least one shipment of guns and explosives was intercepted, but there are strong indications that perhaps three other shipments also got through to the IRA.[4] One smuggling attempt was intercepted in March 1973 when the Irish navy captured the vessel *Claudia* not far from the County Wexford coast, packed with five tons of Russian-made rifles, pistols, ammunition, and explosives.

On board was a man who from then onward personified the IRA-Libyan links: the IRA's then chief of staff and overall military commander, a West Belfast veteran, Joe Cahill. With him was the IRA's quartermaster general, Denis McInerney, the figure who had charge of the IRA's weapons department.

The first liaison between Libya and the Provisional IRA was, however, doomed and destined to break up in acrimony. The weak link in the relationship was to be Mister Eddie, who turned out to have more independence of mind than the IRA leadership would have liked.

In 1974 he organized a conference designed to bring the Provisionals together with the largest loyalist paramilitary group in Northern Ireland, the Ulster Defence Association (UDA), ostensibly an enemy of the republican group. The UDA had helped organize a general strike of Protestants earlier that year, which brought down a political agreement that had established a government in Belfast in which nationalists and unionists shared power and a Council of Ireland was set up, which was aimed at bringing the two parts of Ireland closer together.

According to those who knew him, Mister Eddie was intrigued by the loyalist leadership's ideas for an independent Northern Ireland state and later became a close friend of the UDA supreme commander, Andy Tyrie. In the weeks after the general strike, Mister Eddie hit upon the idea of inviting delegations from the UDA and the IRA's political wing, Sinn Fein, out to Tripoli along with businessmen from his native County Monaghan to discuss an economic aid package to facilitate the execution of UDA's independence ideas.

He also had new ideas about the IRA's relationship with the Libyans and proposed that, instead of receiving cash and guns from Qaddafi, the IRA be given exclusive rights to handle trade between Ireland and Libya. In view of Libya's insatiable appetite for beef and Ireland's thriving cattle industry, it was an arrangement he believed would swell the IRA's coffers.

The problem was that Mister Eddie had arranged all this behind the backs of his IRA commanders in Ireland. When they learned of his plans, especially the invitation to the UDA leadership to visit Tripoli, they were furious.

The conference went ahead in November 1974 and was promptly leaked to the media back in Ireland. The Sinn Fein delegation refused to attend, and the UDA returned home to Belfast, triumphant and claiming that they had driven a damaging wedge between the Qaddafi regime and the IRA. The Libyans, they said, had come to see that the Northern Ireland problem was not as simple as the IRA maintained, that there was a majority in favor of the union with Britain in Northern Ireland. As result, the UDA claimed, the Libyans had said they were rethinking their relationship with the Provos.

The view that the UDA was responsible for terminating the IRA-Libya alliance has become widely accepted as the reason why Qaddafi ended his dealings with the IRA at that time. And there is no doubt that the relationship with Mister Eddie did end in dramatic fashion, when in May 1975 Libyan police picked him up from his luxurious villa and, with sirens wailing and lights flashing, drove him to the Tripoli airport, where they deposited him on a plane bound for Rome. The message to Tripoli's diplomatic community was again clear.

But the truth about what happened was more complicated, as one IRA source explained: "The Libyans were always doubtful about [Mister Eddie] and wanted assurances that they were dealing with real Provos, which was why Cahill was on the *Claudia*. After the [UDA] conference the Libyans were furious with him and suspected him of being a British agent and even of having compromised our operations. They actually offered to bury him in the desert, but the Provos said leave him alone, he's harmless but just foolish."[5] Even so, Mister Eddie could not relax. The last words he heard from his Libyan handler as he headed for the airport were ominous: "Beware the Irish, Mister Eddie. Beware the Irish!"[6]

Mister Eddie was eventually replaced as the IRA ambassador by a more loyal and reliable figure, but the experience had soured the Libyans. The public statements of senior Libyan figures thereafter painted a confusing and erratic picture of their links with the IRA, sometimes disowning the IRA, sometimes supporting it.

The truth was that the Libyans had put the relationship on the back burner, as the same IRA source explained: "The link with Libya that went back to Joe Cahill's day . . . had never been broken, although there had been a period of quiet for a long time."[7] Libyan intelligence had been alarmed at Mister Eddie's freelance antics, and the Qaddafi government had lost its trust in the IRA. They decided to keep the IRA at arm's length.

The event that revived the Libya-IRA axis was the death on hunger strike in 1981 of ten prisoners from the IRA and a related republican splinter group, the Irish National Liberation Army, in the Maze prison outside Belfast. The death fast marked the culmination of a protest against the withdrawal of special category or political status, which had been granted to IRA and other paramilitary prisoners in the 1970s. The prisoners' leader and the first to die was Bobby Sands, who had been elected a British MP before his death.

The 1981 hunger strikes received widespread international publicity and generated headlines around the world for much of the year. The Libyans watched with fascination and mounting interest. According to one senior IRA figure, "The Libyans saw the numbers coming out on the streets, the tens of thousands who came out for Bobby's [Sands] funeral, for instance, and they thought the revolution was starting. They were also very impressed with the way the hunger strikers handled themselves. I think it had something to do with the martyrdom thing in Islam. Anyway that's when the money flow restarted."[8]

The two IRA men responsible for reactivating the Libyan link were both former senior figures in the organization—Joe Cahill, who had been the contact on the *Claudia,* and Daithi O Conaill (David O'Connell), a twenty-six-year veteran and strategist whose republican credentials were impeccable. Both men had known the Libyans since the early 1970s and were trusted by them. In late 1981, following a renewal of contacts with Libyan intelligence, Qaddafi agreed to help the IRA once again. But there were to be no arms shipments, only modest amounts of money. Over the next three years or so they sent some $1.5 million to the IRA, a fraction of their contributions in the 1970s. Qaddafi was being cautious.

The event that changed all that took place in London in April 1984 just yards from the Libyan embassy, in St. James's Street off Hyde Park. A crowd of anti-Qaddafi dissidents from the National Front for the Salvation of Libya (NFSL) were staging a protest against the Qaddafi regime when all of a sudden a burst of automatic gunfire split the air. When the noise subsided, a twenty-five-year-old London policewoman, Yvonne Fletcher, lay dying.

The shots had been fired from within the embassy; of that there could be little doubt. British police then placed the embassy under a state of siege for eleven days, but because of its diplomatic immunity no policeman or soldier could enter the building. Eventually a deal was made, and as the siege ended thirty Libyans were driven to Heathrow Airport and a flight home to Tripoli.

Behind the shooting incident was a story of worsening relations between Libya and Western governments, especially those of Ronald Reagan's United States and Margaret Thatcher's Britain. The CIA, under the aggressive leadership of its director, William Casey, believed Qaddafi was sponsoring anti-American terrorism throughout the world—including hijackings of aircraft and ships and massacres in the Vienna and Rome airports. He and Reagan set out to undermine and overthrow the Libyan leader.

To Qaddafi the evidence that the West was plotting against him was obvious. A month after the killing of Constable Fletcher, anti-Qaddafi elements inside and outside Libya linked up in Tripoli and launched a fierce, but unsuccessful, military assault on the army barracks where the Libyan leader had his headquarters. The Libyans suspected that the dissident groups were being sponsored by CIA allies in Sudan, Egypt, Iraq, and Saudi Arabia and that Britain was giving them a secure base.

The evidence was strong. Four months before Fletcher's death the Libyan ambassador to Rome had been assassinated by anti-Qaddafi elements, and the Libyan consulate in West Germany was bombed. When the Libyan embassy in London was besieged, the staff inside suspected it might be a cover for another attack and, according to Qaddafi's own account, decided to strike first. Qaddafi had already demonstrated his willingness to hit back ruthlessly at his enemies; perhaps fifteen dissidents died in shootings ordered by the Libyan leader at this time.

Qaddafi's war with the Western powers intensified in the mid-1980s. In 1985 the United States concluded that Qaddafi was subsidizing some thirty "insurgent, radical or terrorist groups" around the world and in June of that year decided to support exile Libyan groups in executing a strategy of sabotage, violence, and propaganda.[9] Despite an earlier White House ruling forbidding political assassination, the various U.S. intelligence agencies hoped that "disaffected elements in the military could be spurred to assassination attempts . . . against Gaddafi."[10]

U.S. warplanes twice attacked Libya, once in 1981, when the United States asserted its right to send military vessels into the Gulf of Sirte, and again in March and April 1986, when Tripoli itself was targeted. Nearly eighty people were killed, one of them Qaddafi's adopted baby daughter, Hana, who died when the planes bombed the family home. On that occasion the U.S. jets took off from British air bases with the full approval of Margaret Thatcher.

The impact of all this on Qaddafi and his view of Thatcher's Britain need not be guessed at. "Thatcher is a murderer," Qaddafi protested. "She allowed planes to be sent from her country knowing that they intended to attack me, to attack my home and family. . . . Thatcher is a prostitute. She sold herself to Reagan and now she has sold her country too."[11]

It was strong language, soon to be matched by deeds. The IRA and Qaddafi now had a common enemy in the British prime minister. Qaddafi accused her of complicity in the death of his baby daughter. The IRA loathed Thatcher too, blaming her for callously allowing the ten hunger strikers to starve to death.

In late 1984 and early 1985 the Libyan Intelligence Service moved to put the relationship with the IRA on an entirely different and much deadlier footing, this time offering the organization much more than cash to wage its campaign.

At this stage the IRA's ambassador to Libya was Ivor Bell, a former chief of staff and a veteran West Belfast activist who for years had been a close political and military ally of Gerry Adams. An important IRA leader in his own right, Bell, along with Adams and Martin McGuinness, had been flown to London by the Royal Air Force for secret cease-fire talks with British ministers in 1972. He was an experienced and well-respected member of the organization.

Bell was working for the IRA's GHQ and his job was to scour Europe for weapons, but when it came to the dealings with Libya, he reported directly to the chief of staff. The story of Bell's relationship with the Libyans is a complex one that is still a matter of argument and debate within the IRA. Bell eventually fell out with Adams, and so the account given by the IRA leaders is tainted by their need to paint him in dark colors. The version they have circulated has

Bell failing to get on with his Libyan contacts and, possibly for reasons having to do with his own leadership ambitions, refusing offers of weapons and explosives, much to the surprise and anger of Libyan intelligence.

The authorized version of events credits Joe Cahill with rectifying this state of affairs and for laying the foundations for the Libyan arms shipments. Whatever the truth of that, his links with Libya were long-lasting and deep; he would claim to colleagues that over the years he had become a personal friend of the Libyan leader, and according to this account, it was Cahill who asked the Libyans to come to Ireland to discuss the most ambitious arms-smuggling enterprise in the history of Ireland's centuries-long conflict with Britain.[12]

The person Cahill invited to Ireland for face-to-face meetings with the IRA's ruling Army Council was Nasser Ashour, the number three man in the Libyan Intelligence Service. Ashour was well known to British intelligence from the 1984 siege of the London embassy. He was the Libyan official who negotiated the safe departure of diplomats, including the gunman who had shot Constable Fletcher.

Ashour took a risk coming to Ireland, but he traveled on a false passport and under various pretexts, once to meet Libyan students studying in Dublin; on another occasion he pretended to be a trade official on a mission to negotiate a cattle deal with the Irish government. The ruses worked, and he was able to meet the Army Council without being detected.

The deal Ashour offered was extraordinary. The Libyans would give the IRA $10 million and three hundred tons of modern sophisticated weaponry, as long as both were used against Margaret Thatcher's government. If the arrangement worked out, Nashour hinted, there could be more money and weapons and Libya might introduce the IRA to other sympathetic governments. Nashour's offer was immediately and gratefully accepted. Not only would the money help relieve strains on the IRA's always overstretched budget, especially as the Royal Ulster Constabulary Special Branch was then targeting some of the organization's more dubious ways of fundraising, but the weaponry would put the armed struggle on an altogether higher military plane.[13]

At the moment Ashour turned up knocking at its door, the IRA was in desperate need of assistance. By the mid-1980s it was experiencing great difficulties getting its hands on the sort of weapons that could put the British under serious pressure. During these years the organization had two agents roaming Europe in the search for guns from sympathetic groups and often treacherous arms dealers, but their efforts met with mixed results.

Weapons came in dribs and drabs, and frequently the arms dealers double-crossed the IRA, taking the organization's money for weapons and ammunition that was either dud or mismatched and sometimes betraying entire consignments to the Irish or British authorities.

The only reliable source for guns was, as it always has been for Irish insurgents, the United States, where large Irish-American communities, especially on the East Coast, began providing generous amounts of sympathy, money, and guns once the "Troubles" broke out in 1969.

In those early days guns were easy to come by. The IRA had a network in place in the United States in the 1950s and it was a simple task to reactivate it when violence erupted in 1969. Headed by George Harrison, an IRA veteran from County Mayo, the network was headquartered in New York, where Harrison's links to a Mafia-associated arms dealer introduced the IRA to a steady supply of guns and ammunition.[14]

Harrison was the single most important source of weapons in these years. His consignments, many of which had been sold to his contact in the arms business by soldiers stationed at the massive marine base Camp Le Jeune, in North Carolina were running at up to 300 guns a year. One estimate suggests that he sent a million rounds of ammunition to the IRA during his career, spent over $1 million of the organization's money, and dispatched up to 2,500 weapons across the Atlantic. A key link man to Harrison was the ubiquitous Joe Cahill, part of whose job was to collect funds raised for the IRA in the United States and hand it over to the gunrunner.

In those early days the American security agencies, especially the Federal Bureau of Investigation (FBI), paid little heed to the Irish-American communities and their political activities. It was not until the late 1970s and early 1980s that pressure from Margaret Thatcher on the Reagan White House persuaded the FBI to turn its attentions to the IRA.

Harrison's network was the first casualty. It was rolled up in the summer of 1981 and some of its key members arrested and indicted. Although Harrison was acquitted, along with Michael Flannery, the eighty-year-old head of Irish Northern Aid (Noraid), the body that ostensibly raised money for IRA prisoners' families, the network was lost for good. It was the first of a number of paralyzing blows. A year later the IRA's commander in New York, Gabriel Megahey, and four other men were arrested as they tried to buy a Red-eye missile from an FBI agent posing as an arms dealer. Two years later an ambitious plan to smuggle weapons from Boston by sea foundered when a high-level informer in Southern Command, Sean O'Callaghan, betrayed it to the Garda Siochana, the Irish police.

After the destruction of the Harrison network, arms supplies to the IRA from the United States were infrequent and erratic. "There was very little stuff coming in," recalled one veteran.[15] All too often weapons, sometime purchased over the counter in gun shops, would make their way to Ireland in twos and threes, only to be intercepted or captured by the authorities, who would then be able to trace them back and arrest and charge the sympathizers responsible. The IRA was never again able to construct a network in the United States as productive as Harrison's.

So when the Libyan Intelligence Service offered the IRA three hundred tons of the most up-to-date military equipment with no strings attached, it was the paramilitary equivalent of a lottery win. There could be no question of the IRA's refusing the offer, but its leaders were troubled by other issues. The smuggling operation was bound to be highly dangerous, and questions surrounded the IRA's ability to handle such a difficult enterprise. Even if the weapons were landed safely, the IRA then faced the problem of hiding vast amounts of equipment from the prying eyes of the security forces. But the biggest uncertainty confronting the IRA leaders was how to use such an enormous windfall to the best military and political advantage.

These issues raised a range of awkward questions, and the very first one was whether or not the quartermaster's department was up to such an ambitious task. The weapons would have to be transported hundreds of miles by sea, across the Mediterranean, along the western coast of Europe, landed in Ireland, and then hidden. It was a complex, dangerous, and time-consuming operation and was going to require careful, detailed planning.

At the time the IRA's Quarter Master General, the man who would have the job of organizing the enterprise, was Kevin Hannaway, Gerry Adams's cousin, but there were doubts about whether he could handle such a big challenge. After Nasser Ashour's negotiations with the Army Council, Hannaway had, along with Joe Cahill, traveled to Tripoli to view and select the weaponry that was on offer. But he was a poor traveler, and it soon became evident he was in bad health, the legacy of sensory deprivation during interrogations by police and army carried out when internment was introduced.

The Army Council decided to replace him and instead made him adjutant general. Not long afterward Hannaway quit the IRA altogether. For the new quartermaster general the Army Council turned to Micky McKevitt, a County Louth–born activist who by 1985 was the quartermaster for Northern Command, charged with ensuring that Northern IRA units were well armed. "McKevitt was younger [than Hannaway] and was full of fire," recalled a contemporary, "and he had a big countrywide operation going. The [Army] Council believed he had what was necessary to do the job."

McKevitt, who was in his mid-thirties at the time, agreed to take on the job and was soon traveling to Tripoli to assess the scale of the operation and his own needs. The same IRA source recollects, "When McKevitt returned, he was staggered at what was involved. But he cut a deal with the leadership and got what he wanted. If it hadn't been for that deal, the IRA would have lost a great deal more than the *Eksund*."[16]

The Army Council agreed to a simple plan. The entire operation would be run solely by the QMG's department, and only it would be privy to the details. The Army Council would know in general what was happening, but precise arrangements—such as the landing spots, the modus operandi, means of distributing the weapons, and so on—would be known only to McKevitt and handpicked members of the QMG's department.

The QMG's department was split into two. One section would continue with its routine work, arranging other arms shipments, finding hiding places for guns and explosives, and transporting weaponry northward to the Active Service Units (ASUs). Another section, hidden from the rest of the IRA, would concentrate on the Libyan operation. Chief of Staff Kevin McKenna, a taciturn, guarded figure whose base was in County Monaghan, readily agreed to McKevitt's scheme.

Through Henry Cairns, a forty-seven-year-old bookstore owner from Bray, County Dublin, and a republican sympathizer, the IRA made contact with the man who could supply them with vessels large enough to transport the Libyan weaponry. Adrian Hopkins, then fifty-two, was a man whose business had gone bankrupt, a man who was in great need of money.

In the mid-1960s Hopkins had started a travel agency, Bray Travel, which for a year was a great success, but in 1980 it went bankrupt, stranding 6,000 Irish vacationers in the Canary Islands and costing a further 1,500 their holiday deposits. Creditors were owed some $1.5 million. The collapse hit Hopkins hard. Bray Travel had supported a comfortable middle-class South Dublin lifestyle. He was a trustee of Wicklow tennis club, refereed rugby matches, and was active in the social life of one of Ireland's most affluent areas. He needed money badly to sustain all this.

The IRA gave Hopkins the chance to make a lot of money quickly. The deal he cut with the IRA earned him £50,000 for each shipment he organized, half paid up front, the rest when the mission had been successfully completed. He was also allowed to keep the vessels afterward and to pocket the proceeds of their sale. The operation began in a modest way. The IRA decided the wisest thing was to test its systems by sending a small consignment of weapons in the first shipment. If all went well, the next shipment would be larger, the one after that even larger, and so on until it was time for the *Eksund*'s cargo to arrive.[17]

Hopkins bought a sixty-five-foot Irish fishing boat, the *Casamara*, which he sailed to Malta in July 1985. The next three smuggling trips took more or less the same form. Each journey involved Hopkins's sailing the vessel to Malta, where he picked up the IRA crew members. They normally made their way to Malta by circuitous routes, taking in several European capitals, notably Paris, Athens, and Belgrade, in an effort to throw off any surveillance.

Together they then sailed the boat out to sea, where they met a Libyan mother ship that transferred its weaponry to the IRA. On board the Libyan vessel was Nasser Ashour from Libyan intelligence to make sure everything went smoothly. Only the *Eksund* was loaded in Tripoli docks.

Each IRA ship then made its way back to Ireland, where off the east coast, at a beach called Clogga Strand, the weapons were transferred to inflatable dinghies powered by outboard engines. These ferried the Libyan arsenal to shore, where it was loaded onto trucks and then taken to dumps throughout Ireland.

The *Casamara* brought seven tons of arms, including Taurus automatic pistols and AK-47 rifles, on that first trip. The trip went smoothly, and so two months later the next shipment was dispatched, consisting of some ten tons of arms, including one hundred AK-47s, general-purpose machine guns, Webley revolvers, and several tons of ammunition.

Bad winter weather conditions, the small size of vessels at its disposal, and the need to maintain security meant that the IRA had a relatively small opportunity each year, between February–March and October, to bring over Qaddafi's weapons. For that reason it was not until nine months later that the next consignment came.

Hopkins gave the *Casamara* the new name *Kula* for its July 1986 trip. Fourteen tons of weapons were shipped on that journey, including the first consignment of SAM-7 missiles. For years the IRA had sought the means to bring down the British army helicopters used to ferry patrols and supplies throughout rural areas of Northern Ireland, and now it was within its grasp.

For the next, much larger shipment, Hopkins found a bigger vessel, a former oil rig standby vessel called the *Sjarmar*, which Hopkins renamed the *Villa*. The *Villa* sailed in October 1986 with the largest shipment yet, a massive 105 tons of weaponry. On board were 40 general-purpose machine guns, 1,200 AK-47s, 130 Webley revolvers, over a million rounds of ammunition, 26 heavy Russian-made DHSK machine guns, RPG-7 rocket launchers with grenades, and more SAM-7 missiles. The most important item in the shipment, however, was five tons of Semtex, the highly destructive plastic explosives developed by the Czech arms industry.[18]

The stage was set to bring in the last and largest consignment, the 150 tons scheduled to be the cargo on the ill-fated *Eksund*.

As a result of detailed and careful planning and the failure of British or Irish security to detect the operation, the IRA had been able to get four shiploads of Libyan weapons safely into Ireland. The vital question, though, was what the IRA was going to do with them all.

British security sources estimated the value of the shipments at the time at nearly $40 million, equivalent to five times the IRA's total annual budget. Allowing for attrition through accidental losses, usage, and security forces successes, the *Villa*'s cargo meant that the organization had enough weapons to keep going for a further twenty years.

The IRA now had the wherewithal to fight a really long war, as it had been committed to doing since the late 1970s. But the evidence was that even though it was not losing that struggle, it certainly wasn't winning it. The truth was that though IRA violence by the mid-1980s was a major problem for the British it was on nowhere near the scale needed to force Britain into rethinking its presence in Northern Ireland.

The IRA leadership, represented by the seven-person Army Council, had a choice. The leadership could continue at the current, more or less containable level of violence for another two decades and hope that an unexpected event or piece of luck would transform the IRA's fortunes. Or it could opt for something much more dramatic, a daring strike that would compel British public opinion to demand a radical change in their government's Irish policy. It was this second option that the IRA chose.

So it was that, as the Libyan venture was being organized, the IRA set about planning a major escalation of violence, something that would jolt Britain into reconsidering its options. The plan was modeled on the Tet offensive launched by the Vietcong in January 1968, the lunar New Year in Vietnam, when guerrilla forces mounted a widespread and unexpected assault on U.S. forces throughout the country. The Tet offensive is credited with beginning the end of American involvement in that part of Southeast Asia by convincing a decisive section of U.S. public opinion that the war against North Vietnam was unwinnable. The IRA hoped to do the same with the British public.

The Army Council made a number of adjustments in its battle order to facilitate the strategy. In February 1985 the South Armagh IRA leader and cross-Border smuggler Tom "Slab" Murphy, a fixture on the Army Council for many years, was promoted to the post of director of operations and given the task of drawing up the detailed plans for the offensive. Over the next few months he traveled regularly to Libya to inspect the Libyan army's arsenals and to assess which weapons were best suited for his plans. There was another key change. Martin McGuinness was promoted from adjutant of Northern Command to Northern commander, replacing Murphy. Although it would be his job to put Murphy's plans into operation, McGuinness's new job meant that he would have considerable influence over how and where the weapons were used.

The IRA Southern Command meanwhile set about making preparations for training IRA volunteers in the use of the Libyan weaponry. Sophisticated underground firing ranges, some lined with concrete and soundproofed, were constructed all over Ireland. When the *Eksund* was intercepted and the Irish security forces launched a nationwide search for the other shipments, a number of apparent "bunkers" were unearthed, and the assumption was that they had been constructed to store the *Eksund*'s cargo. In fact they were these meticulously prepared practice ranges.

Later, selected IRA operatives, perhaps as many as thirty, traveled secretly to Libya for training in specialized weapons like the SAM-7s, Ireland being judged too small to perform such training undetected. The arrival of the Libyan shipments was also staggered to dovetail into the plan. The first four consignments were dispatched to dumps in the most southerly, westerly, and northerly parts of the country, to be held in reserve for later use. "The principle was to start outwards and work in," said one IRA source.[19] None of the Libyan weaponry was to be used, the leadership decided, until all the Libyan shipments had safely arrived.

The first shipments were to be stored in reserve and the "Tet" was to be fought with the *Eksund*'s cargo. Once unloaded, it was to be stored temporarily in a single bunker in Arklow, County Wicklow, and then distributed to the ASUs who would lead the offensive north of the Border and elsewhere in Britain and Europe.

The thinking behind the offensive was to cause so much damage in the first two weeks that the momentum would keep the IRA going for another eighteen months. "The idea," said one IRA Volunteer privy to the plan, "was to take and hold areas in Armagh, Tyrone, and Fermanagh and to force the British either to use maximum force or to hold off."[20] Four areas on the Border, security bases and posts, had been earmarked for IRA units to hold and, in theory at least, defend for days.

The SAM-7s were to be used against British helicopters, ideally cutting off South Armagh and leaving it under the effective control of the IRA. The threat against helicopters would force the British to ground their aircraft throughout Northern Ireland and to use armored ground transport, which, in rural areas especially, would be vulnerable to the heavy Russian machine guns and rockets now in the IRA's hands.

Spectaculars were also planned: 106-millimeter canons, whose presence on the *Eksund* has never been acknowledged by the Irish or British authorities, were to be mounted on motorboats and used to bombard and sink the British naval patrol boat that policed the waters of Carlingford Lough dividing Northern Ireland from the Irish Republic. There were plans, too, to blow up a ship in Belfast harbor, thus blocking access to the city from the sea.

Later the campaign would be carried to military and high-prestige government targets in Britain and Europe. At one stage the IRA even contemplated launching rocket attacks on British embassies throughout Europe. But the real offensive was to be a short and very sharp affair in Northern Ireland.

The IRA leaders had calculated that the British would probably respond to their "Tet" by introducing internment without trial and would press the Republic's authorities to follow suit. It was not the first time that the IRA had attempted to provoke the British into draconian and potentially counterproductive security measures. The organization had long believed that it thrived on British repression.

The offensive was daring and ambitious, but it suffered from a single flaw. Its success hinged on the IRA's preserving the element of surprise—if the British ever got to hear of the IRA's plans, all would be lost. For that reason the Army Council resisted the temptation to dip into its Libyan hoard until the *Eksund* had safely delivered its cargo. Not even Semtex, a relatively common explosive, was to be used, so eager was the IRA leadership to capitalize on the surprise factor.

"You were all supposed to wake up one morning, switch on the radio, and discover that mayhem had broken out everywhere," recalled one IRA activist. "The impact was supposed to have been earth-shattering."[21]

But whoever betrayed the *Eksund* robbed the IRA of a priceless asset; the surprise factor vanished the moment the French customs police boarded the vessel. Afterward Hopkins talked freely to his captors, giving them precious detail about the contents of the earlier shipments. The British soon knew exactly what weapons had been brought in, and they were able quickly to put countermeasures in place.

From there it was all downhill for the IRA. Not only had the *Eksund*'s precious cargo been captured and the weapons destined for the "Tet" campaign lost, but the Libyans reacted angrily to the discovery. They were particularly annoyed when they discovered that Hopkins and Cairns had not been members of the IRA. The agreement Libyan intelligence had reached with the Army Council was that only IRA members would take part in the shipments. Almost immediately after their arrest, Hopkins and Cairns confirmed Libyan involvement to French and Irish intelligence officers, much to the embarrassment of the Qaddafi regime.

The Libyan leader immediately canceled the promised cash payments to the IRA; half the promised $10 million had been paid, and the rest would have been sent once the *Eksund* safely made it to Ireland. Now the IRA's coffers were suddenly empty, its ability to intensify its campaign severely curtailed by a shortage of cash.

When the IRA attempted to use some of the Libyan weaponry, it found out what the loss of the surprise factor meant. The SAM-7s had been rendered useless when the British installed electronic countermeasures on helicopters. Two SAM-7s test-fired in South Armagh whistled harmlessly past their targets. The IRA then attempted to compensate by deploying the Russian-made DHSK machine guns against helicopters, but this too was a failure. The weapons were far too heavy to be lugged around the countryside, robbing the IRA ASUs of vital speed and mobility. The British also took to flying their helicopters in groups of up to five, so that if one was attacked the others could respond. Moreover, they reinforced the armor on their vehicles to withstand the IRA's new capabilities. The British knew the IRA was coming, and they were ready.

The only part of the shipment still of major concern to the British was the tons of Semtex explosives that the IRA's engineering department proceeded to deploy in a series of improvised weapons. Infinitely malleable and virtually impossible to detect, Semtex was used in a variety of inventive ways ranging from coffee jar bombs and deadly mercury-tilt booby-trap devices that were attached to the underside of vehicles, to drogue bombs—small, hand-thrown parachute-guided devices that burned through armor plating.

While the security forces in both parts of Ireland were naturally concerned about the IRA's new and staggering military strength, the IRA leadership was, as it is to this day, consumed with the search for the identity of the informer who had betrayed the *Eksund* and sabotaged the "Tet offensive."

The task of unmasking the traitor was made all the more difficult by the variety of available explanations. It was possible, for example, that the British had just been good at their detective work. The Libyans left enough public clues lying around suggesting that they were once again dallying with the IRA, and it would have been seriously deficient of the various British and Irish intelligence agencies to have ignored them.

In June 1986, for instance, Qaddafi's deputy Major Ahmed Jalloud told a group of German Euro MPs that Libya planned to resume aid to the IRA.[22] In March 1987 Qaddafi informed the *Observer* newspaper in London that he had increased arms supplies to the IRA in retaliation for U.S. bombing raids the preceding year.[23] The following month Qaddafi's teenage son, Sadi, made it known at an international conference in Tripoli, to which Sinn Fein had sent two representatives, that Libya would open an office for the IRA in its capital.[24]

There was also a strong possibility that the authorities had simply guessed what was going on. A briefing paper prepared by the State Department in Washington in 1986, declassified and obtained under the Freedom of Information Act, shows Assistant Secretary J. Edward Fox noting with some perspicacity that Constable Yvonne Fletcher's killing in 1984 "had increased [Libya's] political motivation for supporting the IRA."[25] Fox also pointed to another piece of evidence suggesting that Libya had resumed giving weapons to the IRA. That was the discovery by Irish police in November 1985 of arms and ammunition on a Libyan-leased airliner at the Dublin airport.

If the authorities hadn't guessed, they should have. In January 1986 Irish police raided a farmhouse in County Sligo and discovered a large haul of weapons, sixteen semiautomatic AK-47 rifles made in East Germany and fourteen made in Romania, along with bayonets, magazines, cleaning kits, and 7,560 rounds of ammunition, that had originated in Yugoslavia. The haul was packed into six boxes stored in the attic of the farmhouse and was marked with the words "Libyan Armed Forces" and "Destination Tripoli." In two other related raids at separate locations in Counties Roscommon and Sligo, police unearthed another eighty rifles and handguns and 12,000 bullets.

The weapons were part of the August 1985 consignment smuggled on the *Kula,* and were on their way to hiding places in County Donegal when they were intercepted. In an incident that was later to cast a baleful light on Martin McGuinness, a member of the quartermaster's department in

McGuinness's hometown of Derry had betrayed the guns. The British and Irish intelligence agencies should have explored the possibility that the weapons had come from Libya, but they were apparently thrown off the scent because among the weapons were ten West German–made Heckler and Koch rifles stolen in Norway. This and the fact that their informer, Frank Hegarty, who worked for the QM's department in Derry, had been excluded from the Libyan operation and been given a false cover story to explain the origin of the weapons meant that the British missed the Libyan connection altogether.

Although there were compelling reasons to think the British or Irish authorities had chanced on the Libyan enterprise, the IRA automatically assumed that its secret had been betrayed, and the obvious suspects were the two non-IRA men on board the *Eksund*, Adrian Hopkins and Henry Cairns.

Both had reasons to betray the IRA. Cairns was penniless and may have been tempted to sell his precious information for cash. But an internal IRA inquiry concluded that Hopkins was the culprit. The *Eksund*'s skipper had two counts against him, not least that he had stolen IRA money. According to sources familiar with the details of his arrangements with the IRA, he had overcharged the Army Council for the *Eksund*, swindling the organization out of tens of thousands of pounds.[26] It also became clear that he had talked freely to French and Irish police, telling them all about the previous shipments and pinpointing the Arklow bunker that had been built to hold the *Eksund*'s arsenal.

There were also signs that he had made a separate deal with the authorities when suddenly the French granted him bail, enabling him to flee to Ireland, where there were no extradition arrangements with France. The suspicions that a deal had been cut hardened when Hopkins came to trial in Ireland. Eleven of twelve charges against him were dropped, and he received a relatively lenient sentence, three years, compared with the five-to seven-year terms handed down in Paris to the *Eksund*'s other crew members.

Some in the IRA wanted to shoot Hopkins, but friends spoke up for him. The *Villa* had nearly sunk during a terrifying storm in the Bay of Biscay during its 1986 voyage, and but for Hopkins's seamanship its cargo of 105 tons of arms and the IRA crew would have sunk without a trace. Doubtless conscious of the bad publicity that would attach to any effort to kill Hopkins, the IRA leadership let him off with a warning to abandon rumored plans to write a book about his exploits.

Nonetheless, the belief took hold among IRA leaders that Hopkins was the man who had put Gabriel Cleary's TPU out of action, and that at some point in the affair he had been turned by either the Irish or the British authorities. But suspicions that the *Eksund* had been betrayed by another informer, a much more important figure at a high level in the IRA, persisted elsewhere in the IRA's highest reaches long afterward, overshadowing and souring the movement's tortuous trek on the peace process. The IRA leadership would later split and divide over the peace process, but the fault line can be traced back to the doubts and distrust generated by the betrayal of the *Eksund*.

In the immediate wake of the *Eksund*'s loss and long afterward both the IRA and the British and Irish security authorities behaved as if the informer was still around. The IRA leadership has never admitted that the vessel was betrayed and has done everything to encourage the view that its capture was a piece of bad luck. "It was kept very, very quiet," explained one IRA source. "The Volunteers were just not told."[27]

The IRA's stance was understandable. To admit that an informer had gotten so close to the heart of such a vital operation would cause enormous embarrassment to the leadership, as well as the doubts at grassroots level that would inevitably grow, fester, and eventually sap morale. Saying nothing about the betrayal left the rank and file still thinking that, the loss of the *Eksund* aside, the Libyan venture had been a success. After all, the IRA had imported unimaginable quantities of heavy weaponry, and it was clear that the leadership had successfully managed to outwit the British for most of the Libyan enterprise. Only a very few activists would know that the loss of the *Eksund* had scuppered the "Tet offensive." In the eyes of ordinary republicans and IRA activists, the Libyan operation had been a success. The 150 tons of guns and explosives meant that the war could be fought almost indefinitely.

Equally, the British and Irish authorities went to great lengths, and did so for years to come, to pretend that the capture of the *Eksund* was an accidental event caused by the vessel's faulty rudder and a vigilant French customs service. At the time British army and RUC sources encouraged the media to take the view that this is exactly what happened, and they made no attempt to disguise their apparent surprise at the scale of the IRA operation. Some security force spin doctors even went so far as to suggest that the *Eksund*'s cargo was far too big for the IRA to handle and that it had to be sharing the consignment with another terrorist group.

A consensus emerged that was reflected in media coverage: the *Eksund* episode was a piece of pure luck, and the failure to detect the Libyan shipments to the IRA was a major disaster for British intelligence. One respected observer, reflecting a common media view, later wrote, "The shipments . . . revealed an international intelligence lapse of mammoth proportions."[28]

Within the IRA suspicions of a high-level leak persisted, however. The problem was that Hopkins was too small a fry to deserve such an impressive level of official protection. In any case the ruse was clumsy; Hopkins was bound to be at the top of the IRA's list of possible culprits, so why would the authorities go to such extreme lengths to protect him? Some IRA members asked another question: Would British or Irish intelligence really forgo the public credit for the *Eksund*'s capture, keep silent when accused by the media of incompetence, just to shield a relatively low-level agent who was the IRA's number one suspect anyway?

These were not the only reasons for suspecting that the real informer was not Hopkins. In late 1986, not long after the IRA leadership had decided to try to ship the last 150 tons of weapons, there were two serious lapses in the security surrounding the Libyan venture. They happened when Martin McGuinness, chairman of the Army Council and the IRA's Northern commander, sought and obtained permission from the Council to give two crucial briefings and by so doing broke the strict rule of secrecy that had been agreed and imposed on the operation.

An IRA source explained, "The agreement was that people outside the Army Council would not be told anything about the Libyan shipments until the *Eksund* was in, but when Slab [Murphy] and Micky [McKevitt] were out of the country on one of their mysterious trips, the Council gave the go-ahead. When they got back and heard what had happened, they were livid."[29]

McGuinness gave the first briefing to the IRA Executive, the thirteen-member body elected by the rank and file at IRA Conventions, the occasional conferences that determine both the IRA's politics and its military policy. The Executive chooses the members of the Army Council and selects replacements when vacancies occur; but its more important role is to act as the voice and conscience of ordinary IRA Volunteers. Most of its members were new to the job; the bulk of the previous Executive had resigned from the IRA in protest against a decision to recognize the Irish parliament in elections, and McGuinness was addressing a group whose loyalty to the Adams leadership was still untested. The split had sapped morale and McGuinness had cited the need to lift the Executive's spirits when he sought the Army Council's permission to tell it about the Libyan weaponry.

McGuinness was given the go-ahead, but in the circumstances the Army Council's decision was extraordinary. By the time the briefing was arranged, the Army council had learned to be circumspect in its dealings with the Executive. There were strong suspicions that there was an informer in its ranks, and the Council had decided to carefully control what its members were told about IRA policy and decisions. The suspicions were well-founded, for in 1994 an MI5 agent on the Executive was exposed. A Sinn Fein councillor and adjutant of Southern Command, he was spared execution because of the public embarrassment to the republican leadership that would follow his exposure. In that context the decision to brief the Executive about the Libyan shipments was an astonishing lapse.

McGuinness's briefing included the revelation not just that shipments had arrived safely but that the biggest prize of all was on its way. "He told the Executive that a lot of gear [weapons] had come in, but that the cream on the cake was still to come," said the source.[30]

The next briefing was given in County Donegal to the small group of IRA commanders who had been chosen to lead the IRA's Active Service Units (ASUs) into the "Tet offensive" after the *Eksund* had safely delivered its cargo. They were from all over the North, and their job would have been to liaise with the ASUs and outline the operations to be carried out. The briefing, also given by McGuinness, covered the quantities and type of weaponry that would be available and detailed the cargo that was supposed to come on the *Eksund*, the weapons that would give the "Tet offensive" its cutting edge.

Once again McGuinness was addressing a group with a link to an informer. Among those briefed was an IRA veteran from the St. James district of West Belfast called Harry Burns. His career in the IRA went way back to the start of the Troubles when he was interned on the *Maidstone*, a ramshackle prison ship docked in Belfast harbor which had been pressed into service when the numbers of IRA suspects being arrested far exceeded the ability of the Northern Ireland prison system to house them. Burns was trusted, but not so one of his associates. A close friend of "Big Harry," as Burns was known to his IRA colleagues and friends, was Joe Fenton, a West Belfast real estate agent and wheeler-dealer, who turned out to be one of the most important agents ever recruited by the RUC Special Branch. Fenton was so close to Burns and trusted by him that, contrary to the organization's strict security regulations, he would regularly drive him to supposedly secret IRA meetings.

Fenton came under suspicion when the leadership first began shipping the Libyan weapons to the Northern ASUs. A number of consignments headed for Belfast were mysteriously intercepted by the RUC, and it was

obvious that an informer was at his or her work. The common link in all
the losses was Fenton, who turned out to have been directly or indirectly
involved in the purchase or acquisition of the vehicles used to transport
weapons from Southern dumps.[31]

Eventually, in February 1989, and only after he had fled to England but
then inexplicably returned, Fenton was arrested by the IRA's security unit,
the specialized team whose job it was to ferret out informers from the ranks
of the IRA, interrogate them, and, if it found them guilty, shoot them dead.
What happened after Fenton's arrest has taken its place in republican
legend as one of the most far-reaching and squalid scandals in the history
of the Belfast IRA.

Fenton was abducted by the security unit and held for interrogation in
a house in Andersonstown, West Belfast, but after only two days he was
taken out and shot dead. His body, with a single bullet wound to the head,
the IRA's customary punishment for those caught informing, was dumped
in an alley in nearby Lenadoon.

The speed with which Fenton was killed caused a major row within the
IRA. An informer as important as Fenton should have been taken away for
lengthy interrogation and debriefing so that the damage he had done could
be assessed. Fenton had been working for the RUC Special Branch since at
least September 1984, when in an attempt to ingratiate himself with the
IRA's Belfast Brigade (BB) and apparently on the instruction of his Special
Branch handlers, he betrayed two other informers, a young married couple,
Catherine and Gerard Mahon, who were shot dead by the IRA for betraying arms dumps.

Fenton had a great deal to tell his interrogators, but he was never given
the opportunity. Said one angry Belfast IRA member, "Fenton was a huge
fish, and the BB squandered a great opportunity to uncover a network of
agents. Through his estate agency he was getting homes for people and
arranging fraudulent mortgages, helping people to defraud Building
Societies by manufacturing income statements for people who were registered as unemployed. The [Special] Branch would have had a field day
blackmailing his clients into becoming informers."[32]

It also emerged that Fenton had been supplying allegedly "clean" cars to
members of the IRA's England department, that section of the IRA which
was responsible for carrying out bombing missions in England. He had also
provided safe houses for the IRA in Belfast where meetings were held and
presumably bugged by the Special Branch. Between one activity and another
Fenton provided the police with vast amounts of priceless intelligence.

When questioned as to why Fenton was killed so quickly, the Belfast Brigade claimed that a huge manhunt mounted by the RUC and British army was closing in on the house where Fenton was held and that there was no time to arrange his transfer to South Armagh, where his interrogation could be carried out in a more leisurely manner. But there were suspicions that Fenton was killed for other reasons, that senior figures in the Belfast Brigade and elsewhere did not want the full story of his dealings with them to be revealed to the rest of the organization.

Fenton had performed various private favors for selected Belfast Brigade staff, one of which was to provide meeting places, usually vacant houses he was trying to sell, where secret love affairs could be consummated. One such tryst was between a former Belfast commander and the wife of one of his senior staff officers. The estate agent cum informer would give the senior IRA man the keys of a house he had on his books, and the pair would meet. It can only be presumed that the RUC Special Branch recorded their exertions and used the tapes productively. There was every possibility, in other words, that Fenton had helped the RUC to "turn" very senior Belfast Brigade figures.

There are also strong suggestions that Fenton and the IRA commander took part in a freelance, unauthorized jewelry robbery in County Fermanagh that also involved loyalists and criminal elements in Drogheda, County Louth, and Dublin. If IRA weapons had been used in such an unauthorized operation, the consequences, under the IRA's rulebook, could have been severe for the former commander. Although rumors and allegations about the commander's activities were rife in the Belfast IRA at this time, nothing was ever done. The former IRA commander had powerful family connections in the republican movement. That his brother sat on the Army Council and was a senior member of Sinn Fein may have saved his life.

Whatever the reason, Fenton was condemned to an early death, and the IRA's security unit never got the chance to properly question the informer about his long and eventful career as a Special Branch agent. Nor was it able to quiz him about his knowledge of the Libyan shipments and in particular whether or not "Big Harry" Burns had let slip any of the contents of the briefing he and the other IRA specialists had been given by the Army Council figure. Burns always denied he had said anything to Fenton. Burns, who had been severely injured some years beforehand when a mortar bomb he was attempting to fire exploded prematurely, died of cancer in February 1999. Ironically he died a fervent supporter of Gerry Adams's peace strategy.

But afterward, when the dust thrown up by Joe Fenton's killing had settled, the IRA's security unit conducted a more thorough investigation of the informer's activities and found a sophisticated bug hidden in a light fitting in the front room of Burns's house. Someone in the world of British intelligence was very interested in what Harry Burns was up to.

The net effect of the two briefings was that when the *Eksund* was betrayed, the suspicions about the identity of the traitor were more generalized. Since the circle of knowledge about the Libyan shipments had been widened beyond the Army Council, so too had the range of candidates for the role of informer. In fact, by mid-1987 the circle of knowledge had expanded to include a group of activists sent to Libya for training in the weapons as well as a small number of key personnel whose support for major political shifts was needed by the Adams camp.

The special briefings nonetheless sowed distrust in the IRA's higher reaches. But they were as nothing compared with the subsequent suspicion that the real culprit responsible for giving up the *Eksund* and with it the IRA's war plans may have been at the very top of the organization.

"The October [1987] trip was not the first time the IRA tried to bring in the *Eksund*'s cargo," said one knowledgeable IRA source. "The original plan had been to bring it in all in one go sometime in April or May, in the spring of '87. But in February that year the IRA got information that Free State army units had been put on standby from Cork to Carlingford in anticipation of an arms ship coming in sometime in the coming weeks. Someone had leaked the operation. The Free Staters didn't know where it would land, but they knew something was up. The IRA had no choice but to postpone the operation."[33]

When the *Eksund* was captured, it therefore came as no surprise to the IRA leadership. As a result of the February leak, it was half expecting the venture to fail.

The question then became this. If the Irish government had a rough date for the spring 1987 plan but no precise intelligence about where the cargo would be landed, who in the IRA was in possession of just that level of information? The answer appeared to rule out Adrian Hopkins as the main suspect. He knew exactly where the planned shipment was to be off-loaded—at Clogga Strand on the Wicklow coast, where the other four shipments had been unloaded and where the *Eksund* was headed some five or six months later. If Hopkins had been the informer in February 1987, the Irish authorities would have had no need to put their forces on alert along the entire eastern coast; they would have known exactly where to go.

These claims appear to exonerate Hopkins, although he was still suspected of being the man who tampered with Gabriel Cleary's timing power
unit. "Some believe that [it was only] after the February leak [that] Hopkins
was turned by the Brits," said one IRA source.[34]

The finger of suspicion for the source of the February leak, the main
informer, appears to point elsewhere, to someone whose knowledge of the
February plan was much less specific, whose information, although priceless, could not pinpoint the cargo's destination.

Among those who knew that the last cargo was on its way but were
unaware of the details of the operation were those members of the Army
Council not involved directly in organizing the Libyan shipments. The
Council members' state of knowledge was this: they were aware that a boat
was moored in Malta awaiting final arrangements to bring the last shipment to Ireland and that it was due sometime in the late spring. They
needed to know that in order to make plans for the "Tet offensive." But
they were unaware of vital details, such as the precise destination of the
cargo, the spot where IRA members would unload it.

Ironically the *Eksund*'s fate was sealed by an uncharacteristic act of reck-
lessness urged on their Army Council colleagues by Gerry Adams and
Martin McGuinness. Against the advice of even those most intimately
involved in planning the Libyan adventure, both men insisted that the
Eksund's deadly cargo be transported to Ireland as quickly as possible, and
in one shipment, so that the "Tet offensive" could go ahead on schedule.
Others on the Council counselled that a wiser course would be to transport
only a small part of the *Eksund*'s payload to Ireland. If it got through safely,
then the IRA could be confident that there had been no serious infiltration
and the *Eksund* could set sail as planned. If it was intercepted then they
would know for certain there was a traitor in their midst, while the loss of
weaponry to the IRA would be minimal. Alternative plans could then be
drawn up to bring the rest of *Eksund*'s cargo to Ireland at another time and
by a different way. But both Adams, whose customary caution in all matters was legendary, and McGuinness argued successfully that the IRA's
urgent need to launch the big military push demanded otherwise and that
the *Eksund*'s voyage should proceed as planned. They got their way, but
had they not prevailed then the story of the IRA's war against the British—
and with it the peace process—might have been very different indeed.

The question of who betrayed the *Eksund* has never been satisfactorily
settled, but suspicions that there was—and possibly still is—a high-ranking

traitor in the IRA have nevertheless festered for years, poisoning relations and fueling distrust as the peace process gathered pace.

THE YEAR 1987 ended on a disastrous note for the IRA. In November, only days after the capture of the *Eksund,* an IRA bomb exploded at the cenotaph in Enniskillen, County Fermanagh, as local Protestants gathered to remember their war dead. Eleven were killed and over sixty injured. The bomb helped ratchet up public hostility to the organization in the Republic to unprecedented levels.

In the wake of the *Eksund*'s capture, the Irish government ordered a nationwide search, code-named Operation Mallard, for the four other shipments. Some sixty thousand homes and farms were raided and searched. Although none of the weaponry was discovered, the IRA nevertheless suffered several other serious setbacks. The officer in charge of training ASUs in the use of the Libyan arms was captured, and documents unearthed during the search led the FBI to a key IRA operative in the United States, Richard Johnson, a skilled Boston-based electronics engineer with federal security clearance who was helping the IRA develop homemade surface-to-air missiles.

The mood of the IRA as the year turned was mixed. Recalled one activist:

> Despite the *Eksund* and [the] Enniskillen [bombing] the mood of the rank and file was quite good. They knew, thanks to Hopkins, what had come in—they were especially delighted to get the AK-47s—and they were upbeat, even jubilant. Don't forget, for years the cry had been to get heavy gear in, and here it had happened. From mixing with the leadership, however, you could see things were very different there. The mood was much more somber. They knew they had lost the vital element of surprise, and it was back to the drawing board.[35]

The betrayal of the *Eksund* condemned the IRA to military stalemate with the British. The successful Libyan shipments certainly made the IRA a more dangerous enemy than it had been for years, dangerous enough eventually to persuade the British that talking to the IRA might be more productive. But the chance of securing a decisive military advantage over the British—the aim and purpose of the "Tet offensive"—had been lost forever.

It was in such an atmosphere that the idea that politics might be an acceptable, even unavoidable, alternative to armed struggle took hold and was nurtured. When Gabriel Cleary inspected the sabotaged firing unit on the bridge of the *Eksund* and realized that its precious cargo was doomed, he was not to know that the spy who had betrayed his mission had also boosted another secret operation then under way, an operation that not even the Army Council knew about but which the world would soon know as the Irish peace process.

PART ONE

The Dogs of War

British troops take cover from an IRA bomb attack in Belfast in the early 1970s.
(Pacemaker Press, Belfast)

ONE

Roots

The Northern Ireland state created by the Anglo-Irish war of 1919–21 and the subsequent settlement agreed by the British prime minister, Lloyd George, and Irish republican leaders was not much more than a quarter of a century old when, on October 6, 1948, Annie Adams gave birth to her first son and christened him Gerry after her husband. The centuries-old struggle for Irish independence had burst into violent guerrilla warfare between the IRA and the British just as the First World War ended, and although the rebellion was widespread and popular in a way unmatched in Irish history, it was only partially successful. When the two sides, exhausted by their bloody efforts, finally agreed to sit down and negotiate a settlement, the deal that emerged, the Treaty, as it would forever be known, eventually gave most of Ireland—twenty-six of its thirty-two counties—political freedom from Britain. But six counties, Northern Ireland, stayed British at the insistence of their large Protestant and unionist majority. By October 1948 Northern Ireland was enjoying peace, albeit an uneasy one. But trapped inside the state into which Gerry Adams was born was a significant Catholic and nationalist minority, a third of Northern Ireland's one and a half million people, whose oppressive treatment at the hands of the unionists ensured that there would always be a role for the IRA and an audience for its seditious gospel.

To say, however, that violent republicanism was the predominant sentiment among Northern Ireland's Catholics would be wrong. By far the bulk of them supported constitutionalist politicians, principally the conservative and strongly pro–Catholic Church Nationalist Party. Support for the IRA was a minority activity; membership was even more so. Nevertheless there was a republican tradition in Northern Ireland, and by the standards of early postwar Belfast the Adams family were in its blue-blood line. It was this political lineage that would ordain what the newborn Gerry Adams would do in life. As the infant Gerry grew up, he was surrounded by relatives who had fought, been jailed, and, in the case of his father, even shot for the cause of Irish freedom. The IRA—its traditions, history, and values—was imbibed with his mother's milk.

His paternal grandfather, also called Gerry, had been in the highly secretive Irish Republican Brotherhood (IRB), the forerunner of the IRA commanded by the legendary guerrilla leader Michael Collins, during the Anglo-Irish war. His father, Gerry Adams Sr., joined the IRA as a sixteen-year-old and in 1942 was sentenced to an eight-year jail term after an IRA ambush of members of the predominantly Protestant police force, the Royal Ulster Constabulary (RUC), went badly wrong and he was felled by three bullets. Two paternal uncles, Dominic and Patrick, had been interned without trial because of their IRA sympathies, one by the government in Dublin, the other by its Unionist counterpart in Belfast. For a short period prior to the Second World War, Dominic Adams had held the highest rank in the IRA, that of chief of staff, a position his nephew was later to occupy, also briefly but with much more effect.

His mother's family, the Hannaways, had a similar history. His maternal great-grandfather, Michael Hannaway, had been a member of the Fenian movement, which bombed England in the 1860s and 1870s. His grandfather, Billy Hannaway, was Eamon de Valera's election agent when the hero of the 1916 Easter Rising ran for election in West Belfast in 1918. Later he broke with him when de Valera became a constitutional politician.

Adams's mother was a member of the women's branch of the IRA, the Cumann na mBan;[1] she was a "staunch republican," her son was to write many years later.[2] Three of her brothers—Tommy, Liam, and Alfie—were IRA stalwarts in the city. Uncle Liam Hannaway was to play a crucial part in steering the young Gerry Adams toward the Provisional IRA, while Uncle Alfie, a leading light all his life in the IRA's boy scouts movement, the na Fianna Eireann, was a daily communicant at Clonard Monastery, in the heart of West Belfast, helping to establish a relationship between the Adams family and Clonard's Redemptorist priests which proved pivotal many years later when the Irish peace process began.

The Adams and Hannaway families may have been seen as republican aristocrats, but that was only among their own small rebellious circle. In the wider world they were members of a beleaguered minority that had more often tasted isolation and defeat for their dedication to Ireland's cause. In the Northern Ireland of the 1940s and 1950s very few Catholics were in the

IRA or indeed knew much about it. Many were deterred from having anything to do with it by the knowledge that any display of IRA sympathies would be sure to invite the hostile attention of the fledgling unionist government's security agencies, in particular the RUC Special Branch, a detective force that specialized in monitoring political opponents of the Protestant-dominated state.

A draconian law, called the Special Powers Act (SPA), gave the authorities exceptional powers to arrest, detain without trial, and suppress political dissent. So severe were its penalties, which included the death penalty for some firearms offenses, flogging, and the confiscation and destruction of property, that a South African prime minister during the apartheid era once famously remarked that he would swap all his emergency laws for one clause of the SPA.[3] On top of conventional forces, the first unionist government had created an armed paramilitary force, known as the B Specials, manned by thousands of pro-British Protestant supporters, which could be mobilized in emergencies to put down armed revolt. In peacetimes they kept a wary eye on their Catholic neighbors.

Unionism was an ideology that thrived on a sense of siege. Even the creation of a state whose gerrymandered border guaranteed unionists virtually permanent majority rule could not overcome a deep political psychosis. Fear of retribution from their downtrodden and disenfranchised Irish Catholic neighbors was possibly the most potent single factor in their political makeup. It had haunted the Protestants since the sixteenth and seventeenth centuries when English monarchs like Elizabeth I, anxious to create a loyal buffer in rebellious Catholic Ireland, confiscated native-held land in the northeastern part of the island nearest to Britain, in the province of Ulster, and gave it to trustworthy, loyal Protestant planters imported from Scotland and England. Deep inside, many of the planters were terrified at the thought that one day the native Irish would take their revenge and their land back, a communal dread that has survived the centuries.

The idea behind the plantation of Ulster was to make invasion of Protestant England by Catholic France or Spain via Ireland that much more difficult. It was the first expression by England that the occupation and colonization of Ireland served to advance its wider strategic and military interests. But serving England's interests created a poisonous mix of sectarian and political division that was to shape and deform Irish politics for centuries.

Even in the 1940s and 1950s, when Gerry Adams was growing up, many unionists still looked upon their Catholic fellow countrymen in much the same way as white settlers in the nineteenth- and early twentieth-century

American West had viewed the Sioux or Apache or the South African Boer his Bantu servants—that is, with a mixture of fear, guilt, ignorance, and hatred.

The actual threat that the IRA posed to the new state in Northern Ireland was more debatable, especially when the appetite for militant policies south of the Border waned and with it sympathy for the Northern nationalists' plight. Once the 1921 partition settlement had taken root, and especially as Catholic Church influence on the infant Irish Free State tightened, the commitment of Southern republicans to dismantling the Border and freeing Ireland became increasingly rhetorical. As the years passed and they developed their own set of economic and social priorities, the two states in Ireland gradually drifted apart and there was a consequent decline in Southern enthusiasm for the IRA's aims.

A key event in this journey was de Valera's decision in 1926, just five years after the Treaty had been signed, to end the IRA's armed struggle and embrace parliamentary politics. De Valera's supporters had opposed the Treaty and fought a bitter civil war against Michael Collins's forces but had been soundly beaten. Eventually de Valera persuaded most of the IRA to abandon violence—as Gerry Adams was later to do in his day—brought them into his new Fianna Fail party, and eventually entered government. A die-hard rump, from which the modern IRA sprang, refused to compromise and, accusing de Valera of betraying the freedom struggle, vowed to continue the fight. In the North, nationalists and republicans increasingly felt abandoned.

Although Fianna Fail discarded objectionable aspects of the 1921 Treaty settlement, such as the oath of allegiance to the British monarch, de Valera eventually took as tough a line against the recalcitrant IRA as any of his predecessors. The IRA was often divided and at times spectacularly incompetent, but Northern unionists liked to imagine that the IRA was a much more potent threat, that it was an organization swollen with thousands of members, armed to the teeth, just waiting for the word to attack. The truth was much more prosaic. At the time of the arrest of Gerry Adams's father, for instance, the IRA in Belfast could barely muster three hundred members and was poorly armed.[4] Even so, the unionist government did not hesitate to use its formidable powers at any sign or hint of a threat. Sometimes, such as during the "Hungry Thirties," when unemployment rates soared as high as 25 percent, the unionist government found the IRA specter a successful way of scaring its supporters away from cross-community, left-wing politics. Either way, life was made uncomfortable for those Catholics tempted to dabble in the IRA. Republican suspects were regularly arrested and occasionally interned, and detailed records kept of likely sympathizers. Parades, marches, and other expressions of support for the IRA were often banned and the organizers pursued.

Gerry Adams's father became a victim of this system in 1942 after a ban was slapped on the republican parade to Milltown cemetery in West Belfast, an annual event to remember the IRA dead of the 1916 Easter Rising in Dublin. An effort by the IRA to divert police away from the cemetery so that a brief procession could take place failed, and there was a short, sharp exchange of gunfire between the IRA men and the RUC during which one policeman was killed. The six-man IRA unit was captured and sentenced to death, but after pleas and protests, including an intervention from Pope Pius XII, only one of their number, Tom Williams, the officer commanding the unit, was hanged. When the IRA decided to protest against Williams's execution in September that year with further attacks, Gerry Adams Sr. was shot and arrested.

Those who joined the IRA faced other pressures. If they were caught and convicted, a record of their imprisonment would be stamped on their employment records, with the result that republicans often found it difficult to get work even after they had severed all links with the organization. Gerry Adams Sr. was denied entry to Australia with his family because of his prison record. Others discovered they had been declared "politically suspect" even though they had done nothing wrong.[5] Many were forced to emigrate to England or the United States or to move south to Dublin in search of a living.

Not surprisingly, involvement in the IRA was confined to a few. Nationalists in Northern Ireland may have secretly supported the aims for which the IRA fought even if they had qualms about its methods, but very few would go so far as to join. The risks and potential burdens were too great.

The result was that republican involvement tended to be an inherited rather than an acquired activity. Gerry Adams's background was a classic of its type. His parents, like those of many other republicans of this time, would pass on to their children their political views as well as a special, exclusive sense of shared suffering. The IRA in places like West Belfast, where the Adamses and Hannaways came from, grew heavily dependent on a small, often interrelated network of extended families.

West Belfast republicanism was dominated by three families: the Adamses, the Hannaways, and the Burnses. They were all intermarried, the consequence of the imprisonment of their male members. When figures like Gerry Adams Sr. emerged after having served their jail terms, they found girls of a marriageable age either already spoken for or reluctant to marry into the IRA. Inevitably they drifted into relationships with the sisters of their IRA comrades.

The family was always an iconic and powerful image for the Provisional IRA. Years later when the IRA's war with Britain raged, the organization's leaders would routinely refer to their supporters and members as "the Republican family." Later during the peace process, when Sinn Fein organized gatherings to brief supporters on the latest developments, these were called "family meetings." The image that was evoked, one of benevolent parents nurturing loving, obedient, but united children, was deliberate. And like children, the IRA's supporters were not expected to ask too many awkward questions or disobey their elders; the leadership treated those who did in much the same way as a wayward son or daughter who had offended his or her parents.

One characteristic that the young Gerry Adams did share with his non-republican Catholic contemporaries was poverty, deprivation, and the consequences of state-sponsored anti-Catholic bigotry. In the one-party state that was Northern Ireland, Catholics routinely found themselves the victims of economic and social discrimination.

Anti-Catholicism was built into the state ideology and promoted by its leaders. On occasions unionist government ministers would urge their supporters to employ, wherever possible, only "good Protestant lads and lassies."[6] One prime minister, James Craig, famously described the parliament at Stormont, an extravagant neoclassical pile set on a hillside in East Belfast, from where he ruled Northern Ireland, as "a Protestant Parliament for a Protestant state."[7] There was little or no room in the new Northern Ireland state for Catholics.

The message was reinforced by occasional sectarian violence. Riots, burning, shootings, and bombings—carried out mostly by Protestant mobs—had been a regular feature of political life in the north of Ireland since the mid-nineteenth century, when Irish nationalists first began to agitate for Home Rule and a degree of separation from Britain.

In 1912 the unionists rebelled against the British when a Liberal government at Westminster threatened to grant Ireland Home Rule. Protestant leaders recruited and, with the support of British Conservative leaders in London, organized a private army that they called the Ulster Volunteer Force and threatened to resist Home Rule by armed force facilitated by thousands of rifles smuggled into the Ulster port of Larne from Germany. The first Irish paramilitary group, the first effort to import weaponry from

Britain's enemies, came not from Irish republicans but from people who loudly proclaimed their loyalty to Britain.

The Anglo-Irish war of 1919–21 brought fresh communal violence, as did the Treaty settlement when unionists faced the problem of stabilizing their new state. Previous manifestations of nationalist rebellion, such as the bids for Irish Home Rule in the 1880s, had been met with often terrible violence, and now that Northern Ireland's political leaders were presented with the problem of constructing a political order that was opposed by up to a third of its citizens, they and their supporters in organizations such as the Orange Order turned to old, reliable methods. The early 1920s saw scores killed in riots, gun battles, and burnings; in the early 1930s violence erupted again. Catholics made up a disproportionate number of the fatalities.

Faced on the one hand by official state forces that regarded them as hostile and on the other by irregular Protestant mobs that often went on the rampage while the RUC and B Specials turned a collective blind eye, Catholics inevitably came to look on the IRA as a defensive force first and foremost.

The Northern Ireland that Gerry Adams was born into was a society in which most Catholics were at the bottom of the heap, at best tolerated, at worst regarded as a fifth column intent on undermining the state. The best-paid and most skilled jobs, such as those in the Belfast shipyards where the *Titanic* was built or in engineering factories like Shorts, went mostly to Protestants.

Years later, in the 1970s and 1980s, when official statistics were first recorded, this pattern of discrimination was confirmed. Catholics were found to be at least three times more likely to be unemployed than Protestants and disproportionately represented in the poorest-paid, least-skilled, and most insecure jobs.

To buttress their economic domination, Protestants banded together in a semisecret society known as the Orange Order. Founded in the eighteenth century by the Anglo-Irish middle classes, the Orange Order saw its primary role as resisting Catholic and radical Protestant demands for independence that were modeled on the French and American revolutions.

From the mid-nineteenth century onward industrialization transformed the north of Ireland and politics on the island as a whole. The desire to retain access to British markets fueled Protestant resistance to Irish independence, while the flood of rural Catholics into Belfast attracted by the new work opportunities brought competition with Protestants, and sectarian tensions rose.

As unionism developed into a coherent political ideology, the Orange Order, whose ranks were open only to those who had been born Protestant, acted as an umbrella under whose generous frame factory boss and factory worker could both find shelter. The order's ranks swelled. Orangeism became an instrument of sectarian division and privilege. By the end of the 1940s, when Gerry Adams was taking his first, faltering steps, no unionist politician could aspire to elected office if he or she was not a member. The prime minister and all his cabinet were usually Orangemen. Huge parades of Orangemen were held annually on the Twelfth of July. These would see tens of thousands of men wearing bowler hats and orange sashes marching in formation in Belfast and elsewhere behind military-style bands to celebrate the victory at the Battle of the Boyne by the Protestant King William over the Catholic King James in 1690. The Williamite triumph was a major event in British and European history, but by the middle of the twentieth century these annual celebrations had become archaic and incomprehensible to the outside world. They were, though, demonstrations of Protestant domination, designed to remind Catholics of their subordinate place in the political, social, and economic order.

Gerry Adams's parents were not untypical of many Catholics of the day. His mother, Annie, was a doffer, replacing spools of thread in one of the dozens of linen mills that dotted West Belfast, while his father, when he was not unemployed, was an unskilled building laborer. Although the Catholic working class was large, for the first thirty to forty years of partition the Catholic middle class was inconsequential, confined to a few thousand schoolteachers, bar owners, and lawyers who serviced mostly their own communities.

The Catholic clergy held a disproportionate sway over their flock. Once the unionist government handed over control of non-state schools to the Irish hierarchy, the Catholic Church's interest in the status quo became almost as strong as that of the unionist cabinet. Most Catholics, including the young Gerry Adams and most of his contemporaries, had little chance of rising much above their appointed place in life.

What prospect Gerry Adams did have of upward economic mobility came courtesy not of the Northern Ireland government or the Catholic Church but was due to huge political changes across the Irish Sea in postwar Britain. At the end of the war with Nazi Germany, Britain's voters turned against Winston Churchill and the Conservative Party with such determination and numbers that what happened approached a social revolution.

The Labour Party was swept into power on a platform of social equality that included the nationalization of railways, utilities, heavy industry, and coal and the provision of a free national health service. Arguably the most radical social measure was in the field of education, where college education was thrown open to working-class children. Those who were bright enough and could pass an intelligence test when they were eleven years old were streamed into an academic education. For the first time ability dictated how far children could go.

No other factor was more responsible for causing the Troubles. The Eleven Plus, as the exam became known, opened the door to the middle classes and introduced a significant element of social mobility into British society. This was also the case in Northern Ireland, but the state's Catholic population encountered an extra obstacle, the built-in systems of discrimination that had been constructed to preserve unionist privilege. As more Catholics obtained a college education, their economic, their social, and ultimately their political expectations soared. It was unionism's refusal and inability to satisfy these expectations that finally unplugged the Northern Ireland volcano.

Gerry Adams's early life, like that of his peers, was a tough one. After a brief period living with his maternal grandmother in the Falls Road in West Belfast, the family moved to the northern outskirts of the city, to Greencastle on the picturesque shores of Belfast Lough, where they rented a one-room flat. The family grew, each year bringing a new addition and added strain on living space and financial resources.

The family, which eventually numbered five boys and five girls, hankered to be back in West Belfast, where the rest of the extended Adams and Hannaway clans lived, and so in the early 1950s, and largely thanks to his mother's efforts, Gerry Adams made a move that was to have significant consequences for Irish history.

At the end of the Second World War, Belfast had a huge homeless problem. German bombers had twice raided the city but missed their economic and military targets and devastated inner-city housing estates instead. The unionist government was forced to build public housing projects, and it was into one of these, a sprawling estate known as Ballymurphy on the slopes of the hills overlooking West Belfast, that the Adams family moved.

Home at 11 Divismore Park, Ballymurphy, gave the growing Gerry Adams much-needed social stability, comfort, and welcome contact with family as well as a new circle of friends. But it was also to provide him less than two decades later with a base that he would use first to dominate the IRA in West Belfast, next the city, and then the entire organization. If Annie Adams had not insisted on making the move to Ballymurphy, the IRA might

...ave been led by Gerry Adams, and Irish history would now look very different.

His parents were conscious of the opportunities offered by the Eleven Plus, and they encouraged their eldest son to sit for the exam. At the second attempt he passed and was granted a place at the boys-only St. Mary's Christian Brothers Grammar School, situated on what was then the more affluent fringe of West Belfast. Most St. Mary's boys were expected to stay at school until the age of eighteen and would be encouraged to go on to college or enter a profession. The Adams family's hopes for Gerry Jr. were naturally high. Family photographs of the day show a gangly, if not awkward, teenager whose thick spectacle frames reinforced a bookish image.

But the family's hopes were to be dashed. By 1964 he was flirting with republican politics and had helped campaign for the Sinn Fein candidate during an election in West Belfast, the highlight of which was two days of stone-throwing between RUC riot squads and local nationalists and republicans, including the adolescent Gerry Adams.

Adams's studies suffered, and by Easter 1964 he was at the bottom of the class.[8] With many contemporaries in Ballymurphy already working and a growing number of mouths to feed at home, he left St. Mary's in early 1965 and took a job as a bartender, first in a Catholic-owned pub on the Loyalist Shankill Road and then in one of Belfast's most famous hostelries, the Duke of York, home at the time to what passed for the city's artistic and left-wing intelligentsia.

A year later, when he reached eighteen, Adams's career in the IRA began. He was sworn in to D Company (D Coy) of the Belfast Brigade, the unit his father had belonged to and whose members came from the Falls Road and West Belfast.[9] Within six years D Coy was to be known as one of the most ferocious and active units in the emerging Provisional IRA, earning its members the nickname "the Dogs," after "the dogs of war."

Adams had chosen a period of tumult within the Republican movement to join the IRA. Always prone to ideological, military, and personality disputes, the IRA was again on the verge of a bitter and bloody split when the Belfast officer commanding took Gerry Adams through the IRA oath and welcomed him into D Coy.

The history of the IRA both before and after it tasted defeat in the 1921–23 Irish civil war is essentially the story of military failure followed by retreat and introspection. After each reverse the remnants of the IRA would divide into two camps, those who retreated to their firesides and dreamed of better days to come and a second chance to take up the gun and bomb, and those who advocated a new and radical change of direction. Invariably that would involve advocating heresies, usually that the IRA should ditch its almost mystical distaste for parliamentary politics, and an internal row, possibly a split, would follow.

Virtually every twentieth-century republican leader had trodden this path. Michael Collins walked down it, and Eamon de Valera did as well. So too would Gerry Adams, although in circumstances that were to make the efforts of Collins and de Valera appear amateurish and clumsy.

After the 1921 Treaty the IRA divided into those who stayed loyal to Michael Collins and those who supported Eamon de Valera, and a bitter civil war followed. The split was not caused by the partition of Ireland. The Treaty had set up the Boundary Commission to draw the borders of the new Northern Ireland state, and even anti-Treatyites firmly believed that when nationalist areas were removed from the six partitioned counties, as the British had implied during the Treaty negotiations, the truncated remnant would not be viable and the new state would collapse into their hands.

The Treaty had imposed on members of the new Irish parliament and the "Free State" government an obligation to swear an oath of allegiance to the British crown, and it was this that divided the IRA. Collins's men argued that the oath did not matter. Ireland had secured the freedom to achieve freedom, bit by bit, county by county, and that was all that mattered. Predictably his supporters became known as stepping-stoners. De Valera eventually agreed to sign the oath but claimed this was not the same as swearing it, an elasticity of attitude to such matters that Gerry Adams was to imitate and incorporate wholesale into his own peace process strategy.

The resulting Irish civil war was an unequal battle. Armed by Britain and facing an opposition that hesitated to strike the first decisive blow, Collins's "Staters" put the IRA on the defensive almost from the beginning. The war was over by 1923. The IRA leadership, on de Valera's urging, ordered its members to dump arms.

Three years later "Dev" abandoned military methods. He resigned from Sinn Fein and announced the setting up of a constitutional republican party known as Fianna Fail, or Soldiers of Destiny, a name that was chosen to appeal to the militarist tradition from which the party sprang.

The vast bulk of the IRA followed de Valera, and IRA units were transformed almost overnight into Fianna Fail branches, or *cumainn*. Those who rejected Fianna Fail did not like what they saw but were confused about what to do. Some were content to wait and see whether or not de Valera did deliver on the republican rhetoric, especially after election victories brought the party to power. Others, like Peadar O'Donnell, argued that republicans should eschew establishment politics, move to the left, and take up radical social and economic policies. Many IRA men who thought as O'Donnell did later went to Spain to fight against Franco.

At first de Valera welcomed IRA support, not least because the civil war had left deep divisions in Irish society. Trust was hard to find, old civil war enmities simmered just beneath the surface, and Fianna Fail needed friends wherever it could get them. But the alliance was to be short-lived. In 1932 de Valera won enough seats to form a coalition government, and within four years he moved against the IRA and declared it an illegal organization.

By this stage the IRA was once again turning its attention to the older enemy. The British had reneged on promises made in 1921 when the Boundary Commission was set up. In a majority report the commission brushed aside nationalist concerns and recommended that all six partitioned counties be incorporated in the new Northern Ireland state, and the fledgling administration in Dublin had little option but to acquiesce. The decision made the new entity a viable one but at the cost of sowing the seeds of future conflict. Nearly half a million Catholics and nationalists, a third of the population, had been forced against their will into a state with which they did not identify and whose leaders were openly hostile to them.

Nationalist Ireland was unsure about what tactics to adopt. De Valera's answer was to turn up the rhetorical heat. He drafted a new constitution in 1937 which set the goal of reuniting Ireland in legal stone. Physical-force republicans advocated a more traditional approach and urged renewed war against the British but not against de Valera. The IRA ended its conflict with the Southern state. It was a seminal development because it started a process that eventually led to the IRA's formally recognizing the Southern state and then participating in its institutions. From then on, the main goal of the IRA was to get the British out of the North rather than to eject the impostors in Dublin.

By 1939 the IRA felt confident enough to declare war against Britain, and under the leadership of Sean Russell, a veteran of the 1916 Rising and an opponent of O'Donnell's socialism, a bombing campaign was launched. As republicans had done before the 1916 Rising, lines were opened with Germany, whose Nazi leaders were themselves at war with Britain. Although the IRA hoped for all sorts of assistance, little came of the relationship.

The Forties Campaign, as the IRA's war came to be called, forced its own split. Sean MacBride, son of the legendary Maude Gonne MacBride and himself a former chief of staff, broke with Russell. When the Second World

War ended, the future Nobel laureate quit the IRA and formed his own political party, Clann na Poblachta, which enjoyed considerable, but brief, electoral and political success.

The IRA was the author of its own defeat in the Forties Campaign. In the sort of botched operation that would play such a crucial role in the modern peace process, a bombing in Coventry in the English Midlands at the start of the campaign went badly wrong, and five civilians were killed and another sixty wounded. At around the same time the IRA in Dublin raided the Irish army's weapons reserves and, much to its own surprise, netted a dozen truckloads of guns and one million rounds of ammunition, most of which the IRA promptly lost when the police discovered their hiding place.

The Coventry debacle roused the English police, which used harsh methods against IRA suspects, while the Dublin arms raid permitted de Valera the political space to seek emergency powers, which he used to intern IRA leaders. De Valera was concerned that the IRA's attacks on Britain and its overtures to Hitler's Nazis could give the British the excuse to force him to take Britain's side in the "Emergency," as the Irish government termed the Second World War. Chief of Staff Russell had journeyed to Germany in a bid to get arms and other assistance from the Nazis, while the Germans hoped to use the IRA network to facilitate espionage operations against the British. It was just the sort of activity that gave de Valera nightmares, but luckily for him the Germans had grossly overestimated the IRA's capabilities and virtually all the spies they sent to Ireland were exposed and arrested. Russell meanwhile died during a journey on board a German submarine not long after the Coventry bombing, and the IRA campaign soon petered out. By 1945 the IRA had effectively ceased to exist. Its structures and leadership had evaporated. Not even a membership list had survived the defeat. For a short while it seemed as if the long history of violent Irish republicanism had come to an end.

But the movement was not quite extinguished. By 1947, after a slow, painful reconstruction effort, the IRA was showing signs of revival. Structures were rebuilt and a leadership of veterans, headed by the new chief of staff, Tony Magan, put in place. Recruitment was under way, as was training in the hills outside Dublin, and a monthly newspaper was being published. A year later, in 1948, the year of Gerry Adams's birth, the IRA was large enough to hold a Convention, the gathering of IRA representatives that the organization's constitution decrees exerts supreme authority over its policies, ideas, and military direction.

The Convention decided that Oglaigh na hEireann, as its own members called the IRA, was to make plans for a new military campaign to end the

British occupation of Northern Ireland. There would be no repeat of the mistakes of the Forties Campaign, its leaders determined; this time the campaign would be in the North itself, not in Britain.

It was at this point that the IRA leadership took another small but significant step toward accepting the existence and legitimacy of the southern Irish state, whose creation it had once declared illegal. It forbade units from making any attacks on the Irish police, the Garda Siochana, or any other military forces of the state, for fear that Dublin government reprisals would undermine the offensive against Northern Ireland. The IRA's ruling body, the seven-man Army Council, issued General Army Order no. 8, forbidding such military action. From then on the South was to be the IRA's logistical base, while the North would be the war zone.

Preparations for the campaign began with a series of arms raids in Northern Ireland and Britain. In 1955 came a sign that Northern nationalists might be receptive to an IRA campaign when, in the midst of agitation over the arrest of suspected IRA activists, two republicans, one of them an IRA man imprisoned for his part in an unsuccessful arms raid, were elected to the Westminster parliament. The Nationalist Party had stood aside to give Sinn Fein a free run, and overall the republicans won 152,000 votes, an unprecedented level of support, which the politicized Adams movement took twenty years of political work and a major ideological U-turn to better.

Thus boosted, the IRA campaign, code-named Operation Harvest but known popularly ever since as the Border Campaign, began in earnest. In December 1956 a series of cross-Border raids on security and government installations signaled the start. The campaign was strictly limited to areas outside Belfast. The IRA leadership feared that the city's Catholic population was vulnerable to Protestant attack and might be held hostage by the unionist government for the IRA's good behavior elsewhere. In practice IRA actions were confined to the Border counties of Fermanagh, Tyrone, and Armagh.

The Northern authorities introduced internment within days of the first acts of violence, while the Gardai harassed the IRA leadership unmercifully. By mid-1957 de Valera was back in power, and when an RUC officer was killed in an IRA booby trap bomb in Tyrone, he introduced internment and later set up military tribunals that handed out draconian sentences. More seriously for the IRA, the public support evident in 1955 failed to materialize on the ground. The bulk of Northern Ireland Catholics simply ignored the IRA's call to arms.

The Border Campaign limped on for a further five years but was effectively over at that point. In February 1962 the IRA leadership finally acknowledged defeat, ordered its units to dump arms, and admitted the great part played by Northern nationalist indifference to the campaign in the decision to end hostilities.

Twelve people had been killed in the 1956–62 campaign; six were RUC members and six IRA men. Another thirty-eight people—civilians, IRA men, and Northern security personnel—were wounded.[10] At the time unionists were alarmed at this level of IRA activity, but by the standards of the coming conflict it was a tame affair. In 1972, for instance, the worst single year of the Troubles, the entire casualty list for the five-year Border Campaign could be compressed into an average ten-day period.

Exhausted and demoralized, republicans retreated once more. Most quit and took up normal lives, but others returned to the fray determined to rescue something out of the wreckage of defeat. Among them was a forty-six-year-old Dublin painter and decorator called Cathal Goulding, who had several qualifications for leadership. He was one of the small number of IRA men who in 1945 had met in Dublin and agreed to start the slow process of rebuilding the IRA from the ashes of the Forties Campaign, and he was possibly the most enthusiastic of the group. A good friend of the playwright Brendan Behan, with whose widow he was later to father a child, he had a family background that was impeccable from a republican standpoint. His father had "been out" in the 1916 Rising, while his grandfather had been a Fenian revolutionary.

Goulding had also proved his mettle. In 1953 he led a high-profile raid on a British army base in Felsted, Essex, in southeast England, along with the Derry IRA man Manus Canning and a London-based ex-RAF member, Sean MacStiofain, who was later to become the first chief of staff of the Provisional IRA. The raid netted a huge haul of weaponry but so loaded down the men's getaway van that a routine police patrol became suspicious and stopped them. They were later sentenced to eight years' imprisonment each. Goulding was released in 1959 and returned to rejoin the IRA's Army Council and become its quartermaster. But because he had been in an English jail in the early years of the Border Campaign when the most serious setbacks were suffered, he escaped blame for its dismal failure. As a neutral figure amid factions fighting in the ruins of a failed war, Goulding became, in 1962, the IRA's new chief of staff.

The collapse of the Border Campaign provided a major punctuation mark in the history and development of the IRA. In the space of forty years the organization's fortunes had ebbed and flowed. At its peak the IRA enjoyed the backing of a majority of the Irish people, and it had fought a long and bloody campaign, which had brought the British to the negotiating table. But that brief success was followed by division, civil war, and disillusionment while the numbers remaining true to the faith of Pearse and Connolly dwindled, as did public support for and even tolerance of the IRA's activities. The two partitionist states continued to glower at each other across a heavily militarized border, but they also grew roots and developed their own legitimacy. As they did, the IRA was forced to slowly soften and even abandon its hostility to the Southern state and shift the emphasis of its conflict with the Treaty settlement to the existence of Northern Ireland. The Forties Campaign had failed miserably to shift Britain's support for the unionist state, and then the Border Campaign had disintegrated in the face of Northern nationalist indifference. Smarting from failure and lacking any clear sense of future direction, the IRA in 1962 was at a crossroads.

REPUBLICAN ACTIVISTS surveying the scene at the dawn of the sixties would have seen little to be cheerful about. As the prisoners were released from the internment camp at the Curragh just west of Dublin and from Crumlin Road jail in Belfast, they returned to communities whose indifference to their fate was as pronounced as it ever had been. The internees and sentenced men had hoped for and some even expected popular demonstrations and protests when they were arrested, but there were none, just as there were no crowds to stage welcome-home celebrations upon their release. The depth of demoralization could be measured by the numbers who had agreed to "sign out" from prison as the Border Campaign petered out, men who had given their hated jailers written promises never to take up arms in the IRA's cause again in return for their freedom. And of those who did not become "signees," as they were termed, a similar number voted with their feet and refused to report back for duty. The hearths to which many of the IRA retreated after 1962 were cold and lonely places to dream of what yet might be. Few of the released IRA men, surely, could have imagined that in just seven years Ireland would be plunged into the most violent cataclysm in its history.

The 1960s were a period of change for Ireland as for the rest of the Western world. Although the Cold War still raged, other and older enmities were fading. In the United States, John F. Kennedy conquered what many feared was an overwhelming prejudice to become the first ever Catholic president. In Rome fundamental reform was under way. Under the radical leadership of Pope John XXIII the Catholic Church had opened a dialogue with the Church of England, and in 1961 the pontiff met its head, Queen

Elizabeth II, whose ancestors had led the English Reformation. Religious ecumenism began to flourish.

In Ireland ancient enmities appeared to be softening too. In 1963 Lord Basil Brookeborough, the conservative, diehard defender of unionism, finally retired and was succeeded by a young Anglo-Irish aristocrat, Captain Terence O'Neill, who could trace his lineage back to sixteenth-century landowners. Despite this conventional, establishment background, modernizing reform was also on his agenda.

In both parts of Ireland the new postwar realities were beginning to make their impact. In the North old traditional industries like linen and shipbuilding were in decline, and their replacement was a matter of urgency. The Northern Ireland government was forced to turn to the outside world for new investment. The need for political stability and the requirement to present a less distasteful image to foreign investors—which in practice meant building bridges to the nationalist community—acquired a new if unfamiliar importance.

O'Neill was also aware that there was now a Labour government in London that was more likely to listen sympathetically to nationalist complaints of discrimination and human rights abuses. Slowly, gingerly, and with frequent glances over their shoulders at their own hard-line grassroots, some unionists began to reach out to Catholics.

O'Neill's approach infuriated hard-line Protestants, but it was resented by some nationalists, who called it cosmetic, patronizing, and at times insulting. On one famous occasion he explained his approach in almost racist terms:

> It is frightfully hard to explain to Protestants that if you give Roman Catholics a good job and a good house they will live like Protestants because they will see neighbours with cars and television sets. They will refuse to have eighteen children but if a Roman Catholic is jobless and lives in the most ghastly hovel he will rear eighteen children on national assistance. . . . If you treat Roman Catholics with due consideration and kindness they will live like Protestants, in spite of the authoritarian nature of the Church.[11]

Nevertheless many Catholics welcomed O'Neill's conciliatory policies, and hope of real change was in the air. The Southern state was also in transformation. The era of de Valera ended in 1959 with his retirement as taoiseach, and he was succeeded by another, albeit younger, veteran of the

1916 Rising, Sean Lemass, who quickly discarded Dev's protectionist economics in favor of attracting foreign investment. The era of the technocrat, North and South, had arrived.

The two governments in Ireland were on a similar course, and it made sense for them to examine ways of improving cooperation. In 1965 the political ice cracked when O'Neill invited Lemass to Stormont and a month later made a return trip to Dublin. The journeys continued when Jack Lynch succeeded Lemass as Irish prime minister.

Throughout the continent of Europe, a wave of liberalism brought new power to the Left in a way that had not been seen since the 1930s. In Britain a dozen years of uninterrupted Conservative rule were brought to an end when Labour's Harold Wilson swept into power on a ticket of economic modernization. In Ireland the Left made gains in both jurisdictions. The Northern Ireland Labour Party was winning seats to Stormont, while in the South the Labour Party was shedding its conservative Catholic image and beginning to talk more openly of the merits of socialism.

In Europe, as a whole, moves were afoot to dismantle economic borders and to bury old hatreds. Inspired by the American civil rights movement and the excitement brought on by an era of unprecedented sexual liberation, among other factors, the movement toward the left grew increasingly strong.

And that is certainly what Cathal Goulding discerned. Under his leadership the IRA made the most radical and determined move to the left in its history, embracing a doctrinaire Marxist analysis of Northern and Southern Irish politics that would eventually split the organization and spark the most violent upheaval in modern Irish history. The manner in which Goulding failed to take a united republican movement down his chosen path was to provide Gerry Adams with one invaluable lesson when he made his own very similar journey some twenty years later. Preventing the sort of split that destroyed Goulding's hopes became a strategic imperative for Adams.

The greatest obstacle blocking Goulding was the immense conservatism of the Republican movement. Overwhelmingly rural and lower middle class in their makeup, most IRA members were people of a traditional Catholic outlook. This was reflected in the rituals and the ways in which the IRA was organized, many of which had changed little in forty years.

Men and women, for instance, were still segregated into separate military units, as they had been in 1916 when Patrick Pearse sent out a female Irish Volunteer from the GPO in Dublin with a white flag of surrender to present to the British army. The IRA of the 1960s, like Irish society at large, was slow to accept gender equality. The IRA had always been an exclusively male organization, and its members were the soldiers who did the actual fighting when there was any to be done. The women were organized into the Cumann na mBan (Women's Group), with their own distinct structures and leadership. Their role was the IRA equivalent of being stuck in the kitchen and the bedroom; they carried messages and smuggled weapons and explosives and they nursed wounded IRA Volunteers. They could be useful for gathering intelligence and carrying weapons, but they did very little, if any, actual fighting. Nor did they play any part in the formulation of IRA policy or strategy. That was a male preserve, the privilege of the seven-man Army Council, to which Cumann na mBan was subservient.

Catholic Church ritual permeated IRA ceremonials. It was commonplace for a decade of the rosary to be said, often in Irish, at the start of IRA ceremonies, such as the annual Easter commemorations of those who were killed in the Rising of 1916 and other phases of the struggle. It would be difficult to imagine a more effective way of confirming unionist prejudices about the IRA.

Most IRA members had a simplistic set of motives for joining. They believed that only armed force could remove the British from Ireland and that people who advocated parliamentary methods had sold out the struggle. As one commentator put it, "To go into the Dail [the Irish parliament], to seize power, was not only an invitation to corruption, a tainted tactic already proven sterile, but also, and most important, outrageous immorality."[12]

Their history was full of examples of IRA leaders who had abandoned physical force for parliamentarism, yet had failed to force the British out of Ireland, North or South. They viewed with suspicion, therefore, the motives of any who advocated such a course. As one account put it, "They believed no one ever went into politics except a failed revolutionary."[13] Their opposition was not just practical but almost spiritual as well.

The only parliament to which they gave allegiance had by the 1960s long since disappeared. That was the Irish parliament of 1921, the so-called Second Dail, the last gathering of representatives chosen in a pre-Treaty, all-Ireland, thirty-two-county election. The Second Dail had a Sinn Fein majority elected on a platform of support for the 1916 Easter proclamation of independence, and republicans regarded the mandate as almost sacred. Although the Second Dail later voted narrowly for the Treaty, it became an article of faith among the recalcitrant IRA that no other parliament, no other government, could claim the legitimacy bestowed on that parliament. After the Treaty was endorsed, the Second Dail ceased to exist as far the

IRA was concerned, and its partitionist successor, the Northern parliament at Stormont as well as the new parliament in Dublin, was regarded as illegal.

The rump of the Second Dail, those surviving TDs who had voted against the Treaty, were deemed to be the only legitimate government of Ireland, but they were dying off, year by year. In 1938 the dozen or so survivors passed on their authority to the IRA's Army Council to safeguard until all the people of Ireland could again freely choose their own government. To the outside world it may have looked absurd, but it was on this basis that the IRA leadership framed its claim to be the sovereign government of Ireland.

Because of this, one of the most hallowed principles of traditional republicanism was the refusal to recognize or take seats in either Stormont or the Dail. It followed that any republican who betrayed this principle was implicitly recognizing the Treaty and by so doing betraying the Irish people and all those IRA men and women who had laid down their lives in the fight to free Ireland. The logic of all this was that republicans had to deny legitimacy to the other institutions of the state as well. Republicans refused, for example, to ask either police force in Ireland for permission to parade or raise funds. IRA standing orders forbade prisoners from entering a plea in criminal courts—that was the same as recognizing the state—although an exception was made when IRA men faced a capital charge. Abstentionism was the defining characteristic of Irish republicanism, and it was written in legal stone in the constitutions of both the IRA and Sinn Fein. Any IRA or Sinn Fein TD or MP who took his or her seat in a partitionist body or even suggested discussing the idea would be liable to automatic dismissal or expulsion.

These were the uncomfortable realities that faced Goulding and the small number of radical advisers and confidants he had gathered around him. And it was the left-wing background of this coterie that produced the first signs of internal unrest. With the IRA laid low after the Border Campaign, Goulding had turned to new men and new ideas for inspiration. There was already a sentiment in favor of moving leftward. IRA prisoners in the North's largest jail, Crumlin Road in Belfast, had produced a journal called *Saoirse* (Freedom) under the editorship of a young County Cork militant called Daithi O Conaill, which had published an article, "Quo Vadis Hibernia?" ("Whither Ireland?"), advocating involvement in social and economic agitation.[14] Not for the first or last time prison was a crucible in the development of IRA politics.

The move to the left accelerated in 1963 when two radical intellectuals put their stamp on the movement. One was a young computer scientist called Roy Johnston, who had returned to Dublin from England, where he had been prominent in the Communist Party of Great Britain–linked Connolly Association. The other was Anthony Coughlan, a young lecturer at that most Anglo-Irish of bastions, Trinity College, Dublin, who had been national organizer of the Connolly Association in Britain.

The Connolly Association members had been urging on the IRA what they called "a new departure" prior to the 1962 cease-fire. Long before Johnston and Coughlan were able to exercise direct influence over Goulding, their program had been spelled out. One chronicler of the period wrote, "[The IRA was] advised to work through a broad alliance for the displacement of the Unionist regime and for political democracy in the North and for social progress . . . in the South. They were also advised to end their abstentionism and seek to work through parliamentary institutions."[15]

Johnston, who was quickly appointed to the IRA's Army Council by Goulding as a sort of political adviser cum commissar, was the inspiration for the establishment of a debating society named after the eighteenth-century Protestant founder of modern Irish republicanism, Wolfe Tone. With branches in the main universities and in Belfast and Dublin, the Wolfe Tone clubs discussed and advanced the Connolly Association's agenda. Left-wing veterans like Peadar O'Donnell and George Gilmore re-emerged from obscurity to contribute to the debate.

The political program developed by Johnston and Coughlan was borrowed directly from a former Soviet leader, none other than Joseph Stalin, who had died a decade before. Called the "stages theory," it mapped out a rigid, dogmatic path to Irish socialism in which Ireland would pass through three distinct phases before reaching the goal of a workers republic.

The first would be the creation of a normal liberal, parliamentary democracy in the North, which would be achieved through agitation on civil rights issues. The employer class in the North would cooperate with this, since it was in its economic interests to do so, and, Johnston predicted, there would be growing working-class Protestant and Catholic cooperation and unity as workers realized how much their interests coincided. In the second phase, revolutionary links would stretch across the Border as radicalized and increasingly united Northern workers would make common cause with their Southern counterparts, who themselves were being radicalized by Sinn Fein agitation. The third phase would be revolution and final victory.

It followed that clinging to abstentionism was an absurdity. How could Sinn Fein hope to relate to the social and economic problems of the Irish working class, Johnston and his allies asked, as long as it refused to address those problems in the only forums available to Irish workers, their parliaments and governments? The people accepted the partitionist arrangements, and so should the IRA, they urged.

The "new departure" had implications for the IRA and the direction of its armed struggle. Gradually the emphasis of its activities shifted to economic and social agitation and away from the traditional goal of waging war against Britain. The IRA and Sinn Fein became involved in rural cooperatives, and in Dublin they set up a housing action committee that staged sit-ins to highlight poor living conditions and overcrowding.

A campaign was launched against foreign ownership of mining and fishing rights. The IRA organized illegal "fish-ins" on exclusive salmon runs in the west of Ireland and offered manpower to help striking workers. Foreign landowners, mostly Germans, were targeted and buildings torched. In Limerick the IRA burned a bus transporting strikebreakers to an American-owned company. In Kerry a foreign-owned lobster boat was sunk.

Some twenty years later Roy Johnston explained the reasoning behind the leftward shift: "The idea was that if links could be cultivated between the movement and the people, the roots would be firmly in the ground and a principled, political stand would be made, even in 'illegal assemblies' such as Leinster House [the Dail] without automatic corruption."[16]

While all this naturally alarmed the Fianna Fail governments of Sean Lemass and his successor Jack Lynch, the implication was that the need to wage armed struggle against Britain had moved farther and farther down the IRA's list of priorities. That meant downgrading the IRA itself, and when the split finally came there were bitter accusations from his critics that the Goulding leadership had deliberately run down the organization, dismantling command structures, discouraging or diverting promising recruits, scaling down training, and—worst of all—diminishing the IRA's stores of weapons.

The logic of the "stages theory" was that if Northern Protestants were going to cooperate in the democratization of their own state, then the idea that Catholics needed arms to defend themselves against the Protestants was nonsense. Weapons acquisition, once a priority for the IRA, was virtually abandoned. Money that would have been earmarked for this was devoted instead to political activities.

The last defining characteristic of the Johnston-Goulding strategy was the notion that all this could best be achieved if the IRA and Sinn Fein cooperated and perhaps even merged with similarly minded, progressive political parties. It was the classic broad-front strategy so beloved of left-wing groups: Johnston and his associates called it the National Liberation Front

(NLF), a term with echoes of the Vietnamese resistance then beginning to radicalize American youth. The other members of the NLF, at least those mentioned most often as candidates for partnership, were the Communist Party of Northern Ireland, its Southern counterpart, the Irish Workers Party, the Connolly Association, and the Connolly Youth Movement. It was this proposal which fixed the notion in conservative, dissident minds that the IRA was being slowly taken over by godless Marxists.

And there was resistance to the Johnston agenda. The IRA had always distrusted outsiders, especially those preaching foreign ideas. Most of its members were God-fearing, Mass-attending Catholics who had been reared in an Ireland thoroughly dominated by a deeply conservative Catholic Church. It was, though, the manner in which Goulding pursued the Johnston-Coughlan strategy that finally fractured the IRA as much as the ideology he and his supporters espoused. He made two fatal errors. First, he tried to push his ideas onto the IRA at too early a stage. Not only did he not have enough support before he moved; he had failed to isolate his opponents first. Gerry Adams would never make this basic error. Goulding moved too early, and when he met failure his frustration grew and propelled him into confrontation with his opponents. That was his second mistake— and Adams learned from that too.

Having decided upon a strategy of open confrontation, Goulding set the stage for a series of damaging rows within the IRA during the mid-1960s that were destined to end in a damaging and, as it turned out, bloody split. The battles were fought at IRA Conventions and at Sinn Fein's annual conferences as Goulding and his allies attempted to push through the Johnston-Coughlan agenda, only to find their way blocked by traditionalists and conservatives. Rebellious branches, particularly in rural areas, were expelled, as at one stage was the entire branch of the women's IRA, the Cumann na mBan. Frustrated at failure, Goulding turned to tactics that sometimes verged on the ludicrous. At one point he expanded the Army Council from seven to twenty members in a bid to secure a majority for his policy. The normally highly secretive body, which went to great lengths to hide its meetings from the authorities, was now so large that it almost had to hire a hall for its gatherings.

Of the Council's usual seven members, Goulding could count on the support of only three. On his side were Sean Garland, a fellow Dublin republican and a hard-line Johnston supporter, and the quixotic County Wicklow republican Seamus Costello. Opposing him were Ruairi O Bradaigh (Rory O'Brady), a County Roscommon schoolteacher who had been chief of staff when the Border Campaign ended in 1962; Daithi O Conaill, who had been badly wounded in County Tyrone during the campaign; and Sean MacStiofain, Goulding's IRA comrade on the ill-fated Felsted arms raid in 1953 and the IRA's then director of intelligence. Between them, holding the balance of power and uncertain as to his sympathies, was Tomas MacGiolla, the lofty president of Sinn Fein who doubled as chairman of the Army Council. He did not finally throw in his lot with Goulding until the summer of 1969.

Goulding and his allies resorted increasingly to the tactic of purging their enemies. Senior Northern IRA figures were forced out or left in disgust at the tactics being used against their friends. Among them were men who would play key roles in the formation of the rival Provisional IRA a few years later, characters like Jimmy Steele, who had spent twenty years in jail for IRA activity, and Sean Keenan from Derry, a republican stalwart for years. With other Belfast men who had left or were eased out during this period—people like Joe Cahill, Jimmy Drumm, Billy McKee, the Kellys of North Belfast, the Hannaways, and Seamus Twomey—they were to form the core of a bitter opposition just biding their time to strike back at Goulding. If Adams learned another lesson from all this, it was to divide and discredit opponents lest they unite against him.

It was into this maelstrom of conflicting political ideas and personalities that Gerry Adams plunged when he joined the Belfast IRA's D Company, although for a while it did not impinge much on his life. As he was to say himself many years later, all this ferment was "going on, if you like, above my head."[17] He was only sixteen when he joined the republican movement, and the debate within it was taking place far away, at leadership level and mostly in Dublin, where the IRA policymakers were based. But within four or five years events were to force Adams to take sides in their quarrel, and that decision would have unforeseeable consequences for Anglo-Irish politics.

The failure of the Border Campaign had set the scene for the tragedy that has always befallen Irish republicanism in the aftermath of defeat, when the ambitions of those who were convinced that fresh directions had to be taken clashed with the stubborn belief of others that change and compromise were indistinguishable and that deviating from principle meant devaluing the sacrifices of dead comrades. And so it was as the 1960s unfolded; the IRA was on the verge of another rupture.

IDEOLOGICAL, generational, and personality differences had set the scene for internal republican division, but they were not the only factors at work. Beyond the control of the IRA's leaders, beyond the control even of its unionist governors, social and economic change was remolding Northern Ireland and in the process creating the circumstances that would bring political instability. Two factors in particular destabilized Northern Ireland in the 1960s and helped plunge it into the most violent and sustained conflict in Irish history.

The first and most damaging development was the furious reaction within unionism to the moderate reformism of Prime Minister Terence O'Neill. This took three forms. Some within O'Neill's Ulster Unionist Party saw his modernizing policies as a threat to the union with Britain and argued that softening hostility to nationalists was a fatal weakness, while others saw the turbulence as providing the opportunity to snatch the prime minister's crown from his head.

The second group coalesced around the powerful, hectoring frame of the Reverend Ian Paisley, a young Protestant street preacher with political ambitions who combined a fundamentalist biblical view of the world and a hatred for the Roman Catholic Church with a fiery opposition to all things ecumenical, religious, and political. Paisley's oratorical skills made him a formidable opponent. He could sway a mob with a few well-chosen words. He also represented a virulent strain within unionism that could trace its roots back over a hundred years, to Belfast street preachers who would regularly incite crowds to riot, burn, and kill their Catholic neighbors.

Paisley's violent rhetoric had a similar effect in the Belfast of the 1960s. On the Shankill Road in North Belfast, one of the city's toughest loyalist areas, a group of men led by a former British soldier called Gusty Spence met to form a paramilitary group they called the Ulster Volunteer Force (UVF), after the huge private Protestant army that early unionist leaders like Edward Carson had mobilized in 1912 to resist Home Rule. Convinced that the IRA was planning a new violent campaign to mark the fiftieth anniversary of the Easter Rising, in 1966, and inspired by Paisley's oratory, Spence's UVF launched a pre-emptive strike.

They aimed to kill IRA leaders but, like their counterparts when the Troubles intensified, were content to accept any Catholic target. By the summer of 1966 they had killed three times. One victim was a seventy-seven-year-old Protestant widow who died when a gasoline bomb intended for a Catholic-owned pub engulfed her house instead. Another was a tipsy twenty-eight-year-old Catholic pedestrian shot dead on the street; like so many of the victims of the oncoming Troubles, he happened to be in the wrong place at the wrong time. The third was an eighteen-year-old Catholic barman, Peter Ward, who had the misfortune of choosing a Shankill Road bar frequented by Spence and his colleagues for an after-work drink with friends. The deaths were the peals of thunder that foretold the impending storm.

Unionist and Protestant reaction was mirrored by Catholic and nationalist assertiveness. By the early and mid-1960s that new mood, fueled by a growing educated and frustrated middle class, took two forms. On the one hand Catholics began to participate in a state that they had initially boycotted. The first sign of this came in 1965 when, in response to the O'Neill-Lemass meetings, the Northern Nationalist Party entered the Stormont parliament for the first time since 1930 and became the official opposition, a step that signified recognition to the Northern Ireland state.

The other sign of the new mood was an increasing willingness of Catholics to stand up and demand their rights. Although Catholic and nationalist politics had been characterized for many years by meekness in the face of unionist strength, some in that community were well aware that they were the victims of discrimination in jobs and public housing. In the 1960s they set about compiling the evidence. The Campaign for Social Justice was started by a County Tyrone doctor and his former teacher wife, Con and Patricia McCluskey. Their research showed that Catholics were hugely underrepresented in places like the central and local government civil service. Soon the idea was mooted of setting up a civil rights body based on the NAACP in the United States, which had fought for the rights of blacks.

In 1967 the Northern Ireland Civil Rights Association (NICRA) was formally launched at a public meeting in Belfast and drew up a list of reforms. Its most important demand was for the scrapping of a rule that restricted to property owners the right to vote in elections to the local councils. The rules gave some businessmen, most of them unionists, up to six votes, while thousands of working-class Catholics, who did not own their homes, were disenfranchised. The councils exercised considerable power. Not only did they give employment, but they were responsible for building public housing projects. That meant they could decide who, Protestant or Catholic, got decent public housing.

NICRA also sought the scrapping of gerrymandered electoral wards that, in places like Derry, Northern Ireland's second city, gave unionists control over the local council even though the Protestants who voted for them were in a minority. The disbanding of the B Specials and the removal of the Special Powers Act, the law that gave the unionist government unprecedented powers and a points list for public housing, completed the roll call of reforms demanded. Significantly none of NICRA's demands touched directly on the existence of the Border. Composed of a mixture of liberal and radical opinion, NICRA's leadership had a simple attitude: if Nationalists were obliged to be British citizens, then they should have British rights.

These stirrings soon showed themselves on the streets. In June 1968 republicans in Caledon, County Tyrone, organized a sit-in at a house allocated by the local council to the unmarried secretary of a local unionist politician, and they demanded that poorly housed Catholic families take precedence. The protest drew wider publicity when a Nationalist MP at Stormont, Austin Currie, joined the sit-in. Two months later NICRA helped organize a protest march from the nearby nationalist village of Coalisland to Dungannon, Tyrone's largest town, where protesters found their way blocked by a flag-waving crowd of Paisley supporters.

Standing up to demand community rights also meant that nationalists were more and more ready to resort to physical force to defend themselves. The early part of the 1960s had seen two examples of this. In October 1964 the lower part of the Falls Road, the main Catholic artery leading into Belfast city center, was convulsed by a two-day battle when, after threats from Paisley, the RUC invaded the area to remove an Irish tricolor from the offices in Divis Street of the Sinn Fein candidate in the Westminster general election. The trouble resulted in fifty civilian and over twenty RUC injuries. Eighteen months later, in June 1966, a month after Spence's UVF started to kill, Catholics again fought hand-to-hand battles with the police when Paisley brought a mob through the nationalist Markets area en route to a city center protest against ecumenical Protestants. The tinder was in place and was dry; it needed but a spark to set it ablaze.

The spark came on October 5, 1968, when a poorly attended civil rights march in Derry was batoned off the streets by a force of RUC officers who appeared to have lost all control of their emotions. Derry had been chosen for protest because it was in nationalist eyes the capital city of injustice. Not only were the majority Catholics prevented from taking control of their city, but years of unionist rule had condemned them to appalling housing conditions and disproportionately high unemployment.

The unionist government reacted with alarm to the proposed civil rights march. In the eyes of its hard-line supporters, the walled city had been the symbol of Protestant supremacy over nationalist Ireland ever since its inhabitants had withstood a terrible siege in 1688 and helped the Protestant King William of Orange defeat the Catholic usurper, King James II. Its official name was Londonderry, after the City of London companies that had financed its reconstruction as a planter city. In celebration of its heroic resistance during the siege, unionists christened Derry "the Maiden City," and any violation of its walls had to be resisted. The civil rights marchers wanted to parade right into the walled center, and unionists saw that as a bid to ravage the maiden. After an obscure and unheard-of loyalist group threatened a counterprotest, the unionist home affairs minister, William Craig, promptly banned the march.

The marchers assembled and found themselves blocked on all sides by riot police who laid into the crowd with batons flying. Eighty-eight demonstrators were injured and thirty-six arrested. Two British Labour MPs had turned up as observers, guests of West Belfast's Republican Labour MP, Gerry Fitt, who was himself batoned around the head. Later the police turned a water cannon on dispersing protesters, in a violent scene reminiscent of police brutality in Alabama just five years earlier. The whole scene was captured by a camera crew from RTE, whose film was also screened on British TV and around the world. So was an interview with a blood-bespattered Fitt. These scenes seemed more appropriate in South Africa, but Northern Ireland was British and such things were not supposed to happen in Britain. Derry on October 5 sent a shock wave through both Ireland and Britain at the realization that "John Bull's Other Island," a headline borrowed from Shaw by one London newspaper to describe Northern Ireland, was a political slum.

It rapidly became an unstable slum as well, as events took on their own momentum. The nationalist pressure intensified in November after a repeat march in Derry brought fifteen thousand onto the streets and the RUC, hopelessly outnumbered, allowed the protest through. That in turn fueled more unionist anger at Terence O'Neill, and the crowds attending Paisley's rallies grew. As NICRA held more marches and mobilized protests throughout the North, the British Labour government applied pressure on O'Neill to move faster and further to satisfy nationalist demands for change. The government in London led by Harold Wilson had been horrified and alarmed by the events of October 5, and the British prime minister demanded action from the unionists. At the end of the month O'Neill relented and announced a package of reforms and followed this up with a televised appeal for a break in the civil rights agitation.

NICRA obliged, but a small left-wing, radical student group, the People's Democracy (PD) based at Queen's University in Belfast, responded to O'Neill's package with scorn and announced plans for a seventy-five-mile trek between Belfast and Derry to start on New Year's Day 1969 to protest about the inadequacy and slowness of change. The route would go through some tough unionist areas, and trouble was inevitable. On January 4, as the march reached the outskirts of Derry, Paisleyite supporters ambushed the marchers with stones and cudgels. In response fierce bloody rioting between nationalists and the RUC broke out in the Bogside, the main Catholic area of Derry, in reality a slum that nestled at the foot of Derry's walls.

As unionist discontent grew, O'Neill's cabinet colleagues deserted him one by one, and in February he called a sudden and unexpected election to the Stormont parliament, hoping it would strengthen his hand—but if anything the result strengthened his opponents while bringing more able nationalists into political life. In March bombs exploded at an electricity substation and punctured a pipeline that supplied Belfast with most of its water. The bombs were really the work of loyalists, but at the time most people assumed a resurgent IRA had planted them. The subterfuge worked, and O'Neill was undermined even further.

In April the radicalization of nationalists continued apace when the student civil rights leader Bernadette Devlin was elected to Westminster in a by-election in Mid-Ulster, overcoming Catholic divisions to capture the seat. Unlike the republicans, she had no qualms about taking her House of Commons seat to highlight her community's grievances, although her appetite for parliamentary politics quickly waned. In the same month O'Neill's cousin Major James Chichester-Clark, a fellow Anglo-Irish aristocrat, quit his cabinet in protest of the prime minister's policies, and an exhausted O'Neill surrendered and resigned. Chichester-Clark, whose ancestors had planted Ulster in the seventeenth century, promptly succeeded him as prime minister.

The fire was well alight, and soon the explosion came. During July so-called loyalist vigilante groups appeared on the streets in Belfast. They claimed that their role was to defend Protestant areas, but in reality they were there to attack Catholic districts. One group in particular, the Shankill Defence Association, led by an ally of Paisley, was involved in vicious clashes with Catholics in North Belfast, as were RUC riot squads. Reports of Catholics being intimidated into leaving their homes began to circulate.

The focus switched back to Derry when the Apprentice Boys, an offshoot of the Orange Order, made it clear they would go ahead with that year's annual march on August 12 despite predictions of disaster. The march duly went ahead and calamity came in its wake. After skirmishes on the edge of the Catholic Bogside, ferocious rioting broke out between nationalists and the RUC. The rioters repulsed wave after wave of baton-wielding policemen with rocks and gasoline bombs, but soon the RUC turned to CS gas and flooded the narrow streets of the Bogside with acrid clouds that choked indiscriminately. Chichester-Clark mobilized the B Specials while the Irish prime minister, Jack Lynch, warned that his government would not "stand by" and watch as nationalists were attacked. Northern Ireland was moving rapidly toward the edge of civil war, and it looked as if the conflict might engulf the whole island. By August 14 the police were exhausted, and the Stormont government was forced to request military assistance from Britain. That day the first contingents of British soldiers took to the streets of Derry. Thirty years would pass before they left.

As the riots raged in Derry, civil rights leaders tried to ease the pressure on the Bogsiders by appealing to nationalists elsewhere to stage protests and demonstrations so as to stretch RUC numbers and resources. The ploy succeeded but with consequences that few could have foreseen. In Armagh a thirty-year-old Catholic man was shot dead by a party of B Specials in riots that had followed a civil rights rally. But the worst trouble was in Belfast, where that night five people died in gun battles between the RUC, loyalists, and republicans.

There were two trouble spots. In Ardoyne, a small nationalist enclave in North Belfast, two Catholics were shot dead by the RUC in clashes that were to follow a classic pattern. First rival crowds gathered to exchange insults and the occasional stone. The RUC arrived and almost immediately clashed with nationalists. As the clashes worsened, Catholics built barricades and threw gasoline bombs and stones at police, who invariably replied with baton charges. Behind the police came mobs of loyalists, many armed with guns and gasoline bombs, setting fire to homes and public houses as they swept through. Soon gunfire was echoing through the small streets, and mobs fought hand-to-hand battles.

The worst trouble was where it had always been worst, in the jungle of side streets that linked the nationalist Falls Road with the fiercely loyalist Shankill Road, the setting for regular outbreaks of rioting that dated back a hundred years. The two roads, with their crowded streets of small two-story homes, converged in a V-shape near the city center, and it was here, where they were closest, that the worst violence took place. The trouble began outside a police station on the Falls Road when a republican crowd protested and continued with clashes between the RUC, B Specials, and loyalist crowds on one side and nationalists on the other in and around Divis Street where the V of the Falls and Shankill narrowed. A Protestant member of a crowd trying to break through onto Divis Street was shot dead by one of two IRA gunmen firing from the roof of a nearby school. The RUC returned fire, and a gun battle ensued that left three policemen wounded. The RUC reaction to this was dramatic. Senior officers deployed armored cars fitted with Browning heavy machine guns. The weapons could fire high-velocity bullets over a range of 2.5 miles and were completely inappropriate for use in a heavily populated urban area. The results were again grimly predictable. A nine-year-old Catholic boy was killed when a bullet tore through the walls of his bedroom in an apartment block in Divis Street and removed the back of his head.

The next day the situation deteriorated dramatically. A local-born British soldier home on leave was shot dead by the RUC near his home in the Divis Flats complex. Earlier in the day serious rioting had broken out in the mid-Falls area when a Protestant mob invaded the Clonard district, burning homes as they came. Their target was Clonard Monastery, home of the Redemptorist order, whose priests later played such a significant role in the peace process. There was fierce street fighting and a lot of gunfire. One teenage boy, Gerald McAuley, was shot dead. A member of the republican youth wing, the Fianna, he was the first IRA member killed in the Troubles. The loyalists were eventually repulsed, but not before they had burned down much of Bombay Street under the shadow of Clonard Monastery, forcing its terrified inhabitants to flee. Earlier six hundred soldiers from the Third Battalion of the Light Infantry had taken up positions in Catholic and Protestant districts between the Falls and Shankill Roads but were seemingly unable to stop the destruction. Belfast's infamous peace line had been drawn; soon it would take a more solid form and a twenty-foot-high wall would eventually be erected, making the division permanent. The Troubles had begun.

After two days of rioting and disturbances across Northern Ireland, eight people lay dead—two Protestant, the rest Catholics. Much of West and North Belfast resembled a war zone. Barricades blocked dozens of streets in nationalist areas, erected to prevent loyalist incursions and to keep out the RUC; scores of houses had been torched, bars lay wrecked and looted, and public transport had ground to a halt. Some seven hundred people had been wounded or injured and nearly three hundred buildings destroyed or badly damaged. Belfast was no stranger to such sectarian conflict. Throughout the second half of the nineteenth century and again during the 1920s and 1930s, there had been fierce rioting, burnings, and gun battles, but the scale and intensity of the violence of 1969 was beyond living memory. Everywhere anxious Catholics organized street defense committees and began patrolling their areas. Less visible but more traumatic was the intimidation and forced evictions that had occurred throughout the city. The British government later set up a commission of inquiry into the events, headed by a senior judge, Lord Scarman, which concluded that 1.6 percent of all households in Belfast had been forced to move between July and September 1969 and that Catholics had suffered most. Over fifteen hundred Catholic families, Scarman said, had been forced from their homes, five times the number of Protestants. That summer hundreds of Catholic families sought refuge in the safety of ghettos like West Belfast, as the biggest forced population movement in Europe since the Second World War began.

These were the events that finally forced the festering divisions within the IRA into the open. The riots and gunfire, the threat to their neighborhoods and communities, had brought back into circulation republicans who had quit in disgust at the Goulding-Johnston leadership, and now they had a serious charge to lay at their opponents' door. The move to the left, they angrily protested, and the leadership's obsession with politics had led to a military rundown of the IRA, and this had left Catholic areas defenseless. The emphasis given to politics over military matters by Goulding and his henchmen, they argued, meant that the IRA had failed in its primary role in the North, to protect its own people. The anger within this relatively small group of disgruntled former IRA men would simmer throughout the autumn and early winter of 1969 before bursting to the surface in the most serious split in the ranks of physical-force republicanism since the awful Irish civil war.

Throughout the years leading up to the tumultuous events of August 1969, Gerry Adams suffered, as he wrote years later, divided loyalties within the warring IRA: "I was in a strange position, one of a small cadre with contacts in both factions."[18] His father, his uncle Liam Hannaway, and many family friends like the future Provisional IRA chief of staff Joe Cahill sided with the traditionalists. But Gerry Adams, a generation younger, clearly took with enthusiasm to some aspects of Goulding's strategy, especially the emphasis on political activity, and was ambivalent about others like the dropping of abstentionism. Most important, he stayed in the Goulding-led IRA and refused to follow the example of his father's friends, many of whom had quit the organization in protest against its policies.

In many respects his track record as a young republican was a model of what Roy Johnston had in mind; indeed in one interview he recalled attending lectures given by Johnston to the Wolfe Tone Society in Belfast, saying he had found them "excellent."[19] Adams threw himself into the sort of agitational activity that the new leadership firmly believed would win them working-class support. He was to the fore in housing campaigns like that in 1966 which opposed the building of high-rise apartments in Divis Street in the Lower Falls Road section of Belfast. He advocated other forms of political work that traditional IRA members frowned upon, such as producing local news sheets to deliver door to door. This was not the sort of work of which soldiers approved. The young Adams also supported Goulding's notion of the National Liberation Front, the left-wing alliance that his father's generation suspected had opened the door to Communist influence. In 1967 Adams could be found attending the inaugural Belfast meeting of NICRA, whose activities gave substance and meaning to Goulding's strategy.

On the defining question of dropping abstentionism, Adams adopted a position that in years to come would be the hallmark of his approach to such internal controversies. "Although I was opposed to dropping the traditional abstentionist policy, I had no objection in principle to developing a debate on electoral strategy or abstentionism. . . ."[20] The distinction between the two was sometimes difficult to discern, since urging "debate" about abstentionism could be regarded merely as a way of creating the space within which the "debate" could be won. It was a clue that he was much more pragmatic about the issue than many of those who helped him found the Provisionals.

Adams's sole disagreement with the Goulding-Johnston approach was over their idea that Northern Ireland could be transformed into a normal democratic society, one in which left-wing issues could unite Protestant and Catholic, Unionist and Nationalist, in common cause. His experience on the streets of Northern Ireland, he believed, flew in the face of this. That view was formed, according to his own account of events, early on in his political activity when along with other Sinn Feiners he had forged links with Protestants living on the New Barnsley housing estate, adjacent to his native Ballymurphy, in a campaign to demand a pedestrian crossing at a spot on the busy main road dividing the estates where a child had been killed by a car. The campaign was successful, but the Protestant-Catholic unity proved to be short-lived when a Paisleyite politician from the Shankill Road arrived to stir up fears of popery and republicanism among the Protestants of New Barnsley. Adams later commented acidly on the episode: "If the State would not allow Catholics and Protestants to get a pedestrian crossing built together, it would hardly sit back and watch them organising the revolution together."[21]

As the civil rights campaign gathered pace and sectarian tensions were sharpened, Adams's conviction that cross-community unity was a chimera hardened, as did his misgivings about the way the IRA leadership was handling the gathering crisis. "Riot situations were beginning to develop," Adams wrote, "but neither the Belfast nor Dublin [IRA] leaderships were able to understand what was happening let alone to give proper direction."[22] As 1969 wore on and street conflict loomed, some republicans, North and South, began to agitate about the need to prepare for defense but found the Dublin leaders unsympathetic and wholly absorbed in their coming internal battles with the traditionalists. That summer IRA dissidents demanded to know from Goulding how much weaponry existed to defend the Northern nationalists. "When we asked what gear there was the reply was enough for one job, i.e., one rifle, one Thompson submachine gun, two short-arms [handguns], training stuff in other words," recalled one.[23]

Goulding and his allies ignored dangerous signals from Belfast. In late August a group of former IRA men, people who had long disagreed with the leadership and had either left or been expelled, met in the New Lodge Road district of the city to decide what they should do about the Belfast leadership of the IRA then in the control of a Goulding loyalist, Billy McMillen. They were angry about McMillen's failure to organize the August defense and they blamed Goulding for the Catholic deaths. Among them were Jimmy Steele, Joe Cahill, Billy McKee, John and Billy Kelly, Jimmy Drumm, Seamus Twomey, and a Southern ally, Daithi O Conaill. Gerry Adams was the only serving Belfast IRA man invited.

The old guard resolved to oust McMillen, and in September its opportunity came when McMillen called a meeting of IRA commanders in the Lower Falls Road area. Armed men led by Billy McKee were sent to demand his resignation. McMillen refused, and after heated arguments a compromise was hammered out. The Belfast IRA would withdraw from Dublin control for three months, McMillen would add some of McKee's men to his operational staff, and weapons would be sought. If Goulding had not abandoned his strategy by the three-month deadline, McMillen would be replaced and Belfast would be run by a separate Northern Command. Meanwhile the Belfast units would play no part in the coming debate about abstentionism, effectively opting out of it.

The old guard clearly believed that Adams would be on its side not least because his father and all their family friends were. Adams had been deeply angered by the events of August. He had toured the city on August 16 to view the destruction and been appalled by what had happened in and around Bombay Street. He met his cousin Kevin Hannaway and others who had been in the thick of the violence. "The fighting here had been at very close quarters," he later wrote, "yet the poorly armed defenders had repelled a large, much better armed group of attackers. What particularly incensed us was that Bombay Street was burned despite the presence of British troops who had been deployed around the area sometime beforehand."[24]

Even so, Adams still had a foot in both republican camps. He had a soft spot for McMillen, liked much of Goulding's political approach but deplored his failure to defend Belfast's Catholics. As the August riots subsided, it was the fear among republicans that their people were still vulnerable and needed proper defense that was really stirring opinion in their circles. For once republican fears were shared in the city's working-class nationalist areas, and it was this harmony that fueled support for the Provisionals and eventually persuaded Adams to throw in his lot with them.

Despite the violence and trauma of that summer and the divisions all this brought, the Goulding leadership proceeded with the plan to drop abstentionism. Goulding had set up an internal IRA commission under Sean Garland to examine the movement's attitude toward the issue, and predictably it recommended that republicans take their seats in all three parliaments. The enlarged Army Council endorsed this by a vote of twelve to four, with four absentees. Ruairi O Bradaigh, John Joe McGirl, a friend of Adams from County Leitrim, Sean MacStiofain, and one other Northern republican were the dissenters, all of whom were to be to the fore in the impending split. An IRA Convention was called for December, and Goulding prepared well for it, ensuring that this time a majority of the delegates would be in his camp. They were, by a majority of thirty-nine to twelve. The anti-Goulding faction walked out and, with MacStiofain as its leader and new chief of staff, elected a caretaker IRA Executive and Army Council that would be loyal to the traditional principles and doctrines of republicanism.

The new dissident IRA bodies were interim and temporary; the Executive and Army Council could be ratified only by a General IRA Convention, which was not scheduled to meet until September of the following year. But until then they would represent the new group. News of the split and the formation of the rival IRA was leaked to the press by Goulding's people in late December 1969, and in a statement confirming the story the new group claimed that already a majority of IRA units had sworn allegiance to the Provisional Army Council and Executive of the IRA. The tag "Provisional" stuck not least because it was a handy way for the media to distinguish the new group from those who had remained loyal to Goulding. His faction became known, inevitably, as the Official IRA. The two groups would later feud violently and bloodily about whose members had the right to call themselves republican, but there was little doubt that the new IRA, the Provos, as most activists would soon call the group, had arrived.

Adams's criticism of the leadership's handling of this episode, written admittedly after he himself had successfully and painlessly accomplished in 1986 what Goulding had failed to achieve in 1969, suggests that his reservations had more to do with their clumsy tactics than with any qualms he might have had that Goulding was traveling in the wrong political direction. "At the very least," he wrote, "the leadership should have recognised the need for new priorities and suspended its pursuance of the new departure in republican strategy until a more settled time." He added, "For many of the dissidents the issue was not abstentionism itself but what it had come to represent: a leadership with a wrong set of priorities which had led the IRA into ignominy in August."[25]

Having secured the IRA Convention, Goulding pressed Sinn Fein to follow suit at its conference, or Ard Fheis, in Dublin in January 1970. A motion to drop abstentionism was carried but narrowly failed to secure the two-thirds majority needed to change the party's constitution. A Goulding supporter then proposed a motion of confidence in the IRA leadership, a roundabout way of achieving the same thing. Realizing they were about to be defeated, the dissidents walked out. Later that evening they met to set up an Executive for their own version of Sinn Fein and elected Ruairi O Bradaigh the first Provisional Sinn Fein president.

Adams's own account has him missing the crucial debate, barred from the venue, Dublin's Intercontinental Hotel, by a Sinn Fein official because he didn't have the proper accreditation. Instead he went off to join an anti-apartheid protest at a rugby match between Ireland and the South African Springboks. His version of events is controversial not least because the only witness, the official who allegedly barred him, is long since dead. At the very least Adams's memory of events is hazy since the walkout took place on a Sunday and the Springboks match was played the day before. Jim Sullivan, McMillen's adjutant and one of those who stayed loyal to the Goulding faction, has claimed not only that Adams was present during the Sunday session but that he was sitting beside him when the walkout happened.[26] Adams, he asserts, stayed in his seat and remained loyal to the Goulding leadership. Adams has denied this, but if his version of events is accurate and he was among those who did walk out, then he should have been at the meeting that set up the caretaker Sinn Fein Executive. But according to

Ruairi O Bradaigh only two Northerners were present when the Provisional Sinn Fein came into being: Mary McGuigan from Ardoyne in Belfast and Liam Slevin from Beleek, County Fermanagh.[27] Adams, he says, was definitely not there.

Whatever the truth, Adams does concede that he did not immediately align himself with the Provisionals, and that admission is consistent with the Sullivan–O Bradaigh version of the 1970 Ard Fheis rather than his own. Before the December Convention, Ballymurphy republicans had asked for a meeting with Sullivan, which debated the IRA's internal differences, and afterward Adams told Billy McKee, the leader of the Belfast dissidents, that the Ballymurphy unit had decided to sit on the sidelines "until we saw what way things were going to break."[28] This led to accusations at the time that Adams was waiting to see which side came out on top before joining it. It was not until four months later, in April 1970, that Adams officially brought the Ballymurphy IRA into the Provisionals, by which time the vast bulk of IRA companies in the Belfast Battalion, fifteen out of sixteen, according to one estimate, had deserted the Goulding leadership for the new organization.[29] He had joined the winning team.

TWO

The Defenders

The new Provisional IRA was led by men who represented traditional, conservative, republican values, who believed that armed struggle was the only way to rid Ireland of the British presence and that parliamentary politics was an endeavor best viewed with suspicion and treated with disdain. A majority on the caretaker Army Council, and later the Army Council elected after the first IRA Convention, had seen active service during the 1956–62 campaign, and most of them came not just from the twenty-six counties that made up the Irish Republic but from predominantly rural counties as well. Only two of the seven were from the North, from where the impetus for the new IRA had come; there was no representative from Dublin, where Goulding's influence had been strongest. They were all men, all approaching middle age, and all Catholics, some devoutly so.

No one exemplified these characteristics better than the new IRA's chief of staff, Sean MacStiofain. The son of an Irish mother and English father who was raised in South London, MacStiofain was forty-one years old when he attained the highest rank in the IRA. He had been involved in radical Irish politics since his teenage years and became a fluent Irish speaker. Heavily influenced by his mother's strongly nationalistic views, he joined the IRA's English unit in 1949, at the age of twenty-one, but later moved to Ireland and eventually settled in County Meath, where he worked for the Irish language body, Conradh na Gaeilge.

Infused with the special zealotry of the convert, he angrily resisted British media attempts in the early years of the Troubles to anglicize his name to John Stephenson, the designation on his birth certificate. His arrest and imprisonment with Goulding for the Felsted raid meant that, like Goulding, he avoided the internal warring that had plagued the IRA at the end of the failed Border Campaign and escaped blame for the fiasco of 1956–62. His decision to remain inside the organization despite the differences with the Goulding leadership, meanwhile, put him at a great advantage when the split came.

The way MacStiofain chose to express his opposition to Goulding appealed to a very broad section of dissidents, not all of whom were as directly affected by the events of August 1969 as were the Belfast men. He had two celebrated clashes with Goulding, both of which endeared him to the Catholic, conservative center of the republican movement, even though each time Goulding got the better of him.

Not long after Roy Johnston had been installed as adviser to the Army Council, MacStiofain confronted Goulding with Johnston's past membership in the Communist Party (CP) and its Irish offshoot, the Connolly Association. The IRA's rule book, known as General Army Orders, specifically prohibited Volunteers from joining the CP; it was the product of an age in Ireland when Sunday Mass would end with a prayer for the conversion of Russia. MacStiofain demanded that Goulding dismiss Johnston, but the chief of staff stood up to him and said if Johnston went, then so would he. MacStiofain was forced to back down.[1] The new IRA commander later explained why he took such a hard line: "We opposed the extreme socialism of the revisionists [the Goulding faction] because we believed that its aim was a Marxist dictatorship which would be no more acceptable to us than British imperialism or Free State capitalism."[2]

Anticommunism was to become a recurring obsession of the new IRA. The editorial in the very first edition of *Republican News*, the Provisionals' Belfast weekly newspaper, set the tone. *Republican News*, or *RN,* as it became known, had been set up in February 1970 by two IRA veterans, the dissident leader Jimmy Steele and Hugh McAteer, a former chief of staff from Derry. IRA men thought of it as "the Belfast Brigade newspaper."[3] Outlining the malign influence of the Goulding supporters, *RN* railed against them in language that would not have been out of place in a speech by Senator Joe McCarthy: "Gradually into executive posts both in the IRA and Sinn Fein, the Red agents infiltrated," the paper complained, "and soon these men became the policy makers. Young men and girls were brainwashed with the teachings and propaganda of the new policy makers and well-trained organizers were sent into different areas to spread the teachings of the Red infiltrators."[4] The same paper, edited by someone who many years later became a leading light in the Irish Tridentine Mass movement, later described the mission of the IRA's youth wing, na Fianna Eireann, in simple terms: "Our allegiance is to God and Ireland. . . ."[5]

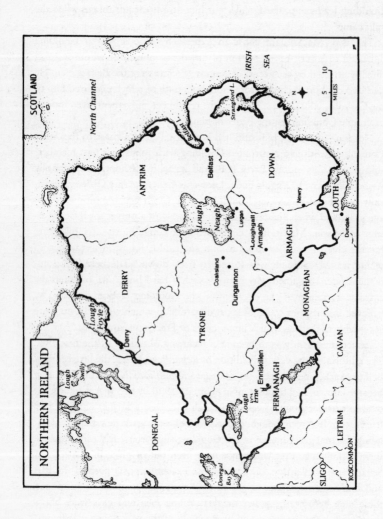

These views persisted well into the 1970s when more and more IRA members found themselves in jail, where debates on left-wing politics became more frequent. Those who espoused such views would be hounded. One former prisoner can recall a member of the IRA jail staff sending a priest to see him because he had been spotted reading a book by James Connolly.[6] The 1916 leader, badly wounded in the Rising and then strapped into a chair and executed by a British firing squad, was in the pantheon of IRA martyrs, but he had been a Marxist and trade union leader as well. The Provisionals' rivals in the Official IRA revered Connolly, and so any Provo Volunteer who showed an interest in his writings automatically came under suspicion. Even as late as 1975 the leadership had a knee-jerk attitude to left-wing politics. When some IRA inmates of Long Kesh internment camp started dabbling with socialism, an order was issued, according to the former Belfast IRA commander Brendan Hughes, to burn all Marxist books.[7]

MacStiofain regarded men like Roy Johnston as godless atheists who were more interested in undermining the influence of the Catholic Church in Ireland than in ending British occupation of the North. When Johnston wrote a letter to the Sinn Fein paper the *United Irishman* criticizing the practice of reciting the rosary at republican commemorations, calling the practice "sectarian," MacStiofain, then living in County Kerry in the deep southwest of Ireland, stopped the offending issue from being circulated and sold, for fear that the letter would be used against the IRA by its enemies. Interfering in the distribution of the *United Irishman* cost MacStiofain his place on the Army Council, the automatic consequence of a six-month suspension from the IRA imposed by Goulding as punishment.

MacStiofain's tilts against Goulding earned him plaudits south of the Border, but in the North the way to the hearts of the hard men in Belfast was by a different route. Throughout the eventful and threatening year of 1969 MacStiofain liaised closely with the dissident Northerners and shared their concerns that the increasingly demilitarized IRA would be unable to defend Belfast's Catholic areas. At one point, according to his own account, he went behind Goulding's back and secretly supplied guns to some Belfast units.[8] A shrewd if somewhat uncomplicated tactician, MacStiofain realized that the engine of the upcoming war would be in Belfast, and throughout his IRA career, until his fall in 1972, he strove to ensure that his relations with the Belfast IRA were always the best.

Two other figures dominated the new Army Council, both then in their thirties and both Southerners who had distinguished themselves during the Border Campaign. Ruairi O Bradaigh, a schoolteacher from County Roscommon in the west of Ireland, was chief of staff at the end of that campaign. He had written the famous IRA statement ending the campaign and ordering IRA units to dump arms, conceding that lack of popular support from Northern nationalists had dealt the IRA the final blow. O Bradaigh inherited his republicanism from his father, who had been badly shot up by the Royal Irish Constabulary in 1919 and who died when O Bradaigh was only ten. O Bradaigh's military credentials were impeccable—he had led an arms raid in England that netted five tons of British army hardware—but he was not as opposed to political activity as others were. In 1957 he was one of four Sinn Fein members elected to the Irish parliament on an abstentionist ticket, and throughout his career with the Provisionals he favored selective and tactical electoral interventions. In 1970 he became the first president of Provisional Sinn Fein, and as the custom was that Sinn Fein always had one seat on the Army Council as of right, O Bradaigh automatically qualified.

The other major personality was Daithi O Conaill from County Cork, also a schoolteacher by profession. Unlike Sean MacStiofain, his new chief of staff, O Conaill did not mind if people used the English form of his name, and most Provisional associates and the media called him Dave O'Connell. Like O Bradaigh's, his military record was beyond criticism. He was interned by the Dublin government early on in the Border Campaign and was incarcerated in the Curragh camp in County Kildare, once the British army's headquarters in Ireland, and there he met O Bradaigh. In 1957 the pair devised a successful escape plan, and they went on the run together. When O Bradaigh became chief of staff, he chose O Conaill to be his director of operations. It was the start of a long and close relationship.

O Conaill was a hands-on commander and fought in Counties Fermanagh and Tyrone, where he was badly wounded by the RUC. Confined to Crumlin Road prison, Belfast, he appears at first glance to have been an unlikely candidate for leadership of the Provisionals. In jail he had edited the *Saoirse* magazine, which had first floated the idea of IRA involvement in social and economic agitation, and after the campaign he became interested in the cooperative movement, often a route into left-wing politics. But his time in Belfast jail had also convinced him that the removal of partition had to be the republican priority, and he believed strongly in the need for armed struggle. The job he undertook with the new IRA emphasized that; he was the Provisionals' first quartermaster general, charged with rearming the organization and giving it the sinews to fight the impending war against the British.

The remaining four Army Council members were also veterans of the 1956–62 campaign: Sean Tracy from County Laois; Leo Martin from West

Belfast, who was OC of the Northern IRA; Patrick Mulcahy from Limerick; and Joe Cahill from Belfast. At a second Convention, held in September 1970, Billy McKee joined the Council. The presence of three Northerners on the Council, all Belfast men, serves to dispel the myth that the Provisionals were Southern-dominated from the start and that it was not until Adams and his allies captured the Army Council in the late 1970s that the Northern voice was allowed to be heard at the IRA's highest levels.

The first Provisional leaders were sure of the rightness of their cause and the reasons for breaking with the Officials. The initial statement from O Bradaigh's breakaway Sinn Fein in January 1970 listed five reasons for splitting with Goulding: his recognition of the Irish and British parliaments; the move to embrace extreme socialism; illegal internal disciplinary methods; the failure to defend Belfast; and the policy of defending the Northern parliament at Stormont.[9] The list demonstrated that the Provisionals were essentially a coalition of differing grievances; for some, Marxism was the major problem with Goulding, and for others the military rundown of the IRA. One characteristic of the new IRA above all others that united the coalition—the glue that held it together—was a distrust of politics, parliamentary politics in particular, and an unshakable belief in the correctness of armed struggle.

The early Provisional leaders were determined that they would not stray down the path of parliamentary reformism trod by other nationalist and republican leaders. Each previous generation of freedom fighters had been betrayed, they believed, by leaders seduced by the siren call of parliamentary politics. They would be the exception. For this reason they defined the relationship between Sinn Fein and the IRA in simple and traditional terms. The military wing, the IRA, was in charge, and Sinn Fein would obey and be subservient to the Army Council. That was the case in the South and also in the North, where, according to one veteran party activist, Sinn Fein was secondary to the IRA from the outset: "Sinn Fein was the poor relation. It wasn't worth bothering about. Sinn Fein in the 1970s was an organization without clout; it supported the 'campaign' and held lofty ideas of a united Ireland but nothing else. The IRA was boss."[10]

As the war intensified and more and more Northerners joined up, the antipolitical nature of the Provisionals intensified, as one of the Provisionals' founding members recalled:

When the resistance began, Northerners came in droves, and they were reacting to events for a number of years. The Northern guys were quite slow to be politicized. They looked down on Sinn Fein and dismissed it saying, "We're Army men," I shared a cell with them in Mountjoy, and that was their view. They were quite happy sitting in their cells reading the *Sun* or the *Mirror* boasting about operations. They were purely militaristic—hit, hit, keep on hitting.[11]

Whereas the first IRA commanders were Southerners, the foot soldiers in the war, the Volunteers, came overwhelmingly from the North and at first mostly from Belfast, where the attempted loyalist pogroms of August 1969 had taken place. Many IRA units elsewhere in the North, in republican heartlands like Tyrone, Armagh, and Derry, were slower to take sides in the republican split; in some cases months went by before they decided whether to follow Goulding or MacStiofain. The Provisionals were born in Belfast and sustained by the city's bitter sectarian politics.

Some of those outside Belfast were repelled by the Provisionals' simplistic politics. Typical of this category was the Derry republican Mitchel McLaughlin, who stayed with the Officials for several months before joining the Provisionals, later rising to become a key Adams aide and advocate of his peace strategy. "At the time of the split," he once told an interviewer, "I actually stayed with the Official Republican Movement. Mainly because of their politics which undoubtedly were more progressive than the more kind of nationalistic rhetoric that I was hearing [from the early Provisional leaders]."[12] Gerry Adams and the Ballymurphy unit were not the only IRA members to hesitate before taking sides in the split. Not surprisingly, many were waiting to see who came out on top, and so what happened in Belfast was crucial. When Belfast republicanism went over to the Provos, as it did during the crucial year of 1970, many of the rural units followed, and soon if angry young Northern Catholics wanted to hit back at either the loyalists or the British army, they knew they would find a warm welcome in the Provisionals.

The IRA before August 1969 was an organization kept going by family tradition. Membership was passed from father to son, mother to daughter, but the recruits who flocked to the ranks of the Provisionals were a new breed, motivated by an atavistic fear of loyalist violence and an overwhelming need to strike back. Known as Sixty-niners, they joined the IRA literally to defend their own streets, were resolved that the near-pogroms of August 1969 would never be repeated, and were ready, if the opportunity arose, to retaliate. They joined the Provos because the Officials had failed to defend their communities in the way that was expected, and they automatically associated the Officials' obsession with politics with military weakness and betrayal. From the outset abhorrence of politics and the requirement for defense and armed struggle were just different sides of the same coin.

Typical of the new Provisional IRA Volunteer was Bernard Fox, an apprentice coach-builder from the Falls Road who joined the IRA in 1969, when he was just eighteen years old. He is now a senior figure in the leadership and was named in 2001 in the British media as a senior figure in the Provisional IRA's GHQ staff. In 2006 he was appointed to the Army Council. He spent nineteen years in prison, either jailed or interned, for IRA activity. His motive for signing up was straightforward, as he once explained in a newspaper interview after the peace process reforms had secured his release from prison: "I was almost shot in a gun attack at Norfolk Street. I came away wanting a gun. It was survival. You wanted to protect your own people . . . my family and myself. When the barricades went up I wanted a gun so I approached this fella who was in the IRA and asked for gun and he said: could I shoot a British soldier? At that time I hadn't the idea that it was the British government's fault. . . ."[13]

Brendan Hughes from the Lower Falls Road district, a figure who later became an IRA legend, was similarly affected by the violence of August 1969. "At that time it was simply 'Here we are being attacked by Loyalists, by B Specials, by the RUC, by the British army,' and there was a need to hit back," recalled the former Belfast commander. "I mean I was in Bombay Street the morning after it was burned out, helping people out, and I went to the bottom of the Falls Road and seen all the burnt-out homes. I had relatives in Bombay Street who were burnt out, and I felt the desire to get back at these people who were doing it."[14] Micky McMullen, a former long-term IRA prisoner, came under similar pressure but managed to resist it: "Up to 1969 there was nothing, but August 1969 was the turning point. I became involved in community defence you know and stuff like that, helping families to move after they had been burned out. At that time a lot of my friends would have been trying to join the IRA and the rationale would be just to get stuck into the 'Orangies' you know. It was a defence thing but something stopped me from getting into that."[15]

Fox, Hughes, and McMullen and the many hundreds who followed them into the Provisional IRA in the first years of its existence were part of a Northern Catholic tradition that went back nearly two hundred years, when another armed uprising had very nearly ended British rule in Ireland. The United Irishmen's rebellion of 1798 is celebrated as the moment when modern, secular Irish republicanism was born, but it also coincided with the birth of sectarian politics in Ireland and left a scar that would mark Northern society for centuries to come.

The United Irishmen were mostly Presbyterians whose determination to sever the link with England had been partly inspired by the American and French revolutions but which was also forced upon them by the penal laws, harsh anti-Catholic measures that also penalized Protestants who were not members of the established Anglican Church in Ireland. The leader of the United Irishmen, the Dublin-born lawyer Theobald Wolfe Tone, defined his objectives in heady language that inspired future generations of Irish freedom fighters: "To break the connection with England . . . and to assert the independence of my country—these were my objects. To . . . substitute the common name of Irishman in place of the denominations of Protestant, Catholic, and Dissenter—these were my means."[16]

These were noble sentiments, but the reality on the ground in the late eighteenth century was the reverse of what Tone wanted to happen. Ireland was beginning to divide very deeply on religious and sectarian grounds, nowhere more so than in the North. The cause was simple—land. Protestant planter tenant farmers in the North had enjoyed superior rights over native Catholics since the 1600s when the plantation settlement had accelerated. A practice known as the Ulster Custom gave them security of tenure as long as they kept up their rent payments, and it also entitled them, if they decided to quit the land, to receive compensation for improvements they had made to the land or property. They had an incentive to work and invest that was denied their Catholic countrymen, and the rewards made their sacrifice worthwhile. But in the early 1780s the English began to relax the penal laws, Catholics were allowed to hold leases on the same terms as Protestants, and the planters' privileged lifestyle came under threat. Catholics, who were used to a lower standard of living, were also ready to pay higher rents, with the result that Protestant planters saw more and more of their farms falling into the hands of their native rivals.

Around the mid-1780s the worm began to turn. The first secret Protestant societies appeared and announced that they were dedicated to preserving privilege and driving the Catholics out. The largest was the Peep O'Day Boys, so called because its members would appear at dawn to burn or intimidate Catholic families. This Protestant violence stimulated a Catholic response, and rival secret societies devoted to defending Catholics were formed. Inevitably they became known as Defenders, and as they toured the countryside raiding for arms and skirmishing with troops, they adopted a strategic dictum that would have been familiar to the Provisional IRA leadership: the best means of defense, they preached, was attack. Although their roots lay in what are now the Border counties between the

Irish Republic and Northern Ireland, the Defender phenomenon spread throughout Ireland. The objectives of the Defenders varied from place to place; in the South discontent over high rents and low wages combined with an insurrectionary and defiant politics animated by events in America and France to swell their ranks. But the Defenders were less inspired by the idea of freeing Ireland from British rule and more by the hope that life in Ireland could be improved.

In the North there was a sharp sectarian edge to the Defenders' activities, and as Protestant anxiety over land losses intensified, clashes with the Peep O'Day Boys became more and more frequent and bloody. One confrontation was to have momentous consequences for Ireland's history. In September 1795 just outside the city of Armagh, at a place called the Diamond, over twenty Defenders were killed in a pitched battle with a much smaller force of Peep O'Day Boys. The victorious Protestants then decided to re-form themselves into the Orange Society, later called the Orange Order, named after the Protestant hero King William of Orange, who had defeated the Catholic King James in the late 1690s and secured the Protestant crown and succession in England and Ireland.

As the thoughts of the leaders of the United Irishmen moved increasingly to violent rebellion, they turned to the Defenders for the muscle they would need to take on the English redcoats, and the two groups coalesced in 1796. The ensuing rising in 1798 was brutally put down by Lord Cornwallis, who had just lost the American colonies and was determined not to suffer another humiliating defeat at the hands of impudent rebels. Too late to help his associates, Wolfe Tone returned to Ireland with a force of French troops but was captured, arrested, and sentenced to death. Determined to cheat the English hangman, Tone took his own life in prison. The 1798 rebellion went down as another glorious defeat, and Wolfe Tone became known as the founding father of Irish republicanism. His grave at Bodenstown, County Kildare, has become a place of pilgrimage for all shades of Irish republicanism. The Provisionals' commemoration takes place each June, and the keynote speech is invariably used by the Army Council to spell out current IRA policy.

Tone's influence survived his death, and so too did that of the Defenders. The Defenders and the early recruits to the Provisional IRA two centuries later shared a number of important characteristics. In both organizations the prime motive for taking up arms was to defend their people from Protestant attack, not to free Ireland. The Defenders organized themselves to protect Catholic farms and land in rural Ulster; the early Provisionals did so to defend Catholic streets and ghettos in Belfast. Both believed that the best defense was attack, and both put the need for guns or other instruments of defense before political ideas.

Both were reactive responses to the iniquities of British rule. In 1795, for instance, a Kildare schoolteacher, Laurence O'Connor, sentenced to death for administering a Defender oath, told his judge, "[P]rosecutions were not the means of bringing peace in the country but if the rich would alleviate the sufferings of the poor, they would hear no more of risings or Defenders and the country would rest in peace and harmony."[17] Two hundred and five years later Eamonn McDermott, an IRA Volunteer from Derry sentenced to life imprisonment in 1979 for killing a policeman, expressed not dissimilar sentiments: "Its a cliché now but the British Army created the IRA. . . . They brought the national question into it, before then it wasn't really an issue. Republicans would argue that it was there from the start, but that's a load of rubbish. Initially [we] were trying to reform the state; the national question and partition came later."[18] In their different ways both men were saying the same thing: if the British had behaved sensibly and fairly, they and their communities would probably have been content.

AS CATHOLIC Belfast recovered from the shock and bloodshed of August 1969, the need for defense was uppermost in the minds of republicans in Ballymurphy, where in November 1969, after the death in a car accident of the local IRA commander, Liam McParland, Gerry Adams took charge. In those days the vast sprawling Ballymurphy housing project was divided by the Springfield Road, one of the city's main arterial routes. The lower, southern side was Catholic, while the upper, northern side, New Barnsley, which dominated the rest of the district from the slopes of hills that overlook the city, was Protestant. Tension, suspicion, and fear were rife after the August riots, and barricades set up then by Catholics were still in place. Ballymurphy Catholics were worried that loyalists could direct sniper fire on them from the high ground of New Barnsley. Eager to acquire weapons of their own, locals turned to the as yet nonaligned IRA unit, as Adams later recalled: "Many people involved with the defence committees flocked to the IRA, which speedily mushroomed out of all proportion to its previous numbers."[19] There was little doubt that in Ballymurphy defense against loyalist attack was the main motive for those who joined the local unit, as one Volunteer explained: "It was a gut reaction. The Loyalists were attacking our ones and we knew that sooner or later it would come to the 'Murph. The Brits didn't really figure in those days. They just didn't belong in the fight."[20]

At its first meeting, in January 1970, the MacStiofain-led Army Council devised a three-stage strategy that initially placed the emphasis on the need to defend the Catholic areas of Belfast. "All our energies would be devoted to providing material, financial and training assistance for the Northern units," MacStiofain later explained in his autobiography. "The objective was to ensure that if any area where such a unit existed came under attack, whether from Loyalist extremists or British forces, that unit would now be capable of adequate defensive action."[21]

As soon as possible thereafter, according to the MacStiofain plan, the IRA would go into a second phase, a mixture of defense and retaliation, the latter designed to deter loyalists from mounting attacks. When the IRA was strong enough and political circumstances suitable, the IRA would move into the third phase, an offensive war designed to bring Britain to the negotiating table to agree to the final withdrawal of its forces from Ireland. Within weeks the Army Council also approved the design for the new IRA's icon, one that would symbolize the determination that the killings and burnings of August 1969 would never happen again; a phoenix rising from the ashes—meant to be the ashes of Bombay Street—soon adorned lapel badges and ties worn in bars and drinking clubs in West Belfast.

The political circumstances quickly began to move in the Provisionals' favor. The deployment of troops ended half a century of effective British non-engagement in Northern Ireland. The Harold Wilson cabinet in London realized it had no choice but to force the pace of political change. A reform program was announced. The B Specials, hated by the Catholics, would be disbanded and replaced by a militia to be drawn from both communities. It would be called the Ulster Defence Regiment. The RUC would be disarmed and reorganized in the hope of attracting more Catholic recruits. The allocation of public housing and other powers were taken away from Northern Ireland's unionist-dominated local councils, while plans were laid to outlaw public expressions of sectarian hatred and to improve community relations. The British home secretary was given oversight of Northern Ireland, and that was a dark hint to Unionists that London could take away their powers entirely; if they didn't clean up their act, their parliament at Stormont could be suspended and the days of exclusive Protestant rule brought to an end. Although the government of Major James Chichester-Clark had little choice but to accept Wilson's diktat, the unionist grassroots were alarmed and restive. The disarming of the RUC had led to rioting on the Shankill Road, and three people were killed in gun battles between British troops and loyalist snipers. One of the fatalities was an RUC constable, the first police death of the Troubles. Early in 1970 the Reverend Ian Paisley, already a fairly reliable barometer of grassroots Protestant discontent, won Terence O'Neill's old seat at Stormont in a by-election called after the unseated prime minister's retirement from politics. Chichester-Clark was under constant attack from right-wingers on his backbenches, some motivated by hostility to the reform program, others by fear of losing their seats to Paisley supporters. Events on the streets also contributed to the sour unionist mood. In the wake of the August riots, the RUC had been expelled from nationalist areas in Belfast and Derry, and the British army had taken over control of law and order. The defense commit-tees—in many cases controlled by either the Provisional or the Official IRA—banned the police from their areas and refused to dismantle the August barricades. Their behavior infuriated the unionists.

There is little doubt that most Northern nationalists welcomed Britain's reinvolvement in Irish affairs, especially since it came from a British Labour government, some of whose leaders were known to be sympathetic to the nationalist cause. To the discomfort of many early Provisional leaders, rela-tions between Catholics and British soldiers were, if not friendly, then cer-tainly not hostile, mirroring this new, hopeful mood.

As unionist angst grew, the need to buttress Chichester-Clark against his right-wingers brought a change in British policy. The honeymoon between nationalists and the British began to end in Easter that year, when there were clashes between British troops and republicans at commemorations of the 1916 Rising in Armagh and Derry. But the worst trouble was in Ballymurphy in riots that finally forced republicans there to align with the Provisionals. As in other parts of West Belfast, day-to-day control of law and order in the estate was in the hands of the British army, at first the Royal Scots Regiment, which set up headquarters in a deserted school on the Springfield Road. To the astonishment of Ballymurphy Catholics, at the end of March the commander of the Royal Scots gave Orangemen from New Barnsley permission to parade down the Springfield Road past their estate. As outraged nationalists heard the flute-and-accordion bands striking up sectarian, anti-Catholic tunes, the first stones were thrown. This time the troops sided with the Orangemen. As Catholic rioters hurled rocks and gasoline bombs, the troops replied with CS gas, which seeped through the housing estate, disabling young and old, rioter and non-rioter indiscrimi-nately. Military snatch squads charged the crowds to arrest and beat stone throwers. Ballymurphy nationalists contrasted this tough response with the more low-key and measured reply to loyalist rioters. Chichester-Clark's critics had demanded that the British army remove its kid gloves in Catholic areas, and this had now happened.

The Easter 1970 Ballymurphy disturbances were significant not just because they pushed the local unaligned IRA unit into the arms of the Provisionals but because, for a sizable section of Belfast Catholic opinion, they began to put British soldiers on the same side as the unionists and Protestants. It was this development, repeated elsewhere with increasing frequency and ferocity in the coming weeks and months, that transformed matters to the advantage of the Provisionals. And no one was better able to take advantage of this than Gerry Adams, the new commander of the Ballymurphy IRA.

By the time of the Easter 1970 riots the Provisional IRA in the city had grown so quickly that it was obliged to reorganize. At that time the IRA operated at three levels. At the bottom were local defense committees, in effect vigilantes who patrolled areas at night to warn of loyalist incursions. Above them was the Auxiliary IRA, men whose job was to defend their own areas, should the loyalists attack. They were in practice part-time IRA members whose services could be called upon in an emergency and who, in the meantime, provided the IRA with ears and eyes. Above them was the full-time IRA unit or company, modeled on the British army's structure. Each company was recruited from within its home area.

With their ranks swollen by new recruits, the IRA expanded from one Belfast battalion to three, each with its own complement of companies. The First Battalion was based in Andersonstown and the Upper Falls Road area. The Second Battalion encompassed Ballymurphy and the Lower Falls Road area. The Third Battalion took in the rest of Catholic Belfast, principally the isolated and often besieged ghettos of Ardoyne in North Belfast, the Short Strand in East Belfast, and the Markets district in South-central Belfast.

Nearly all Gerry Adams's family went with the Provisionals. Only one sister, Margaret, whose husband was in the Official IRA, refused; the rest—father, mother, siblings—all gave their allegiance to the reborn phoenix. Adams was well placed to rise in the new movement. At the time of the split there were no more than forty to sixty IRA members in the whole of Belfast and even fewer of Gerry Adams's youth and ability. The Provisional leadership in Belfast naturally turned to able republicans to show the way to the newcomers, among them Adams. Talent-spotted by the pre-split Belfast commander, Billy McMillen, the young Adams was already headed for leadership, but the Troubles gave him the opportunity to utilize his special skills with deadly effect. Other IRA leaders rose because of their record as "operators," as gunmen and bombers. But not Adams. Although he was to dominate the IRA for the next thirty years, there is no evidence that he ever fired a shot in anger against the British or their local allies. "I have never met anyone who has ever been on an operation with him," recalled one early colleague. "Usually you get to hear about people, that so-and-so is a nerveless operator or this one's a wreck and so on, but never with Adams. He was never on a robbery, never on a gun crew, a bombing or anything."[22]

The key to his rise lay in other qualities, prime among them the skills of a ruthless general. The first opportunity to display his strategic dexterity came during the Easter riots of 1970. The new Provisional Belfast commander was Billy McKee, a confirmed bachelor and devout Catholic who had devoted his life to the republican cause. Like other conservative critics, he had quit the Goulding IRA in protest against its policies but rejoined when the riots of August 1969 broke out. He became the first commander of the Second Battalion and then, after the split, took over command of the entire Belfast Brigade.

Deeply affected by the IRA's failure to defend nationalist areas in August 1969, McKee was determined that the Provisionals would make up for that lapse. When the Ballymurphy riots erupted, he ordered an armed unit from D Coy in the Lower Falls Road to go to Ballymurphy and take on the British army. When Adams found out, he was furious and detained McKee's men at gunpoint. "Adams put us all in this house and wouldn't let us out," recalled an IRA colleague who was impressed by this first encounter with the Ballymurphy leader, "and there we sat with all our guns stacked against the wall. McKee wanted a gunfight, but Adams didn't. Adams wanted ordinary people involved in the rioting as a way of radicalizing them. That impressed me. He seemed to be very competent and capable; he knew what he was talking about."[23] The rioting lasted for four days and affected thousands of West Belfast people. Had the IRA opened fire on the first day, the trouble would have possibly been over in a few hours and could have ended with the IRA's defeat at the hands of superior British firepower and Ballymurphy's substantial Catholic community rendered less angry, less willing to take up guns.

Three months later the chance came to repeat the exercise. The months of June and July 1970 were to witness a series of historic blunders by the British military and the unionist government which catapulted the Provisionals into an organization large and strong enough to embark on the second and third stages of MacStiofain's strategy. The riots of that summer also made the Ballymurphy IRA the most militant in Belfast and helped ensure that Gerry Adams would rise through the ranks.

The spark that lit the fire came on June 18, when in Britain a general election ousted Harold Wilson's Labour government and installed a Conservative administration led by Edward Heath. The result buoyed the unionists in Northern Ireland. Harold Wilson's cabinet had been openly sympathetic to the civil rights agenda, whereas the British Tories had historical and cultural ties to unionism. Encouraged by the result, unionists began to press for harsher security measures, including internment, the measure that they believed had crushed the IRA during the 1956–62 campaign. But there were warning signals from the election as well. The Reverend Ian Paisley was elected to the Westminster parliament at the expense of a more moderate unionist, and there was a fear that mainstream unionism might lose control unless it was bolstered. It was in this atmosphere that Chichester-Clark secured the agreement of the British army commander in Northern Ireland, Lieutenant General Sir Ian Freeland, that a number of impending Orange parades would be allowed to go ahead. The unionist premier believed he could not survive much more grassroots antagonism, and the British, desperate to sustain Chichester-Clark, agreed.

Two controversial parades were scheduled for June 27. One was due to march past the Ardoyne district of North Belfast, where some of the worst loyalist violence of August 1969 had happened. Another would go through Ballymurphy, as the Easter march of that year had done with such disastrous consequences. Predictably both marches degenerated into violence. In Ballymurphy fierce rioting broke out, again between British troops and local Catholics, but in Ardoyne things took a more serious turn. The Ardoyne parade was attacked with stones and gasoline bombs, and the guns quickly came out on both sides. In August 1969 the loyalists and RUC had given local nationalists a bloody nose, but this time it was the Provisionals who meted out the punishment. Three loyalist snipers were shot dead by gunmen from the IRA's Third Battalion and several more were wounded.

As news of the killing spread, angry loyalist mobs gathered in East Belfast and began moving in on the small Catholic ghetto of Short Strand, situated on the banks of the river Lagan. Inexplicably the British army made no effort to stop them, although it was clear that the loyalists were intent on death and destruction. It was a heaven-sent chance for the Provisionals to demonstrate they could defend their community, and a small group of IRA Volunteers took up position in the grounds of the local Catholic church, St. Matthew's, and opened up on the Protestant crowds. Loyalist snipers returned fire, and soon a full-scale gun battle was raging. The IRA squad was led by the Belfast commander, Billy McKee, his presence testimony not just to his devotion to the Catholic church but to his determination to expunge the shame of August 1969. Although McKee was badly wounded in the five-hour-long exchange, his mission succeeded. The loyalist mobs retreated, carrying two of their number home dead. One local Catholic, who IRA leaders claimed was a member of the Auxiliaries, was also killed, but there was no doubt that the events in Ardoyne and the Short Strand— "the siege of St. Matthew's" in Provisional folklore—had established the Provisionals as the Catholics' only reliable defenders. The British army was discredited. The importance of the gun battles did not escape the IRA, as one of those involved in the Short Strand battle recalled: "It was very significant. On our way over to the [Short] Strand that night there was a lot of Brits and peelers [police] just sitting outside the area. Did they allow that battle to develop to sicken the Protestants and Catholics? A lot of people joined the Republican Movement after St Matthew's. It finished the business of IRA equals 'I Ran Away.' If that trouble had not broken out the IRA was dead."[24]

The IRA's success cleared the way to implement the offensive stage of MacStiofain's battle plan. In the past small Catholic areas like Ardoyne and the Short Strand had been held hostage by unionism for the good behavior of republicans elsewhere. This was one of the reasons the IRA had confined its 1956–62 campaign to rural Border areas. But now that the loyalists had been repulsed in East Belfast, the most vulnerable Catholic district in the city, the IRA could contemplate taking the war to the British, knowing areas like it could be adequately defended.

There then followed one of those events that historians may never be able to properly explain but whose consequences were plain for all to see even at the time. On Friday, July 3, British troops descended on a small, four-room house in the Lower Falls Road district and began tearing it apart in a search for arms. These they soon discovered, and it was obvious they had been tipped off. The puzzling question, though, was why the military had acted on the intelligence. The arms dump belonged to the Official IRA, the Provisionals' rivals, and the area was at the time largely sympathetic to the Goulding faction. Although forced by events to adopt a more militant pose, the Official IRA's leadership was not spoiling for a fight with British troops. The arms raid risked forcing the Officials into retaliation but did the Provisionals no harm at all. If the British were unable to distinguish between the two IRAs, as some observers have suggested, then they made a monumental blunder, for it was the Provisionals who gained most from the ensuing events.

As the troops prepared to leave the Falls Road, they came under heavy stone-throwing from a large and angry crowd. Some soldiers were trapped in the maze of narrow unfamiliar streets, and reinforcements were sent for. Soon three thousand troops were deployed in the area that was now cloaked in CS gas and littered with rubble and exploding gasoline bombs. Freeland ordered a curfew, and troops began house-to-house searches, in many cases wrecking homes, bars, and businesses. The soldiers looted virtually every public house in the area. Gun battles broke out between the Official IRA and the British, and then the Provisionals' D Coy joined in. The curfew lasted until Sunday afternoon, when it was broken by over one thousand women, many with babies in carriages, who marched from Andersonstown with milk and bread to feed the besieged inhabitants. Four men, all civilians, were killed by the British army that weekend, three by bullets and one crushed by an armored car in circumstances that made the Provisionals' violent strategy seem unavoidable, appealing, and even necessary to many West Belfast Catholics. The Falls curfew, as the events of that weekend became known, marked a victory for the tactic of armed struggle.

Provisional IRA gunmen had opened up in the Falls Road, Ardoyne, and East Belfast; in Ballymurphy, however, Gerry Adams's constraining order on the local unit still applied. As the Protestants of New Barnsley evacuated their homes, the riots that had started on June 27 continued almost nightly and lasted for the next six months. Ballymurphy republicans were in the thick of the fighting, but not once did they break open their arms dumps. The Belfast Brigade was unhappy at the rioting and wanted to see some armed action, but Adams persisted, determined to radicalize his own people.

The strategy was effective, but it was also ruthless. During the six months of riots that followed, hundreds of people were injured or arrested and imprisoned; others, old and young alike, suffered from the effects of CS gas. Dozens of young people joined the IRA to seek revenge against the soldiers; some were to end up in jail, others in early graves. But the effect of the rioting was profound, as Adams later boasted: "Every man, woman and child was involved. They didn't fire a shot but for months, the British army had the hell beaten out of them. The women were humiliating and demoralising them. The kids were hammering them. You had the whole community organised right down into street committees, so that you had a sort of spider's web of regular coordination."[25]

The result was that Ballymurphy became the most militant republican district in the city, and its IRA units made the Second Battalion area the most active and ferocious in the Belfast Brigade. One crucial consequence of this was that, as the IRA's war intensified, the brigade leadership in Belfast relied heavily on figures drawn from the Second Battalion area. This was Gerry Adams's route to the top of the IRA.

BY CHRISTMAS 1970 the Provisional IRA was just a year old, but it was a vigorous and rapidly growing infant. A unique combination of events had come together to create the Provos, and during its first year of existence another series of extraordinary, unpredictable incidents—the siege of St. Matthew's, the Falls Road curfew, and the Ballymurphy riots prime among them—had given the organization an undreamed-of boost. It would be tempting to conclude that fate was playing an awful trick on the people of Northern Ireland by arranging matters in such a disastrous fashion, but there was a common factor in all these happenings that explained why events were spiraling out of control. Just as unionist obduracy had played the role of midwife to the new IRA, so the same need to placate Protestant extremism and prop up the Stormont government led Britain to take an increasingly tough line against the communities from which the IRA sprang. As that conflict worsened, the notion that as long as unionists held power and were supported by Britain, nationalists could expect no fair dealing gained more support and sympathy. The events of 1970 nourished the view that Northern Ireland was incapable of being reformed and that only its destruction could end the nationalists' nightmare. For the first time in the history of the state the extreme republican agenda and the IRA's violent methods were winning the allegiance of a sizable section of the Catholic community. Unionists had created the Provos, and now they were sustaining them. Only in Ballymurphy had republicans manipulated events; everywhere else there was no need to.

THREE

"The Big Lad"

The year 1970 was without doubt a seminal one for the IRA, as an early Volunteer recalled in vivid terms: "At the start of it I remember picketing outside British Army dances with placards and being spat at by local [Catholics] who attended those dances. We were nothing at that point. By the end of the year we had an organisation capable of taking on the British Army."[1] A few months later the war between Britain and the Provisional IRA was raging, and the most violent conflict in the tangled and tragic history of Britain and Ireland was under way.

As 1970 drew to a close, the IRA's leaders could be confident that their fortunes were improving and that 1971 would almost certainly see that trend continue, although not even the wildest-eyed IRA man could have foreseen just how sharply the curve would rise. In Gerry Adams's home estate in Ballymurphy, as elsewhere in Belfast, the realization that a new plateau had been reached forced a change in tactics.

The riots in Ballymurphy faded around Christmas 1970, but in the middle of January 1971 they flared again with greater ferocity. Now, however, Adams and the Ballymurphy republicans were ready to bring them to an end, to patch up their differences with the Belfast Brigade leadership, and to unleash the gunmen. The local historian Ciaran de Baroid explained why: "The Ballymurphy republicans felt that [the riots] had served their purpose; the people were cemented together; the British army was humiliated and demoralised; alienation between the people and the state was complete and irreversible; and self-confidence and an efficient infrastructure of organisation had been developed within the area."[2] Ballymurphy IRA members moved to quell the rioting, and British army commanders were not slow to notice the change in tactics.

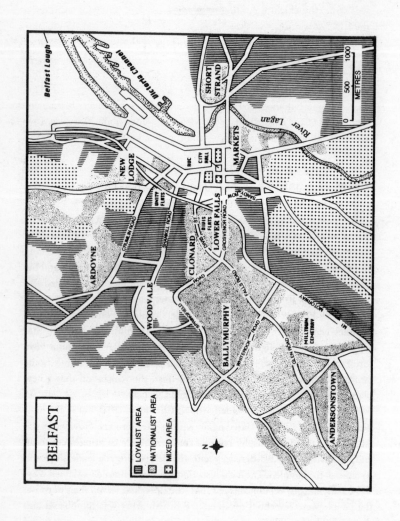

BELFAST

LOYALIST AREA
NATIONALIST AREA
MIXED AREA

N

Belfast Lough

Victoria Channel

SHORT STRAND

River Lagan

MARKETS

NEW LODGE

RUC
CITY HALL

UNITY FLATS

LOWER FALLS

MCDONNELL'S

ARDOYNE

CRUMLIN ROAD

SCHOOL ROAD

CLONARD

WOODVALE

DIVIS ST
DIVIS FLATS

GROSVENOR ROAD

SPRINGFIELD ROAD

FALLS ROAD

WHITEROCK ROAD

BALLYMURPHY

GLEN ROAD

MILLTOWN CEMETERY

ANDERSONSTOWN

ANDERSONSTOWN RD

1000

500

0

METRES

Discreet negotiations were opened up between them and a policing deal was struck in which, according to the IRA version, the Army agreed that the RUC would stay out of the area, and policing in the Second Battalion area would be left to the IRA. The British would also evacuate the area. Almost immediately the deal, if such it was, fell apart, and seven hundred troops invaded the estate and began searching for arms. Fierce rioting once more engulfed Ballymurphy. Then the Reverend Ian Paisley announced that he had found out about the secret talks, while an increasingly beleaguered Chichester-Clark extracted a pledge from the Tory home secretary, Reginald Maudling, that British troops could now take "the offensive" against the IRA.

On February 2, 1971, in response to pressure from unionists and ministers in London, British soldiers cordoned off the Clonard area of West Belfast, the scene of the burning of Bombay Street in August 1969, and began a punitive series of house searches. These sparked vicious riots, in which loyalist workers from a nearby engineering factory joined. Clonard was in the Second Battalion area and was supposed to be covered by the secret policing deal. IRA commanders saw this as evidence of British army bad faith and responded accordingly. The Clonard riots spread to other Catholic districts, and soon the IRA went into action. British troops came under gun and bomb attacks in North Belfast, and then on the night of February 6 an IRA unit under the command of Billy Reid from the New Lodge Road area ambushed a British patrol, killing one soldier, Gunner Robert Curtis, and wounding four of his colleagues. He was the first of 503 British military personnel to die in the Troubles.[3]

By the end of 1970 support for the Provisionals in Belfast was increasing in direct proportion to the weight of the British military presence in nationalist areas. The unionist government's answer to every downward twist in the cycle of violence was to ask Britain to send more troops to police nationalist districts. Invariably the British refused the more outrageous demands, but unionists still got a good deal of what they wanted. Chichester-Clark was in a strong position. Without him the British would have been forced to intervene directly in Northern Ireland's affairs and might well have had to abolish the local parliament and government and rule directly from London, a leap in the dark that no British leader yet wanted to take. That might have had to happen at some stage, but in the meantime, the British calculated, the only viable policy was to give the unionist leader what he needed to stay in office.

Sending more troops into nationalist areas was, however, a bit like throwing gasoline on a fire. The troops were trained battle soldiers, not policemen; their instinct was to hit every problem on the head with a club, and, with some exceptions, few of their officers showed much understanding of the political cauldron in which they had landed. Some, like the Parachute regiments and the Marines, were particularly ill suited to the delicate task of keeping peace and quickly developed a name for casual, horrific brutality. For some incomprehensible reason the British insisted on sending into some of the worst troublespots, like Ballymurphy, Scottish regiments, many of whose recruits came from Orange backgrounds in Glasgow and elsewhere and were every bit as staunch as their Belfast brethren. If the riots in Ballymurphy were particularly bitter and bloody, it was due in no small measure to this ingredient.

The troops were also operating in a political environment that became more and more warlike, not least because the views of their commanders were hardening. During 1970 British commanders had given their troops permission to open fire and shoot dead any gasoline bombers who ignored warnings, and after the death of Gunner Curtis, Chichester-Clark declared that his government was at war with the Provisional IRA. As the rhetoric grew more bellicose, the troops on the ground became more aggressive, and increasingly the operational distinction between ordinary Catholics and IRA activists became blurred. Belfast Catholics repaid the soldiers' hostility and anger with interest, and a self-perpetuating, self-nourishing cycle began that no one seemed able to break. It was all a boon to the fledgling IRA, as MacStiofain recognized: "The fact was that . . . the British soldiers caused friction, resentment and problems that had not been there before."[4]

By 1971 there were unmistakable signs that the Provisional IRA was getting bigger and more dangerous than Goulding's Officials. In June 1970 some five thousand people had attended the Provisionals' Bodenstown ceremonies; within twelve months the crowd had nearly tripled, to fourteen thousand. This was reflected in growing IRA recruitment figures. The IRA Convention of September 1970, which regularized the makeup of the Army Council and Executive, was, in MacStiofain's opinion, the largest he had ever attended, as was the following month's Sinn Fein Ard Fheis.[5] In Belfast the Provisionals had scored two moral victories over their rivals in the Officials, both in Adams's Second Battalion area, and these resulted in a shift of support to them in a key district of the city.

It was Adams's old colleagues in D Coy in the Lower Falls Road area who swung matters the Provisionals' way. The members of D Coy had performed well against the British army, better than the Officials, some believed, during the Falls curfew, even though the fighting had taken place in an Official

IRA stronghold. Then, in March 1971, D Coy's commander, Charlie Hughes, was killed by the Officials in circumstances that strongly suggested duplicitous dealing by the Goulding supporters. A feud had broken out between the two groups, and each side had kidnapped hostages. Negotiators intervened and patched together a settlement, but just as rival leaders endorsed it, Hughes was shot dead. Hughes was widely respected in the area; he had fought off a loyalist mob with a Thompson machine gun during the August 1969 riots, and it looked as if the Officials had killed him out of resentment at his local standing. The Officials claimed that the responsible gunman had not been told of the mediation in time, but few in the Lower Falls believed them and local sentiment shifted to the Provisionals.

With the political and military circumstances shifting in their favor the Provisional leaders decided to intensify the campaign, to move from defensive mode into retaliation and attack. The way the IRA signaled the change was also a harbinger of the depths to which the violence could and would descend in the years to come. On the evening of March 8 three young members of the Royal Highland Fusiliers, two of them brothers aged seventeen and eighteen from the Scottish town of Ayr, were lured from a bar in central Belfast and taken to a lonely mountain road overlooking the northern suburbs of the city; there they were each shot in the head, apparently as they were relieving themselves after the night's hard drinking. The extreme youth of the victims, the fact that the killers would likely have known that two were brothers, and the supposition that girls may have played a part in enticing them to their deaths made it an operation that the IRA was not keen to boast about. The IRA issued a statement actually denying responsibility, and the episode was written out of the organization's annals. The killings, for instance, did not feature in MacStiofain's own account of this period or in the IRA's official history of its early years,[6] but the truth was that the operation had been authorized by the Belfast Brigade and was carried out by personnel from the city's Third Battalion.[7]

Such ruthlessness paid off. The loyalist reaction was instant and widespread, fueled in no small way by the cultural and ethnic links many Protestants had with the part of Scotland the soldiers hailed from. Thousands of Protestants marched to the center of Belfast, where the Reverend Ian Paisley led them in an impromptu memorial service; angry Protestant workers in the shipyard laid down tools and joined them. Teenage loyalist bands calling themselves Tartan Gangs in tribute to the dead soldiers appeared on the streets, adding a violent and unpredictable element to the growing unionist unease. Within days the beleaguered

Chichester-Clark resigned. The shipyard workers and other loyalists had demanded that IRA leaders be immediately interned, and the Ulster Unionist Party's choice for their new leader was evidence that this measure was now on the agenda. Brian Faulkner, an ambitious member of both O'Neill's and Chichester-Clark's cabinets, had been minister of home affairs during the IRA's 1956–62 campaign when the use of internment on both sides of the Border had helped end the IRA's violence. Convinced that internment could and would work again, he promised his hard-line supporters that his would be a law-and-order administration.

The prospect of internment also alarmed the IRA leadership, especially in Belfast, where the killing of the three Scottish soldiers and Faulkner's elevation combined to produce leadership changes that would have profound and lasting effects on the course of the Troubles. In April, days after the killings, the Belfast commander Billy McKee and his adjutant, Proinsias MacAirt, or Frank Card, as the British insisted on calling him, fell foul of a new get-tough approach. They were stopped by a military patrol in West Belfast, and their car was searched both by the soldiers and by Scotland Yard detectives, who were on secondment to the military because of the RUC's inability to operate in nationalist districts. One of the detectives triumphantly brought out an automatic pistol. McKee and MacAirt were arrested and charged. The IRA alleged that the men had been framed. Both men had participated in the secret talks about policing Ballymurphy, and the British knew exactly how important they were. They were also under constant surveillance. A powerful British army searchlight nightly illuminated the front of MacAirt's house in the Lower Falls, where early brigade staff and other IRA meetings had been held. The pair knew how foolish it would be to drive around the city carrying arms. Their defense, however, was rejected and each was sentenced to five years in jail.

McKee's removal created gaps in the Belfast leadership's battle order. The Second Battalion commander, Joe Cahill, took charge of the Belfast Brigade while Seamus Twomey replaced MacAirt as second in command and was made brigade adjutant. Cahill took McKee's position on the Army Council, thereby preserving the precedent set at the September 1970 IRA Convention that the Belfast Brigade leadership would be heavily represented at leadership level. Twomey, a veteran of the 1940s' IRA campaign, had been in charge of building up the Auxiliaries, but now he was set on a course for national prominence. Known as Thumper because of his habit of slamming the table with his fist when angered, Twomey would later leave an indelible imprint on the history of the Troubles.

McKee's departure opened opportunities for Gerry Adams. McKee disliked Adams and distrusted his motives for joining the Provisionals, believing that he was secretly sympathetic to the Goulding faction. The April 1970 riots in Ballymurphy had soured relations between them even further; Adams's defiance had angered McKee, and it was clear that as long as McKee was in charge of Belfast, Adams's chances of promotion would be slim. "He always thought of him as a Stick,"* recalled a contemporary.[8]

Temperamentally the two were at opposite poles. McKee was first and foremost an operator and believed that the best way to lead was by example. When the Short Strand was under attack in June 1970, he immediately drove over from West Belfast to take his place beside the East Belfast IRA, crouching behind crumbling headstones to return the fire of loyalist snipers. The wounds he received that night left him with a permanent illness. Adams on the other hand led more from behind, earning a name not for his physical courage or operational valor but for his organizing abilities and tactical canniness.

The British army had unwittingly cleared the way for Adams to rise through the ranks. Not only was McKee now out of the picture, but the elevation of Joe Cahill, a longtime IRA contemporary and friend of Gerry Adams Sr., meant that Adams had a friend at the top of the organization. As new Belfast commander, Cahill had the right to appoint his own commanders, and so in April 1971 he put Adams in charge of the Second Battalion. Adams had been Second Battalion adjutant when Cahill was battalion commander and according to one contemporary had managed to exercise "great influence" over his superior officer.[9] Now Cahill's old job was his, while Seamus Twomey became Cahill's new deputy, the adjutant of Belfast Brigade. Twomey was another friend of the Adams family, and both he and Cahill looked to Adams as someone who knew the minds of young Volunteers who were now flocking to the IRA. Adams's influence over Cahill and Twomey gave him a line right into the Army Council. Only fourteen months after the birth of the Provisional IRA, Gerry Adams's voice would be heard, albeit indirectly, in its highest councils.

The appointment of Faulkner and events on the streets combined to put the Belfast Brigade, and in particular the Second Battalion, in combative

---

*After the 1969 split the Officials designed a new Easter lily emblem, which republicans traditionally sport on their lapels to commemorate the 1916 Rising. Instead of using the customary pin to affix the paper emblem, the Officials backed theirs with adhesive, thus earning themselves the sobriquet "Stickybacks" or "Sticks." A locally recruited regiment of the British army, the Royal Ulster Rifles, were also known by this nickname; in the world of republicanism the term thus acquired a subtle double meaning.

mode. It was clear that Faulkner would press the British to introduce internment, and since the IRA itself, from bitter experience, knew how effective a
weapon it could be, it was important that the threat was met correctly.
Adams realized that the great weakness of the British was their lack of hard
intelligence on the burgeoning IRA. The no-go areas in Belfast limited the
ability to mount searches, screenings, and various other surveillance and
information-gathering exercises while the IRA itself had changed radically,
expanding way beyond the small, well-known family networks of the 1940s
and 1950s to include people who had no republican background and were
unknown to the RUC's intelligence wing, the Special Branch.

Adams decided to force the pace, as a contemporary recalled:

[I]n the Second Battalion, the leadership, which was making much of the
running at that time, were aware that internment was on the way in so we
took a strategic decision to force the British hand on the matter. We
mounted a concerted bombing campaign against the barracks in the battalion area. Some of them we bombed two or three times. We could not
afford to allow them to bring in internment when they were ready. Had it
been introduced a year later the British would very probably have had
their intelligence act together and would have hit us badly. We knew at the
time that their intelligence was bad so it was to our advantage to force
internment much sooner than they would have liked.[10]

The official explanation given by the IRA for launching its bombing campaign in April 1971 was twofold—it would stretch the British army on the
ground, and it would inflict economic damage, which the exchequer in
London would have to pay for.[11] But the truth was that the IRA wanted
to force Britain into premature and hasty action. The number of bombing
operations, mostly in Belfast, steadily rose: 37 in April, 47 in May, 50 in
June, and 91 in July. The targets were not just military and police bases but
increasingly included government and commercial premises.

As the summer progressed, the pressure for internment and on Faulkner
grew. In the early hours of the Twelfth of July, ten bombs exploded along
the route in Belfast to be used by Orangemen later in the day. During the
same week a brand-new printing plant built on the western edges of Belfast
for the Irish edition of the popular British tabloid the *Daily Mirror*
was destroyed in a daylight raid by a large IRA force. The bombing was a
serious blow to Faulkner's policy of attracting foreign investment to his
ailing economy. By then the number of British troops on duty in Northern

Ireland exceeded ten thousand, and the Tory home secretary, Reginald Maudling, declared that a state of "open war" now existed between the IRA and British forces. Faulkner calculated that if he did not get internment he was doomed, while the British still saw propping him up as preferable to dismantling unionist rule, a course they feared would cause more Protestant unrest.

On August 9, 1971, a day earlier than planned because of widespread rioting in Belfast, troops raided hundreds of homes in the hope of arresting and interning IRA leaders and activists. But the operation was every bit as disastrous and counterproductive for the British as Gerry Adams and his colleagues in the Second Battalion had hoped. As they had forecast, RUC Special Branch and British army intelligence on the IRA was either hopelessly out of date or inaccurate, and only a few handfuls of activists were rounded up in the initial swoop. Forced into premature action, the British army seized people who were in no significant way central to the IRA's war effort. The IRA also had excellent intelligence and knew several days beforehand that the raid was about to happen. "Those capable of running an effective war machine escaped," recalled one of Adams's Second Battalion colleagues, "and went on to direct the war."[12] To rub salt in the British wounds, Joe Cahill held a press conference in the heart of Ballymurphy right under the noses of patrolling troops to declare that the IRA was intact. The press conference was organized by Gerry Adams, who had taken on the role of media adviser to the Belfast commander. It was evidence of Adams's great media and PR skills, which he would put to good use throughout his career.

Internment was a triumph for the IRA in political terms as well, not least because it had been introduced in such a completely one-sided way that its effect was to enormously increase nationalist alienation on both sides of the Border. Although loyalist violence was also growing, the operation was directed solely against republicans, and even then political activists who were in no way associated with the IRA, student civil rights leaders, for instance, were included in the swoop. In Dublin the prime minister, Jack Lynch, had been toying with the notion of introducing the measure in tandem with Faulkner but the one-sided nature of the Northern operation meant he had little choice but to abandon the idea. As sympathy for their cause in the Republic exploded, IRA fugitives could now find sanctuary across the Border, safe in the knowledge that the Gardai would not throw them behind bars. Internment also pushed the levels of violence to record heights. Sectarian rioting flared across the city, driving up to seven thousand Catholics and two thousand Protestants from their homes, while for several days fierce gun battles raged, in many cases pitting loyalists and British soldiers together against the IRA. Once again the IRA could boast that it had answered the call to defend Catholic areas.

The figures spoke for themselves. In the whole seven months up to August 9, 34 people had been killed in conflict-related incidents, but in just three days following internment 22 people died violently. The death rate continued at a high level afterward; a further 118 were to die during the rest of the year, an average of nearly one a day. In Ballymurphy, British troops were involved in two days of savage gunfire and violence, which left a Catholic priest and 7 civilians dead, shot in circumstances that led to allegations the troops had killed with wanton abandon. There was little doubt that internment had exacerbated the violence.

The consequent alienation and anger in the Nationalist community took two catastrophic forms. Scores of young men and women, eager to strike back, flocked to the IRA, while older and more moderate nationalists registered their disgust by resigning from public positions. At Stormont, the nationalist opposition party, a pro-reform coalition called the Social Democratic and Labour Party, or SDLP, had already withdrawn in protest against British security policy, but now its leaders announced plans to establish a rival parliament. Internment had united Northern Catholics against the state in a way nothing else had done since 1921. It also soiled Britain's name abroad and brought protests from respected human rights activists and intellectuals. Special interrogation methods used against twelve of those arrested landed Britain in the European Court of Human Rights, accused by the Republic of Ireland's government of breaching the human rights charter and found guilty, the first of many occasions in which events in Northern Ireland would see an embarrassed British government carpeted at the international tribunal.

As the violence intensified and it became clear that internment had failed, unionists looked elsewhere for scapegoats and revived an old favorite—the IRA, they said, was still active because the Border with the Irish Republic was wide open. This simplistic conclusion flew in the face of the reality that most of the violence was taking place in Belfast, at least forty miles from the Irish Republic and rather too far for lightning cross-Border raids. Nonetheless in mid-October the British army obliged unionist anxieties and began to crater Border roads with explosives in an effort to make them unusable. In response, angry members of local farming communities who needed the road links to conduct day-to-day business promptly filled in the craters. The British army would arrive to stop them and there would be riots, often spread across fields.

The effect of all this was to antagonize a broad swath of rural Catholics and to energize the IRA outside Belfast, in Counties Tyrone, Armagh, and Fermanagh in particular, where new units, battalions, and brigades of Provisionals were formed or expanded. Existing units that were still unsure of their allegiance after the 1969 split now decided to plump for the Provisionals. Internment enlarged the IRA into a six-county-wide army and transformed it into a force that could now seriously challenge British rule in Northern Ireland.

Inasmuch as Gerry Adams's Second Battalion had, by its bombing and his strategic foresight, helped to precipitate this disaster for British policy in Northern Ireland, the IRA had benefited from his strategic talents, and this enormously boosted his standing within the IRA. Cahill and Twomey became even more dependent upon his advice. Not the least of the effects of internment was that the IRA's ranks were filled with new, angry, young recruits. The folklore of the IRA at this time is full of stories of young men and women rushing to join, some returning from as far away as North America and Britain. Numbers in the Second Battalion in particular soared, and soon its four companies were each able to field up to 100 volunteers. D Coy led the way with 120 members on active service at one point. By the end of 1971 the IRA in the whole of Belfast was more than 1,200 strong, a far cry from August 1969 when the entire organization was hard-pressed to mobilize more than 50.

With its ranks bloated, the IRA went on the offensive. All units, not just those in Belfast, were encouraged to take part in a commercial bombing campaign against businesses and offices. IRA operations multiplied. The number of bombings rose to nearly 200 in September 1971, the first full month after internment. In its official history the IRA claimed that all but a tiny number of the violent incidents, shootings as well as bombings, logged by the British after August 9 were its responsibility: 999 in September, 864 in October, 694 in November, and 765 in December.[13] One weekend in November saw no fewer than 100 IRA attacks, 60 of them carried out on the first day.[14] The death toll also soared. Killings by the IRA climbed to 86 in 1971, more than four times the number in the preceding two years, while those ascribed to the British army rose by more than sixfold, to 45. Forty-four soldiers were killed in 1971, more than two-thirds of them after August 9, while IRA casualties rose threefold, to 23, all but 4 of whom died after internment. Civilians made up the largest category of violent deaths, as they would throughout the Troubles; 92 died in 1971, compared with 16 since 1969.[15]

During all this time Gerry Adams led a highly furtive and clandestine existence. This was especially so after August 9, when British troops raided widely in West Belfast in the hope of catching those who had escaped the first swoops. Like other senior IRA figures, he moved from one safe house to another to sleep and eat—"billets," in IRA language—and not always in the Second Battalion area. It was during this period that some IRA leaders realized that South Belfast, a mixed, mostly middle-class area with a large transient student population, was an ideal hiding ground, and they based themselves here. When it was necessary to talk to other members of his battalion staff or to pass on instructions, Adams used "call houses," operational HQs in the houses of sympathizers in West Belfast, where it was considered safe to meet but not to stay overnight.

Generally, as he related in his autobiography, he rarely ventured onto the streets during daylight hours. As a result Adams was something of a mystery figure to the British army. The Ballymurphy riots had made him a well-known IRA personality, but his precise rank and status in the organization remained a puzzle to the authorities. One former British intelligence officer recalled the poverty of intelligence on him. "We had a trace on Adams as Second Battalion staff, Lower Falls, St. James, the Rock, and Ballymurphy, but not much more than that. We had no trace of his involvement in any act of violence except what you would call B2 grade; in fact we didn't have much intelligence on him at all. We certainly didn't know where he was when he was 'on the run.'"[16]

The British army was not even very sure what Gerry Adams looked like. Only one photograph of him existed; it showed a bespectacled, clean-shaven figure wearing an IRA beret at the funeral of the Provisional icon Jimmy Steele, whose coffin he had helped to carry. Now that he wore a beard his appearance was an even greater mystery. Adams's own story seems to bear this out. In his autobiography he writes that British soldiers kidnapped his pet dog, which they took with them on patrol around Ballymurphy, apparently in the hope that the animal would identify him. Had they been sure what he looked like, that would not have been necessary. His account of his life in this period is littered with stories of near-escapes, of being stopped, questioned, and let go by British patrols who failed to recognize that one of the most senior figures in the Belfast IRA had just slipped through their fingers.

At rank-and-file level in the IRA it was a different story. Adams was beginning to acquire a celebrity status that he strengthened by placing a distance between himself and ordinary IRA Volunteers. He was never one to go for a drink with the lads or to hang around the many illegal drinking clubs that were sprouting up all over West Belfast. And he acquired a prestigious nickname to fit his image, as one IRA contemporary remembered: "Adams was talked about with great reverence. It was 'The Big Lad says this and the Big Lad says that.' Adams loved being called the Big Lad because it evoked images of Michael Collins, the Big Fella."[17]

If the Second Battalion and the Ballymurphy IRA had acquired a fearsome name by mid-1971, it was due largely to the activities of a small group of "operators" Adams had recruited to A Coy in Ballymurphy. Jim Bryson, Tommy "Toddler" Tolan, and Paddy Mulvenna were Ballymurphy's equivalent of Dan Breen and Sean Treacy, legendary gunmen of the 1919–21 Anglo-Irish war, and their often bloodcurdling exploits helped to construct the Adams myth. "They were the brawn, he was the brain," remembered a contemporary.[18]

The most fearsome of the three was Bryson, who took command of A Coy when Adams was promoted to lead the Second Battalion. A terrifying and even reckless figure, Bryson would think nothing of patrolling the streets of Ballymurphy armed to the teeth on the off-chance of meeting a British patrol. Other members of A Coy lived in terror of being ordered to accompany him. "He was a controlled psychopath, someone with ice water in his blood. He would do things no sane man would ever consider," concluded an IRA colleague.[19] His favorite weapon was a vintage Lewis machine gun, known as Big Louie, with which he terrorized the British army. But he also earned a name as a deadly one-shot sniper. His relationship with Adams was complicated. Since Bryson's death Adams has claimed him as "a dear friend of mine,"[20] but contemporaries say the friendship was not returned. "Bryson didn't trust Adams, because he had never fired a shot," remembered one. "He was such a hard bastard, and I think Adams was basically frightened of him."[21] When Adams needed to curb Bryson, to put him on a leash, he would send someone else, usually a fellow operator for whom Bryson had respect. He never did the job himself.

Bryson died in September 1973, a few days after being shot by an undercover British army unit in Ballymurphy. He was on the run at the time, as was Toddler Tolan, who survived him by a mere four years. The pair became IRA legends when in January 1972, along with five other IRA prisoners, they succeeded in escaping from the prison ship *Maidstone,* which had been berthed in Belfast docks first as military accommodation and then as an overflow to the city's Crumlin Road prison, where there was just not enough room to hold the scores of IRA internees. Within hours their feat was being celebrated in song. Tolan was shot dead during a vicious Provisional IRA–Official IRA feud in 1977, while the third member of the group, Paddy Mulvenna, a brother-in-law of Gerry Adams, was killed by the same covert unit that fatally wounded Bryson. Following the escape Bryson had insisted he stay in Belfast to fight. He was recaptured in September 1972 but made another extraordinary escape, overpowering prison guards and fleeing in a stolen uniform. After a short spell across the Border, he came back to Ballymurphy and to his death. "He was born to be killed," concluded an associate.[22] Bryson was just twenty-six when he died, Mulvenna twenty-two, and Tolan thirty-one.

Adams's leadership of the IRA during these early years received much of its shape and direction from his relationship with two influential comrades, both of whom were to leave lasting marks on IRA history. One was Ivor Bell, his adjutant in the Second Battalion, and the other, Brendan Hughes, an early commander of D Coy. Bell had been in the IRA during the 1956–62 campaign but disagreed with the decision to call a cease-fire and had quit. As much an anarchist as a republican, he rejoined in 1970 and became commander of B Coy in the Kashmir Road area. "Ivor and Gerry were a team. We looked to them for political direction, for strategy, and for interpretation," recalled a colleague.[23] Hughes, from the Grosvenor Road, was an early recruit to the Provisionals and a disciple of the slain Charlie Hughes. Known as the Dark because of his swarthy features, Hughes was happier as a rank-and-file "operator" than as a leader and often teamed up with Bryson for operations. After Cahill's elevation to the post of Belfast commander, he became Adams's Battalion operations officer. Together, Adams, Bell, and Hughes were synonymous with the Belfast IRA of the early 1970s.

After internment the trio played an even more crucial role in the Belfast IRA. MacStiofain decided that leaving Joe Cahill in charge of Belfast was a public relations risk too high to take. Cahill had humiliated the British command with his Ballymurphy press conference a week after the failed internment swoop, but he was now a marked man and, as a result of the media coverage, well known too. It would only be a matter of time before he was arrested, and the British would be sure to make much of his capture. MacStiofain ordered Cahill down to Dublin, where he combined his Army Council position with the post of GHQ director of finance. Twomey was promoted to Belfast commander, and Adams became his adjutant, effectively his second in command. Bell became Brigade staff operations officer, while Hughes took over the Second Battalion. The trio had each moved up a step on the IRA's ladder.

INTERNMENT USHERED IN a new phase in the IRA's development, especially in Belfast. Its ranks were flush with new and angry members eager to strike back at the British, supplies of cash and weapons increased, particularly from Irish-American communities in the United States that had watched unfolding events with a mixture of astonishment and mounting atavistic fury, and soon IRA violence was at an unprecedented level.

The defining characteristic of the IRA in the weeks and months after internment was the utter spontaneity and unpredictability of its violence. There was virtually no central control from Dublin or even the Belfast Brigade. Aside from special operations that required coordination and planning, IRA companies were encouraged to go their own way. "There was an incredible amount of activity at this time," remembered one activist. "We would mount five or six operations every day—a bank would be robbed, a bomb downtown, a booby trap for the Brits, snipes, a float."[24] A float was a particularly hazardous operation in which three or four heavily armed IRA members would drive randomly around their streets in the hope of encountering a British army patrol to fire upon.

At the start the British army was naïve and suffered badly in the unfamiliar warren of tiny streets that made up much of West Belfast. The first armored cars, Saracens, which were nicknamed Pigs by military and IRA alike, came onto the Falls Road with pictures of the Virgin Mary or Christ pinned to their radiators, apparently in the belief that the IRA would then not dare shoot at them. Their knowledge of where they were or whom they were dealing with was fashioned by ignorance and bigotry. Early on, the IRA discovered that they could easily trick soldiers into firing at their own patrols: "Whenever the Brits came in they would come in big 'duck patrols.' They would patrol in parallel and we would snipe at one, and before you knew what was happening the Brits would be shooting at each other and we would withdraw and watch them."[25] Such naïveté did not, however, last long.

Adams kept one or more steps ahead of the British army for months after August 1971, but eventually he made a mistake. In July 1971 he married Colette McArdle, an activist who came from a well-known republican family, whose mother, Maggie, was a republican veteran and a friend of Joe Cahill. Gerry Adams and Colette McArdle had met in 1970 at a point when republicans were mounting pickets outside British army bases where discos were being held and Ballymurphy girls were fraternizing with the troops. Adams had a progressive attitude toward female involvement in military matters, but he barred Colette from involvement in them, although he encouraged other women to join his Second Battalion on the same terms as men, much to the fury of Cumann na mBan leaders, as one female member recalled. "That was in the days when the Cumann na mBan came under the authority of the IRA; in fact even a Volunteer in the IRA could give orders to a ranking Cumann na mBan woman. The Cumann na mBan stopped taking orders from the IRA when he [Adams] allowed women to join it; they wouldn't take orders from other women; they were very resentful of them and refused to work with them." Adams was, by contrast, keen to ensure that Colette never got involved in activities that could put her in danger, which her association with him might well have done, as one contemporary remembered. "We were told that he had given a direction [to Cumann na mBan leaders] that Colette was not to go on any operations, not even to carry a weapon or papers, nothing."[26] The purpose may well have been to make it more difficult for the British to track him and other IRA leaders down, but the order unsettled some colleagues.

The newlyweds had a difficult first few months, always on the run and constantly afraid that at any moment they could be parted by Adams's arrest or worse. Colette suffered a miscarriage, and the pair were rarely able to spend more than a few hours or at most a day or two in each other's company before Adams had to move on to a safer "billet." Regularly changing habits, routes, and lifestyle was the key to survival for IRA leaders in 1971 and 1972. Despite the strain Colette appeared delighted to have married the IRA leader, as an associate recalled: "I remember once going to a call house where we had to meet Adams, and as we were sitting there in the midst of an Army meeting Colette came bursting in and sat down on Adams's lap, and it all got kissy-kissy, stroking his hair and so on. We had to change the conversation to general things, and someone asked, 'What would you do if your partner was unfaithful?' And I remember Colette flourishing her hand and pointing to the wedding ring, saying this is all I care about, as long as I've got this, and Adams was giggling."[27]

In a bid to create some stability in the relationship, Adams arranged to rent a terraced house in Harrogate Street in the Clonard district, where at least Colette, now pregnant, but destined not to go the full-term, could be assured of a more settled life even if her husband could visit her only occasionally. They moved in, but they were "hardly there," to use Adams's words, when the house was raided at dawn on March 14, 1972, by British troops and he was taken away to Springfield Road RUC barracks. Adams suspected that an informer had betrayed the house, because the troops knew whom they had come to get, although they were not really sure he was the Gerry Adams on their list.[28] He chose to play on this by claiming he was someone called Joe McGuigan. The soldiers believed him, but when they brought in a veteran RUC Special Branchman, Harry Taylor, who identified him, Adams was transferred to the main military interrogation center at Palace barracks in Holywood, on the eastern outskirts of Belfast. Palace barracks had a terrifying name among IRA members; it was where the special interrogation methods had been used in the first internment swoops and the victims, Adams's cousin Kevin Hannaway included, suffered long-term psychological and physical damage.

Adams was given a rough time by his interrogators. He was beaten badly and subjected to mental terror; his captors pretended they were about to kill him, and an attempt was made to inject him with what he was told was a truth drug. Years later Adams would be credited with introducing the IRA to systematic anti-interrogation training, which had at its core the principle that if IRA Volunteers stayed silent and avoided creating any relationship with their interrogators, they would survive the experience. But during his own interrogation he chose the dangerous course of conversing with his questioners and persisted with the attempt to pass himself off as Joe McGuigan even though Harry Taylor had destroyed the ploy. In his autobiography he claimed the tactic helped him withstand the experience, but in the end he admitted who he was after the Special Branch told him that if he was interned under the name Joe McGuigan, he would not be able to get visits from Colette. Once the police and army were satisfied they had seized the right man, he was transferred to the *Maidstone,* where he found his maternal uncles Liam and Alfie Hannaway waiting. Later, when the *Maidstone* was closed down as a prison ship, he was moved to a World War II prisoner of war–style internment camp at Long Kesh, on the western outskirts of Belfast, where his father and brother Paddy were imprisoned. There was no shortage of Adams family members in jail.

SECURITY SUCCESSES like the arrest of Gerry Adams were slowly restricting the IRA, but the British military was still denied the sort of face-to-face confrontation that its generals were confident could deal a knockout blow to the republicans and give the politicians the time and space to construct a deal. Since the IRA was unlikely to make a gift of such an opportunity to the British, it was left to the British to create one or at least to take full advantage if even half a chance came along. On January 30, 1972, in Derry, an opportunity did present itself, but far from providing the British with an opening to give the IRA a bloody nose, the horrific events of that day were to be a watershed in Irish history, one that would propel the Provisional IRA measurably closer to the goal of forcing the British to withdraw entirely from Ireland.

The event on January 30 was a march organized by NICRA to protest against the continuing use of internment, a march that was bound to attract many thousands of demonstrators and lead to the sort of stone-throwing confrontation that might tempt the IRA to come out into the open. The British chose to send one of their crack outfits, the First Battalion of the Parachute Regiment, to police the march in the apparent expectation that its battle skills would be needed.

Later IRA leaders concluded that the British were hoping that the presence of the First Para would lure the IRA into a gun battle that the Provisionals would surely lose. If that was the plan, it was misconceived; the IRA had no intention of falling into such an obvious trap. Ten thousand people marched to the Bogside, and just after a small section broke off to throw stones, bricks, and iron bars at the troops, the Paras went into action. An hour later thirteen men lay dead and seventeen wounded, one of whom died a few weeks later. None were in the IRA, and eyewitness testimony said they had been killed in cold blood. The deaths on Bloody Sunday outraged nationalist Ireland. A wave of anger swept through the entire country. In Derry the local SDLP leader, John Hume, said that the mood in the Bogside was now for "a united Ireland or nothing," while at Westminster the civil rights MP Bernadette Devlin physically attacked the British home secretary, Reginald Maudling, in the chamber of the House of Commons. In Dublin a crowd of twenty thousand besieged the British embassy before IRA members arrived to bomb and burn it down. Even ministers in Jack Lynch's Fianna Fail government in Dublin were moved to unaccustomed militancy by the bloodshed. As he arrived in New York to speak at the United Nations, the Irish foreign affairs minister, Dr. Patrick Hillery, declared, "From now on my aim is to get Britain out of Ireland."[29] In the Bogside, meanwhile, young people were said to be queuing up by the hundreds to join the IRA.

The most significant outcome of Bloody Sunday is that it sounded the death knell for unionist rule at Stormont. Within weeks the British finally concluded that the cost of sustaining Faulkner in power was too high. On March 24, 1972, after a contrived dispute with Faulkner over control of the security forces, the British prime minister, Edward Heath, announced a yearlong suspension of the Stormont parliament pending an agreed political settlement. In the meantime Britain would take direct responsibility for governing Northern Ireland on a day-to-day basis. A cabinet minister would run the government until the suspension was lifted, but everyone knew that in practice the suspension would be much longer than a year.

The fall of Stormont was a major victory for the Provisionals, but it also marked a watershed in their campaign. Most nationalists were jubilant. Stormont symbolized unionist domination and Catholics' second-class status. Its collapse was a reason to celebrate and also to suspend the violence. This dramatic change in the psychological climate coincided with a series of badly bungled republican military operations, the combined effect of which was to stimulate demands for a cease-fire.

The botched operations followed one upon the other. On February 22 the Official IRA bombed the Paras' headquarters in Aldershot, England, in revenge for Bloody Sunday, but instead of killing soldiers, five cleaning women, a British army chaplain, and a gardener were blown to smithereens. On March 4 a bomb exploded without warning in the middle of a busy Saturday afternoon in the Abercorn restaurant in downtown Belfast, killing two women and injuring seventy people, mostly shoppers, some of them terribly. The IRA was blamed for the bombing, and while it strongly denied the charge, the allegation stuck. Sixteen days later the IRA loaded two cars with bombs and parked them in Belfast city center. A number of conflicting phone warnings were given, with the result that police moved fleeing crowds in the direction of one of the bombs in Lower Donegall Street; it exploded and killed seven people, five of them civilians. The Provos had engineered their own Aldershot. Then, on May 21, the Official IRA in Derry kidnapped and killed a local Catholic, William Best, a nineteen-year-old member of the locally recruited Royal Irish Rangers, a regiment of the British army barred from serving in Northern Ireland. Ranger Best was seized while he was on home leave from Germany, and there was a strong local reaction against the killing, which affected the Provisionals as much as the Officials. As small peace groups, many led by women, sprang up in nationalist neighborhoods, the Official IRA leadership declared a cease-fire, and this in turn added to the pressure on the Provisionals.

THE SUSPENSION of Stormont and the imposition of direct rule from Britain represented a major victory for the IRA. In its own account of the period, the IRA described the day when Heath suspended the Stormont parliament as "one of the most momentous . . . in Irish history."[30] The IRA had good reason to celebrate. The destruction of the Stormont parliament had been a declared Provisional IRA war aim from the outset, as Sinn Fein's president, Ruairi O Bradaigh, made clear when he told a July 1971 rally in Derry, "We're on the high road to freedom, and what we need to do now is to rock Stormont and to keep it rocking until Stormont comes down."[31] Most Catholics, moderate as well as militant, heartily agreed—but with an important qualification. Many Catholics believed that, having achieved this success, the IRA should then at least review its options. There was also war weariness in many Catholic districts of Belfast. The shootings and bombings had transformed many nationalist areas into terrifying war zones, where people ran a daily risk of running into gun battles or being caught up in nerve-jangling bomb explosions. The collapse of unionist rule brought the hope that this could all be near an end, as one commentator noted: "This major victory having been won, the feeling grew in the Catholic community—fostered by the SDLP, the clergy and the Dublin government—that the Provos ought now call a halt to their campaign. At the very least, thought many nationalists, we deserve a bit of a respite from the past six months of non-stop violence."[32]

While the moderate nationalist party, the SDLP, welcomed the arrival of the new British minister for Northern Ireland, the avuncular and genial gentleman farmer William Whitelaw, and showed an eagerness to re-enter political dialogue, the IRA greeted the fall of Stormont by stepping up its violence. With its ranks swollen by the anger at Bloody Sunday and other instances of state violence, the IRA carried out twelve hundred operations in May 1972, many of them in rural areas, and more the following month. While the IRA leadership hoped that this would drive the British to the negotiating table, the truth was that the fall of Stormont had opened up a fault line within nationalism that would never really close. Moderate nationalist opinion now sought a political deal and reform, while the IRA fought on for revolution and the elusive republic.

From all the available evidence it seems that the subsequent truce was entered into halfheartedly by both the British and the IRA and in an atmosphere of intense mutual suspicion and distrust. After weeks of maneuvering, the cease-fire began on June 26, 1972, and ended just thirteen days later, on July 9, only two days after Whitelaw and an IRA delegation had met in London. It appears that neither side was all that sorry when it ended. A squalid sectarian dispute over the housing of Catholics in a loyalist-controlled part of West Belfast was allowed by the British to get so serious that it broke the cessation. If the British were secretly glad to see the truce end, so was the IRA in Belfast. Fears that the longer the cease-fire lasted, the more damage it would cause the IRA were very strong. The halt in hostilities had tempted hitherto unknown IRA members to break cover; they were mixing in public with known IRA men, and this was all very visible to the British. Something similar had happened during the 1921 truce. The IRA then had greeted the Treaty negotiations as a victory and celebrated accordingly, emerging in public to receive the adulation of their communities. Collins's negotiating hand had been badly weakened as a result. Nevertheless the 1972 cease-fire gave something to both sides. The British got an opportunity to take a close look at the key Army Council and military leaders, while the IRA could now say to nationalists that at least it had tried to negotiate terms with the British, and if it had failed it was no fault of theirs.

It was a measure of Adams's status within the IRA even at that early point that part of the truce preconditions included a demand that he be released from Long Kesh to join the IRA leadership delegation and to assist Daithi O Conaill in making the detailed arrangements for the Whitelaw-IRA summit. According to one account the cease-fire would not have happened had Adams not been freed: "The leadership of the Belfast Brigade at this time was heavily made up of those who commanded the Second Battalion in the run-up to internment. When MacStiofain announced internally that we were going for a truce he was told by that element in the Belfast leadership that there would be no ceasefire in Belfast unless Gerry Adams was released from internment."[33]

It was men from Adams's Second Battalion who fired the shots that ended the truce, a fusillade directed at troops stopping homeless Catholics from occupying houses in the Lenadoon housing estate. One of them recalled it vividly: "I remember quite clearly, Jim Bryson, Tommy Tolan, and another figure were told by Twomey to go up to Lenadoon with a Lewis gun—Big Louie—and two Armalites. They were told to wait for a signal from Twomey, who was negotiating with the Brits. When he raised his arm they were to open fire, and the cease-fire would be over. He couldn't, because of the crowd that was confronting the Brits, but eventually Twomey got them back, and they opened up followed by the Andytown men."[34]

MacStiofain, ever eager to keep on good terms with the Northerners, had packed his London team with hard-liners from Belfast and Derry. Adams was joined by Seamus Twomey, Ivor Bell, now Belfast adjutant, and Martin McGuinness, the young leader of the Derry IRA who had risen through the ranks since internment. MacStiofain and O Conaill were the sole Southern IRA leaders on the delegation. Conspicuously absent was the Sinn Fein president, Ruairi O Bradaigh.

Afterward only MacStiofain appeared positive about the encounter, a view with which Adams openly disagreed. Adams and the Belfast IRA men suspected that Britain was seeking to draw the IRA into a long cessation, as an associate recalled: "The reasoning of the Belfast leadership . . . was that the British wanted the truce to continue. One of the delegation saw previously unknown Volunteers sitting outside pubs drinking with known IRA people, and he was deeply concerned. [The IRA's] guard was dropping, and he was determined to see the truce broken. As far as I recall, the Belfast delegation left the Whitelaw talks with the clear intention of breaking the truce."[35] Adams sided with the hawks, according to a contemporary. "Adams and Bell were very, very skeptical about the cease-fire, they warned us that things weren't good, they didn't trust the Brits and thought they were playing for time. They were fully in favor of breaking it. If Adams had been opposed, it wouldn't have happened."[36] The truce duly broke down amid violence that claimed twenty lives over the next three days.

The Belfast IRA had its own reasons for wanting to break the truce. There had been developments on the military front that gave the IRA in the city reason to believe that it could stretch the British further. The IRA, they calculated, was not yet at its strongest and, if things went well, could put more pressure on the British before returning to the negotiating table in a more powerful position. In both cases Adams's contribution was crucial.

The first was the decision by the Belfast Brigade to import quantities of the American-made Armalite rifle, a powerful semiautomatic weapon that came to symbolize the IRA of the 1970s. The Belfast Brigade first heard of the gun when a Falls Road seaman showed a member of Second Battalion staff a U.S. magazine article about the weapon, known as the AR-15, in the autumn of 1971. Weighing only seven pounds and fitted with a collapsible butt, the Armalite was easy to hide and could even be dumped in water. It fired a high-velocity .223 round, which tumbled through the air with the same deadly effect as a dum-dum bullet, and it was highly accurate. When brigade staff heard about the weapon, the decision was instantaneous: the Armalite could make the IRA better armed than the British army. The conclusion was simple, as one source familiar with the episode recalled: "If we could lay our hands on these guns [maybe] we'd win the war."[37]

Adams ordered his operations officer, Brendan Hughes, to travel to New York to arrange for the purchase and shipment of the guns. The Americans involved in gunrunning for the IRA had old-fashioned ideas about what the best weapons were, and GHQ in Dublin agreed with them. They were the weapons of their age. GHQ instructions were to acquire standard World War II U.S. infantry weapons, principally MI Carbines, Garand rifles, and the ubiquitous Thompson submachine gun. When Hughes arrived in New York looking for a completely different sort of weapon, he met enormous opposition from the locals. It strengthened a growing view at the top of the Belfast IRA that many in the Dublin leadership, especially in GHQ, were out of touch with the needs of those fighting the war in the North. Adams's orders, however, were that the Armalites had to be acquired even if that meant bypassing GHQ. By the spring of 1972 the Belfast Brigade had organized its own supply route, and the Armalite began to appear in the city, where it was tested in combat by D Coy in gun battles with the British. The weapon was judged a huge success, and arrangements were made to import larger quantities. In May and June 1972, when preparations for the truce were in progress, two hundred AR-15s arrived in Belfast, smuggled aboard the transatlantic liner *QE2* and then transported to Belfast from Southampton in England.[38] There were enough Armalites to equip every active-service unit in the city. As Adams and Bell flew out on board the RAF plane to meet Whitelaw, they knew that back in Belfast the IRA was better able than ever to take on British troops.

The second military advance was the development of the car bomb, another weapon synonymous with the IRA of that era. The car bomb was discovered entirely by accident, but its deployment by the Belfast IRA was not. The chain of events began in late December 1971 when the IRA's quartermaster general, Jack McCabe, was fatally injured in an explosion caused when an experimental fertilizer-based homemade mix known as the "black stuff" exploded as he was blending it with a shovel in his garage on the northern outskirts of Dublin. GHQ warned that the mix was too dangerous to handle, but Belfast had already received a consignment, and someone had the idea of disposing of it by dumping it in a car with a fuse and a timer and leaving it somewhere in downtown Belfast. "It was a bomb in a car rather than a 'car bomb,'" recalled a Belfast IRA source familiar with the episode. "A young Volunteer took it in [to the center of Belfast] and we could feel the rattle where we stood. Then we knew we were onto something, and it took off from there."[39] The car bomb enabled the IRA to increase significantly the amount of explosives it could deliver in each individual operation while exposing fewer operatives to arrest or premature death.

The "black stuff" mix was perfected and made safer to handle within weeks of McCabe's death, and this meant that the IRA now had unlimited supplies of homemade explosives. It no longer had to depend on gelignite, supplies of which were gradually being cut off by the British and Irish intelligence authorities. The car bomb was, however, a double-edged sword. The sheer size of the devices greatly increased the risk of civilian deaths in careless or bungled operations. The IRA bombs that killed seven people in Little Donegall Street, for example, were among the very first car bombs deployed, and no one could doubt that the episode was a public relations disaster for the Provisionals.

The new explosives mix could be used outside the city as well. It was an ideal explosive to use in rural land mines, which were usually hidden in culverts, or drainpipes, which ran under country roads at regular intervals to draw off rainwater. The land mine came into its own during the early summer of 1972, making military and police patrols in Tyrone and Fermanagh hazardous and eventually rendering South Armagh a no-go area for motorized British units. The truth was that among Armalites, car bombs, and land mines, the IRA felt it was on a string of successes when the 1972 cease-fire was called. Seen in that perspective, the chances that IRA leaders would enter talks with Whitelaw in a mood of compromise were virtually nonexistent.

WITHIN TWO WEEKS all had changed utterly. The IRA had forced the destruction of the Stormont parliament and fought the British to the negotiating table. Not since 1920 had the organization wielded such power or been so well placed to influence and shape events. But in a trice all that was to disappear. On Friday afternoon, July 21, the Belfast Brigade sent twenty of the new car bombs into the city and detonated them in just over an hour, killing 9 people and injuring 130, in one of the worst days of violence yet seen during the Troubles. At the height of the bombing the center of Belfast resembled a city under artillery fire; clouds of suffocating smoke enveloped buildings as one explosion followed another, almost drowning out the hysterical screams of panicked shoppers. Six people, two of them soldiers, were killed by a car bomb at a bus station, and three civilians, two women and a fourteen-year-old schoolboy, died when another device was detonated in North Belfast. Television pictures of firemen shoveling human remains into plastic bags compounded the horror.

The deaths were not deliberate but the result of careless planning by the Belfast Brigade leadership. Brigade commanders made the fatal error of assuming that the British army and RUC could deal with so many bomb alarms all happening more or less at the same time in different parts of the city. Bloody Friday, as the day was called, was the unionist equivalent of Bloody Sunday, and it was an unmitigated disaster for the IRA. The IRA later tried to blame the British for deliberately ignoring telephoned warnings, but that cut little ice with anyone except its most loyal supporters. Most people accused the IRA of using sheer terror tactics. Bloody Friday had a speedy political impact. Moderate nationalists put even more distance between themselves and the IRA and intensified efforts to seek negotiations with the British and Faulkner's unionists.

It took years for the IRA to admit that Bloody Friday was its fault. "We put it down to the Brits allowing bombs to go off, but the real reason was it was too much for the Brits to cope with, the bombs went off too close together, the town was too small, people were being shepherded from one bomb to another," conceded an IRA activist of the time.[40] Bloody Friday had been planned by Twomey and his staff before the June 26 truce and was intended to pressure the British to come to the negotiating table.[41] Adams was in jail at the time and played no role in its conception, but after the collapse of the truce he was back at the center of events, acting with Bell once again as adviser to Twomey.[42] The plan was revived to demonstrate that the IRA was still in business, but it backfired badly; Adams did not initiate Bloody Friday, but he was involved in its organization. The British quickly realized that events had moved to their advantage. Ten days later, on July 31, in an operation code-named Motorman, hundreds of British troops invaded the no-go areas of Derry and Belfast, an action that would have been unthinkable before Bloody Friday. Within weeks military forts were constructed right on the IRA's doorsteps, and the organization's freedom of movement was severely curtailed. Now able to put the IRA under close surveillance in both cities and to screen thousands of civilians for IRA sympathies, British army intelligence on the IRA improved markedly. Within two years the British grip on areas like West Belfast was so tight that the Belfast Brigade was forced to move its operational headquarters to the southern outskirts of the city, to the affluent Malone area.

Bloody Friday was the one great black mark against Adams's strategic record in the early 1970s. The man himself was incandescent with rage after the botched bombings, according to IRA sources. "Most of the bombs that day came from the Third Batt area, from Ardoyne and the Markets, and some from the Second Batt; it was a BB [Belfast Brigade] operation though. Afterwards the word was that: 'the Big Lad's doing his nut, about the warnings not being phoned in or being bungled.' There was an undercurrent of blame being put on the Third Batt leadership."[43] In his autobiography Adams played down the implications of Motorman, saying that it merely required the IRA to readjust its tactics. But the reality was that Bloody Friday and its aftermath marked a watershed in the IRA's fortunes. From then on the organization would be on the defensive both politically and militarily.

The first IRA casualty of Bloody Friday was the Belfast commander Seamus Twomey. Adams and Bell were convinced that Twomey was "too fiery" for the new circumstances, and they combined to persuade him to quit Belfast and to move to Dublin, where he would be better placed to look after the Northern IRA's interests. In September, Twomey acquiesced. Adams replaced him and appointed Bell as his adjutant, and Hughes became his operations officer. In the view of some IRA members Adams was merely formalizing what already existed: "Twomey was commander in name only; Adams [always] really called the shots."[44]

Soon Adams would have an ally at the very top of the organization. In November 1972 Sean MacStiofain was arrested as part of the Dublin government's accelerating crackdown on the IRA leadership. Sentenced to six months in jail on IRA membership charges brought on the basis of a radio interview he gave to the Irish broadcasting service, RTE, MacStiofain immediately embarked on that most traditional of IRA protests, a hunger strike, which ended fifty-seven days later, inconclusively and amid charges that the Provos' chief of staff had cheated during the fast. Upon his arrest MacStiofain immediately lost his IRA rank, and thanks to the opprobrious circumstances of his fast's conclusion, his republican career effectively ended. A tough and uncompromising leader, MacStiofain had overseen the birth and development of a formidable fighting machine, and for that Northern IRA leaders retained for him a degree of affection and respect that survived his ignominious departure. Joe Cahill took over as the Provisionals' second chief of staff. Second Battalion veterans now occupied the two most important posts in the IRA, its national leadership and the command of Belfast, the cockpit of the IRA's war against Britain.

GERRY ADAMS was to be Belfast commander for the next ten months, during which time his already established reputation as the IRA's key strategic thinker was significantly enhanced. But he also earned a name for ruthlessness that would make many a potential rival pause for thought before considering any challenge to his authority.

One event marked out Adams's period in command as special in the eyes of other IRA members, and that was a strike against British military intelligence that was reminiscent of the triumphs organized by IRA leaders during the Tan War. It looked like an astonishing counterintelligence coup, but in reality what happened was more a chance affair, which owed much to the alertness of an observant junior IRA member. But the operation that followed persuaded many that the new Belfast commander had penetrated the core of British intelligence.

The story of what became known as the affair of the Four Square Laundry began with an admission by a rank-and-file volunteer in the Second Battalion's D Coy that he had been working as an informer for the military. The volunteer, Seamus Wright, from the Lower Falls Road area had come under suspicion because he was so often absent from Belfast, apparently spending much of his time in England. Under interrogation by Second Battalion staff, Wright admitted that all the time he had actually been in the company of a special military unit based at Palace barracks in Holywood, County Down, where IRA suspects were taken for routine interrogation before being interned. The unit was known by the initials MRF, which the IRA believed stood for Military Reconnaissance Force, a group subsequently alleged to have been involved in two drive-by shootings in the summer of 1972 that were blamed at the time on loyalist gangs. Wright admitted he had agreed to work for the MRF.

The MRF ran plainclothes military patrols in republican areas of the city, but it also had built up an agent-running capacity and had set aside a special section of Palace barracks to house informers where debriefings were conducted and operations planned. A favorite tactic was to drive these agents through nationalist districts in military vehicles to identify and photograph other IRA activists through the slits in armor plating. Wright named another D Coy volunteer as a fellow MRF agent. The IRA arrested Kevin McKee, and his questioning added significantly to the IRA's knowledge of MRF operations.

McKee revealed that the MRF had constructed an intricate undercover intelligence network that included a massage parlor, ostensibly run by English prostitutes, an ice cream business, and the Four Square Laundry, which operated in West Belfast. The Four Square operation was simplicity itself: a van would tour housing estates offering cut-price laundry sevices so as to acquire clothing to be analyzed for traces of explosives and gunpowder and so to identify IRA houses. Within the roof space of the large van used to collect and return laundry lay two British operatives who would photograph suspects on the streets. By the standards of later British intelligence operations against the IRA, it was an amateurish operation but also an indication of how little the British knew about the IRA in those early days.

After McKee's interrogation, the Belfast Brigade—Adams, in other words—took over the operation from Second Batt, and plans were made to ambush the various MRF teams. During the midmorning of October 2, 1972, gunmen ambushed the Four Square Laundry van as it made its rounds in Twinbrook, a sprawling housing estate on the edge of West Belfast. The driver was shot dead and the roof compartment sprayed with automatic fire. At the same time in North Belfast gunmen from the Third Battalion shot up the massage parlor. The third premises identified as an MRF front, city center offices, turned out to be vacant when the IRA arrived. At the end of the day the IRA claimed to have killed five undercover British soldiers, but the British would admit to only one dead, the van driver killed in Twinbrook. Despite this uncertainty the IRA regarded the day's work as a major victory over British intelligence, and Adams compared the operation—and implicitly himself—to the counterintelligence exploits of Michael Collins, whose famous "squad" had wiped out the bulk of Britain's secret agents in Dublin in one violent day, the first Bloody Sunday, fifty-two years earlier: "It was a devastating blow, on a par with Michael Collins' actions against British Intelligence in November 1920 . . . ," Adams later wrote.[45]

A devastating blow it certainly was, but the incident was no less serious for the IRA. Although badly hit by the Belfast Brigade, the episode had demonstrated that the MRF had clearly managed to infiltrate the IRA's crack Second Battalion, and that this had only been discovered by chance. It was also apparent that, thanks to Wright and McKee, British intelligence now knew the names of all D Coy's members and many of the Second Battalion's secrets. The chances of there being other Second Battalion agents on the MRF's payroll, recruited as a result of intelligence passed on by the pair, had to have been high. More than anything else the penetration demonstrated that the IRA had no systematic counterintelligence capability. After all, Wright and McKee had been caught by luck, not by any IRA system. While the task of pursuing traitors was part of the Coy intelligence officer's job, it was only one part of a substantial job description—more time and energy went into identifying targets than into uncovering agents. The Four Square Laundry affair exposed major deficiencies in the way the IRA conducted its business and it raised embarrassing questions. Not least it exposed the damaging consequences that would result if the intelligence officer himself or herself had been turned by the British. Without a foolproof counterintelligence capacity, the IRA had no protection against that level of penetration. The Four Square Laundry operation was loudly praised, and Adams basked in the adulation, but the hard questions were just not asked. Instead, the accidental discovery of the MRF's penetration and the weaknesses in IRA command and control which it had exposed were literally covered up.

The IRA sentenced the MRF agents Wright and McKee to death after courts-martial, but in an unprecedented twist the Belfast Brigade ordered that they be buried in secret after execution and their treachery kept hidden.[46] This was contrary to one of the central principles of the IRA's informer-hunting practice, which was that those found guilty of working for the British must be exposed publicly in order to discourage others from imitating them. In practice that meant that the bodies of dead informers must be left literally by the roadside and a public explanation given for the killing. The thinking behind this was that anyone tempted to follow suit would be persuaded to think again. That in this case, contrary to IRA rules, Wright and McKee were put in secret graves suggests another motive.

The justification for "disappearing" the men that was put forward at the highest levels of the Belfast Brigade—at the level of Adams, Bell, and Hughes—was disarming. Since Wright and McKee were both members of influential republican families, it was agreed, the IRA would be sparing their relatives considerable embarrassment if they were just quietly buried and news of their fate kept hidden.[47] Wright was related to the Hickey family, and a sister-in-law, Eileen Hickey, went on to become a senior figure in the Belfast Brigade and the commander of IRA prisoners at Armagh women's prison. McKee was a nephew of Billy McKee, Adams's old adversary. Secret executions and burial would spare their familes embarrassment, although anguish at their unexplained disappearance would surely outweigh that. But the secret manner of their deaths served another purpose; the extent of British intelligence penetration of Adams's IRA units, particularly in his own Second Batt and D Coy, went to the grave with them and the luster of the Four Square Laundry operation left untarnished. The pair were ferried secretly down to South Armagh, where they were held for six weeks before the orders to kill them arrived. By that time their jailers had built up such a strong rapport with them that the South Armagh IRA requested that others do the deed. IRA men from Belfast, in fact from Adams's old IRA unit in Ballymurphy, were sent down to carry out the killings.[48] The execution and burial of the two agents was kept a secret until March 1999 when the IRA, under pressure from relatives and the demands of the peace process, finally admitted part of the story of what had happened. Despite intensive efforts their graves have never been located. Seamus Wright and Kevin McKee carried to their secret graves the untold story of how British intelligence bested Gerry Adams. Their fate ensured that the story would never see the light of day.

THE CLANDESTINE BURIALS of Wright and McKee set a precedent that was repeated at least seven more times in subsequent years. The Belfast Brigade, under Adams's leadership, had set a grisly precedent. From there on, if the IRA had an informer on its hands whose existence would embarrass the organization or its supporters, it would think little of disposing of the problem under the clay that covered a secret grave. The third secret interment during Adams's reign as Belfast commander fell into that category, although the circumstances of the disappearance of Jean McConville were to leave a much more lasting and damaging stain.

The death and disappearance of Jean McConville was made possible by another important military innovation pioneered by Gerry Adams. With an eye on the special "squad" that Michael Collins had constructed in 1920 to subvert British intelligence operations in Dublin, Adams did the same thing in the Belfast of the early 1970s when he got Twomey's go-ahead to set up two secret cells in the city to carry out special operations on behalf of the Belfast Brigade. These cells reported directly to Adams and received their instructions only from him, a chain of command that was formalized when Adams replaced Twomey as Belfast commander. They became known in IRA folklore as "the unknowns." One unit was located in West Belfast and led by the brigade staff intelligence officer, a figure from the Turf Lodge area. The other was in the Third Battalion area in North Belfast and commanded by a renowned IRA leader, who was later shot dead at his home by loyalists. The cells were very small at the start, consisting of only three members each, later expanded to four. The idea was that "the unknowns" would be self-sustaining and independent of the rest of the Belfast IRA; they carried out their own intelligence work and acted on it themselves, although from time to time they borrowed personnel from other units for larger operations, especially D Coy in the Lower Falls.

Jean McConville was a thirty-seven-year-old East Belfast Protestant who had married a West Belfast Catholic and converted to Catholicism after their wedding. In 1972 she had been living for two years in the Divis Flats complex in the Lower Falls area with her ten children. Her husband, Arthur, a former soldier in the British army who had quit in 1964 to become a builder, had died a year before. Now widowed and poverty-stricken, Jean McConville was struggling to raise her family. In December 1972, suddenly and without any reason, she disappeared from the face of the earth. One widely accepted and repeatedly given explanation for her disappearance was that she had angered the IRA by comforting a seriously wounded British soldier who had been shot by a sniper outside her front door. In revenge, the story continues, the IRA abducted her and took her to a house in the Beechmount district of West Belfast, where she died during interrogation, allegedly suffocating when her questioners placed a plastic bag over her head in a bid to make her talk. Rather than admit what they had done, the IRA then decided to bury her quietly and afterward spread stories that she had deserted her children and run away to England with a British soldier.

The truth was much more complicated, as it tends in such stories to be, although there is no doubt the IRA lied about what happened to Jean McConville—and continued to lie for many years thereafter. The real story behind McConville's death, the sad and squalid truth of her killing pieced together from sources in the IRA active at this time, is that she died because she was a small and not very important cog in the British army's intelligence-gathering machine who had the misfortune to cross paths with two ruthless men. One was the British officer who ran her as an agent; the other was the senior IRA figure in Belfast who decided that her secret death would suit his purposes.

THE BACKGROUND to the tragedy of Jean McConville was set in Divis Flats, then a large sprawling complex of apartments and tower blocks whose stairways and corridors provided a perfect stage for snipers and bomb throwers. In the early 1970s the IRA operated virtually openly in Divis. "Everyone knew who the IRA in Divis Flats were; they walked around with guns and so on," remembered one of their number.[49] For the British army it soon became a priority to place a reliable spotter in the flats who could warn them of IRA activity and planned ambushes. Jean McConville agreed to be one of those spotters, but by all accounts she was not very good at her job and showed a too obvious interest in the IRA's affairs. It was not long before the local unit tired of her unending questions and began to suspect her. Her apartment was raided, and sure enough the IRA found a radio transmitter that she had been using to communicate with the British army. "It was taken off her, and she was warned never to do that again; she was a woman and the mother of a large family, and so we let her off," explained one IRA member familiar with the events.[50] But it was just that, a warning. Next time, she was told, there would be no warning.

Inexplicably McConville went back to spying on the IRA, this time with fateful consequences. Although by this stage the British army must have been aware that the IRA knew all about her activities and that she was now in terrible danger, her handlers carried on regardless and supplied her with a second transmitter. Her spying recommenced, and it did not take long before the IRA worked out that she was back in business, once more betraying IRA volunteers and operations. The Belfast Brigade decided that this time she had to die, but its senior members disagreed violently about what to do with her body. The question bitterly divided the Belfast Brigade staff. Some argued that her body should be dumped in the street so that her fate would act as a deterrent to other would-be informers in accordance with IRA custom and practice. But one figure disagreed, arguing that the publicity attached to her death, the fact that she was a widowed mother of ten, would work strongly against the IRA, and he urged that she be buried in secret and effectively disappeared.[51]

The job of "disappearing" Jean McConville was given to "the unknowns" in a move that guaranteed that the story of what had really happened to her would be confined to the smallest number of IRA activists. According to one well-informed source, the order to "disappear" McConville was given to the Turf Lodge-based commander of one of the "unknown" units by a senior member of the Belfast Brigade. Whether, as alleged by one well-informed source, or not the order was given by Adams himself, it is inconceivable that such an order would have been issued without his knowledge. Her court-martial had been held—although McConville was not present to defend herself—she had been found guilty and sentence pronounced. The task of the "unknown" was to fetch her and carry out the sentence.[52] McConville was taken down to a beach near Carlingford just across the County Down–County Louth Border, where she was shot in the back of the head and her body buried in the sand.

Jean McConville's death and disappearance came back to haunt Sinn Fein during the height of the peace process in the mid-1990s. A campaign to discover her fate was launched by her children, all of whom had been dispersed to foster homes after her abduction, and their efforts won the support of President Bill Clinton and the Irish government, two of Adams's strongest allies in his new foray into constitutional politics. Adams met the chief campaigners, McConville's daughter Helen McKendry and her husband, Seamus, but initially denied all knowledge of events. Only after Clinton's intervention did he and the IRA admit that she had been "disappeared" by the organization. Even then strenuous efforts were made to distance Adams from the affair. Sinn Fein spin doctors suggested that he had been in Dublin at the time of the killing, implying that he had played no part in the decision to kill and secretly bury Jean McConville. Adams himself, according to her son-in-law Seamus McKendry, tried to claim that he could not have been involved, since he had been interned at the time: "He told Helen and I [sic]: 'Thank God I was in prison when she disappeared.' "[53] In fact Adams was very much at large at the time of Jean McConville's disappearance and must have known all about the circumstances at the time. He was not arrested and imprisoned until July 1973, more than six months after her abduction and execution.

Public disquiet over the IRA's treatment of the "disappeared," especially Jean McConville, forced the Irish and British governments to set up a cross-Border commission to coordinate the search for missing remains. The IRA's Army Council appointed its director of intelligence, Bobby Storey, a close ally of Gerry Adams, to revisit each case and to question the IRA members involved in an effort to discover where bodies had been hidden, while the police on both sides of the Border dug up bogs, beaches and basements. In the case of Jean McConville, extensive searches and excavation of beaches in the Carlingford area by Irish police in 1999 and the following year failed to find anything. But in August 2003 her remains were discovered, apparently by chance, by members of the public walking on a nearby beach that had not been searched. A postmortem examination revealed she had been shot once in the back of the head. While many in Sinn Fein were relieved to see this grisly and embarrassing case apparently closed, for others the killing and disappearance of Jean McConville had become an enduring metaphor for the Adams stewardship of the Belfast IRA. It also seems likely that McConville's "disappearance" will haunt the Provos and Adams for some time. In July 2006, Police Ombudsman Nuala O'Loan said that an investigation by her office, launched at the request of the McConville family, had failed to find evidence Jean McConville had been an informer, a claim that forced the IRA to publicly repeat its assertion that the dead woman had been executed for spying on behalf of the British army. With the McConville case thus re-opened and an unwelcome spotlight directed at himself, Gerry Adams felt obliged to express concern at the IRA's past behavior, although managing to avoid mentioning the word "disappeared" or his own possible knowledge of events: "Whatever about the circumstances surrounding Jean McConville's killing, the burial of her remains was a great injustice to the family." He also urged the Irish government to "act speedily" so that more excavations to find others who had been "disappeared" by the IRA could take place.

THE IRA'S FORTUNES had waxed and waned in the two years since the Ballymurphy riots ended in December 1970. By the end of 1972 the political and military balance was swinging in the British favor and the IRA was very much on the defensive. Not least of the factors now working against the IRA was that the British military's intelligence was improving all the time, thanks to the recruitment of a growing number of informers. Since the IRA was increasingly restricted on its home patch, the idea grew among Belfast activists that it should try to break out of the straitjacket, to take the war directly to the enemy. The idea came not from Adams himself but from others in Belfast Brigade, although in IRA mythology it is credited as his and recorded as yet another example of his military and strategic skill.

"Towards the end of 1972 we started working on the plans," recalled a well-placed IRA source.

> The first priority was to recruit unknown Volunteers with no records. It was Adams who went to the three battalions to get them; he told them that the operation was a very big one, that it could be a hanging offense, as it was treason. There were rooms full of Volunteers, and when he said that and that anyone who didn't want to go should leave, he was nearly knocked down in the rush. The result was that the team ended up with red lights, people like Gerry Kelly who was on the run for murder and others who had been interned.[54]

Elaborate planning went into the bombs that would be placed in London. Although Chief of Staff Sean MacStiofain was told about the plan and approved it, GHQ's involvement from Dublin was kept to a minimum, not least because the clannish Belfast IRA did not fully trust their Southern colleagues. The date of March 8 was chosen deliberately, for it was the day on which a British government-organized poll to decide whether the Border should be retained was to be held. With the result a foregone conclusion, thanks to Northern Ireland's built-in Protestant majority, it was the IRA's way of showing contempt for the idea that unionist consent should ever be a precondition of Irish unity.

The choice of bombing team was to prove controversial. Among the six IRA members who went to London were two young sisters, nineteen-year-old Marion Price and her twenty-two-year-old sister, Dolours, from a staunchly republican family in West Belfast. They had been among the first to volunteer for the mission. The Price sisters had been brought up in a family atmosphere in which sacrifice to the republican ideal had been sanctified. An aunt had been cruelly maimed in the cause, losing her sight and both hands in a bombing that had gone wrong in the 1956–62 campaign. MacStiofain objected, saying that they were too young and that both couldn't go, because they were sisters. He relented only when one of them became visibly upset.[55] The operations organizers in Belfast, by contrast, had expressed no such qualms, and they were sent on the mission.

The bombings duly went ahead. Car bombs were driven over on the Dublin–Liverpool ferry and taken down to London, where at 9:00 A.M. they were parked beside their targets. March 8, 1973, was not an abnormal day by the standards of the time in Northern Ireland. That morning a twenty-one-year-old British soldier was shot dead by an IRA sniper as he guarded a polling station in West Belfast; a thirty-one-year-old soldier shot earlier in the week in South Armagh died in hospital of his wounds; and the body of a forty-five-year-old married Catholic man was found in a Protestant district of North Belfast, shot in the head, apparently by loyalist gunmen. Six bombs exploded in Belfast that day and five in Derry, but it was the blasts in London that captured the world headlines. One car bomb detonated outside the Old Bailey courthouse and another exploded in Whitehall, at the epicenter of the British government. One man died of a heart attack and 180 people were injured. The IRA had bombed targets in England before, during the Forties Campaign, but never on this scale in London. Now, as a result of the efforts of the Belfast Brigade, the IRA's war had come to Britain, and the extent of the subsequent media coverage taught the IRA a lesson its members would never forget: one bomb in London was worth a dozen in Belfast.

The bombing team had, however, made a simple error that caused its downfall. The group had fitted false British license plates to the cars ferrying the bombs before they arrived in Liverpool but had made them up randomly. What they had failed to realize was that British plates were year coded, and the age of the cars did not match the code on the plates. An alert police patrol noticed that a car parked outside Scotland Yard, the headquarters of the London metropolitan police, had the wrong plates and raised the alarm. The second car bomb, parked in the West End, was discovered in the same way, and both devices were defused several hours before they were due to go off. The police headed straight for Heathrow Airport, where they found the bombing team queuing for the flight to Belfast. The plan had been that the bombers would all be safely back in West Belfast by the time the car bombs detonated, but it had all gone badly wrong.

It looked as if a simple oversight at the planning stage had landed the London bombers in jail, but there is evidence to suggest that the operation

had been compromised somewhere in Ireland. The Belfast Brigade's original plan had been to take ten bombs over to London, but that was scaled
down to six, one for each member of the team. Two days before the bombs
were set, a decision was made to reduce the number to four, after British
customs officers had taken a close interest in one of the car bombs as it was
driven off the Dublin–Liverpool ferry. A message was sent to the Belfast
Brigade to leave the fifth and sixth car bombs in Ireland, just in case the customs interest was more sinister.[56]

It later became clear that the British knew all about this change of plan.
At the bombing team's trial, depositions from the prosecution side revealed
that British police had sent out a bomb alert warning of four devices—not
the six or ten in the IRA's original plans—and had sealed ports and airports
at 6:00 A.M. on the day of the bombings, long before the bombs had even
been put in place. The intelligence was very specific and suggested the existence of an agent somewhere at the top of the organization. In addition, the
police had distributed photographs of the Price sisters with instructions to
stop them—it was clear that the police in Britain knew not only that a
bombing was planned but who was involved. The evidence appeared to
point to a serious leak somewhere in the Belfast Brigade, but attempts to
hold an internal investigation into the affair were resisted.

THE NET HAD CLOSED over the London bombers, and in a wider sense
it was also closing in on the Provisionals. On the political front the fracture
within nationalism brought about by the fall of Stormont deepened. Whitelaw cajoled the SDLP into talks and won the party's support with a promise that any deal negotiated would need to embrace "the Irish dimension"
and that other nationalist concerns would have to be addressed. In March
1973 Whitelaw published a white paper that recommended a power-
sharing form of government that would give the SDLP a guaranteed say in
running Northern Ireland. There would also be a Council of Ireland to give
meaning to the Irish dimension.

The principle of consent—the doctrine that Northern Ireland would stay
British as long as a majority wanted—was reaffirmed, but there were other,
balancing concessions for Catholics. Oaths of allegiance to the British crown,
which were obligatory for civil servants, teachers, and local councillors and
which Catholics considered discriminatory, were abolished. Most nationalists found Whitelaw's proposals to their liking, and gradually the middle
classes dropped their post-internment boycott of the state and returned
to public life. There were other positive developments to encourage the

Catholic middle class. In mid-1973 the first loyalist paramilitaries were interned, thus answering a long-standing nationalist complaint that the implementation of internment had been biased and one-sided.

The Provisionals meantime sought refuge in ideological purity and as a consequence became more isolated. In January 1973 Sinn Fein announced that it would boycott local council elections planned for later in the year. These went ahead, and the SDLP managed to establish itself as the North's largest nationalist party. In June an SDLP councillor became mayor of Derry, once the capital city of unionist discrimination. When elections were held to Whitelaw's power-sharing Assembly, the IRA urged nationalists either to boycott the poll or to spoil their votes. Another Stormont parliament would hinder the achievement of "a just and lasting peace," it said.[57] Most nationalists ignored the IRA and voted. The SDLP got a mandate, 22 percent of the votes and one-fifth of the seats. When the results came in, the SDLP leader in Derry, John Hume, declared, "The IRA have now heard the voice of the people and it is time they listened."[58]

Operation Motorman had meanwhile tightened the British army's grip on the previously unchallenged no-go areas of republican Belfast and curtailed the IRA's freedom of movement. The numbers of IRA suspects arrested and either interned or charged with criminal offenses increased steadily, according to official claims: one hundred by November 1972, a thousand by the following April. In June 1973 the Northern Ireland Office claimed that 500 IRA members had been convicted and sentenced since Motorman, eight of whom had been given life sentences, the rest an average of four years in jail apiece. Slowly the number interned fell—it stood at 450 in early 1973 but at 330 in June—as the British relied increasingly on the courts to put their adversaries out of action.

By this time Adams had found a safe billet in the University area in neutral South Belfast where he lived with Colette, by now expecting their first son, Gearoid. Like some sort of revolutionary commuter, Adams traveled daily from the safety of his middle-class hideout into the war zone of West Belfast to direct IRA operations. The fact that the IRA's senior figure in Belfast was now unable to live among his own people was eloquent testimony to the extent to which events had put the IRA on the defensive.

On July 18, another signal that the IRA's fortunes were slipping came when the Northern Ireland Constitution Bill, a product of Whitelaw's political negotiations, became law and enshrined once again in section 1, part 1, the principle of consent, that Northern Ireland would remain part of Northern Ireland unless and until a majority of people voted otherwise in a poll. The passage of the bill symbolized the gravity of the political reverses suffered by the IRA since the suspension of the Stormont parliament in March 1972. The British move to strip unionism of power had succeeded in dividing nationalism and diluting opposition to the state, while the IRA's stubborn support for violence alienated more and more Catholics.

The largest section of nationalism, represented by the SDLP, which was supported by the Catholic middle classes and church hierarchy, welcomed British direct rule and quickly entered into talks with the British and eventually the unionists about a deal that at its core would, inevitably, recognize the constitutional integrity of Northern Ireland. It was a decisive break with the Provisionals. The Catholic middle-class boycott of the institutions of Northern Ireland, which had begun in sympathy with and protest against the internment of IRA men in August 1971, slowly evaporated, and soon constitutional nationalist politicians and Catholic clerics would be condemning IRA violence with the gusto and vehemence they had once reserved for British excesses.

PART TWO

Taking On
the Old Guard

Gerry Adams speaks to jubilant supporters after his election as Westminster MP for
West Belfast in June 1983. *(Derek Speirs/Report, Dublin)*

FOUR

Cage 11

At around the same time on July 18, 1973, that Queen Elizabeth signed Whitelaw's Constitution Bill into law, a British army patrol was briefed to carry out one of the most important arrest operations of the Troubles so far: the capture of most of the Belfast Brigade's key staff. Early the following morning Adams, his operations officer, Brendan Hughes, and another staff officer, Tom Cahill, arrived at the appointed call house in the Iveagh district of the Falls Road, and this was the signal for the soldiers to swoop. Adams, Cahill, and Hughes were dragged off to Springfield Road RUC barracks, where another senior brigade officer, Owen Coogan, joined them not long afterward.

Adams was stripped and for several hours was badly beaten by his interrogators. Eventually the beatings ended, and Adams and his comrades were trussed up and then photographed, almost as if they were prize trophies, before being flown by helicopter to Long Kesh internment camp. When Adams was welcomed once again by IRA comrades into the huts and cages of Long Kesh, it was two days short of the first anniversary of Bloody Friday.

The IRA was never quite sure how the British army knew about the brigade staff meeting in Iveagh, but it was clear that a well-placed informer had been at work. The loss of the Brigade staff made this a disastrous day for the IRA, but worse was to come. Only hours after the capture of Adams, Hughes, Cahill, and Coogan, the entire Third Battalion staff was arrested at a house in Ardoyne in North Belfast. That day the Belfast IRA saw at least sixteen of its most skilled and experienced leaders incarcerated by the British.

It was not until two years later that the identity of the informer responsible for these losses was established with any certainty, and by then the damage he had done elsewhere to the Provisional IRA's personnel, resources, and structures was irreparable. The informer's activities were to have major long-term significance for the IRA, but they were also eloquent testimony to the IRA's failure in Belfast to sustain the brief counterintelligence successes enjoyed under Adams's command. The Four Square Laundry operation of late 1972 had been a flash in the pan.

The name of the informer was eventually pieced together in the Long Kesh prison camp, where IRA inmates worked out that their brigade quartermaster in Belfast, Eamon Molloy, was the one figure who had featured in each of their sad stories. A message was smuggled out to trusted colleagues suggesting that he should be closely questioned, and Molloy was tricked into admitting his secret role. Under interrogation he confessed that he had been working for the British since early 1972 and had betrayed dozens of IRA members and revealed the whereabouts of enormous amounts of arms and equipment. After a court-martial in the summer of 1975, Molloy was killed, felled by a bullet to the back of the head, and, like Seamus Wright, Kevin McKee, and Jean McConville, his body was buried in a secret grave, by now the Belfast IRA's established way of dealing with its embarrassing secrets.

Molloy's remains were recovered by the IRA, placed in a coffin and left in a graveyard near the Irish Border in May 1999, a year after the Good Friday Agreement was signed. The scandal of the "disappeared," which surfaced as the peace process gathered pace, had forced the IRA to end years of lying and admit that it had abducted, killed and hidden nine people, mostly in the early and mid-1970s, and all but one from Belfast. To that list have been added five other names who were "disappeared" by the IRA in later years. Some sources have hinted that there is yet another category of such victims, people who could be said to have been "double-disappeared," i.e. their secret executions and burials have never been acknowledged by the IRA. There may be two or even three such victims, the first of whom was executed and "disappeared" after his alleged misuse of IRA procedure, weapons and personnel led to a serious clash with the rival Official IRA and the death of one Official IRA member. Another of the possible "double-disappeared" was an alleged undercover MI5 agent killed by the IRA in County Kerry. The remains of only five of the fourteen people that the IRA admit to having "disappeared" have been recovered despite claims from the IRA to have provided details of the location of their bodies to the authorities.

That Molloy was able to inflict such damage was due in large measure to the refusal of his immediate superior to believe that one of his own men could be a traitor. It was a weakness in IRA commanders that the British learned to exploit well. Brian Keenan, the IRA's quartermaster general at this time and Molloy's commander, has entered IRA mythology as one of its

IRA OPERATIONAL AREAS—
NORTHERN AND
SOUTHERN COMMAND

Legend
Northern IRA Command
Southern IRA Command

hardest men, a skilled and ruthless commander who was as determined a revolutionary as existed anywhere in the IRA—but like many military-minded men he had a weak spot in his vanity, and Molloy's handlers in British intelligence exploited this flaw with consummate skill.

The problem for the British was simple but not straightforward. Molloy had been picked up by the military and had quickly broken during interrogation at Castlereagh RUC station in East Belfast, which was fast becoming the major holding center for IRA suspects, and had agreed to work for military intelligence. But if he was to be of any value to the authorities, he had somehow to be put back into circulation, back into the IRA's higher circles in Belfast—and fast. The difficulty was that too many of Molloy's senior IRA colleagues knew he had been arrested, and since the fate of most IRA men who fell into the hands of the authorities was usually immediate consignment to an internment cage, Molloy's reappearance in West Belfast would automatically attract suspicion. A way had to be found to explain away his safe return from Castlereagh. Molloy's handlers devised an audacious cover story that worked only because Brian Keenan fell for it, although it required nerves of steel on Molloy's part when he explained it to the IRA's quartermaster general. The story concocted by British intelligence was extraordinary: Molloy would tell his IRA colleagues that during a break in questioning one of his interrogators had carelessly left the key to his cell in the lock on the outside of the door. He had spotted this, he said, slipped a sheet of paper taken from the detectives' carelessly discarded notepad under the door, and using the policemen's similarly abandoned pen then worked the key free, and fortuitously, it fell onto the paper. He slid this back, unlocked the cell door, and calmly crept out of the station unnoticed by any of his jailers. It was a measure of the hold that his captors had over him that Molloy was prepared to return to the IRA with such a fanciful tale. But incredibly it worked. "Keenan gave him a clean bill," recalled a colleague.[1]

At the time of Molloy's arrest and "escape," Brian Keenan was already one of the IRA's most important leaders and a key ally of Gerry Adams. Throughout his long IRA career, even during fourteen long years spent later in the high-security sections of various British jails, Keenan, whose IRA nickname was "the Dog," would stay loyal to Adams and was always there to give support to whatever new direction Adams was advocating. At one point in the peace process he appeared to back dissidents who were plotting Adams's downfall, but this, it later appeared, was a ruse devised to infiltrate and undermine the Sinn Fein president's enemies. This hard-line image was a huge asset to Adams. When it came to selling a strategy that filled the republican grassroots with doubt and uncertainty, Keenan's support helped to win over skeptics. Had he seriously opposed Adams, the outcome of the peace process might have been very different.

Born in Swatragh in rural South Derry in July 1940, Keenan had been in the republican movement since his early twenties. He came from a much more eclectic background than most other Northern republicans of his time and was certainly more politically aware than the scores of recruits flooding into the organization after 1969. The son of a junior member of the British Royal Air Force, Keenan left home when he was just sixteen and emigrated to England, where he worked for a while as a television repairman. Accounts of his early life conflict. One version says that when he went to England he joined the Communist Party and embraced left-wing politics, while another says that he got the name for holding Marxist views only because he was a Goulding supporter when he joined the IRA in the early 1960s.

Much has been written about Keenan's links to radical Middle Eastern and former Soviet satellite countries in Eastern Europe—he is said to have had extensive links with East German intelligence, for example— but little has ever been substantiated in the way of definite links to such regimes. He has often been portrayed as the sole, uncompromising Marxist revolutionary in the IRA leadership, but this portrait suffers from one major flaw. It was the Goulding group, the Official IRA, which obtained political, financial, and other assistance from the Soviet Union and its allies, not the Provisionals. The Officials received cash, guns, and other aid both from East Berlin and from Moscow, but no evidence has ever been produced to indicate that the Provisionals enjoyed such generosity, which presumably would have been the case had Keenan been as close to these governments as has been suggested. Occasionally Keenan revealed his politics publicly. In an article written in the February 1988 edition of the IRA prison journal *Iris Bheag*, Keenan, writing under the penname Pow-Wow, revealed that he got his real political inspiration from the neocolonial struggles of South and Central America rather than from the dull orthodoxy of Eastern Europe.

At thirty years of age Keenan was considerably older than most other IRA recruits when he switched to the Provisionals, but he quickly rose through the ranks. By 1971 he had become Belfast quartermaster and two years later was made quartermaster general, succeeding the rebel Catholic priest Father Patrick Ryan, who had been promoted when Denis McInerney was captured on board the *Claudia* as it made its way from Libya packed with Colonel

Qaddafi's weapons. Keenan's elevation was another piece of evidence that Northerners were not as excluded from the IRA's upper reaches in those early days as the Adams camp would subsequently claim. His appointment as QMG also gave Adams another important ally at leadership level, one who was also in charge of a crucially important IRA department.

Keenan's impact was felt very quickly. While his predecessors in the QM's department had mostly turned toward conservative Irish-America, the Clann na Gael, and other support organizations for supplies of arms and cash, Keenan was not afraid to seek assistance from revolutionaries elsewhere, even those in strange foreign lands. He was one of the first to realize that the strongly anti-British regime of Libya's Colonel Muammar Qaddafi could be a rich and regular source of weaponry. By 1972 Keenan was importing RPG-7 rocket launchers and missiles from Libya to add to the IRA's already fearsome arsenal of Armalite rifles, car bombs, land mines, and endless supplies of homemade explosives.

Keenan had overseen and approved Eamon Molloy's rise through the quartermaster's department, from deputy QM to brigade QM, and in 1972, after his arrest and apparently remarkable escape from Castlereagh police station, cleared him of all suspicion of treachery, apparently unwilling to believe that someone he had mentored could turn against him. The British double agent was now free to wreak havoc on such a scale that within two years his activities played a major role in forcing the IRA to call a cease-fire.

Molloy's treachery led to important arrests. In February 1974 Ivor Bell, Adams's successor as Belfast commander, was arrested in Andersonstown on the basis of information that was subsequently shown to have come from Molloy. Bell soon escaped by swapping places with a prison visitor on April 15 but was recaptured less than a fortnight later, hiding out in a flat in the affluent Malone Road section of South Belfast. In December 1973 Brendan Hughes also managed to escape from Long Kesh, hidden in an old mattress, and returned to active service as Bell's adjutant. When Bell was captured, Hughes took over the Belfast command and moved into the IRA's operational headquarters in Myrtlefield Park, also in the Malone area, where he posed as a toy salesman. He lasted until May 10, a fortnight or so after Bell's second arrest. The IRA later learned from Molloy that the British had placed Hughes and the Myrtlefield Park house under constant surveillance and could have moved against him at any moment—but did not.

This aspect of Molloy's spying activities convinced Adams, Hughes, and Bell that the British were using his information to shape and mold the composition of the Belfast Brigade staff to their liking. This was done, they suspected, to boost elements in favor of a cease-fire, by releasing more pragmatic figures from internment while simultaneously rounding up the IRA's so-called Young Turks, those identified as hard-line associates of Adams, Bell, and Hughes. That way the brigade staff would be composed of figures more amenable to a peace settlement. The evidence for that, they later claimed, was the cease-fire of December 1974, a disastrous cessation that helped seriously debilitate the IRA. That cease-fire opened a fault line between the Belfast IRA and the national leadership, the basis for which was the conviction in the Adams camp that the new Belfast Brigade leaders and the national leadership of the IRA had been the victims of a British intelligence sting.

The British, however, may have had other reasons to put the youthful militants behind bars. In late 1973 the unionist leader, Brian Faulkner, had agreed to share power with the moderate nationalist SDLP and the middle-of-the-road Alliance Party and also to establish a cross-Border Council of Ireland to foster cooperation between the two parts of Ireland.

The Provisionals opposed the deal, known as Sunningdale, after the English civil-service college where the parties hammered out the deal, seeing it as something that had the potential to sideline and defeat the IRA—but it was also bitterly opposed by hard-line unionists who saw the deal as a plot to destroy Northern Ireland. There was widespread agreement within the republican movement that the IRA had better move to kill off Sunningdale before Sunningdale killed it, as a key strategist of the time recalled: "Our objective was to ensure that the Sunningdale Agreement would not succeed. [Daithi] O Conaill was pushing us to blow up [the] Stormont [parliament] with a massive bomb and the Belfast leadership was trying to devise a method of getting a bomb onto a ship and blow it up in order to block the main channel in Belfast harbour. We wanted to make our presence felt as a force without which there could be no solution that was not to our liking."[2] But before these plans could be put into place, the British, very possibly armed with intelligence from Molloy, moved against the Belfast Brigade. Just four days before loyalists began a general strike aimed at killing off Sunningdale, the Myrtlefield Park headquarters were raided and troops arrested the brigade commander, Brendan Hughes.

The timing of Hughes's arrest convinced the Adams camp that the British were manipulating the IRA leadership in Belfast and elsewhere. The Young Turks later discovered that secret contacts with the British were being opened behind their backs, contacts that eventually formed part of the negotiations for the 1974 cease-fire. Hughes learned that Jimmy Drumm, a veteran from the 1950s and a member of the IRA Executive, was talking indirectly to the Northern Ireland Office; Drumm was arrested by the Belfast Brigade and questioned, but he denied the story. Nevertheless Hughes complained directly to the Army Council. A week later he was arrested.[3] Among the Adams dissidents the view hardened that Hughes had been kept under surveillance but removed only when he started to threaten the British plans for the new cease-fire.

The conspiracy theorists found evidence from elsewhere to support their suspicions. From inside Crumlin Road prison—then a peeling, overcrowded Victorian hulk used to hold paramilitary remand prisoners—it emerged that the MRF, the British undercover group, had re-formed and was once again dabbling in black operations in a bid to destabilize the organization. The IRA staff in the jail uncovered what they were convinced was evidence of a plot to poison senior IRA figures who were in the jail awaiting trial, as well as plans to sow suspicion and distrust within the ranks. The story began when a young remand prisoner confessed that he had taken part in a number of MRF-type operations carried out on behalf of British intelligence. "They were involved in dirty tricks, MRF sort of stuff designed to get a sectarian war going or to discredit the IRA," recalled a source familiar with the episode. "They planted a bomb in Corporation Street in a Protestant bar that killed two children and that was wrongly blamed on the IRA. A woman was raped and shot, garages robbed, and so on, all of which was blamed on the IRA."[4] The remand prisoner, eighteen-year-old Vincent Heatherington from Andersonstown, claimed that British intelligence had trained and armed him and then given him, along with other double agents, a free hand to carry out shootings, bombings, and robberies that would be blamed on the IRA.

Heatherington named his alleged co-conspirators to the IRA leadership in Crumlin Road, many of whom were interned or imprisoned in Long Kesh. His claims were believed, and a reign of terror began in the jails. Those named by the young prisoner were tortured into making confessions to even the most far-fetched wrongdoings against the IRA. "They created paranoia in the ranks . . . ," admitted one of those involved in the affair.[5] It was of course a classic sting operation, as the IRA staff in Crumlin Road and Long Kesh eventually realized. The aim was to set the IRA prisoners at each other's throats, and the ploy worked.

The British operation did more than that. Outside the jail it divided the IRA leadership in Belfast between those who took Heatherington's allegations seriously and those who were either deeply skeptical or who believed that torturing people into confessions was fundamentally counterproductive. This division coincided with the fault line that had long existed in the

Belfast leadership and that was now, as the 1974 cease-fire approached, asserting itself with a vengeance. The split was between those associated with Adams, Bell, and Hughes, who had all fallen for the British sting, and Billy McKee, at this point commander of IRA prisoners in Long Kesh, who had tried but failed to stop the torture and mistreatment of the IRA inmates named by Heatherington. The effect of the British operation was to discredit the Young Turks and strengthen the traditionalists who proposed and supported the coming cease-fire. When, in September 1974, McKee finally came to the end of his sentence on the 1971 arms charge and was released, he was not interned, as happened to many released IRA prisoners, but allowed to return to the IRA, where he slipped easily and unopposed back into command of the Belfast Brigade.

Eamon Molloy's activities were meanwhile having a devastating impact on the IRA's ability to sustain its war effort in Belfast. The loss of hard-to-smuggle weaponry in particular enervated the organization, and the cease-fire came as something of a relief, as one former IRA officer recalled:

> The cease fire was a godsend. We had no weapons. In the Second Battalion of the Belfast Brigade there were three weapons. In fact the situation was so bad that at the start of 1975 while we were still waiting on [a] shipment [from the Irish-American gun-running ring] to come in we went to a member of the Sticks [Officials] and we told him that we felt there was going to be a repeat of the 1969 pogroms but on a larger scale. We asked him for weapons which he refused to part with. We told him that it would be on his conscience if such a situation developed. He then agreed to sell us twenty weapons without the knowledge of his leadership.[6]

The cease-fire arrived hesitatingly. Secret contacts with the IRA leadership were opened up by a group of liberal Protestant clerics, and there were other indirect conversations between the Army Council and the British government, mostly though its Secret Service, MI6, which produced a short-lived truce over the Christmas holiday of 1974 and early new year of 1975. The cease-fire was renewed in early February 1975, and there were reasons to believe that this time it would not be like 1972, and that the British wanted to hold serious talks. Although the IRA was not able to raise its violence to the levels of 1972, when nearly five hundred people had died, 1974 was nevertheless a bad enough year. Killings had risen by nearly 20 percent compared with 1973, and the notion that, in the bleak winter of 1974–75, in the wake of the collapse of Sunningdale and with no other viable options available, a frustrated British government might seriously contemplate talking to the IRA about withdrawal was not that far-fetched.

IF THE IRA LEADERS agreed to the 1974–75 cease-fire with high expectations that it would end with a British commitment to withdraw, they were to be sadly disappointed, although it was easy to see why at the time the Army Council might have entertained such thoughts. The collapse of the Sunningdale agreement sent British policymakers into despair. The power-sharing deal had offered something to everyone, yet it had been decisively rejected both by the Protestant working class—and less ostensibly by much of the unionist middle class as well—and by the supporters of the Provos. In a way the collapse of the Sunningdale experiment seemed to symbolize to the outside world the addiction of the parties in Northern Ireland to their ancient quarrel and spoke to an almost inherited inability on the part of the belligerents to entertain reasonable solutions. With IRA and loyalist violence continuing apace and no political settlement in sight, the British might, it seemed, be inclined to contemplate even the most extreme solution. So it was when, at Christmastime 1974, Sinn Fein's president Ruairi O Bradaigh received an extraordinary message from an intermediary in Derry that the British wanted to talk about ways of disengaging from Northern Ireland, the Army Council did not hesitate in recommending that the advance be followed up.

As things turned out, the cease-fire was to be just another punctuation mark in a long story, a pause during which the British regrouped their forces and improved their intelligence in preparation for an assault on the IRA that very nearly brought its total defeat. But the cease-fire was to have other unexpected consequences, the most significant of which was that it paved the way for Gerry Adams and his allies to take control of the IRA.

Adams and a small group of like-minded activists grouped around him in jail led the opposition to the cease-fire, and the manner in which they did so created one of the most abiding myths of his career—that he rescued the IRA from the near defeat precipitated by the cessation. The Adams camp would argue that the Army Council of 1974 foolishly led the IRA into a carefully laid trap, the objective of which was to tempt the IRA into lengthy and inconsequential talks designed to buy the British enough time to construct the method of the organization's downfall. From the confines of their cages in Long Kesh, Adams and his supporters not only put forward the political arguments against the cease-fire and those who had advocated it, but, the myth continued, they designed the practical changes and political-military strategies needed to drag the IRA back from the edge of the abyss.

A crucial part of their case was that the blame for the cease-fire disaster lay with an Army Council that was dominated by Southerners who had no feeling for those fighting the war in the North. But the facts suggested a massaging of the truth. Of the seven Army Council members who sanctioned the 1974–75 cease-fire, no fewer than five came from the North. These included the chief of staff, Seamus Twomey, who had been Belfast commander when Adams was his number two, while another key Council member, Joe Cahill, was a family friend and an ex-Belfast commander who had been particularly close to Adams. There were three other Northerners on the Council: J. B. O'Hagan from Lurgan, Kevin Mallon from Coalisland, County Tyrone, and Seamus Loughran, from West Belfast. The anti-Northern accusation was a potent, if unfair, charge which greatly appealed to the prejudices of those who made up the bulk of the fighting units north of the Border, while serving to undermine the position of Army Council members Daithi O Conaill and Ruairi O Bradaigh, two of the three major IRA figures who stood between Adams and his supporters and their bid to win absolute control of the organization. The third member was Billy McKee, who rejoined the Council upon his release from Long Kesh late in 1974 and who was a figure with whom Adams had repeatedly clashed ever since the Ballymurphy riots of 1970. That McKee was a fellow Northerner and a West Belfast veteran was later forgotten as Adams and his allies portrayed the struggle for the IRA's soul as a battle between compromising, armchair generals pontificating from the safety of the South and those who actually had to take on the British in the mean streets of Belfast and Derry.

Adams exploited the divisions within the IRA to his own advantage, but so too did the Army Council in its efforts to commence talks with the British. In the run-up to the cease-fire the Army Council held discussions with a group of liberal Protestant clerics in the County Clare village of Feakle, and one of the clergymen vividly recalled the IRA leaders playing the Adams card: "O Conaill told me at the time that we would have one bite at the cherry, no more. He said, 'That's because behind every one of us on the Army Council there's a young man with a gun in his hand who still has to make his name for Ireland and write his name in the history books. And when they take over there will be no more cease-fires.'"[7]

The 1974–75 cease-fire had three major negative consequences for the IRA, each of which would be critiqued by Adams during his subsequent bid to capture the organization. The first was the debilitating effect on the organization caused by both the sheer length of the cessation and the failure or refusal of the British to put flesh on the bones of the secret offer to talk about "structures of disengagement" from the North, as O Bradaigh had been promised by the Derry intermediary.[8]

Talks took place between the two sides, but nothing concrete ever seemed to emerge. There were three levels of contact. At the lowest level, incident centers were set up that linked Sinn Fein and British government monitors in Belfast, where there were seven such offices, and in Derry, Armagh, Newry, Enniskillen, and Dungannon. These were supposed to monitor the truce to ensure there was no 1972-style breakdown. Sinn Fein figures and British officials, communicating mostly via telex machines, would try to make certain that small problems did not become big ones. The enterprise was given an appropriate code name, after the mock-Gothic pile, Stormont Castle, which housed the British administration in East Belfast. Operation Ramparts conjured up a picture of British spies crouched over keyboards at the top of spiral stone staircases as they waited for the latest message of complaint from their IRA counterparts.

At the next level there were regular meetings in Belfast between the IRA Executive members Jimmy Drumm and Proinsias MacAirt and British officials that were held at a British government house called Laneside, in the affluent County Down seaside town of Hollywood. The Laneside talks happened quite frequently, much more often than the highest level of talks that were held in Derry between Army Council delegates, O Bradaigh and McKee, and senior officials from the Northern Ireland Office (NIO). One authoritative account of the contacts depicts the British as quite open about their wish to withdraw but reluctant to spell out the details, even resorting to evasion in response to IRA questions.[9] There were constant squabbles and complaints about breaches of the terms of the cease-fire by either side. The British could produce only one piece of evidence to support the notion that they wanted to be out of Northern Ireland, and that was the exclusion from British plans to nationalize the shipbuilding company of Harland and Wolff, the Belfast shipyard where the *Titanic* had been built some sixty-five years before. Nonetheless the Army Council perservered.

The British failure to make good on the secret promises gave the Adams camp powerful ammunition. The allegation he and his allies leveled was simple: the Army Council had been fooled into taking part in bad-faith negotiations and tricked into calling a cease-fire that was designed to last so long that it seriously eroded the IRA's fighting ability. The result was that the British were given a breathing space in which to devise ways of inflicting even more damage on the IRA. With IRA members relaxing visibly as the cease-fire dragged on, the British built up their intelligence on the organization in preparation for major changes in security policy, the central feature of which was that control of operations against the IRA passed from the British military to the Royal Ulster Constabulary and a new emphasis was put on legal methods to put IRA members behind bars. The use of internment was phased out, and instead more conventional judicial methods were employed, primarily the processing of IRA suspects through the courts, albeit courts that had no juries and in which verdicts and sentences, fashioned by a barrage of new antiterrorist laws, were handed down by a single judge. The change affected the prisons as well; special-category status, which had been granted to IRA prisoners as part of the 1972 cease-fire deal and which recognized a political motive for paramilitary activity, was scrapped, and instead IRA inmates were to be officially regarded and treated as common criminals.

The British strategy was known variously as Ulsterization, normalization and criminalization, but whichever word was used the result was the same. The British had put in place a system that, from 1976 onward, saw IRA suspects trundled along a sort of conveyor belt that began with arrest and lengthy questioning in new RUC interrogation centers where confessions would be extracted, often amid claims of brutality. The next stage was in the courts, where, despite their often dubious integrity, the confessions were invariably accepted, and the last stage was in the Maze prison, the renamed and rebuilt Long Kesh camp but soon known to the world as the H Blocks, where IRA prisoners were to be treated in the same way as thieves and rapists. The new security policy cut swaths into the IRA, bringing it to the verge of defeat. The fault for this, the Adams camp was to insist, belonged to those who had negotiated the cease-fire.

Terrifying and cold-blooded loyalist violence, most of it directed at ordinary Catholics, particularly in Belfast, was the second result of the 1974–75 cease-fire. Unnerved by the IRA's contacts with the British, loyalist paramilitary groups began murdering Catholics in an often gruesome fashion and in a way that challenged the Provisionals' claim to be the defenders of their community. As the loyalist killing increased, the pressure to hit back in like manner intensified.

The loyalists' logic was terrifyingly simple: the more Catholics they killed and the more horrible the manner of their deaths, the stronger the pressure would be on the IRA to stop its activities. The cease-fire was the trigger for the bloodshed. When the British and the IRA announced the terms of their truce, the loyalist groupings, especially the UVF, reacted with unusual violence. Within seven days they had killed five Catholics, and many more were to follow.

AS 1975 UNFOLDED, Northern Ireland, and Belfast in particular, entered what is arguably the darkest period of the Troubles, nearly two years of slaughter in which the loyalists and the IRA vied with each other in an often indiscriminate sectarian killing game, the latter refusing to admit its activities or seeking refuge behind fictitious cover names, the former glorying openly and proudly in the carnage. These were the years that saw the rise of chilling loyalist gangs with names like the Shankill Butchers, a group of UVF killers who specialized in cutting their victims to death with surgically sharp knives and axes. The IRA responded with bombings of Protestant pubs that invariably killed uninvolved civilians. Increasingly the IRA imitated the loyalists by kidnapping and killing innocent Protestants. The violence spread to rural areas of Tyrone and Armagh, where IRA members using cover names such as the South Armagh Republican Action Force to disguise their bloody deeds enthusiastically joined the slaughter. By the end of 1976 loyalists had killed nearly 250 people, most of them innocent Catholics, while 150 Protestants, similarly unconnected to those who were directing the murder campaign, had also met violent deaths, a majority of them at the hands of the IRA, however disguised or renamed.[10]

The upsurge in loyalist killing put the IRA in a quandary. To respond in kind threatened to drag republican values into the gutter, making a nonsense of IRA claims to be a nonsectarian movement in the tradition of the Protestant founder of republicanism, Wolfe Tone. Yet if the Provisionals stood aside, this would be to deny the atavistic forces that had brought them into being in the first place, the need to defend their streets and communities. Most Provisionals agreed, some with less enthusiasm than others, with the view of one IRA leader of the day: "Republicans had to hit back at the Loyalists. It was as simple as that. They were slaughtering the Nationalists. There was no other way round it."[11]

The Adams camp chose to see things in a more negative light and courtesy of the same conspiratorial prism through which they had viewed the arrests of Hughes and Bell and the treacherous activities of Eamon Molloy and Vincent Heatherington. The sectarian warfare, they claimed, was being sponsored by the British, whose aim was to pull the IRA into a brutal but diverting tribal conflict in which the British could depict themselves as "the piggy in the middle," as neutral arbiters, whose only interest was to stop the irrational violence of mad Irishmen. For this state of affairs Billy McKee, the defender of St. Matthew's and once again Belfast commander, was held to blame. His motives were regarded as beyond justification. "McKee just wanted to get into a war with the Orangies," concluded one of the Adams camp at the time.[12]

The third consequence of the cease-fire was an outbreak of vicious feuding between rival republican groups, a hangover from the split of 1969, but something the Adams camp also maintained to be in the British interest. Billy McKee was, in their mind, guilty of allowing the IRA to get involved in sectarian killings, and they blamed him for the feuding as well. The worst piece of internecine slaughter between Provisionals and Officials broke out in Belfast at the end of October 1975. It started with around a dozen attacks mounted by the Provisionals in the course of an evening during which one member of the Official IRA was killed and sixteen were wounded. Up to ninety Provisional IRA members were said to have been involved in the night's violence. The feud ended a fortnight later with a total of eleven dead, including a six-year-old girl, fatally shot during an attack aimed at her father, a member of the Official IRA. Feuds between the Provisionals and the Officials were not unknown, but this was by far the most serious outbreak of such violence. McKee justified the attacks by arguing that the Officials were acting as an arm of the British in areas controlled by the Provisionals, passing on information about IRA activists, facilitating British community policies, and undermining Provo influence. But the feud, coming on top of the loyalist onslaughts, was deeply demoralizing inside nationalist areas, and Adams seized on this to criticize McKee, as he later recorded: "Republican feuding contributed significantly to feelings of alienation on the part of the Nationalist people, who had long provided the essential support for the IRA. It also coincided and dovetailed with a sustained British propaganda campaign to portray IRA members as 'common criminals.'"[13]

The long-standing hostility between Adams and McKee, which had its roots in the Ballymurphy riots of 1970, came bursting to the surface again but this time in surrogate form. Even so, the dispute can with hindsight be seen as the first shot fired by Adams in his campaign to oust McKee and to engineer his takeover of the republican movement.

The target chosen by Adams was David Morley, the commander of IRA prisoners in Long Kesh. The former leader of the Provisional IRA in the County Down Border town of Newry, Morley took over the job of camp commandant from McKee just prior to McKee's release in the autumn of 1974. The two men were on close terms, and when McKee assumed command of the Belfast Brigade and rejoined the Army Council, Morley became the principal point of contact between the leadership and the Long Kesh prisoners.

Largely because of McKee's patronage, Morley had been elected camp commander by the rank and file in the jail, but his style was not universally popular. "Morley came from a British army background and ran the prison, much as McKee had done, on very militaristic lines," remembered one former IRA prisoner who supported the Adams line. "There were roll calls, parades, tight discipline, and so on, all of which rankled with many people, especially young lads. Morley introduced a new IRA salute, two salutes to the head rather than one, so as to distinguish the IRA from the British army. Staff members wore Sam Browne belts and a holster with a wooden gun stuck in it." Adams would describe it all as a cross between George Orwell and Spike Milligan.[14]

To the astonishment of many in the camp, Morley told the prisoners that McKee wanted them to scrap existing escape plans and not to bother hatching any more. "The Army Council told us that we were all going to get out, internees and sentenced men," recalled one former prisoner. "First there would be 50 percent remission, then two-thirds, then all out."[15] This was, the Morley-McKee critics complained, the ultimate in naïveté for at the same time this advice was being given, the IRA leadership was fully aware that the British were planning the construction of a brand-new prison, the H Blocks, to house IRA inmates. Morley had toured the first H Blocks, so named after the shape of the cell wings, and could see they were intended for something much more permanent. He was also allowed out of the jail on parole for talks with Jimmy Drumm and with British officials. "Mixing at this level with senior Brits went to his head," suggested one critic.[16]

Morley's elevation coincided with changes to Adams's own prison circumstances. He had initially been housed in the internee section of Long Kesh, in Cage 6, which he shared with some one hundred other inmates in three huts. But after two unsuccessful escape attempts, Adams was sentenced to three years' imprisonment and was moved to the sentenced-prisoner section of the camp, into Cage 11. Coincidentally, hostility to the leadership line had been growing over the cease-fire and the leadership style in jail; a large number of prisoners had been suspended from the IRA for disputing Morley's authority. When Adams arrived in Cage 11, it was decided that a challenge should be made against the camp leadership, and Ivor Bell ran against Morley in the election for camp commander and fared surprisingly well. "The purpose of the exercise was to show there was unease with what was happening," recalled an Adams supporter. Morley won but by a margin of just a handful of votes. Adams later stood in a separate poll and again ran Morley close, so close that the result badly scared the IRA leadership.[13]

One outcome of the election was that the Army Council changed the rules governing the selection of prison OC. From then on the rank-and-file IRA inmates could nominate whomever they liked, but there would be no election. Instead the Army Council would choose the commander it wanted out of the list of candidates submitted by the prisoners. The idea was to prevent splits from coming out into the open, but it enormously strengthened the leadership's hand in the jail; ironically, this was later to greatly benefit Adams when he assumed control of the IRA and wanted to be sure of the loyalties of the prison leadership. Although he had been a victim of the change, he made no alteration in the rule when he and his allies assumed control of the IRA.

From early 1975 until Adams's release in February 1977, two cages in Long Kesh were the focus for dissident criticism of the leadership in Dublin. One was Cage 11, where first Adams and then Brendan Hughes was OC, and Cage 9, commanded by Ivor Bell. But as the new British security strategy swung into action and the Castlereagh conveyor belt gathered speed, disgorging more and more IRA members into prison, Cages 11 and 9 also became think tanks devoted to planning new structures and policies designed to rescue the IRA from what every activist, inside and outside the jails, could see was imminent defeat.

The period was vividly symbolized by the British Labour government's choice for Northern Ireland secretary in 1976, a blunt and diminutive former coal miner called Roy Mason, who saw his job in simple terms. He had come to Belfast not to indulge in dangerous political experiments like power-sharing but to crush the IRA. In one of his earliest public pronouncements he delighted unionists with a promise to roll up the IRA like "a tube of toothpaste." And such was the initial success of the new police interrogation centers at Castlereagh, at Strand Road in Derry, and at Gough Barracks in Armagh in extracting confessions from IRA Volunteers that he felt strong enough to predict, "My view is that [the IRA's] strength has waned to the point where they cannot sustain a campaign."[18] The security statistics appeared to support his boast. The death toll for 1977 went down to 116, about a third of what it had been the year before. Even though this reflected a lower level of loyalist activity, there was no doubt IRA operational capacity was being undermined. Shooting incidents in 1977 were down 45 percent from 1976 and bombings by more than half.[19]

IRA MEN have always used their time in prison well. After the 1916 Rising in Dublin the defeated rebels were jailed in Britain, and one of their leaders, a young Michael Collins, used the time, leisure, and opportunity provided by his spell in the Frongoch internment camp in Wales to restructure the Irish Republican Brotherhood in preparation for the coming conflict with Britain. Gerry Adams, Ivor Bell, and Brendan Hughes spent their days in Long Kesh sixty years later doing something remarkably similar for the Provisional IRA. There was one major difference, however. The ideas produced in Cages 11 and 9, many of which Adams outlined in a lengthy report to the IRA leadership in 1976, were more than a rescue plan for the IRA; they were also a blueprint for his takeover of the movement. Their significance does not stop there. Within the plans can also be found the seeds of what, only a few years later, would become the Irish peace process, although it is doubtful if any of those responsible for drawing them up could see that at the time.

The conceptual foundation stone of the takeover plan was the doctrine that the war against the British was going to be a long-drawn-out affair and that the heady days of 1972, when the IRA could realistically imagine forcing a speedy military defeat on the British, were gone forever. As with other controversial ideas, Adams employed junior allies to float the notion first, a ploy that allowed him to gauge grassroots reaction before declaring his own hand. In this instance his choice was Danny Morrison, a bright young West Belfast IRA member who had been interned but then released as part of the 1975 cease-fire deal. Morrison, who had initially backed the McKee leadership against Adams and then switched sides, eventually replaced Daithi O Conaill as the IRA's director of publicity and went on to become a strong ally of Adams on the Army Council.

One IRA activist of the mid-1970s can remember when Morrison first expounded Adams's "long war" doctrine.

He was the first I heard it from sometime in 1975. We had one or two mini- [IRA] Conventions, one in Clare and one in Donegal involving twenty-five or thirty of the top people, and Morrison was saying we have sold the people a false bill of goods with slogans like 'Victory in 74!' and so on. People were getting cynical, and we would have to say instead that it is a long war. It grated with a lot of us. None of us believed it would be a long war. We were of the opinion that we could win it, we could force the Brits to pull out. We were young and in our twenties, we had seen the fall of Stormont, burned down the British embassy in Dublin, ran the Brits

ragged in the countryside. We were of a generation that had seen Saigon
fall and the U.S. defeated in Southeast Asia.[20]

The "long war" became IRA policy, but estimates of just how long the
Long War would have to last varied enormously. Writing in the Belfast IRA
paper under the pen name Brownie, Adams envisaged the conflict lasting
for just seven more years, that is, until 1983.[21] But privately he and his allies
talked of a twenty-year conflict.

Whatever the reservations, the "long war" doctrine was really just a
statement of the obvious. Roy Mason had nearly defeated the IRA, and it
was going to take years of careful rebuilding before it would again be in a
position to challenge the British, if ever. The signal that this had been formally accepted by the Army Council as IRA policy came only four months
after Adams's release from Long Kesh, at the Bodenstown commemoration
of June 1977, the highlight of the republican calendar. Adams's choice of
speaker to give the address sent its own signal. Jimmy Drumm, who had
been one of the senior IRA figures involved in the secret Laneside dialogue,
climbed the podium beside Wolfe Tone's grave to declare that he and the
other leaders associated with the 1974–75 cease-fire had all been wrong. In
a script composed by Adams and Morrison, Drumm declared, "The British
government is not withdrawing from the Six Counties. Indeed the British
government is committed to stabilising [them] and is pouring in vast sums
of money . . . to assure loyalists and to secure from loyalists, support for a
long haul against the IRA."[22]

The speech crafted for Drumm went further and contained a hint of what
was to come, although few of those present at Wolfe Tone's graveside that
day would have realized the full significance of his remarks. "We find," he
went on, "that a successful war of liberation cannot be fought exclusively
on the backs of the oppressed in the Six Counties, nor around the physical
presence of the British Army. Hatred and resentment of the army cannot
sustain the war . . ."[23]

Heavily coded though these remarks were, the import was clear. The first
message was that if republican activists wanted to sustain the war effort,
they would have to expand their support base in the North by becoming
politically active. Adams had already described how he saw this being done,
in a series of articles written in Long Kesh and published weekly in
Republican News under the Brownie pen name. Dropping abstentionism,
recognizing the partitionist parliaments, and running for office, at least in
the North, was still forbidden territory, but Adams nevertheless put the idea

onto the Provisionals' agenda, albeit in a more subtle way. He called his approach "active abstentionism," a philosophy that in theory involved republicans' building alternative governmental structures and becoming relevant to the needs of ordinary people.

Borrowed from his days as a Goulding republican, "active abstentionism" was just another way of encouraging political activity in an organization in which "politics" was still a dirty word. The plans to construct alternative structures never really got off the ground, but the idea that republicans should "do things for the people" took root and later found more tangible expression when Sinn Fein started to fight elections and in an approach that was christened the "Armalite and ballot box" strategy. The really significant feature of the move was the way Adams sold it to his colleagues, largely on the basis that increasing political support would enable the IRA to intensify and sustain its war effort. It would not be the last time that he justified political activity in military terms even if, in the end, the effect was to undermine the IRA's war effort.

The same military argument was used to justify another major theme in the Drumm speech, the idea that the republican movement should try to build political support in the South. Increasing political support south of the Border, Adams argued, would translate into more safe houses for the IRA to use, more money, and more recruits. The argument was uncritically accepted internally, even though it flew in the face of the reality of the Ireland of the mid-1970s. The truth was that by that point in the Troubles, the conflict in the North was something most Southerners wanted nothing to do with, and no amount of political work by Sinn Fein was likely to change that. Nevertheless the Adams dictum became IRA policy, and with hindsight it seemed a highly significant move. Its effect was to introduce a contradiction into Provisional politics that played a major role in the evolution of the peace process. Political ambition south of the Border and armed struggle in the North were mutually exclusive. One or the other could prosper but not both. The contradiction was sharper in the South but it also restricted Sinn Fein's room for growth in the North, even though the IRA's campaign had created a sizable support base. Adams had set the republican movement on a journey that would eventually reach a crossroads, where it would have to choose between politics and the gun.

When it came to putting flesh on the theory of "active abstentionism," Adams and Bell turned to the Libyan regime of Colonel Muammar Qaddafi for inspiration. Qaddafi had outlined a system of people's committees or popular congresses to help govern Libya. Organized in a pyramidal fashion, the people's committees oversaw different aspects of government and elected delegates to a general people's congress, Qaddafi's version of the Libyan parliament. This system, Qaddafi wrote, is "the only means to achieve popular democracy."[24] Adams and Bell copied the idea and suggested that people's committees be established separately from British government structures in republican areas of the North. Adams extolled the idea in a Brownie article: "We need an alternative to the British administration in our country. Especially now in the 6 Counties and when the Republican movement has control and administration to some degree in all the Nationalist areas. So why not cement this into local government structures. In Belfast alone could not the three or four big Nationalist areas be organised into community councils?"[25]

The concept of people's committees made a brief appearance after Adams's release from jail, but by mid-1979 talk of building alternative government structures had virtually disappeared. The reason given was the arrest of the group of Sinn Fein activists charged with bringing them into existence, but the idea had proven to be simply impractical. One bit that did survive, however, was the Civil Administration, or Administrative IRA, which was created to police the areas within which the IRA had influence. With the Troubles now nearly a decade old, law and order had broken down in many nationalist districts and established value systems had been upturned. Crime, vandalism, and joyriding were endemic, and there was a demand for a policing system. Rather than see the RUC back in their areas, the IRA began to dispense its own system of rough justice and to mete out punishment shootings, beatings, and expulsions.

While it appears that some of Adams's associates, Bell in particular, were motivated by an admiration for Qaddafi, the Long Kesh dissidents were also trying to ingratiate themselves with the Libyan leader in the knowledge that he had the wherewithal to arm and finance the IRA beyond its wildest dreams. This consideration was evident in two other structural changes advocated by Adams and Bell.

One was the Revolutionary Council, which came into being in 1976–77 and took its name from a central part of the Libyan system of government. In Libya the Revolutionary Council was the executive branch of government that sat atop the people's committees. It consisted of Qaddafi, a general people's committee chosen from the People's Congress, and the ministers of the principal government departments. The IRA's version was a sort of mini-Convention, a sounding board of IRA opinion representative enough of the grassroots, yet small enough to be able to meet safely. The regular IRA General Army Convention could draw as many as a hundred delegates, and the risks attached to convening such a large gathering were considered too great in the mid-1970s. The last Convention had met in September 1970, and much had changed in between. Adams and Bell saw the Revolutionary Council as a way of bringing the IRA leadership into touch with the rank and file, among whom their influence ran strongly.

A mini-Convention held in late 1976 agreed to set up the Revolutionary Council and determined its makeup. It would consist of the seven-man Army Council, the GHQ staff, and the commander, adjutant, and quartermaster of the Belfast, Derry, Mid-Ulster, East Tyrone, South Derry, and South Armagh Brigades. Allowing for overlapping at Army Council and GHQ level, the Revolutionary Council had perhaps thirty to thirty-five members.

Bell had intended the Revolutionary Council to effectively replace the Army Council as the IRA's primary decision-making body. As a radical—some would say a Marxist, others an anarchist—Bell distrusted the middle-aged conservatives who dominated the Army Council, and he wanted to sideline them by subjecting them to IRA democracy. Adams, however, used the Revolutionary Council in a very different way, to control and bend the Army Council to his way of thinking but not to replace it. In his hands the Revolutionary Council became an instrument for taking over the leadership of the IRA, but the Army Council, a smaller body and thus easier to manipulate, remained, under his direction, the supreme decision-making body. The Revolutionary Council was phased out when Adams's control of the Army Council was complete, although it was revived, to perform a similar function, during the peace process many years later. "It was at this stage that a gap started to open up between Adams and Bell," observed a contemporary.[26] While Bell wanted to broaden and radicalize the IRA, Adams sought merely to curb and then control the Army Council.

Qaddafi had outlined his political philosophy, a compromise between communism and capitalism that he termed "the third way," in a three-volume publication called the "Green Book," so called because green is the color of Islam. Again in imitation of their putative arms supplier, Adams and Bell proposed that the IRA should have its own "Green Book," which all IRA recruits would be obliged to read and digest before being admitted as full-fledged Volunteers. Thereafter such IRA members would be described as having been "Green-Booked."

A cross between a political manifesto and a training manual, the hundred-page "Green Book" set out the IRA's fundamental beliefs and political and military strategies. It also included a copy of the most up-to-date IRA constitution, often an extremely sensitive and revealing guide to the organization's political disposition and intentions, which IRA leaders strove to keep secret. The result was that the Green Book's circulation was unnecessarily restricted, bestowing upon it, in the public mind, a sense of mystery and importance beyond its merit. The IRA, it said, was the lawful inheritor of the First Dail and was the legal government of Ireland. The Dail in Dublin and any parliament at Stormont were thus bogus and illegal, the "puppet governments of a foreign power and willing tools of an occupying force," according to the text.[27] The IRA's long-term aim was to create a democratic socialist republic, and Volunteers had the moral right to kill to achieve it, not least because they were acting on behalf of the true Irish government. IRA strategy would be based on a number of tactics, the Green Book said, including a war of attrition against "enemy personnel," a bombing campaign to deter inward investment, opposition to all attempts to create internal political stability, and a propaganda campaign in Ireland and abroad aimed at broadening support for the war effort.[28]

To most rank-and-file IRA members, however, being "Green-Booked" really meant they had gone through training in the anti-interrogation techniques outlined in the manual. The RUC's holding centers at Castlereagh, Gough barracks, and Strand Road were having a devastating impact on the IRA, and there was an urgent need to instruct Volunteers in ways of resisting police questioning, as one member recollected: "Men were breaking in the police stations. We'd hear of people handing over twenty-five to thirty names at a time. In the first twelve to eighteen months of Castlereagh we suffered great damage."[29] The lectures in the "Green Book" on anti-interrogation methods, which basically boiled down to tutoring IRA members—seasoned activists as well as novices—in how to remain silent during questioning, came into effect around late 1978 and early 1979. From then on the only defense that an IRA member could make to a proven accusation of informing was that he or she had not been "Green-Booked."[30]

The Army Council chose a brutal way of demonstrating to Volunteers the importance it attached to the "Green Book" and its admonition to stay silent during interrogation. In July 1979 Michael Kearney, a twenty-year-old IRA Volunteer from Lenadoon, was found dead near Newtownbutler in County Fermanagh with a bullet wound to the head. In a statement the IRA said he had been killed "for breaches of general army orders in that he imparted information of vital importance to the British war machine."[31] Later the organization's spin doctors suggested Kearney had betrayed a major bombing operation in East Belfast aimed at destroying oil depots and industrial plants. But within the IRA the strong belief was that Kearney had been killed only because he had broken during RUC interrogation and that his death was meant as a warning to others. A few years before, when such examples of weakness had been commonplace, the worst that most IRA members could expect was to be boycotted and isolated by colleagues in jail. Kearney's death was intended as a signal that this leniency had gone and that others should take the "Green Book" with deadly seriousness.[32] In September 2003, the IRA finally admitted that Kearney had not been an informer, thereby implicitly conceding that he had been killed only because he had violated the Green Book's admonition to stay silent during police questioning.

British informers were high on the dissidents' target list. In their reorganization scheme, Adams and Bell suggested the creation of a specialist counterintelligence unit, known as the security department, which was initially charged with debriefing IRA members who had been in police custody with the aim of discovering whether they had talked to their interrogators or been turned by them; initially confined to Belfast, the security department was eventually extended to Northern Command and, over the years, its powers to probe IRA affairs were expanded. The security department was also responsible for arresting, interrogating, and ultimately arranging the deaths of informers, a great number of whom would end their days hooded and trussed at lonely roadsides in places like South Armagh. After 1977 the number of deaths of alleged informers rose steeply; one estimate suggests that as many as 70 percent of all informers caught by the IRA during the entire Troubles were killed after that date.

The security department proved to be a double-edged weapon, however. Infiltrating the new department became a priority for the RUC and British intelligence for one very simple reason. The security department's members knew many of the IRA's most intimate secrets, including the identity of key gunmen and bombers, and a double agent placed within their ranks could cause havoc. The years since the department was set up have been characterized by persistent suggestions that this is just what happened.

The idea for the internal security department came in part from the special "unknown" cells set up by Adams in 1972. Part of the task of "the unknowns" had been to lure alleged informers to their deaths and to engage in counterintelligence work. "The unknowns" were also the inspiration for another part of the reorganization plan, and that was the refashioning of the IRA into secret cells and the dismantling of the old company and battalion structures. Modeled on the British army, the IRA's old system of companies and battalions were based in well-defined geographical areas, and this made it relatively simple for the British to work out which units were responsible for what operations. The structure also made easier the task the RUC Special Branch and other intelligence agencies faced in mapping and identifying the IRA's battle order so that when the interrogation centers swung into action the organization quickly buckled.

Adams was asked by the Army Council to design the reorganization plan, a draft copy of which was found by the Gardai when they arrested Chief of Staff Seamus Twomey in Dublin in December 1977. The kernel of Adams's scheme was the creation of secret, four-man active-service units (ASUs), which would specialize in activities such as sniping, bombings, assassinations, and intelligence work. They would have a roving commission and could operate anywhere in the IRA's war zone so that the British would find it more difficult to identify which ASU had been active where.

The restructuring of the IRA, its new political-military strategy, the "Green Book," the internal security unit, and the course of anti-interrogation lectures for recruits and veterans were all parts of a strategy designed to facilitate the conduct of the "long war." The theory was that between them the changes would enable the ASUs to ward off penetration by British intelligence and resist RUC efforts to force confessions out of the activists, thus enabling the IRA to survive and fight for years to come. At the same time the IRA's new political activism would, again in theory, expand the support base and provide a steady supply of new recruits, safe houses, and so on.

On top of all this Adams proposed another major innovation, the idea that the IRA should have "permanent leadership" at all levels. The argument put forward in favor of this innovation was that the IRA lacked consistency at the commander level and was too easily disrupted by arrests and harassment. Since the start of the IRA campaign, Adams and his allies argued, there had been too many chiefs of staff, too many changes in Army Council and GHQ personnel, and, lower down too high a turnover at the brigade staff level. Each time a top commander was arrested and jailed, valuable talent was lost, and precious experience and knowledge would disappear and have to be replaced in a lengthy and often difficult process.

Adams's proposal was backed by a powerful group of activists, including Danny Morrison, Brian Keenan, Martin McGuinness, and Adams's cousin Kevin Hannaway. They got their way, and while the change was not always implemented, where it was enforced it did not come cost free. In an important way the concept of "permanent leadership" made the IRA more vulnerable to British penetration; a commander turned by the RUC or MI5 could be in place for a very long time. There was another unforeseen consequence. In practice the only way "permanent leadership" could work was for commanders to become operationally inactive so as to avoid any risk of arrest. That was a significant break with Provisional IRA tradition and practice, in which leaders had often led by example, fighting alongside Volunteers. One outcome was the development of a self-perpetuating elite at top- and middle-level ranks whose composition was often the result as much of loyalty to the political strategy of the Army Council, and ultimately to Gerry Adams, as of battle skills. The concept, the fact that leaders put away their guns, also paved the way for hitherto secretive senior figures to emerge as public personalities, an essential prerequisite for a successful electoral strategy.

Much of the Adams-Bell blueprint was beginning to be implemented before Adams's release from Long Kesh. With Adams, Bell, and Hughes in jail, the task of selling the restructuring plans both to the Army Council and to the middle leadership fell in part to Martin McGuinness, the Derry IRA leader who had spent much of the cease-fire period in Portlaoise prison after a conviction for IRA membership. But it was mostly Brian Keenan who toured the country preaching the Cage 11 gospel to IRA members. "More than anyone else," remembers one former IRA man, "Keenan was a roving ambassador for Adams."[33]

The most important and meaningful part of the restructuring scheme was also its most controversial. Adams proposed the division of the IRA into two separate geographical entities. A Northern Command would be set up, comprising the six counties of Northern Ireland and five Border counties in the Irish Republic (Louth, Cavan, Monaghan, Leitrim, and Donegal), an area that coincided with what was effectively the war zone where military operations were planned and carried out. A separate Southern Command was proposed in the remaining twenty-one counties that would specialize in providing the logistics necessary for conducting the campaign in the North. The Southern Command would supply three essential elements: most of the IRA's arsenals would be hidden there, most of the "factories" churning out homemade explosives and the IRA's often ingenious improvised weaponry would be based there, and so would the organization's training camps, often situated in isolated mountainous countryside or in underground firing ranges painstakingly excavated in lonely farmland and forests.

Important though these functions were, there is little doubt that the proposal for a Northern Command would herald a significant switch in the internal balance of power. The IRA's principal business was to fight a war against British forces in Northern Ireland, and those who controlled how that war was conducted—and those who appointed them—would inevitably wield the greatest influence in the organization. The Northern Command would have its own staff, which would shadow that in GHQ, which promptly lost its responsibility for conducting operations in the North and was thus weakened. Thereafter GHQ's direct military role was confined to the IRA's international activities, principally in Britain and Europe. The construction of a Northern Command would make the position of Northern commander one of the most important positions in the organization. Not least of the Northern commander's powers would be that of having a major say—in later years the final say—in deciding who became brigade commanders and who made up their staff.

The idea of creating a Northern Command was always going to be a contentious proposal, and so it was, especially with older republicans who had bitter memories of the last time, aside from the brief period before and after the 1969 split, when the Northern and Southern parts of the IRA had gone their separate ways. A Northern Command, composed of the six Northern Ireland counties and County Donegal, was established in 1939 just after the outbreak of the Second World War when cross-Border communication difficulties made the change necessary. The IRA had begun a bombing campaign in England around the same time, but within two years arrests by the British police had brought it to a halt. The IRA in the South, meanwhile, was enfeebled by arrests and arms seizures. The police forces in Ireland and Britain clearly had good intelligence, which the Northern commander, Sean McCaughey, and his allies suspected was being supplied by a traitor in the Dublin leadership. They kidnapped the chief of staff, the Wexford man Stephen Hayes, and held him for several weeks, during which time he was tortured, starved, and repeatedly questioned about failed operations and alleged Garda successes. After a court-martial, which predictably convicted and sentenced him to death, Hayes was forced to write out a lengthy confession. He managed to drag this out until an opportunity arose to escape. Hayes turned himself in to the Gardai and survived the ordeal, but McCaughey was captured and later died on a hunger and thirst strike. The Hayes affair and its consequences deeply divided the IRA on North–South lines. Many activists of the day blamed the Northern Command experiment for the acrimony and vowed never to repeat it.

The "Forties men" were the strongest opponents of Adams's proposal, among them Joe Cahill, Proinsias MacAirt, and Billy McKee, who was probably the most bitterly against the idea. Their common fear was that a Northern Command would precipitate a split. But Seamus Twomey, the chief of staff and, in the words of one IRA militant, "Adams's pet Rottweiler,"[34] backed the proposal, and Brian Keenan did the rest. Most of Belfast supported the idea, as did Martin McGuinness in the Derry Brigade, while Keenan, still the IRA's QMG, won over crucial middle leadership people in three other vital areas, South Derry, East Tyrone, and South Armagh. Keenan's argument was simple: a Northern Command would be responsive to the needs of the men who were fighting the war. "He told us we wouldn't have to wait to see someone from Kerry," explained a Northern activist. "We asked would a Northern Command mean that we would get more gear, and Keenan would say bigger, better, longer guns and then it was okay."[35]

Another rural Northern IRA member takes up the story:

Adams was still in jail at this time, so Keenan was really the John the Baptist to Adams's Christ. Into our midst during our perennial quest for gear would come Brian Keenan. Unlike other leaders he was an activist. He would arrive in jeans and denim jacket and would sleep in the ditches along with the Volunteers. He was good fun, clever, likable and would always arrive with a bit of gear wrapped up in plastic, fifty or a hundred rounds for some weapon. Brian could always turn up stuff for esoteric weapons. I remember we had a Chinese version of the AK-47 called the SKS, which used short 7.62 mm ammo as opposed to the British-NATO standard long round, and he got some for us. He would sit and talk things over with us; we'd go and get a carryout to eat; he charmed us and won us over.[36]

Keenan and Adams were knocking at an open door, and the establishment of the Northern Command became a foregone conclusion. In late 1976 a meeting of the Revolutionary Council passed a resolution recommending to the Army Council that the change be made; faced with the united voice of the fighting units in the North, the Army Council had little choice but to agree. Martin McGuinness was appointed the first Northern commander but on Billy McKee's insistence the powerful Belfast Brigade was excluded from the new arrangement. McKee was still OC of Belfast Brigade, albeit hanging on by his fingertips, and correctly saw Northern Command as an effort by the Adams camp to extend their power base. Only when Ivor Bell took over from McGuinness, when he was appointed chief of staff in early 1978 in succession to Gerry Adams, was Belfast integrated into Northern Command.

The creation of the Northern Command had important and long-lasting consequences for the IRA. Not only did it facilitate coordinated Northern Ireland-wide attacks and make rapid alterations in military tactics more feasible, it established and refined central control over the IRA's cutting edge. This was especially the case outside Belfast in militant areas like East Tyrone and South Armagh where the local IRAs were really under the control of clan chieftains—Kevin Mallon in Tyrone and later Tom "Slab" Murphy in South Armagh were examples—rather than part of a structured, centrally directed organization. "The leadership would never try to give them orders," recalled a rural activist. "There was virtually no control from the center. They mounted operations against the British, and the job of leadership was to provide resources, training guns, explosives, etc. You just could not guarantee that they would vote at a Convention for the leadership's political strategy. That independence all but disappeared with the Northern Command."[37] Creation of the Northern Command marked a vital staging post on the road to Adams's establishing control not just of the IRA's military tactics but of its political direction as well.

The new structure also standardized the IRA in another important way. Prior to the Northern Command each area in the North had organized its own training camps and procedures. Separate camps had existed for Belfast, Tyrone, Derry, and Armagh IRA units, but after the change training was centralized and procedures regularized and, inevitably, improved. This development had its negative side. If a training camp was stumbled upon or betrayed to the Garda, Special Branch surveillance would now reveal much more about the IRA than before.

There were other adverse consequences from the creation of the new body. The IRA lost a great deal of the spontaneity and unpredictability that had made it such a difficult quarry to corner in the early 1970s. After Northern Command was set up, Adams sent emissaries throughout the countryside to propound the new gospel, with the result in some instances that well-protected safe houses were revealed and local command structures disclosed to outsiders. Some areas were forced to share hitherto jealously guarded technology. The IRA in South Armagh, for instance, had developed radio-controlled bombs but had refused to allow other areas to use them, for fear that the British would capture them and work out countermeasures. Once the Northern Command was set up and the technology shared, that is precisely what happened.

IN FEBRUARY 1977, after the best part of four years spent in the Long Kesh prison camp, Gerry Adams was released into the loving arms of Colette and Gearoid, his three-and-a-half-year-old son, who had been born while he was in jail. Adams had seen his young son grow up but only in the visiting rooms of the jail and under the watchful and often intrusive eyes of the prison guards, the hated "screws." Now for the first time they could be a proper family, inasmuch as an IRA leader ever had a proper family life. Despite the risks associated with the IRA lifestyle, at least they knew that the fear of arrest no longer hung over the head of the family. The phasing out of internment meant that if the British wanted to put Adams back in jail, they would have to assemble a case that would pass the scrutiny of a court, even if it was one where only a single judge also acted as the jury.

Adams could be well satisfied with the fruits of his work in jail. Given the agenda devised in Cage 11, the IRA had been set on a course that would have lasting consequences for Anglo-Irish politics and for Adams himself. Reorganized to revive its flagging military fortunes, the IRA now had a political program to guide it, one that would ultimately propel it into electoral politics. It also had a structure that would inexorably and increasingly concentrate control and power in the hands of Gerry Adams and those he chose to have around him.

Adams did not emerge from Cage 11 and return to his IRA comrades empty-handed. As far as some Army Council members were concerned, the disastrous cease-fire of 1974–75 had been partly forced on the leadership by a weapons shortage in the Belfast Brigade area that was so severe that many doubted if the organization in the city could conduct anything approaching a sustained campaign. Within weeks of Adams's release, however, a cache of sixty Armalite rifles, a batch smuggled by Irish-American sympathizers, was being distributed to grateful and astonished active-service units in the city. The sudden abundance of weaponry was credited to their released leader. To many activists, it seemed that Gerry Adams had not only the ideas to rescue the IRA from defeat but the means as well.

What none of them could have known was that the Armalites had arrived in Belfast well before the weapons famine hit the IRA in the city, before the resulting cease-fire, and had been secreted in five sealed dumps under the supervision of Brian Keenan and hidden even from Eamon Molloy's prying eyes. The weapons had been put aside in case of an upsurge in loyalist violence, but when Adams was arrested and imprisoned along with many of his brigade staff, and eventually replaced by Billy McKee and his allies, no one told the new Belfast leadership that the weapons existed. Had they known about the guns, it is almost certain that the pressure to call the cease-fire would have been considerably less than it was. And if there had been no cease-fire, Gerry Adams would have been deprived of the cause around which to build his bid for control of the IRA.[38]

FIVE

"Our Dreyfus"

Gerry Adams's release from Long Kesh was eagerly anticipated by the IRA in Belfast and in the rest of Ireland. It was clear to even the most junior Volunteer that the organization had lost its sense of direction by the spring of 1977, that it had come out of the cease-fire in a battered and damaged state, and that its leadership was largely directionless and bereft of new ideas. Defeat stared the IRA bleakly in the face, and it was to Gerry Adams and the group around him that republicans now looked for salvation. The grassroots were aware of the divisions inside the jail, knew of the critique Adams had made of the Army Council's policies, but they also knew that he had a reputation for strategic innovation, and although only a few were privy to the detail of his plans, most expected Adams to come out of jail with some sort of blueprint for regeneration.

He was supposed to go on a vacation south of the Border with his family immediately after his release from Cage 11, but within hours of being reunited with Colette, Gearoid, and the wider Adams clan in Ballymurphy, he changed his plans. Seamus Twomey, the IRA chief of staff, who was still in hiding in Dublin after his dramatic escape from Mountjoy jail, had sent a message summoning him to an urgent meeting. Adams had been able to communicate with Twomey and the Army Council from Long Kesh but only within limits. Written messages as well as the occasional typewritten document were smuggled out by visitors, and these had included a lengthy critique of the cease-fire and the state of the IRA that Adams had composed. His trip to Dublin after his release gave Twomey and Adams the first chance to discuss fully all the momentous events of the preceding four years and to bring Adams up to date on the implementation of the IRA reorganization plans hatched with Ivor Bell inside Long Kesh, not least the creation of Northern Command.

By the end of 1977, less than a year after his release from Long Kesh, Adams had become chief of staff in succession to Twomey, but not before another spell as Belfast commander. Debilitated by the 1975 cease-fire and a series of security successes by the British, the Belfast Brigade had corroded badly under McKee's stewardship. Both the quality and quantity of IRA operations in the city had seriously deteriorated and when McKee was finally ousted, Gerry Adams was drafted in to reorganize and revive the organization.

Recapturing the Belfast Brigade from Billy McKee was an important milestone in Adams's quest to dominate and mould the IRA nationally. In the late 1970s, as at the outset of the Troubles, Belfast was the engine for the IRA nationally. If the IRA in Belfast prospered so did the entire organization; if it faltered in the city, it faltered everywhere. And whoever dominated the IRA in Belfast, especially when it was doing well, inevitably carried huge clout in the national leadership.

Following his release from jail, Adams was armed with a powerful critique of the McKee leadership and had crafted a far-reaching plan to revive the IRA. But he also encountered stiff resistance to his agenda, even from those who had been part of his circle before his arrest. The explanation was very simple. The McKee leadership had taken pains to ensure that their supporters were in key positions throughout the Belfast Brigade and elsewhere in the IRA. No matter how convincing Adams's case was against the cease-fire leadership, it made little impact on men who owed their positions and status to that leadership. Adams had to move with guile and caution to advance his agenda.

Assuming command of the Belfast Brigade brought Adams the breakthrough he needed. McKee's allies in Belfast were removed and replaced with figures sympathetic to Adams and his reorganization plan. He also had the support of Seamus Twomey, the IRA's chief of staff, who managed to get Adams on to the Army Council later in 1977. These developments paved the way for a decisive shift in the IRA's direction that was cemented when Adams succeeded Twomey as the IRA's military commander.

By 1977 two important allies from the North had joined the Council, and they would greatly assist the project. One was Martin McGuinness, the Derry IRA commander, whose IRA career had been launched when he was talent-spotted by Daithi O Conaill in 1971, and Brian Keenan, who by 1977 was IRA quartermaster-general, in charge of acquiring, hiding and distributing the IRA's weapons.

McGuinness had spent much of the 1975 cease-fire either on the run across the Border or in Portlaoise prison, where he had been jailed after a conviction for IRA membership. Unlike Gerry Adams, he was not yet a national figure in the IRA but was known in Derry as a fearless and talented commander. Whereas Adams had a family history of association with the IRA, McGuinness's parents were strong supporters of the old Nationalist Party and were typical of the vast majority of Catholics in a city never known for its adherence to the republican cause. Street violence, first involving the RUC and then the British army, had driven McGuinness into the IRA, initially the Goulding Officials, who had the greater support in the Derry of 1969–70. Unhappy at the Officials' military timidity, McGuinness switched to the Provisionals just before internment removed the bulk of its activists. He suddenly found himself a general in a tiny army, but one that quickly mushroomed in numbers as conflict with the British intensified.

McGuinness had managed to stay out of the controversy caused by Cage 11's campaign against the truce but had strongly supported Adams's reorganization scheme and was rewarded with a place on the staff of the new Northern Command, first as operations officer ("double O," in IRA parlance) and then as northern commander. Adams's release and elevation to the Army Council meanwhile encouraged Keenan to abandon a long-standing reluctance to involve himself in the IRA leadership. Senior colleagues had often complained about Keenan's repeated refusal to throw in his lot with them by joining either the Council or the IRA Executive, the twelve-person body whose main function was to select the Council's members. But with Adams now on the Council, Keenan's reservations dissolved. The effect of this crucial move was to strengthen Adams's hand significantly.

The rest of the Army Council was a different matter. All the key figures were either obstacles to Adams's ascent or ideological foes. Two in particular, Daithi O Conaill and Ruairi O Bradaigh, were major roadblocks. In 1977 the pair were still powers in the republican movement despite widespread criticism of their handling of the truce. Both men had enthusiastically backed the cessation and had played leading roles in bringing it about and nurturing it, and when it failed Cage 11 blamed them. O Conaill had acted as spokesman for the Army Council when senior Irish and English Protestant clerics had met the IRA leaders in an isolated hotel in Feakle, County Clare, in December 1974 to broker the cease-fire terms. His importance to the cease-fire was recognized by the British, who chose to send messages down the clerical pipeline to the IRA via O Conaill rather than anyone else. O Bradaigh was a member of a three-man Army Council delegation that met secretly with British officials in Derry throughout the cessation. His commitment to a successful resolution of the IRA's campaign was more personal. When asked by the Feakle clergymen why he wanted a settlement, O Bradaigh had replied that the war could consume a second generation if it wasn't brought to a halt.[1] There was no doubting the disappointment of both men when the cease-fire failed to secure the deal they had hoped for.

Notwithstanding that failure, O Conaill and O Bradaigh had an IRA record that ensured they had considerable support at grassroots level, particularly in the South, where they were well known and respected. If they had a weakness, it was that they were largely unknown quantities north of the Border, where the attentions of the British security forces meant it was too risky to circulate frequently among the rank and file. To most of those IRA activists who had joined since the early 1970s, they were distant figures, a weakness Adams would later exploit to his great advantage.

Soon Adams would have two close allies by his side in the Army Council. One was his old Second Battalion and Belfast Brigade comrade Ivor Bell; the other was Danny Morrison, the republican movement's able public relations guru and editor of *Republican News*, who first handled publicity relations for Northern Command and then became the IRA's overall director of publicity. According to one account of this period, Adams, McGuinness, and Bell tightened their control of the Army Council by taking advantage of a clause in the IRA constitution that allowed the Council to co-opt people to fill vacancies in its ranks as long as the Executive ratified the appointment later. But in practice, knowledgeable sources say, no ratification was ever sought, a snub to the Executive that exacerbated internal divisions.

As Adams and his allies consolidated their hold on the IRA leadership, Billy McKee emerged as the first target. McKee had become president of their Army Council during the 1975 cease-fire, a post separate from that of chief of staff, whose occupant normally fulfilled a plenipotentiary role on behalf of the leadership. Along with Ruairi O Bradaigh, he had led the secret Derry negotiations with British officials on behalf of the Army Council, and like O Bradaigh and O Conaill, he desperately wanted the cease-fire to work. A confirmed bachelor who lived with his elderly mother and later his sisters, McKee was a deeply religious man who attended Mass daily. A quiet talker, he was described by one of the Feakle clerics as looking "like a Baptist pastor or a Sunday school teacher." The reason McKee gave the Protestant clergymen for wanting the cease-fire to succeed revealed much about his politics. "He was fed up with the fight because it was doing more harm to the Catholic Church than enough," recalled one. "When [the war] started at first all the boys went to Mass, but now they weren't going. He said, 'I'm not fighting to destroy my church.'"[2]

Adams's attack on McKee centered on his direction of the IRA during the cease-fire, in particular alleging that he had encouraged the IRA to fight a sectarian war and to feud with other republican groups. McKee, the Adams camp said, had fallen into a double British trap. The sectarian killings allowed Britain to say that the Troubles were a communal conflict, not an anticolonial war, while the shooting wars with the Officials just spread demoralization in the nationalist community, something the British welcomed. It was the latter that provided the reason for Billy McKee's fall.

McKee's approach to conflicts with Goulding's Officials was simple, as an IRA activist of the day recalled: "His attitude was that 'if any of my men are hit, I'll hit back.'"[3] The 1975 feud had claimed eleven lives, and scores more were injured. This and the killings of Protestants had enraged the Cage 11 dissidents. "When I first met Adams, he was very angry over what had been happening outside while he was in jail," remembered the same IRA source. "He was pointing out that we started the '75 feud. Yobos in the Provos would get drunk, start fights, and away you go, and we are supposed to be surprised when it started up. In that feud a score or more 'Sticks' shot in one and a half hours, then retaliations. Meanwhile 150 Catholics are killed by loyalists, more retaliations but no British being killed. It was a total waste."[4] The hostility toward McKee from the Cage 11 dissidents ran to such feverish levels that some even argued that they should arrange to get the Belfast commander shot dead.[5]

While Adams and those who thought like him undoubtedly saw McKee as a political and military liability, he was still a formidable opponent. When Adams was released from Long Kesh, McKee still had iconic status among the IRA grassroots, particularly in Belfast. McKee had two strikes in his favor. He had helped to defend St. Matthew's Church in East Belfast against a loyalist mob, and his long hunger strike had, in IRA eyes at least, secured political status for IRA prisoners in the jails. As long as Billy McKee still held a leadership position in the IRA, Adams's ambitions would be stalled.

The Revolutionary Council, the gathering of twenty to thirty IRA commanders and senior officers devised in Cage 11, was the instrument Adams used to purge McKee from the Army Council. McKee's downfall began with yet another feud between the Officials and the Provisionals which broke out not long after Adams's release from Cage 11.

AT THE EASTER commemorations in Belfast on April 10, 1977, a parcel bomb exploded just as the Official IRA parade was about to leave for the

republican plot at Milltown cemetery from the assembly point at Beechmount Avenue in the mid–Falls Road area. A ten-year-old boy whose father
was a member of the Officials' political wing, the Republican Clubs, was
killed, and several other Official IRA members and sympathizers were
injured. The Officials assumed that the Provisionals had placed the bomb,
and they set out to exact revenge. When the Officials' parade eventually
arrived at the gates of Milltown, the Provisionals were just leaving and the
angry crowds clashed. Violent fistfights broke out, and shots were fired.
Later that afternoon the dead boy's uncle was shot dead by the Provisionals,
and others were wounded. The feuding was stemmed when Catholic priests
mediated a settlement, but the bad feelings simmered on for weeks even
when it became clear that it had been loyalists, members of the UVF's notorious Shankill Butchers gang, who had planted the Beechmount bomb, not
the Provisionals. Nevertheless, at the end of July the Provisionals struck
again, when gunmen killed a top-ranking Official IRA officer from North
Belfast. Over the next four hours three more people were killed, two of
them Provisionals and one a civilian mistaken for a member of the Officials.
The last to die was Adams's old friend Tommy "Toddler" Tolan, who along
with Jim Bryson had helped make the Ballymurphy IRA unit such a formidable outfit back in the early 1970s.

His alleged failure to secure Army Council permission for striking against
the Officials was the charge leveled against McKee at a Revolutionary Council meeting later that autumn. The accused IRA leader had no defense and
appears to have been taken by surprise at the strength of the assault. According
to one account McKee told the meeting that he could not remember the details
of what had happened, and he was heavily criticized by one speaker after
another, many of them members of the Adams camp. At a meeting of the Army
Council held afterward, the censure continued, and he was out. Of the Council
members present, only O Bradaigh spoke up for him. One version of what happened says that he resigned, another that he was asked to go.[6]

Whatever the truth, Billy McKee's days as an IRA leader were over, and he
was badly affected by the experience. "I saw him the next morning, and he
was a shrunken man," recalled a GHQ member who was at the Revolutionary
Council meeting.[7] Shortly afterward he was admitted to hospital first in
Belfast and then in Drogheda over the Border, and his illness was the official
reason given to fellow republicans for his departure from the leadership.

Adams had chosen the right issue on which to confront McKee. Had he criticized McKee for allowing the IRA to kill Protestants, the outcome might have
been very different. While important IRA leaders, Twomey in particular, were

ready to accept that feuding with the Officials played into British hands, striking back against the loyalists was a different matter. The truth was that many IRA leaders, particularly those from Belfast, found little wrong with McKee's uncompromising attitude to the loyalist gangs and had raised no objection when the retaliations were at their worst in 1975 and 1976. "Twomey was all about protecting Belfast from the Prods," explained one contemporary.[8]

Adams's criticism of the 1974–75 cease-fire was accompanied by promises that if he and his supporters had their way there would never be another cessation unless and until the British had committed to withdrawal, and it was this dual approach that appealed most to the Revolutionary Council. There had been a great deal of resentment within the republican grassroots at the way the 1974–75 cease-fire had been handled, and the Adams camp expertly exploited the unease. The IRA leadership had never spelled out the terms of the cease-fire or made public any of the promises allegedly made, and broken, by the British. Even the way the cease-fire had ended was never satisfactorily explained. Above all there was a suspicion that the Army Council had been tricked and manipulated by the British, who had used the breathing space afforded by the cease-fire to reorganize and refocus their drive against the IRA. The overwhelming sentiment after the truce among activists at all levels in the IRA was that never again must a cease-fire be called unless the IRA had the British on the rack. It was against this strident background and distaste for cease-fires that Adams and his supporters made their pitch.

The message that they delivered was that as far as he and his supporters were concerned, there would be no more cease-fires, no repeat of the disaster of 1974–75. Presenting a hard-line, militant face was a strategy that Adams was to use again and again to take his leadership colleagues and the IRA rank and file down paths they otherwise would have shunned.

The anti-cease-fire message was repeated in public as well as privately. Using the Brownie pen name he had adopted in 1975, Adams had started sending it out as early as May 1976, using a *Republican News* critique of the leaders who had declared the 1921 Truce to make a thinly veiled denunciation of those behind the 1975 cessation. An admission of IRA membership in one Brownie column led Sinn Fein spin doctors during the later peace process years—when Adams was emphatically denying any association at all with the IRA, past or present—to claim that others in Cage 11 shared the Brownie by-line with Adams and that the offending article had actually been penned by Richard McAuley, Adams's aide and constant companion during the peace process. Cage 11 veterans insist, however, that Brownie's work was the product of only one hand, while the Republican movement as a whole regarded the Brownie articles as carrying Adams's imprimatur. "The weakness of the IRA of that period," wrote Brownie,

> was that instead of pursuing the war to its bitter end come what may, they allowed unscrupulous politicians and so-called "Peacemakers" to gain the upper hand. The result was the betrayal of the Fight for Freedom followed by a vicious and brutal Civil War and of course partition. It is to be hoped that the lesson of that period will not be lost on today's leaders. There is only one time to talk of peace and that is when the war has been won not while it is raging. The time to talk of peace is when the British have left Ireland, otherwise they will find some excuse to remain.[9]

Within two years the message had become much more explicit while public condemnation of the 1975 leadership was barely concealed. In an interview with Vincent Browne, the editor of *Magill* magazine, a GHQ spokesman was blunt. Asked what attitude the IRA now had to talks with Britain of the sort that had happened during the truce, the spokesman replied, "We now regard such talks as entirely futile and the only time we will talk to the British again is when they come to us and ask our help to secure their immediate departure from Ireland." Pressed on whether or not any consideration had been given to another cease-fire, the spokesman did not mince his words: "None. There is absolutely no question of another ceasefire or truce. In my opinion the last one went on far too long and it would be almost impossible for anybody to persuade the Volunteers that another one would be in the interests of the Movement or its objectives. Our aim now is to win the struggle on this occasion and we are prepared to make whatever sacrifices are necessary to achieve this."[10] To drive the message home, *Republican News* reproduced the *Magill* interview in a special double-page center spread.

The American writer Kevin Kelley was given the same story in, if anything, stronger terms:

> [T]he IRA today asserts that almost certainly it will not enter into a cease-fire agreement again, no matter what the bait might be. The Provos' post-mortem on the truce of 1975 is that, on balance, it proved to be seriously damaging to the movement, politically as well as militarily. As one volunteer observed . . . , "Even if the Brits reintroduced internment tomorrow and managed to pick up most of our guerrillas and all our weapons, we still wouldn't ask for a cease-fire. The attitude would be, 'Right, let's get

some new recruits and some more guns and keep fighting.' Cease-fires are just not on."[11]

It was hardly surprising that, presented with such uncompromising sentiments, the Revolutionary Council was so ready to give Adams his way and the Army Council so unwilling to oppose him.

The other reason was that the new leadership was quite simply delivering the goods. Although the IRA was never able to reproduce violence on the level and scale reached in the early 1970s, the years immediately after Adams joined the Army Council nevertheless saw a significant recovery in its fortunes, one which even the British were obliged to concede.

In 1977 Roy Mason had boasted of squeezing the IRA like a toothpaste tube, but eighteen months later, after the changes introduced by Adams had begun to take effect, his successor, Margaret Thatcher's nominee Humphrey Atkins, was forced to admit to the British House of Commons that the situation had changed radically. In July 1979 he told MPs, "The first six months of this year have shown a marked rise in the level of terrorism and have demonstrated that we are up against a more professional enemy, organised on a system of self-contained, close-knit cells which make it difficult to gather information. Their weapons are more powerful and their operations have a different emphasis."[12] Atkins was not saying that the IRA was able to present the sort of threat it had posed in the early 1970s, but his words were an acknowledgment that the defeat of the IRA was no longer within easy reach.

Toward the end of 1977 Adams's grip on the IRA leadership strengthened. In November, Belgian customs officers, possibly acting on an intelligence tip-off from the police in Dublin, discovered six tons of Russian- and French-made automatic pistols, explosives, mortars, rockets, and rocket launchers and ammunition hidden in electrical transformers on board the MV *Towerstream,* which had docked at Antwerp after a voyage from Cyprus. The weapons had been smuggled from the Middle East and were being sent to a front company in Dublin established by a GHQ officer called Seamus McCollum. The Garda Special Branch put him under surveillance and on December 2 swooped on a house in Martello Terrace in the scenic Sandycove area of South Dublin, where McCollum was arrested. The operation was a singular success, but the detectives got two apparently unexpected bonuses. In the flat detectives found a draft of the cellular reorganization plan put together by Adams at the request of the Army Council, while outside they found Seamus Twomey sitting in a parked car.

After a frantic car chase that ended outside Fianna Fail's headquarters in central Dublin, Twomey was captured. Four years earlier he and other IRA men had made world headlines when a helicopter had swooped into the exercise yard of Mountjoy jail in Dublin and carried him off to freedom. It was one of the most dramatic jail breakouts in the IRA's history. Now he was back behind bars.

The circumstances surrounding the capture of Twomey have long been a matter of conjecture and controversy within the IRA, not least because his departure paved the way for Adams to become chief of staff for the first and only time. Adams was the sixth chief of staff in the Provisional IRA's history, and his tenure is distinguished by two features: his reign as military commander was the only one that can be precisely dated, and it was also the shortest. He took over immediately after Twomey's arrest but lost the post seventy-eight days later, on February 18, 1978, when he was arrested by the RUC along with over twenty other republican suspects, as a wave of condemnation swept Ireland following one of the most horrific IRA incidents of the Troubles.

THE BOTCHED BOMBING of the La Mon House hotel on the south-eastern outskirts of Belfast was one of the worst atrocities of the IRA's campaign, its twelve uninvolved victims exceeding the death toll of Bloody Friday. The bombing was a political and public relations disaster for the IRA, tarnishing its attempts to present a new efficient military face to the world and once again marking the IRA with a sectarian stigma—all twelve of the dead were Protestants. The La Mon bombing also held up the implementation of the Adams military and political agenda by nearly a year, much to the dismay of his supporters and allies.

The dead, seven of them women, had been attending the annual dinner dance of the Irish Collie Club when a blast incendiary bomb hung on a window of the restaurant exploded, sending a huge fireball billowing through the room and incinerating everything and everyone in its path. The IRA later admitted that the warning it had phoned to the RUC was inadequate. The bombers could not find a public phone box nearby, and by the time they did, the bomb was just minutes away from detonation. There was simply not enough time to evacuate the building. The outrage caused by the size of the death toll and the horrible manner in which the victims met their end was intense and widespread, and orders were issued to arrest Adams. He was picked up by the RUC in West Belfast, questioned at Castlereagh holding center, and then held in Crumlin Road jail in Belfast on an IRA membership charge for the following seven months. But the case against him collapsed before it reached a full trial. It had been based on what proved to be flimsy evidence, principally clips from a BBC TV *Panorama* program featuring him making a Sinn Fein Ard Fheis speech in which he used words like "billet" and "war zone." Much to the anger of the British, the North's senior judge, Lord Chief Justice Sir Robert Lowry, threw out the case.

Adams was once more free, but he would never again hold the post of chief of staff. The disaster at La Mon had happened on his watch as chief of staff, and while he was clearly not responsible for the bungled warnings that caused the deadly inferno, the use of La Mon-style incendiary bombs had been approved by an IRA leadership of which he was then a crucial part. As soon as he was arrested, his place had been taken by Martin McGuinness, who occupied the position for the next four years while Ivor Bell replaced McGuinness as Northern commander; on his release Adams became McGuinness's deputy, the IRA's adjutant-general. The takeover of the IRA begun inside the cages of Long Kesh was complete and the Adams—McGuinness era had begun.

The months after Adams's arrest were quiet as the IRA attempted to recover the swaths of political and propaganda ground lost after La Mon. Operations diminished in both number and scale, and the use of the deadly blast incendiary bomb virtually ceased. But in November 1978, two months after Adams's release from jail and his assumption of the Northern Command post, the IRA offensive resumed. On the night of November 30, sixteen towns were bombed in the space of a one-hour period; altogether that month more than fifty bombs exploded across Northern Ireland, injuring nearly forty people. At the same time the Army Council authorized a new bombing campaign in England, and that Christmas police leave in London was canceled in expectation of a bombing blitz. By coincidence or otherwise, Adams's release from prison signaled an upsurge in IRA violence.

Humphrey Atkins's view that the post-1977 IRA was becoming a greater menace received its most powerful endorsement from one of the British army generals charged with combating the organization. An assessment of the IRA threat written in November 1978 by Brigadier James Glover, an intelligence specialist who later became the British army's commander of land forces in Northern Ireland, fell into the IRA's hands and was released by the IRA's publicity department in May 1979. If Gerry Adams had been asked to write Glover's report, he could hardly have done a better job. The brigadier's central conclusion was an alarming one for the British government but music to the IRA's ears. The Provisional IRA, he wrote, "has the dedication and the sinews of war" to maintain the then current levels of violence for the foreseeable future. He went on, "The Provisionals cannot attract the large number of active terrorists they had in 1972–73. But they no longer need them. PIRA's organisation is now such that a small number of activists can maintain a disproportionate level of violence . . . though PIRA may be hard hit by Security Force attrition from time to time, they will probably continue to have the manpower they need to sustain violence. . . ." He also paid a compliment to Adams's skills in revamping the IRA: "[B]y reorganising on cellular lines PIRA has become less dependent on public support than in the past and is less vulnerable to penetration by informers."

For years the official British propaganda view of the typical IRA Volunteer painted a picture of thugs motivated by subhuman criminality, but Glover recognized not only that this was rubbish but that the IRA itself was a great deal more sophisticated than was ever publicly admitted. "Our evidence of the calibre of rank-and-file terrorists does not support the view that they are mindless hooligans drawn from the unemployed and the unemployable. PIRA now trains and uses its members with some care. . . . They are constantly learning from mistakes and developing their expertise . . . there has been a marked trend towards attacks against the Security Forces and away from action which, by alienating public opinion, both within the Catholic community and outside the province is politically damaging." Glover's final judgment underwrote the entire Adams project: "The [republican] Movement will retain popular support sufficient to maintain secure bases in the traditional republican areas," he wrote.[13]

Meanwhile Adams was using his post as adjutant-general to consolidate his standing in the eyes of the rank and file. His brief included enforcing discipline and reviewing IRA unit strength all over the country. The circumstances of the late 1970s were very different from those of 1973, when Adams was last on active service. Internment had been phased out, and while the authorities would dearly have loved to put him back in jail, they lacked the evidence to convict him in court, as Roy Mason had learned to his cost. Adams was now able to move around freely, and as he did so his influence outside Belfast grew, as a contemporary recalled:

Unlike any of his predecessors he was by this stage not on the run. He could go anywhere and spend days at a time reviewing units. He would arrive at a house, for instance, where there had been a death in the family and sympathize, telling them that he and Colette had prayed at Clonard for whoever it was, you know, showing a charming, personal touch. He made contact at a human level in a way his predecessors couldn't, and that helped him to disseminate his message and win support.[14]

LORD LOUIS MOUNTBATTEN was arguably the best-known and possibly best-respected member of the British royal family. A naval hero, he had served with distinction during the Second World War, commanding a British destroyer, the HMS *Kelly,* which was torpedoed several times in an incident immortalized in Noel Coward's 1942 film *In Which We Serve.* He went on to serve as Supreme Allied Commander in Southeast Asia between 1943 and 1946, after which he was named viceroy of India, in which capacity he oversaw the turbulent and violent handover of power to the Congress Party and the partition of India into separate Muslim and Hindu states. It was, however, his role as adviser and confidant of the British royal family that really marked him out as a significant figure. As cousin to Queen Elizabeth II and mentor to Prince Charles, the heir to the throne, Mountbatten was eagerly sought out for his advice and experience by a dynasty going through painful and unwelcome changes in the media-conscious, iconoclastic latter half of the twentieth century.

The seventy-nine-year-old Mountbatten had a soft spot for Ireland. Since the early 1970s he had vacationed for part of each summer at Mullaghmore on the Bay of Donegal between Bundoran and Sligo on the northwest coast. It was a dangerous spot for such a high-profile member of the British establishment to spend his vacations. Bundoran was a popular resort with Derry folk, and inevitably the summer crowds enjoying a vacation break would include IRA members and sympathizers who would be bound to hear of Mountbatten's presence and might be tempted to strike a spectacular blow against the British royal family. But Mountbatten ignored the security advice to think twice about spending time there and continued to enjoy his fishing and boating expeditions off a section of the Irish coastline that everyone agreed was spectacularly beautiful.

His stubbornness cost him his life. On August 27, 1979, he died instantly when a fifty-pound radio-controlled bomb exploded on his thirty-foot pleasure craft, reducing the vessel to matchwood. Mountbatten died alongside his fourteen-year-old grandson, his daughter's mother-in-law, and a fifteen-year-old boat boy from Enniskillen. It was clear that the IRA had known all about Mountbatten's vacations for some time but had deliberately chosen this moment to move against him. The new British prime minister, Margaret Thatcher, had just taken office. She was a hard-line opponent of Irish republicanism who was known to sympathize with the unionists and whose close friend and adviser on Northern Ireland matters, Airey Neave, had been killed by a bomb planted by the violent splinter group, the Irish National Liberation Army (INLA), during the 1979 British general election campaign. Mountbatten's killing, as the IRA must have known, could only drive the new prime minister to adopt tough security measures of the sort that in the past had sustained and nourished the IRA.

The British establishment and media were only beginning to digest the enormity of this disaster when, later the same day, news of another catastrophe came in. On the shores of Carlingford Lough, a picturesque stretch of sea that divides County Down in the North from County Louth in the Republic, a two-truck convoy of British paratroopers was making its way from the soldiers' base in Ballykinler to Newry when a huge bomb, hidden beneath hay on a trailer parked by the roadside, was detonated by a radio signal. The explosion devastated the convoy. Six soldiers died instantly, and when their shocked and disoriented colleagues came under sniper fire from across the bay, they sought refuge in the ruins of a gate lodge at a spot called Narrow Water. The frantic survivors radioed for assistance, and within twenty-five minutes a large Wessex helicopter carrying soldiers from the Queen's Own Highlanders arrived and cautiously landed in a nearby field. No sooner had the reinforcements disembarked than another huge bomb, hidden near the gate lodge, was detonated. Another twelve soldiers were killed and a score or more seriously injured. Among the dead was the CO of the Queen's Own Highlanders, Lieutenant Colonel David Blair, who was so close to the explosion that his body was literally vaporized by the force of the blast. It was a classic guerrilla ambush that drew the grudging admiration of the British, but there was no concealing the scale of the calamity. The death toll was the highest of the Troubles for the British army and represented the worst casualties suffered by the Paras since the Battle of Arnhem in 1944. In the annals of Anglo-Irish conflict it equaled or surpassed the famous Kilmichael attack of November 1920 in which the West Cork IRA commanded by the legendary guerrilla leader Tom Barry had ambushed a convoy of auxiliary police and, depending upon the version of the incident, killed seventeen or eighteen of their number.[15]

Between them the combined slaughter at Narrow Water and the assassination of Earl Mountbatten threatened to pitch Northern Ireland into the sort of security crisis relished by the IRA. There were rows between the RUC and the British army over who should lead the security battle against the IRA, and Mrs. Thatcher was forced to referee. She appointed Sir Maurice Oldfield, a former head of the British Secret Intelligence Service, MI6, as security coordinator in an effort to improve interservice intelligence operations. Despite the provocation, the incident did not, however, tempt Thatcher into the sort of precipitate response the IRA had hoped for. The IRA, under Adams as under any of its leaders, operated on the principle that the more Britain resorted to crude repression, the greater the degree of sympathy and support, passive and active, the organization could count on from nationalists. The classic example of that was the one-sided internment operation of 1971, which had boosted IRA ranks enormously. For years afterward the IRA lived in hope that the British would repeat that mistake. But Thatcher disappointed them.

THE REAL LONG-TERM significance of the events of August 27, 1979, was that they enormously fortified Adams's status in the IRA and thus his control of and influence over the republican movement's political direction. In its review of 1979, *An Phoblacht–Republican News* gave the credit for Mountbatten, Narrow Water, and other military successes to the changes pioneered by Adams: "Last year was one of resounding Republican success," crowed the paper, "when the IRA's cellular reorganisation was operationally vindicated, particularly through the devastating use of remote-control bombs."[16] The IRA had been delivered from the disaster of 1974–75.

It has become an accepted part of the mythology of this period in the IRA's development that Adams's reorganization plan rescued the organization from certain defeat and was responsible for a dramatic turnaround in its fortunes between 1977 and 1979. The truth may be more complex. To begin with, the cell system was largely a Belfast phenomenon. Some rural areas successfully fought to maintain their old structures and the operational spontaneity and local control that came with them. The South Armagh Brigade, whose members had planned and carried out the Narrow Water attack, was perhaps the best example of this. Even in Belfast the reorganizing was far from complete or universal, as one former battalion commander recalled: "The cells in Belfast were never really divorced from the old company structures, because they [the companies] were needed for logistics, safe houses, call houses, and so on."[17]

Those involved in fighting the war believed that a much more important factor in reviving the IRA after the 1975 cease-fire was the fact that the British had ended internment, and as a consequence scores of released IRA prisoners returned to active service. Internment was brought to an end officially in December 1975 as part of the cease-fire deal, and after this IRA suspects began to be processed through the courts and treated like ordinary criminals. As far as the Cage 11 dissidents were concerned, the criminalization policy that followed internment represented a major political setback, but according to another IRA commander it brought an unanticipated bonus for the organization:

> Myself and [Billy] McKee analysed the political situation at the time [late 1974]. Internment had decimated the ranks of the IRA and in Ardoyne we had only four active Volunteers. I was never consulted about the possibility of a ceasefire and I near blew a gasket when I heard in prison that the Feakle talks had taken place. But I can't understand these people who say that the truce wrecked us. In my view it strengthened us. We had a lot of internees coming back in for active service. It was so unlike the situation in 1974 when we had four active Volunteers. By the start of 1976 we were bursting at the seams.[18]

Nevertheless Adams received most of the credit for the IRA's resurgence, and as his position strengthened he set his sights on removing the last obstacles in his way to unchallenged control of the republican movement. With Billy McKee ousted, the two most formidable remaining opposition figures were Daithi O Conaill and Ruairi O Bradaigh. The Belfast leader had once confided to a colleague on the Army Council the tactical approach he favored when going about the destruction and removal of political enemies, and it was this line of attack that he adopted to remove the Southern veterans: " 'You don't confront people,' he would say. 'You isolate and marginalize them and then get rid of them.' I often heard him say that," the figure recalled.[19] It was to be a long, arduous, and at times painful campaign against O Conaill and O Bradaigh, but in the end it succeeded—the pair was isolated, marginalized, and then discarded.

Gerry Adams's drive against O Conaill and O Bradaigh had actually started before the purge of McKee when, in July 1977, the Revolutionary Council was convened to expel a fellow West Belfast man, Gerry O'Hare, a former public relations man for the republican movement in Belfast who had risen to become editor in Dublin of An Phoblacht, the Provisionals' Southern weekly paper. There were two reasons for the heave against

O'Hare; one was his political friendship with O Conaill and O Bradaigh, and the other was the fact that as long as the editorship of *An Phoblacht* was in his hands, Adams would be unable to influence republicans south of the Border. The pretext for O'Hare's removal was, however, a much less straightforward matter.

O'Hare's wife, Rita, one of the first women to join the male-dominated IRA and a formidable activist in her own right, had been badly wounded during an ambush of British soldiers in Andersonstown in 1972 in which she had taken part. She was arrested and charged, but because of her severe injuries she was given bail. On the eve of her trial she absconded across the Border and took up residence in Dublin. Like many IRA relationships, the O'Hare marriage had been battered by the Troubles and weakened by separation and worry. Gerry had been interned in the North and jailed in the South while the authorities relentlessly pursued his wife in the Republic and attempted to have her extradited back to Belfast for trial. Under the stress and strain, the couple had begun to drift apart. In 1975 the marriage was dealt a devastating blow when Rita attempted to smuggle a stick of gelignite into Portlaoise prison during a visit to an IRA prisoner and was caught. The three-year jail term meted out by the Special Criminal Court in Dublin sounded the death knell for their relationship.

With the couple now married in name only and Rita confined to Portlaoise prison, sixty miles south-west of Dublin, Gerry O'Hare struck up a relationship with Grainne Caffrey, Daithi O Conaill's sister-in-law and a first cousin of Ruairi O Bradaigh, and it was this that Adams and his allies seized upon to undermine the *An Phoblacht* editor. Internment and imprisonment had badly weakened family life in republican areas in places like Belfast, and one of the most divisive problems faced by IRA leaders was the constant allegation that prisoners' wives were sleeping around, often with IRA men still at liberty. At a Revolutionary Council meeting in July 1977, O'Hare was accused of setting a bad example to IRA Volunteers because of his relationship with Grainne Caffrey, and he was dismissed from the editorship of *An Phoblacht*. "O Bradaigh defended him saying that but for the absence of divorce legislation they [Gerry and Rita O'Hare] would have regularized their situation, but Adams and Co. were pitching their appeal to Twomey and McKee, who were both very conservative Catholics," recalled one delegate.[20]

The merciless ousting of O'Hare was the first move in Adams's push to take control of the Provisionals' public relations arm. O'Hare was replaced as editor of *An Phoblacht* by the Dubliner Deasun Breathnach, a member of a distinguished republican clan, but in reality control fell into the hands of Adams and his allies. While Breathnach became editor, power was transferred to an Adams appointee, Mick Timothy, who became manager of the weekly, and soon there were loud and bitter complaints about its content from the O Bradaigh–O Conaill wing.

The takeover of *An Phoblacht* was interrupted by Adams's arrest and imprisonment after La Mon, but following his release in September 1978 the campaign resumed with vigor, and the Army Council authorized what was officially termed a fusion of *An Phoblacht* and *Republican News*. The new weekly, *An Phoblacht–Republican News (AP-RN)*, was unveiled on January 27, 1979, and its first lead story announced that the purpose of the fusion was to "improve reporting of the war in the North." But there was a hint of another objective, one that would pitch the organization into ideological turmoil. "We also intend to provide an improved and widened forum for Republican debate on building a new Ireland," it declared.[21]

The fusion was a logical move from a number of viewpoints. It made economic sense to produce and distribute one rather than two weeklies, and the existence of separate Southern and Northern papers flew in the face of the republican objective of destroying partition. All these points were made in a paper prepared for the leadership by Danny Morrison, who was slated to be the new paper's first editor. But the real significance of the merger became clear only after it had happened. It was at first not so much a merging of the two papers as a takeover of *An Phoblacht* by the Belfast paper, to the extent that the new weekly even looked and read like *Republican News*. "Effectively the *Republican News* people came down from Belfast and took it over," recalls one spectator.[22] Even so the real control of the new paper would lie in the hands not of its editorial board, or even the Sinn Fein Ard Comhairle, or Executive, but with the IRA leadership, and as a result the paper would become a powerful vehicle in the effort to undermine the remaining influence of O Conaill, O Bradaigh, and their allies. *Republican News* had started life as the news sheet of the IRA's Belfast Brigade, and *AP-RN* would be the creature of the Adams-dominated Army Council. Having captured the IRA Army Council, Adams was now determined to remove O Conaill and O Bradaigh's influence from the last forum where their voice was still strong, in the leadership of Sinn Fein. The takeover of *AP-RN* was a vital first step in that drive.

THE FOUNDERS of the Provisional Republican movement had devised a policy program that they believed would satisfy the two unresolved issues from the 1921 Treaty settlement. Known as Eire Nua, or New Ireland, the program was designed to create political structures that, its architects believed, would calm Protestant fears that a united Ireland would mean their subjugation and eventual absorption by nationalist and Catholic Ireland, while its economic ideology was intended to correct the grave wrong wrought to those who had done most to give Ireland its freedom back in 1919–21. The great economic imbalance that gave the east coast, and especially Dublin, such a huge advantage over the rural west, south-west, and north-west, where much of the IRA's 1919–21 campaign had been fought, had to be rectified, and the sacrifice made by lower middle classes, particularly the small farmers, who had provided the manpower for the independence struggle, would be recognized in the new order.

No republican policy was more personally identified with O Conaill and O Bradaigh than Eire Nua. It had been adopted as IRA policy in June 1972 when the Army Council endorsed it. Sinn Fein followed suit, and at that year's Ard Fheis the party's constitution was changed to encompass the plan. Eire Nua outlined a decentralized federal scheme that would consist of a central government drawn from a federal parliament, half of whose members would be elected nationally via a system of proportional representation and half drawn from four provincial parliaments that would have strong powers over economic policy. The provincial parliaments would be based on the four ancient provinces of Ireland—Munster, Leinster, Connaught, and Ulster—and underneath them would be two further structures, a series of regional development councils and a system of district councils.

The important layer was at the provincial level, and the keystone of the whole edifice was the Ulster parliament. Although based on the pre-1921 province of nine counties, and not on the six counties of Northern Ireland, the Ulster parliament, or Dail Uladh, was intended to safeguard Protestant rights in an independent Ireland and to sweeten the bitter pill of British withdrawal. "Dail Uladh would be representative of Catholic and Protestant, Orange and Green, Left and Right," declared the Eire Nua document. "It would be an Ulster parliament for the Ulster people. The Unionist-oriented people of Ulster would have a working majority within the Province and would therefore have considerable control over their own affairs. That power would be the surest guarantee of their civil and religious liberties within a New Ireland."[23] At the same time the inclusion of Counties Cavan, Monaghan, and Donegal, with their significant nationalist majorities, meant that the overall Protestant majority in Ulster would be a thin one and that compromise with Nationalists would be necessary to make the scheme workable.

Eire Nua held other attractions for the republican movement of the early 1970s. By creating strong provincial governments, Eire Nua intended to adjust the economic and political imbalance that had developed in the Republic as a result of the overdevelopment of the east coast and in particular the spectacular growth of the greater Dublin area since the 1960s. One result of this was that the west of Ireland and the southern and northern edges of the Southern state, including the Border counties, felt excluded and discriminated against. Eire Nua promised to change that. It was no accident that the bulk of Provisional supporters in the South came not from the east coast or from Dublin but from these poorer and more isolated fringes of the country.

A profile of the typical rural Provisional supporter of that time would show him or her to be a member of the small landowning and small business class, what one of their number called "peasant proprietors"[24] and an Adams supporter once scornfully dismissed as "Fianna Failers with guns."[25] These were the people who stored weapons and explosives for the IRA's Northern war, raised money, gave shelter to fugitives, and allowed their land and farms to be used as training grounds, meeting places, and bomb factories. Family ties to the losing side in the civil war motivated many, and few had shared in the benefits of Irish independence; above all they were overwhelmingly Catholic and conservative in their outlook. Eire Nua's social and economic program appealed to all these elements. Based on the ancient philosophy of Comhar na gComharsan, Eire Nua decreed that the main instrument of economic policy would be the cooperative. A firmly neutral Irish state would control the finance sector and major industries; large ranchers would be dispossessed and their land broken up, and even though private enterprise would still play a role, it would be subservient to the cooperative principle. Non-nationals would be barred from owning a controlling interest in any Irish industry, while the strengthening of the Irish language and culture would be a priority in the new order. All this was, as the Eire Nua document boasted, a compromise between individualistic Western capitalism and the Soviet socialist system, a spot on the political spectrum that ideally suited the Provisionals' Southern support base.

Both O Conaill and O Bradaigh strongly supported the Eire Nua policy and firmly believed that it was the only scheme that stood a chance of winning Northern Protestants to the idea of Irish unity and independence. But, for Gerry Adams and his allies, hostility to Eire Nua became the route by which they would undermine the O Conaill–O Bradaigh leadership. The assault on Eire Nua that followed took place on two fronts, one within the IRA and the other inside Sinn Fein, and in each case the tactics were markedly different.

Winning over the IRA was the easy part. With the organization now dominated by Northern Command, support for the Eire Nua policy was sapped by appealing to the most sectarian of sentiments—namely that the federalist scheme would leave Northern nationalists in the same subservient situation vis-à-vis the unionists as had existed before British withdrawal. The very reason for waging armed struggle would be questioned in the minds of many Northern and Belfast IRA activists if Eire Nua was implemented. It was, its critics claimed, a sop to loyalism.

Once again the Revolutionary Council was employed to win the argument for Adams. Now dominated by his allies, it rejected Eire Nua at a meeting in Donegal in July 1979 and shortly afterward the Army Council endorsed the decision. Eire Nua was no longer IRA policy, although it was still Sinn Fein's program. The extraordinary situation now existed where the military and political wings of republicanism held diametrically opposed views on what shape Ireland should take after the British had been forced out of Northern Ireland. Within weeks the Army Council attempted to exert its authority over the Sinn Fein leadership on the issue, and that is when the trouble began, as a participant recalled:

> One fine day we were sitting in an Ard Comhairle meeting when a certain gent appeared and announced he had a statement to read, that we had to listen and it was of vital importance that it shouldn't go outside the room. There was to be no discussion, and after he had read what he came to read we were to move on to the next business. He had been asked to deliver a message saying that the Army Council no longer supported Eire Nua, and all documents and leaflets, stocked and on shelves [dealing with Eire Nua], were to be taken away and boxed.[26]

A fissure had opened up in the Provisionals that was unseen by the outside world but starkly visible to those at the top of the movement. While Sinn Fein continued to support the idea of Irish federalism, the IRA leadership and increasingly the organization's weekly paper An Phoblacht–Republican News opposed it. Furthermore, O Conaill and O Bradaigh showed every sign of fighting to hold the precious ground of Eire Nua, playing on what they perceived to be Adams's fear of a public and damaging split that could cost Northern Command much of its logistical support in the South. At the 1979 Ard Fheis, Sinn Fein delegates overwhelmingly passed a motion proposed by the County Kerry republican Richard Behal and seconded by Daithi O Conaill urging that Eire Nua be "retained, promoted and publicised." The 1980 Ard Fheis the following November endorsed a similar motion. The two resolutions were as near to an open defiance of the IRA leadership as it was possible to get. That Easter the Army Council replied with a declaration that deliberately omitted any mention of federalism, saying instead that only a unitary state—"a 32 County Democratic Socialist Republic"—could bring unity and peace between Catholics and Protestants.[27] The two sides were at war, and occasionally, as at that Easter time, their skirmishes became publicly visible.

The warfare was fought on a number of fronts, political and organizational, but at one Sinn Fein Ard Fheis after another O Bradaigh and O Conaill were slowly but firmly sidelined. The determination of the Adams camp to destroy its enemy was absolute. To establish their militant credentials the Adams camp first persuaded Sinn Fein to back a policy of demanding "immediate" British withdrawal from Northern Ireland and the simultaneous disbandment and disarming of the mostly Protestant RUC and Ulster Defence Regiment. This was pie-in-the-sky stuff of course—there was little chance of republicans ever being able to enforce it—but that was not the purpose. The intention was to contrast Adams's militancy and determination with the vacillation of O Bradaigh and O Conaill, whose own preference was for a phased and gradual British withdrawal so as to lessen the chances of a violent Protestant reaction, causing a civil war to break out. Meanwhile on the organizational level Adams and his allies pushed through measures that allowed for the co-option of their allies to Sinn Fein's ruling executive. He also secured approval for the appointment of deputies to the party's officers, a measure that soon brought charges that Adams's allies were being placed strategically in places that would allow them to undermine the old guard.

The effect of all this was to gradually strengthen Adams's grip on the Sinn Fein leadership. In 1977 he could count on the support of at most three other members of the party executive, but five years later he and his supporters had a total of ten out of the sixteen Ard Comhairle members elected by the Ard Fheis on his side and perhaps half or more of the twenty-one co-options.

It was, however, the turn to the left, charted and pioneered by Adams and his supporters, that sharpened the divisions almost to the breaking point. The Adams camp was picking at an ancient scab with this move. It was the extreme socialism of the Goulding leadership that had motivated many of the Southern republicans to side with the Provisionals in 1969 and 1970, and their views had not changed much in the intervening years. The reintroduction of socialist ideas by the Adams faction in the late 1970s deeply unsettled O Conaill, O Bradaigh, and their allies, but it also created a dilemma for them. Goulding's leftward movement was accompanied by a scaling down of the IRA and military methods and was thus easier to denounce, whereas Adams presented his socialism as part of a revolutionary agenda of which an enhanced armed struggle was a vital and integral part. Opposing Adams's socialism in these circumstances made O Conaill and O Bradaigh appear as if they were against the IRA at a time when many of those doing the fighting in the North identified fully with other revolutionary movements elsewhere in the world and saw the IRA's struggle as fully consistent with them. As one of their number recalled, "[We were] . . . delighted to see the Khmer Rouge take over Phnom Penh, reveled in the liberation of Saigon, thought it fantastic when the Cubans chased the South Africans out of Angola, and identified with the Left in Europe, the ANC, and the Zimbabwe liberation struggle."[29]

THE MOVE TO THE LEFT was first signaled not by Sinn Fein but by the IRA in bloody and dramatic fashion on the evening of February 2, 1977, when fifty-nine-year-old Jeffrey Agate, the English-born managing director of the giant multinational chemical company Du Pont, arrived home after a day's work to find IRA gunmen waiting for him. He died instantly in a hail of bullets. Agate was the first businessman shot dead in the IRA's new campaign of assassination aimed against the employer class. He died just before Adams's release from Long Kesh. A month later, after Adams had joined the Army Council, the IRA killed its second businessman victim when forty-five-year-old English-born publicity consultant James Nicholson was shot dead as he made his way to Belfast airport following a one-day business trip to a struggling hi-fi factory on the edge of nationalist West Belfast. The killing of Agate and Nicholson and possibly as many as eight other locally based business figures in subsequent weeks and months[29] was justified by Chief of Staff Seamus Twomey. Employing the unfamiliar left-wing rhetoric of Cage 11, Twomey told a French TV interviewer, "All British industrialists are targets. They are exploiting the Irish working class . . . everyone directly connected with British imperialism are definite targets."[30]

The move to the left was announced at same time as the "long war" doctrine was spelled out, at the 1977 Bodenstown commemoration. Declaring

"We need to make a stand on economic issues and on the everyday struggles of people," the Army Council spokesman Jimmy Drumm called for "the forging of strong links between the Republican Movement and the workers of Ireland and radical trade unionists." The alliance, he predicted, "will ensure mass support for the continuing armed struggle in the North."[31] Two years later it was Gerry Adams's turn to give the Bodenstown address, and he amplified the message, this time not as a Belfast troublemaker fresh from the Long Kesh prison camp but with the authority of a former chief of staff and current Northern commander.

The move to the left became the backdoor way of attacking the Eire Nua policy. The target became not the federalism of Eire Nua itself but the economic and social program attached to it. To transform Eire Nua's mild radicalism into a left-wing revolutionary program, Adams relied heavily on advice from outside the republican movement and in particular from a figure who quickly became, in the eyes of the O Conaill–O Bradaigh camp, the new version of Roy Johnston, Goulding's éminence grise. Phil Shimeld was an English writer on the Trotskyist weekly *Red Mole*, the newspaper of the London-based International Marxist Group (IMG). He had made contact with IRA prisoners during the mid-1970s and they had invited him to Belfast and asked him to write for *Republican News*. Much to the irritation of the republican old guard, Shimeld supplied leftist-oriented articles, often under the nom de plume Peter Dowling, a tactic that enraged allies of O Conaill and O Bradaigh.[32]

The IMG was the British section of the Fourth Socialist International and traced its political roots to Leon Trotsky himself. Among the group's leading lights was Tariq Ali, a left-wing celebrity of the 1970s who had hit the headlines when he helped organize mass demonstrations in London against American involvement in the Vietnam War. Although the IMG was hostile to the Soviet Union, as most Trotskyist movements were, the distinction was lost on the older republicans, who saw Shimeld as Adams's version of Roy Johnston and Tony Coughlan. The allegedly baneful influence of Goulding's pro-Communist aides had badly divided the IRA and Sinn Fein in the 1960s, and although they may have been unaware of these niceties of Marxist ideology, O Conaill and O Bradaigh suspected that history was about to repeat itself.

Following the IRA's rejection of Eire Nua, Adams came under pressure from the old guard on the Ard Comhairle to come up with an alternative policy, which eventually he presented to his senior colleagues late in 1979. It became known as "the gray document" because a fault in a photocopy machine in Belfast had darkened the copies made for the rest of the Sinn Fein leadership. It was a slim document—at most two pages long—that still advocated the decentralization that characterized the Eire Nua document but strengthened central government at the expense of the provincial parliaments. Adams reserved his assault on Eire Nua for its economic and social program. The alternative he advocated was unequivocally socialist, and it appalled the conservatives in the Sinn Fein leadership.

Declaring that political control in a post-British Ireland would be worthless without control of the country's wealth and economic resources, the Adams document continued:

> Furthermore with James Connolly, we believe that the present system of society is based upon the robbery of the working class and that capitalist property cannot exist without the plundering of labour, we desire to see capitalism abolished and a democratic system of common or public ownership created in its stead. This democratic system, which is called socialism, will, we believe, come as a result of the continuous increase of power of the working class. Only by this means can we secure the abolition of destitution and all the misery, crime and immorality which flow from that unnecessary evil.[33]

This was strong meat for the rural Southerners, but worse was to come. The new program would also abolish the right to own land; under Adams's plan the state would be the only entity allowed to possess the title to Irish land, and those who were working the country's farms, no matter how small the holding, would enjoy only "custodial ownership." That touched a nerve in rural Ireland, for among other things it meant that inheritance rights would be lost. If Adams had his way, the family farm, the mainstay of rural Ireland, would be no more. It was a formulation designed to strike fear and anger into the bulk of republicans outside Belfast and Derry, and it did.

The fight back came in October 1979 at a special Sinn Fein conference held in Athlone. That year's Ard Fheis had been postponed and was not scheduled to meet until the following January, and so a stopgap weekend gathering involving two hundred or so of the faithful, mostly from the South, was held instead. Someone had decided to leak the story of the internal turmoil to the press, and a story was published in the Dublin tabloid the *Sunday World* under the byline of the left-wing journalist Eamonn McCann. The story claimed that federalism was to be ditched and that the Provisionals were about to move sharply to the left under the influence of Marxist sympathizers. The story, which was uncomfortably accurate, also talked about the waning influence of O Conaill and O Bradaigh. The reaction of many of the delegates, who included the party's thirty councillors in the Republic, was an angry one. According to one report of the meeting, some would have staged a walkout had Adams not intervened during the Sunday morning session to deny the report.[34] The identity of the deep throat was never established despite an inquiry ordered by the Ard Comhairle, although the Adams camp let it be known that it suspected the ousted *An Phoblacht* editor, Gerry O'Hare.

The *Sunday World* story put Adams on the defensive. Within ten days both the Army Council and the Sinn Fein leadership had been forced to issue statements denying the story, claiming that it was the result of British and Irish government efforts to raise a Red scare against them.

THE MARXIST ALLEGATION persuaded Adams to give an interview to the author, then a junior reporter with the Dublin weekly magazine *Hibernia*, to underline in person the IRA and Sinn Fein denial. It was the author's first meeting with Adams and took place in a council house in the West Belfast housing estate of Andersonstown over a large tray of tea, sandwiches, and cake provided by an obviously adoring middle-aged hostess. Dressed in sports jacket and light trousers, sporting fashionably long hair and a somewhat unkempt beard, Adams still puffed on a pipe in those days. Anyone unaware of his real identity could easily have mistaken him for a visiting lecturer at a New England women's college or a left-wing sociology professor at a red-brick English university. He was charming and impressively attentive and, displaying even then the consideration of the veteran political operator, stayed long enough to clear away the tray and wash the dishes when the interview concluded. Our matronly hostess beamed with pleasure and adoration when finally he left.

If he had his tongue stuck in his cheek during our conversation when he dismissed the left-wing allegations, it did not show. "First of all there's one thing which should be said categorically," he declared. "There is no Marxist influence within Sinn Fein; it simply isn't a Marxist organisation. I know of no-one in Sinn Fein who is a Marxist or who would be influenced by Marxism."[35] The *Hibernia* interview was reproduced in full in *An Phoblach–Republican News*, and the following two issues carried more reassuring stories, one describing a pilgrimage Adams had made to the home of the decidedly non-Marxist hero of the 1916 Rising, Patrick Pearse, and another applauding the ultraconservative head of Irish Northern Aid in New York, seventy-two-year-old Michael Flannery.

Emboldened by all this, Adams's opponents blocked the "gray document," and in a compromise deal a special subcommittee was set up by the Ard Comhairle to marry the radical program with the original Eire Nua in time for the postponed 1979 Ard Fheis. While Adams had been forced to draw in his horns, the compromise document did contain concessions to his hard-line approach. For instance, while the original Eire Nua program envisaged that private enterprise would still have a role to play in the new Ireland, the compromise paper said it would have "no role to play" at all in key industries, and that small local businesses would be permitted only "provided no exploitation occurs."[36] Adams also got included a proposal to wage an "economic resistance campaign" that would commit Sinn Fein to work with radical trade unionists. Custodial ownership of land survived but became the clumsier and somewhat contradictory concept of "family or co-operative custodial ownership." Even so, many of the delegates regarded the compromise program as an attack on small farmers, and the veteran and respected Leitrim republican John Joe McGirl had to intervene to assure the Ard Fheis that this was not the same agenda as that espoused by Goulding. "Ten years ago I parted ways with people whose policies I disagreed with," he declared. "My politics have not changed and I support this document."[37] The document was jointly proposed by O Bradaigh and Adams and was passed, but by a margin that suggested serious divisions among the rank and file: 65 percent were for, 30 percent, against, and 5 percent undecided. "That was too close for comfort," recalled O Bradaigh.[38]

The year 1980 ended on a positive note for the Adams camp. By November it shared control of the Sinn Fein ruling executive with the old guard, and the Northerners guerrilla tactics had forced one key opponent, Sean O Bradaigh, brother of Ruairi, to quit the leadership in protest against the radicalism of the compromise Eire Nua document. His shadow as SF publicity director, Danny Morrison, took over his job. Morrison became the confrontational, belligerent edge of the opposition. "Adams made the snowballs but Danny threw them," commented one of his victims. The Adams grip on Sinn Fein had tightened immeasurably.

THERE THEN FOLLOWED one of those events that no one had anticipated or could have anticipated. For the previous four years republican prisoners had been staging a protest designed to preserve special-category or political status. Frustrated by the failure of the protest and angry at their treatment as common criminals, IRA and INLA prisoners in the Long Kesh jail, now renamed the Maze prison, finally decided to bring matters to a head. The protest had begun with inmates refusing to don prison uniform, insisting that they wear only their bed blanket instead, and then they had refused to slop out their cells every morning, instead smearing the cell walls with excreta and pouring urine under their doors. As Catholic Church intermediaries tried but failed to broker a settlement with the British and the violence of the prison staff against inmates intensified, the prisoners finally decided in the autumn of 1980 to embark on a hunger strike in a bid to win recognition that their imprisonment was politically motivated.

That protest, which ended in confusion and defeat a week before Christmas, and the second, fatal fast, which began three months later, had the effect of temporarily uniting the Provisionals and papering over the widening cracks. The anti-Adams camp called a halt to the undeclared warfare, as one of their number recalled: "Ruairi and Dave avoided stand-up rows with Adams in order to prevent a split, especially during and after the hunger strikes when what we had was a very united and very strong movement."[39] They could do nothing else.

The feud was on hold, but the way the hunger strikes were run actually served to strengthen the Adams leadership, not least because the profile of the Northerners was heightened considerably, while that of Southerners like O Bradaigh and O Conaill was reduced. The campaign in support of the hunger strikers was largely directed from the North. Adams and colleagues like Danny Morrison were regarded very much as spokesmen for the protesting prisoners, and when republicans began winning elections, first as H Block prison candidates and then as Sinn Fein members, they were seen as the architects of that success, not O Bradaigh and O Conaill.

There was another, possibly more potent factor. As IRA coffins started to come out of the jail, the argument that federalism was a sop to the forces ultimately seen as responsible for the prison conflict became more and more appealing to grassroots activists. The pressure mounted on O Conaill and O Bradaigh. By the time the 1981 Ard Fheis met in the autumn, the two veterans had lost all control of the Sinn Fein leadership. A motion proposed by the Ard Comhairle and by the party organizations in Belfast and Dublin called for the Sinn Fein constitution to be changed so that the party's aim was no longer a "federal" state but a "democratic socialist republic" instead. The motion, a head-on tilt at Eire Nua, was passed but just failed to win the two-thirds majority necessary to change Sinn Fein policy. The following year, by which time Adams and Martin McGuinness had been elected as abstaining members of a new Northern Assembly, the motion got the backing needed to alter the constitution. The O Conaill–O Bradaigh camp had lost the war with Adams. O Conaill quit as vice-president of Sinn Fein, a post he had shared uncomfortably with Adams, and O Bradaigh would step down from the party's leadership a year later, in November 1983, and be replaced by the West Belfast man.

The old guard had fought on in the hope that Adams and his colleagues would grow weary of the battle, but they badly underestimated their reserves of patience. Adams quite simply outlasted them, and each time they promised to bring matters to a head—for instance, by threatening to resign en masse, which happened more than once—Adams would temporarily retreat, only to regroup for another debilitating round a few weeks or months later. It was the old guard who tired first, not Adams. They also forgot just how ruthless he and the other Northerners could be.

SIX MONTHS OR SO before the changes at the top of Sinn Fein (some date it at around April or May 1983), a tall, willowy, dark-haired woman in her midthirties boarded a flight at Dublin airport bound for Toronto, in the Canadian province of Ontario, and said farewell to Ireland forever. It would have been surprising had any of her fellow passengers recognized her or been aware of the part she had played in the drama unfolding inside Sinn Fein. Christin Elias was not a figure who had been much in the public eye despite her prominence in republican politics, but the extraordinary circumstances of her exile and Gerry Adams's rise to the summit of Sinn Fein were inextricably linked, if well hidden and only rarely discussed, events.

Christin Elias was by common admission an enigmatic figure who appeared on the Provisionals' stage in the mid-1970s without any obvious tie to Ireland or its political ferment. About the only thing that fellow Republicans knew about her was that she hailed from somewhere in Eastern Europe; some believed that she was Hungarian, others that she was Russian or Ukrainian. Another version was that her mother was Irish and her father a Lithuanian who had been a high-ranking official in the Communist Party of the Soviet Union. In fact she was born in Canada of a Canadian-Irish mother of Methodist stock and a Bulgarian father. She had been educated in Sofia and spoke Bulgarian fluently, a skill she learned from her émigré father. She and her mother traveled a lot and had ended up more or less by chance in Dublin in 1974, where, attracted by the conflict then raging in the North, she offered her home in Churchtown in South Dublin to the IRA as a "safe house" where meetings were held and fugitives took refuge. She worked in an engineering plant by day, but at night was an enthusiastic Sinn

Fein worker; both she and her mother joined the party's Cumann in Churchtown. She soon adopted the Irish version of her name—Christin ni Elias meant Christin, daughter of Elias—and moved gradually toward the leadership of Sinn Fein.

An enthusiastic supporter of Eire Nua's federalist program, she befriended O Bradaigh, O Conaill, and other members of the Ard Comhairle and generally made herself indispensable. "She was a very clever, efficient lady, who ate work and was totally committed to Eire Nua," remembered one of them. "She had studied behind the Iron Curtain and was the one who kept on pointing out the left-wing stuff of Adams's people, predicting what would happen next."[40] By 1978 she had risen to membership of the Ard Comhairle and was Sinn Fein's national education officer, charged with, among other things, promoting Eire Nua among the rank and file. When the hunger strikes started in 1980, she almost single-handedly ran the national committee formed to publicize the prisoners' cause. One activist remembers that she often met the bills for printing hunger strike posters and leaflets out of her own pocket.[41]

It was perhaps inevitable that such a strong-willed woman would clash with Gerry Adams, but when she did the violence of the collision startled everyone. One witness vividly recalled the occasion:

In the months after the [July 1979] Army Council message dismissing Eire Nua, every Ard Comhairle meeting was getting more and more painful, the divisions were intense. We wanted to know that if the policy wasn't to be Eire Nua what was it to be? So at this particular Ard Comhairle meeting Adams pulled a document out of his jacket pocket, but it was only two pages long, typed on each side. Behal laughed, everybody tittered as he started to read from it. When he finished, we thought it was just an introduction, it was so short. O Conaill said,"Are you sure that's all?" and O Bradaigh asked when we would see the documents behind it all.

Christin sat back, drew on her cigarette and said, "Well, Gerry, isn't this a rather slim document to produce after two years of turmoil? This is not even a foundation, we'd have a job to build on that. Surely this is a rather threadbare document?" Adams lost the rag. "What do you expect," he exploded. "I had only twenty-four hours to produce the document!" We were all sitting there with our mouths open. Christin then replied, "In that case, Gerry, it was a very poor presentation." Adams hit the table with rage, shouting that she was putting words in his mouth. From that day on her cards were marked.[42]

Other witnesses agree that Elias had made a dangerous enemy that day. "You could see the spark in Adams's eyes; he had been hurt by her," said one.[43] "Boy was he mad, and all his lieutenants were mad! I pulled at her sleeve because I knew how vicious they could be," remembered another.[44]

It was around the time of this famous confrontation that Christin ni Elias was approached by an official attached to the British embassy in Dublin who asked her out on a date. His interest was ostensibly romantic, and he asked if he could see her on a regular basis. It was an implausible story, and despite his assurances that he was not from MI5, she was suspicious and feared that he was an agent for one or other branch of British intelligence. She went straight to a senior member of the Sinn Fein leadership, who passed her on to the IRA. "They established an ongoing situation," explained one source familiar with the story. "Belfast people in the GHQ Intelligence Department handled the operation, and they told her to meet the guy and they briefed her on what to say."[45] The relationship began in August 1979, and the pair would meet about once a month, usually for lunch at venues in Dublin or Belfast: "The IRA instructed her to report back on the meetings, and when she met them she gave them a written report, all typed out and in triplicate, which was typical of her."[46]

Much to Christin ni Elias's frustration there seemed to be no end to the affair. The IRA wanted her to continue meeting the official, but she was, as she told one Sinn Fein friend, "totally sick of the arrangement, it went on so long." After more than two years, by the end of 1981 there was still no sign of the IRA operation coming to an end. "She was always hoping that she would be 'interrupted', that the IRA would abduct him," recalled the friend.[47]

In early 1982 the IRA attitude to Christin ni Elias suddenly turned hostile, and it was not long before the reason was a subject of republican gossip. "The word got out that she was a British agent, a whispering campaign was started, and attempts were made to stop her being elected to the Ard Comhairle," said one source.

Eventually in July that year, it was announced at the Ard Comhairle that there would have to be a court of inquiry into her, that she was suspect. It went ahead, but the truth was that it was a foregone conclusion, that the Army had already judged her and found her guilty.

The biggest charge against her was that she had sabotaged one of their operations. The background was that she had been told by the IRA to have lunch with the official in a certain Belfast hotel on December 22 or 23,

1981, and she agreed. But what Christin didn't realize was that as it was Christmastime the hotel was full of office parties, so when they turned up there were no free tables and they had to go elsewhere. The IRA arrived to find no British official in the restaurant, and they immediately accused her of sabotaging their operation.

I told her she had been lucky, that they were probably going to kill both of them and accuse her of being a spy and meeting her handler. She paled. After that they came and searched her house. They held her blindfold for three days, all of them men, and they even accompanied her when she went to the bathroom. They questioned her all the time, and I believe they were looking for the blacks [copies] of the intelligence reports she had typed up for the IRA.[48]

Ruairi O Bradaigh arrived in the midst of the affair and was held at gunpoint until the IRA took ni Elias away, eventually abandoning her several miles from Dublin in the middle of the countryside.

ni Elias was expelled from Sinn Fein in November 1982, at almost exactly the same time as the party's annual conference finally ditched her beloved Eire Nua policy. Those who were her political friends had little doubt that the timing of the purge against her was intimately connected to the internal battle being waged over federalism. It seemed the only explanation for the IRA's dragging out the intelligence operation so long and then deciding to move when they did. "The incident really tore the curtain of trust," commented a friend of ni Elias. "We felt they used the incident to get at her and to scare off everyone else. She was too articulate, too politically skilled, too astute to be allowed to survive."[49] Another commented, "The message was quite simple. If they could get at her, they could get at anyone. No one was immune."

The atmosphere on the Ard Comhairle soured after the incident. Not long afterward the Ard Comhairle asked for a special meeting with the IRA to discuss Eire Nua, and the Army Council sent along two of its members, Chief of Staff Martin McGuinness and his deputy Ivor Bell. "The whole meeting was dominated by what had happened to Christin and their litany of complaints about the 1975 cease-fire," recalled a participant. "The two Army men did all the talking. The meeting was full of bad vibes, the tenor was that if you criticized the opponents of Eire Nua and the O Bradaigh–O Conaill leadership you were anti-Army. Things started to get bad on a personal level after that. Before, everyone would go for a drink together in Conway's pub after Ard Comhairle meetings, but after that they would go to Conway's and we would go to Mooney's up by Parnell Square."[50]

The reality was that the Christin ni Elias affair had struck fear into Adams's critics. The Ard Comhairle was told that the three members of the Sinn Fein court of inquiry into the allegations had unanimously found against her, but one of the tribunal, Kevin Agnew, a solicitor from Maghera, County Derry, wrote privately to a party official, saying that this was not true; he had voted for her, and as a lawyer he was horrified at what had happened. But he beseeched the official to burn the letter after it had been read in case it fell into the hands of the Adams camp. Her friends were appalled at what had happened, but no one wanted to stand up and publicly make an issue of it; they were too frightened. When the author, then Northern editor of the *Irish Times*, revealed in September 1982 that ni Elias had been dismissed from Sinn Fein on security grounds, there was a rush to deny it. The Ard Comhairle, which still included some of her closest political friends, called the article "a piece of scurrilous journalism." Those who had been dismayed at the way the IRA had behaved chose to stay silent.[51] A few months later Christin ni Elias left quietly with her ailing mother for Toronto, where she has lived ever since. Aside from a few Christmas cards and letters she has had little or no contact with her friends in Ireland since the trauma of 1982. "She was our Dreyfus," confessed one of them.[52]

SIX

A Long, Hot Summer

By the start of the 1980s, Adams's struggle to oust the O Conaill–O Bradaigh leadership had been virtually won. The IRA Army Council was at this stage completely under his control and had rejected Eire Nua, and it would just be a matter of time before the last vestiges of the old leadership had been swept out of Sinn Fein. The blueprint drawn up and refined in Cage 11 of Long Kesh had been almost fully implemented, thanks in no small measure to the patience, skill, and determination of its architect.

The IRA was, however, no nearer its goal of expelling the British from Northern Ireland than it had been in 1969 when its war had begun. While it was true to say that the Adams plan had rescued the organization from virtually certain defeat, and an ignominious one at that, the IRA still lacked the strength and resources, both political and military, to make the British change their Northern Ireland policy in any significant way. The IRA's violence had fallen off dramatically from the heady days of the early 1970s when victory over the British did truly seem possible, dropping from an average of some 160 killings a year to fewer than 80, a decline of exactly half. Military stalemate reigned, with nothing on the horizon to suggest that major change was possible. The IRA could not be beaten, that seemed certain, but neither could the British.

It was in these circumstances that Gerry Adams led the republican movement into one of the most extraordinary and complete political volte-face in its long history in a bid to break this stalemate, executing a move that involved adopting some of the very same tactics and ideas whose espousal by the O Conaill–O Bradaigh leadership had made them such objects of hatred and scorn. The shift took many forms, but none was as dramatic or unequivocal as the decision to give the fighting of elections the same priority as the waging of war against Britain.

Those who knew Adams well during these years say that the episode not only demonstrated the utter pragmatism that governed his approach to politics but revealed a determination that neither he nor his generation of republicans would suffer the same sad fate as his father and his contemporaries. When their IRA project ended, in the case of Adams's father in the late 1940s, they had retreated to their hearths demoralized and directionless, bereft of community support, to dream of what might have been and sustained only by the hope that a new generation would one day rise up, take on the torch, and succeed where they had failed. Old comrades would meet on Friday nights to drink and sing stirring ballads of war and sacrifice, of battles fought and lost—but rarely won. His father helped found the Felons Club, a social and drinking club on the Falls Road where membership was open only to those who had been imprisoned for the cause. There, old IRA comrades could gather and reminisce and help each other out when sickness, bad luck, or death struck. In some ways it almost seemed as if defeat suited them better than victory, for there was a sense in which Irish republicanism thrived on oppression and the isolated exclusivity that came with it. This had been the story of one generation of IRA men and women after another, and it was the atmsphere within which Adams was born and reared. Unlike his father and his generation, however, Adams would not settle for such paltry spoils.

One Cage 11 veteran remembered Adams once putting all this into words. "There was no way he was going to fade back into the obscurity of Ballymurphy. He hammered it home to all of us that something had to come out of all of this during our lifetimes, that no matter about previous campaigns this struggle was not going to be for nothing."[1]

For this to be possible, ideas and policies once regarded as sacrosant could and would be discarded when necessary. The "move to the left," which Adams had launched to isolate the old guard in Sinn Fein, was eventually reversed, as were other policies that characterized and even defined the Provisionals under his leadership in the 1970s and much of the 1980s. The opposition to federalism, once thought of as a core Adams value, faded and was forgotten, and so too was the opposition to electoral politics, to the idea that Sinn Fein should run in elections and thereby give establishment politics even that small level of recognition. The Adams camp had fiercely resisted electoral politics when its feud with O Bradaigh and O Conaill was raging, but once they had been vanquished, that too was abandoned and reversed.

Running in elections was a tactic on which republicans had historically taken a pragmatic stand and past IRA leadership often justified the practice as a way of advancing the struggle against Britain when military methods were no longer viable. Frequently, electoral success was used to vindicate later violence. As long ago as the 1870s, the Irish Republican Brotherhood (IRB) had authorized its leaders to run in elections and take seats in the Westminster parliament in London as part of a strategy to obstruct the business of government in Britain. In December 1918 Sinn Fein's victory in the general election in Ireland paved the way for the IRA's war of independence. After partition and the split with de Valera, anti–Fianna Fail republicans regularly contested elections in both jurisdictions, although always on an abstentionist basis. Mostly they were beaten, but on two celebrated occasions they scored remarkable victories. In 1955 Sinn Fein ran for several Northern seats in the Westminster general election and won in two, Mid-Ulster and Fermanagh–South Tyrone, while in 1957, a year after the IRA had launched its Border Campaign, the party contested the Republic's general election and ran in nineteen constituencies. They were successful in four: Fergal O'Hanlon won in Monaghan, J. J. Rice in South Kerry, John Joe McGirl in Sligo-Leitrim, and Ruairi O Bradaigh in Longford-Westmeath. There was nothing in republican ideology that forbade the organization from fighting elections. The only iron rule was that successful candidates could never take their seats in what were regarded as illegal and corrupt parliaments. In practice, as well, republicans ran only occasionally, when there was a particular advantage to be gained. Otherwise, as a matter of doctrine, priority was given to the strategy of armed struggle.

That pragmatic stand changed at the time of the 1970 split with Goulding. Those who left to form the Provisionals had a long list of grievances with the Goulding leadership, but high on that list was suspicion about its parliamentary intentions. Goulding's move to leftist, agitational politics and his gradual erosion of the abstentionist principle were seen as parallel tracks leading in the same direction, toward participation in elections and the recognition of the partition parliaments in Dublin and Belfast. "Elections" became a dirty word.

Not all those who went with the Provisionals thought that in such simplistic terms. O Bradaigh had been an abstentionist member of the Irish parliament and knew the propaganda and political value of electoral success. He was also aware that, no matter how successful the IRA's military campaign in the North was, the absence of elected representation was a serious weakness that the British would be foolish not to exploit. O Conaill likewise developed a more mature attitude to elections with the passage of time. By the third or fourth year of the war in the North, around 1972–73, republican leaders knew that they could count their support in the tens of thousands and that if this could be properly harnessed, they could produce a respectable republican vote. The commonly held view at this time was that the IRA had at most the support of 1 or 2 percent of the North's nationalist community, but republican leaders knew better. They knew, for instance, that they could not sustain the war effort at the levels it had reached in those years without considerable grassroots support. The days when republican gatherings could attract at most a few score hardy veterans were long gone. The war in the North had radicalized people by the thousand. Some had joined the IRA, but many more were ready to help in other ways. IRA leaders knew from annual events like the Bodenstown commemoration, for example, that if thousands of people could turn out to publicly show their support for the IRA, then there were probably many more who would vote for Sinn Fein in the privacy and safety of the polling booth. The republican movement was like an iceberg; the visible tip was the IRA's violent campaign, but the rest was hidden beneath the surface.

But opposition to contesting elections was fierce in the Northern IRA. O Bradaigh and O Conaill wanted to fight two elections in the North during 1973, but Northern IRA leaders stopped them. The first was for local councils, and that opportunity arose when the British abolished the oath of allegiance that unionists had made mandatory for such contests. The pair argued that Sinn Fein should field candidates but not take seats. It would be a protest against internment, they said, that involved no loss of principle. Likewise when elections were announced for the new power-sharing Assembly, they urged that these should also be fought on an abstentionist basis so that the SDLP, Northern Ireland's moderate nationalist party, would not have a clear run. But powerful forces on the Army Council, led by Chief of Staff Seamus Twomey, vetoed both proposals. An ally of O Bradaigh remembered the strength of Twomey's opposition: "In early 1973 at a joint meeting of the Army and Sinn Fein, Sean O Bradaigh and Twomey had a serious row. Sean felt that we were allowing the SDLP to make all the running. Twomey's response to that was: 'Fuck you! You never fired a shot in anger all your life.' The SDLP were allowed to get off the ground as a result of Twomey and after that we missed a beat in publicity terms. It was very noticeable that the traffic in journalists to Kevin Street [Sinn Fein's Dublin office] diminished in the summer of 1973."[2] When polling for Northern Ireland's power-sharing assembly took place on June 28, 1973, an IRA unit from Gerry Adams's old Second Battalion fired an RPG-7 rocket at a polling station in the Lower Falls Road area. It was as if the IRA could not contain its contempt for electoral politics. From then on, ballot boxes had to be taken from polling stations by military guard so that the IRA could not destroy them.

The pro-election camp was again outvoted by the IRA leadership when the British announced elections in 1975 to a new body, a constitutional convention, which was to replace the power-sharing Assembly brought down by striking Loyalists the year before. Thereafter opposition to fighting elections became part of the general Cage 11 critique of those members of the 1975 Army Council highest on their target list, like O Bradaigh, O Conaill, and McKee. During the 1975 truce the British secretary of state, Merlyn Rees, had legalized Sinn Fein in the hope that it would encourage republicans to enter electoral politics. This failed because a majority on the Army Council suspected that the British were really trying to suck the movement into constitutionalism. But Adams and his allies seized on this and linked O Bradaigh and O Conaill's flirtation with elections to the same alleged failing that had brought the IRA into a near-fatal cease-fire in the first place. Talk of fighting elections became the next worst thing to discussing surrender.

The next opportunity to fight an election came after Ireland's accession to the European Economic Community. The first direct contest for the European parliament was due to occur in 1978 but was then postponed for a year. O Bradaigh and his allies had prepared the ground to fight the election on a quasiparticipatory basis. "We thought we would have won one seat," recalled an O Bradaigh ally. "Neil Blaney [a former County Donegal–based Fianna Fail minister] had contacted us to offer to stand down in Connacht-Ulster if we had stood while O Bradaigh and O Conaill would have stood in Munster."[3] O Bradaigh spent two years persuading Sinn Fein and the IRA to agree to a proposal to take seats in Europe on what was called "a controlled basis," that is, limited to using the offices and facilities in the Strasbourg parliament for propaganda purposes.

Adams led the opposition to this proposal, arguing that this was the thin end of the wedge. If Sinn Fein took seats in the European parliament, then the way would be opened, no matter what the proponents said, to taking seats in the Irish parliament or at Westminster, he said. A defining republican principle would be breached. He turned to the Revolutionary Council as a way if undermining O Bradaigh, and on the eve of the November 1978 Ard Fheis, IRA commanders by a single vote came out against contesting the Euro election. Even so, the first subsequent meeting of the Army Council backed the idea, but then the Adams camp once more intervened and a second meeting was called. "The Army Council was got at and the vote went four to three against," recalled a prominent activist. "One person, Joe Cahill, was got at on the grounds that the move would open the way to constitutionalism, to taking seats in Leinster House and Stormont."[4] Adams also spoke against, and the motion was lost. "It was one of the turning points," commented the same source. "We went back into the doldrums. It was like we had been knifed."[5]

The Sinn Fein–IRA squabbling opened the way for the former student civil rights leader Bernadette Devlin to contest the Northern Ireland Euro constituency, and on an issue the Adams group considered the exclusive property of republicans. The motive for her decision was the deteriorating situation in the H Blocks of Long Kesh, where IRA prisoners were into their third year of a blanket and no-wash protest, heading inexorably, it seemed, toward a hunger strike. With the assistance of women activists from the Relatives Action Committees, a support network set up by families of the protesting prisoners, Bernadette, as she was simply known in republican circles, raised the issue of intervening in Europe in early 1978. Her intervention split the Provos. While the Sinn Fein leadership in Dublin backed her and even offered financial support, the Northerners, led by Adams, fiercely opposed her.

The Belfast Sinn Fein leadership and the IRA's Northern Command joined forces to disrupt Devlin's campaign, using her reluctance to give "unequivocal support" for the IRA's armed struggle as a stick to beat her. Even though she was running to publicize the cause of the IRA prisoners, the Adams leadership mobilized the H Block protesters against her. A statement issued in their name called on republicans to boycott her campaign and declared, "We know only too well that the only way to remove the H Blocks forever is to boot both them and the people who build H Blocks out of the country at the point of a gun . . ."[6] Privately Devlin was accused of using the prisoners' plight to advance her personal political ambitions, while on the ground leading figures campaigned against her. The IRA's chief of staff, Martin McGuinness, followed her around Derry, urging people to boycott the election with the slogan "Back the prisoners, back the war!"

Despite the public and often vindictive opposition of Adams and his supporters, Bernadette, running under her married name, Devlin-McAliskey, won just shy of 34,000 votes in the June 1979 contest, a performance that far exceeded expectations and amounted to a serious rebuff for the Adams camp. The lesson was clear—if Bernadette Devlin could get that result in the face of republican antagonism, what could she have gotten had the IRA and Sinn Fein thrown their weight behind her? It was evident that there was untapped and not insubstantial electoral support for republican candidates. Her vote was dwarfed by the 140,000 votes won by the SDLP leader, John Hume, but her performance nevertheless indicated a far higher level of sympathy for republican-type issues than conventional wisdom had imagined possible.

Adams has never admitted that his opposition to Bernadette Devlin's European campaign was mistaken or that it was the spur for his own turnaround on electoral politics. In his autobiography he claimed that it was "around 1978–79," that is, before the Euro poll, that it was decided "simply and in principle that there would be a positive attitude towards an electoral strategy by Sinn Fein."[7] If a "positive attitude" toward elections had been taken at that time, there is scant evidence of it; in fact the evidence is that the Adams camp actually hardened its opposition to electoralism at this time. At Sinn Fein's November 1980 Ard Fheis for instance, held only five days after the first hunger strike had started, Adams's allies forced through a motion barring the party leadership from even considering running in the following May's Northern local elections. Two of his close supporters, the IRA and Sinn Fein director of publicity Danny Morrison and IRA Executive member Jimmy Drumm delivered the telling speeches. The result was that when the election was held, two weeks after the death of Bobby Sands in May 1981, Sinn Fein could field no candidates and other, smaller groups like the Irish Republican Socialist Party, the Marxist People's Democracy, and the Irish Independence Party, a greenish breakaway from the SDLP, cashed in on republican anger.

By the time of the next Ard Fheis, in November 1981, the situation had changed. The deaths of ten hunger strikers and the political turmoil that accompanied them had changed everything. Bobby Sands's victory in the Fermanagh–South Tyrone by-election in April 1981 and the success of H Block candidates in the Republic's general election earlier that year cleared the way for Adams and his supporters to openly argue for electoral politics. The scale of their flip-flop was huge. While O Bradaigh and O Conaill had argued only for occasional electoral interventions, Adams and his allies pushed for a permanent strategy of fighting elections, a strategy that would coexist, albeit uncomfortably, with the IRA's armed struggle.

Once again it was done by first giving assurances to the republican grassroots about the leadership's total commitment to the tactic of IRA violence. Adams's ally Danny Morrison told the assembled faithful that the lessons of history "show that the only effective campaign is that of armed struggle."

He went on, "[T]here is no one and no argument that can convince republicans that Britain, as she often asserts, cannot eventually be broken."[8] Having genuflected toward the altar of armed struggle, Morrison was delegated to lead the charge in the opposite direction and in favor of electoral politics a few months later at Sinn Fein's annual Ard Fheis, this time arguing that military force on its own could not do the job of forcing Britain out of Ireland. It was as if the Bodenstown speech had never been given. "Who here," he asked the delegates in what became one of Irish republicanism's most famous speeches, "really believes we can win the war through the ballot box? But will anyone here object if with a ballot paper in this hand and an Armalite in this hand, we take power in Ireland?"[9]

The so-called Armalite and ballot box strategy had been born, but the deep contradictions inherent in the approach, the built-in tendency for one to always inhibit and damage the other, would soon set Adams and others in his confidence on an expedition to seek a way out of armed struggle altogether. Adams was almost at that point in his political journey reached years before by Cathal Goulding and others who had led the republican movement in his youth, the point at which seeking votes and fighting a war would become mutually exclusive options.

The trek toward electoral politics had been a slow and cautious one, but with hindsight it appears to have been predetermined by the political program put together in the cages of Long Kesh. The key moment was when Adams won the argument in favor of the IRA's involvement in political agitation. Once that was accepted and the IRA set out to capture and hold public support, the logical dynamic pushed republicans more and more toward contesting elections as the most effective way of measuring and demonstrating that support. And the more the IRA sought public approval, the more it had to examine how its military tactics and its violent actions contributed to or inhibited the task. The Cage 11 agenda was sold to the IRA on the basis of its republican purity and military ruthlessness, but the truth was that it imposed political restraints on the IRA which became tighter with the passage of time and with Sinn Fein's deeper involvement in electoral politics. Eventually the contradictions would be too great to sustain.

WHEN ADAMS and his allies moved into the leadership of Sinn Fein in the late 1970s, the party they found was by and large unsophisticated and conservative. Movement into political activity was blocked by people who were instinctively antipolitical in outlook and who were content to allow a secret and unaccountable IRA leadership, the seven-man Army Council, to decide their politics for them. If the Adams agenda was going to succeed, that had to change; new and young blood would have to be brought into the party, if only to dilute the influence of the old guard.

Recruitment to the Provisionals had come in two great waves in the 1970s. There were first of all the Belfast Sixty-niners, as they were called, those who had joined the IRA in the wake of the August 1969 burnings and riots. Another surge of support followed the internment operation of August 1971 and Bloody Sunday nearly six months later. The next wave would come with the 1981 hunger strikes, but this time with a difference. The previous surges had all been into the ranks of the IRA; this time Sinn Fein would be the major beneficiary.

Even before the prison deaths Adams had been throwing Sinn Fein open to activists whose roots lay not in the IRA or even in Defenderism but in radical, left-wing politics. The first manifestation of this was the decision to introduce Sinn Fein to feminist politics, a ploy that enjoyed the extra advantage of infuriating the O Bradaigh and O Conaill camps.

Until the late 1970s the IRA and Sinn Fein had what would now be termed a traditional attitude toward women. Although individual women, often on the coattails of their husbands, did rise to leadership positions—the assassinated Maire Drumm, wife of Jimmy Drumm and at one stage a vice-president of Sinn Fein, being a prominent example—the republican movement was male dominated. Adams had encouraged the recruitment of women into the mainstream IRA and in the late 1970s he encouraged them to join Sinn Fein. Not least of their qualities was that many of them detested the O Bradaigh–O Conaill leadership more than he did. Sinn Fein then adopted a women's program and, much to the horror of the old guard, set up the women's department, which approved the use of contraception and began to address, gingerly at first, the vexed and divisive issue of abortion, eventually putting the Provos closer to a pro-abortion stance than any other Irish political party.[10]

Bringing women's issues into republican politics became part of the heave against the O Conaill–O Bradaigh leadership. It was intended to enrage the conservative old guard, and this it succeeded in doing, as one of their allies angrily recalled: "Radical feminism was married to republicanism, and for a long time I couldn't work out whether we were a national liberation movement, a radical feminist group, or republican revolutionaries!"[11] But the move also had the effect of broadening Sinn Fein's appeal to a new layer of political activists who might otherwise have found the Provisionals' single-issue program of armed struggle in the North suffocating. These were just the sort of people who would be most open to electoral politics.

Adams also introduced republicans to broad-front politics, the tactic of making alliances with other groups and individuals on single issues, the essence of which implied a willingness to compromise core beliefs. The principle behind the tactic was that different groups would come together on the basis that, even though they could not agree on everything, there would be one or two issues on which they could find common cause. The benefit was that it brought greater political strength; the downside was that each group was required to bury the issue dearest to it. In the IRA and Sinn Fein's case this meant that their insistence that everyone else was obliged to sign up to the armed struggle had to go. It was another important stage in the dilution of the influence of IRA militarism, and ironically it was the prisoners' struggle in the H Blocks of the Maze prison to be treated as politically motivated prisoners that became the principal vehicle for another key and defining political turnabout.

BY OCTOBER 1980 the IRA and INLA prisoners on protest in the H Blocks of the Maze prison had reached the end of their tether. They had been refusing to wear prison unforms for the best part of four years in protest against the British attempt to treat them like criminals, and for over two years, clad only in a thin blanket, the prisoners lived, ate, and slept in their own dirt and stench. From time to time they were transferred to clean parts of the jail and guards moved in with steam hoses to decontaminate their cells, but soon their new accommodation was as foul and putrid as the one they had just vacated. The moves were often accompanied by violence, meted out by prison staff acting as if they were under orders to break the men's morale. There had been nothing to compare with it in Irish history, and participating in the protest required special qualities and conviction on the part of the prisoners. The protesting prisoners numbered some three hundred, only around a half of those serving sentences in the Maze for IRA offenses, and their numbers sometimes grew but more often shrank as the protest showed no signs of achieving success.

The IRA and Sinn Fein leadership had, with reluctance, been persuaded to mount a campaign of street marches and demonstrations to advertise their cause, but it was clear that key figures were afraid that the prisoners' plight would not attract the public support needed. The prison protest had the potential to bring about a great defeat, and those around Adams knew it.

Senior Catholic Church figures, notably the Irish primate, Cardinal Tomas

O Fiaich, had intervened in a bid to persuade the British to relent, with no success. He dealt directly with Margaret Thatcher, the British prime minister, but had found her totally inflexible on the issue. Although human rights lawyers had taken a case to the European Commission on Human Rights, its outcome held out only the slimmest possibility of a settlement. The IRA had stepped up its campaign on behalf of the prisoners, singling out prison guards for assassination. But nothing, it seemed, would move the British.

As the prisoners' leaders surveyed the situation in the early fall of 1980, they realized the time had come to embark on the ultimate protest, the hunger strike to death. Their commander, Brendan Hughes, the old Cage 11 ally of Gerry Adams who was still serving out his sentence for the Malone Road arms finds, asked each wing on the protesting IRA Blocks to send in lists of volunteers prepared to go on the protest. Scores of names came back, and from the list Hughes chose himself and six others, five from the IRA and one from the smaller INLA, to go on the fast. They began refusing food on October 27, 1980.

There is little doubt that the Adams leadership was opposed to that hunger strike. Popular support for the prisoners was still too low, and it was clear that Mrs. Thatcher would not only resist the prisoners' demands, the key one of which was that they be allowed to wear their own clothes, but might relish the chance to do the IRA serious damage by allowing the protesters to die. Should the fast end in deaths but no concessions, Thatcher would have won a great victory.

The timetable agreed by Hughes and his prison colleagues meant that at some point six of the hunger strikers would have to decide whether the seventh should die. It was highly unlikely that all seven would reach a crisis point at exactly the same time, and inevitably the weakest prisoner would die first. It soon became clear that the British had rejected the option of forcibly feeding the men, on the grounds that this tactic, redolent of British behavior during the 1919–21 conflict, would only anger opinion south of the Border. The men would either die or somehow be persuaded to relent. Just before Christmas 1980 the crisis point was reached when the Newry-born IRA man Sean McKenna started to slip in and out of a coma. It was certain that he had only hours to live. Just at this psychological crux, a British government document appeared, presented to Brendan Hughes via a Catholic Church intermediary. It offered what seemed to be a compromise on the prisoners' five demands, and the protest was called off. But even on a superficial reading the document was full of imprecision. Hughes and his five semiconscious comrades knew that rejecting the document meant that

Sean McKenna would die. There was really no choice.

The ambiguity in the document was apparent to all who read it, and most who did concluded that the protest had failed. Despite that, the Belfast Sinn Fein leaders attempted to present the document as a victory, but their efforts were less than convincing. A celebration march held in West Belfast attracted only a paltry crowd. Morale at grassroots level was low and confusion widespread, not helped by the refusal of Adams's allies in Belfast to show the British document to party members, claiming that their one and only copy had been sent to Dublin.

The British document was the result of secret negotiations between the IRA in Belfast and Michael Oatley, an officer in the British Secret Intelligence Service, MI6. Code-named Mountain Climber, Oatley liaised with two figures, one the Derry-based businessman Brendan Duddy and the other a member of the Redemptorist Order, Father Meagher, who ferried his messages to and from the Belfast IRA men. With Adams and his allies opposed to the hunger strike and fearful that it would end calamitously, the circumstances behind the appearance of the British document raised dark questions elsewhere in the Provisionals, suggesting that the Belfast leaders would go to any length to end the protest.

"The deal was done behind the backs of the national leadership by Northern Command," claimed a well-placed spectator of events in Dublin.

Just as Sean McKenna was approaching his end, I heard there had been a message from the Belfast people, and I hotfooted it round to Parnell Square [Sinn Fein's headquarters], where Joe Cahill opened the door. Eventually I was ushered in, and there they all were, Christin ni Elias, Ruairi O Bradaigh, Dave O'Connell, and Piaras O Duill. They said they had received a message from Belfast which said the British had conceded four and a half demands and that the only thing missing was an acknowledgment of political status. This was the first they had heard of it. The deal had been done behind their backs and behind the backs of the National H Blocks Committee; they didn't know a thing about it.

Bernadette McAliskey and Piaras O Duill were dispatched to Belfast to meet Adams to find out what was going on and specifically whether or not the British paper was as generous as had been claimed. They were kept waiting from 3 A.M. until 8 A.M. before Adams and Morrison agreed to meet them. "The message the pair from Dublin had for them was to get their ass across the Border. But Morrison's reply was 'come and get us.' There were tears in the National H Blocks office that day. If we had won, why were we crying? It was a deception which fired the second hunger strike."[12]

THE FAILURE of the first hunger strike meant that a second protest was not only inevitable but would this time end in either victory or death for the IRA prisoners. Once again the pressure for the fast came from the prisoners and specifically from Hughes's successor as IRA jail commander, Bobby Sands, a twenty-seven-year-old coach builder who had been drawn into the IRA when he and his family were expelled from their home in North Belfast by loyalist mobs. Known by his IRA colleagues as Geronimo, more for his resemblance to the Apache chieftain than for his hot temper, Sands was serving a fourteen-year-term for possession of weapons when fate propelled him into the history books.

A self-educated poet and a songwriter of some distinction, Sands had been in Cage 11 with Gerry Adams and was, by all accounts, a keen disciple of the Adams gospel. He was bright and a brilliant publicist who excelled at writing letters soliciting support for the prisoners' cause from prominent personalities. He was popular with his prison colleagues, trusted, and, as events were to prove, brave as well. The new IRA commander designed the second protest in such a way that death, his own in particular, was almost guaranteed. The protest would be staggered. Sands started by himself, a lone protester whose fate, the decision to live or die, lay in his own hands. He began refusing food on March 1, 1981, just two-and-a-half months after the first hunger strike had collapsed. After him other prisoners, usually in groups of two, joined at two- or three-week intervals. If any hunger striker died, the moral pressure on those who followed to continue through to the end was huge. The fast also guaranteed that if there were deaths, the North would be pitched into a crisis every fortnight or so until the end. As an instrument for destabilizing political life in Ireland, it was beyond historical comparison.

Ten hunger strikers died agonizing deaths in jail, and sixty-eight people were killed on the streets of the North, before it all ended eight turbulent months later. Sands's death was probably the most traumatic. He slipped away in the early hours of May 5, and within minutes the darkened streets of nationalist Belfast were echoing to the crash and thump of exploding gasoline bombs tossed by rioters and the thud of plastic bullet guns being fired by police and troops. Sands's funeral three days later was the largest political demonstration probably in living memory, as tens of thousands of nationalists poured in from all over Ireland to pay homage to the dead IRA man, by now rapidly assuming an iconic status. It was as if people had difficulty believing that Mrs. Thatcher could have allowed him to die.

Sands's death divided Irish society. Constitutional nationalists in the North, like the SDLP, as well the main parties south of the Border feared the potential for instability posed by the hunger strike deaths, while the Catholic Church wrestled with the moral questions raised by a protest that some theologians insisted was a form of suicide. International interest in the hunger strikes was intense. Media from all over the world poured into Belfast that summer, and Sands's photograph, a flattering portrait showing a good-looking, long-haired youth, became a symbol of revolution. In Teheran a street was named after him, as was one in New York. The Irish diaspora was radicalized. Demonstrations took place in New Zealand, Australia, and Canada and in many American cities. In New York, Noraid supporters mounted a picket outside the British consulate on Third Avenue that lasted for years.

The months from May to September that year were unusually balmy by Irish standards, but a sense of crisis and of impending doom permeated life as one coffin after another was carried out of the jail to funerals that, although they drew smaller crowds than had turned out for Sands, were as emotionally intense as ever. The impact of the hunger strike deaths was felt throughout the island. That summer the author regularly and repeatedly drove around Northern Ireland, in and around the Border counties and down to Dublin, in the Republic, covering the protest for the *Irish Times,* and there was scarcely a crossroads in a nationalist area in either jurisdiction that was not draped with mourning black flags or did not have rows of telephone poles adorned with protesting placards. During that long, hot summer of 1981 as nationalist Ireland, North and South, vented its anger at Mrs. Thatcher's government in London, a new phrase entered the island's political lexicon—"nationalist alienation."

Again the evidence is that the Adams leadership, fearing a second defeat, which would be impossible to dress up in any but the thinnest of garments, also opposed the second hunger strike. But that was only at the beginning. As events unfolded, the Sinn Fein and IRA leadership realized that the political potential from the prison protest was immeasurable. It was a realization that would propel the organization into serious electoral politics and herald a phase in the Provisional's department that would usher in the peace process.

To the surprise of many observers, the hunger strike deaths did not lead to the enormous upsurge in IRA violence that many observers had predicted. The widespread expectation was that the organization would cause mayhem when their imprisoned colleagues began to die, but although there was considerable street violence and some continuing IRA violence, including one devastating land mine attack by the South Armagh Brigade that killed five British soldiers, the organization resisted the temptation to throw everything into war. The relatively restrained response to the prison protest surprised even IRA activists. To those with long memories, however, the summer of 1981 carried echoes of the summer of 1970 in Ballymurphy when, at Adams's urging, the IRA was held back while increasingly vicious but well-organized rioting between Catholic civilians and the British army alienated thousands of people, drove scores into the ranks of the IRA, and transformed this slice of West Belfast into the strongest republican redoubt in the city. Something similar happened throughout nationalist Ireland during the summer of 1981.

In October the hunger strikes came to an end as more and more of the prisoners' families brought their sons off the protest, usually when they had slipped into comas and were unable to stop them. The end also came not long after the appointment of a new, more accommodating British secretary of state, Jim Prior, who announced concessions on prisoners' clothes and other issues. As the prison settled, Sinn Fein began to prepare for elections. In an interview with the author shortly after the protest ended, Gerry Adams announced that he would recommend that Sinn Fein embrace electoral politics when the party met for its November Ard Fheis.[13]

Writing in *An Phoblacht–Republican News* in 1984, three years after Bobby Sands began his hunger strike, Adams revealed that the main effect the hunger strikes had was to fast-forward the move toward electoralism. It made it "easier to argue for an electoral strategy within Republican ranks," he wrote, effectively admitting that this had been his ambition and goal for some time.[14] Before the hunger strikes, one of Adams's leading advisers had confided to the author that resistance from rank-and-file IRA activists meant that persuading people to fight elections would be a slow and lengthy business. Sinn Fein might be permitted by its conservative membership and by the IRA to fight elections at the council level, but the prospect of larger-scale contests, for seats at Westminster, was probably some years down the line.[15] The election of Bobby Sands in the Fermanagh–South Tyrone by-election of April 1981 transformed that scenario and made it possible, much sooner that anyone had imagined, for Sinn Fein to fully embrace electoral politics.

The idea of making some sort of electoral intervention on Sands's behalf appears to have originated with Bernadette Devlin-McAliskey. If Sands was to stand for the Westminster parliament, there was only one seat that he could conceivably win, and that was Fermanagh–South Tyrone, which had been held by the independent nationalist Frank Maguire since 1974. There were other nationalist seats but both, West Belfast and Derry, were held by Gerry Fitt and John Hume, respectively, bitter political enemies of the IRA who would do the prisoners no favors. Maguire, on the other hand, was effectively a republican MP, although his official designation was Independent. A former IRA commander in Fermanagh, he had been interned during the 1956–62 Border Campaign and took a more or less abstention-ist attitude to the Westminster parliament. He never got around to making his maiden speech, for example, and he rarely attended the House of Commons, although his vote did keep a minority Labour government in office at key moments.

Devlin-McAliskey conceived the idea of asking Maguire to temporarily relinquish the seat to allow an H Blocks candidate to run. Confident that he would respond positively, she made plans to visit him, and, if he agreed to go along with the proposal, Sinn Fein would be presented with a fait accompli. The idea of "borrowing" the seat was born. Just before her trip and only five days after Sands had begun his fast, Maguire suddenly died and the whole situation changed. The seat was now vacant, and a race began to fill it. Maguire's family and the local Catholic church wanted his brother Noel to run in the by-election, and McAliskey let it be known that if that happened she would run against him on the H Block ticket. Some Sinn Fein leaders, Ruairi O Bradaigh in particular, were keen to run her in the seat, but O Conaill suggested running Sands instead, and Bernadette Devlin-McAlisky agreed to stand aside. Sinn Fein leaders, virtually the entire Ard Comhairle along with the Fermanagh republican Owen Carron, met in Clones, County Monaghan, to discuss the idea but initially rejected it. Locals feared that because Sands was an outsider in this most parochial of areas, nationalist voters would stay at home. The convention ended, but no one would leave. "People hung about talking, having little discussions and were clearly dissatisfied with the outcome," remembered one delegate. "The outcome was a second convention, and the proposal went through. Adams had to be convinced. O Conaill was the main mover. He was con-vinced Sands could win. He had been IRA organizer there in the 1950s, he knew the area, knew the people, he'd even been shot there. He convinced everybody."[16]

The drama was not quite over. The SDLP's Austin Currie, a local man and a fierce opponent of the Provisionals, toyed with the notion of stand-ing against Sands, but he relented after enormous pressure was applied by his SDLP colleagues to dissuade him. The SDLP feared that it would be blamed if Sands was beaten and then died, and no one in the SDLP, no matter how much he or she despised the Provos, wanted to carry that burden. Noel Maguire also flirted with the idea of running, but amid dark hints of threats against him he withdrew at the last moment. As the deadline for nominations neared, Adams hid in a nearby Catholic church ready to withdraw Sands if another nationalist candidate decided to run. It wasn't necessary. Sands had a clear run against a local unionist farmer, Harry West. In the charged atmosphere of the time, nationalists swallowed whatever reservations they had about the IRA's violence and elected Sands.

Caution was again the overriding consideration in Adams's mind when the next opportunity arose to put hunger strikers before the electorate, this time in the Republic's general election of June 1981, a month or so after Sands's death. After much bickering between rival republicans, the decision was made to run nine prisoners in selected constituencies, four of them hunger strikers. The National H Blocks Committee had been divided over the issue. Some wanted to run nonprisoner candidates who would take their seats in the Irish parliament, where it was possible they could hold the balance of power and determine who made up the next government. But Adams vetoed the idea. No one on the committee could give him a guarantee that they would be able to hold the next Irish government to ransom. "He wouldn't take the risk of any dissension within Sinn Fein about abstentionism," recalled a member of the committee.[17] It was a missed opportunity. Two prisoners won seats to the Dail, the hunger striker Kieran Doherty in Cavan-Monaghan and Paddy Agnew in Louth, who actually topped the poll. The result took Ireland's media completely by surprise and threw Irish politics into turmoil. The broader election had produced a virtual dead heat between Fianna Fail and its opponents, Fine Gael and Irish Labour, who wanted to form a coalition government. The two seats won by IRA prisoners came at the expense of Fianna Fail; had Doherty and Agnew been able to take their Dail seats, or if nonprisoner candidates had run, the pro–hunger striker candidates would have held the balance of power and the history of the prison protest and much subsequent Anglo-Irish history might well have been very different.

While caution had dictated Adams's attitude to the first two hunger strike elections, his demeanor changed after Sands's death when a by-election to replace the dead prisoner loomed. His principal concern was to ensure that Sinn Fein held on to the prize of the Fermanagh–South Tyrone seat, but there were problems. Following Sands's election the British had changed the electoral law to prevent serving prisoners from seeking election, so nominating another prisoner was out of the question. That was not all. Nationalist voters in Fermanagh–South Tyrone had been won over to support Sands with the promise that the hunger striker would merely "borrow" their votes in order to publicize the prisoners' cause. Once the hunger strike was over, the seat could again be contested freely by mainstream nationalists. Under British parliamentary rules the writ for any by-election had to be moved by another serving MP, but no one at Westminster wanted to see another contest held while the prison fast was still under way. In June the Welsh nationalist MP Daffyd Ellis Thomas phoned the National H Block's Committee to say that he would move the writ for the by-election whenever they wanted, but the committee demurred. Sinn Fein was not quite so backward. Behind the committee's back, Thomas was contacted and he agreed to set the by-election machinery in motion. Sinn Fein then imposed Owen Carron as a "Proxy Political Prisoners" candidate, and in August he romped home, easily beating the local ex-UDR officer Ken Maginnis and actually increasing Sands's majority.

Carron's victory was the perfect springboard for Sinn Fein's entry as a party into electoral politics, standing in its own name and not that of hunger-striking prisoners. Carron's victory came, however, at a price. Throughout the hunger strikes the Army Council had refused to intervene and order the prisoners to quit, even when it became clear that, despite election victories and widespread international publicity for the prisoners' cause, Thatcher would not bend and that any more deaths would be futile. The Army Council had that power and had used it in the past. The former chief of staff Sean MacStiofain had been ordered to end his fast in 1972, for example. As the hunger strikes intensified, so did the demand from some that the IRA leadership should intervene to end the deaths. In early August 1981, after the seventh hunger striker had been carried out of the jail in a coffin, Adams agreed to go into the jail to speak to the hunger strikers. He had come under enormous pressure to do this from prisoners' families and their Catholic Church adviser, Father Denis Faul, and eventually he relented, or so it seemed.

According to the accounts of those who were present, Adams met six of the hunger strikers in the prison hospital canteen and gave them a frank assessment of their situation. He told them that it was likely Mrs. Thatcher would let them die, and he went on to describe what was on offer from the Mountain Climber, Michael Oatley. But he left it up to the prisoners themselves to decide whether or not to end the protest. The IRA would support and understand them, he said, if they agreed to end the hunger strike either individually or collectively. But it was evident that neither he nor the IRA would order or even ask them to call a halt.[18] With the weight of Bobby Sands's sacrifice and the agonizing deaths of other comrades bearing down upon them, the prisoners unsurprisingly decided to continue their protest. Their decision meant that when the second Fermanagh–South Tyrone by-election was held two weeks later, prisoners were still dying in the H blocks, and with nationalist emotions running high, Owen Carron's victory was assured. The SDLP once again stood down in his favor, and with a clear run against the sole unionist candidate he won by an even greater margin than Bobby Sands. When Adams addressed the next Sinn Fein Ard Fheis in the winter of 1981 to urge that they fight elections, he had in Carron a real live MP standing beside him as proof of the potency of fighting elections. Adams had spurned the opportunity to order an end to the prison fast, but by doing so created the most favorable circumstances for Sinn Fein's change in political direction.

As the hunger strike headed toward its conclusion, Sinn Fein threw away any pretense that the National H Blocks Committee was an independent organization. At a conference in Dundalk in September, chaired by Adams's Army Council colleague Ivor Bell, block voting removed all but two of its non–Sinn Fein members. By this stage of the protest the National H Blocks Committee had created a national structure of support groups throughout Ireland that rivaled and even exceeded Sinn Fein's, and once the protest ended, a concerted effort was made to absorb these local committees into the party.

Then, with not even a whimper, the eight-month-long hunger strike ended. On the morning of Saturday, October 3, a brief statement announced that the most traumatic prison protest in IRA history was over. The end came as a relief. One hunger striker's family after another had intervened to take their sons off the protest as unconsciousness overwhelmed them, and it was clear that further fasts were pointless and even counterproductive. The stage had been reached where the motives of Provisional leaders like Gerry Adams for not ending the protests were being openly questioned by clerics like Father Faul, once a sympathetic friend of the IRA prisoners but now a bitter opponent of the Sinn Fein leadership. Ten men had died awful deaths inside the jail, many more perished outside; nationalist politics had been radicalized in a way not seen since the 1916 Rising when the British had executed its leaders, while Mrs. Thatcher had become a hate figure beyond parallel in Irish history. The stage had also been set for Sinn Fein to

1. The *Eksund*, docked at Brest harbor in November 1987. With its betrayal, the IRA lost 150 tons of Libyan weapons, but the peace process was saved. (*AFP*)

1-A. The *Eksund*'s captain, Adrian Hopkins, was wrongly accused by some IRA leaders of treachery. (*AFP*)

2. Gerry Adams as a young teenager in Belfast. *(Pacemaker Press, Belfast)*

3. Gerry Adams accompanies his father *(wearing suspenders)* on a republican march in Belfast at Eastertime, 1997. *(Kelvin Boyes, Belfast)*

4. The IRA's first Belfast commander, Billy McKee *(seated)*, and Proinsias MacAirt, photographed in Crumlin Road jail, 1971. McKee and Adams were later bitter rivals for the leadership of the IRA. *(Pacemaker Press, Belfast)*

5. BELOW: IRA snipers engage British troops in West Belfast in 1972. *(P. Michael O'Sullivan)*

6. Joe Cahill officiates at an IRA funeral in 1971. A former IRA chief of staff and family friend, he could always be counted on to support Gerry Adams's ideological shifts. *(Victor Patterson Archive, Linen Hall Library, Belfast)*

7. Jean McConville, with three of her ten children. She was killed and then "disappeared" in December 1972 by "the unknowns," a secret IRA unit created by Adams. *(Pacemaker Press, Belfast)*

8. Maire Drumm (*far right, carrying bat*), leader of the IRA's women's section, Cumann na mBan, marshals her supporters in Belfast. *(P. Michael O'Sullivan)*

9. A young Martin McGuinness, then Derry commander, joins IRA leaders for a press conference in June 1972: (*left to right*) McGuinness, Daithi O Conaill, Chief of Staff Sean MacStiofain, and Seamus Twomey, the Belfast commander. *(Victor Patterson Archive, Linen Hall Library, Belfast)*

10. Gerry Adams, photographed by the British army after his arrest in July 1973. *(Victor Patterson Archive, Linen Hall Library, Belfast)*

11. Cage 11 inmates pose for a secret photograph. Standing to the left of Adams *(who is seated, front right)*, and wearing a mustache, is Brendan "Darkie" Hughes. Also standing, far right, the IRA icon and hunger-striker Bobby Sands. *(Kelvin Boyes, Belfast)*

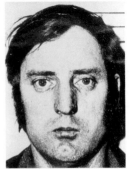

12. Ivor Bell, pictured in 1974, was once Adams's closest ideological ally, but the two men fell out when Sinn Fein began contesting elections. *(Victor Patterson Archive, Linen Hall Library, Belfast)*

13. The Sinn Fein Executive member Christin ni Elias in October 1981. Detested by the Adams camp, friends believed she might have been the target of an IRA assassination squad in December 1981. *(Derek Speirs/Report, Dublin)*

14. A police poster published after the La Mon massacre in February 1978. *(Pacemaker Press, Belfast)*

15. Public smiles but private strife: (*left to right*) Daithi O Conaill, Gerry Adams, and Ruairi O Bradaigh hide their bitter conflict from the cameras at Sinn Fein's annual conference in 1980. *(Derek Speirs/Report, Dublin)*

16. Gerry Adams oversees the burial of the IRA hunger-striker Bobby Sands. Standing behind the masked IRA guard of honor, with folded arms and wearing glasses and a beard, is Tom Hartley, a leading member of Adams's think tank. *(Pacemaker Press, Belfast)*

17. The body of the UDR sergeant Thomas Cochrane lies dumped beside a South Armagh hedgerow in October 1982. His kidnapping by the IRA led Father Reid to visit Gerry Adams to plead for his life. The contact prompted discussions about political alternatives to violence which developed into the peace process.

18. Cardinal Cahal Daly. When bishop of Down and Connor in 1984, he refused to support Father Reid's diplomacy but agreed not to undermine it. *(Pacemaker Press, Belfast)*

19. Cardinal Tomas O Fiaich, an enthusiastic supporter of Father Reid's initiative. *(Derek Speirs/ Report, Dublin)*

20. Archbishop Justin Rigali of St. Louis, Missouri. A former secretary of the College of Cardinals in Rome, he kept Pope John Paul II and key American bishops informed about the Irish peace process. *(Courtesy of the Archdiocese of St. Louis, Missouri.)*

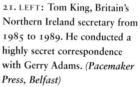

21. LEFT: Tom King, Britain's Northern Ireland secretary from 1985 to 1989. He conducted a highly secret correspondence with Gerry Adams. *(Pacemaker Press, Belfast)*

22. RIGHT: Peter Brooke, King's successor in Belfast. His overture to the IRA in November 1989 was partly inspired by the Father Reid–Gerry Adams diplomacy. *(Pacemaker Press, Belfast)*

emerge as an electoral force in Irish politics, at first in the North but eventually in the South too. Quietly, meekly, and with almost no notice taken by the media, the National H Blocks Committee voted itself out of existence, and scores of its supporters moved over to Sinn Fein. "The fact was that after the hunger strikes the republican movement was swamped by new young members," explained one former Sinn Fein leader. "Some H Block committees just became SF branches overnight."[19] The decision by Sinn Fein to contest elections and to embrace this as a strategy was a formality.

THROUGHOUT the early part of the next year, 1982, the new British secretary of state, Jim Prior, spent his time constructing a new political initiative that he termed "rolling devolution." Under Prior's scheme the unionist and nationalist parties would be rewarded by a gradual and increasing return of powers to a local elected Assembly at Stormont if they could show they were able and willing to share power. Despite objections from both camps and lukewarm support from Margaret Thatcher, Prior pressed ahead with his scheme and announced elections for that October. In April, Sinn Fein declared that it would definitely field candidates on an abstentionist basis, and that rattled the SDLP, worried by the alienating impact on their supporters of the lengthy hunger strikes. After weeks and months of agonizing, the SDLP then decided that, while it would contest the election, it too would not take seats in Prior's Assembly. The hunger strikes had made both nationalist parties in the North abstentionists.

Adams had great difficulty persuading the IRA to allow him to stand for election to the planned new Assembly. At an Army Council meeting in July 1982, he and McGuinness indicated their interest in running, Adams in West Belfast and the chief of staff in Derry. But the Army Council voted four to three against, on the grounds that neither man could be an elected representative and be able to carry out his IRA role at the same time. But Adams came back. At a second meeting in August, Joe Cahill, who had voted against, was absent on vacation, and Adams put the proposal once more. In the meantime Adams had won over one key figure, a County Donegal–based member of the Council, and the vote went in Adams's favor, four to two. McGuinness and Adams were, however, forced to make a concession to the skeptics. Both men were allowed to run but on condition they give up their IRA roles, McGuinness as chief of staff and Adams as adjutant-general. McGuinness's departure paved the way for Ivor Bell to become chief of staff.[20] Adams's ally Brian Keenan, by now a prisoner in England, wrote from his cell in Leicester jail that he "emphatically" supported the move and endorsed the

Army Council's decision. Keenan wrote, "It is not enough for Republicans to say, with reference to the Army, actions speak louder than words. We must never forsake action but the final war to win will be the savage war of peace. To those of us who have struggled for years in a purely military capacity, it must be obvious that if we do not provide honest, recognisable political leadership on the ground, we will lose that war for peace."[21] Not for the first or last time, Keenan sided with Adams at a critical juncture.

To again reassure the IRA, that November's Sinn Fein Ard Fheis obliged election candidates to "be unambivalent in support for the armed struggle." But in the run-up to Prior's Assembly election there was a subtle shift in the rhetoric. Again *An Phoblacht–Republican News* was the first to reflect the change. In a front-page editorial the paper declared that, while "Irish freedom will only be achieved by armed struggle . . . it needs to be said loudly and unequivocally that freedom, unity and the creation of conditions by which we can proceed to the democratic, socialist republic will not be achieved by armed struggle alone and that armed struggle of a revolutionary nature cannot even be sustained without popular logistical back-up and support."[22] A few months earlier armed struggle alone had been the only way forward. Now that would not be enough. The contradictions between the Armalite and the ballot box were beginning to be acknowledged. The hunger strikes had wrought many deep changes in Irish society, but it would be some time before the effects of this would become visible.

PART THREE

A Secret Process

Father Alec Reid giving the last rites to a British soldier killed by an angry mob after he had stumbled into an IRA funeral procession in 1988. Reid's secret diplomacy, in conjunction with Gerry Adams, laid the foundations for the Irish peace process. *(Trevor McBride, Belfast)*

SEVEN

"Behind the Scenes"

It was Friday, October 22, 1982, just two days after Sinn Fein's first outing as an electoral party in the contest for seats to Jim Prior's new "rolling" Assembly in Belfast, and the Irish media and political establishment were just beginning to digest the implications of a stunning Sinn Fein performance. The party had won the support of 10 percent of the electorate, some 64,000 votes, and had secured five seats to the new parliament, one won by Adams in West Belfast, another by McGuinness in his native Derry. As horrified constitutional Irish nationalists and stunned British politicians grappled with the meaning of all this, in the rolling countryside that surrounds the historic cathedral city of Armagh, not far from the town of Markethill, members of the South Armagh IRA drove up beside fifty-four-year-old Thomas Cochrane and with one swipe of a wooden club sent him flying off his motorbike. Known as Tommy to his friends and family, Cochrane was a part-time sergeant in the local unit of the Ulster Defence Regiment (UDR), the mostly Protestant local militia that had replaced the B Specials way back at the outset of the Troubles. He was also an Orangeman, a member of the Lurgyross Orange Heroes Lodge, which met near his home in Bessbrook.

Cochrane was on his way to work at Glennane linen mill that morning when the IRA struck. The police later found his motorbike in a hedge. His crash helmet, and gloves and the club used to fell him were found nearby. There were also signs of a violent struggle. Although the facts surrounding his fate have never been definitively determined, Cochrane was almost certainly overpowered and then bundled into a car and driven deep into South Armagh, an area the British media had long since christened Bandit Country.

In its first statement the IRA said it had abducted Cochrane and was holding him for "interrogation because of his crimes against the Nationalist community."[1] This was an unusual thing for the IRA to do; normally the IRA killed UDR members whenever and wherever they could. Targeting members of this locally recruited, mostly Protestant, and overwhelmingly part-time force for death was an integral part of IRA strategy; such killings kept ordinary unionists angry and in no mind to seek a political settlement with their nationalist neighbors. In the unfortunate case of Tommy Cochrane it seemed that the IRA had decided to exploit a chance to gather some possibly valuable information about the security forces. Cochrane's motorbike journeys along a regular and predictable route provided the IRA with an ideal opportunity to kidnap and question him about his colleagues in the UDR and any other intelligence in his head. If such was the case, then the terrors that Cochrane went through can only be imagined. Members of the South Armagh IRA had a name for ill treating and even torturing those they questioned, but the truth was that they mostly didn't need to; their terrifying reputation loosened most tongues almost immediately. Tommy Cochrane could not even have guessed at that, but he did know with stomach-churning certainty that he was going to die; the only question was when.

The knowledge that Cochrane was suffering an almost indescribable ordeal reverberated around Northern Ireland. Most Catholics knew instinctively that there would be retaliations for his kidnapping, and the fear in that community was almost palpable, heightened by a communal memory of the scores of co-religionists kidnapped and killed by loyalist paramilitaries in the terrible mid-1970s. In all likelihood the loyalists would take an eye for eye, and soon some innocent, uninvolved Catholic would die a terrible death in revenge. That afternoon, Cochrane's wife, Lilly, and their grown-up son, Glen, made an impassioned appeal for his release. The plea was ignored by the IRA in South Armagh, but it was heard in West Belfast, by a Redemptorist priest based in the congregation's huge Clonard Monastery, which sprouted amid the tiny terraced streets that formed the heart of the Falls Road.

That afternoon Tipperary-born Father Alec Reid decided he would journey the short distance from Clonard to talk to the president of Sinn Fein and the newly elected Assembly member for West Belfast, Gerry Adams, to argue for Cochrane's freedom. An active mediator during some of the worst years of the Troubles, Reid had employed his negotiating skills to help end vicious republican feuds and had often intervened between the worlds of the IRA and the loyalist paramilitaries. He would say himself that he operated mostly at street level and had built up a unique relationship with the Adams leadership. "Al's power in the peace process," confided one fellow participant, "derived from the trust that he had built up with Adams. I know he believed that no one else, certainly no other priest, had more close and continual contact with him than he had, and because of that he was able to sense the opportunity and the time to move."[2] But Father Reid, then in his late forties, was not a well man. He had suffered a nervous breakdown two years before and only now was beginning to function normally again. His mission to Adams, a man whom everyone knew to be a major power in the IRA, was his first significant expedition since his illness. His plea was to get the IRA to release Tommy Cochrane or at the very least to tell his family what his fate had been. The Redemptorist priest knew enough about the IRA's affairs to know that Adams carried sufficient clout to do that.

Protestants reacted with horror and anger to the news of Cochrane's abduction—horror because they could imagine with awful clarity what the UDR man was going through, and anger because it was their old enemy the IRA that had kidnapped him. Like their Catholic neighbors, Protestants knew there would be retaliation. Around midnight on that Friday night one of the most cold-blooded loyalist killers ever spawned by the Irish Troubles briefed his gang members at a drinking club deep in the Shankill Road in the heart of Protestant North Belfast. They were going to kidnap a Catholic and hold him for Cochrane's release, he told them. A handsome man with a fondness for fast women and the high life, thirty-year-old Lennie Murphy was the leader of a gang of loyalist killers that had struck terror into Catholic Belfast in the mid-1970s. Known as the Shankill Butchers, Murphy's gang had earned its terrifying name because of a series of almost ritual torture-murders during a sixteen-month period between 1975 and 1977 when they dispatched a number of randomly kidnapped Catholic victims with axes, cleavers, and butcher's knives. In one killing, a man was almost decapitated, in another all but three of the victim's teeth had been ripped out with pliers; three died when their throats were slit open. Murphy himself was regarded by the police as "a psychopath"[3] and was suspected of involvement in up to eighteen murders. He had killed with gun, poison, and knife; he consigned four Catholics to eternity in one single incident and wielded a sharp cleaver during the Butchers' throat-slitting killings.

It was just after midnight that Friday when Joe Donegan finally left the Pound Loney drinking club in the Lower Falls Road. An unemployed carpenter, forty-eight-year-old Donegan lived with his wife and their seven children in the Brittain's Parade district of Ballymurphy, but he had been born and spent most of his life in the Lower Falls. Only when the violence got just too bad did he decide to move his family the two miles or so out of the area to the relative safety of Ballymurphy, but he still spent a lot of time in his old haunts, where he would meet friends for a drink and a game of pool. When that night's drinking was done, he made his way by foot onto the main Falls Road, meaning to hail one of the many black London-style taxis that ferried people to and from the city center. The black taxis had been imported to Belfast in the early days of the Troubles when riots and barricade burning meant that the regular Corporation bus services were suspended, sometimes for days at a time. The black taxis were operated mostly by former IRA prisoners, and soon the loyalist Shankill Road copied the idea. The UVF ran the service in most Protestant districts of the city.

Joe Donegan must have realized almost immediately what a terrible mistake he had made when he clambered into the back of the taxi that answered his hail. Within moments Lennie Murphy was battering him so viciously that by the time the taxi arrived at its destination on the Shankill Road, its back windows were spattered with Donegan's blood.[4] Like Tommy Cochrane, Joe Donegan must have guessed that he was about to die, and his end too must have been unimaginably awful. The taxi had been stolen on the Shankill by Murphy's gang with the intention of duping the first vulnerable Catholic they encountered. The ploy worked with terrifying simplicity. By two in the morning Donegan was dead. Dragged semiconscious into a house once used by Murphy as his home, he was tortured and beaten repeatedly by the loyalist leader and his associates; he was finally finished off with a series of blows to the head with a garden spade. These blows were so violent that the wooden shaft snapped.

Joe Donegan was dead, but Murphy kept up the cruel pretense that he was still alive. Over the weekend the UVF killer made a series of calls to nationalist politicians and Catholic clerics, threatening to kill him if the IRA didn't release Tommy Cochrane. The fate of the UDR man was still not known. One account suggests that the IRA held him for several days and that he may still have been alive when Murphy made his calls.[5] But the truth remains unknown. The pretense ended, however, on the Monday morning when Joe Donegan's battered corpse was found, wrapped in a blanket and dumped in an alley off the Shankill Road. Later that night the IRA phoned the nationalist newspaper *Irish News* to say that it had killed Cochrane and that his body would be returned "when security allows."[6]

Father Reid's effort to get Gerry Adams to arrange Tommy Cochrane's freedom had failed, but it seemed that the Sinn Fein leader had tried to intervene in some way. At least that is what he said he had done. On the

Sunday, Adams released a press statement claiming that "since Friday evening, Sinn Fein have attempted to get clarification on the condition of UDR Sgt Cochrane and of the IRA intentions towards him." But this had been made impossible, he went on, by the heavy security presence on either side of the Border. As soon as it was possible, Sinn Fein would urge the IRA to make a public statement. Later, after it had admitted that the UDR man had been killed, the IRA attempted to persuade nationalists that it would have spared Cochrane's life if the offer to exchange him for Joe Donegan had been genuine. In an off-the-record briefing the IRA told the *Irish News* that its GHQ in Dublin had ordered South Armagh to release the UDR man but that the message "was not received in time."[7]

The weeks after the deaths of Tom Cochrane and Joe Donegan were the most violent of the year as the full significance of Sinn Fein's election victories sank in. Despite more than a decade of killing, shooting, and bombing, the IRA's political wing had won significant support among the Catholic population, and for many, not least loyalist paramilitaries, that was a message of despair, a signal that violence could pay off. A further 39 people were killed between then and Christmas, bringing the death toll for the twelve months to 112. There were to be many more years of bloodshed before the IRA declared its first cease-fire, but never again would the numbers of deaths reach the level of 1982.

Republicans reveled in the election successes, and when three policemen were killed in a huge IRA land mine explosion near Lurgan, County Armagh, a few days after the Assembly elections, *An Phoblacht–Republican News* hailed the deaths as evidence that the Armalite and ballot box really did complement each other despite what the skeptics might say. The police deaths set off another round of retaliations, this time carried out by specially trained RUC units in which six people, five Republican activists and a Catholic civilian, were shot dead in circumstances that poisoned relations between the nationalist community and the RUC for years afterward.

On November 16, the IRA wreaked revenge for Joe Donegan's death when Lennie Murphy was cut down in a hail of automatic IRA gunfire as he drove up to his girlfriend's house. The carefully planned assassination had been arranged by a double agent in the rival Ulster Defence Association, a notorious racketeer called Jim Craig, who was working for his own side and the Provisional IRA at the same time.[8] Then, on December 7, came one of those incidents that will be remembered as a sort of gruesome high-water mark of the Troubles. That night as crowds of young people flirted and danced at a disco in the Droppin' Well public house near Ballykelly, not far from Derry, a bomb placed near the dance floor by the Irish National Liberation Army exploded without warning. The blast killed seventeen people, eleven of whom were off-duty soldiers based in the garrison town. The remaining six dead were civilians, five of them women.

In between all this slaughter there were, by the standards of the Northern Ireland of that day, the routine killings of policemen and off-duty UDR soldiers by republicans and loyalist killings of uninvolved Catholics. On the same day that Lennie Murphy died, his UVF colleagues in East Belfast singled out a sixty-four-year-old Catholic shopkeeper for death. A lone gunman walked into Patrick Murphy's greengrocers and opened fire with a handgun, fatally wounding the father of six three times. He was the fourth victim of violence that day. Four days later the UVF in East Belfast claimed another Catholic life when twenty-five-year-old Michael Fay was abducted as he made his way to the hospital to visit his young daughter. He was taken to a nearby loyalist housing estate and shot in the head. The UVF claimed he had been killed in retaliation for Lennie Murphy's death.

The bloody violence of the autumn of 1982 was to leave its mark on Northern Ireland in unexpected ways. The killing of Patrick Murphy and Michael Fay had roused a group of liberal Protestant clergymen to action. Some forty of them, including three former Presbyterian moderators, decided to attend their funerals as a mark of solidarity. Their spokesman was another Presbyterian cleric, the Reverend Kenneth Newell, a former Orange chaplain turned ecumenist whose community in Fitzroy Avenue in South Belfast had the year before forged links with Father Reid's Redemptorist colleagues in Clonard. Asked to explain what had motivated the group, Newell had answered, "We want to show that people still have the ability to scream out at murder."[9]

The Protestant initiative was to be a short-lived one that fell victim to Northern Ireland's unrelenting sectarian politics. But the trip to Gerry Adams made by Father Alec Reid was, by contrast, to have much more long-lasting consequences. A few years later the Redemptorist cleric was to tell friends that the kidnapping of Tommy Cochrane was the event that had persuaded him to play a more active and effective role in trying to end the violence. As a result, he would say, he decided to take up peace work again.[10] From that decision flowed the often highly secret and protracted dialogue and interaction with Gerry Adams that ultimately led to the Provisional IRA's decision to quit armed struggle. In a very real sense the IRA's decision to kidnap Tommy Cochrane was the moment at which the peace process could be said to have been born.

TO SAY THAT Father Alec Reid is the unrecognized inspiration of the Irish peace process would be an understatement. Long known as a confidant of the Sinn Fein leader, Reid is accorded in most accounts the role of message carrier for Adams during the odyssey to peace, but the full story reveals him to be a much more substantial figure, who initiated, devised, and nurtured many of the ideological innovations that made Gerry Adams's journey possible. Passionate about his project, secretive, trustworthy, but at times gullible and naïve, Reid persisted at times when others in the British and Irish governments were close to giving up—his reward was the IRA cease-fires and the political settlement that eventually came more than a decade after his bid to save Tommy Cochrane's life. To those who supported his efforts, he is the unsung and largely unrewarded hero of the peace process; to those who do not, he is the crafty Wolsey to Adams's Henry VIII.

To the British civil servants who had secret dealings with Reid in later years, the Catholic priest seemed a curious choice for a go-between for Adams. "When I first met him, I thought he was a strange intermediary, with his black leather jacket and, if I'm right, I recall his nose was dripping," remembered one.[11] For his work as a mediator, Reid dispensed with the standard Redemptorist garb—a black cotton gown circled by a thick leather belt, garlanded with heavy rosary beads—and dressed in jeans and bomber jacket like many of the people, especially republicans, he was dealing with.

But it was not this that made him such a valuable intermediary for Adams. His years of work intervening between squabbling republicans or trying to calm IRA-loyalist tensions had created a bond of trust between him and the West Belfast republican leader. Posted to Belfast in 1967, a year after Gusty Spence's UVF had spilled the first blood of the Troubles, Reid emerged as a serious peacemaker at the time of the 1975 feud between the Provisional and Official IRAs and first got close to Adams in 1977 when again he mediated between the two groups during the bloody dispute that saw Billy McKee meet his nemesis. The relationship blossomed, and soon the word was out among Belfast Provos that they should regard Reid as Gerry Adams's friend. "You could say anything you liked to the Provos, but if you criticized Alec Reid their backs went up," recalled a member of the rival INLA in the city.[12]

Reid was also discreet to the point of reticence and avoided the media assiduously, both qualities that Adams valued. When, in early 1989, the author heard rumors of Reid's part in secret peace talks and wrote to him asking for an interview, he replied, politely declining. ". . . I trust that what I have already mentioned about the relationship which every pastor must observe towards the media will explain why it would not be feasible for me to accept [your request for a meeting]. The pastor must be above suspicion in these matters and, for that reason, over the past twenty years or so, I have continually refused to appear on the media or to give interviews in circumstances that might give rise to such suspicion or the appearance of it."[13]

After the IRA declared its 1994 cease-fire, Reid went into virtual hiding. When the author tried to contact him at Clonard Monastery, a secretary would say only that he was not in Belfast and that she did not know where he was. He had left a simple message on her typewriter that read, "Father Reid is not and will not be speaking to members of the press or media."[14] Whatever clandestine comings and goings the Redemptorist priest got involved in on his behalf, Adams could be sure that Father Reid would keep them secret.

Illness had laid Reid low in 1980 at a crucial moment in the IRA's prison protest. When delicate mediation between the Catholic Church and the Thatcher government broke down, Reid blamed himself for the hunger strike that followed, according to those who knew him then. He believed, they said, that he had wrongly raised the prisoners' expectations of a settlement and that this had dangerously exacerbated their disappointment and anger, possibly propelling them into a death fast. Reid's brief from his superiors in the Redemptorist Congregation allowed him to engage in peace and reconciliation work, and it was natural, given the gravity of the prison protest, that he would find himself visiting IRA prisoners, especially their leaders in the years 1979 and 1980.

He struck a sympathetic figure in the eyes of the republican protesters. Generally nationalist in his outlook, he rejected the IRA's violent methods but believed it was important to understand why it was that people joined the IRA and supported the use of violence. He believed it was vital that he talk to republicans, and in those days very few Catholic priests did. The IRA prisoners liked and respected him. "He was seen as a gentle, hopeful, optimistic man, continually giving us comfort," recalled one former protesting prisoner.[15] When asked by Sinn Fein before he started his own fast to the death which priests he trusted and was most friendly with, Bobby Sands gave Reid's name as one of only three he could list. "Not much use that, is it?" he asked acidly in a smuggled communiqué to Danny Morrison just before he went on his hunger strike.[16]

The prisoners may have trusted Reid, but the authorities suspected him of ferrying messages to and from the IRA leadership. "The screws would never search [Father] Toner, who brought in tobacco and stuff, but on two occasions Reid was strip-searched," said the same ex-prisoner.[17] Although his search did not entail the humiliating examination of the anal passage, either by hand or mirror, routinely meted out to IRA inmates, it was nevertheless an embarrassing and insulting experience. The priest bore his ordeal without protest.

The IRA prisoners respected Reid, but they were sometimes frustrated by his naïveté, a criticism the British would share later when his joint diplomacy with Gerry Adams began to get serious. "He told us once," remembered the former prisoner,

that he'd been to the American consulate in Belfast to try to drum up support [for the H Block protesters]. I asked him who was there, and he said the ambassador, officials, and an English guy. I said who was the Englishman, and he said someone called Oldfield. "My God!" I said, "that was Maurice Oldfield of MI6." It turned out that they had asked him a lot of questions about Brendan Hughes and others in the prison leadership. They were trying to build up a profile, and he was innocently helping them.[18]

All the priests who visited the jail or who got involved in the protest were given nicknames by the IRA prisoners. Father Denis Faul, who said Mass every Sunday in the prison, was initially admired by the prisoners and his nickname, Denis the Menace, indicated a certain endearment that turned to bitter hostility when he opposed the hunger strike and the Adams leadership in late 1981. Father Tom Toner, the official Catholic chaplain, was Index, after the F(inancial) T(imes) Index. Cardinal O Fiaich was Saggart Mor, literally "big priest" in Irish. Father Alec Reid became known as Behind the Scenes. "He was always telling us not to worry, things were going on behind the scenes, and it would all turn out okay," recalled the same IRA inmate.[19] He said it so often that the prisoners, half cynically, renamed him.

Reid put enormous faith in secret talks that had been opened with Thatcher by Cardinal O Fiaich and the bishop of Derry, Edward Daly. The threat of a hunger strike in March 1980 prompted the dialogue in which O Fiaich and Daly argued with the British that a small concession on scrapping the prison uniform, just one of the IRA's five demands, could avert a great disaster. Of all people in Ireland, the republican-leaning Catholic primate and his colleague from Derry knew just how destabilizing and emotional an IRA hunger strike could be. In late October 1980 the crisis came to a head. The prisoners announced their plans for a hunger strike, and O Fiaich and Daly frantically pressed the British for the concession on prison garb. The British responded with a piece of smoke and mirrors that greatly embittered the clerics. The prison uniform would be scrapped, Margaret Thatcher's Northern Ireland secretary, Humphrey Atkins, told them, and be replaced by "civilian-style clothes." It did not take much probing to discover that "civilian-style clothes" were just the old prison uniform renamed and redesigned. Disappointed and disillusioned, the clerics withdrew. Four days later the first hunger strike began.

The prisoners remember Reid as being extremely optimistic about O Fiaich's efforts. The cardinal had visited the H Blocks in July 1978 and was so upset by the sight of prisoners living in their own excreta that he issued an angry statement comparing the conditions in the H Blocks to the sewers of Calcutta. The prisoners now had a powerful friend, and after the Calcutta remarks Reid assured the prisoners that O Fiaich would see Thatcher and "could sort it out." So it was that the failure of the O Fiaich–Daly mission hit him hard. He fell ill and suffered a nervous breakdown. Disappointed, guilty, and fearful, Reid decided to quit his prison diplomacy, but before he left he made one last attempt to stop the protest, as the prisoner's leader, Brendan Hughes, recalled: "When the hunger strike was planned, he begged me not to start it, and when I said no, he asked to speak to someone else to try to persuade them. So I sent Sands to see him, and Bobby was as strong as I was."[20]

IT WOULD BE IMPOSSIBLE to understand the relationship that was built up between Gerry Adams and Father Alec Reid without first appreciating the extraordinary influence that the Redemptorist Congregation exercised on the Catholic population of West Belfast during the Sinn Fein president's childhood. When Reid visited Adams to plead for Tommy Cochrane's life in October 1982, he came not as just another Catholic cleric but as a member of a community that for nearly a hundred years had shaped and molded the views and attitudes of Adams's family and those of the rest of his community.

Founded in 1732 by Alphonsus Liguori, the lawyer son of wealthy aristocrats from Naples, the Redemptorists, whose official title is the Congregation of the Most Holy Redeemer, are the Jesuits for the poor and working classes. Bound by vows of poverty, chastity, and obedience and steeped in the Irish Marian tradition, they are renowned for a "hellfire and damnation" style of preaching that is designed to strike fear of death and an eternity spent in the fiery pits of hell into the hearts of waverers. They are often invited to conduct intensive missions in parishes where the church authorities believe the congregation has become lax. "We provide a 64,000-mile service for the faithful," a member of the order once told the author.[21]

The Redemptorists set up their first base in Ireland in 1853 but did not come to Belfast until 1896, when a surge in the city's Catholic population, the result of rapid industrial growth and an influx of linen workers from rural areas set alarm bells ringing amongst the Irish hierarchy. Concerned that his burgeoning flock, numbering some 100,000 by the turn of the century, would fall prey to the droves of assiduous Protestant evangelists who roamed Belfast in those days, the then bishop of Down and Connor, Dr. Henry Henry, asked the Redemptorists to set up shop, and they readily agreed. They chose to establish their base in the area around Clonard off the Falls Road in West Belfast, a crowded district of small terraced streets where many of the migrant Catholic linen workers had been housed.

The growth in Belfast's Catholic population drew an increasingly hostile Protestant reaction, and from the mid-nineteenth century onward, animosity to and intolerance of the newcomers grew. A series of vicious citywide riots gradually imposed a sectarian and political segregation on the map of Belfast. Protestants in the adjacent Shankill Road area particularly resented the arrival of the Redemptorists in Clonard. During the construction of the first church building, there were threats of violence. "This threat became very real in the winter of 1899," the congregation's official history recorded, "and for several days and nights, local men patrolled the area to defend the Monastery should it be attacked."[22] These tensions were replayed seventy years later during the violent August of 1969, when loyalist mobs invaded the Clonard area and burned down Bombay Street, only yards from the monastery buildings. It was said their real target was the monastery church, from whose tower, according to Protestant mythology, IRA snipers could fire down on the Shankill. No one knew or understood, and perhaps even sympathized with, the Defenderist roots of the Provos better than the Redemptorists of Clonard.

The West Belfast that Gerry Adams grew up in was steeped in the influence of the Redemptorists. The most direct influence on the future IRA leader, his friends, and family was exerted through the confraternities that the congregation had run for many years. There were three "confos," as Adams and his contemporaries called them, one for "ladies," one for men, and another for boys. A society of lay Catholics, usually led by a

Redemptorist priest, the confos would meet separately every week to say prayers, sing hymns, and hear a stirring sermon on Catholic doctrine from one of the Clonard priests. The confraternities were the Redemptorists' way of ensuring that the faithful stayed faithful. The societies had flourished in West Belfast. By 1957, when Adams was old enough to join, the male confraternities had hit record numbers; nearly 9,300 West Belfast males were on the books that year.

Adams himself has nothing but fond memories of his days as a confrater. "One night a week," he wrote in his autobiography,

> we used to go for our religious instruction to confraternity down in Clonard Monastery and if we left early we could spend the bus fare on sweets. We cut down the Springfield Road and joined hundreds of other boys in the chapel. To me Clonard was a wondrous place with high, high ceilings and a huge high altar. The altar boys wore long, red soutanes and white gowns. The priest's incense spiralled upwards through the shafts of sunlight which came slanting down from stained-glass windows at the very top. It wasn't a long service. Father McLaughlin, who was in charge of the confraternity, got up and made a joke or preached a sermon and then we sang a few hymns. I didn't mind it all; in fact I found parts of it good fun.[23]

The Redemptorists adapted well to the conditions of West Belfast and had little difficulty relating to the often violent world that some of their flock inhabited. A not untypical example of this coexistence of muscular Catholicism and physical-force republicanism was Gerry Adams's maternal uncle Alfie Hannaway. An active republican from 1936, Alfie was first an organizer for the IRA boy scouts, na Fianna Eireann, and was responsible for recruiting Tom Williams, the legendary IRA man hanged in 1942. Alfie Hannaway was later promoted to the staff of the IRA's Second Belfast Battalion, and in the early 1940s, as the IRA's "English campaign" was fading, the Stormont government interned him. But Uncle Alfie wore another hat, which he donned weekly on behalf of the Redemptorists, as an obituary recorded:

> His strong faith which was nurtured alongside his Republican beliefs led him to a strong association with the Clonard Monastery and a lifelong friendship with the Redemptorist priests. A member of both the boys' and men's confraternities for over 60 years, he earned the nickname "The Bishop" among his work mates, and when he was seen approaching the

comment came that there must be another retreat in the offing and he was looking for people to enrol.[24]

The association between the Redemptorists of Clonard and the republicans could be seen in other ways. The Redemptorists' celebrated annual novenas in West Belfast, nine intensive days of prayer, sermons, and services intended to refresh and strengthen religious belief, attract tens of thousands of local Catholics and transform the Clonard area into a huge religious carnival site. The novenas are held each June at around the time of the republican Bodenstown commemoration. The more spiritual republicans, like Alfie Hannaway, would spend the month of June first renewing their Catholic convictions in Clonard and then they would travel to County Kildare to reinvigorate their political faith at Wolfe Tone's graveside.

Gerry Adams may not have been as pious as Uncle Alfie Hannaway, but he too forged a close relationship with the Redemptorists, which worked to his benefit when he had to convince skeptics of his peaceful bona fides, as the New York–based insurance mogul Bill Flynn recalled when he met Adams at Clonard in 1991: "I'm a Catholic," he told the writer Conor O'Clery. "Adams is a Catholic, a communicant. I would see these priests and brothers, living there, trying to help people, under poor conditions. To see them, and their respect and friendliness for Adams, I knew he had to be a man of peace."[25]

FATHER REID would later say to others who participated in his peace enterprise that the only chance of getting the IRA to the point of ending its campaign lay in putting together a process that had the imprimatur of the Catholic Church firmly stamped upon it. "Al would say over and over again that the church was the only body which could pull something like this off and that if she didn't do it no one ever would," recalled one confidant.[26] Reid advanced a number of reasons why the church should get substantially involved. The first was that the IRA trusted Catholic intermediaries in a way it did not trust others. There was an encouraging record. Priests, many of them Redemptorists, had acted as messengers or go-betweens during the prison hunger strikes as well as in feuds between rival republican groups. Adams had himself been party to a lot of this activity and trusted the individuals concerned, especially Reid. The Redemptorist was not modest about his influence over the Adams's leadership: "He told us, and I think we came to believe him, that he had more close and continual contact with them than any other priest and possibly more than any person outside the IRA," said one government contact.[27]

Reid also contended that the church would bring a special flavor to the effort arising from its extraordinary, centuries-old influence over Irish society. This, he would say, would bestow a moral authority and stature on the enterprise that would both legitimize it and add to the pressure on republicans to respond positively. Reid's third point followed on from this. He argued that the church's role in providing a neutral setting for the process would give cover to any other political parties who were talking to Adams and his colleagues. "The point he made, and John Hume grasped this particularly well, was that if there was a leak, responsibility could be shifted onto the church," recalled an Irish participant.[28]

Had news of Reid's 1982 overtures to Adams leaked out at the time, there is little doubt that in the prevailing climate the Irish political and media establishment would have been aghast at the revelation of any contact between the church and the Provos. But the news would have shocked many republicans as well. The hunger strike scars were still fresh when Reid approached Adams and the memory of the role played by the church still rankled with rank-and-file Provos. During the prison protest, republicans had bitterly accused the Catholic hierarchy of betraying the hunger strikers and of kowtowing to the Thatcher government. The church's stance, they claimed, had been supine and had encouraged Thatcher to take an unbending line on the prison protest, contributing in no small measure to the ten hunger strike deaths. While the reality may have been much more complex, the belief was strongly held. When the protest was finally abandoned, the IRA prisoners issued a public statement attacking the church with unprecedented acrimony. Accusing the church of being "intricately immersed in the field of politics and deceit," the prisoners went on, "We contend that their position has at all times been established by political consideration rather than the Christian values of truth and justice. Therefore their stance has been extremely immoral and misleading."[29]

It was ironic therefore that it was to the head of the Catholic Church in Ireland, Cardinal Tomas O Fiaich, and through him the Vatican that Alec Reid, and, indirectly, Adams, turned for assistance in advancing his peace project. O Fiaich responded warmly to the suggestion from Reid that they hold talks with Gerry Adams. "Reid was convinced, and in turn persuaded Tom O Fiaich that the church should get involved in devising an alternative to the IRA's violence, that her resources, influence, independence, authority, and the lines of communication open to her all meant that the church should encourage and even initiate talks with Adams," recalled one peace process confidant.[30] Once Reid was able to tell the cardinal that Adams wanted to find a political alternative to violence and that he could deliver the IRA, O Fiaich agreed to take part. From then on, Reid could accurately describe his initiative as a church enterprise.

IT WAS REID'S and Adams's good fortune that at this time the occupant of Ara Coeli (House of Heaven), the Irish primate's official residence in Armagh, was Tomas O Fiaich. Had it been anybody else, the Reid initiative would perhaps have fallen at the first hurdle. Born in Cullyhanna, one of the most republican villages in South Armagh, O Fiaich was a staunch Irish nationalist, although one strongly opposed to the IRA's armed struggle. An academic who for many years had headed St. Patrick's College in Maynooth, County Kildare, the Irish church's principal seminary, O Fiaich was appointed archbishop of Armagh in October 1977, in succession to the late Cardinal Conway, the Belfast-born conservative who had led the church during the turbulent years of civil rights protests and the birth of the Provisionals. Within two months O Fiaich was embroiled in controversy when, in an interview with the Dublin-based *Irish Press* newspaper, he showed his political colors. "I believe the British should withdraw from Ireland," he said. "I think it is the only thing that will get things moving."[31] The comment stirred the DUP leader, the Reverend Ian Paisley, to dub O Fiaich "the IRA's bishop from Crossmaglen."[32] Although Paisley got O Fiaich's birthplace wrong, the label, in unionist eyes, was accurate and it stuck. O Fiaich was eventually elevated to the Irish primacy but only after a reportedly concerted British diplomatic effort to persuade the Vatican to choose someone else.

O Fiaich's decision to back Reid's enterprise was bound to animate controversy in the Irish church, not least because it came at a time when political pressure to isolate Adams and Sinn Fein was growing. The origin of much of this pressure elsewhere in Ireland as well as Britain lay not in London but in Dublin. After Adams's success in the 1982 Assembly election, the British let it be known that he and his four colleagues would have full access to Northern Ireland Office ministers to discuss constituency matters.[33] Adams actually got to meet one of them, Housing Minister David Mitchell, with whom he raised the subject of poor living conditions in his native Ballymurphy. But it was to be one-shot event. The incoming coalition government in Dublin, headed by Garret FitzGerald, had followed these events with growing dismay. FitzGerald believed passionately that the Provos should be isolated and that to talk to them would only encourage IRA violence. He had angrily condemned the British for engaging in past cease-fire talks with the IRA, on one famous occasion going so far as to recruit U.S. Secretary of State Henry Kissinger to his cause, and so he successfully lobbied the NI secretary, Jim Prior, to reverse the decision. Sinn Fein was banished from respectable company and stayed that way for over a decade.

The principal supporter of this view in the Catholic Church was the second or third most important bishop in the country. Dr. Cahal Daly, who occupied the see of Down and Connor, centered in Belfast, was technically responsible for the spiritual welfare of Gerry Adams and most of the West Belfast IRA. He was, though, as violently opposed to what Adams represented as O Fiaich was critical of British policy in Ireland. Unlike FitzGerald, Daly rooted his objections in Catholic theology and moral teaching—namely that the IRA's armed struggle was a sinful activity and thus abhorrent—but the effect was the same. In one typical onslaught he called the IRA "an evil and barbaric organisation,"[34] which should be shunned until such time as its leaders accepted the church's moral teachings on the use of violence. He regularly urged Catholic voters not to support Sinn Fein.

Cahal Daly was a formidable opponent of the IRA. Born in County Antrim in 1917, he was ordained in June 1941 and spent most of his early years in the priesthood as an academic. An accomplished linguist and scholar who held separate doctorates in theology and philosophy, Daly had taught Scholastic philosophy at Queen's University, Belfast, for twenty years. When he was elevated to the diocese of Ardagh and Clonmacnois in County Longford, the Catholic Bishop's Conference was to discover that this thin ascetic figure was possessed of one of the ablest minds in Irish Catholicism. The other bishops soon asked him to compose their pastoral letters, thus giving Daly the opportunity to shape Catholic attitudes to a whole range of social and moral issues during the 1970s and 1980s. "He was streets ahead of the other bishops in intellectual ability," recorded a contemporary.[35] While the Provisionals returned Daly's hostility with interest—"They cordially detested him," recalled one of Adams's closest advisers[36]—the widespread respect for his intellectual abilities, in Rome and farther afield, meant that his opposition could not be ignored.

Before he embarked on his initiative, Alec Reid had been careful to secure the approval of the Redemptorist Congregation, both in Ireland and in Rome. Cardinal O Fiaich and Bishop Edward Daly of Derry, an often stringent critic of the IRA who nevertheless argued for dialogue with its leaders, agreed to write him letters of comfort, stating that his proposed talks with Adams had their approval. Armed with these letters, Reid won over his superiors. But he needed more. Constitutionally the Redemptorists were independent of Bishop Cahal Daly, even though the Clonard Monastery and their retreat house, St. Gerard's in North Belfast, both later used as venues for peace talks, lay within Daly's diocese of Down and Connor. The Irish Redemptorists answered to their superiors in Dublin and Rome, not to Down and Connor, but nevertheless the situation was awkward. After all, they were proposing church involvement in a process of which their local bishop heartily disapproved. In the councils of the Catholic Bishops' Conference, the Southern bishops had left the issue to their Northern colleagues to debate and decide, but if support for the enterprise was to be found in Rome, Reid would have to have to answer Daly's argument. Reid needed a heavyweight to counter Cahal Daly.

He found him in the shape of a fellow Southern Irish Redemptorist, Father Sean O'Riordan, from Tralee in County Kerry. Just a year older than Cahal Daly, O'Riordan matched the Belfast bishop in academic prowess, in Reid's view. The professor of moral and pastoral theology at the Redemptorist-run Alphonsian Academy in Rome, O'Riordan also held a double doctorate, in theology and in history. A liberal theologian, he was a scholar of world renown who together with other academics in the Alphonsian Academy had crafted key documents for the Second Vatican Council.

By 1983 Reid had recruited O Fiaich to his cause but his attempts to persuade Cahal Daly to join his enterprise foundered.[37] All this brought the division within Irish Catholicism out into the open. In December 1983 Adams had written to Daly asking for a meeting. "During the last 12 months," he wrote, "a number of people [had] suggested to me that you and I should have a meeting and that discussions between us would be of benefit to the people of West Belfast."[38] Adams said that the unnamed intermediaries—meaning Alec Reid—had discussed with Daly the possibility of a meeting, and he had expected to hear from him. In the absence of an approach from the bishop, he was making himself "available" if Daly was interested.

Daly replied and marshaled the moral argument against dialogue. Adams's membership of Sinn Fein and that party's "unambiguous support" for the IRA's violence was "completely contrary" to the church's moral teaching, he wrote. If there was a change of heart on Adams's part, he would be glad to meet, but otherwise, no, the meeting could not happen.[39] In January 1984 Adams responded, "Whilst accepting your desire for confidentiality I cannot, in honesty, accept any other conditions, no more than I would expect you to accept conditions set by me. We all have a duty to seek ways to resolve the present conflict. This can only be done by means of dialogue and by an honest and frank exchange of views."[40]

Daly's reservations about the enterprise were not just theological. He also distrusted the Provos and feared they would deliberately leak news of their meeting to cause him embarrassment and weaken his influence with unionists. When Adams made their correspondence public in April 1984, it seemed his doubts had been well founded. "He was not hostile to what was happening, nor did he ever try to stop it, but he wanted nothing to do with it himself," explained a source close to Daly.[41] Seven years later, when Cahal Daly succeeded Tomas O Fiaich to the archdiocese of Armagh and was able to learn much more about the years of secret diplomacy, he became an enthusiastic supporter of the process. But in 1983 and 1984 his views were fixed. Nonetheless, the correspondence with Adams had set out the theological case against dialogue; the Redemptorists were obliged to respond, and they looked to O'Riordan for an adequate reply.

The opportunity came a year later, in January 1985, when again Adams and Daly clashed publicly. In a speech Daly had castigated the IRA's campaign as immoral and counterproductive, and in response Adams published an open letter asking the bishop what his alternative to violence was. Adams posed a series of questions to Daly, and it was to these that O'Riordan addressed himself, as one figure familiar with the debate recalled. "Adams had asked Daly that if he was advocating a peaceful struggle, then was he ready to spell out an alternative, and O'Riordan basically said that Adams was justified in asking the question," the source said. "He unequivocally backed Reid's opinion that the church should talk to anyone and everyone and had a duty to help in the process of devising an alternative to armed struggle. He also welcomed a remark by Adams that he himself would be pleased to consider any alternative to armed struggle, and that was an important thing to say."[42] O'Riordan tape-recorded his analysis in Rome and sent it to Clonard, where it was transcribed. Whenever Reid needed to recruit politicians or other influential figures to his enterprise, O'Riordan's document was at hand to strengthen his case.

In January 1985 the Irish peace process was just over two years old, and by this stage the Vatican was being kept fully informed by Cardinal O Fiaich of the progress of the dialogue with Gerry Adams. One channel of communication was the papal nuncio in Ireland, Archbishop Gaetano Alibrandi, a figure whose sympathy for Irish republicanism was a constant source of friction between the government in London, which resented Alibrandi's perceived interference in Northern Ireland's affairs, and the Vatican. Valuable though Alibrandi's support was, the Redemptorists and O Fiaich had more direct access to the Vatican through a contact who was often at Pope John Paul II's elbow.[43] Archbishop Justin Rigali had been talent-spotted early on in his church career as a potential Vatican highflier and by 1985 had spent virtually all his life as a priest in Rome, immersed in the high politics of the church. By that stage he was well placed to shape papal thinking and Vatican policy.

Born into a devout Catholic family in Los Angeles in 1935 and ordained in 1961, Justin Rigali was, at just thirty-five years of age, appointed director of the English-language section of the Vatican's Secretariat of State. The job description meant he liaised on behalf of the papacy with the church in Britain, Ireland, the Antipodes, and North America, all powerful and wealthy outposts of Catholicism. His elevation brought him right into the inner councils of the papacy. He became English-language translator for Pope Paul VI during his trips abroad, and when John Paul II ascended the throne of Saint Peter, it was Rigali who organized and accompanied the new pontiff on his many international trips, including his visit to Ireland in September 1979. It was during this journey that Rigali and Cardinal O Fiaich became friends, and as his influence with John Paul II grew, so the Clonard Redemptorists could be more certain of a friendly reception for Alec Reid's diplomacy. Rigali, like John Paul II a theological conservative and a strong supporter of the pro-life lobby, rose irresistibly through the Vatican hierarchy, each move strengthening his influence in papal circles. During the years 1985 to 1990 he sat on no fewer than seven Vatican commissions; in December 1989 he was named secretary of the Congregation of Bishops and a year later secretary of the College of Cardinals, one of the most powerful posts in Rome. In 1994, as a reward for his years of loyal service and as a possible precursor to the red cardinal's hat, John Paul II made him archbishop of St. Louis, Missouri. The esteem in which the pope held Rigali was illustrated in January 1999 when he chose St. Louis as the only venue for the U.S. leg of his trip to the Americas.

Rigali gave the fledgling Irish peace process vital access to the papacy, but, no less important, he also opened doors to the politically powerful U.S. church, especially to those in the hierarchy of Irish-American ancestry. "Rigali was a key man in influencing people like Cardinal O'Connor and Cardinal Law," recalled one church source. "The Americans were involved long before Clinton came on the scene."[44] Cardinals John O'Connor of New York and Bernard Law of Boston both received their red hats at around the same time, in 1984 and 1985, respectively, just as Alec Reid's enterprise was picking up speed. Both men were to play crucial parts in persuading U.S. political opinion of Gerry Adams's bona fides and greatly assisted his efforts to woo and then win over important figures in corporate Irish-America.

BY 1985 AND 1986 small glimpses of the secret diplomacy were occasionally visible, and with hindsight it is possible to discern the direction in which the talks were heading at this time. Three elements went together to make up the embryonic peace strategy. One was a proposal to forge an alliance of Irish nationalists which would replace the IRA's violence as the cutting edge of the republican struggle. The second was the idea that a conference should be held to which all shades of opinion in Ireland would be invited and which would hammer out a political settlement. The third was a declaration of neutrality from the British, a statement that said they had no desire to impose a settlement on anyone in Northern Ireland and would be content to accept whatever political representatives could agree in negotiation. Taken together, the peace strategy outlined a way in which Adams could accept the principle of consent in relation to the political future of Northern Ireland while being able to say that none of the core republican doctrines had been abandoned or compromised.

The tip of the iceberg soon became visible. Gerry Adams first broached the idea of pan-nationalism at Sinn Fein's November 1984 Ard Fheis when he called for "a firm, united and unambiguous demand from all Irish Nationalist parties" for an end to the unionist veto. This he said would create a new situation in which future arrangements could be worked out in "business-like negotiations" with all the parties in Ireland.[45] A few months later, in February 1985, during the course of a radio current affairs program, Adams asked the SDLP leader, John Hume, for talks to establish "a united nationalist approach" to the British.[46] In March he again called for "a united and dogmatic Irish nationalist approach" to the North.[47] These were all clues to the direction of the still-secret diplomacy. Cardinal O Fiaich meanwhile was treading similar ground. In January 1984 the Catholic primate urged the convening of a political forum either in Belfast or in Dublin where "representatives of all sides" could meet to discuss the future of the North.[48] Three times in 1985 he called on the British to indicate that they would not be staying in Northern Ireland forever and in the meantime to use their good offices to "try to bring Protestants and Catholics together."[49] It is possible to discern in his remarks the germ of what soon became recognizably the Adams peace strategy.

It was all very tentative stuff, and only those who were privy to what was going on behind the scenes could be aware of its real significance. The rest of Ireland, distracted by the ferocity of the IRA's campaign, dismissed the comments either as irrelevant or as deliberate distractions. The idea that the SDLP, Fianna Fail, or any other constitutional nationalist party in Ireland would want to link up with the Provisionals at that time or that the British would somehow agree to such far-fetched proposals was simply unimaginable.

It was also an impossible concept for most Provisional activists and supporters to grasp, at grassroots or even at leadership level. The common IRA/Sinn Fein view of the SDLP and Fianna Fail, the hatred at the core of their relationship, had been expressed in a bitter statement by the IRA prisoners at the end of the 1981 hunger strike—the same statement that had so bitterly excoriated the Catholic Church. Attitudes had changed little since then. Fianna Fail and the other Southern parties, the prisoners had said, were "accessories to the murder" of the ten hunger strikers for failing to confront Thatcher, while the SDLP was merely "an amalgamation of middle class Redmonites, devoid of principle, direction and courage."[50] The enmity between the Provos and the Irish establishment was deep and seemingly unbridgeable.

Even if Gerry Adams had wanted to confide in his senior colleagues, it is highly questionable that he would have received a sympathetic hearing. Most IRA activists at this point believed unwaveringly in the armed struggle and tolerated electoral politics only because it seemed to offer, as Adams and others had told them it would, a way of increasing logistical support for the IRA. Had they thought that the political path down which Adams had taken them would lead into negotiations that threatened to dilute dearly held republican beliefs, most would have seen it as treachery.

So it was that the diplomacy of Alec Reid and Gerry Adams was kept a tightly guarded secret even from the IRA Army Council. Although Adams was slowly to win over key members of the council to his strategy with the passage of time and did confide in the small group of advisers around him in Belfast, his enterprise with Reid was never discussed or formally approved by the body charged with deciding IRA policy and strategy.[51]

What the reaction of IRA leaders would have been had they been fully aware of the ideological territory being traversed by the still-secret peace process can only be guessed at. The logic of the entire initiative was, of course, to produce an alternative to the IRA's armed struggle. The goal of Reid's diplomacy, the reason for its existence, was to achieve a cease-fire, and not long after it was launched, that possibility was being actively canvassed, as one senior Protestant cleric remembered:

> It was around 1983 or 1984 that I became aware through Alec Reid that Adams was asking three questions, a sort of testing-of-the-water exercise in my view. The first question was "What would the parameters of a political settlement be if there was an IRA cease-fire?" Second, "Would the unionists and the British just pocket the cease-fire and return to the trenches?" and third, "How influential would people like me be with unionists? How proactive was I prepared to be?"[52]

THE REID-ADAMS INITIATIVE had gotten off to a moderately encouraging start. Adams himself was clearly willing to discuss an alternative to the IRA's violence, and to contemplate huge ideological shifts. There was no shortage of Catholic Church figures, at very senior levels, eager to assist him in his difficult journey. But the real problems lay elsewhere, in persuading and cajoling and otherwise moving the Provisional support base in the same direction. By the mid-1980s, however, other events were combining to make that task a little less daunting than it appeared.

The Provisionals' foray into electoral politics had been a triumph at the start, but Sinn Fein soon discovered that this new weapon was a two-edged sword. As long as electoral support for Sinn Fein was growing, as it was in the first two years, everything was fine, but once the vote started to slip and falter, this would be bound to be seen as a verdict on the IRA's armed struggle. Sinn Fein's electoral strategy made each poll a popularity or unpopularity contest for the IRA. The election of Adams to the West Belfast Westminster seat in the British general election of 1983 was the high point of the strategy. A total of nearly 103,000 people voted for Sinn Fein in that poll, almost 43 percent of the nationalist electorate, and the party came close to a second seat when Danny Morrison lost by just 80 or so votes in Mid-Ulster to the Paisleyite cleric Willie McCrea. But after that, it was a gentle but unstoppable slide downward. The Sinn Fein vote was being pinched in two directions. The novelty wore off for many Sinn Fein voters, and it became more and more difficult to cajole them into the polling booths, while the IRA's continuing violence put a natural limit on Sinn Fein's appeal. There was a broad swath of Catholic voters who just would not vote for Sinn Fein while the IRA killed and bombed. In the 1984 Euro election the SDLP leader, John Hume, easily outpolled Danny Morrison, and the SF share fell to 37 percent of the nationalist vote. A slight rise to 39 percent was recorded in the council elections the following year, but then two results, a series of Westminster by-elections in 1986 and the full British general election in 1987, saw the SF vote settle at around the 35 percent mark. As the SF vote dipped, Adams and his allies slowly but surely put more and more of the blame on botched IRA operations, which, they said, sapped support for Sinn Fein. And as the pressure grew on the IRA to refine, dilute, and ameliorate its campaign, it became easier to sell the idea of a political alternative.

Another key reason for the fall in the Sinn Fein vote was the Anglo-Irish Agreement of November 1985. The agreement, signed by Margaret Thatcher and Garret FitzGerald, gave the Irish Republic a formal if only advisory say in Northern Ireland affairs, which Dublin's diplomats skillfully used to smooth the rough edges of Britain's security policy, thereby reducing the grievances that nourished Catholic support for the IRA. The product of two tortuous years of diplomacy, the Hillsborough agreement was regarded North of the Border as a triumph for the SDLP's John Hume and the politics of persuasion. A vocal unionist reaction against the agreement, which saw a burst of loyalist street politics and a temporary withdrawal by unionist parties from constitutional politics, helped persuade nationalists that they had won some sort of victory. It injected new life into the SDLP and stabilized nationalist politics. The Irish political establishment's nightmare scenario, Sinn Fein outpolling the SDLP, evaporated. From then on it was clear that, short of another hunger strike or a repeat of Bloody Sunday, Sinn Fein's vote would never rise much above the 80,000–90,000 mark again. The Anglo-Irish agreement had created a stalemate in the competition between the two nationalist parties, and this was to make it easier for Adams to argue among his close advisers that only a radical departure could break the logjam.

ELECTORAL SETBACKS raised questions about the direction Sinn Fein and the IRA could and should be taking, and that, in general, was of great assistance to the Reid-Adams project. But the IRA was still full of formidable men and women whose standing made them dangerous to have as opponents, who almost certainly would have stenuously resisted the infant peace process had they known of its existence. Fortunately for the Adams camp, some of the fiercest of these rivals were removed or otherwise fell at around the time that the peace process was beginning to develop its own sense of direction.

The first to go was Kevin Mallon, who had become director of operations after Brian Keenan's arrest in 1979. Mallon, who also sat on the Army

Council and was on the same ideological wavelength as O Conaill and O Bradaigh, was a powerful figure in the IRA whose record went back to the Border Campaign, during which he was tried and acquitted on the capital charge of murdering an RUC man. The IRA in Tyrone was extremely loyal to him, and many of its members there would have sided with him in any political dispute with the Adams camp. It was Adams's great fortune that Mallon self-destructed and that he did not have to confront him.

Mallon's downfall came over a number of botched kidnapping operations in the Republic that he had organized to help fill the IRA's depleted coffers. One was the abduction of the racehorse Shergar, whose owner, the Aga Khan, refused to pay the ransom demanded by the IRA. As it was, Shergar was an uncontrollable, highly strung animal, and his kidnappers were forced to put him down. Worse was to follow in November 1983 when the IRA kidnapped the English-born supermarket executive Don Tidey in Dublin and demanded a seven-figure sum for his return. Three weeks later Tidey was rescued in a forest near Ballinamore, County Leitrim, but only after a fierce gun battle with the IRA in which an Irish army private and a Garda recruit were shot dead. The killings outraged opinion in the Republic, and for a while there was speculation that the government of Garret FitzGerald would actually proscribe Sinn Fein. In the following days, one senior republican after another emerged to express criticism of the kidnapping tactic, while Adams privately castigated "militarists" in the movement.[53] Mallon was finished.

The other upheaval in the Provisional IRA leadership was a much more serious affair for Adams, on a number of grounds: it was the first direct challenge to his political leadership of the Provisionals, it originated in his home base of West Belfast, and it was led by a figure whose regard in the IRA was beyond criticism. Ivor Bell had become chief of staff in the autumn of 1982, when Martin McGuinness stood aside to participate in the Assembly elections. Bell's collaboration with Adams went back to the early 1970s, when both held staff positions in the Second Belfast Battalion and the Belfast Brigade. When the pair ended up in Long Kesh, they cooperated in the campaign against the Billy McKee leadership and together devised the plan to reorganize the IRA. The names Adams and Bell went inseparably together in the 1970s in the same way that those of Adams and McGuinness would twenty years later. Initially an enthusiastic supporter of electoralism—he had argued to run non-abstentionist candidates during the 1981 general election in the Republic—Bell developed reservations when he saw the negative impact on the IRA's armed struggle, especially in Belfast, where

IRA operations had been scaled down to facilitate Adams's bid for the West Belfast seat and then for Morrison's European contest.

In 1983 and 1984 the Belfast IRA, once the cockpit of the organization, had accounted for only eleven of the IRA's ninety-five victims. Bell's fears that the campaign was being run down and that resources that should have gone to the IRA were being diverted to Sinn Fein were shared by senior figures on Northern Command, including his partner, Anne Boyle, and the operations officer, Sean McIlvenna, and in the Belfast Brigade by its commander, Eddie Carmichael, while two other senior Belfast figures, Anto Murray and Danny McCann, sympathized with the criticism. Bell's tenure as chief of staff came to an abrupt end in September 1983, when the Belfast Brigade adjutant, Robert "Beano" Lean, became the latest in a series of embarrassing and damaging IRA supergrasses to agree to testify against former comrades, and the damage he could do to the IRA was enormous. Although Lean later retracted, his evidence led to the arrest and brief imprisonment of Bell and some twenty-seven other senior figures. Under IRA rules Bell lost all rank in the organization, and Kevin McKenna, a key figure in the Tyrone IRA, took his place as chief of staff. On his release Bell got back onto the council, but his power had been eroded. He was given the task of liaising with Libyan intelligence and also joined the IRA Executive, from where he began plotting against the Adams strategy.

The Belfast Brigade meanwhile was intent on causing trouble for Sinn Fein. Angered by the amounts of money channeled to Sinn Fein from IRA coffers to finance election campaigns, the IRA leadership in the city carried out a number of killings and other actions intended to embarrass and damage Adams. Just before the June 1983 general election, the Belfast Brigade detonated a huge bomb outside Andersonstown RUC station, which devastated local homes right in the heart of the West Belfast constituency. The bombing angered many voters but, owing mostly to the fact that the opposition to Sinn Fein was split two ways, failed to deprive Adams of victory. In December 1983 the up-and-coming Ulster unionist politician Edgar Graham was shot dead outside the law department of Queen's University, Belfast, where he taught. In April 1984 Mary Travers, the daughter of a leading Catholic magistrate, Tom Travers, was shot dead and her father seriously wounded when an IRA gunmen opened fire as they left Mass in an affluent area of South Belfast. Travers later claimed the gunman had also tried to shoot his wife in the head but that his weapon had misfired.[54] The author was in the home of one of Adams's closest advisers not long after the shooting happened when Adams phoned from Donegal, where he was on vacation. It was clear from their exchange that the Sinn Fein president was dismayed to hear what had happened and seemingly did not know that the operation was in the pipeline. An attack such as that on Travers should have been cleared at the highest political level and Adams, or at least those close to him, should have been told about it. Two months later, in the midst of Danny Morrison's Euro campaign, the Belfast IRA shot dead a minor criminal, Jimmy Campbell, as he sat drinking in a social club off the Falls Road. The punishment was out of all proportion to Campbell's transgressions—he was just a petty thief—but the killing had been done to embarrass Sinn Fein, and it led to protests and pickets outside one West Belfast polling station.

It is not clear just when Bell and his colleagues began their attempt to overthrow Adams. The version put around by Adams's allies afterward was that it started when Bell's partner, Anne Boyle, was dismissed from Northern Command, allegedly for endangering the security of a Northern Command staff meeting, and that this led an angry Bell to set the plot in motion. Another says that the spark was the death in December 1984 of another Bell ally on Northern Command, Sean McIlvenna, a North Belfast IRA man who had been operating on the Border for some years. McIlvenna, thirty-three, was killed by a single bullet in the back when, by chance, the RUC came across him and other IRA men shortly after a land mine attack in County Armagh.[55] The dissidents complained that while Adams and his Sinn Fein coterie were able to buy bulletproof jackets to shield them from loyalist attack, the IRA could not afford to give men like McIlvenna the same protection, and this is why the police bullet had felled him.[56] Bell was convinced that a majority of IRA Volunteers were unhappy with the electoral strategy, and he had come close once before to successfully challenging it. A majority of the Council had indicated their sympathy for him when he was chief of staff, but he had been unseated just as he was about to move against Adams.

Whatever the truth, when Bell began to canvass fellow members of the Executive in late 1984 and early 1985 to call for an extraordinary Army Convention in a bid to abandon or severely limit Sinn Fein's electoral strategy, it did not take long for Adams to hear about it. He moved swiftly and resolutely against the dissidents. Bell, Boyle, Carmichael, McCann, and Murray were court-martialed and expelled from the IRA, although two, McCann and Murray, were later readmitted. Charged with treachery, Bell faced a possible death sentence, but Adams interceded, no doubt aware of the adverse publicity and speculation that would follow the discovery of his corpse in a South Armagh laneway, the customary dumping ground for such victims. Nevertheless the death threat continued to hang over Bell. He and Anne Boyle have lived quietly in West Belfast ever since; both have stubbornly refused to talk about the events of that time, least of all to journalists. The Ivor Bell rebellion was over, and in the space of a few months Adams had seen Kevin Mallon and Ivor Bell, two potentially serious obstacles to his leadership—and to the infant peace process—removed.

By the end of 1985 the peace process was just over three years old, and already it was clear what the driving force behind it was. Sinn Fein's success in the 1982 Assembly election had opened up intriguing possibilities. The results of that election and especially Adams's own election to the West Belfast seat a year later meant that Sinn Fein was now a major political force on the island, confounding and dismaying its critics and enemies in both Ireland and Britain. The Sinn Fein achievement had alarmed supporters of the political status quo and had forced Britain and the Irish government to put together the Anglo-Irish agreement, the most ambitious attempt to stabilize Northern Ireland in ten years.

Sinn Fein's improved circumstances meant that when, in the aftermath of Sergeant Cochrane's kidnapping, Father Alec Reid visited Gerry Adams, he found the Sinn Fein and IRA leader in a much more receptive frame of mind than ever before to discuss options to violence. On any prior occasion such discussions would have taken place in a vacuum. Now, after the electoral successes, there was something real to talk about.

Success at the hustings fueled the peace process but so, paradoxically, did setbacks. Unwittingly, perhaps, the Sinn Fein and IRA grassroots had backed a strategy that almost precisely measured popular disenchantment with the IRA's violence. In the days before Sinn Fein fought elections, the IRA could afford to disregard such considerations and take refuge in the thought that while the Irish people might not vote for republicanism, deep down they secretly supported it. Now there was no such fantasy in which to seek refuge.

As 1986 dawned, much of the groundwork in the peace process had been done and Adams's own internal problems had been eased with the departure of key rivals. But a peace process with only one participant was worthless. The next key questions were about the British and Irish governments and the extent to which they would be prepared to deal with Adams. The answer to those questions would determine the success or failure of the whole enterprise.

EIGHT

Dealing with the Brits

The history of contacts between the IRA and the British government was, by 1986, a long but unhappy one. British ministers, including the then Northern Ireland secretary, William Whitelaw, had met a delegation of IRA leaders, including Gerry Adams and Martin McGuinness, in London as far back as June 1972 during the first IRA cease-fire. In 1975 there were further contacts, although this time no British politicians were directly involved, and instead the talking was done between British officials and representatives of the Army Council. The talking in both cases ended in angry recrimination. In 1972 the cease-fire was abandoned within days of the contact amid IRA accusations of British bad faith, while in 1975 Adams and others alleged that the British had tricked the IRA into the cessation in order to buy time to devise the IRA's defeat. Officially the Army Council was in 1986 so hostile to the notion of a cease-fire that it was committed never to talk to the British again, unless it was about their withdrawal from Ireland.

All this meant that when Gerry Adams decided to open a dialogue with the British about the burgeoning peace process, he chose Father Reid to act as his go-between and representative. The Redemptorist acted as a sort of clerical cutoff, providing cover to all involved, both republican and British, and it was a task he performed with diligence and discretion when, finally, the moment came for Adams to move. Precisely when the pair made contact with the British government is not known, but the evidence strongly suggests that sometime in 1986, courtesy of Father Reid, a highly secret line of communication was opened between the Northern Ireland secretary, Tom King, and the Sinn Fein leader.

In the intervening years both the British and the Sinn Fein leadership have, for reasons best known to themselves, gone to considerable lengths to persuade the outside world that the first contact between them did not take place until much later, in 1990, when British intelligence made contact with the IRA and commenced a dialogue with Martin McGuinness.[1] But both parties have been extremely economical with the truth about the full extent of their dealings with each other.

They each had very good reasons. Adams had not told his Army Council colleagues about his dialogue with Father Reid, much less the indirect contact opened up on his behalf with the British through the Redemptorist priest. Had they known just about the talks with Reid, Adams would have faced some hard questions from other IRA leaders. But knowledge that Adams was talking to the British government, especially one led by the woman most Republicans blamed for the 1981 hunger strike deaths, and was doing so without their sanction, would have set off alarm bells in the Army Council, possibly with serious consequences for Adams. The government of Margaret Thatcher had equally compelling reasons to keep a tight lid on the story. Mrs. Thatcher's hatred and contempt for the IRA was renowned and although she had allowed MI6 officers to speak to the IRA during the hunger strikes, by 1986 there was another reason to keep her government's contact with Adams, albeit filtered through Father Reid, a tightly guarded secret. Two years earlier, in October 1984, a 20-pound IRA bomb exploded in a bathroom of the Grand Hotel, in the south-eastern English coastal resort of Brighton, during the annual Conservative Party conference. The bomb exploded just before 3 a.m. and came very close to killing Thatcher and other members of her Cabinet. Five people were killed, including Sir Anthony Berry MP, while Thatcher's hard-line Trade and Industry Secretary, Norman Tebbit, was badly injured in the blast. Mrs. Thatcher herself had a narrow escape; a bathroom she had been in a few minutes before the explosion was destroyed. In a statement the IRA said: "Today, we were unlucky, but remember, we only have to be lucky once—you will have to be lucky always." In fact this statement was mostly bluster; the IRA never again attempted to kill Mrs. Thatcher, while senior figures, including Adams, were said by colleagues to be privately thankful that the effort had failed in its primary aim. Even so, the Thatcher government was taking an extraordinary political risk by opening up communication with Adams. Common sense suggests that someone in British officialdom with sufficient influence and knowledge of the background may have advised that the risk was worth taking.

As can now be revealed for the first time, confirmation that Gerry Adams was in indirect conversations with the British government as early as 1986, or at least 1987, has been given in interviews with the author by two former British secretaries of state for Northern Ireland who conducted these dealings with the Sinn Fein leader. One was Tom King, who came to Belfast in September 1985, just before the Hillsborough agreement was signed, and the other was his successor, Peter Brooke, secretary of state between 1989 and 1992, a figure whose term of office is most identified with the emergence of the first public clues about the secret diplomacy that lay behind the peace process. Both men have since been elevated to the British House of Lords.

A scion of the British establishment, Brooke came to Northern Ireland with what seemed like impeccable unionist credentials. His father had been a Tory home secretary in the early 1960s when the unionist and British Conservative parties were as one, and his family roots in Ireland went back 250 years to the heyday of the Anglo-Irish ascendancy. Although welcomed at first by unionists, he was viewed with some unease and doubt by the end of his term, since his sometimes less than forthright approach to the Provisionals unsettled them. Their alarm bells were triggered very early on in his ministerial term when he took a soft line on the defining question of how the British would respond to an IRA cease-fire. A charming and often amusing man, Brooke was well liked by the media and became extremely popular with nationalists, not least because unionists distrusted him.

In an interview given to a press agency in November 1989 to mark his first one hundred days in office, Brooke conceded that the British and the IRA were in a military stalemate. He then made remarks that came so unexpectedly that they confounded observers at the time. Now, in the knowledge of the secret Reid-Adams diplomacy, they make perfect sense. "There has to be a possibility that at some stage debate might start within the terrorist community," he said. "Now, if that were to occur, then you would move towards a point, if in fact the terrorists were to decide that the moment had come when they wished to withdraw from their activities, then I think the government would need to be imaginative in those circumstances as to how that process should be managed."[2]

In an interview at his office in Westminster, many years later, Brooke explained to the author what lay behind his words. "That 1989 interview was based on a mixture of what I had heard from John Hume, MI5, and military intelligence and finally what I had heard about Reid," he said. "I had heard about Reid during a briefing I got from Tom King. What Reid was saying to us was that there was an opportunity here to end it, and one of the aims of what I said in the interview was to communicate my attitude on talks to Sinn Fein."[3]

What Peter Brooke learned about the Reid-Adams diplomacy suggests that the dialogue had begun not long after Tom King had become secretary of state. "I . . . saw intelligence [on Reid-Adams]," he told the author, "going back as far as 1986, intelligence which underlay my November 1989 interview."[4]

Tom King also confirmed the existence of the Reid-Adams pipeline to the author during interviews conducted at Westminster in 2000. A former British army officer and gentleman farmer-businessman turned MP for one of England's more affluent shire constituencies, King was fortunate to have been made a minister. A close friend of Michael Heseltine, a major critic of Thatcher's right-wing ideology, King was on the wrong end of the Tory Party spectrum for many of Thatcher's allies, but when he arrived in Belfast he made efforts to get in the unionists' good books. He hit the headlines when a few weeks after the Hillsborough pact had been signed, he said the Irish prime minister, Garret FitzGerald, had "accepted that for all practical purposes and into perpetuity there will never be a united Ireland."[5] The remark ruptured relations with Dublin but delighted unionists.

King could not say whether or not the Redemptorist pipeline to Adams was in place before he arrived in Belfast, but he did confirm that it was working while he was there. "I became aware of it," he said. "I may have asked questions, but I think I knew there was a Clonard connection."[6] King also confirmed that Margaret Thatcher was aware of the contact with Adams and had approved it.

King said that he was first active in the communication "at the turn" of 1986–87; in other words, that the dialogue did begin sometime in 1986.[7] This accords with Peter Brooke's memory of the intelligence briefing he received, which also suggested that the pipeline was opened sometime in 1986—at the very least. The matter is important not just because it fundamentally challenges other accounts of the peace process, which have the first contact between republicans and the British happening much later, but because it suggests that the British must have had an invaluable insight into the mind and intentions of the republican leader on the eve of what proved to be a turbulent and violent period in Northern Ireland, encompassing the smuggling of huge amounts of Libyan arms to Ireland and an intensification of IRA violence. The knowledge that Adams was at least prepared to talk about peace at this time was priceless information.

Other evidence suggests that the Adams-King dialogue continued until late 1987 or mid-1988 when spectacular bursts of IRA violence—the postponed "Tet offensive"—caused the British to cool the diplomacy. Either way, it is clear beyond contradiction that secret talks between the British and Adams began much earlier than any of the participants have so far admitted, a disclosure that demands a fundamental reassessment of the genesis and origins of the Irish peace process.

This disclosure also challenges another long-held belief about the peace process—namely, that it was the Irish government in Dublin with which Reid and Adams first made contact and that this was followed, in an admittedly lengthy and tortuous manner, by attempts from Dublin to coax the British to join the process. That is clearly not true. It is now evident that at the very least the British were contacted at the same time as Dublin, and that, far from having to be cajoled by Dublin into joining the process, the British, very possibly, were engaged first. What also emerges from this account is that the peace process was well advanced by the time the *Eksund* set sail from the Mediterranean and into the trap laid between them by British intelligence and the well-informed IRA traitor. Had the vessel and its deadly cargo gotten through and the IRA been able to launch its "Tet offensive," then a well-developed peace process would have been its first casualty. Whoever betrayed the *Eksund* saved the process, whether wittingly or otherwise.

It is also clear that the Reid-Adams dialogue with Tom King played an enormously important part in the evolution of the peace process even if the Provisional representation was confined to Gerry Adams and his close advisers and did not, at that stage, embrace the rest of the IRA leadership. Both Brooke and King believed, they told the author, that Adams was acting with the approval and knowledge of the Army Council. They were wrong, but they were not to know that. Adams was engaged in an enterprise of which the Army Council knew nothing, and had it been privy to these events it is likely that it would have heartily and angrily disapproved. The Reid-Adams initiative was a hugely dangerous exercise for the Sinn Fein leader.

A crucial moment in the secret contact came early on when King received a lengthy letter from Adams, which posed a number of questions about Britain's policy in Northern Ireland and its attitude toward the Provisionals. King has confirmed that this happened and indeed believes there may have been two letters from Adams. "I had one or two letters but I can't remember the detail, just the opening, 'A Chara,'" he said.[8] "A Chara" or "friend" is the traditional Irish opening to a letter and the equivalent of "Dear so-and-so."

In an earlier interview King said that he had received a series of questions from the Reid contact, and it is apparent that this was a reference to the

Adams letter. "We received questions," he said, "asking us, 'Is this right?' 'Is that right?' 'How can that possibly be?' 'Surely there are strategic and economic reasons to hang on in Northern Ireland?'"[9]

There were six questions in Adams's letter. Although Tom King says he has forgotten what they were, another well-informed participant in the peace process does remember. They were the following:

1. What is the nature of the British government's interest in Ireland?
2. What is the British government's attitude toward self-determination, and what will it do to ensure that there is no veto exercised which would militate against the exercise of self-determination?
3. Will the British government play a positive role in persuading unionists toward self-determination?
4. Will the British government publicly state its position, assuming the appropriate replies to these questions?
5. Will the British government accept that the republican movement will represent itself in any negotiations?
6. In the context of dialogue free from interference, will the British government publicly state its intention to withdraw from Ireland and give a date by which such withdrawal will be complete?[10]

Taken at face, the questions contained nothing that any of Gerry Adams's IRA colleagues could have quarreled with. They were all seemingly embedded in traditional IRA dogma, all apparently predicated upon the analysis that Britain's presence in Northern Ireland prevented the Irish people as a whole from freely deciding their own future. But the questions opened the way for the British to offer Adams an exit from armed struggle by redefining what was meant by concepts such as "self-determination" and "withdrawal."

Tom King has declined to say whether he or someone else wrote the document that was sent in reply to Adams, but that there was a reply is not in doubt. It came in an undated, unsigned statement, twelve paragraphs and nearly a thousand words in length, that responded to four of Adams's six questions in the order in which they were asked.[11]

The British answers set the agenda for the rest of the peace process and created a template for negotiations that after delays and many failures of nerve were to lead some ten or so years later to the Good Friday Agreement of April 1998. Most of the concepts and much of the language that characterized the process during the long years of its gestation and development were contained in the secret British reply to Gerry Adams's letter to Tom

King. If the peace process has a philosophical fountainhead, this is it.

The British reply, now revealed for the first time, is possibly one of the key, historic documents of the peace process. It reads in full:

The Provisional IRA say they are fighting a war of independence to win freedom and self-determination for the people of Ireland. They maintain that force must be used to persuade the British government to acknowledge such a freedom because it has a colonial self-interest in remaining in Northern Ireland and in exercising authority there. This interpretation of the political situation in Northern Ireland is based upon the false assumption that Britain has some interest of her own in remaining there and is therefore engaged in some way in defending those interests by force of military strength.

Britain of course has an interest in Northern Ireland which is to respond with a warm goodwill and friendship to the needs of the people of Northern Ireland as a whole. (We respect and admire the contribution which they have made to the union in peace and war.) But let me be very clear! In the second half of the 20th century no matter what has been the position in the past the British government has no political, military, strategic, or economic interest in staying in Ireland or in the exercise of authority there that could transcend respect for the wishes of the majority in Northern Ireland.

The political and security situation as it has now developed in Northern Ireland is due to the historical, political, religious and cultural divisions which separate the people of the nationalist tradition from the people of the unionist tradition in Ireland. These divisions are at the root of the conflict there and not any self-interested dominion policies of the British government.

The central issue in the conflict therefore is not to persuade the British government to decide on the question of self-determination in Ireland but to bridge the divisions between the people of both traditions there in a way that will enable them to decide it freely and democratically for themselves. The political consensus and agreement which would bridge these traditional divisions and so open the way to a peaceful resolution of the questions of Irish self-determination can only be achieved through the processes of political debate and dialogue between the peoples of both traditions.

Should they through their political representatives agree to engage in such dialogue the British government would do everything possible to accommodate and facilitate it. It would, for example, provide the necessary framework and forum which could take the form of an ongoing conference or convention composed of the official representatives of the people of both traditions. It would confine its own role in such a dialogue to that of facilitator and so would not officially take part in it or, much less, seek in any way to dictate to it.

This means the British government is prepared to withdraw from the central area of historical, political, religious and cultural conflict and from the central forum of political debate that would seek to resolve it so that the parties to the conflict, namely the people of the nationalist tradition and the people of the unionist tradition can engage freely, independently and democratically in the political dialogue and in agreement-making which would bridge their divisions.

Should this dialogue result in agreements based on the consent of the people of the two traditions which would bridge the political divisions between them and to define the forms of new political structures which would embody, institute and organise such agreements the British government would respond with the necessary legislation.

We hope that this statement will clarify our present policies in Northern Ireland. We also hope that it will prompt the Provisional IRA to review their present policies and to see that the use of violent tactics against "colonial interests" which in fact do not exist is a mistake and a tragedy beyond words not only for the people of Ireland generally but also for themselves.

Questions about Irish political self-determination can only be answered by the people of the nationalist and unionist traditions in democratic conference among themselves. Britain can assist them but she cannot answer for them because the problem is not that the British government will not agree to Irish self-determination but that the people of the two divided traditions do not at present agree amongst themselves on how to exercise it.

It is our fervent hope that what we have said in our statement will convince the Provisional IRA and the Sinn Fein party that the political divisions between the people of the two traditions in Ireland which are at the heart of the conflict cannot be bridged much less healed by force. Their use of force is, in fact, holding back the day of justice and peace for the people of both traditions because the political debate which would bring that day forward cannot take place freely and democratically while they or indeed any significant section of either tradition are using the argument of the gun.

We accept that the republican tradition within the nationalist community should be represented at the peace conference table but we cannot and will never accept that the Provisional IRA and the Sinn Fein party should be represented there while they continue to use the tactics of violence. Apart from other considerations they themselves would never really expect to sit down with representatives of the unionist tradition to confer and decide about the political future while unionists feel as they do that Republicans are holding a gun to their heads.

The strategies of peacemaking are the strategies of political dialogue, political persuasion and political force. These alone can create the political agreements whatever their developing or final form which would breach the divisions between the people of the nationalist tradition and the people of the unionist tradition in Ireland. Only on such a bridge can the conflict be ended and the foundation of a just and lasting peace for both traditions be soundly and progressively established.[12]

The secret British document made three significant and important statements to Adams. It said first that, contrary to IRA dogma, Britain had no interests in Northern Ireland, no selfish reason for remaining there, and was indifferent about the nature of any settlement as long as it was not imposed by force and did not offend the principle of consent. Britain was also prepared to allow Sinn Fein to have a part in the forging of any settlement, but that would be conditional on an IRA cease-fire. That was not a departure from policy. Britain had always made it clear that IRA violence was the obstacle to Sinn Fein's taking part in normal political life. What made this offer interesting was that Britain also offered to convene the sort of conference that Irish nationalists had long asked for and promised that it would not attempt to impose its will upon its deliberations. Sinn Fein could attend, providing the IRA ended its violence, while Britain also gave a pledge to implement any settlement in legislation, a hint that the 1920 Government of Ireland Act, which upheld the partitionist settlement, could be significantly amended and even replaced.

The most intriguing and momentous part of the British reply came with the novel redefinition of what British withdrawal would actually mean. The traditional republican interpretation of this was straightforward. The British would physically leave, their troopships would sail from Belfast harbor, and their politicans and officials would decamp while Irishmen, Protestant and Catholic, got on with the business of constructing a new government for the whole of Ireland. Irish and British constitutional politicians had long rejected this scenario as unworkable, largely on the grounds that Protestants would resist it probably to the point of civil war. But now the British came up with an ingenious reworking of the idea. Britain would not physically withdraw but it would withdraw politically, that is, it would promise not to interfere or intervene in the decision-making process—the all-party negotiations in other words, aimed at securing a final settlement. Irishmen would be allowed to construct the deal while the British acted as impartial facilitators.

Two of Adams's questions went unanswered, and many of the ensuing problems faced by the peace process would be caused by this. The British did not respond to Adams's request to make their position public—that would not happen for two or three years, until Peter Brooke gave his neutrality speech. Nor would the British name a date for the end of the process, the point at which they would finally leave Ireland. At the time of this writing the answer has still not been given.

Nevertheless, it is possible to see in the secret British letter the blueprint for the peace process as it unfolded in the coming years. Armed with this redefinition of British disengagement and a statement of neutrality, Adams could happily continue the secret diplomacy with Reid while the road map showed that all-party negotiations, an IRA cease-fire, and adherence to the principle of peaceful consent were the way forward. This is precisely what did happen, although it would be nearly eleven years before the destination was reached. The argument that the peace process was a precooked deal and that much of what happened in the process was about managing the various forces involved, not least the IRA and Sinn Fein rank and file, finds its origin in this document.

AT THE START of their dialogue Tom King had responded diligently to the Reid-Adams pipeline, but other diplomacy was under way as well, albeit more tentative. Sometime in early 1987, and separately from the more considered response to Adams's letter, King authorized a statement to be delivered to the Sinn Fein leader saying that there was no strategic or economic interest in staying in Northern Ireland as far as Britain was concerned, nothing "that would override the democratic will of the people of Northern Ireland."[13] According to King this was in response to an overture from the SDLP leader, John Hume, rather than the Reid-Adams pipeline, and King's memory is that it happened in early 1987. "It was before Loughgall [the SAS ambush that killed eight IRA members] because after Loughgall things slowed down, and we were annoyed by this," he recalled.[14]

Tentative peace talks may have been opened with Gerry Adams, but the latter's colleagues in the IRA continued with their armed struggle regardless. Unaware of the secret diplomacy, certainly ignorant of the correspondence between Tom King and Adams, the Army Council authorized the

launch of the much delayed and reduced "Tet offensive." It was this decision, later on in 1987, that brought the dialogue between King and Reid-
Adams to its first crisis.

At the end of August 1987, three Irish people—two men and a woman,
all with Dublin addresses—were arrested in the grounds of King's estate
near Bridgeport, Wiltshire, and later charged with conspiracy to murder the
Northern Ireland secretary. Paramilitary-style equipment, notes of King's
car registration numbers, and a large cash sum were found in their camp-
site nearby. The three were initially convicted but later cleared on appeal.
Nevertheless, King was convinced that all the while he was sending messages to and receiving them from Gerry Adams, the IRA had been plotting
to kill him, and he was furious. A few months later, in March 1988, the
attentuated "Tet offensive" was launched with an attempt to bomb the
Mediterranean colony of Gibraltar, and that was followed by a wave of
violence culminating that September in an effort to kill the head of the
Northern Ireland civil service, Ken Bloomfield, in a bomb attack on his
home outside Belfast.

The alleged IRA surveillance of his home caused an incandescent King to
cut the cord to Alec Reid. "He told Adams to get stuffed," recalled one
informed source. "He took Bridgeport as a very personal affront, and I also
suspect that he was getting a lot of support from Mrs. Thatcher for cutting
off the talks."[15] In autumn 1988 the Thatcher government responded to the
IRA upsurge with a tough package of security measures, which included a
ban on radio and TV interviews with members of Sinn Fein, a change in the
law that eroded the suspect's right to silence during police interviews, and
a mandatory oath of nonviolence for all candidates in local elections in
Northern Ireland. What brought matters to this point was the stark difference between the desire for peace of which Reid and Adams talked and the
reality of the IRA's violence, a difference the British might have better
understood had they realized just how secret the Reid-Adams diplomacy was.

From then on and for years ahead, there were two distinct British views
of Adams's and the Provos' motives, as one participant with a ringside seat
remembered:

> At the start Tom King saw this as something that had to be pursued, that
> it was an historical chance. He saw it as the IRA going through their dying
> throes, and they were looking for a way out. It was only after what hap-
> pened at Bridgeport that he concluded they were spoofing. The Foreign
> Office was very positive all the way through. I can't remember a time when

they were negative. In the Northern Ireland Office it depended very much on who was there, but the prevalent view was that they were doing something new but for the same purpose. The difficulty was that it was so hard to take Reid seriously; he was so passionate about things [but] with no evidence of change.[16]

The letter from Adams to King that produced the remarkable British reply was undated—as is the secret reply itself—but public comments by the Sinn Fein leader suggest that the ideas contained in the British correspondence were circulating inside Adams's head toward the end of 1986 and the beginning of 1987. In a December 1986 interview with the *Irish Times*, for example, he stated, "I say the British still have an interest in this country. If they don't, let them say it. What they should be saying, quite simply, is that they have no interest in Ireland and they're going to leave. That would have the effect very quickly of bringing everyone—and people might say that includes us—to their senses and starting to work something out."[17] That point was dealt with in the secret British answer.

Three months later there was more of the same. In a speech to the Oxford Union, Adams called "for the establishment of an all-Ireland constitutional conference consisting of elected representatives of the Irish people that would draw up a new constitution for an independent Ireland and organise a new system of government open to all significant organisations of political opinion in Ireland."[18] The British reply also dealt with that matter. With hindsight it is difficult not to conclude that these comments were an intriguing public glimpse of a still very secret diplomacy.

One unresolved question concerns the identity of the British civil servants who were dealing directly with Father Alec Reid, those who very probably drafted the secret answer to the Adams letter. The conduit between Tom King and those who were talking to Alec Reid was Ian Burns, then the deputy under secretary of state at the Northern Ireland Office, who retired in the early 1990s.[19] According to informed sources, Burns was a consistently optimistic influence on NIO thinking during this period, and to some of his colleagues this suggests he was privy to much of Adams's thinking. There is also evidence that he was the conduit to King for highly confidential information coming from a second source in or near to the Provisionals, this time in Derry. The contact civil servant in that case was Mark Elliott, a Foreign Office official seconded to the NIO who was in charge of the British side of the joint Irish-British secretariat, which had been set up as part of the 1985 Anglo-Irish Agreement. Elliott made regular monthly trips to Derry, and his subsequent reports were considered so sensitive that for security reasons he wrote them out by hand and delivered them directly to Burns.[20]

Elliott's role had its roots in the bureaucratic structure erected by the British when the outbreak of violence in August 1969 and the deployment of British troops forced a more direct involvement by London in the day-to-day running of Northern Ireland's affairs. To keep an eye on the increasingly volatile situation, the British sent over a senior civil servant to be its official representative, a sort of ambassadorial figure, to liaise with the unionist government. Over the years the office became the regional headquarters of British intelligence, and it was eventually located in a secluded villa called Laneside, in the pleasant seaside town of Hollywood, east of Belfast. It was from Laneside that British officials like Michael Oatley of MI6 made discreet contact with the IRA in 1974 and 1975 on the eve of the cease-fire, and it was there that secret meetings with IRA leaders were held. Laneside was the nerve center of British policy in Northern Ireland.

Eventually Laneside was closed down. Some of the office's functions were transferred to the Political Affairs Bureau (PAB) at the Northern Ireland Office, and the interest of Whitehall was signified by the presence of a Foreign Office official at its head. In later years the job was given to Mark Elliott. The intelligence section of Laneside went its own way and was later housed in a new office block in the Stormont complex along with MI5.

Neither Tom King nor Peter Brooke can say, will say, or can remember who on their staff dealt with Father Alec Reid. "I don't know who was dealing with Reid," said King bluntly; "probably the political relations side."[21] But the evidence is that the Political Affairs Bureau in the NIO was kept firmly in the dark about the secret communications with Gerry Adams, as one former British official explained: "I never had the slightest wind of it, no hint of it all. I can't believe that the way the office was organized it could have been possible. No one would have thought of doing it that way, because it would have got out almost immediately," he said.[22] This official, like other of his former colleagues interviewed by the author, is convinced that the intelligence services must have handled the contacts.

We were very much part of the ordinary office, and it's conceivable that one person could have been up to it, but I just find it impossible to believe that. I think it was done through other channels. And frankly I suspect if you were doing something like that, you would have left it to someone who perhaps had some training and background. They are the sort of people who are trained to do that sort of thing, and they are probably better placed for that sort of endeavor. What you also have to remember is that when this started (a) it was not stated government policy, and (b) it easily could have gone very, very pear-shaped, and I would have thought whichever minister or ministers [were] involved would have wanted some cover.[23]

Some aspects of the diplomacy suggest that it embraced a strong "need to know" element of the sort that usually indicates an intelligence role rather than the conventional duties of a mainstream government department. Both King and Brooke denied all knowledge of the secret British reply to Gerry Adams and said they had never read the document until shown a copy by the author. Had they known about it at the time, the political risk to them would have been enormous. The document was explosive, its content an absolute contradiction of stated British policy toward the IRA in the mid- to late 1980s, which was to shun and isolate both it and Sinn Fein. Had the document or any of its contents leaked, the sitting secretary of state, either King or Brooke, would have been forced to resign.

The piece of evidence that suggests that both King and Brooke may have been kept in the dark about the secret reply to Adams is that one of them, Peter Brooke, had no knowledge at all of Adams's original letter to Tom King until this writer told him. He had not been told about it during his ini- tial briefing as NI secretary from civil servants, and Tom King had not dis- closed it to him either, even though, according to Brooke, King had briefed him on the Reid-Adams conduit. It seemed that someone, somewhere in the NIO or possibly in the intelligence apparatus had decided it would be bet- ter if Brooke remained ignorant about the correspondence. When the author told Brooke about the King letter during lunch in Westminster, he was astonished and frankly incredulous. It was the first he had heard of the letter.[24] But the existence of the Adams correspondence is undisputed by King himself, even if he disavows all knowledge of the reply. The British politicians, it appears, were only partly aware of the full picture.

There is another clue that strongly suggests intelligence involvement. It also comes from Peter Brooke's memory of events. Previous accounts of the peace process have told how in late 1990 a senior MI5 officer called John Deverill met Brooke with a proposal to initiate secret talks with the IRA leadership and that when Brooke gave the go-ahead, back-channel negoti- ations began.

In an interview with the author in June 2000, Brooke explained that what really happened was that Deverill came to see him not to get author- ity to start talks with the IRA but to inform him that a different intelligence officer would be taking over day-to-day handling of what appeared to be an already ongoing operation.

> What was put to me in relation to political cover—and I was being told because of a change in personnel—was that a channel existed, represented by an individual in Derry, there was a vehicle or conduit under which British intelligence services acting on behalf of the British government was in a position to say things to him by which Sinn Fein could test if they wished what we meant by some action by us. The circumstances suggest that the dialogue with the IRA had been going on for some time.[25]

If British intelligence was conducting covert conversations with the IRA behind the backs of British ministers, then, equally, it could have been sending secret letters to Gerry Adams, and figures like Peter Brooke and Tom King would have known nothing about them. Although this is necessarily conjecture, there is no doubt that there was a British letter to Adams and that it laid the foundations for the Good Friday Agreement. Someone in the British administration wrote it.

By the time the secret Reid-Adams pipeline to the British was opened, the Redemptorists and British intelligence were not exactly strangers to each other. During the 1980 hunger strike a Redemptorist priest, Father Brendan Meagher from the congregation's Dundalk House, had acted as a messenger between Michael Oatley of MI6 and leading Provisionals, Gerry Adams, Martin McGuinness, and other IRA figures in Belfast, as well as the leader of the hunger-striking prisoners, Brendan Hughes. According to one account, members of the Provisional leadership who wanted a settlement to the protest[26] had initiated the contact, and some republicans believe that had Father Alec Reid been fit and healthy, he would have performed the role played by Meagher. Code-named Angel, Meagher met Oatley, code-named Mountain Climber, at Belfast airport to receive a copy of last-minute British proposals to settle the prison dispute.[27] Meagher took the document to the prison and then to a house on the Falls Road to show to Adams, McGuinness, and Danny Morrison.

Five years later, in 1986 and 1987, another Redemptorist priest, this time Father Alec Reid, would shuttle between Gerry Adams and the British government. But this time his mission was much more historic than settling a hunger strike. This time it was about ending the IRA's ancient war with Britain.

NINE

"Stepping Stones"

Few twentieth-century Irish politicians have aroused such powerful passions as Charles Haughey and none whose political legacy has been so fiercely argued over, even during their lifetime. If Ireland had a Richard Nixon figure, then it was Haughey. Once banished into the political wilderness, tarnished with allegations of gunrunning, Haughey made an extraordinary comeback, rising to become leader of Ireland's largest political party, Fianna Fail, and on three occasions Irish prime minister, or taoiseach. Like Nixon's, his years in office were dogged by scandal and controversy until finally he was driven out of office and hounded by disclosures and allegations of corruption and venality. But just as the passage of time and reflection caused Nixon's period to be reassessed, so Haughey's role in the Northern Ireland peace process, a story never before fully told until now, may well place his own stewardship in a different light.

Charles Haughey had never met Gerry Adams, but the men were not entirely strangers either. They first started talking to each other, albeit indirectly, during the 1981 hunger strikes when Haughey was taoiseach and trying to negotiate a settlement of the prison protest with the British prime minister, Margaret Thatcher. The go-between was an old friend and confidant, Padraig O hAnnrachain (O'Hanrahan), whose Fianna Fail credentials were impeccable. A County Clare man, O hAnnrachain had been recruited by de Valera in the 1950s and became the great man's private secretary. In the days of Lemass and Lynch, he headed the Government Information Service, and was responsible for ensuring that the taoiseach got the best media coverage possible. Discreet and affable, O hAnnrachain, who died in 1988, was trusted by Haughey to handle the secret phone calls to and from Gerry Adams during the turbulent spring and summer of 1981. Had Adams wished, he could have destroyed Haughey with a judicious leak about their dialogue, but the contact was never revealed and trust between the men grew.

Five years later Haughey was no longer ensconced in Government Buildings in Dublin, but he was still the leader of Fianna Fail, despite the best efforts of rivals to unseat him. In August 1986, a few months before he was once again elected taoiseach, Father Alec Reid came to see him at Kinsealy, the splendid Georgian estate owned by the Haughey family on the northern outskirts of Dublin. It was the start of a dialogue that would culminate just nine months later in an extraordinary offer of an IRA cease-fire from Gerry Adams and later in the creation of a strategy that enabled the republican leader to coax, direct, and otherwise persuade his followers to take a path that would lead to the ending of the Provisionals' long war against the Northern Ireland state.

BY THE TIME the Provisional IRA Army Council ordered the second cease-fire of the peace process, in July 1997, a decade or so after Father Reid's journey to Kinsealy, it seemed, as one erstwhile loyal fan put it, that "the pathological anti-Haugheyites" had won the argument about Haughey's place in Irish life.[1] The former Fianna Fail taoiseach had been mired in one of the worst corruption scandals ever to hit Irish politics, and it seemed that it would be this rather than the achievements of office that would shape history's judgment of him.

It was the Provisional IRA that was indirectly responsible for Haughey's plight. Back in October 1981 the IRA was strapped for cash, and so the Army Council authorized the kidnapping of Ben Dunne, one of Ireland's wealthiest and most flamboyant supermarket tycoons. It was a risky operation, for it was sure to attract the anger of the Irish political establishment, but despite that the IRA went ahead. The task was given to the IRA in South Armagh, and it went about the kidnapping with typical flair and careful planning. Just north of the Border at Jonesboro the IRA staged a fake car accident, and when Dunne stopped to give aid, armed men pulled him from his car. He was held for a week and then released into the hands of a local journalist. Both Gardai and the Dunne family denied reports that some £300,000 was paid to the IRA for Dunne's life, but the suspicion persisted.

Whatever the truth, the experience scarred Dunne and in no small measure contributed to a serious cocaine habit, which finally surfaced eleven years later in a bizarre incident at the Grand Cypress hotel in Orlando, Florida, when the supermarket boss threatened to jump from the seventeenth floor. Other members of his family were appalled and angered, in particular his sister Margaret Heffernan, who ordered an investigation into the financial affairs of their supermarket chain, Dunnes Stores. The probe revealed secret payments to Charles Haughey and led directly to the government of the day setting up a tribunal to inquire into the former taoiseach's past financial dealings.

Further investigation by the tribunal established that Haughey's expensive lifestyle, which included not just his ownership of Kinsealy but also an island retreat off the County Kerry coast, had been bankrolled by a small group of wealthy Irish businessmen. The tribunal calculated that the businessmen had donated £8.5 million in the seventeen years since 1979, when Haughey first became taoiseach. Ben Dunne, who gave some £2 million, turned out to be the single most generous donor. Although no evidence was ever produced at the tribunal to suggest that Haughey had returned favors to the businessmen while in office, the suspicion lingered and was strong enough for many in Irish public life, the media in particular, to consign him forever to the rogues' gallery of Irish politics.

It was difficult, in watching the pursuit of Haughey, not to be aware that many of his enemies fell upon him with the sort of glee and venom that characterizes the patient hunter who at long last has cornered an elusive prey. For years significant sections of political life and the media in the Republic had held Haughey responsible for the creation and birth of the Provisional IRA, and there were some who had long hoped for the day when he would be brought low. It is, though, one of the great ironies of the peace process that no single Irish politician did more than Haughey to start the Provos on the path that eventually resulted in the cease-fires.

His contribution was twofold. The first was that many of the political ideas on Northern Ireland developed during his time as Fianna Fail leader were incorporated almost wholesale into the strategy worked out by Adams and Reid. In many important ways the strategy was Haughey's, not theirs. The second contribution was that by the time he left office in 1992, the theology of the peace process had been fully worked out, and the completion of the enterprise was then only a matter of internal management and negotiation. Whatever about Haughey's role as midwife to the Provos, there is no doubt that he was in there at the beginning of their end.

The story begins at the start of the Troubles. When the violence flared in the summer of 1969, forty-four-year-old Haughey was the ambitious minister for finance in a badly divided Fianna Fail government led by the former Cork hurling star Jack Lynch. The street violence in the North would make those divisions worse and finally propel the Southern state into what one experienced commentator later described as "arguably the most serious political conflict since the Civil War."[2] Lynch's cabinet was riven by personality differences and by competing ambitions, but these coincided with a deep ideological fault line. Lynch had been won over by the influential Irish civil servant Dr. T. K. Whitaker to a much more moderate policy on Irish reunification than normally was Fianna Fail policy. It was one that stressed the need for unionist consent to change,[3] a view echoed later by constitutional nationalists in the North and in particular by John Hume, the leader of the SDLP. The approach implied that partition was not the sole responsibility of the British and that an attitude of confrontation with the government in London or the unionists was unlikely to be productive. Whitaker preached the need for slow, gradual, peaceful change, a breaking down of barriers between unionist and nationalist, Protestant and Catholic, and Lynch agreed.

Not everyone in Fianna Fail accepted the Whitaker-Lynch analysis. For large sections of the party the violence of 1969 signaled an opportunity to complete the unfinished business of 1919–21 and to make right the wrong that had been done to Irish sovereignty by the imposition of partition. The principal spokesman for this viewpoint in Lynch's cabinet and the Fianna Fail party was Neil Blaney, the minister for agriculture, whose base in County Donegal was adjacent to riot-torn Derry. It was perhaps no accident that Blaney hailed from a part of Ireland that had suffered most from the partition settlement, for the Border meant that Derry lost its natural hinterland while Donegal was stranded between two states and often felt abandoned.

Haughey seemed an unlikely member of the Blaney camp, but he did have excellent family credentials. He was born in Castlebar, County Mayo, in 1925, although his parents were both Northerners who had left Northern Ireland not long after partition. They hailed from the County Derry village of Swatragh, and his father, Sean, joined the local unit of the IRA at the outbreak of hostilities, becoming adjutant of the Second Derry Battalion. Like most Northern IRA men, he sided with Collins after the Treaty, but he appears not to have actually fought in the subsequent civil war.

By 1922 he had risen to be Brigade OC of the Second Northern Division, but then the family moved to Mayo, where Haughey Sr. took a regular commission in the new Irish army. The young Charles Haughey did not follow his father's footsteps into the IRA, but he did the next best thing and joined Fianna Fail. An accountant and lawyer by training, Haughey was first elected to the Dail in 1957 and four years later was promoted to the post of minister for justice. Within a month he had dealt the final blow to the IRA's dying Border Campaign, when he introduced special military courts to try republican activists. The secretary to his department, Peter Berry, later credited him with having made the move that "broke the back of the organisation."[4] That and the fact that only once before the crisis of 1969 had Haughey mentioned Northern Ireland in a speech[5] led many to conclude that he held no noticeably strong views on the national question. Haughey had made a bid for the Fianna Fail leadership when his father-in-law, Sean Lemass, retired as taoiseach but withdrew when Lynch was adopted as the compromise candidate acceptable to most tendencies in the party. But such was the impact of the violence of August 1969 in the Republic that the leadership question seemed ready to be reopened.

The violence forced the Lynch government to make some sort of response; the television scenes of blazing Catholic houses and refugees flooding across the Border had roused public opinion in the Republic. Lynch managed to resist efforts to send the Irish army across the Border but agreed to set up a special cabinet committee to relieve "the distress" suffered by Northern nationalists, whose control he placed in the hands of his enemies, Blaney, Haughey, and another cabinet hawk, Kevin Boland. As minister for finance, Haughey was charged with administering a fund of £100,000 to spend on the North, a considerable sum in 1969–70. Haughey and Blaney also liaised with Captain James Kelly, an officer in Irish military intelligence who was mixing with Northern republicans and nationalists on behalf of the government.

From these circumstances came two extraordinary allegations. One was that Haughey, Blaney, and others, including a senior Belfast IRA man, John Kelly, had tried to import weapons from Europe to supply defense committees in Belfast. The allegation was all the more staggering given the size and quality of the arsenal supposedly involved: 200 submachine guns, 84 light machine guns, 50 general-purpose machine guns, 50 rifles, 200 pistols, 200 grenades, and 250,000 rounds of ammunition, enough to equip a battalion of the British army.[6] Since the defense committees were under the sway of either the Official IRA or, in more cases, the new Provisional IRA, it meant the weapons were headed for republicans who would not hesitate to use them, and not necessarily in a defensive mode.

Haughey, who along with Blaney was later sacked by Lynch when the affair became public, was charged with conspiracy to import weapons. The subsequent hearing, known simply as the Arms Trial, was one of the most sensational in Irish history, but it ended with Haughey's acquittal, while the charge against Blaney was dropped at an earlier stage. Although spared shame and imprisonment, Haughey was banished to the Fianna Fail equivalent of a political Siberia. John Kelly was similarly acquitted.

The other allegation was that, along with Captain Kelly and Blaney, Haughey had conspired to foment a split in the IRA with a twofold aim: to neutralize or weaken the politically radical and increasingly violent Goulding leadership in Dublin, while creating an instrument in the North that would be more amenable to Fianna Fail control. Cabinet papers of the day that have recently been published acquit Haughey of this particular charge; they reveal that this was a policy agreed upon by all Lynch's ministers in April that year, long before the August riots. The papers show that the Department of Justice had recommended a policy of dividing the IRA's rural conservatives from the urban radicals and that the cabinet endorsed this. Even so, the working out of the policy put Haughey and Blaney at the center of the scheme, almost as if it was their private, freelance plan.

In the wake of the Arms Trial, Haughey was dispatched to the political wilderness, but he turned this into an opportunity. He cultivated the grassroots and discovered that the rank and file responded well to a tough republican rhetoric. In 1977 Fianna Fail won a thumping majority in the general election, unseating the strongly anti-IRA Fine Gael–Labour coalition. Lynch was obliged to include Haughey in his cabinet, making him minister for health and social welfare. Within two years Lynch was gone, forced to quit by a series of by-election reverses, and Haughey narrowly won a hard-fought leadership contest with the retired taoiseach's preferred successor, George Colley.

The day after his election as Fianna Fail leader, on December 7, 1979, Haughey signaled a new assertive direction regarding Northern Ireland matters, an end to Jack Lynch's tractable approach to London. Not only did the new Irish leader flag a more confrontational line with the British, but he hinted that the way forward was for the two governments to bypass the unionists altogether and deal directly themselves with a shared problem. The government's line, he announced, would revert to the traditional Fianna Fail program that called on the British to encourage Irish unity and to declare their commitment to implement "an ordered withdrawal" from the North.

His first Fianna Fail Ard Fheis, in February 1980, gave an opportunity to signal the changes in a way the ordinary grassroots would more readily understand. Haughey was piped into the Royal Dublin Society's auditorium, not far from the British embassy in affluent Dublin 4, by a trade union band to the air of "A Nation Once Again," the hymn of nationalist Ireland. He followed that with a speech that for the first time rejected the traditional goal shared by the British and the Irish governments of securing an internal settlement. Northern Ireland, he told the wildly cheering delegates, had "as a political entity, failed and . . . a new beginning was needed."[7]

ACCOMPANIED BY cabinet colleagues, Haughey traveled to Downing Street for talks with the new British prime minister, Margaret Thatcher, in May 1980. This teapot diplomacy, so named after the silver-plated gift that Haughey brought as a present for Thatcher, launched the Anglo-Irish approach to Northern Ireland. Although it was to culminate five years later in the Hillsborough agreement, the diplomacy also contained the germs of ideas that would re-emerge during the peace process dressed in Sinn Fein garments. In a Dail debate after the Downing Street summit, for example, Haughey obliquely introduced the idea of an all-party conference if the British were to make a declaration expressing their interest in ultimate Irish unity. "If that interest were declared," he told TDs, "we could then start working together, the Government here, the British Government and Irishmen of every tradition in the North towards a solution which will guarantee permanent peace and stability."[8]

The proposal for an all-Ireland conference was hardened up between 1983 and 1984, during sittings of the New Ireland Forum in Dublin, a body set up by constitutional nationalists to meet what was widely perceived to be the burgeoning threat from Sinn Fein's growing electoral strength in the North and its alarming potential to cause political instability in the South.

In his contribution to the forum report, Haughey made clear that in his view the way to achieve unity would be for Britain to respond positively to proposals for an all-party conference at which unionists and nationalists would thrash out the institutional details and constitution for the whole island. Sinn Fein could attend, but only if the IRA ended its violence and the party renounced violence. This was one of the central proposals contained in the later secret British correspondence with Adams. It had been borrowed wholesale from the Fianna Fail leader and made British policy, at least in the private diplomacy with the Sinn Fein leader.

But that was not all. During one private, unreported session of the forum in October 1983 Haughey produced a formulation on the crucial issue of unionist consent whose ambiguity was later borrowed almost entirely by Gerry Adams. Its significance was that it opened the door to a reinterpretation of the consent principle that would allow Adams to accept the unionist right to self-determination and thus to accept, if only in a de facto sense, the existence of the Northern Ireland state. In his address to the forum,

Haughey said, "As regards the veto—the constitutional guarantee [to unionists]—we should make a clear distinction on consent. Consent is only applicable to arrangements on a new Ireland. But consent by the Unionists to British action to find a solution is not required."

By the end of 1984 Haughey had articulated three of the principal features of what would eventually become the Sinn Fein peace strategy. His denunciation of Northern Ireland as a "failed entity," his call on the British to declare their interest in seeing Ireland united, and his proposal for an all-Ireland constitutional conference were all vital ingredients in the mix.

But it was Haughey's assertive style with the British that gave his politics the color that Adams and Reid needed. In 1982, for instance, he had refused to endorse Britain's military expedition against the Argentinean invaders of the Malvinas, or Falkland Islands, and when the SS *Belgrano* was sunk he reasserted Irish neutrality at the United Nations, much to the fury of Mrs. Thatcher and the delight of Irish republicans, of the Provisional as well as the Fianna Fail variety.

His opposition to an internal Northern Ireland settlement was given tangible expression that same year when he appointed the SDLP deputy leader, Seamus Mallon, to the Irish Senate, even though British law barred Mallon from sitting in the locally elected Stormont Assembly at the same time. An embarrassed British administration was forced to expel Mallon from its own parliament. He publicly accused the Duke of Norfolk of being a British spy and regularly lambasted the Fine Gael leader Garret FitzGerald for a weak-kneed attitude to the Thatcher government, on one occasion accusing him of colluding and secretly collaborating with the British on security matters.

A year after the Hillsborough agreement had been signed, Haughey was the first mainstream politician to complain that the deal had not only failed in its declared objective of improving the lot of Northern Nationalists but that "the position of Nationalists in the North has, in fact, seriously worsened." Whatever the private thoughts of Gerry Adams and his closest colleagues about the Hillsborough deal, this was an echo of what they too were saying in public.

By December 1986, two months before Haughey was to take power for the fourth and last time, Adams was able to tell Fianna Fail's newspaper, the *Irish Press*, that he regarded the taoiseach-to-be as "a genuine Nationalist."[9] Haughey's role during the 1981 hunger strike—an accessory along with Fine Gael's Garret FitzGerald "to the legalised murder of ten true and committed Irishmen,"[10] according to the IRA prisoners' statement at the end of the protest—was forgotten.

Haughey's forceful brand of Irish nationalism appalled significant sections of Irish political society, but it was precisely this quality that allowed Adams and Father Reid to contemplate advancing the fledgling peace process in the mid- to late 1980s. Haughey was the right man, in the right place, at the right time. Had any other recent Fianna Fail leader, from Jack Lynch onward, been taoiseach at this time, it is likely the project nursed by Adams and Reid would have been stillborn.

HAUGHEY'S LEADERSHIP of the Irish government and his forceful brand of nationalist politics made possible the next seminal moment in the Irish peace process, one kept a tightly guarded secret until now by all the participants, not least because once again, as with the secret British diplomacy, it signaled not just the private desire of Gerry Adams for an end to the IRA's violence but his willingness to accept a settlement that fell short of what most republicans would find acceptable, from the Army Council to the Volunteers on the streets of Belfast, Derry, and South Armagh.

So it was that sometime in the second week of May 1987, the editor of the *Irish Press*, Tim Pat Coogan, delivered a lengthy written message from Father Alec Reid to Charles Haughey, containing Gerry Adams's terms for an IRA cease-fire. It was a remarkable document whose message said not just that an opportunity existed to call an IRA cease-fire but that if the enterprise was handled properly, the proposal brought by the Redemptorist priest on behalf of the Sinn Fein leader could mean taking the gun out of nationalist politics forever.

As Reid explained the initiative, it became clear that he was communicating not just on his behalf or on Adams's but on behalf of the Irish Catholic Church as well. The enterprise, he explained, had been endorsed by the Redemptorist order in Ireland and by other senior church figures, most notably Cardinal O Fiaich, who would give political cover to Haughey if the dialogue were ever publicized. It had been developed after lengthy thought and debate, Reid said, which involved church figures talking widely to key figures in the nationalist and unionist communities. The message the church had received, he said, was the same from everyone. As the body with the required resources, influence, and access to power centers, it should and would try to get this peace initiative under way.

Since the church's aim was primarily to bring the IRA's violence to an end, it had made a priority of approaching Gerry Adams, Reid explained. Adams also had told them that the church could play an important role in finding the ways and means of ending the armed struggle but that there was no

chance of persuading the IRA to do this unless there was unrestricted dialogue with fellow nationalists aimed at formulating a strong political alternative to the armed struggle involving all Ireland's nationalist parties. Only
in that way, Adams had told them, could the peace initiative succeed.

This was the kernel of the Reid-Adams initiative: the creation of a pan-
nationalist axis whose political clout would be greater than the IRA's and
sufficiently strong to persuade the hard men of the organization to lay
down their weapons. For this reason Haughey was being approached in his
capacity as Fianna Fail leader, Reid explained, not just because he was
taoiseach. The dialogue, if it ever happened, would initially be between Sinn
Fein and Fianna Fail, with the church acting as a neutral host and facilitator. Even the start of such a dialogue, Reid suggested, would be sufficient to
influence the course of the armed struggle, and once it was under way, he
believed, the IRA would respond and cooperate positively.

Sinn Fein, he said, had consistently told him that republicans would fully
cooperate with the church in the search for what became known as "the
alternative method" to armed struggle. They, or rather Gerry Adams, had
also given a number of pledges, should the dialogue start. Adams would not
insist on any preconditions either officially or unofficially and promised
that all their dealings would be treated in the strictest confidence; there
would be no question of Sinn Fein's leaking embarrassing details for political advantage. The peace initiative would be given the highest priority by
the Sinn Fein leader, the necessary resources and energy would be devoted
to it, and Sinn Fein promised to "engage constructively"[11] with anyone the
church decided should be involved in the dialogue.

Reid went on to tell the Fianna Fail leader that Sinn Fein would accept
any settlement that came out of a properly structured process, even if it fell
short of its stated aim of achieving a socialist Ireland. The goal of the IRA's
armed struggle, he had been told, was not the creation of a thirty-two-
county socialist republic; rather, it was to establish the right of all the Irish
people to decide their own political future in free negotiations, the so-called
right of national self-determination. The goal of socialism was a political
one that Sinn Fein would pursue by political methods only.

This was an important and revealing concession. The move to the left
during the 1970s had been constructed by Adams and his allies in Cage 11
as part of a strategy to capture the movement. By 1987, however, the need
to make an alliance with Fianna Fail dictated a compensating move in the
other direction—socialism would be discarded in the interests of advancing
this new Adams strategy. The underlying message to Haughey and others

involved in the process was that pragmatism would determine the flow of events, not dogged adherence to political ideology.

Adams did have certain bottom lines in negotiation, however, Reid explained. The most crucial was that nationalists and unionists should be able to negotiate their political and constitutional future free of dictation from the British, and as long as this principle was honored, Sinn Fein would be content with whatever shape the agreed settlement took.

It was at this point that the Reid-Adams enterprise dovetailed with the secret British correspondence with the Sinn Fein leader. The British had told Adams that while physical withdrawal from Northern Ireland was out of the question, they would promise not to interfere or dictate the terms of any settlement reached by unionists and nationalists; they would withdraw politically, in other words. It was all very Jesuitical, but by the late spring of 1987 Adams was approaching Haughey with the very same idea and sought his cooperation in making this a public and formally acknowledged policy of the British government.

Adams wanted the British to implement this promise, Reid said, in a practical fashion by declaring in some convincing way their willingness to set aside section 75 of the Government of Ireland Act (1920), the legislation that formalized the partition settlement. This section gave the British parliament supreme authority over Northern Ireland, in effect saying that Britain could veto the wishes of the people of Northern Ireland even if their representatives reached political agreement. As long as a majority favored staying in the union, this was not an issue, but theoretically it could be used to thwart a vote in favor of Irish unity.

This was to be the revised and reinterpreted version of British withdrawal, the centerpiece of the Reid-Adams initiative: a declaration of constitutional disinterest and a promise not to dictate or influence the outcome of the all-party talks. If the British withdrew the legal claim of veto over the people of Northern Ireland, in other words, then Sinn Fein would be content to view this as the culmination and realization of the IRA's goals, for which, by that time, it had waged some seventeen years of killing, shooting, and bombing.

In practice, Reid said, Sinn Fein would accept a promise from the British to repeal the offending section of the 1920 act after agreement had been reached in negotiations between unionists and nationalists, not before. The traditional republican model for British withdrawal foresaw the all-party conference happening once the British had at least declared their intention of leaving Northern Ireland. In Adams's new version, the conference would happen first, and then the British would make good their declaration.

The Sinn Fein leader had added an important qualification to all this, Reid told Haughey. The British did not have to withdraw immediately or even in the foreseeable future. In fact Sinn Fein wanted the British to remain, and would insist that they did, in order to oversee the practical details of implementing any agreed settlement.

Then came the central message from Reid to Haughey: if the British agreed to do this, the IRA would declare a cease-fire. The IRA's long war would come to an end, and in a much more definitive fashion than any of the short-lived and doomed cease-fires of the 1970s.

Once representatives of nationalist and unionist opinion were able to meet freely without a British veto hanging over their heads, then, as far as Sinn Fein was concerned, all options for a settlement of the national question would be on the table. Sinn Fein would at that point abide by negotiating arrangements that would guarantee unionists their heritage and culture in accordance with their right of consent and the right of consent of the Irish people as a whole. This was Gerry Adams's way of recognizing the integrity of the Northern Ireland state and of opening the way to Sinn Fein eventually helping to govern it.

IT WAS AN EXTRAORDINARY offer. The Reid-Adams principle married the separate and conflicting concepts of all-Ireland and Northern Ireland–based self-determination, and in practice that would mean accepting the outcome of separate referenda held in the two divided parts of Ireland, albeit on the same day, which is precisely what happened in the weeks following the signing of the Good Friday Agreement in April 1998, eleven years after the astonishing offer to Haughey was made. Traditional republican theology held that self-determination had to mean the Irish people voting as one unit; in the message from Father Reid, Adams was saying that he would accept two separate votes and, crucially, that they would have equal value. If the North voted differently from the South, then he would accept this. It was setting established republican dogma on its head, and substituting heresy for orthodoxy.

Although senior republicans like Gerry Adams continue to deny to this day that they have conceded the right of a majority in the North to maintain the link with Britain, in practice the unionist majority,[12] the subtle, ambiguous formula devised by Father Reid and the Sinn Fein president meant that they had. Sinn Fein, under Adams, was a little like a team of soccer players who strongly object to the offside rule but agree, nevertheless, to play in the cup final.

There was an important sense in which the proposal was based on fantasy. It assumed that the British would want to frustrate the will of the people of Northern Ireland, even if they did vote themselves into a united and independent Ireland. It was clear from a variety of public statements over the years of the Troubles that they would do no such thing. They had said as much in 1973, before the Sunningdale agreement, and again in 1985 when the principle of consent, both for the union and against it, had been written into law when the Hillsborough Agreement had been signed by Margaret Thatcher and Garret FitzGerald. But the great achievement of Adams and Reid was that they had fashioned a wording that enabled Sinn Fein to join the ranks of constitutional nationalism while preserving the outward aspects of the party's traditional uncompromising brand of republicanism. As an instrument for keeping the Provisionals united and the rank and file unaware of the true implications of the peace process, it was almost perfect.

All this was a preamble to the core proposal that Reid had brought from Belfast. It was for what the rest of the world would soon call a pan-nationalist front, an alliance of Irish nationalist parties, North and South, that would try to agree a common policy on the North. What this meant, said Reid, was that the three principal parties—Fianna Fail, the SDLP, and Sinn Fein—must agree at a minimum to press the British to remove their right of veto from the Government of Ireland Act.

Reid outlined two ways in which the enterprise could be advanced. Either the church could host face-to-face talks between Sinn Fein and Fianna Fail, whose confidentiality the church would underwrite, or the church could mediate between Fianna Fail and Sinn Fein in a bid to devise ways in which direct dialogue between them could begin.

There was one immediate problem with the Reid-Adams proposal. It was not entirely clear in what circumstances the IRA would declare a cease-fire. Reid seemed to outline two scenarios for an end to armed struggle—one when the British agreed to remove their veto from the Government of Ireland Act, the other when the pan-nationalist alliance was formed. It was clear that the chronology outlined by Reid-Adams envisaged the latter happening first, but just when would the IRA cease-fire start?[13] It was a loose thread in an otherwise finely woven garment.

This, in its essentials, was the blueprint of the Irish peace process, and with variations and amendments, and not necessarily in the order originally envisaged, it was the plan that was eventually implemented.

It would be quite wrong to say that with this message from Alec Reid the peace process was full-fledged, but its shape had been sketched out, a road map of sorts indicated, and the parameters of the historic but still secret ideological compromise that Gerry Adams was prepared to make clearly identified. There was a great deal of distrust to overcome, much of it caused by the IRA's post-*Eksund* campaign of violence. Like the British, the Haughey government noted the gulf between what Gerry Adams and Alec Reid preached and what the IRA practiced.

At the time, according to one informed source, it never occurred to Haughey or his advisers to ask Adams if he had the backing of the Army Council for the initiative. Like the British, they assumed Adams would never take such a dangerous course unless he had the informed support of his leadership colleagues. Had they known that the process was, at this stage, as much a secret from the IRA leadership as it was to everyone else, the Reid enterprise might well have suffered an early and precipitate ending. But as it was, the question was never asked.

The process was full of difficulties, not least the need to overcome Irish and British government doubts about the IRA's real intentions. One great obstacle was Margaret Thatcher. Few of those involved believed that movement along the lines sketched by Reid-Adams would be possible as long as she was British prime minister, as one of Haughey's key aides, Martin Mansergh, was to write later: "I was always fairly clear that there was little hope of an end to belligerence in Ireland while she remained British prime minister."[14] He and everyone else would have to wait until November 1990 before she left the political stage. But the important point about Father Reid's overture to Haughey was that it contained an unmistakably strong signal that Adams knew where he wanted to go, and even if the how was still a little hazy, the ending of armed struggle by the IRA was clearly now on the agenda.

Faced with two options by Father Reid—one of direct dialogue with Adams, the other indirect dialogue facilitated by the Redemptorist order—Haughey chose the safer and, as he had in 1981, chose to talk to Adams indirectly. With the history of the Arms Trial hanging over him, Haughey calculated that the risk of exposure was too great and that the slightest leak could destroy him. He kept the Reid approach secret from cabinet colleagues and particularly from his coalition partners, the Progressive Democrats, who were led by his deadly enemy, Des O'Malley, a determined foe from the Arms Trial days.

Haughey's decision caused the first crisis in the enterprise. Adams made a desperate plea to Haughey for face-to-face meetings, but to no avail, as one well-informed source told the author. "Adams was looking for [face-to-face talks] on the basis that if he was going to go to the IRA—and he said he would go to individual active-service units if necessary—he would have to be able to tell them that he had looked Haughey in the eye and that Haughey had assured him that this would be the policy of the Irish government."[15] Cardinal O Fiaich even offered a room at Maynooth College, Ireland's principal seminary, where the two men could meet discreetly. But the proposal was too risky, and Haughey declined. The prospect of a speedy IRA cease-fire receded.

Known as *An Sagairt*, the Irish word for priest, in the code language worked out by Adams and the Redemptorist priest, Reid had come to see Haughey armed with a detailed, worked-out strategy, which he called "A Concrete Proposal for a Political Strategy for Justice and Peace."[16] Spread over three documents, "A Concrete Proposal" drew together all the various strands of the secret discussions between the Reid group, Sinn Fein, and the British, as well as the ideas developed by Haughey.

One paper set out the six fundamental principles that would underpin the strategy. Two of these crucially redefined the principle of Irish national self-determination to embrace the need for unionist consent. The idea behind Reid's proposal was that if the project went ahead, then the three nationalist parties would agree to subscribe to the principle. The real significance of this is that it meant that Sinn Fein and the IRA would agree to abide by something that republicans had traditionally abjured and waged war to resist. Another key principle encapsulated the new definition of British withdrawal. By agreeing to this, republicans would formally abandon the IRA goal of ejecting Britain from Northern Ireland by force.

A second document suggested twelve "stepping stones,"[17] as they were called, toward an agreement among Irish nationalists on a peace strategy.

These were as follows:

- An agreement in principle that there should be a joint Nationalist strategy
- An agreement in principle that peace can only come with the free, independent and democratic consent of the Irish people
- An agreement in principle that the aim of the strategy should be to design and create a New Ireland with a new Constitution
- An agreement in principle that the Irish people as a whole should design this new Constitution in unfettered dialogue amongst themselves
- An agreement that the Irish people consist of two traditions, Unionist and Nationalist

- An agreement in principle that consent must be two-fold in nature, requiring agreement from both Unionists and Nationalists
- An agreement in principle that this two-fold consent can only be achieved by political dialogue
- An agreement in principle that the framework for dialogue would be a Constitutional Conference that would sit on a semi-permanent basis until final agreement about Ireland's future had been reached. Membership of the Conference would be through direct election and it was hoped that both Unionist and Nationalist parties would attend. The British, the Irish government, Sinn Fein, other Irish Nationalists and the Unionists would agree the arrangements for the Conference.
- An agreement in principle that the British would withdraw from the central decision-making process in Northern Ireland
- An agreement in principle amongst Sinn Fein and the other Nationalist parties that they would agree to try to persuade the British to make a declaration containing five points:
    (i)   That they will set aside the 1920 Government of Ireland Act when agreement is reached in the Constitutional Conference;
    (ii) That they will say they have no selfish interest in remaining in Ireland
    (iii) That they will facilitate the Constitutional Conference;
    (iv) That they will not interfere in or dictate to the Conference;
    (v)   That if there is an agreement then the British will implement it in law.
- An agreement in principle that an advisory committee representing the leadership of the main Nationalist parties be set up to examine how best to implement and propagandise this strategy and win support for it in Ireland and abroad
- An agreement in principle, although couched in more discreet language, that Sinn Fein would try to win approval for the strategy from the IRA.[18]

All twelve "stepping stones" would in time be incorporated into the peace process, though with variations and modifications. The British declaration, for instance, became a British-Irish joint declaration after it grew clear that the British would make no promises about the fate of the Government of Ireland Act until the Irish agreed to amend articles 2 and 3 of Eamon de Valera's 1937 constitution, which formally expressed the Republic's territorial claim over Northern Ireland.

The leaders' advisory committee would, in later documents, become first a nationalist "Convention," which would advise on the steps necessary to achieve democratic self-determination, and then finally the Forum for Peace and Reconciliation, set up in Dublin after the 1994 IRA cease-fire. An entirely nationalist body, the forum was designed to introduce Sinn Fein to the civilities of constitutional politics.

The problem of how Charles Haughey should proceed with the dialogue with Gerry Adams yet keep him at arm's length was a difficult one, but the solution was eventually found in the structure of the strategy itself. Reid and Adams wanted to involve the main Northern nationalist party, the SDLP, and in particular its leader, John Hume, in the enterprise, and it was through Hume that Haughey's difficulty was overcome.

At the same time that Reid had sent his lengthy message to Haughey, in May 1987, he dispatched a similar document to the Derry office of the SDLP leader. Hume responded cautiously. He had done one favor for Reid before, according to Tom King, when he had pressed the then NI secretary to give a private assurance of Britain's neutrality to Adams, but the Reid letter was the first formal request to Hume to involve himself fully in the process.

Hume met Reid several times, first in June 1987 and then in August and again in September, before agreeing in December 1987 to meet Adams. Like the Fianna Fail leader, Hume was cautious about supping too close to the Provos. As all this was happening, Haughey was putting together his own alternative to the face-to-face dialogue demanded by Adams. The proposal was simple: he would suspend his direct involvement and instead nominate John Hume to represent him and to act as a sort of go-between for the Irish government. This would solve the problem of having to meet Adams directly while preserving the initiative. Adams protested angrily, but he had little choice. He agreed, on one condition, to which Haughey readily assented: the communication line between him and Haughey through Father Reid would remain active, while Haughey would promise to reinvolve himself if and when necessary.[19] There was another condition that Haughey insisted upon. The dialogue between him, Reid, and Adams was to be kept hidden from the SDLP for fear that it would be leaked and Haughey ruined. Hume was deliberately not told about the contacts and for long afterward believed that his subsequent meetings with Adams marked the start of the peace process. In retrospect this was a key moment, for it gave the peace process an identity it did not entirely deserve. Thereafter the process would be known as the Hume-Adams process, and with that the SDLP leader was set on the path that would eventually lead to a Nobel Peace Prize and international acclaim. The choice of Hume as Haughey's representative had an unexpected bonus. The SDLP leader's association with the Reid-Adams enterprise gave it a level of acceptability it otherwise would have lacked, especially in the Republic, where Hume's standing was exceptionally high. Haughey began the Irish part of the peace process, but Hume gave it respectability.

It was at this point that Haughey brought in his talented Northern adviser, Martin Mansergh, a former diplomat in the Department of Foreign Affairs whom Haughey had made his principal point of communication with Northern parties. There then began a partnership that was to last for more than a decade in which the Redemptorist priest would carry written and oral messages between Adams in Belfast and Mansergh in Dublin, who would in turn analyze and pass them on to his political master, Haughey at first and, in later years, Albert Reynolds and then Bertie Ahern.

Much to the anger of the unionists and the great surprise of the rest of the world, the first of a series of talks between Sinn Fein and the SDLP took place on January 11, 1988, at Clonard Monastery. It was the public working out of the secret agreement arrived at by the nationalist leaders. For two hours Hume and Adams discussed and agreed arrangements for wider negotiations involving delegations from each side. The meeting had been requested by "a third party interested in creating political dialogue," the two men said in a veiled reference to Alec Reid. As always the Redemptorist's role would remained cloaked in shadow.

In March the delegations met at the Redemptorists' retreat house, St. Gerard's on Belfast's Antrim Road. Adams was accompanied by three key allies—Danny Morrison, a fellow Army Council member and director of publicity for both the IRA and Sinn Fein; Mitchel McLaughlin, a veteran Sinn Fein member from Derry; and Tom Hartley, a former Sinn Fein press officer from West Belfast and a driving force behind the bid to politicize the Provisionals. It was a carefully balanced delegation. Adams and Morrison represented the Army, but the image presented by McLaughlin and Hartley to the outside world and certainly to the SDLP was of figures who had spent their republican careers entirely in Sinn Fein with no or next to no involvement in IRA matters.

Hume came with his own top team: Seamus Mallon, his County Armagh-born deputy; the university lecturer Sean Farren, one of Hume's closest confidants; and Austin Currie, a somewhat independently minded figure from County Tyrone who could trace his political genesis back to the old

Nationalist Party. There were five more meetings that year, in March, May, June, July, and September. One meeting was a private head-to-head between Hume and Adams; otherwise the party delegations were involved. Haughey agreed to send Mansergh and a junior TD, Dermot Ahern, to low-level meetings with Sinn Fein, which took place in the Redemptorist house in Dundalk with Father Reid present. Two such meetings happened, one in May, the other in June.

With hindsight the curious feature of the talks is the extent to which they were conducted in public. In sharp contrast to the secret diplomacy that had occurred from 1982 and 1983 onward, each session of the 1988 Sinn Fein–SDLP talks was known about almost as soon as it had taken place, courtesy of detailed briefings to the media. After the first meeting, both Hume and Adams readily agreed to be interviewed by the author and other journalists. Adams, for instance, used the interviews to call speculation that a cease-fire was on the agenda "mischievous and erroneous" and denied that Haughey knew about the meeting beforehand or that Hume had come armed with what he termed "concrete proposals."[20] In April documents that had been exchanged by the parties were leaked at a high level to the author and published in the *Sunday Tribune*.[21] In September, when the talks officially concluded, both sides made their respective papers public, and these were reproduced in full in the *Irish Times*.[22]

The structure of the talks raised questions about the reason for the publicity and whether more would have been achieved had the two parties kept their dialogue secret, as they very soon did. Not least of the advantages of maintaining secrecy was that both Hume and Adams would have avoided the very extensive unease that emerged in their respective parties as a result of the publicity surrounding the meetings.

The Sinn Fein–SDLP talks did, however, make one significant achievement; activists in both parties became accustomed to the notion that once deep and bitter enemies could sit around the same table and talk. The dialogue also managed to introduce into nationalist and republican political discourse many of the key concepts and language of the peace process. Seen as a conditioning process, the 1988 talks between the SDLP and Sinn Fein make a great deal of sense.

ALMOST AS SOON AS the public talks ended, the private dialogue between Adams and Hume started, and this continued in secret for five years, until one Saturday morning in April 1993, when Gerry Adams and Father Alec Reid met John Hume in his house in Derry, on the edge of the

Bogside and in circumstances that almost guaranteed that someone would see them. They were spotted and the story was made public. A statement subsequently issued by the two men used the precise language of Reid's "Concrete Proposal." They were engaged, they said, "in a political dialogue aimed at investigating the possibility of developing an overall political strategy to establish peace and justice."[23]

Although hopes were high that progress could still be made, the reality was that the year 1988 had seen the process falter. The promise of an IRA cease-fire held out in Father Reid's first messages to Haughey and to Hume in the spring of 1987 had not been fulfilled. The intensity of the IRA's military campaign was such as to deter the British from taking any more risks, while in nationalist Ireland the conviction grew, as Martin Mansergh was to say later, that the Provisionals still had some distance to travel. "Both the SDLP and Fianna Fail," he wrote, "formed the view separately that northern republicans were not then ready to end their campaign, and that the primary aim of any continuing dialogue was to end their political isolation and build a broad front."[24] Neither party was prepared to accept that outcome, he added.

ALTHOUGH CONSIDERABLE progress had been made in advancing the theology and in shoring up the political foundations of the peace process, the truth was that Adams and his supporters still had an enormously long way to go before they could persuade, maneuver, or cajole the IRA to accept a cessation. None of the mainstream nationalist parties were aware that the Army Council had been kept in the dark about much of the process prior to the talks with the SDLP or that the details of the Reid-Adams proposals were still a secret to all but Adams and his close advisers. It had taken Adams and his supporters in the Provisionals five years to overthrow and remove the O Bradaigh–O Conaill leadership and to move the Provisionals into electoral politics. It would take a lot longer to end the armed struggle.

The peace process did not quite end when the SDLP and Sinn Fein concluded their public dialogue. Not only did Hume and Adams continue to meet regularly and in secret—the first meeting, at the invitation of the Redemptorist superior in Ireland took place in the order's Dublin house within weeks of the official ending of the dialogue—but in October an extraordinary event by the standards of 1988 took place at a private conference in the German town of Duisburg in the Ruhr valley.

Four of Northern Ireland's senior politicians were there. Peter Robinson, the shrewd, ascetic deputy to the Reverend Ian Paisley, represented the hard-line DUP; Jack Allen, a gregarious publican from Derry, came from the largest unionist group, the Ulster Unionists; Austin Currie came from the SDLP; and Gordon Mawhinney, the deputy leader of Alliance, represented the moderate, middle-of-the-road liberals. The weekend conference had been organized by Irish and German churchmen in an attempt to get peace talks going back in Belfast. The meeting had the blessing of the party leaders, and hopes for a breakthrough were high.

What made the gathering doubly significant was the attendance of Father Alec Reid, who participated as the representative of Gerry Adams, albeit an unofficial one. All the participants knew beforehand that he was to be there as someone familiar with the views of Sinn Fein, and so did their party leaders. His presence kept the unionists in terror of discovery for months afterward. At that time, talking to Sinn Fein was possibly the most unforgivable sin in the book, and even being in the same room as a surrogate figure like Reid would have caused an outcry.

At that stage the prospect of participating in political talks did not concern Sinn Fein or Gerry Adams—the IRA's raging war ruled that out. But Reid was there to give the unionists a highly important message, as one account of the weekend conference recorded:

> Alec Reid spoke of the two traditions and how essential it was to enter into a dialogue with the right spirit. It was a Republican tradition to use violence but if we do [sic] enter dialogue he was certain that we would find that they were not so difficult. In his view the Republican Movement must be dealt with—it represents the views of the Nationalist people. They are pursuing the right of the Irish people to determine their own future and would pursue that right by political means if given reasonable opportunity.[25]

As a political event the Duisburg conference was a sideshow, but its significance was twofold: the Sinn Fein leadership was signaling a willingness to join the mainstream, while the readiness of unionists to accept Father Reid showed that they were not entirely appalled at the prospect. Everyone knew that if Sinn Fein wanted to become constitutional politicians, the IRA's campaign had to end.

The peace process hadn't stopped, but it had slowed down, and further movement was spasmodic. Hume and Adams met only four times in 1989, as the IRA's post-*Eksund* "Tet offensive" worked its way through failure and one setback after another. In February 1989 Haughey made another bid to advance the "stepping stones" strategy when he told the Fianna Fail

Ard Fheis that an end to the IRA's violence could dramatically change things. Using language that could have been taken wholesale from the Reid document, Haughey said that such a development

> would open up, as it did in the New Ireland Forum, the possibility for a broad consensus among Nationalists on how to achieve political stability based on justice. Our efforts, supported by a large majority of Irish people everywhere, could then be constructively directed to persuading our Unionist countrymen that their future lay with us in a partnership of equals and in convincing the British government that the future of Ireland could and should be left to all the Irish people to decide for themselves.[26]

This was the Reid-Adams formula for national self-determination, almost word for word.

Later that year Hume incorporated Reid's twofold consent formula into a practical proposal, suggesting to his party conference in November that any political settlement agreed by the Northern parties and the two governments should be put to the whole Irish people in twin referenda, held in the separate jurisdictions on the same day. Such a proposal, which Hume had first floated way back in 1981, would mean, he said, that from a nationalist/republican viewpoint "for the first time the people of this island would have expressed self-determination on how we live together."[27] It would also remove, at a stroke, the basis for the IRA's opposition to the 1921 settlement, rooted as that was in the fact that the unionists had flouted the principle of all-Ireland self-determination.

It was around the same time that the Northern Ireland secretary, Peter Brooke, chose to make his neutrality speech, directing it at Gerry Adams and his allies from the heart of his constituency in Westminster. Such a public declaration had been the missing part of the secret British correspondence, but now Brooke was rectifying that omission. Offering Sinn Fein a full political role in Northern Ireland's affairs if the IRA's violence ended, Brooke tackled two of the issues raised in Alec Reid's "stepping stones" document. "The British Government," he said, "has no selfish strategic or economic interests in Northern Ireland; our role is to help, enable and encourage. Britain's purpose, as I have sought to describe it, is not to occupy, oppress or exploit but to ensure democratic debate and free democratic choice."[28] Reid had said the British would need to declare their neutrality and agree to sponsor a dialogue with which they would not interfere. Peter Brooke had delivered. Slowly the "stepping stones" were being laid.

ALTHOUGH THE PEACE PROCESS was moving forward, its speed was not much faster than a glacier's, and nearly everyone agreed on the reason for that. As long as Margaret Thatcher was British prime minister, Adams could never deliver the IRA leadership or grassroots. IRA supporters would condemn even the suggestion of a deal with Thatcher as surrender. Nor could the participants be confident that a declaration of the sort outlined in the Reid-Adams proposal from Thatcher's lips would carry any weight in the Provo heartlands. The hatred between them was just too deep. Suddenly, three weeks after Brooke's "neutrality" speech, the logjam was removed and the glacier picked up speed. An internal Tory Party crisis forced Thatcher to resign, and with her went the last, great obstacle to an IRA cease-fire.

Thatcher's departure revived the process. Her successor, John Major, was by and large an unknown quantity on Northern Ireland, but in its way this was an advantage. The fact that he carried no political baggage on the Northern Ireland issue meant that he could, if he wanted, be more flexible and even imaginative in his approach. There was also an important change in the bureaucracy. At the Northern Ireland Office, John Chilcot became the new permanent secretary. A former British Home Office official, Chilcot had little difficulty buying into the theory of the peace process and quickly grasped what Adams was attempting to achieve. He constructed his own pipeline into the process via John Hume, and through that contact Chilcot would also get to know Adams's mind. Along with his talented deputy, Quentin Thomas, and the British cabinet secretary, Sir Robin Butler, the three officials were to make up the British negotiators during the tortuous road to the 1994 cease-fire.

Despite Thatcher's fall and Brooke's neutrality declaration, progress was still painfully slow. In Dublin the process had stalled. Haughey and Hume distrusted Adams's motives, made suspicious by his failure to deliver on earlier promises of an IRA cease-fire, and the talking had slowed down. Neither man was aware at that stage that Adams's foray into the peace diplomacy had been undertaken *without* the Army Council's knowledge or approval and that his every step had to be carefully measured. By 1990 the Redemptorists wanted to withdraw Father Reid from the process amid fears about his health, but Haughey had urged them to persist and they relented.

Finally, in the early part of 1991, Haughey was spurred to action. He assembled his own team of Irish civil servants to spearhead a new initiative, choosing to extend knowledge of the peace process beyond his private office. Dermot Nally, an experienced diplomat whose involvement in Northern Ireland matters went back twenty years, headed the team. He was secretary to Haughey's cabinet, the Irish equivalent of Sir Robin Butler. Despite his distaste for the Department of Foreign Affairs [DFA], Haughey decided to include two of its senior officials, Noel Dorr, who headed the DFA, and Sean O hUiginn, a senior official in the Anglo-Irish division whose remorseless logic would irritate the British and earn him the sobriquet "The Dark Prince." O hUiginn, from Boho in County Mayo, had been the first Irish joint secretary to the Anglo-Irish secretariat. Opposite him, representing the British, sat Mark Elliott, the Foreign Office official whose trips to Derry were so secret only manuscript records were made of them.

In the autumn of 1991 Hume and Adams produced the first draft of a model joint British-Irish government declaration incorporating, inasmuch as they affected the British, Reid's "stepping stones." Mansergh and O hUiginn made changes, and when John Major traveled to Dublin for his first Anglo-Irish summit in December 1991, Charles Haughey handed him a copy of this document, known as "Draft 2."

According to its terms the British would say that they had no "selfish, strategic, political or economic interest" in staying in Northern Ireland and that they wished only to see the Irish people live together "in unity and harmony." Dublin would accept that Irish self-determination was subject to Reid's twofold consent principle and agreed to set up a permanent convention that would advise on ways to exercise self-determination.[29] This would convene whether or not the British agreed to put their name to the declaration. Thus began the complex and often tortuous intergovernmental negotiations that would lead in a mere two years to the Downing Street Declaration.

HAUGHEY'S OFFICIALS had prepared a lengthy list of speaking points, sixteen in all, to present to Major in an effort to win the British premier over to a fundamental reappraisal of Northern Ireland policy. These dwelt on the financial, human, political, and social costs of a conflict that seemed to be unending and that ultimately was in the interests of both governments to resolve and stabilize. Although each politician knew more about the secret peace process than he was prepared to admit, there was only one veiled reference to the clandestine diplomacy that had been going on in the background for over five years. "There are factors working for progress," said one account of the exchange. "There is a strong tide of public opinion in favour of peace in both communities in Northern Ireland and in Ireland as a whole. The futility and horror of violence must surely become more evident even to its proponents with every passing year and we know that at least some of these elements are reflecting on this."[30] Haughey's arguments succeeded, and Major agreed to initiate a comprehensive internal review that the two leaders would consider in the early part of 1992.

The meeting between them never took place. An old scandal concerning the tapping of politicians' and journalists' telephones resurfaced, and in early February 1992 Haughey was forced to resign. Albert Reynolds was chosen by the Fianna Fail parliamentary party to succeed him, and a day later the group of British and Irish civil servants charged with considering the new initiative met at the Cabinet Office in London. Butler, Chilcot, and Thomas told their Irish counterparts there could be no further movement on the initiative until after that year's British general election. Various problems were raised by the British, not least their unwillingness to talk directly to the Provisionals and the difficulties of selling the language contained in "Draft 2" to the unionists.

Those on the British side were less than forthright with the Irish officials about their own lengthy dialogue with Gerry Adams, and made no mention of their complete familiarity with the concepts and language that permeated "Draft 2." The British said they wanted an assurance of an end to violence before committing any more resources to the project. But there was a way ahead, they said. It lay in a British declaration of neutrality and an assurance by the Irish concerning the principle of consent in Northern Ireland. The meeting ended with agreement on those points and on a strategy to deal with any leaks to the media of John Hume's role as an intermediary. But it was a doubtful, uncertain meeting; no one quite knew what the political landscape would look like in a few weeks' time.

As it turned out, Albert Reynolds embraced the peace process with enthusiasm and John Major survived the British general election. Haughey had fully briefed the new taoiseach on the state of play, and Reynolds had immediately agreed to keep Martin Mansergh on his staff. Alec Reid's visit to Government Buildings in Dublin increased, as did the number of meetings between Hume and Adams. In December 1993, after months of exhausting, often frustrating negotiations with the Major administration, the Downing Street Declaration was finally unveiled by the two leaders to a curiously mixed reception in Northern Ireland.[31] While unionists were relaxed about its contents, rank-and-file Provisional supporters were bewildered. Some feared that their leaders had been drawn into a deadly trap from which there could be no escape; none suspected that the declaration had emerged from the secret initiative launched by their own leader.

The reason for their confusion was contained in the declaration's paragraph 4, which incorporated Alec Reid's consent principle, although none of the IRA's supporters who read it could have been aware of that. "The British Government," it said, "agree that it is for the people of the island of Ireland alone, by agreement between the two parts respectively, to exercise their right of self-determination on the basis of consent, freely and concurrently given, North and South, to bring about a united Ireland, if that is their wish."[32]

The declaration was an astonishing document and one of the seminal pieces of Anglo-Irish diplomacy. The fact that it elevated the principle of consent and dictated that this had to be a cornerstone of any Northern Ireland settlement was secondary. The two governments had long agreed on that. What made the Downing Street document exceptional was that it was modeled on ideas and concepts evolved, initiated, and developed in a secret dialogue whose instigator was the head of the political organization pledged to overthrow the principle by gun and bomb.

In June 2006, after a lengthy illness, Haughey finally succumbed to the rigors of prostate cancer and died at his home in Kinsealy where some twenty years earlier he and Father Reid had met to begin the peace process. Haughey's supportive role in the peace process at its most vulnerable and crucial period—at its birth—had rarely been acknowledged in Irish public life, perhaps because it conflicted so starkly with the dark image that his political enemies and many in the Irish media preferred to project. But at his graveside Haughey's protégé and successor as Fianna Fail leader and taoiseach, Bertie Ahern—once famously described by Haughey as "the most clever, the most cunning, the most devious of them all"—paid an overdue tribute to the role Haughey had played in ending the Troubles in the North: "His courageous decision to open a secret channel of communication with the Provisional leadership paved the way to the banishing of the bomb and bullet, North and South, in our time."[33]

TEN

"No Idle Boast"

D ublin's Mansion House has witnessed many dramatic and historic
moments in its nearly three hundred years of life. Built as a town
house in 1710 in the middle of Georgian Dublin by a wealthy
County Derry property developer, Joshua Dawson, it has been the official
residence of the city's lord mayors since 1715. Its famous Round Room,
added to mark the visit of King George IV in 1821, has been the venue for
some of Ireland's most momentous political gatherings. In January 1919 the
First Dail, dominated by the revolutionary Sinn Fein party, met there to ratify the 1916 proclamation and adopt Ireland's Declaration of Independence.
Only twenty-six of the sixty-nine successful Sinn Fein candidates were at liberty to attend the session, and although the British authorities permitted the
rebel parliament to meet, the proceedings were closely monitored from a
building across the road, by the inspector general of the Royal Irish Constabulary, Sir James Byrne, and his Dublin counterpart, Colonel Wedge-
worth Johnston. The Second Dail also convened in the Mansion House more
than two years later but was dissolved after only a year as civil war gathered Ireland in its terrible grip. And it was in the Mansion House that Eamon
de Valera had presaged the civil war when he told delegates to the Sinn Fein
Ard Fheis of October 1921 that "Ireland's representatives will never call
upon the people to swear allegiance to the English King." When a few weeks
later Collins and the Treaty delegates brought home from Downing Street
an agreement requiring just that, Irish republicanism was convulsed by violent division.

More than sixty years later, on November 2, 1986, as once again the
forces of law and order watched events from a safe distance, the Mansion
House was witness to another great Irish political rupture when Provisional
Sinn Fein delegates, after nearly five hours of tense and at times emotional

debate, elected to drop the party's long-standing opposition to taking seats in the Irish parliament. To some in the hall this formal act of recognizing the hated partitionist settlement was a case of déjà vu. The same issue had split the movement in 1969 and 1970, with the IRA and Sinn Fein taking separate but equally divisive stands on the issue. The resulting quarrel had torn the movement apart, and the consequences were violent and long-lasting, leading not just to the formation of the Provisional IRA but also to the creation of a feud culture within republicanism in which ideological differences were often settled by the shedding of blood.

There were, however, key differences this time that would make this split less divisive and provide evidence that Gerry Adams had learned important lessons from the mistaken way Cathal Goulding and his allies had handled the issue in their day. In 1970 Goulding had advocated entering all three partitionist parliaments at the same time—the Dail in Dublin, or Leinster House, as republicans preferred to call it; Stormont in Belfast; and the House of Commons at Westminster.

In 1986 Adams made a much less ambitious proposal to the republican movement. He wanted Sinn Fein to enter only the Irish part of the 1921 settlement, Dail Eireann; the British parts, Stormont and Westminster, would still be off limits. There was no ideological reason for this, since once the principle of abstention was ditched for one assembly it applied to all three. But by advocating entry first into the Dail, a far-off place about which Northern republicans knew little and cared less, Adams minimized likely opposition from Northern IRA units.

Goulding's move also came at a time when his internal critics were complaining that he was running down the IRA's military capacity and had failed to ensure that Catholic districts of Belfast were adequately protected against loyalist attack. No one could level that charge against the Adams-led IRA. The debate on dropping abstentionism came just as the IRA was receiving huge shipments of weaponry from Colonel Qaddafi. Far from running the IRA down, Adams and his colleagues were promising an escalation in both the quality and the quantity of IRA operations, and on such a scale that they could possibly tilt the military and political balance in the IRA's favor. In 1969 the IRA had split after a general Army Convention had voted in favor of the policy switch, but at a similar Convention, held in County Donegal in September 1986, delegates were able to reconcile their differences without a rupture. Reassured by the leadership's promise of an intensified war, most of the delegates who voted against the motion stayed in the IRA's ranks. In 1970 they had walked out.

In 1986 some of those attending the Sinn Fein Ard Fheis did walk out in protest, but they never presented the threat posed by the dissidents of 1969. Led by Ruairi O Bradaigh and other veteran activists, they went on to form Republican Sinn Fein (RSF). Despite the purity of their beliefs, the O Bradaigh wing failed to persuade enough Provisionals to join them. The split was small and contained, confined largely to older republicans, many of whom were based south of the Border miles away from the war zone, where the Provisional IRA still carried the greater appeal for grassroots militants. Although RSF supporters did set up a military wing, such was the fear of reprisals from the Provisionals that it was years before the Continuity IRA revealed its existence. That in itself was a comment on the new group's frailty.

To most delegates and nearly every media representative crammed into the Mansion House that day, there seemed little doubt that the underlying reason for that was the Adams leadership's apparently unswerving support for armed struggle. It had been clear to all in 1969 that Goulding was intent on demilitarizing the republican movement. There was, apart from members of the O Bradaigh–O Conaill wing, no such suspicion by 1986. The debate about abstentionism seemed to be about what the leadership said it was about, an attempt to make Sinn Fein more relevant on the southern side of the Border by abandoning a policy stance that was unpopular with the bulk of voters there.

What only a few in the Mansion House could know was that the Adams leadership had already commenced a secret diplomacy with the leadership of Fianna Fail and that dropping abstentionism was a key part of the strategy. Changing Sinn Fein and IRA policy was in fact vital to the prospects of creating an alliance with Charles Haughey; after all, how could the Fianna Fail chief even contemplate a relationship with Adams as long as the Provisionals rejected the legitimacy of the state he led? The shift would undoubtedly help Sinn Fein win votes, but that would take many years to happen and require an IRA cessation. Primarily, the ending of abstentionism prepared the way for constructive dialogue with Haughey.

When Father Reid sent Haughey his lengthy message in 1987, he cited the outcome of the 1986 Ard Fheis as evidence of the strength of the Sinn Fein leadership and the freedom it had to initiate and organize its own policies. Adams, in other words, was the man with the skills and the trust of the rank and file needed to do the job. "Alec would say," recalled one participant in the peace process, "that not even de Valera or Collins was able to accomplish such a huge shift in policy and get away with what was really an insignificant split and no upheaval worth the name."[1] What he meant, of course, was that while de Valera and Collins had both steered the IRA of their day into constitutional politics, it had been at the cost of serious and bloody splits. Adams was doing the same but largely kept the organization intact. That meant that he might even be able to deliver a fully intact IRA into the peace process.

To the outside world, dropping abstentionism seemed to be the logical conclusion of Adams's efforts to politicize the Provisionals. He had started to move the organization in this direction during the Cage 11 days in the mid-1970s, when he had argued in favor not only of social and economic radicalism but of republican involvement in agitational politics in the South. Throughout the development of this strategy, Adams and his allies had justified it on military grounds. The argument was disarmingly simple; the more republicans identified with the lives and needs of the poorest sections of Southern society, the more support, tacit or otherwise, the IRA would get for the war of national liberation in the North. Adams would use the same argument to urge that abstentionism should be dropped.

In practice, however, it worked the other way around. When Sinn Fein tested the electoral waters in the Republic, the party discovered that the violence of the IRA's campaign and Sinn Fein's associations with the Northern conflict were liabilities. The early toleration of the IRA's campaign in Northern Ireland had virtually disappeared by the late 1970s and had been replaced by a fear that the conflict would spill over the Border, as it had in May 1974, for instance, when loyalist bombs killed thirty-three people in one day in Dublin and Monaghan. Many Southerners blamed the Northern republicans for this and strongly resisted voting for Sinn Fein. Although Sinn Fein attributed this to state censorship, particularly section 31 of the Broadcasting Act, which banned the party from radio and television, the truth was that the IRA and its violent activities were the reason for the party's electoral failure.

Adams's push for involvement in Southern politics began in 1977, not long after his release from Long Kesh. It was there in Jimmy Drumm's "long war" Bodenstown address in June that year and was made explicit in January the following year, by which time Adams had become IRA chief of staff.

As in the North, it was the hunger strikes of 1981 that strengthened Adams sufficiently to enable him to accelerate Sinn Fein's electoral activity south of the Border. H Block candidates had done well in the Republic's general election of June that year when nine of them won nearly 43,000 votes, some 2.5 percent of the electorate, and two won seats, both taken by Long Kesh prisoners. If nonprisoner candidates, pledged to take their seats, had run instead, they would have held the balance of power in the new Dail. Flushed with these victories and the separate successes in the North, delegates to the 1981 Ard Fheis had given the party leadership a free hand in deciding whether to contest future elections, North and South. The first opportunity to do that south of the Border came in February the following year when the FitzGerald government elected in the turbulent summer of 1981 suddenly collapsed.

As it turned out, the election was a disaster for the republicans. Sinn Fein ran in seven constituencies, two fewer than in 1981, and selected a decidedly military-leaning slate. Two of the best-known candidates were IRA prisoners. Joe O'Connell, the leader of the Balcombe Street IRA unit, which had bombed and shot its way around southern England and central London in the mid-1970s, ran in Clare, while Seamus McElwaine, an IRA leader from the Monaghan-Fermanagh Border, then on remand in Crumlin Road jail, Belfast, ran in Cavan-Monaghan. His agent was Caoimhghin O Caolain, a former bank clerk from Monaghan town, who had been talent-spotted by Adams during the hunger strike and subsequently groomed for the seat. He eventually became TD for the constituency in 1997. The overall result revealed a collapse in the H Block vote, from 43,000 votes, or 2.5 percent, to just under 17,000, or 1 percent. The message was clear: Southern voters might come out at an emotional moment and support dying hunger strikers, but otherwise they would spurn the IRA and its political wing. By way of contrast, republicans who had run on a platform of taking their seats did well. Bernadette Devlin-McAliskey tripled the H Block vote in Dublin North-Central, while Sinn Fein's old rivals in the Goulding's Officials, now calling themselves Sinn Fein–The Workers Party, won three seats.

Sinn Fein drew in its horns in 1982 after that poor first result. That Easter the Army Council reaffirmed the traditional disdain of constitutional methods: "Only through armed struggle will we be listened to . . . ," it said.[2] When another Dail election was called in November 1982, Sinn Fein decided not to contest it, conserving its resources for the election to Jim Prior's "rolling" Assembly in Belfast, which was held the month before. Nevertheless, the move toward dropping abstentionism in the South continued apace as Adams and his allies chipped away at the opposition at one Ard Fheis after another. First Sinn Fein agreed to contest European elections—a proposal Adams had resisted when O Bradaigh had suggested it—and to take its seats in the unlikely event of winning. Then it agreed to register as a political party in Dublin, a move that de facto recognized the hated Southern state. At the next conference a motion declaring abstentionism to be a tactic, not a principle, was passed, although short of a large enough majority to change the party's constitution. Slowly, incrementally, the party was moving to end its ban on taking seats in the Irish parliament and recognizing the state that the IRA's predecessors had vowed to destroy.

THE IRA held one of the keys to winning the issue, or rather Colonel Qaddafi did. By October 1986, a month before the Ard Fheis and just after the IRA Convention, the IRA had smuggled some 130 tons of Libyan weaponry into Ireland in four separate shipments and had successfully hidden these in secret dumps in some of the most isolated parts of Ireland. As the Army Convention and the Sinn Fein Ard Fheis neared, the number of key IRA activists who knew that substantial amounts of arms had been successfully landed slowly grew. "People were told there was big gear come in," remembered one IRA member, even if only a select few knew the details.[3] The origin of the arms, the fact that they were a gift from Qaddafi, was still a secret to all but the Army Council. With tons of weaponry stored away and many middle-ranking IRA activists aware that a big offensive was in the pipeline, the notion that Adams was about to sell out just seemed absurd. Colonel Qaddafi had helped make the outcome of the abstention debate a foregone conclusion.

Before going to the Sinn Fein conference with the proposal, Adams first had to win over the IRA. Once that was done, Sinn Fein would be easier to handle. In early 1986 the Army Council set up a special subcommittee to examine the possibility of holding an IRA Convention. When the decision to go ahead was made, it moved very fast. "It was done very hurriedly, in less than two weeks, when normally it would take a month to organize," remembered one delegate.[4] Before the Convention met, the ever-reliable Brian Keenan, by then into his seventh year in various English jails, made his support for Adams known publicly. In a letter to *An Phoblacht– Republican News*, co-signed by three other IRA prisoners held in Britain, Keenan wrote, "It is time for a change to enable elected representatives to carry out revolutionary work in the corridors of power. We do not believe any republican principle is involved in this issue."[5] A secret letter went to the Army Council saying the same thing.

At the Convention, the Adams camp, including Adams himself, argued that a yes vote would assist the armed struggle by broadening the base and producing more safe houses for the IRA. Martin McGuinness predicted that Sinn Fein would win up to five or six seats, and if that happened no government in Dublin would dare move against the IRA. The IRA could launch attacks in the North safe in the knowledge that its rear was secure against assault. Danny Morrison claimed that the dead hunger strikers, especially Bobby Sands, would have voted yes, and Seamus Twomey declared his support for the change. Opposition was strongest from around the Border in South Armagh, Louth, and South Down. But the message from the outgoing IRA Army Council was that the war was going on regardless of how the vote on abstention went, and this swayed the meeting. "The way Adams did it was to say to the IRA men, 'This is politics. You get on with your thing—the war—and it won't be affected,'" remembered another delegate.[6] The Convention was held in a room that sloped downward from the back rather like a cinema; somewhat disconcertingly for the delegates, the leadership sat in the rear seats, watching and noting the speeches and who voted which way.

The vote went three to one in favor, comfortably exceeding the required two-thirds majority. There were two bonuses. The Convention once again upheld General Army Order no. 8, which had prohibited IRA actions against the security forces in the Republic for some forty years. The effect of this would be to reinforce Father Reid's conciliatory message to Haughey. Adams also got a restructured Executive, the first to be elected since 1970 and one much more sympathetic to his politics, at least initially. A small minority eventually left the IRA after the vote, but there was no walkout from the Convention, as there had been in 1969.

ADAMS'S PROBLEM was not with the IRA but with Sinn Fein. The IRA had been under the sway of the Belfast leadership ever since the establishment of Northern Command, and since it was larger in the North the units there would always have a greater say at a Convention. But Sinn Fein was as numerous on the ground in the South as in the North, and feelings in the South were stronger against change. Many of the Southern members of Sinn Fein came from families and backgrounds shaped by the bitter divisions of the civil war in 1922 and they literally hated the system of government in Dublin. The Southerners had stymied Adams at the 1985 Ard Fheis when a move to declare abstentionism a tactic rather than a principle failed to get a two-thirds majority. Having foiled Adams once, they could do it again. The difficulty that Adams and his allies faced was the possibility that they would end up with the same result that Goulding had got in 1969 when the

IRA had voted for the change, but Sinn Fein was against. If sufficient numbers split from Sinn Fein, they could act as a magnet for military dissidents, and the division could worsen. With Father Reid's approach to Haughey building up speed, Adams's need to avoid a big public split in Sinn Fein assumed greater significance.

Just before the Ard Fheis, Adams moved to try and neutralize O Bradaigh, and he used the Libyan weapons to lure his opponent, hinting that a number of big arms shipments had been brought in and that the war effort would be intensified. "Ruairi was told there was good news in that regard," said one source familiar with the meeting.[7] But Adams's efforts to win over O Bradaigh failed. On the day of the debate he again asked to see O Bradaigh and his supporters. They met backstage in the Mansion House at lunchtime, both accompanied by supporters, for what turned out to be a bad-tempered and fruitless encounter. Adams had brought Micky McKevitt along as evidence that even though the powerful quartermaster's department had voted against the change at the Convention, it was nevertheless prepared to stick by the Adams leadership afterward, once more hinting at the arms shipments and the coming IRA offensive. Daithi O Conaill had been barred by the Adams camp from the meeting, and it ended with a threat to the dissidents: if they set up a rival Army, the Provisionals would take O Conaill out.[8] One of O Bradaigh's supporters, Des Long from Limerick, slammed a table with his walking cane in anger, and they stormed out.

THE ARD FHEIS DEBATE started just before 11:00 A.M. on the Sunday morning, but many believed the key contribution had been made the evening before, when Gerry Adams gave his presidential address. His speech set out the classic arguments for change. The IRA had met in Convention and approved the move without staging a walkout, he said. It followed that anyone who opposed a yes vote was actually opposing the IRA. Critics had gone to the establishment media with accusations that the leadership was going down the same road as Goulding's "Stickies." "To compare us with the 'Stickies' is an obscenity," he protested. "For anyone who has eyes to see, it is clear that the Sticky leadership had abandoned armed struggle as a form of resistance to British rule as part of their historic departure into British and Free State constitutionality. For our part, this leadership has been actively involved in the longest phase ever of resistance to the British presence. Our record speaks for itself. We have led from the front and from within the occupied area."[9] And, he added, the armed struggle would continue until victory. "We all have a part to play in it and those of us who remain committed to it will ensure, regardless of the dangers it holds for us, that this struggle is going to continue until Irish independence is won. That is no idle boast."[10]

Others echoed the military arguments. Another Adams ally, County Donegal man Pat Doherty, opened the Sunday debate on the abstention motion and argued that the major difference between Sinn Fein and other republicans who had entered parliament in the past was this leadership's commitment to the IRA's armed struggle. John Joe McGirl, a former chief of staff, repeated the message. He had gone to other veterans, J. B. O'Hagan, Joe Cahill, and Seamus Twomey among them, he told the delegates, and they all supported the change. "We have an army fighting 16 years which will continue to fight until British rule is defeated," he declared.[11] Joe Cahill said that the Goulding leadership "had sold out the military spirit," but he was confident that by the time the election after next came, the deadline for progress set by Adams, "the freedom fighters of the IRA will have forced the Brits to the conference table."[12] Speaker after speaker who backed the move invoked the IRA and the leadership's commitment to the armed struggle.

It was left to Martin McGuinness to deliver the hardest and most uncompromising military message of the debate, establishing a precedent for the peace process in which McGuinness's militancy would be regularly flourished to reassure the rank and file that there would be no sellout. A large enough number of the delegates would have known exactly who Martin McGuinness was—that he was the current Northern commander in charge of the day-to-day war against the British. That day the Derry man was the voice of the IRA.

He began his speech with a commitment on behalf of the leadership never to enter Stormont or Westminster and then turned to allegations that he and other Republican leaders had plans to abandon the armed struggle. "I reject any such suggestion and I reject the notion that entering Leinster House would mean an end to Sinn Fein's unapologetic support for the right of Irish people to oppose in arms the British forces of occupation," he said. "That, my friends, is a principle which a minority in this hall might doubt but which I believe all our opponents clearly understand. Our position is clear and will never change. The war against British rule must continue until freedom is achieved."[13] The opposition to the change, he continued in a less than subtle reference to O Bradaigh and O Conaill, was not about abstentionism but about the 1975 cease-fire. "The reality is that the former leadership of this Movement has never been able to come to terms with this leadership's criticism of the disgraceful attitude adopted by them during the disastrous 18 month ceasefire in the mid-1970's."[14] In other words, the only people who were talking about the war's being ended had themselves nearly brought the IRA to defeat through a foolish cease-fire. How could anyone think that this leadership, which had rescued the IRA then, could or would make the same mistake?

At around four-thirty that afternoon the debate ended, and the Mansion House, which had been packed with media and spectators, waited expectantly for the result of the vote. When it came, the sigh of relief from the Adams camp was almost audible. Fully 429 delegates had voted for the change, 161 against, and 38 abstained. A two-thirds majority was 418, and the Sinn Fein leadership had made it by the votes of just 11 delegates.

In the excitement of the moment no one noticed that the number of delegates attending the Ard Fheis had inexplicably doubled from its usual figure. At the 1985 conference, the year before, the motion seeking to define abstentionism as a tactic and not a principle had been lost by 181 votes to 161; a total of 341 delegates had cast their votes. Yet just a year later the number of delegates at the Ard Fheis soared to 628, almost double; the following year, in 1987, it reverted to its normal 350 or so delegates. That was also the number of SF delegates, more or less, who voted overwhelmingly to back the Good Friday Agreement when Sinn Fein held a special Ard Fheis in May 1998, twelve years later, to discuss the political deal. Each year after 1986 and before 1998 had seen more or less the same number of delegates at each Ard Fheis. The puzzle is why the number of delegates suddenly jumped to over 600 in that one crucial year.

The explanation, according to a number of republican sources, is that the 1986 Ard Fheis vote was really organized and manipulated by the IRA, with all the care and preparation normally reserved for a military operation. This exercise, which began as early as 1984, had been twofold in character. One well-placed Belfast Sinn Fein source active at the time described what happened:

They went about it in two ways. Over a two-year period beforehand released IRA prisoners loyal to Adams were ordered to join Sinn Fein *cumainn* [branches] and take them over by replacing hostile or unsympathetic officers. In one instance in Andersonstown that I remember, two of these people got themselves chosen as delegates to the 1985 Ard Fheis and just point-blank refused to propose a motion that was seen as critical of Adams.

The other way was that they just invented Sinn Fein *cumainn*. All you needed was five names, and you got two delegates to the Ard Fheis. They were set up all over the country and in Belfast. I personally saw faces at the '86 Ard Fheis I had never seen before or since. There must have been a hundred or more of these *cumainn* but after '86 they just petered out. It was done over a two-year period with a big push in 1986, slow at first, but then it became obvious.[15]

No one noticed the disparity in numbers, or if anyone did, they chose to remain silent. The reality was that afterward the reason for the sudden surge in membership hardly mattered. The Ard Fheis result had objectively changed republican politics in two ways: Sinn Fein, and by extension the IRA, had been edged significantly closer to constitutionalism, while the Redemptorists' mission to Charles Haughey had been armed with a crucial piece of evidence about the bona fides and skills of the Adams leadership.

Within six months of the Ard Fheis and in great secrecy, Reid delivered the cease-fire offer to Haughey, and his trips to Kinsealy on behalf of the Sinn Fein leader increased. The peace process was accelerating, and the 1986 Ard Fheis and its historic political turnaround had played a crucial part in achieving that.

ALTHOUGH SINN FEIN was by now well on the way to an even more comprehensive political transformation, its leaders continued to assure the rank and file that the IRA's armed struggle would remain sacrosant, no matter how unsettling the changes. Between 1987 and 1989 Adams, McGuinness, the IRA GHQ, the Army Council, *An Phoblacht–Republican News*, and other influential figures and bodies gave one promise after another that the IRA would carry the war to the British until they agreed to leave Ireland and that whatever the talks with the SDLP were about, they did not encompass an IRA cease-fire.

At the same time this was happening, the Adams leadership gradually introduced some of the key elements of the still-secret "stepping stones" agenda into the republican vocabulary. But not all of them, by any means. Some concepts, like the redefinition of British withdrawal, were just too heretical to be allowed into the public domain. Nor were the rank and file, or for that matter the Army Council, told about the secret strategy that underlay the new concepts. To call what happened between this point and the declaration of the first IRA cease-fire in 1994 a "debate," as more than one observer has, would be something of an exaggeration. Ideas were certainly put into circulation, but the ideas belonged mostly to a Sinn Fein leadership that preferred to talk at rather than to or with their base. Dissension was frowned upon. One internal theoretical magazine, *Iris Bheag* (Little Magazine), which had been thrown open to the rank and file, was quietly suppressed around 1990, after IRA prisoners had used it to criticize aspects of the Adams strategy. *Iris Bheag* was replaced by two glossy productions, *The Captive Voice*, for IRA prisoners, and *The Starry Plough*, which featured mostly articles written or approved by SF headquarters. If there was a debate, it was mainly on the leadership's terms.

In April 1987, just before Tim Pat Coogan carried Alec Reid's letter to Haughey, Sinn Fein issued an eight-page discussion paper entitled "A Scenario for Peace." Couched in the traditional idiom of republicanism, the document repeated the conventional demand for British withdrawal, called for the disbanding of the RUC and UDR and the release of IRA prisoners, and demanded reparations for British misrule. It seemed to be a routine repetition of republican dogma and was ignored by the media and most political rivals. But "A Scenario for Peace" did two things. It scrapped the simplistic and rigid "Brits Out" slogan of the 1970s and replaced it with the much more subtle and flexible phrase "national self-determination" (NSD), a concept that was one of the cornerstones of the Reid-Adams strategy. NSD was a formulation within whose generous frame two utterly conflicting definitions could coexist quite happily, one the traditional republican one, which envisaged physical British expulsion, and the other Reid's version, which said that any move by the British to leave Northern Ireland had to be with the consent of unionists, not just nationalists. One other "stepping stone" idea was contained in the paper, the proposal for a constitutional conference at which elected representatives from all the Irish traditions, nationalist and unionist, would hammer out a settlement. Again worded in republican language, this idea nevertheless could happily sit alongside the Reid-Adams formulation. Adams's efforts to move Sinn Fein away from its ban on taking seats in the Dail had been a slow, cautious, and incremental journey; it would be the same with the bid to make the Reid-Adams diplomacy republican policy. Slowly, the building blocks for a settlement based on the constitutional status quo, by and large, were being laid—and Sinn Fein would be part of that settlement.

Within two years another plank in the Reid-Adams strategy, pannationalism, fell into place when the notion of an alliance with constitutional nationalism became de facto Sinn Fein policy. The groundwork had been done in the months before. Against a background of regular assurances throughout the spring of 1988 from Martin McGuinness that talks with the SDLP had nothing to do with an IRA cease-fire, a troop of Adams's supporters, Mitchel McLaughlin, Tom Hartley, and Danny Morrison among them, made public calls urging the adoption of a pan-nationalist strategy. It was all in preparation for a special internal conference of Northern Sinn Feiners at the end of June 1988 that would consider a special report prepared by the SF general secretary, Tom Hartley, arguing for an alliance with the SDLP.

This was unfamiliar and unfriendly territory as far as many Provisional activists were concerned. Most still shared the scathing view of their constitutional rivals that had been expressed by IRA prisoners at the end of the 1981 hunger strike, and six years of electoral rivalry between the parties had, if anything, deepened the hostility at grassroots level. The June 1988 conference also heard a critique of the IRA's armed struggle from a Belfast councillor, Martin O Muillear, a post–hunger strike, non-IRA recruit to republicanism who told the delegates that there were contradictions between "the armed struggle and our political work," not least in the area of job creation. As a councillor he wanted jobs for his constituents, but the IRA was pledged to deter inward investment with its bombing campaign. "[L]et's have enough savvy to tell the difference between what is a position of political suicide," he told the 150 delegates, "and what is an intelligent and pragmatic political position."[16] O Muillear's message was clear: the IRA was becoming an electoral liability, while Hartley's message, the need for an alliance with the SDLP, offered an alternative.

Leadership figures were pushing the new ideas, but at the wider grassroots level reservations about dealing with the SDLP at such close quarters were deeply held and seemingly staunch. In the mostly pseudonymous columns of *Iris Bheag*, Tom Hartley's discussion paper "Towards a Broader Base," was given a dusty response by republican activists and IRA prisoners alike. Hartley's principal contention that "Britain can only be moved on the National Question if the British state is confronted by the combined forces of Irish Nationalism"[17] implied a compromise that went too far for many. In August 1988 one group of IRA prisoners identified the central danger of the approach, as they saw it. "We don't believe that Britain can be moved 'only by the combined forces of Irish Nationalism,' mainly because we feel that no constitutional party will agree to 'formal' alliances with us unless we reject the use of armed struggle (and we don't believe such is possible) . . ."[18] The same prisoners also complained about the inconsistency in Hartley's approach, recalling the long-held Provisional view that the SDLP's role in Northern Ireland was to support British strategy. "We cannot simply tell our membership today 'SDLP bad—Sinn Fein good' and then tomorrow tell them 'maybe SDLP not so bad, Sinn Fein good.'"[19]

IRA prisoners in H5 of the Maze prison were equally dismissive: "The central position of an alliance with the SDLP is impracticable," they complained, "given the class position and interests of their leadership, and their stance on Hillsborough was a conscious reinforcement of imperialist rule. Neither the SDLP (nor the Dublin government for that matter) were pushed into this treaty, they jumped! Do we seriously believe we can force Hume or Haughey to adopt a more 'Republican' position?"[20] Tony Doherty, SF education officer in Derry, put it more bluntly: "The Republican Movement is clearly identified as the arch-enemy of the SDLP. We [must] show them that we make a very formidable enemy."[21] *Iris Bheag* was closed down not long afterward.

Although Adams and his closest allies continued throughout 1988 to urge pan-nationalism on the republican base, the level of internal hostility toward it and the fact that in the autumn of that year Gerry Adams and John Hume took the Sinn Fein-SDLP talks into private and secret mode forced a more cautious and circuitous approach on the leadership. At the Ard Fheis of January 1989 talk of pan-nationalism had disappeared, replaced by a slogan calling for the setting up of a left-wing "anti-imperialist" mass movement that would bring together "nationalists, patriots, socialists, republicans and democrats" to press for national and economic self-determination.[22] The Adams leadership—Tom Hartley, Martin McGuinness, Jim Gibney, Mitchel McLaughlin, and Adams himself—lined up to recommend the new slogan to the delegates, and it was easily approved. Although one agitational group, the Irish National Caucus, did emerge, little resulted in terms of long-term practical initiatives. As a strategy it disappeared from the leadership's lexicon not long thereafter, replaced once again by pan-nationalism, albeit rechristened "the Nationalist consensus." Not for the first or last time, Adams used the appeal of radical politics to bring his supporters to the desired goal.

The 1989 "anti-imperialist front" proposal got the rank and file accustomed to the notion of Sinn Fein's working with other parties in broad fronts, an essential prerequisite for an alliance with the SDLP. The motion, Adams told the Ard Fheis, was a recognition of the republican movement's weakness: "[W]e can't win this struggle alone . . . ," he said.[23] This would reemerge years later as the central argument for calling a cease-fire. Crucially the strategy also envisaged Sinn Fein's making alliances with parties that were opposed to the IRA's violence. "Participation in this movement," a leadership document stated, "should not be dependent on one's attitude to armed struggle. Those involved in the movement would have the right to their own individual positions on armed struggle."[24] In practice, as a moment's reflection would have revealed, prospective constitutional allies would refuse to consider a relationship with Sinn Fein unless ending the armed struggle was on the agenda. The H Block prisoners were, in their terms, right. In an important sense this was history repeating itself. It was precisely this fear that constructing alliances with non-Republicans would dilute the armed struggle that had persuaded the founders of the Provisionals to reject Cathal Goulding's version of broad-front politics, the "National Liberation Front," exactly twenty years before.

The move to drop abstentionism contained a hugely significant message for Haughey and the British, but it was by no means the only signal sent in these crucial years. In March 1987, a month before the publication of "A Scenario for Peace," the IRA's Northern commander, Martin McGuinness, bowed to Catholic Church pressure in Derry and announced that the IRA would review the practice of firing volleys over the coffins of IRA Volunteers in church grounds. McGuinness's retreat came in the wake of a public protest from the bishop of Derry, Edward Daly, after two masked men had fired handguns over the coffin of Gerard Logue, a twenty-six-year-old from the Gobnascale area of the city who had been killed accidentally by his own weapon while on active service. Logue's funeral cortege had been surrounded by police and soldiers in a bid to prevent a paramilitary display, but at the door to St. Columba's Long Tower church the IRA had seized the chance to give their fallen comrade the traditional farewell salute. Daly accused the IRA of reneging on an understanding not to violate church grounds in this way, and he said that in the future the bodies of paramilitary members would not be allowed on church premises in the city.[25]

Bishop Daly, unlike his namesake in Belfast, had supported the secret diplomacy of Father Alec Reid and was an enormously popular figure in Derry. Television coverage of him waving a bloodstained handkerchief as an improvised flag of truce at heavily armed British troops as he tried to secure safe passage for one of the fatally wounded civilians shot on Bloody Sunday became one of the visual icons of the Troubles. McGuinness's decision not to seek a fight with Daly over the funeral issue was understandable in the light of all that, but it also served to highlight a largely unnoticed IRA policy change that had significantly demilitarized its funeral rites. The practice of firing volleys over IRA coffins, whether in church grounds or not, had at one time been part of the ritual of defiance, but by this stage had ended in Belfast. The change coincided with the expulsion of Ivor Bell and his hard-line, militarist allies and with the beginnings of Father Reid's secret peace enterprise. Instead the IRA now paid "tribute" to martyred colleagues by firing volleys over their wreath-bedecked photograph, usually after the funeral had taken place. The effect of McGuinness's concession was to extend the change to Derry, the second city of Provisional republicanism. The change had been partly forced upon the IRA by a tougher British security force presence at IRA funerals, but the fact that the leadership chose not to make an issue out of this, when it could easily have sought violent, destabilizing street conflict by staging firing parties, was a subtle signal to both governments and a concession to the Catholic Church allies whose friendship Sinn Fein sought.

Republicans still tried to bury their fallen colleagues with other military trappings. Tricolors and IRA berets and gloves were draped over caskets, and corteges would be accompanied by marching color parties in displays that often led to ugly confrontations with RUC riot squads. These caused violence and tension, but in circumstances less calculated to cause death and more likely to generate sympathy from a wider nationalist audience.

Similar signals were sent by an Army Council decision to demilitarize the color party that led the march into Bodenstown graveyard each June for the annual commemoration of Wolfe Tone. The Goulding leadership had used this public ceremony to advertise its own ideological shifts, and ever since the split in 1969 the Provisionals had insisted that their color party at the annual ceremony be an IRA one, complete with all the customary paramilitary trappings, masks, and uniforms. It symbolized their republican purity and the adherence to armed struggle. In June 1987, however, the color party was suddenly civilianized, much to the disappointment and puzzlement of the rank and file. In the *Iris Bheag* of September 1987, a correspondent called "The Weasel" complained bitterly. "Of all the people I spoke to about the change in policy in relation to colour parties at Bodenstown," he wrote, "not one single person agreed that it was a good policy and nearly all agreed that it was sapping the morale which went with previous parades before the policy change."[26] In the same issue, "Sea Hag" commented, "I wouldn't have seen [the colour party] go by only that someone next to me said it was passing."[27] "The Weasel" unwittingly detected the subliminal message contained in the move: "Defiance was always one of our strong points, without it we will be left to the history books."[28]

There were other adjustments in Provisional theology every bit as significant. In February 1988, a year later, a Catholic civilian, twenty-four-year-old Aidan McAnespie, was shot dead as he walked through a British army checkpoint at Aughnacloy, on the Tyrone-Monaghan Border, en route to a local Gaelic football game. Despite British protestations to the contrary, McAnespie's family alleged the killing had been deliberate and cited a history of harassment and verbal abuse directed at the dead man by soldiers manning the checkpoint. The Irish prime minister, Charles Haughey, chose to cause a diplomatic row with the British over the incident. He ordered a senior Garda officer to investigate the death, and quietly the IRA and Sinn Fein instructed its councillors and supporters to cooperate with him. The importance of the move was enormous; traditional republican dogma forbade cooperation with the Irish police force in such matters on the grounds that the police enforced the laws of what was seen as an illegal state. Again a writer in *Iris Bheag* hinted at the internal controversy this had caused: "Some thought it was wrong because it legitimised what we in Sinn Fein do not see as legitimate."[29] The underlying message to Haughey and to the Southern security authorities was unmistakable. The Army Council, under Adams's direction, was in a very real way conceding to Haughey its traditional claim to be the only legitimate government in Ireland.

A similarly significant signal was sent to the British the following month when, for the first time since the split with Goulding, the organizers of the annual Easter Provisional republican parade to the IRA plot at Milltown cemetery in West Belfast filed for permission from the RUC to hold their march. The traditional refusal to ask official leave carried legal penalties, but rather than extend recognition to the Northern Ireland state that filing for an RUC permit implied, the organizers were normally quite happy to bear the consequences. Later in the year Sinn Fein began to use the courts in Northern Ireland to challenge unionists who were refusing to give the party's councillors seats on committees. It was the first time ever that republicans had resorted to British justice in this way to seek redress.

The effect of all this was to flag an important message that only a few could detect. The bulk of the republican grassroots were distracted by the noise of the IRA's ongoing war, which was by 1988 in the midst of the postponed "Tet offensive," and those who did notice were satisfied with the explanation from Adams's colleagues in the Sinn Fein leadership that it was all a ploy to win sympathy in the South and among the greener fringes of constitutional nationalism in the North. None of them could have guessed the real significance and meaning of the changes.

ELEVEN

Death in Tyrone

Loughgall, County Armagh, Friday, May 8, 1987. It was just after 7:15 on a bright spring evening when the shooting began. Witnesses later said that the gunfire seemed to go on forever, but in such situations the mind often plays tricks and events can seem to happen in slow motion. Nonetheless the shooting was relentless. When finally it ceased, an eerie silence descended over the shattered remnants of the village's police station. The scene that greeted the Special Air Services (SAS) soldiers and policemen as they carefully emerged from their hiding places was shocking even by the standards of a Northern Ireland whose seventeen years of bloody conflict had been regularly punctuated by multiple loss of life. Scattered around the bullet-riddled shell of a Toyota Hiace van lay the bodies of the cream of the Provisional IRA in County Tyrone. The eight-man active service unit (ASU), the cutting edge of the East Tyrone Brigade, had been wiped out in the carefully planned ambush, cut to ribbons in a withering fusillade of automatic fire. Estimates of the number of rounds fired by the British that evening reach as high as twelve hundred.

The East Tyrone ASU's plan had been to destroy Loughgall police station with a huge bomb. The device had been placed in the bucket of a mechanical digger hijacked from a farm near Dungannon and then driven the twenty-five minutes or so to the picturesque village situated deep in Armagh's rolling apple orchard country. Loughgall police station was a part-time post, manned by just three or four RUC officers, which opened only in the mornings and afternoons. The IRA men expected to find it unoccupied when they arrived, and anticipated no resistance. Three of the ASU traveled with the digger, while the remaining five drove ahead in the Toyota van, scouting for patrols and checkpoints. The digger easily broke through the wire mesh rocket-proof fencing that surrounded the police station, and it was rammed into the building so that when the explosion came it would cause maximum damage. The fuse was lit, but just as the bomb detonated the SAS opened fire.

The East Tyrone IRA had walked into a carefully laid trap. More than three dozen British soldiers drawn from the elite SAS regiment were lying in wait for them. Armed with heavy machine guns and automatic rifles, they poured bullets into the startled IRA men from at least four points. Backing them up were scores of officers from the RUC's elite paramilitary wing, the Headquarters Mobile Support Unit, while shadowing the IRA operation as it unfolded that day were many more police and military surveillance personnel. The scale of the British operation spoke eloquently to the quality of intelligence that had come their way. The conclusion was difficult to avoid: someone, somewhere in the IRA had betrayed the East Tyrone Brigade.

The Loughgall ambush resulted in the heaviest single death toll suffered by the Provisional IRA in all the years of the Troubles. The only comparable loss in IRA history had happened way back in the middle of the Tan War in February 1921 when, in an operation characterized by the same military ruthlessness, a fifteen-strong IRA company was pinned down in a cottage in Clonmult, County Cork, by a mixed party of British troops and auxiliary police. After a fierce firefight the IRA men surrendered, but when they did they were set upon and twelve were killed. Although the scale of the slaughter at Loughgall was not as great, it probably dealt a more devastating blow. In fact the ambush had two damaging consequences for the Provisionals. Not only was the morale of IRA activists and Provisional supporters throughout Ireland rocked by the killings, but the organization lost a number of irreplaceable members, skilled and determined operators who had been slated by GHQ to play a key role in the planned post-*Eksund* "Tet offensive."

Even more damaging were the subsequent suspicions that have surrounded the identity and motives of those who apparently betrayed the East Tyrone Brigade. The questions have lurked in the minds of the IRA in the county ever since, hanging over Tyrone republicans like a huge black cloud that threatens to explode into a storm yet never quite does. The years since 1987 may have passed, but the speculation has never ceased about whether the traitor came from Tyrone or from elsewhere in the IRA and, if so, how high up, or, alternatively, whether the British stumbled upon the operation by expert surveillance or whether flaws in the restructured IRA sealed the unit's fate. Even darker and more sinister are the questions that link the ambush to the then growing peace process and the impact on its development.

Whatever doubt exists about the identity or role of the Loughgall informer, there is no doubt that the ambush robbed the IRA of some of its best fighting men. Perhaps the most feared and certainly most wanted by the British was Jim Lynagh from Tully in County Monaghan. One of four-teen children, thirty-one-year-old Lynagh had joined the IRA as a teenager and was soon making his name as a fearless activist. In 1973 he had a nar-row escape when a bomb he was carrying exploded prematurely. He was badly injured but survived and then was sentenced to ten years' imprison-ment, becoming one of the few Monaghan men ever to serve time in Long Kesh. In 1978 he was released, immediately rejoined the IRA, and a year later was elected a Sinn Fein councillor on Monaghan Urban District Council. Three years later he was caught carrying bullets by the Irish police and was sent to Portlaoise prison. Freed in April 1986, he once again resumed active service with the East Tyrone Brigade.

Lynagh was a ruthless IRA gunman, whose politics were simple and straightforward, his belief in military methods as unshakable as his readi-ness to conform to the party line was undependable, as a former colleague remembered:

> He was outside the charmed circle. He was regarded [by Sinn Fein leaders] as not quite respectable enough, a bit too wild for them. He was no saint. He had been involved in the odd punch up, and his brother had been charged with shooting a bouncer. He was also a hard-line republican. I can remember when the word came [from Sinn Fein headquarters] not to men-tion the North or the war on the doorsteps while canvassing [for election] and to concentrate instead on social and economic issues, Lynagh objected and then just ignored it.[1]

Despite the leadership's doubts about Lynagh, GHQ had chosen him to play a key part in the "Tet offensive"; he was one of a small group of trusted operators taken to Libya in 1986 for training in the weaponry being smug-gled from Qaddafi's arsenals.

Lynagh's ideological soulmate was thirty-two-year-old Padraig McKearney, a member of a renowned republican family from The Moy, on the border between Tyrone and Armagh, whom Lynagh had met in jail and befriended. McKearney's maternal grandfather, Tom Murray, had fought with the Roscommon IRA in 1920, and the family tradition lived on with the Provisionals. The oldest McKearney brothers all joined the IRA as teenagers in the early 1970s, and a sister, Margaret, has lived in Dublin, out of the reach of the British authorities, since the mid-1970s, not long after Scotland Yard branded her as "the most dangerous and active woman terrorist" operating in Britain.[2] Their youngest brother, Sean, was killed along with a lifelong friend, Eugene Martin, in May 1974 when a bomb intended for a local garage exploded prematurely as they were transporting it. It was probably his first IRA operation, and he was just eighteen at the time. The oldest brother, Tommy McKearney, rose through the ranks to become a member of the IRA's GHQ until he was arrested in 1976 and processed through the Castlereagh conveyor belt to a cell in the H Blocks of Long Kesh. When the IRA prisoners decided to fast for the return of political status in the autumn of 1980, Tommy McKearney volunteered and was one of the seven inmates chosen to go on hunger strike. When the protest ended in confused circumstances on December 18, he had gone without food for fifty-three days. The Troubles were to touch the McKearney family again more than a decade later when the youngest son, Kevin, was shot dead by Ulster Volunteer Force (UVF) gunmen in the family butcher's business in The Moy and an uncle, Jack, fatally wounded. Later that year another uncle, Charlie Fox, and his wife, Tess, were shot dead in their home by the same UVF. Few republican families had been as devastated by the Troubles as the McKearneys.

Padraig McKearney joined the IRA in 1971, when he was seventeen, and served two spells in jail, the first in 1974, when he was convicted of blowing up a factory, and again in 1980, when he was caught with a loaded Sten gun. He was sentenced to fourteen years' imprisonment for that offense but never served the full term. In September 1983 he and thirty-seven other IRA prisoners broke out of Long Kesh prison in a spectacular escape. Like his close friend and fellow escaper Seamus McElwaine, another republican nonconformist, Padraig McKearney reported back for duty with the IRA as soon as he was safely across the Border.

Along with twenty-nine-year-old Gerard O'Callaghan, Lynagh and McKearney were the senior members of the East Tyrone ASU that day. Their commander was Patrick Kelly, the thirty-two-year-old OC of Tyrone IRA, who drove the Toyota van into Loughgall. Regarded by some as the architect of the IRA's strategy in Tyrone, Kelly was seen differently by the activists. "He was there for diplomatic reasons, to represent the interests of Northern Command and McKenna [the chief of staff]," commented one. But two generations of IRA men were shot dead in Loughgall. Declan Arthurs (twenty-one), Seamus Donnelly (nineteen), Tony Gormley (twenty-five), and Eugene Kelly (twenty-five) were all chums who lived in and around the staunch republican village of Galbally, home of the dead IRA hunger striker Martin Hurson, whose death in 1981 persuaded them to join the IRA. According to those who knew them, their role model and the IRA man they most looked up to was Jim Lynagh.

THE LOSS of the East Tyrone Brigade devastated the Provisional IRA. None could have guessed it back in 1987, but the killings at Loughgall marked the start of a concerted undercover British and loyalist offensive against organized republicanism in the county, its supporters, and uninvolved Catholics which would leave over twenty IRA members and twice that number of nationalists dead within five years. As a contribution to the internal and external pressures on the IRA to go down the peace process road, this slaughter in Tyrone should never be understated.

Tyrone had always played a crucial role in the annals of Irish republicanism, and a setback to the IRA in Tyrone would be bound to damage the cause throughout Ireland. It had been that way for over three hundred years. Ever since the great Tudor campaigns against the remnants of Ireland's Gaelic chieftains, Tyrone had stood out for the strength of its resistance to English rule. The defeat and death in 1648 of Owen Roe O'Neill, great chieftain of the Tyrone clans who had returned from European exile to lead his people into battle, marked the end of opposition throughout Ireland to the English occupation. It was not until a hundred and fifty years later that the flame of Irish rebellion was lit again when a Southern Protestant, Theobald Wolfe Tone, made common cause with the Northern Catholic Defenders to mold the United Irishmen. The defeat of O'Neill also consolidated the plantation of Ulster by lowland Scots and Northern English Protestants whose seizure of Catholic land gave England a buffer against French or Spanish invasion through its Irish back door but left a deep and enduring scar on the Tyrone psyche. "Rural memories are long," commented one Tyrone republican. "People know which land they lost in the plantation and who took it. They can identify their fields, and in all probability the same Protestant families who took it from their ancestors are still living there."[3]

Military defeat and repression created two tendencies in Northern nationalism, based partly on differences in social class, partly on conflicting political interest. One, from which the Provisionals sprang, preached physical resistance to British and unionist rule and the attainment of full independence, while the other, a Hibernian, strongly Catholic tendency, argued for slow constitutional advancement and the placing of sectional before national interest. The Hibernian tendency thrived in most of pre-partition Ulster and was dominant in most counties. Tyrone was the exception. There the two forces were historically more evenly balanced and are even to this day, the advantage tilting in one direction or the other, depending on which is thought better placed to give unionism the hardest time.

Tyrone republicans were to play a significant part in the 1916 Rising and the subsequent Anglo-Irish war, not least because of ties with Irish-American sympathizers on the east coast of the United States. Following the collapse of an alliance between Parnell's parliamentarians and the revolutionary Fenian Brotherhood in the late nineteenth century, Irish republicanism found a new home in New York, where the Fenians regrouped to form the secret, elitist Irish Republican Brotherhood (IRB), whose Military Council in Ireland and the United States plotted and planned the Easter rebellion.

The IRB set up an American wing called Clann na Gael, and Tyrone men would always figure prominently in its affairs. The best known of these was the "father" of the Easter Rising, Tom Clarke, one of the 1916 Proclamation signatories, whose mother was from Tyrone and who had been reared in Dungannon, where he joined the IRB. Clarke emigrated to New York, but the Clann sent him back to Ireland, where he was arrested and then imprisoned in England for fifteen years. After his release he quietly recruited for the IRB in Dublin in preparation for the Easter Rising. Using a tactic that was to be imitated by future republican groups, the IRB infiltrated and ultimately controlled the much larger and open Irish Volunteers, who provided the manpower for the Rising. Clarke paid for his militancy with his life. Along with Patrick Pearse, who was regarded by the British as the leader of the failed insurrection, Clarke was in one of the first groups of rebel leaders executed by a British firing squad in the days after the Rising.

Clarke's activities on behalf of the Clann began a long tradition of Tyrone involvement in the group's clandestine support for militant republicanism in Ireland. In the buildup to the Rising, the Clann was headed by J. J. McGarritty, from Carrickmore in Mid-Tyrone, who sent Roger Casement to Germany in a fruitless search for weapons to arm the 1916 rebels. He later helped raise thousands of dollars for the IRA's 1919–21 campaign and hosted de Valera during his lengthy stay in America. The Tyrone influence in Clann na Gael lived on, and during the Provisionals' campaign most of its leading New York members were from the county, many of them prosperous figures in the city's construction industry. While the media focused on Noraid as the largest U.S. fund-raiser for the Provisionals, the fact was that the secretive and close-knit Clann was a much more significant source of support.

In 1916 Tyrone was chosen by the IRB as the rendezvous point from where the Northern IRA was to mobilize and play its part in the Rising. Fearing that sectarian violence would engulf Belfast and Derry, the IRB had ordered that there be no military action in the North and instead told Northern units to gather in Coalisland, from where they were to link up with Liam Mellowes in Galway. The idea was that they would help hold the west, in a line from Cavan to Limerick. When the orders were counter-manded by the Volunteers' commander in chief, Eoin MacNeill, most of the Tyrone men returned to their homes but some went on to fight.

Tyrone's tradition of militant republicanism went hand in hand with an often stubborn streak of dissent against distant leaderships, whether in Dublin or in Belfast. Liam Kelly was perhaps the best example of this breed. Born and reared in Pomeroy, Kelly almost single-handedly forced the IRA leadership into launching its 1956 Border Campaign. Interned by the Stormont government in the 1940s, Kelly, who had joined the IRA at sixteen, was OC of the IRA in Tyrone, and he was impatient for battle. When he was expelled from the IRA in 1951 because of unauthorized military action, he took most of the Tyrone membership with him and formed Saor Uladh (Free Ulster), which scandalized unionists when it occupied and sealed Kelly's home village of Pomeroy. In 1953 he was elected to the Stormont parliament as an abstentionist MP on a platform of utter simplicity: "I do not believe in constitutional methods, I believe in the use of force; the more the better, the sooner the better—that may be treason or sedition, call it whatever the hell you like."[4] Nearly a quarter of a century later his nephew Patrick would lead the Loughgall unit to their deaths.

Curiously, Kelly's political line mirrored that of the post-1986 Sinn Fein, although his methods were much more violent than those with whom figures like Gerry Adams would ultimately be comfortable. Kelly happily accepted de Valera's 1937 constitution, linked up with Sean MacBride's strongly republican Clann na Poblachta, which was a partner in the 1948 coalition government and was happy to take a seat in the Irish Senate, courtesy of MacBride in 1954. Kelly's quarrel was not with the Irish state but with the Northern state, and his pursuit of that made him an irritating thorn in the flesh of the IRA leadership. In November 1955 Saor Uladh bombed and shot up Roslea RUC station in County Fermanagh. Although Kelly was forced to flee and eventually sought refuge in New York, the unionist government was startled by the attack and the IRA leadership was forced to contemplate advancing its own military plans or risk defections to extremism. A year later Operation Harvest was launched.

The same streak of independence was evident in the years following the 1969 IRA split. Most of Tyrone stayed loyal to the Goulding leadership, if only because the Army Convention of that year had backed it, but the line between the Officials and the Provisionals was always blurred. The ideological differences that had split the movement in the South mattered little in Tyrone. What did count was which IRA was able to hit the British hardest. The killing of the Official IRA OC, John Paddy Mullen, and another member of the Official IRA, Hugh Heron, in October 1972 illustrated the point. British soldiers shot them dead at a roadblock, and there were angry allegations that they had been killed in cold blood. The Officials' failure to strike back, despite Goulding's pledge at their funerals that they would, strengthened support for the Provisionals, and Mullen and Heron were quietly transformed into posthumous Provos. Their names now appear among the Tyrone dead in the republican roll of honor published each Easter in *An Phoblacht–Republican News*. As late as 1977 the local pro-Goulding Republican Club would make no distinction between the Provisional and Official IRA when it contributed to the Prisoners Dependants Fund. Goulding eventually expelled them.

The leading Provisional IRA figure in Tyrone after the split was Kevin Mallon, whose trial during the Border Campaign had been a cause célèbre. Accused of the 1957 murder of an RUC sergeant killed in a booby trap bomb near Coalisland, Mallon was acquitted when evidence was produced showing he had been ill treated by his police interrogators. Mallon had a strong following in Tyrone, but he kept those under his control more or less independent of the Provisional Army Council after the 1969 split until, as a former colleague put it, "he was caught up in the tidal wave"[5] and gave allegiance to the Provos.

Lynagh, McKearney, and other members of the East Tyrone ASU showed the same independent and rebellious streaks. They opposed much of the Adams agenda, especially the dropping of abstentionism, fearing that recognizing and accepting the Irish parliament would lead inevitably to endorsing the Stormont and Westminster bodies too. Had they lived, they almost certainly would have also opposed the peace process and perhaps might have brought significant numbers of the IRA in Tyrone and Monaghan with them. What distinguished their opposition to the leadership was that it was expressed in both political and military terms. Lynagh and McKearney had worked together to oppose the dropping of the abstentionist rule and had used exactly the same arguments as O Bradaigh and O Conaill, principally that it would lead to constitutionalism and inevitably to the dilution of armed struggle. At the Tyrone-Monaghan brigade convention, which chose delegates for the Army Convention, they spoke out against the motion and clashed with the chief of staff, Kevin McKenna, a fellow Tyrone man but at that stage a strong Adams supporter. They were counting on the support of another veteran republican (J.B.) Joe O'Hagan, a former quartermaster general and IRA Executive member from Lurgan, County Armagh, who had found refuge in Monaghan. They believed they had his support, but when the brigade convention voted, O'Hagan, like the majority of delegates, went with Adams. Despite that setback, Lynagh and Paddy Kelly attended the 1986 Army Convention and voted against Adams, although they were in a minority of the brigade delegation.

Their military critique was also calculated to cause friction with the leadership. It opposed two tenets of the Army Council's strategy as it was developed in the mid- to late 1980s, both closely associated with the Adams concept of republican struggle: namely the notion that the IRA's war was a piece of armed propaganda and that Britain would be forced to move when enough soldiers were killed. "[Lynagh and McKearney] didn't believe sending Brits home in boxes would work, because the British army wasn't a conscript army like the Americans in Vietnam," recalled a former associate.

They were working on the basis that a radical departure had to be made. The idea was either total war or no war at all, to force the British out of their bases and to make the place ungovernable. They said that either the IRA should take it to that level or finish with the war; killing the odd UDR man did nothing. They believed the "Green Book" [the IRA manual of tactics and regulations] was shit, that it was based upon the false idea that the IRA would be able to operate from its home base and at the same time be able to resist interrogation at Castlereagh. Their response was that the enemy will not allow you to survive in his bosom. Would Castro have survived if he had been in Havana rather than in the mountains? That was the question they asked.[6]

The pair had gone to Chief of Staff Kevin McKenna with a radical proposal to build a flying column, consisting of perhaps twenty or thirty trusted activists, which would be based deep in the South, with its own dedicated training facilities. The column would never break camp, in a conscious imitation of the flying columns that had run the British ragged in Cork during the 1919–21 conflict. This was meant to ensure that it would be more secure; an informer in the midst of the column would reveal himself if he separated from the group, as an informer would have to do in order to communicate with his or her handlers. The column would strike three to five times a year, aiming to cause maximum damage and disruption to the British administration. Satellite groups of two or three men would all the while attack on a harassment basis and collect intelligence for the bigger strikes.

McKenna turned down the idea, condemning it as too impractical, too ambitious, and not sustainable, and rejected their request for a separate training camp on security grounds. Friction between McKenna and the Lynagh-McKearney team intensified. There were attempts to separate the pair, apparently aimed at weakening their influence. "McKenna tried to put Lynagh in one zone and McKearney in the other," recalled an associate. "It was possibly also an attempt to divide and conquer, to cause rivalry over assets and the like."[7] Another IRA source suggested that McKearney may have been seen as the greater irritant: "Padraig and McKenna had never really got on. After the escape in '83 the men were offered the choice of going to America or back to active service. Padraig got the feeling McKenna would have liked to see him take the boat. For his part Padraig was very strongly opposed to the 1986 decision [to drop abstentionism]. He felt afterward that people who were in favor of running down the war were being pushed forward."[8]

McKenna and the Army Council did not like these militant views, but they could not afford to ignore them. Lynagh and McKearney had powerful friends and allies. Among those who backed their agenda or at least were sympathetic to it, according to IRA sources in Tyrone, were some of the most active IRA gunmen and bombers of the day. The claim is not, it has to be stressed, supported by any independent evidence, but it has been made by sources who claim a deep and close knowledge of the relationship between Lynagh-McKearney and others of a like mind. The other dissidents and malcontents, according to this version of events, included not only the bulk of the Loughgall unit but also Seamus McElwaine and Kieran Fleming, who had escaped from Long Kesh with McKearney in 1983, Antoin MacGiolla Bhride from South Derry, Dessie Grew from Armagh, and the Ardboe men Michael "Pete" Ryan and Liam Ryan, the former OC of the New York IRA who was brigade intelligence officer when the Loughgall ambush happened. The area covered by the dissenters embraced not just East Tyrone but Armagh, South Derry, and Monaghan, the most important and active operational area outside of South Armagh. Like the Loughgall ASU, McElwaine, Fleming, MacGiolla Bhride, Pete Ryan, and Grew were all to be killed in British undercover ambushes, while Liam Ryan died in an expert UVF gun attack on his bar.

Although McKenna had turned down the East Tyrone flying column proposal, Northern Command did order the unit to bomb and mortar police and UDR bases in 1985, although in this case the strategy was a limited one, aimed at frustrating the repair and renewal of security bases. The East Tyrone ASU spearheaded much of this activity, and a sort of flying column was set up—but it came together only for specific operations, and that made it very different from the full-time and secure column Lynagh and McKearney had in mind.

In December 1985 the East Tyrone ASU blew up Ballygawley RUC station and killed two policemen who were stationed inside. Then it mortared bases in Castlederg and Carrickmore. In the autumn of 1986 the police station in "The Birches" near Portadown, County Armagh, was devastated by a bomb carried to its target in the bucket of a mechanical digger. The Loughgall attack was supposed to be a repeat performance. East Tyrone was also to the fore in the offensive against building contractors. Two weeks before the Loughgall ambush, five ASU members took fifty-two-year-old Harry Henry out of his Magherafelt, County Derry, home in his stocking feet and shot him in the head. Henry's brother owned a building firm that specialized in doing work for the security forces.

Although the IRA leadership had moved to meet some of the East Tyrone demands, Lynagh and McKearney felt it still fell far short of the sort of tactic they believed could cause a qualitative shift of fortune in the IRA's direction. Relations between McKenna and McKearney in particular were worsening, and the number of operations carried out by East Tyrone kept to a minimum, as one dissident confidant recalled: "[McKenna] kept on knocking back ideas for operations and separating Padraig from the rest of the [East Tyrone] unit. He was excluded from the attack on The Birches for example, and it was like McKenna was trying to tell the others they didn't need Padraig."[9]

In the months between the 1986 Convention and the Loughgall ambush, McKearney began putting out feelers in Dublin and elsewhere in a bid to acquire weapons that would be used to arm the rebels if they decided to break free of the Provisionals. He was also in touch with the faction that had coalesced around the Provisional IRA renegade turned INLA leader Dominic McGlinchey, whose violent campaign in the South Derry countryside in the late 1970s was matched in its ferocity only by that in East Tyrone. McGlinchey, who had even less regard for the Adams leadership than the East Tyrone men, was in jail at this point, but his formidable wife, Mary, an experienced and ruthless operator in her own right, had assumed leadership of his group. The contacts between McKearney and the INLA were designed to test whether they could find common ground, but when Mary McGlinchey was killed in January 1987, shot dead by unknown gunmen as she was bathing her two infant sons, the liaison ended.

Nonetheless, in the spring of 1987, just weeks before the Loughgall ambush, the dissidents met to discuss their plans. The venue was Seamus McElwaine's family home on the Monaghan-Fermanagh Border. "They sat down in North Monaghan and asked their colleagues whether it would be feasible to break away and form a separate organization which would put their flying column idea into practice," recalled a former associate. "It was an informal meeting, seven or eight of them were present."[10] Naturally, the meeting was kept secret from mainstream IRA loyalists. Another source familiar with these events added, "The gist [of the meeting] was that they [decided that they] could get arms from their own sources and move away from the Provos."[11]

Jim Lynagh and Padraig McKearney did not live long enough to put whatever plans they had made into action. Since their deaths in the Loughgall ambush the search for an explanation of what went wrong that day has obsessed many Tyrone republicans. Was there an informer and, if so, who was he? The obsession caused near-paranoia to grip the IRA in the brigade area. Patrick Kelly's successor as OC, Brian Arthurs, went as far as splitting East Tyrone in two to see if this could isolate the guilty party, and for a long time brigade operations were suspended altogether while internal investigations were carried out.

Certain features of the Loughgall operation suggested the possibility of a more innocent explanation. Glaring mistakes were made in the planning and execution of the bombing which inadvertently could have put the British on the trail, mistakes that spoke of a reckless overconfidence and carelessness. There were, for instance, no probes made around Loughgall before the attack. This was routine practice in South Armagh, where, before ambushes or other IRA operations, sheepdogs were sent into adjoining fields to flush out undercover soldiers. Nor was there any effort to give the attackers the protection of covering fire just in case something went wrong. Such sloppiness at this late stage possibly indicated that other lapses had occurred earlier in the preparatory work and it is conceivable that this is how the British learned of the plan. An internal IRA investigation held afterward concluded that something like this might have happened, and that there had been a leak at the Monaghan end of the operation, although the precise source was never identified.[12] The IRA leadership remains as much in the dark about what really happened as anyone else.

The number of theories suggesting that an informer had betrayed the unit have multiplied with the years. An Ardboe woman, Colette O'Neill, came under suspicion in 1989, for instance, and was briefly kidnapped by the IRA but rescued by the RUC, which seemed to have excellent information about her plight. She later made a deal with the IRA in which she agreed not to give evidence against her abductors if the IRA left her alone. In an interview with the author not long afterward, she denied being the Loughgall informer, although she admitted that a phone call had been made from her home to members of the ASU on the day of the operation, clearing the way for the bomb to be picked up. Another theory blames a ninth member of the ASU, who was supposed to be on the Loughgall mission but missed it. Although the man protested his innocence, not surprisingly he left for England not long afterward and has not been seen since.

Some British sources have claimed that electronic surveillance of the homes of two other Tyrone IRA members, Gerard and Martin Harte, near Omagh, put the British on the trail of the Loughgall operation.[13] The same eavesdropping operation directed against their home led a year later to the death of the Hartes, lured into an ambush near their home by the SAS. The Harte brothers' role in the Loughgall operation was to hijack the mechanical digger, and the sources say that electronic bugs picked up details of this part of the plan. Against this, local sources claim that while this may have happened, it did not necessarily mean the British would have known the target.

"Liam Ryan did the intelligence work for Loughgall, and he insisted that he had compartmentalized everything, that no single participant would have known all the details," recalled a confidant of the Tyrone Brigade intelligence officer. "He felt [the leak] had to be at a centralized level; he would have concluded that it had to be higher up than Tyrone."[14] Other Tyrone IRA sources corroborate this and say that some of the minor members of the Loughgall team were not told about the operation until fourteen or fifteen hours beforehand, not enough time for the British to mount an SAS ambush on the scale of that which destroyed the ASU.[15]

Another factor may have led to the Loughgall ambush. Since the mid-1980s the IRA leadership had exercised tighter and tighter control over the

IRA's day-to-day activity as it became clearer that bad IRA operations, those in which civilians were put at risk or killed, could seriously erode electoral support for Sinn Fein. During the 1983 general election a huge bomb aimed at Andersonstown RUC station had wrecked homes in the streets where Gerry Adams had been canvassing for votes not long before. The Ivor Bell–Belfast Brigade revolt against Adams during 1983 and 1984 had led to the deaths of Edgar Graham, Jimmy Campbell, and Mary Travers, daughter of the Catholic magistrate Tom Travers. Adams had warned of the need for "controlled and disciplined" IRA actions at the 1983 Ard Fheis.[16] After Sinn Fein's poor performance in the June 1984 Euro election, he returned to the theme: "[T]here are a number of people who, while they voted for us in June 1983, may not have been able to tolerate some aspects of IRA operations," he cautioned. "I think it is fair to say there are varying degrees of tolerance within the Nationalist electorate for aspects of the armed struggle."[17] The ballot box was beginning to curb the Armalite.

Just before the death of Seamus McElwaine, killed by the SAS in County Fermanagh in April 1986, Northern Command got permission to vet most IRA operations in Northern Ireland in a bid to forestall further electoral damage. "There had been some bad operations, politically bad operations, and this was done to correct that," recalled one activist. "McGuinness [the Northern commander] got authority from the Army Council to vet operations. Before that, area commanders would run through their plans in very general terms, for example, 'I have a policeman or a British patrol,' with the chief of staff or director of operations. Now people had to go into the detail of the operations."[18]

IRA activists had an almost pathological fear of sharing operational intelligence with people they did not know or who did not come from their area. No one ever suggested that Martin McGuinness or any other senior figures at his level were passing on information to the British, but the very fact that the circle of operational knowledge was widened beyond those chosen to go on the mission heightened fears of leaks, surveillance and even treachery.

The vertical IRA structures introduced by Adams after his Cage 11 days combined with the greater political control exercised over operational matters made it easier, not harder, for British intelligence to penetrate the IRA's nerve centers. The old battalion and company architecture was leaky, for sure, but whatever damage an informer did was usually confined to one small area. Even then it was a relatively easy task to isolate and identify the traitor. A well-placed agent in the remodeled IRA could by contrast cause enormous harm throughout the length and breadth of the organization and be pretty sure of getting away with it. Those on the ground who fought the IRA's war were acutely aware of these dangers.

Loughgall was a case in point. The bombing was a Northern Command–directed operation, but Lynagh objected strongly to having to share vital details of the mission plan with others. Before the go-ahead was given for the operation he traveled to Monaghan to see Kevin McKenna to complain, and the two had a blazing row. "McKenna and Lynagh never saw eye to eye," remembered one associate.[19]

But this alone does not explain the deep gulf of mistrust that separates many Tyrone republicans from their leadership beyond the county. To explain that, it is necessary to go back to the secret meeting of East Tyrone activists who gathered in North Monaghan in the spring of 1987 to discuss splitting from the Provisionals. "They made a big mistake by including someone who really shouldn't have been there," concluded an associate.[20] This was a reference to a Belfast IRA man whose family had a record of long and loyal service to the leadership. No proof or evidence has ever been produced to show that he or anyone else told the leadership about the dissidents' plot, but in the hothouse world of the IRA that hardly mattered. "This is the reason for all the suspicion around Loughgall," said the same source.[21]

FROM THE TIME of the Loughgall ambush onward, it was more or less open season on the Tyrone IRA as far as the SAS and British intelligence were concerned. In August 1988 the SAS killed the Mid-Tyrone IRA members Gerard Harte, Martin Harte, and Brian Mullin. In October 1990 Dessie Grew and a ferocious young gunman from Galbally, Martin McCaughey, were ambushed and killed by undercover soldiers not far from Loughgall. In June the following year the remnants of the East Tyrone ASU died in an SAS trap in Coagh, between Ardboe and Cookstown. Lawrence McNally and Pete Ryan, both Monaghan-based operators, had been lured to the village by a sighting of a UDR soldier who, because of his alleged connections to loyalists, had long been an IRA target, but their car was destroyed in an SAS gun and rocket attack. Their driver, Tony Doris, was an IRA member from Coalisland. "After McNally and Pete Ryan that was it; we had nobody left," commented one Tyrone republican.[22]

The SAS was not finished, however. In February 1992, undercover soldiers cut a swath into the next IRA generation when they killed the twenty-one-year-old student Kevin Barry O'Donnell, twenty-three-year-old Sean

O'Farrell, nineteen-year-old Peter Clancy, and twenty-year-old Daniel Vincent in a set-piece ambush in the parking lot of the Catholic church in Clonoe, between Coalisland and Ardboe. The four died after a particularly pointless machine-gun attack on Coalisland police station mounted from atop a truck as it sped through the town. Once again, according to IRA sources in a position to know, Northern Command had approved the operation.[23] In all four ambushes the British security forces' intelligence had been excellent.

The impact of the British offensive is evident from the war statistics, which reveal a picture of a steady decline in IRA activity in Tyrone. In 1986, before the Loughgall ambush, according to the author's analysis of the weekly IRA "War News" column published in *An Phoblacht–Republican News*, East Tyrone accounted for 21 percent of all IRA operations in Northern Ireland. But in 1987 that dipped to 9 percent. In 1988 there was some recovery in IRA activity to 16 percent; but thereafter the decline resumed: in 1989 to 13.5 percent, in 1990 to 16.4 percent, in 1991 to 8 percent, in 1992 to 11 percent, and in 1993, the year before the first cease-fire, to 9 percent.[24] The IRA death toll tells the same tale. Up to April 2000, the IRA in Tyrone had lost 53 members, the highest death toll for any brigade area. But over half, 28, were killed in the five years between May 1987 and February 1992, compared with 25 in the seventeen years between 1970 and 1987. In other words, IRA deaths in Tyrone increased fivefold after the Loughall ambush.

The SAS was not alone in putting East Tyrone in its deadly sights. The years 1987 and 1988 also saw the beginnings of a concerted UVF assault against republicans and nationalists in the brigade area that in its way was more enervating than the undercover military ambushes. In an important sense the East Tyrone Brigade brought the calamity upon itself. The killings of Harry Henry in April 1987 and then a year later of Ned Gibson, a Protestant sanitation worker who was also a part-time soldier in the UDR, shot dead as he collected garbage in Ardboe, were regarded by Tyrone's unionists as overtly brutal sectarian assaults, and they responded in kind. It was, however, the nature of the IRA's response to the loyalist offensive that made the carnage in Tyrone such a significant milestone on the road to the 1994 cease-fire.

In the first twenty years of its existence the Provisional IRA had a simple if brutal attitude toward loyalist killings. This was to retaliate with excessive but deliberately directed violence against the unionist community. Two notorious incidents stand out as examples of what in practice this policy meant. The first occurred in early January 1976 when Provisional IRA gunmen halted a minibus carrying textile workers home from work near Kingsmills in South Armagh. They singled out the lone Catholic on board, told him to get out of the way, and then lined ten Protestants up against the side of the bus and riddled them with automatic fire. The incident was so horrific that the IRA was reluctant to admit responsibility, and instead a cover name, the South Armagh Republican Reaction Force, was used. The Kingsmills slaughter was the IRA's response to the UVF killing in the days before of five South Armagh Catholics, members of two families.

The second example came in January 1981 when an eleven-man IRA unit, reportedly led by Jim Lynagh, broke into Tynan Abbey, an enormous mansion set in eight hundred acres of lush farmland near the Armagh-Monaghan Border, and killed its two occupants, eighty-six-year-old Sir Norman Stronge and his merchant banker son, forty-eight-year-old James. They then planted incendiary devices that set the abbey alight, destroying it in the fire. The family had been in Tynan for eight generations, and the Stronges were scions of the unionist establishment. Sir Norman had been Speaker of the Stormont parliament for a quarter of a century and his son had been a unionist MP at Stormont; his great-grandfather had been Speaker of the old Irish House of Commons. The reason for the IRA attack was clear. Five days before, UDA gunmen had made an unsuccessful attempt on the life of the Tyrone republican leader Bernadette McAliskey, which had left her and her husband, Michael, barely alive. The UDA attack was the latest in a series of assassinations of prominent nationalist and republican figures. The killing of the Stronges was designed to bring them to a halt.

The point about the Kingsmills and the Stronge killings is that most Provisional supporters believed that they had worked and that a speedy and violent IRA reaction of that caliber was the best, perhaps the only, way to stop such loyalist violence in its tracks. Such retaliations became accepted as part of the Provisionals' view of the world. "It's a lesson you learn quickly on the football field," commented a Tyrone republican and GAA veteran. "If you're fouled, you have to hit back."[25] The reprisal policy was part of what the Provisional IRA was about; it reached deep down into the group's Defenderist roots.

But by the time the Mid-Ulster UVF began its killing in the autumn of 1988, IRA policy had begun to change. In November 1988 the UVF targeted the home of the Moortown Sinn Fein councillor Francie McNally, not far from Ardboe on the shores of Lough Neagh. Shots were fired through the kitchen window, and McNally's younger brother Phelim was fatally wounded as he played an accordion. Three months later, in February 1989, the UVF struck once more against Sinn Fein. This time the target was fifty-eight-year-old Magherafelt SF councillor John Joe Davey, who was cut down in the driveway of his isolated rural home. Davey had been named under privilege in the House of Commons by the DUP MP for Mid-Ulster, the Reverend William McCrea, as an accomplice in the killing of a local Protestant security contractor in 1986. A veteran of the Border Campaign, Davey had twice been interned by the Northern authorities. The UVF was exacting revenge.

Army Council policy in relation to reprisals had changed significantly by this stage. Retaliations of the Kingsmills and Stronge variety were banned, as one IRA source familiar with the policy change explained: "John Davey was the first Sinn Fein councillor to be shot, but there was to be no retaliation because of [an Army Council directive] against political assassinations. Although there could be exceptions—Ken Maginnis [ex-UDR captain and the former Fermanagh–South Tyrone unionist MP] was one—and there could be special requests, basically that type of reprisal was politically unacceptable to Adams and company."[26]

Instead the IRA was allowed to strike back only at named, identified targets, and this meant that only those who could be shown to have been directly involved in the loyalist killings or who were known to be pulling their strings in the background were legitimate targets. Again Northern Command would vet each operation, and local brigades would have to justify the choice of targets. That was necessarily a drawn-out process that delayed the IRA response. "The time frame was crucial, otherwise the message was lost," recalled a Tyrone republican. "Loyalists retaliated fast, while in the IRA they had to battle for permission to strike back. You virtually needed a jury trial."[27]

Retaliation for the McNally and Davey killings came in the first week of March 1989 when East Tyrone IRA members sought out Leslie Dallas, a UVF member and a leading member of one of the four UVF families in the East Tyrone–South Derry area. He was gunned down in a garage in Coagh, not far from Ardboe, but the shooting was a disaster for the IRA. Two elderly Protestant men, Ernest Rankin and Austin Nelson, neither of whom had any association with the UVF, were caught in the gunfire and shot dead.

In Belfast, Gerry Adams distanced Sinn Fein from the killings. Referring to the deaths of Rankin and Nelson, he echoed the Army Council line. "Our position is clear," he said. "Sinn Fein does not condone the deaths of people who are non-combatants. There can be no legitimate reason for any uncertainty about Sinn Fein's attitude to such killings."[28] On the ground in East Tyrone, the Provisionals' grassroots, by contrast, had demanded a much more drastic response. "The cry was a councillor for a councillor, for Willie McCrea or a bomb in the council chamber," explained a Tyrone republican. "That was the gut feeling of the rank and file."[29] They didn't get their way.

After the Coagh shootings, the UVF campaign in the East Tyrone, North Armagh, and South Derry areas intensified. Their targets included not just uninvolved Catholics but IRA and Sinn Fein members and their families, and its effect was to deeply undermine republican morale. "In Tyrone the SAS went for IRA members while the UVF went for the families," was how one republican source described the tactics in these years.[30] The UVF killed twice more in 1989, five times in 1990, and fifteen times in 1991, eight of the victims gunned down in the first three months of the year. Again the facts and figures speak for themselves. Between 1988 and August 1994 eighty-six people died violent deaths in the East Tyrone operational zone, and the UVF was responsible for forty of them, nearly half the slaughter. Davey's death began an open season on Sinn Fein councillors and activists. Fourteen Sinn Fein members were killed in the four years that followed the killing of the Magherafelt councillor, over half of all the Sinn Fein personnel killed since 1970. The IRA was powerless or unwilling to stop it.

Relatives of Republican activists were also picked off, sometimes in exceptionally brutal circumstances, sometimes in circumstances suggesting that the loyalist killers had excellent intelligence. Roseanne Mallon, for instance, shot dead in Lisgallon in May 1994, was related to the most senior IRA figure in the county. In one of the worst examples of this kind of killing, a mother of five, Kathleen O'Hagan, was gunned to death in front of her children at her home near Cookstown in August 1994. Her husband had served eight years for possessing an IRA gun, and that made her a target, as it made by implication the spouses of other IRA personnel. Mrs O'Hagan was seven months pregnant at the time of her brutal death. There were other clues that the killers were well briefed. Patrick Shields, shot dead with his son Diarmuid in January 1993 in his grocer's shop near Dungannon, had been in the IRA in the 1970s but had quit long before. He was, however, still a contact of Kevin Mallon's, by this stage no longer a Provisional but a dissident sympathizer. Not many people would have known that. A month later his son's girlfriend, Julie Statham, overwhelmed by grief, committed suicide.

The IRA's new, restrained retaliation policy had two effects. The IRA concentrated all its energies in the hunt for the head of the Mid-Ulster UVF, Billy Wright, who was based in Portadown and who was believed to have had a hand in most if not all the killings. The IRA made at least five attempts on Wright's life, including a booby trap bomb placed underneath his car, but the UVF leader lived a charmed life and survived them all. He was later shot dead by the INLA under extraordinary circumstances, inside the Maze prison, but the IRA's inability to deal with him or his associates discredited the organization. "They were always talking about a night of the long knives against the UVF, but it never did happen," remembered one Tyrone IRA man.[31] Another recalled approaching a prominent Sinn Fein politician in the county after learning of a UVF threat against his family: "His response was 'I wonder if we could get in touch with the UVF and sort it out.'"[32] A week later the UVF killed his brother.

The IRA's failure to stem the loyalist killings struck at the core of its raison d'être. If it couldn't protect its own, especially in Tyrone, wondered many republicans, how could the IRA expect to drive the British out of Ireland? "As the killings grew, the demand to do something grew as well," recalled one activist. "People were scared because it seemed the loyalists had a free hand. People were afraid to be identified with Sinn Fein, not just the IRA. You could be shot for having the same name as someone in Sinn Fein like poor Tommy Molloy. Meanwhile the IRA was doing nothing to protect people."[33] Molloy was killed apparently because he shared a surname with Francie Molloy, the leading Sinn Fein figure in the area, who later became an Assembly member for Mid-Ulster. By the end of 1990, according to republican sources in the area, Sinn Fein was having great difficulty persuading people to run in council elections.[34] The grassroots demoralization that flowed from all this nourished the psychology of cease-fire, making the peace process acceptable and even welcome, as one astute observer of Tyrone republicanism noted. "People are terrified of going back to war because of their memories of that UVF campaign," he said.[35]

The IRA leadership's new attitude toward loyalist killings sometimes meant that lies were told about the true allegiance of some victims. At least three Sinn Fein councillors killed by the UVF in the area were also key IRA activists, but this was never acknowledged even years later. When Liam Ryan was shot dead by the UVF at his Battery Bar near Ardboe along with a civilian, Michael Devlin, his IRA membership, never mind his role as brigade intelligence officer, was denied by Sinn Fein, although three weeks later an IRA firing party did fire a volley of automatic shots over his grave. The IRA's worst loss at the hands of the Mid-Ulster UVF came in March 1991, when three young IRA members were shot dead as they drove into the car park of Boyle's Bar in the strongly republican village of Cappagh, County Tyrone. Twenty-three-year-old John Quinn, seventeen-year-old Dwayne O'Donnell, and twenty-year-old Malcolm Nugent were cut down in a hail of bullets, and a Catholic noncombatant, fifty-two-year-old Thomas Armstrong, killed by a stray round as he used the toilets in the bar. The IRA did not acknowledge the three for a year, and they were depicted in Sinn Fein propaganda as innocent Catholic victims, the result of an order relayed to the Tyrone Brigade on behalf of Northern Command by Jim Gibney, a senior Belfast-based adviser of Gerry Adams.[36] The deception fooled no republicans in Tyrone and very few in the rest of Northern Ireland, but was aimed at currying sympathy south of the Border, where people were much less likely to be aware of the truth.

"Adams's attitude was always to encourage the view of nationalists as being the underdog, the ones at the receiving end of this sort of violence," recalled a senior IRA source. "He would say we want to be seen as the oppressed, and that was why the Cappagh men were disowned."[37] Denying the Cappagh dead enraged many Tyrone republicans, but the IRA on the ground was assured that there were good reasons. "It was to do with making life easier in the South, particularly in relation to the safe houses and the like which we could get, especially from Fianna Fail people," explained one former senior figure. "After disasters like Enniskillen, houses were shut to the IRA; after Cappagh when what happened [was] seen as security force collusion with loyalists to kill Catholics, the houses open again."[38] There was a political dimension to this as well. If Fianna Fail supporters could open their homes to the IRA, then perhaps the Fianna Fail leadership could do the same at a political level with Sinn Fein. This provided the real reason for the shift in Army Council policy on loyalist killings. The change dovetailed into Gerry Adams's quest for pan-nationalist unity that in 1988 and 1989 was at the center of his secret diplomatic overtures to the Fianna Fail taoiseach, Charles Haughey.

THE FUNERALS of the Loughgall ASU were some of the biggest seen in Ireland since the hunger strikes. Jim Lynagh's removal and burial became an occasion for the Provisional grassroots to demonstrate a disdain for the Republic and its institutions that had been sharpened by suspicions that the Irish police, the Gardai, may have played a part in laying the ambush, possibly by passing on intelligence to the British. Lynagh's body was escorted back across the Border on the Monday after the killings by hundreds of IRA supporters. At Emyvale in County Monaghan the cortege stopped in the main street and was joined by an IRA color party. From a side entry stepped three masked IRA men armed with automatic rifles. They fired three single shots over the coffin and then a wild volley into the air that roused the crowd. As they turned to melt back into the sea of faces, they found their way blocked by a carload of the elite Garda antiterrorist unit, the Task Force armed with Uzi submachine guns. Seeing this, the crowd surged forward and manhandled the police car into an empty drain, upturning it with one of its plainclothes occupants still inside. Other policemen fired wildly in the air, and for a few moments it looked as if a serious confrontation might follow. Later that day a Sinn Fein picket gathered outside Fianna Fail's headquarters in Lower Mount Street in central Dublin. Angered by Fianna Fail denunciations of the IRA in the wake of the ambush, the picketers strung a banner across the footpath which read, "Fianna Fail, 'The Republican Party,' Collaborators with SAS Murderers."

Lynagh was buried two days later, on May 13, and Gerry Adams gave the oration at his graveside and lashed the Fianna Fail government and its leader, Charles Haughey. "A few short months ago," he said,

the people of this State elected a Fianna Fail government of sorts. Their leader made many brave noises about a British withdrawal being a prerequisite for peace in this island. He described the Six-County State as a nonviable social and economic unit. He chose Bodenstown to denounce British policy, [Garret] FitzGerald's collusion in that policy and the actions of the British Crown Forces. That was when he was looking for votes. I have some questions for all Fianna Fail supporters and for all nationalists. Did you elect a government to support Thatcher's terrorism? The British government understands Charles J. Haughey . . . as it understood FitzGerald and Spring. It has always understood the shoneen clan—it bought them off with partition. It does not understand the Jim Lynaghs, the Padraig McKearneys or the Seamus McElwaines. It thinks it can defeat them. It never will.[39]

It would have been later the same day or not long afterward that Tim Pat Coogan was ushered into Charles Haughey's presence to hand over the lengthy letter from Father Alec Reid that outlined Gerry Adams's proposals for an alliance between Fianna Fail and Sinn Fein and the extraordinary offer of an IRA cease-fire. The letter, fifteen pages and 7,000 words long, had been written two days before, when the gunfire over the coffin of Jim Lynagh was still echoing around the streets of Emyvale and the angry shouts of Sinn Fein picketers were ringing outside Fianna Fail's offices.

TWELVE

"The War of the Twilight"

As the year 1988 dawned, there were two sharply contrasting moods in the IRA. At grassroots level, disappointment at the loss of the *Eksund* the previous November was more than compensated for by the subsquent disclosure that other shipments had gotten safely through from Libya, well over 120 tons according to reports in the British and Irish media, and at the realization that the IRA was now better armed than at any other time in its history. Ever since the first shots were fired at British troops in 1970, the Volunteers had dreamed that one day they would have plenty of modern weaponry with which to take on British forces, and now that day had arrived. Whatever doubts they had about the political direction the Adams leadership was taking, whatever questions had been raised by the movement's recognition of the Irish parliament a few months before, now vanished like snow off a ditch in spring.

At the level of Army Council, the mood was entirely different. Those who had spent the previous three years putting the Libyan smuggling venture together and who had been planning the "Tet offensive" knew just what a disaster the betrayal of the *Eksund* was. They knew it spelled military stalemate for the IRA, robbing the offensive of the one element that would have guaranteed a major impact—surprise. But that was not the only disheartening aspect of the *Eksund*'s loss for IRA leaders. On board had been military mortars that could have devastated British barracks and RUC bases throughout the North, enabling the IRA to launch damaging attacks from safe distances. Also gone were the powerful 106-millimeter canons that were to be used to sink the Royal Navy's patrol boat that cruised Carlingford Lough. There had also been plans to sink boats in Belfast harbor with the weapons, blocking access to the city's docks and disrupting trade. But these ambitious schemes too would now have to be scrapped.

Also lost with the *Eksund* was the ambitious political agenda that the Army Council expected would be advanced by the "Tet offensive." The immediate objective of the plan was to force the British into reintroducing internment against the IRA, the weapon last used in 1971 but discredited then as both ineffective and iniquitous. Internment would, the IRA leadership calculated, bring a number of political benefits. The use of the weapon would likely anger and alienate nationalist opinion in both parts of Ireland as it had done in 1971, thereby fueling support for the IRA's campaign, and would also demonstrate the bankruptcy of British policy in Ireland, discrediting Britain in the eyes of world opinion and perhaps provoking public opinion in Britain to search for a more radical and long-lasting solution to the Irish problem.

The Army Council may have miscalculated the IRA's ability to use the Libyan weaponry to the best advantage. Not everyone in the IRA was convinced that the organization had the wherewithal to deliver such an ambitious enterprise, as one middle-ranking commander recalled. "The strategy was to mount a massive campaign, but I had been going around the units and I was not convinced it would work," he said. "We weren't capable of that. There hadn't been enough organization, and our security and training weren't good enough. We didn't have enough intelligence work done either. If we had tried to mount it, I think it would have been a disaster. I believed we needed a lot more time, but people had got carried away with all the heavy gear."[1] In a sense that did not matter, for the purpose of the "Tet offensive" was, like that of its Vietnamese original, to show the world how deep and violent the opposition in Ireland was. After all, the Vietnamese had been given a bloody nose during their offensive, yet the violence had helped transform American public opinion.

The plan came so close to success that the Army Council at one point succumbed to bragging. After the *Villa* had landed 105 tons of arms in October 1986, the leadership's spirits had soared, and at the following Easter's republican commemorations it could not resist dropping a hint of what was in the pipeline. In tune with the military mood, the Council's statement was distinctly dismissive of electoralism:

> We agree with the building of a revolutionary, republican party in the course of the armed struggle and we refuse to be over-euphoric with electoral victories or disillusioned or deterred by electoral setbacks. The British will only be talked out of Ireland through the rattle of machine-guns and the roar of explosives. . . . It has been a long time since the Irish Republican Army has

felt so confident, so sure of victory, so happy about the future even though for many of us the coming fight may mean imprisonment and death.[2]

The move to abandon abstentionism in the South became part of the plan. At the 1986 IRA Convention the leadership sold the notion to the rank and file that recognizing and taking seats in the Dail in Dublin would help neutralize the Republic's government and isolate the British. If Sinn Fein won seats to the Dublin parliament, it was argued, then it would be much more difficult for the Republic's government to join with the British in an assault against the IRA. Furthermore, if Sinn Fein TDs held the balance of power in the Dail, as could happen, then the party would hold the whip hand and the IRA would be free to bomb and shoot at will. "We knew there were going to be major casualties and draconian measures introduced like internment," recalled one IRA source familiar with the "Tet" strategy. "That was the story at the '86 Convention: 'We'll have a couple of TDs by then, and if [the Republic's government] introduce[s] internment we'll be able to block it.'"[3]

There would be other succulent fruits to pluck if all went according to plan. If the British responded by reintroducing internment, the deal agreed with Nasser Ashour of the Libyan Intelligence Service envisaged Qaddafi sending more consignments of weapons to Ireland and pumping more money into the IRA. And there were other, enticing possibilities. "By inflicting such big casualties, you'd get the support of radical governments elsewhere in the world," recalled the same source.[4]

The capture of the *Eksund* changed everything. The more astute among the IRA leaders fully realized the consequences. "We were gung ho before at the prospects, but now it was the war of the twilight," recalled the source. "It was over, and it led directly to a stalemate situation which then fed into the peace process."[5] The IRA's grassroots were jubilant over the organization's newfound strength, but even this was illusory. The IRA had lots of weapons, but it was by no means certain that they were the best that could be had. The value of the AK-47s, for example, had been exaggerated. "The Volunteers thought they could fire round corners," remembered the same source. The heavy Soviet machine guns, the "Dushkies," were pretty much useless. "They took three men to carry and only fired eighty rounds to a belt; they fired too slow," recalled a rural IRA activist.[6] The SAM-7s were virtually obsolete. They dated back to the 1960s, and the batteries in the firing mechanisms were dead and useless. Without Libyan assistance, and that was cut off when the *Eksund* was lost, they could not be replaced, and so the SAM-7s stayed in their dumps while the IRA's spin doctors did their best to exaggerate their threat. The IRA had scores of Webley revolvers, but their ammunition was of too low a caliber for its needs, while many of the millions of rounds of ammunition shipped from North Africa had been rendered unusable by old age. Qaddafi had been generous to the IRA, but his gifts had come mostly from the back shelves of his arms stores.

The IRA had plenty of Semtex, but that, really, was all. In the coming years the inventive resources of the IRA's engineering department would be stretched to the limit as improvised weapons were developed one after the other. Homemade rocket launchers, grenades, coffee jar bombs, booby trap car bombs, and mortars poured out of the IRA's factories hidden deep in the Republic, each device designed to utilize the explosive power of Semtex. At the time all this was seen as evidence of the IRA's ingenuity, skill, and strength, even though in fact it was a symptom of the weakness caused by the loss of the *Eksund*.

The IRA leadership was forced to make do with what was available, but the big military breakthrough was now as elusive as ever. The plan put together by the director of operations, Tom "Slab" Murphy, and approved by Chief of Staff Kevin McKenna before the capture of the *Eksund*, envisaged a three-pronged offensive that would start in Northern Ireland and then spread to continental Europe, where British army contingents in West Germany would be targeted, and to England, where the targets would be military, political, and economic. Following the *Eksund*'s loss, IRA structures in the Republic were disrupted for weeks by the huge twenty-six-county-wide search for the earlier shipments, but nonetheless the go-ahead was given to begin the campaign in Europe.

A probing attack had been made in early 1987, when a 300-pound car bomb exploded outside the officers' mess of the British army's West German headquarters at Rheindahlen, injuring thirty-one people. It looked like a reasonably successful operation, but, in fact, the IRA had had a miraculous escape. The only reason people were not killed was that the ASU had been unable to position the car bomb close to the mess, because the car park was full of vehicles. Unknown to the IRA, most of the vehicles blocking their way were owned by West German military officers who had been invited to spend a social evening with their British counterparts. Had the car bomb exploded as it was supposed to, many of these officers could have been killed and the beginning of the IRA's European campaign would have become a diplomatic and military disaster.

The campaign proper began on as bad a note for the IRA when on Sunday, March 6, 1988, two seasoned IRA activists, thirty-one-year-old

Mairead Farrell and thirty-year-old Danny McCann, and a young, twenty-three-year-old bomb maker, Sean Savage, were gunned down by the SAS as they made their way out of Gibraltar, Britain's quaint cosmopolitan colony perched on the southern tip of Spain. The trio, who were all from West Belfast, were unarmed when shot, and this helped transform their subsequent inquest into a virtual trial of Margaret Thatcher's tough approach to the Northern Ireland problem. A celebrated Thames Television documentary, *Death on the Rock*, produced eyewitness evidence that supported the allegation that the three had been shot down in cold blood while trying to surrender, a contradiction of the version of events put about by the Thatcher government, which implied that the SAS believed they might have been about to detonate a bomb or reach for weapons when killed. An inquest jury cleared the SAS, but the controversy lingered on.

The IRA's plan was to place a large Semtex car bomb in the center of the colony and detonate it just as a British military band assembled for a weekly changing-of-the-guard ceremony outside the governor's official residence. Usually some fifty soldiers took part in the parade, and the target was doubly tempting, offering the IRA substantial casualties in one of the few remaining British colonies. If it worked, the attack would be a military triumph full of political symbolism. The three were on a final scouting mission when they were killed, and had left an empty car in a parking lot near the band's assembly point, presumably to reserve a spot for the real car bomb two days later. On the trio's way back to the border with Spain, the SAS struck.

At the inquest, held amid considerable publicity in Gibraltar itself, it became clear that substantial British intelligence resources had been deployed to forestall the attack, and it seemed there was little that the authorities did not know about the IRA's plans. Apart from the SAS soldiers, teams of MI5 "watchers" had been assigned to follow the ASU in Gibraltar. The Garda Special Branch had watched the team leave Dublin airport for Malaga, but while the Gardai did not inform the British, the IRA later learned, Interpol in Vienna was told. Interpol in turn contacted Spain, and via the Spanish police the British were told the team was on its way. IRA intelligence later established that the Spanish had sought assurances from the British that if they tailed the three and kept MI5 and the Gibraltar police informed of their movements, they would not be killed. The British reneged on the deal.[7]

The Gibraltar operation was a disaster for the IRA, although it probably did win the subsequent public relations battle with Thatcher's government.

The true extent of the calamity for the IRA was, however, never acknowledged by the organization and was kept hidden from the rank and file. The story of Gibraltar is the story of an operation that should never have been allowed to happen.

In the weeks leading up to the operation, warning signals were clearly visible to IRA GHQ and senior Army Council personnel—red flags in military parlance—which indicated that the British had access to the IRA's plans in Europe. They were ignored.

ALONG WITH the Gibraltar bombing, the IRA was planning another European spectacular to open its Continental campaign. The IRA had learned that the British foreign secretary, Sir Geoffrey Howe, traveled regularly to Brussels for meetings of NATO and European Community ministers, and, crucially, there was a regular pattern to his movements in the city. He was driven to his destination by the same route each time. A plan was devised to assassinate him by means of a remote-controlled bomb placed in a car parked at the side of the street. When Howe's car passed, the bomb would be detonated and one of Mrs. Thatcher's most senior ministers blown to pieces.[8] The operation was approved by the IRA leadership, and the bomb put in place. The IRA team charged with carrying out the mission arrived, but Howe's car, for the first time in months, failed to turn up. The IRA concluded that British intelligence had discovered the plan and changed Howe's itinerary. The bomb was dismantled and left in a lockup garage in Brussels where, in January 1988, Belgian police found it.

There was, however, one puzzling aspect to the affair. The British clearly knew all about the IRA plot, but they did not tip off the Belgian authorities, who could easily have arrested the ASU. That would have been something of a coup for all concerned. The reason the British and Belgians let matters lie was that the Gibraltar and Brussels operations overlapped. The IRA chiefs who had planned the Gibraltar attack and two members of the Gibraltar ASU were also involved in putting together the attempt on Sir Geoffrey Howe's life. Had the authorities moved against the IRA in Brussels, thereby indicating that there had been a leak or treachery, GHQ would have been obliged to abandon the Gibraltar operation and Mrs. Thatcher would have been denied the chance to give the IRA a bloody nose in the streets of her colony.

Even so, the evidence suggests that the British knew weeks in advance about the IRA's plans for Gibraltar and that the IRA should have suspected this. The original intention had been to bomb the Rock in December 1987, but the operation had to be abandoned when suddenly and for no obvious reason the changing-of-the-guard ceremony outside the governor's residence was cancelled. But early in the New Year the IRA returned to Gibraltar and found that the parade had been resumed. The intelligence on the operation was resubmitted, and the bombing was once again authorized by the IRA leadership. No effort had been made to discover why the parade had been halted at a crucial point during the execution of the first plan or if this might have indicated that the British knew something about the IRA's intentions. Nor did anyone in the IRA hierarchy link that with the failed attempt on Sir Geoffrey Howe's life.

The Army Council ordered an internal inquiry into what had happened at Gibraltar and blamed loose talk by members of the ASU, three of whom were dead and could not answer back. The investigation claimed there had been a leak in West Belfast and one in County Louth, just across the Border. There was other independent evidence to indicate carelessness on the part of some of the team which suggested there was validity in the complaint. Just after the killings a West Belfast republican told the author that Danny McCann had been seen drinking in a Lower Falls social club a week before, and nearly everyone who knew him could tell he was going on an operation. "He had dyed his hair," the source explained.[9] McCann had been allowed back into the IRA not long before and forgiven for his rebellious liaison with Ivor Bell. The IRA inquest did not, however, consider the possibility that there had been a leak or a traitor at a higher level. Given the occurrence of the Gibraltar debacle within months of the loss of the *Eksund* and after the Loughgall massacre, that possibility should have been considered.

THE CELLULAR REORGANIZATION of the IRA prompted by Adams and his colleagues in Long Kesh in the mid-1970s had been motivated by the alleged looseness of the old company and battalion structure. But the changes had failed to stem security breaches or agent infiltration and recruitment on the part of the British. In fact there has always been a strong school of thought in the Provisionals that held that the centralized control systems introduced in the mid-1970s may have facilitated rather than hindered such penetration. Not least it meant that one well-placed agent in the new IRA could do more damage than a dozen informers distributed around the old company and battalion system. In the months after the betrayal of the *Eksund*, more and more evidence surfaced suggesting that the IRA had been infiltrated in this way, at a high level and in different sections. So serious was the problem that it effectively hobbled the revised "Tet offensive."

The autumn and winter of 1989 provided the evidence. In October a mass breakout of remand prisoners from Crumlin Road jail in Belfast was frustrated by the British. At least thirty IRA men had planned to escape by using smuggled Semtex to blast their way out of the central block. The Belfast Brigade had organized backup. A bomb would blow a hole in a perimeter wall while up to a dozen cars had been positioned around the prison to whisk the escapers to freedom. But on the appointed day the British were waiting in large numbers and clearly knew everything there was to know. A smuggled "comm" from remand prisoners to a colleague on the outside a few months later made the prisoners' suspicions clear. The secret communication, apparently intercepted by the authorities, was quoted in Jack Holland's *Hope against History* and read, "Our conclusion is the BB [Belfast Brigade] may well be compromised."[10] It was one of several bad operations highlighted by the prisoners.

There were other telltale signs of serious penetration by the British. The original plan for the post-*Eksund* offensive had called for the establishment of flying columns along the Border and in Belfast and Derry. The columns, which would be brought together for specific operations and then dispersed until needed again, were to be the cutting edge of the first assaults, but in the wake of the Loughgall and the *Eksund* setbacks, GHQ and Slab Murphy drastically scaled down the plan. Eventually a single, experimental flying column was put together under the command of Michael "Pete" Ryan from East Tyrone, composed of around twenty of the IRA's most experienced and trusted operators from throughout the North who were specially drafted in.

The column's first and, as it turned out, only operation was devised by Northern Command, two of whose staff vetted the details. The plan was shared with the column members just before it was put into action. The aim was to destroy a large British army checkpoint at Derryard, near Roslea on the Fermanagh-Monaghan Border, and kill perhaps a dozen soldiers. While some members of the column sealed off approach roads to prevent civilians from stumbling onto the scene, a truck carrying eleven IRA men was to drive into the checkpoint and attack the base with two heavy machine guns, half a dozen automatic rifles, grenades, and a flamethrower, one of a consignment that the Libyans had added, unasked, to the IRA's shopping list. Under the cover of all this fire the column would then place close to the soldiers' living quarters a 400-pound van bomb, which would cause carnage when detonated. The operation went according to plan, and two soldiers, members of the King's Own Scottish Borderers, were killed in the initial phase. Suddenly the column itself came under attack. Heavy gunfire was directed at its members from fields about fifty yards away, while a British army Wessex helicopter appeared from nowhere over a nearby hill. The column fled, leaving behind the primed van bomb.

To the outside world the Roslea attack looked like a success. Unionists protested angrily and called for a tough security response, while the media pondered the significance of this sudden intensification of IRA violence. But the truth was that the flying column's first outing had been betrayed, and its members were lucky to have survived. "It was a disaster," said a source familiar with the operation."[11] The van bomb failed to explode, and an internal investigation concluded that the detonating mechanism had been sabotaged, a sign that a traitor had been at his or her work. A limited number of people had known about the operation, and although no one was pointing fingers, at least openly, the failure at Derryard illustrated for many IRA activists the dangers of sharing operational details with Northern Command or indeed with anyone outside their tight, trusted circle.

That was the end of the flying column idea. "The fear of a high-level informer made people afraid to go on column operations," recalled another IRA source.[12] Not only had an informer sabotaged the original "Tet offensive," but the revised campaign had been undermined apparently in a similar fashion. The loss of the *Eksund* had dealt a devastating blow to the IRA's ambitions, and now the campaign patched together in the wake of that disaster was falling to pieces. Slowly but surely the IRA's military options were being closed off.

A MONTH LATER one of Gerry Adams's closest advisers and confidants, Danny Morrison, was arrested in a house in Andersonstown, West Belfast. Inside police found the disheveled, exhausted, but extremely relieved figure of Sandy Lynch, a Special Branch agent who had infiltrated the IRA in North Belfast. Financed by the RUC, Lynch had purchased a car, started taxiing, and offered his services to the IRA, who had gratefully accepted. It was one of the oldest tricks in the intelligence book, yet it always seemed to work. Eventually Lynch came under suspicion, and he was lured to the Andersonstown house, where he was interrogated and quickly confessed. Those questioning Lynch were members of the IRA's security department, a specialist counterintelligence unit established as part of the Cage 11 reorganization plan.

The arrest of Danny Morrison proved to be a serious blow to the Adams leadership. A skilled and affable propagandist, Morrison had revamped

Republican News back in the mid-1970s and overseen the "fusion" of the Belfast paper and *An Phoblacht* in Dublin. Regarded as a figure who could always be relied upon to loyally echo the Adams line, Morrison rose through the ranks. A member of GHQ staff, he was the IRA's and Sinn Fein's director of publicity and by 1989 had sat on the Army Council for the best part of a decade.

Morrison found himself in the Andersonstown house because of the activities of another informer, Joe Fenton, or rather because of the Belfast brigade's decision in February 1989 to kill Fenton before he could be thoroughly interrogated and the extent of his treachery—and his dealings with key brigade staff—discovered. The decision had angered senior figures in the IRA, who realized that a golden opportunity to uncover a network of spies had been lost. There were angry accusations of a cover-up and favoritism toward the relatives of key West Belfast figures. To quell the unease, the Army Council ordered that in the future one of its number would have to check whether a suspected informer had been properly and fully questioned before any action could be taken. The British security forces had nicknamed Morrison "The Lord Chief Justice" after he took on this role, and they clearly relished the prospect of catching him red-handed. On January 7, 1990, their opportunity came. Almost as soon as Morrison turned up at the house, soldiers and RUC officers swooped. He was arrested and subsequently convicted and sentenced to eight years.

The significance of the swoop was that it suggested that the IRA department whose job it was to track down and kill informers had itself been penetrated by the British. The RUC Special Branch and British military intelligence had long identified the IRA's security department as a prime target for infiltration and for very good reasons. The security department had an intimate and unrivaled knowledge of the organization's affairs. Its job was to investigate every botched, failed, or aborted operation to see whether or not the IRA had been compromised. It was work that meant that the security department would be aware of the identities and detailed role of IRA members throughout the organization. The department also had the job of vetting recruits. It was the Achilles' heel of the reorganized IRA. An agent placed inside the security department could provide priceless information. There already had been strong suggestions that this had happened. In July 1988, Markets IRA man Brendan "Ruby" Davison was shot dead by the UVF at his home. An irritated RUC later let it be known to the media that the loyalists had killed a key double agent. The RUC would have been grossly negligent had it not made considerable efforts to replace Davison, and Morrison's arrest suggested that it may well have succeeded. The Sandy Lynch affair added to a general sense of paranoia in the IRA, inhibiting its ability to intensify the revised "Tet offensive" to the levels hoped for by the Army Council.

Between them these events pointed to the existence of agents or leaks at leadership, Northern Command, European department, Tyrone Brigade, Belfast Brigade, and security department levels. It was difficult to see how the IRA could have been more thoroughly compromised.

NOT EVERYTHING the IRA touched turned to dust. The European department resumed its campaign on the European mainland and enjoyed immediate success, killing three RAF personnel in one weekend in May 1988, but inevitably, it seemed, there were botched operations leading to civilian deaths, seven in all over the next two years, including that of a six-month-old baby girl and the German wife of a British serviceman. Ten members of the European department were arrested, again suggesting more leaks or treachery. The IRA's England department enjoyed better luck. Between August 1988 and July 1990 its members killed fourteen British servicemen, eleven in a single bomb attack on the Royal Marine School of Music in Deal, Kent. The IRA also assassinated Ian Gow, Margaret Thatcher's close friend and a political ally of Northern Ireland's unionists. In two bombings it came close to causing multiple British army deaths. Later MI5 would make serious inroads into the IRA's English department, so many that the IRA was forced to virtually abandon the use of "sleeper" units, groups sent in to merge with the local population and then activated, but the first two years of the campaign in Britain had shown no obvious sign of agent penetration.

In Northern Ireland, Adams's strategy of encouraging pan-Irish nationalist unity was by this stage formal and public republican policy, although the details of his discussions with Haughey and the contents of the "stepping stones" document remained a closely guarded secret even from the Army Council. Instead Adams argued that pan-nationalism could politically isolate the British and the unionists, and increasingly he urged that the IRA's military strategy be tailored accordingly.

So it was that the Army Council ordered its units to concentrate their energies on attacking British military personnel, to seek out and kill British soldiers in preference to locally recruited and mostly Protestant RUC and UDR members, a change in strategy strongly supported by Adams and his allies.

"Adams's argument was that we needed to build a nationalist consensus and had to tailor the armed struggle accordingly," recalled an IRA source familiar with the debate. "We needed fewer car bombs, more attacks on the Brits, more use of mortars against bases, and so on, but the IRA couldn't deliver."[13] It was this thinking that had shaped the European and English departments' campaigns, and the same would be attempted in Northern Ireland.

Once again there were public clues to the private shift which became evident during the spring and summer of 1988. In June Adams told the *Observer*'s veteran Ireland correspondent, Mary Holland, that it was "vastly preferable" for the IRA to target British soldiers rather than the RUC and UDR. "Callous as it may seem," he told her, "when British soldiers die it removes the worst of the agony from Ireland. . . . It also diffuses the sectarian aspects of the conflict because Loyalists don't see the killing of British soldiers by the IRA as an attack on their community."[14] A month later Adams overtly linked the military tactic with Sinn Fein's quest for pan-nationalist unity. In an interview with the author he said,

> It is a fact which the Dublin establishment might not like to admit, but there is . . . a broad acceptance in the 26 Counties which straddles elements of all the political parties that people don't have any problems about operations against British Crown forces and particularly against what you would call British Army units which are not domestically recruited—no problem whatsoever. If you start off from the basic position that this is morally the right way to do it and add all these other considerations then not only is it the right thing to do but it's also the clever thing to do—to pursue the armed struggle in such a way that it helps either to broaden the base or doesn't obstruct the broader aims of the Movement."[15]

Within the IRA the tactic was justified on the basis that the British would move to leave Ireland if enough soldiers were sent home in coffins. The appalled British reaction to the deaths of two British corporals in March 1988, in the wake of the Gibraltar funeral, was cited as an example. Mistaken for loyalist gunmen about to ambush the funeral of an IRA member, the two men were dragged from their car, beaten by a mob, stripped, and then shot dead by the IRA. Much of the incident was filmed by television crews and the scenes horrified British viewers. Mrs. Thatcher herself turned up at the airport when their bodies were returned to England, testimony to the traumatic impact of the deaths.

The Army Council's endorsement of the Adams analysis was a highly significant move whose underlying message was not detected at the time.

Leaving aside the IRA's capability or lack of it, the notion that Thatcher's government or any British government could be influenced by military deaths was a contentious one. The British army was a volunteer, professional outfit, and the precedent from other colonial-style conflicts, from Cyprus to Vietnam, showed that it was only when conscript armies suffer casualties that domestic pressure to withdraw could become a potent factor, as it was in the United States during the Vietnam War and in Britain during the Cyprus emergency. The decision to scale down attacks on the RUC and UDR, in practice unenforced and unenforceable, disguised a deeper political shift. For years the IRA had targeted local security forces, the UDR in particular, knowing that such attacks, in the words of one Tyrone republican, "stop the unionists doing a deal with the SDLP."[16] In other words, the IRA's attacks on Protestant security force members kept Northern Ireland unstable. Even though the new military tactic was in this regard largely observed only in rhetorical terms, it indicated a subtle change in attitude toward a Stormont-based political settlement on the part of Republican leaders.

The security statistics tell the tale. The number of British soldiers killed by the IRA between 1988 and 1990 rose to fifty-six, as many as had been killed in the six previous years. The IRA's efforts in Europe, Britain, and in Northern Ireland, where in 1988 seventeen soldiers were killed between mid-June and mid-August, meant that the killing rate against the British military doubled. But the IRA could not sustain the campaign. In 1988 military fatalities dropped by over a half, to twenty-two soldiers. The next year there was a slight rise to twenty-four, but then in 1990 the IRA accounted for only ten soldiers. In 1991 British fatalities fell to five, to more or less the level they had been at before the revised offensive was launched. The offensive had proved to be unsustainable and was now over.

The failure of the campaign demonstrated that the British were more or less on top of the IRA. Thatcher had responded to the offensive with a public package of measures, including tougher prison terms, a media ban on Sinn Fein, and a restriction on the right of silence normally enjoyed by suspects in police custody, but a secret package, a vast increase in the Irish budget of MI5 and other intelligence agencies, caused more damage. "Money was being pushed through letter boxes," recalled one activist.[17] Much of the extra finance was directed to recruiting spies in the IRA, but GHQ intelligence noted a sharp rise in efforts to recruit informers in Sinn Fein, so-called "agents of influence," whose job would be to steer the party in certain political directions. There were even attempts to recruit Adams's senior advisers, on one celebrated occasion while the target was on a trip to Barcelona.

The British were ahead of the IRA in technical terms as well. New flak jackets worn by patrolling soldiers could not be penetrated by any bullet in the IRA's armory. Only one weapon could fire a powerful enough round, and that was the U.S.-manufactured Barrett Light 50, an anti-helicopter sniping rifle that fired a huge half-inch armor-piercing slug. Eventually the South Armagh Brigade managed to acquire three of the weapons from its own American contacts, and sent one up to Belfast, where it was promptly lost to the security forces by the Belfast Brigade. But by then it hardly mattered, as the IRA was well on the way to the 1994 cease-fire. The IRA had also lost the battle over radio- and remote-controlled bombs. The British had learned how to block the IRA's radio signals, even though the IRA had learned to modulate its signals. Bombs triggered by landlines could be detected thanks to infrared sensors fitted to British helicopters that were able to detect heat given off by the detonating cables, while culvert bombs, which had once made rural areas a terror for military patrols, had also been mastered by the British. Stuffed into the drains that tunneled underneath rural roads all over Northern Ireland, these land mines had killed scores of soldiers in the 1970s and made South Armagh too dangerous for the security forces to travel in by road. But by the late 1980s every single culvert in Northern Ireland had been blocked with wire mesh, making it impossible for IRA engineers to booby-trap them.

One way or another IRA strategy was in a state of flux. The demands of pan-nationalism had radically changed IRA policy toward loyalist violence, with enervating results on the republican base in Tyrone. Now the objective of building an alliance between Sinn Fein and Fianna Fail had created a demand for military goals that the IRA had been unable to deliver. The IRA was fast running out of military options. The more Machiavellian members of the organization came to a bleak conclusion. "It was a way of running down the war without saying so," deduced one former IRA commander.[18]

IF THE NEEDS of pan-nationalism were pushing the IRA in the direction of politics, then Sinn Fein's electoral reverses were pushing it in the same direction from another. With its constitutional opponent, the SDLP, revitalized by the 1985 Anglo-Irish agreement, Sinn Fein's electoral march upward and onward had been halted. By 1988–89 the party's share of the vote had settled at around the 11 percent mark, almost what it had been in 1982 when the electoral strategy was launched, while the SDLP enjoyed twice that level of support. At the level of council elections the SDLP made gains at Sinn Fein's expense, and then in 1992 disaster struck when the SDLP showed it could repeat that sort of success even against the best that Sinn Fein could field. The jewel in the Sinn Fein electoral crown was snatched away when Gerry Adams lost his West Belfast seat to the SDLP's Joe Hendron, an affable but politically lightweight local family doctor.

In the Republic it was an even sorrier story. There were no signs at all of the power-broking TDs promised by Martin McGuinness at the 1986 IRA Convention, while Gerry Adams's assertion that the second election after the Ard Fheis would be the real test of the benefts of dropping abstentionism showed that Sinn Fein's electoral appeal to Southern voters had collapsed. In the 1987 poll the party won 1.7 percent of the poll and no seats; two years later the Sinn Fein vote fell to a miserable 1.2 percent. In the June 1991 council elections Sinn Fein managed to win only 6 out of the 883 seats at stake and a derisory 0.7 percent share of the vote.

Virtually all the commentators agreed on the cause—a series of botched and bungled IRA operations that began in the autumn of 1987 and continued through to 1992. Each disastrous IRA operation highlighted the glaring contradictions between the IRA's Armalite-based approach and Sinn Fein's espousal of electoral, or ballot box, politics, as it was called. With every botched and bungled operation, with every uninvolved civilian killed, public anger grew and electoral support shrank. Gerry Adams's press aide, Richard McAuley, put it most succinctly in 1992. Once a supporter of the anti-Adams camp led by Billy McKee and David Morley in Long Kesh in the mid-1970s, McAuley had long since joined the Adams camp and later became the Sinn Fein leader's trusted press attaché. In September 1992 he wrote, "We're not going to realise our full potential as long as the war is going in the North and as long as Sinn Fein is presented the way it is with regard to armed struggle and violence."[19]

ON SUNDAY, November 8, 1987, just days after the discovery of the *Eksund*, local Protestants were mingling with members of the RUC and soldiers of the Ulster Defence Regiment at the cenotaph in Enniskillen, the county town of Fermanagh situated in one of the most picturesque spots in Ireland, where the two Erne lakes, the upper and lower loughs, meet. It was Remembrance Day, the annual occasion when the dead of two world wars and the conflict in Ireland were commemorated in a solemn ceremony that culminated in the laying of poppy wreaths at the base of the ornate war memorial. For Protestants it was a sacred day. Suddenly, and without warning, a bomb, hidden in a building overlooking the scene, exploded, sending tons of rubble and brick onto the heads of the crowd. When the dust settled, eleven people lay dead or dying, six of them woman, many of them elderly, and all of them Protestants. It was one of the worst IRA atrocities of the Troubles.

Condemnation was widespread, but it was particularly intense in the Republic. The reason for that was the impact made by Gordon Wilson, the father of the youngest victim, his daughter Marie, a local nurse. Father and daughter had been caught up in the blast, buried together under the rubble. He had survived, but Marie had been crushed to death His emotional, eloquent, but forgiving account of the ordeal, given in a Border brogue, caught the Southern imagination. In many ways Wilson was the South's idealized Protestant—liberal, open-minded, and compassionate. He even read the Dublin-based daily, the *Irish Times*. The fact that the IRA had killed his daughter and had violated a commemoration of Protestant war dead deeply offended many Southerners. Gordon Wilson became an iconic figure in the Republic and was later appointed to the Irish Senate.

The political damage to the IRA was almost beyond calculation, and to compound the disaster the organization had been caught lying in its explanation for the slaughter, falsely claiming that the British had triggered the bomb with a radio sweep for bomb signals. Compelling evidence provided by the British army showed that the device had been set off by a mechanical timer that could have been set only by the hand of an IRA bomber.

It was the start of a catalog of disasters for the IRA. In March 1988 a twenty-one-year-old Protestant woman, Gillian Johnston, died in a machine-gun attack on her car near the Fermanagh village of Beleek that seriously wounded her boyfriend. Again the IRA lied in its account, claiming that the attack had been meant for her brother, a soldier in the UDR. In June the Fermanagh IRA set off a bomb in a school bus near Lisnaskea. The device was meant to kill the part-time UDR driver, but instead it injured children. In July a sixty-year-old Catholic mother and a twenty-four-year-old man, both West Belfast constituents of Adams, were killed in a booby trap bomb placed in the public swimming baths on the Falls Road. A soldier was also killed. Later the same month a land mine meant for a senior Catholic judge as he crossed the Border near Newry instead killed a family driving a similar car. Robert Hanna, a heating contractor, his wife, Maureen, and their seven-year-old son, David, were blown to pieces.

In the nine months since November 1987 the IRA had killed eighteen civilians, not an unusually high level for an organization that had, on the average, claimed the lives of twenty civilians during each year of the Troubles. As in every war, it seemed that civilian casualties were an unavoidable consequence of the Troubles. Two factors, however, made civilian deaths a new and urgent issue for the IRA in 1987 and 1988. The first was the fact that the British had learned from earlier mistakes and no longer killed as many civilians as they used to. In the 1970s and even the 1980s, IRA and British atrocities had more or less canceled each other out. But by this stage only the IRA was killing noncombatants, and there was a public relations and political price to pay for that. The political price was exacted at the polling stations, where bad IRA operations, as they were called internally, lost Sinn Fein support in the voting booths. In fact the damage, the seepage of support for the IRA in effect, could be calculated down to the last vote, and inevitably it had an impact on the organization's politics.

Only a year before the Enniskillen deaths, figures like Adams and McGuinness had promised their grassroots that dropping abstentionism would not weaken or dilute the armed struggle. In one celebrated interview Adams had gone as far as saying that if Sinn Fein ever repudiated the armed struggle, the party would have to look for a new leader.[20] Two years later, as he sought the go-ahead for talks with the SDLP and Haughey's representatives, he had assured the Army Council that military policy would remain supreme. But now, as the armed struggle spawned electoral difficulties, Adams and, to a lesser extent, McGuinness began to criticize the IRA's conduct of the war, criticism that implied the need to curtail and restrict operations.

Adams highlighted the negative consequences of Enniskillen days after the bombing, and he was to return to this theme repeatedly in the next two years. "What is clear is that our efforts to broaden our base have most certainly been upset in all the areas we have selected for expansion," he said. "This is particularly true for the South and internationally. Our plans for expansion will have been dealt a body blow."[21] After the Lisnaskea school bus bomb, Adams said he was "unable to condone" the IRA action.[22] Following the Falls Road swimming baths attack he called on the IRA to "get its house in order,"[23] while the deaths of the Hanna family brought stronger words. He was "very shocked," he told the BBC, and "considerably annoyed."[24] The language of his condemnations grew sharper with each atrocity.

Then, at the Sinn Fein conference in January 1989, Adams took the bull by the horns. "I want to speak directly to the active service volunteers of Oglaigh na hEireann," he told delegates. "You have a massive responsibility. At times the fate of this struggle is in your hands. You have to be careful and careful again. . . . The morale of your comrades in jail, your own morale . . . in the field can be raised or dashed by your actions. You can advance or retard this struggle."[25] Adams's criticism intensified as one botched IRA operation followed another until finally, in June 1990, it reached a sort of watershed. At the launch in West Belfast of a book he had written about his life as an IRA prisoner in Cage 11, his patience ran out. That morning the IRA had placed a booby trap bomb under the car of a retired policeman, sixty-five-year-old James Sefton, in North Belfast. The bomb, fixed by a magnet to the underside of the vehicle and known in the IRA as "up and under," killed Sefton and his sixty-six-year-old wife, Eileen. Asked what he thought of the operation, a visibly angry Adams replied that he no longer believed that Sinn Fein had to explain, justify, or defend every IRA operation. "You can best describe Sinn Fein's position as one of critical support for the IRA," he said.[26] The significance of the remark was that only seven years earlier Sinn Fein's election candidates had been obliged to give unambivalent support to the IRA, lest anyone thought that fighting elections might inhibit the IRA's armed struggle. Now Adams didn't care what the IRA thought. Times had changed.

IT WAS, of course, next to impossible for the IRA to conduct its violence without risking civilian life. Given the conditions under which it fought, especially in urban areas, and the obvious limits on its ability to rehearse operations, civilian casualties were inevitable. Unable to wage the "clean" war that the Sinn Fein leadership demanded and incapable of delivering the quantity and quality of "military operations" necessary to inflict significant casualties on the British army, the IRA saw its war gradually, slowly run down. The preconditions for a public move into the real peace process agenda had arrived.

Adams turned to an institution that he had utilized before when he had wanted to influence the IRA's direction. In the past he had used it to push the Army Council in a radical military and political direction, but now he would use the Revolutionary Council in an effort to steer the IRA away from violence and toward the still-secret peace strategy. In its first manifestation the Revolutionary Council had been an exclusively IRA body, but when Adams again turned to it, he ensured that Sinn Fein was invited to send members to its meetings. The Army Council was, of course, represented at its gatherings, as were the heads of GHQ departments, but this time the Revolutionary Council would also include key members of the Sinn Fein Ard Comhairle in its deliberations, figures who, like Adams, were unhappy at the conduct of the IRA's violence. Composed of some twenty-five to thirty people, the cream of the IRA and Sinn Fein, and chaired by Adams himself, the Revolutionary Council would meet two or three times a year, and although its decisions and opinions were not binding on the Army Council, it was in practice difficult if not impossible for the IRA's leaders to ignore them. Although billed as a way of improving communication and understanding between the IRA and Sinn Fein, the Revolutionary Council would in this form be used by the Adams camp as a tool to rein in and curb the IRA.

One IRA source familiar with its deliberations explained how this worked.

Its function was supposed to be to explore the best way forward. Sinn Fein people raised bad operations, and the IRA people raised criticisms of Sinn Fein statements, but really it was aimed at pointing out to the IRA the error of its ways. It began restricting operations—attacks on school buses were banned, an attempt made to stop killing off-duty UDR men was made but failed, booby traps were restricted and then phased out because they were too indiscriminate, the bombing of factories stopped, and so on. Sinn Fein people said we were putting our own people out of work. They came out against the hoaxes that we were using to cause economic damage. At one stage they were regular Friday events in Belfast, but first they got them banned in the mornings because they were hitting their people going to work and then they were banned in the evening because they affected their people going home. Eventually they were phased out altogether. The Adams faction won the day.[27]

Although the Revolutionary Council was moving the IRA in the direction Adams wished, it was often a hard struggle, and on at least one occasion he was forced to play his ace, in the knowledge that his value to the movement was inestimable. On that occasion, after two Australian tourists mistaken for off-duty British soldiers had been killed in Holland in May 1990, he threatened to quit the IRA and then sought Army Council permission to criticize and condemn IRA operations. When he was refused, he then came up with a second idea. This was to formally and publicly separate Sinn Fein from the IRA, although in practice he and other prominent Sinn Fein figures in the IRA leadership, like McGuinness, would continue to hold their seats on the Army Council. "It lost," recalled one source, "when a consensus emerged that if Adams went down that road, he and others could no longer hold leadership positions in the Army. McGuinness didn't back it either. It would have been a sham division but would have allowed Sinn Fein to criticize the IRA and distance themselves from it. But it was rejected out of hand so strongly that it was never heard of again."[28]

Adams was frustrated but nevertheless later managed to put some formal distance between Sinn Fein and the IRA. Sinn Fein let it be known in January 1991 that the party would no longer act as "proxy spokespersons" for the IRA. A Sinn Fein source told the *Irish Times*, "The IRA can speak for itself."[29] Adams's biographers noted that from this time on it became increasingly difficult to meet the IRA; such meetings were no longer held in Sinn Fein offices, and Sinn Fein stopped faxing IRA statements to the media.[30] The Sinn Fein's publicity machine had been separated from the IRA's. The author had a bizarre personal experience of what this meant. On one occasion an appointment to meet an authorized IRA spokesperson turned into a scene from a B spy movie, complete with instructions on which newspaper to read at which café table. The instructions were too complicated, and the meeting never happened. Prior to this a simple phone call would have ensured a rendezvous.

In 1991 Martin McGuinness joined in the criticism echoing Adams's impatience with IRA mistakes and distancing himself from the organization publicly, even though he was the organization's military chieftain in Northern Ireland.

> Nowhere in the Sinn Fein constitution does it state that if you become a member or supporter of Sinn Fein do you have to support armed struggle. It doesn't say anywhere whatsoever that you have to support the IRA and I think personally from within the republican movement that that is a position which we should be moving towards in the future. That we have to say to people that you can support Sinn Fein and you can support the republican analysis of what's wrong in the six counties and you don't necessarily have to support every single IRA operation which takes place.[31]

Skillfully employing the Revolutionary Council–Army Council mechanism, the Adams camp managed to control and gradually restrict IRA operations, but still the PR disasters—"fuck-ups" as the Provo base called them—continued. The worst of these came in January 1992, when eight Protestant workmen were killed in a 500-pound IRA land mine explosion at Teebane Crossroads on the main road between Cookstown and Omagh in County Tyrone; the blast destroyed their van and tossed their bodies into nearby fields. They had been working for a building company contracted to carry out repairs at the British army base at Lisanelly, Omagh. Opposition to the Provisionals sharpened in the Republic afterward and took tangible form when Dublin City Council banned Sinn Fein from using the Mansion House for its annual Ard Fheis. The council cited Sinn Fein's support for the IRA as the reason.

Despite all the warnings from figures like Gerry Adams, it seemed that the IRA was determined to carry out operations that embarrassed Sinn Fein, demoralized republican supporters and activists, and, arguably, served to undermine the armed struggle itself. To the outside world it sometimes looked as if all this was deliberate, that the IRA was, at best, uncontrollable and, at worst, at odds with Sinn Fein leaders like Adams over the movement's political direction. There was a major difficulty with this view and that was that the IRA leadership did not exist in an insulated, self-contained compartment. Adams was a long-standing member of the Army Council, and the Council, as the supreme IRA body, decided Army policy. Metaphorically, the Army Council's offices were just across the corridor from the offices of the people who ran the war on a day-to-day basis in GHQ, the English department, the European department, and Northern Command and who took their orders ultimately from the Army Council. The heads of these departments were sometimes also members of the Army Council and were often in close, intimate contact with each other. In the latter years of the IRA's campaign, for example, three key figures—the organization's director of operations, its Northern commander, and his deputy, the Northern Command adjutant—all had seats on the Army Council. If all these people had been privy to the peace process strategy—as should have been the case—and appreciated the need for a refined military strategy, Gerry Adams would not have had to lecture them so often about the need to be careful in the way that they fought the war. There could be only two explanations: either the Army Council was deeply divided about the strategy, or its members were largely ignorant of it.

IN THE MID- and late 1980s the Army Council had authorized Northern Command to vet brigade operations in Northern Ireland, and as the years went by that control tightened, much to the irritation of the IRA rank and file, who much preferred to operate on a loose leash. The reason for tightening control was simple. It meant that the leadership could more easily ensure that the IRA's military strategy dovetailed with its political approach, a consideration that assumed enormous importance when Sinn Fein began contesting elections. Despite the requirement for a precisely directed military strategy, the record shows, according to well-informed IRA sources,[32] that Northern Command approved and sometimes initiated the very operations that so often imperiled Sinn Fein's political strategy, operations that frequently claimed civilian lives. They were not the haphazard, ill-thought-out enterprises that the Adams-McGuinness criticism made them out to be. In the case of McGuinness, he sometimes denounced operations that either he, as Northern commander, or his colleagues on Northern Command staff had approved or endorsed. In the case of Adams, he was condemning operations that had been approved in many instances by his closest political ally. Even though much of the criticism by Adams and McGuinness concerned the manner in which the operations had been carried out as much as the concept behind them, it was an extraordinary, not to say bizarre, inconsistency.

According to these IRA sources, Northern Command had, for example, given the go-ahead for the Enniskillen bombing. Attempts by the IRA at the time to blame the disaster on local activists do not square with the fact that there were similar operations elsewhere that day, evidence of the sort of coordination that only Northern Command could organize. A bomb was found at Tullyhommon War Memorial on the Fermanagh-Donegal Border, set to go off at 11:00 A.M., when the Poppy Day service was set to start, while in Belfast a carload of explosives was defused at the headquarters of the Royal British Legion, which organized the annual war tributes.[33] Northern Command had also vetted the Lisnaskea school bus bomb, the bomb at the Falls Road swimming baths, and the Border land mine that had killed the Hanna family, while the deaths of James and Eileen Sefton, which had so exercised Gerry Adams, came as a result of a plan vetted and approved by Northern Command.

IT WAS AGAINST this background, and with the full approval of the entire leadership, that the IRA organized one of the most cold-blooded operations in its history, one that would be imitated years later on a much larger scale in lower Manhattan and on the streets of Jerusalem by Islamic extremists less concerned about the effect of their actions on public opinion. The use of the human bomb did not begin when Al Qaeda hijackers pointed passenger jets at the towers of the World Trade Center or when Hamas bombers blew themselves and scores of Israeli partygoers to pieces. It began in Derry a decade before.

The first use of a human bomb by the IRA was one of those examples of Northern Command initiating an operation rather than approving one suggested by activists lower down the chain of command. In the autumn of 1990, the Command staff won the approval of the Army Council to mount the first of what was to be a series of human bomb attacks, although there was a crucial difference between these and the events that devastated the United States on September 11, 2001. Unlike the Islamic extremists of Al Qaeda, IRA men would not die in their version of the human bomb. The IRA's device instead would be delivered by an uninvolved outsider, usually an innocent civilian, forced to ferry the explosive while his family was held hostage. As an operation calculated to undermine the IRA's armed struggle, alienate even its most loyal supporters, and damage Sinn Fein politically, it had no equal; no other single act of violence perpetrated by the IRA during this phase of its campaign could match it.

Armed and masked IRA men took the family of Patsy Gillespie hostage in the early hours of October 24, 1990, and forced him to drive a car loaded with 1,000 pounds of explosives to the British army checkpoint at Coshquin on the Derry-Donegal Border. Gillespie was chosen to deliver the device because he worked in the canteen of a local British army base, and in the minds of the IRA organizers that made him a legitimate target. He lived in the strongly nationalist Shantallow area of Derry and had refused to relocate even though four years earlier he had been forced to drive another IRA bomb into the city, although on that occasion his life had been spared. As soon as he arrived at the checkpoint, the bomb was detonated by remote control, tearing Gillespie and five British soldiers to pieces. A similar attack later the same day killed a British soldier near Newry, while another human bomb near Omagh was intercepted and defused. Attacks like these continued for a month, culminating in a foiled attempt to destroy the checkpoint at Roslea, County Fermanagh, with a 3,500-pound trailer bomb. In that incident members of a hostage family were tied to a tree while a relative drove the bomb to its target.

Predictably, the human bomb tactic was a public relations disaster. What made the use of the human bomb so difficult to comprehend was that it had been proposed and supported by an IRA leadership that supposedly was in the midst of implementing a strategy aimed at winning political and electoral support on both sides of the Border. That similar attacks were repeated for weeks after Coshquin made the episode even more extraordinary. Adams's lieutenants told journalists they were in despair at what the IRA had done, conveying the impression not only that the Sinn Fein leader had had nothing to do with it but that he was actively opposed to the tactic. One key adviser told the author at the time, "It's gone down very badly with the base from the Ma' [mother] on down. It might be different if it had been a one-off, but because it was done again it has had such a bad effect."[34] But the criticism and public outrage were entirely predictable and raised obvious questions. The IRA leadership, including Adams, was capable of seeing the negative consequences that resulted from, for example, placing a bomb on a school bus, yet they had unhesitatingly supported a tactic that involved forcing a father of three to drive a huge bomb to an army base and then, before he had the chance to escape, blowing him to smithereens.

Only one thing can be said with certainty. The human bomb tactic fortified the peace camp within the Provisionals and weakened the militarists. The BBC journalist Peter Taylor, a veteran reporter of the Irish Troubles, put it well. "By actions such as this and the revulsion they provoked within the community," he wrote, "the IRA inadvertently strengthened the hand of those within the Republican Movement who argued that an alternative to the armed struggle had to be found."[35]

THIRTEEN

The Derry Experiment

The deaths at Coshquin in October 1990 caused outrage in Derry, and there is little doubt the attack marked a low point in the fortunes of the IRA's Derry Brigade. The local nationalist weekly paper, the *Derry Journal*, devoted three pages to the story. The banner headline on the front page called the attack "Bloody Wednesday," and an editorial said the anger in the city was at a level not seen since Bloody Sunday 1972, when British troops had killed thirteen local men, gunning them down without warning or mercy.[1] While nationalist and unionist politicians vied with each other to condemn the atrocity, and the city's Catholic bishop, Dr. Edward Daly, called it "a callous, cynical, crude and horrible deed,"[2] behind the scenes the deaths animated a mini–peace process that was to see the IRA in the city gradually and secretly de-escalate its violence in tandem with the British security forces. Although limited in scope and cautious in its application, this mutual de-escalation made Derry a laboratory experiment where the viability of a wider peace process was tested and the IRA enabled to signal to the British authorities a willingness to bring its long war to a controlled and phased end. In the process, both sides began to build the trust that would be needed if the IRA was to declare a much wider cease-fire.

The IRA's campaign in the rest of Northern Ireland would last for another four years, but in Derry the end came much quicker. Nobody could know it at the time, but the five British soldiers who perished in the Coshquin explosion were the last military personnel to die at the hands of the Provisionals' Derry Brigade. Although seven more people were killed as a result of republican violence in the city before the IRA called its August 1994 cease-fire, only two, both RUC officers, were members of the security forces. Once ranked as the second or third most active brigade in Northern Ireland, the IRA in Derry soon became one of the quietest in the whole organization.

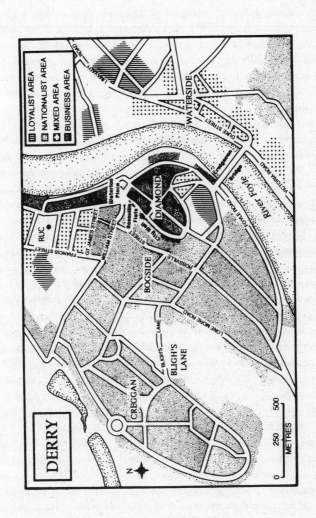

The mechanism that achieved this was modeled on Cold War superpower diplomacy of the sort that for so long had prevented an outbreak of nuclear war between the United States and the Soviet Union. Ultimately it led to both sides' reducing and scrapping much of their arsenals of nuclear warheads. Known by the acronym GRIT (Graduated and Reciprocated Initiatives in Tension Reduction), the strategy was devised when President Kennedy and Premier Khrushchev were in office and it was employed by them a total of sixteen times in the early 1960s.[3] Instead of demanding concessions from each other, GRIT involved one party to a conflict making a unilateral and publicly verifiable concession to the other. The prior agreement of the other party was not necessary for this to happen, and the strategy could be employed in the absence of formal talks or contact. The effect nonetheless would be to invite the other party to do the same. Failure to reciprocate meant that the erring party shouldered the blame for lack of progress, while agreement accelerated the process. GRIT was a safe way of pressurizing each party to de-escalate. Ideally the strategy would be progressive, as one academic expert explained: "With each exchange of concessions, trust grows and tension is reduced."[4]

In the context of Derry's violent past, the IRA's decision even to discuss its participation in such an enterprise was extraordinarily significant. Unlike the Provisionals in Belfast, the IRA in Derry was not driven by sectarian considerations or by the need to defend its community. The Derry IRA was instead created and sustained by conflict between the city's nationalist population and the security forces, first the RUC and then the British army. By agreeing to take part in a process that endeavored to reduce the opportunities for conflict or that softened hostility between its constituency and the British forces, the IRA was in effect offering to cut off the supply of its own lifeblood. It would be difficult to find a more convincing way of signaling a willingness to end the war.

TO GRASP the significance of the events at and after Coshquin, it is first necessary to understand the sanguinary history of Derry itself. Although it is inaccurate to do so, most Northern nationalists place and date the beginning of the Troubles to events in the city on October 5, 1968, when a small civil rights march was batoned and hosed off the streets by a force of RUC men. Their orders from the unionist home affairs minister, Bill Craig, were to stop the crowd marching from Duke Street, on the eastern banks of the Foyle, across Craigavon bridge into the historic, walled center of the city.

The reaction of the police was out of all proportion to the threat posed by the crowd of four hundred or so, but their behavior betrayed the enormous importance unionists attached to retaining their grip on this most nationalist of Northern Ireland's cities. Built and developed as a commercial venture by the City of London companies in the northwest of Ireland in the early 1600s, the walled city was constructed as a Protestant bastion, a garrison of the Scots-English plantation of Ulster. Its fortified walls made the city a place of Protestant refuge during successive Irish native rebellions. A lengthy siege in 1689 mounted by the Catholic King James II won Londonderry, as Protestants always call the city, a special place in loyalist mythology. The fact that it resisted the siege earned it the title "the Maiden City," and hard-line Protestants determined that Catholics would never breach its sanctity.

Catholics had lived outside the walls of Derry from the late eighteenth century in a rat-infested collection of hovels called the Bogside. The population nevertheless grew; by the mid-nineteenth century Catholics were in a numerical majority and by 1920 made up a majority of voters, although gerrymandering meant that unionists held on to control of the corporation. The introduction of proportional representation in the same year changed all that, and for the first time in Derry's history a coalition of nationalists and republicans took control and a Catholic was made mayor. But after partition Derry became part of the Northern Ireland state, and unionists set about reasserting their control. Proportional representation was abolished, electoral boundaries were redrawn so that Catholic votes were devalued, and a property qualification was introduced for elections to local government. According to one estimate, a third of the adult population of the Bogside in 1964 was not allowed to vote in council polls.[5]

Characterized by discrimination and deprivation and with huge male unemployment rates, Derry symbolized nationalist complaints about life in unionist-dominated Northern Ireland. Things did not begin to improve for the city's nationalist community until after the Second World War, when the benevolent effects of the British welfare state, especially the availability of college-level-education, filtered through the Catholic population. A more assertive and impatient generation emerged and demanded change.

Anger at the poor quality of public housing and the unionist-dominated corporation's refusal to build new developments, part of a calculated policy to confine Catholic voters to overcrowded electoral wards, provoked the first mild street protests, led mostly by left-wing activists. The same factors were working on the Catholic psyche elsewhere in Northern Ireland, and in August 1968 the first civil rights march, from Coalisland to Dungannon in County Tyrone, was held but was barred by the RUC from reaching the center of Dungannon. A few weeks later the Derry housing agitators invited the organizers, the Northern Ireland Civil Rights Association, to lead a similar protest in October.

Not everyone in Derry was in favor of such street demonstrations. The Catholic Church exercised the single most powerful influence on the minds of Derry nationalists. The city's bishop at the time, Dr. Neil Farren, one of the most conservative Catholic clerics in Ireland, consistently aligned himself with the forces of law and order, while moderate Catholics expressed alarm both at the radical politics of those behind the civil rights agitation and at its potential for unrest. John Hume, for instance, was ready to lead a motor cavalcade of Derry people to Stormont to protest the unionist government's decision to locate Northern Ireland's second university in the Protestant town of Coleraine but declined to put his name to a document notifying the RUC of the route of the first civil rights march in Derry, something that would have meant accepting legal responsibility for the event.[6] Tensions between these conservative elements and Derry's radicals—and later militant republicans—was to be a defining feature of nationalist politics in the following years, but security force excesses repeatedly drove the moderates into the hard-line camp or neutralized them.

That process began on October 5, 1968. Dozens of marchers were hospitalized by the initial RUC charge, while scores more were forced to run a gauntlet of batons or were drenched by a water cannon operated by policemen whose commander, District Inspector Ross McGimpsie, a local version of Bull Connor, enthusiastically joined the fray. A prominent West Belfast MP, Gerry Fitt, the founder of the Republican Labour Party, was the first to get his skull cracked, while the presence there of a number of British Labour MPs ensured that the events would be impossible to ignore. As it was, a cameraman from the Irish broadcasting service, RTE, captured the police violence on film, and the scenes shocked public opinion in the Republic and in Britain. In the Bogside the events in Duke Street triggered three days of stone throwing, and poorly constructed barricades were erected to keep out the RUC. The October 5 melee was a public relations and political disaster for unionism, but it set Derry's nationalists on a course of increasingly violent confrontation with the state and its uniformed guardians.

The situation only worsened thereafter. In January 1969 some four score radical students from the Belfast-based People's Democracy group staged a march from Belfast to Derry in deliberate imitation of the American black civil rights march from Selma to Montgomery. The seventy-three-mile route took the students through staunch loyalist areas of Counties Antrim and

Derry, and they were constantly blocked and harassed by mobs, some led by associates of the fundamentalist unionist Ian Paisley amid allegations of police collusion. At Burntollet bridge, on the eastern outskirts of Derry, the march was ambushed by an organized gang of stone throwers, many of them off-duty members of the Protestant militia, the B Specials. The RUC fled, leaving the students to the mercy of the loyalist mob. The remnants of the march were again stoned by loyalists as they made their way to Guildhall Square, on the edge of the Bogside, where the arrival of bloodstained survivors sparked five days of fierce rioting. In the early hours of the first night, drunken RUC men went on the rampage in part of the Bogside, smashing windows, shouting sectarian insults, and beating up any Catholic resident unfortunate enough to cross their path. After that, the barricades, this time more effective structures, sprouted throughout the area. Someone painted a slogan on a gable end in the Bogside that read, "You are now entering Free Derry." A myth had been born.

Derry's moderate nationalists had condemned the Burntollet march, as it became known, and eventually talked the barricades down, but events were slipping out of their control. In April there was another outburst of violence, and this time the mostly teenage rioters used gasoline bombs as well as stones to fend off the RUC. Again the police went on a late-night rampage and badly beat a Bogside man, Samuel Devenney. He died three months later, and the conviction grew that RUC batons had hastened his death.

There were more riots on July 12, when Orangemen marched through the city on their way to their annual gatherings, but the real crisis came in August, when the Apprentice Boys of Derry staged their traditional parade through the walled city. Founded in memory of youthful Protestant heroes who had defied attempts by their leaders to surrender the city to the Catholic King James in 1688, the Apprentice Boys parade was always an occasion for sectarian coat-trailing, but in 1969, after a year of accelerating nationalist confrontation with the unionist state, the potential for serious trouble was obvious. Attempts by moderate Derry nationalists to get the march stopped failed in the face of a nervous unionist government's need to appease its extremists. The result was predictable. The ensuing violence pitched not just Derry but the whole of Northern Ireland into the most serious and violent crisis since partition.

In Derry, skirmishes between the Apprentice Boys and Bogside Catholics on August 12 soon developed into a full-scale battle, when the RUC took the side of the loyalists as they made efforts to invade the Catholic area.

This time the Bogsiders repulsed the police charges with volleys of stones thrown from behind barricades and gasoline bombs tossed from the top of a tall block of flats, while the police replied by soaking the area in clouds of acrid CS gas, disabling rioter and innocent resident alike. Roused by a communal fear of what defeat might bring, the resistance offered by the Bogsiders was determined and fierce.

After two days the Battle of the Bogside had been won by Derry's nationalists, and an exhausted RUC was obliged to withdraw. The victorious Bogsiders celebrated as, on the afternoon of August 14, a company of the Prince of Wales Own Regiment took up positions in William Street at the mouth of the Bogside. Elsewhere in Northern Ireland the Derry riots had transformed the political situation. The Irish taoiseach, Jack Lynch, had gone on Irish television the night before to warn that the Republic could not stand by and see innocent people injured and perhaps worse. Lynch's speech raised unionist fears and nationalist hopes that the Irish army would invade, but arguably the real effect was to oblige the Wilson government in Britain to send in the troops. Meanwhile pleas from the besieged Bogsiders that nationalists in Belfast and other towns stage protests aimed at drawing off police resources had been answered with tragic and fatal results. A Catholic man was shot dead by B Specials in County Armagh, and five people were shot dead in Belfast as rioting engulfed interface areas of North and West Belfast.

The arrival of the British army in Derry was greeted by most Catholics as a huge political victory over the unionist government in Belfast, and although some voices warned against giving the troops a welcome, these were in the minority. What everyone did agree on, however, was that in less than twelve months the nationalists of Derry had been transformed from quiescence to militancy, thanks mostly to the actions of the RUC.

IF DERRY PROVIDED proof that nothing radicalizes people quicker than the thump of a police or army club, then it would be hard to find a better example of this than the experience of Martin McGuinness. A nineteen-year-old apprentice butcher at the time of these turbulent events, McGuinness was later to occupy virtually all the top positions in the Provisional republican movement: Derry IRA commander, Northern commander, chief of staff, chairman of the Army Council, Sinn Fein vice-president, Mid-Ulster MP, and Sinn Fein minister of education. Back in August 1969, though, he was just one of the hundreds of so-called Young Hooligans who would throw stones and gasoline bombs at the police. McGuinness's journey to militancy was typical of so many of his contemporaries, and his story is the story of the rise and growth of the IRA in Derry.

Born just at the dawn of the welfare state, McGuinness had a background mirroring that of most families in the Bogside. His mother and father were both devout Catholics and daily communicants. Politics, he remembered in a 1989 interview, were "never discussed" in his family, although, like most Bogsiders, his parents voted for the Derry-based nationalist leader Eddie McAteer with as much devotion as they practiced their religion. Militant republicanism was just not an issue. Back in the late 1960s the number of republicans in Derry could be counted on the fingers of one hand. While Belfast had a large network of republican families, Derry republicanism was dominated by just two veteran figures, Sean Keenan and Neil Gillespie, who could trace their involvement back to the 1940s. In the McGuinness household the IRA was a distant and strange thing. "It was never a subject for discussion," he later recalled.

We had been through what you term the Border campaign, from '56 to '62. I do remember vaguely discussions with my friends about what is the IRA and people were saying the IRA is this and the IRA is that. I had no real interest in it and it meant nothing to me. Our lives revolved around attending Derry City football matches, playing football ourselves, playing Gaelic football and hurling and, when we got old enough, having a good time at the weekend.[7]

Nor were McGuinness and his contemporaries always hostile to the RUC:

The cops were people who came to street corners to chase you away if somebody sent for them because you were playing football on the street . . . they were never seen as a political thing at all. There was actually a cop, I forget his name, who was fairly involved with the local football club here. The cops were strolling around the Bogside and nobody took a second look at them. The older people had a resentment towards them but it was never really discussed or talked about to us young people. I can never recall my father or my mother or any older people saying "these guys are bad news" or "they've done this" or "they've done that."[8]

At the early stage of the civil rights agitation McGuinness shared the moderate views of Catholic leaders like John Hume. Reform, not revolution, was uppermost in his mind:

[I was] very pacifist, absolutely and I agreed with them at the time. I thought it was dead sound because at that time I wouldn't have been saying let's fight back, let's use violence against these people because they're using violence against us. I never felt that the situation had deteriorated so badly that that could be justified. There was always the hope that somewhere along the lines of government would catch themselves on and grant the Catholic people the demands they were asking for.[9]

The beating and subsequent death of Samuel Devenney began a change in McGuinness's attitudes. "The innocuous policeman who was involved in our football club had suddenly overnight become a monster because Catholics were demanding civil rights," he recalled. "So at that stage we regarded our community as being under attack by the RUC, that these people had turned into monsters."[10] After this he began throwing bricks and stones with the best of them.

McGuinness was neutral about the British army when the Prince of Wales Own Regiment replaced the RUC on August 14, and was ready to be influenced by the way subsequent events unfolded. "[T]here were people saying that the troops eventually would be used against the people [but] I never took sides in that debate at all. I never said this side's right, we should welcome them. After they arrived I just went home . . . and took up no position at all on whether the coming of the troops was a good thing or a bad thing."[11]

THE BRITISH TROOPS and the nationalists of Derry enjoyed a honeymoon period after the Battle of the Bogside, but like all honeymoons it was fated to be a short-lived affair. At the end of September, the Derry Citizens Defence Association, set up in anticipation of the August riots by the presplit Republican Club, dismantled the last remaining barricades around the Bogside, but almost immediately there were sectarian clashes that developed into running battles between Protestant youths from the Fountain area and Bogside Catholics. In the riots that followed, a middle-aged Protestant man, William King, was beaten, suffered a heart attack, and died.[12] Local unionists, already deeply unsettled by the events of August, demanded that the British troops react vigorously to this incident and to the continued defiance represented by Free Derry.

The British army's response to the death of King was governed in no small way by the background of the senior military commanders now charged with policing the city. Many had recently served in colonial trouble spots, and this shaped their attitude to the Bogsiders, as the most detailed study of the city at this time noted: "Brigadier Peter Leng, for example, the commander of the British troops in Derry, had been a battalion CO in Aden from 1964 to 1966, when the British withdrew. It is hardly surprising that such officers should draw on their colonial experiences, in Aden, Malaya, Kenya, Cyprus or Oman, when dealing with the situation in Derry."[13] Within days of King's death British troops erected a "peace-ring", which comprised checkpoints and military barriers, that cut off the Bogside and the Creggan above it from the city center, treating it like an Arab souk that had to be insulated from the rest of civilized humanity. Under pressure from unionists, the British army was beginning to isolate and identify Derry's nationalists as the problem. That they did so without taking into consideration the objections of the city's moderate Catholics served only to further isolate this important sector of nationalist opinion and foster the psychological climate for further confrontation.

It was not long after this that Martin McGuinness had his first brush with the law, when he was arrested and charged with a breach of the peace during a confrontation with the RUC and British troops near the Bogside. Accused of shouting abuse at soldiers, he was bound over to keep the peace for two years.[14] Relations between the soldiers and Catholics in Derry gradually worsened in the following months. After clashes between off-duty troops and Catholic youths, often sparked by rivalry over girls at dances, the army banned city center cinemas from showing movies at nighttime. As an example of taking a sledgehammer to break open a nut, it could hardly be bettered.

The number of clashes increased as 1970 wore on. In February a rally by the loyalist leader Ian Paisley sparked confrontations between Catholics and British troops, who pursued stone-throwers into the Bogside, just as the RUC used to do. For the first time the military resorted to snatch squads equipped with long, heavy batons to arrest alleged rioters, often beating them severely. At Eastertime there were more riots and incursions by troops into the Bogside after a protest at Strand Road RUC station, where a Union Jack had been hoisted to coincide with the Official Republican Easter parade. Allegations of beatings, indiscriminate arrests, and the use of fabricated court evidence against accused rioters by British troops multiplied. In one of the most notorious of such cases three teenage girls were jailed for rioting on the word of a soldier whose flirtatious advances, one of the girls claimed, had been spurned some days before.

The worst rioting, three days of it, came in June when the civil rights MP Bernadette Devlin was jailed for her part in the August 1969 violence.

When the RUC reneged on an agreement not to take her into custody until after she had addressed a rally in Derry, the frustrated crowd went wild with anger. For the first time since their arrival, British troops used CS gas against the Bogside.

By mid-1970 support for the new Provisional IRA was growing in Belfast, but in Derry the Officials were still the dominant of the two groups. Despite competition between them, the bitter ideological and personal rivalry that characterized the republican division in Belfast was absent in Derry. As in Tyrone and other rural areas, the two groups often acted as one, and recruits were attracted to one or the other by their sense of which group offered the better chance to hit back at the British troops, rather than by political ideas. As relations between the Catholic population and the British military deteriorated, however, that choice increasingly became the Provisionals.

In June 1970 the small group that constituted the Provisional IRA in the city was virtually wiped out in one fell swoop when a premature explosion killed Thomas Carlin, Joe Coyle, Tommy McCool, and his two young daughters. The three men were making a bomb when it blew up in their faces, and the fledgling IRA was decimated. After this, Provisional IRA activity was sporadic and infrequent. Shots were fired at the British army in August 1970 and a bomb exploded in September, but that was more or less the sum of IRA operations. The Easter 1971 republican celebrations revealed that support for the Officials was running at around twice the level for the Provos. The journalist and left-wing activist Eamonn McCann was able to write, "In the spring of 1971 the Provisional IRA in Derry for practical purposes did not yet exist."[15] Despite the rioting and the bitterness that flowed from it, the threat from either IRA was considered to be so slight that nationalist Derry was still regarded at this time as safe for off-duty soldiers; only in May 1971 were the Bogside and Creggan declared off-limits by British commanders.[16]

The Provisionals' fortunes began to change on July 8, 1971, when British troops used live rounds against rioters and in the space of twenty-four hours shot dead two young Bogsiders, twenty-eight-year-old Seamus Cusack and nineteen-year-old Desmond Beattie. Allegations by the British that the two men had been armed or were about to throw gelignite bombs when shot infuriated the small nationalist community, which knew both men well enough to know this was untrue. For Martin McGuinness the shooting of Cusack and Beattie was a seminal moment. He had joined the Officials but had left, disgusted at their inactivity, and defected to the Provisionals not long after the McCool group were killed. He, like others in the city, sensed a turning point had been reached that shifted nationalist opinion firmly against the British army and set the stage for the Provisionals to eclipse the Officials. "[O]f all the incidents that happened in Derry, the shooting of Cusack and Beattie were [sic] the most traumatic and the most decisive in turning people against the British Army in this city," he recalled.[17] Within days John Hume had led the SDLP out of Stormont, much to the barely disguised anger of the party leader Gerry Fitt in Belfast. It was a testament to the intensity of feelings in Derry that Hume and his moderate allies had little choice; not to have taken the step would have risked the political leadership of their community.

The introduction of internment a month later pushed the pendulum even more in the Provisionals' direction, as Martin McGuinness testified.

> Right up until internment . . . the Provisional Republican movement in the city was in my opinion very, very weak; there wouldn't have been more than a dozen or fifteen people involved in it. And then when internment was introduced the majority of those people were arrested, the vast majority were arrested. After their arrest the strength of the movement in this town would have been almost at zero, apart from a few isolated people. And . . . when [the British] introduced internment the floodgates opened. By the end of the week the Republican movement would have risen from about five to twenty and by the end of the next week would have went to thirty. You were [then] into gun battles at this stage and soldiers being killed and IRA [being killed]. You're talking about membership being into the hundreds then.[18]

The first British soldier killed by the Derry Brigade was shot by a sniper a few days after the August 9 internment operation, and the scale of recruitment to the Provisionals in response to internment can be gauged by the fact that in the following sixteen months twenty-eight more soldiers suffered violent deaths,[19] while the commercial center of Derry was subjected to a clinical economic bombing campaign until, as one account described it, the city "looked as if it had been hit from the air."[20] A significant feature of the recruits flooding into the Provisionals was their extreme youth. Martin McGuinness, for example, was only twenty-one when he became the Derry Brigade's second-in-command, while the adjutant of the Bogside Coy, Eamonn Lafferty, shot dead in August 1971, was only nineteen.[21] The abundance of young recruits meant that the IRA would have the resources to wage a prolonged struggle in the years to come.

THE ROAD to Bloody Sunday five months later was littered with more examples of British army violence driving recruits into the ranks of the Provisionals. In July 1971 a nine-year-old boy was knocked down and killed by an army Saracen speeding through the narrow, confined streets of the Bogside; the vehicle drove on and left the dead boy lying in the street. In September an army sniper shot a fourteen-year-old schoolgirl in the back of the head. The child's funeral provided an opportunity for a huge outpouring of grief and anger, and the size of the mourning crowd—put at some ten thousand people—was eloquent testimony to the speed with which Derry was being radicalized. Later that week a speeding armored car knocked down and killed a three-year-old boy and drove on. As in the earlier fatal vehicle incident, the authorities ignored the death. British troops were later accused of firing live rounds indiscriminately in the Creggan district of the city; the pock-marked walls of houses appeared to substantiate the complaint. Derry's influential Catholic schoolteacher coterie protested as one when it became clear that military operations were being timed to coincide with the passage of children to and from local schools. The teachers alleged that this was being done either to give troops protection or to entice the IRA into mounting operations that could endanger young lives.[22] Meanwhile the military abandoned even the pretense of consulting with moderate Catholic opinion, further eroding the influence of the church and figures like John Hume.

On January 30, 1972, the British army's war against the civilian population of Derry reached its zenith, when soldiers of the First Battalion of the Parachute Regiment, specially drafted into the city for the day, opened fire on a crowd attending a march and rally called by the Northern Ireland Civil Rights Association to protest against the continuation of internment. Within a few minutes thirteen men, mostly young and none of them armed or involved with either IRAs, had been shot dead. A fourteenth man died of his wounds some time later. In the days afterward young men and women literally queued up to join the Provisionals, while the remaining moral qualms about the use of violence against the British vanished. "People made a holiday in their hearts at the news of a dead soldier," wrote Eamonn McCann of the atmosphere in the Bogside afterward.[23]

The story of the growth and development of the Provisional IRA in Derry is the tale not about how ideology triumphed but about how police and military violence created and nourished the need to retaliate. Martin McGuinness himself put it best: "The British developed republicanism. It was nothing we had done to develop resistance to British rule. They brought about resistance to British rule. . . ."[24]

IRA support in Derry was disproportionately high because of the events of 1971 and 1972; one authoritative estimate suggests that a staggering 2 percent of the city's 50,000 Catholic population was imprisoned for IRA activites in the years between 1971 and 1986.[25] Many more evaded capture. The Derry Brigade established itself as one of the most active groups in the IRA. Its involvement in sectarian and civilian killings was possibly the lowest of any group in the IRA. At the same time the brigade's record of attacks against the British army demonstrated vividly that hatred for the military was undoubtedly the strongest force persuading Derry people to join the IRA. Some 17 percent of all British military fatalities during the Troubles in Northern Ireland were caused by the Derry IRA, compared with 30 percent in Belfast, where the pool of potential IRA recruits was perhaps four or five times larger.

THIS HISTORY and the Derry Brigade's central role in the development of the Provisionals make all the more remarkable the fact that the IRA's campaign was scaled down earlier there than anywhere else, albeit secretly and gradually. It was even more significant that the IRA leadership, or at least elements of it, chose Derry as the arena for secretly discussing and implementing mutual de-escalation measures with the British authorities.

The story of how this happened has its roots in an earlier peace movement, one that, far from securing support from the Provisionals, was actively and at times violently opposed by them. Inspired by the tragic deaths in Belfast of the three young Maguire children, killed when the driver of a Provo getaway car was shot dead by British troops in Andersonstown and careered out of control, the Peace People movement of 1976 captured a popular mood of fatigue with the Troubles. Led by Mairead Corrigan, an aunt of the young victims, and a neighbor, Betty Williams, the Peace People held rallies and marches throughout Ireland, one of the largest of which traversed Belfast's Shankill and Falls Roads in a bid to unite Catholic and Protestant. Ultimately the Peace People faltered. The group lost its influence in republican areas when it refused to condemn British and loyalist violence, and it was later embroiled in a financial scandal over the distribution of funds donated by sympathizers across the world and the proceeds of the Nobel Peace Prize awarded to Corrigan and Williams. But enthusiasm for the project in the initial period was intense, and numerous branches were established in both parts of Ireland.

A support group was set up in Derry, but in 1978 it broke off from the parent body in Belfast in protest against the leadership's refusal to consult the grassroots membership, and the Derry Peace People became the Peace and Reconciliation Group (PRG). Comprising around a dozen members drawn from both communities in the city, the PRG included former loyalist and republican paramilitary members, some of whom were still in friendly contact with former colleagues even though they had themselves given up violence.

Quaker influence was strong from the start of the Troubles in much peace work in Northern Ireland. Quakers had run a family center for the relatives of republican and loyalist prisoners at the Maze prison from the early days of internment, and the name they earned for neutrality enabled the Society of Friends to mediate between and within paramilitary groups. The PRG was partly inspired by the work of an English Quaker, Will Warren, who had lived in Derry since the early 1970s. Described as "a very good-hearted and honest man" by those who knew him, Warren built up a network of contacts from church leaders to republican and loyalist paramilitaries and was trusted sufficiently to move freely through the Bogside. Those contacts were to prove invaluable when in the early 1980s two other English Quakers, John and Diana Lampen, decided to make their home in Derry. Financially supported by the Rowntree Trust, a Quaker-oriented charity funded by the famous English confectionery and chocolate company, they joined the group. The role John Lampen and two former paramilitary members of the PRG undertook as mediators between republican leaders and the British security and political authorities was to play a largely unreported but significant part in the IRA's journey to the 1994 cease-fire. Some in the Northern Ireland Office regarded the Lampens "as Derry's version of Alec Reid," as one official recalled.[26]

The PRG was involved in conventional community work, organizing Protestant and Catholic sporting events, vacations, and so on. But it was in their work mediating between the security forces and the Catholic community, especially the IRA, that the real impact was made. Their first moves were meant to improve relations between the Catholic community and the RUC. Derry City Council had established a police liaison committee, but none of the nationalist parties would sit on it. The RUC divisional commander in turn declared that there would be no point in his working with the committee unless nationalists participated, so the PRG chairperson, the County Donegal–born nurse Margaret O'Donnell, and a Catholic friend joined. Their purpose was to persuade the RUC to respond more honestly and intelligently to Catholic complaints of police misbehavior. All too often, the PRG realized, the instinct of the authorities was to treat such complaints as republican propaganda and ignore them.

Slowly the PRG established a reputation among Nationalists as an acceptable and trusted channel of complaints to the RUC about security force misbehavior, often securing results that strengthened the group's credibility. It had tried to establish the same sort of relationship with the various British army regiments stationed in Derry, but for years met a brick wall of refusal. "Community liaison officers were there to keep the public off the backs of regimental commanders not to liaise with the community," complained one source.[27] In 1989, however, the PRG made a breakthrough when the CO of the Royal Hampshire Regiment, Colonel Paul Davies, asked the group to help his soldiers improve relations with the community. Davies welcomed a suggestion from the PRG that they should talk to rank-and-file soldiers about attitudes, particularly those in the nationalist community, toward the military.

"They would meet in the NAAFI canteen, ten to fifteen soldiers about to undertake a patrol together, and they would talk about the issues of the day and explain how people in the Bogside felt about the army," recalled one military source.[28] Another explained, "A lot of it was really basic stuff, like how the kids who threw stones at them weren't being made to do it by the IRA and that most of the general public didn't hate them." There would be question-and-answer sessions and every six weeks a refresher seminar with the PRG. The soldiers related well to the Derry-born members of the PRG, regarding their views as an authentic reflection of the people they met on patrol. Officers, on the other hand, responded well to John Lampen, not just because he was English like them but because he had served as an NCO during the days of national service in Britain and knew the military mind well.

Slowly, under the PRG's guiding hand, the British army began to soften its profile in Derry in the late 1980s. The system of civilian complaints was overhauled. "Before if soldiers misbehaved on the streets or abused people or property during searches and a complaint was made, civilians would never be told what the outcome was," said a source involved in the changes. "Under the new system the CO would ensure that an officer visited the complainants to inform them."[29] Soldiers were discouraged from using the telescopic sights on their rifles to scan streets, a practice that to civilians looked as if they were being aimed at. The local British commanders successfully argued the case for modifying the military instruction that obliged soldiers to wear combat helmets while on duty in Northern Ireland. Troops were allowed to wear soft berets at checkpoints and then gradually the practice was extended to other situations. "The helmets sent a warlike message, so we decided to make our soldiers look more like human beings," said one senior military source.[30]

The British military at all levels in Derry increasingly went to the PRG for advice about operational matters. Army commanders had, for example, toyed with the notion of patrolling the Bogside and Creggan in open jeeps, but the PRG dissuaded them on the grounds that the sight of soldiers careering through housing estates in this way would be provocative and an invitation to stone-throwers. PRG advice was also sought on how best to police public order situations such as IRA funerals and the annual Bloody Sunday commemoration march.

The PRG had cultivated excellent contacts with senior Derry republicans, and both the IRA and the British army were aware that the Lampens and their colleagues were in touch with each other. It was due to this relationship that the war in Derry was slowly and gradually brought to an end. "We had agreed ground rules, and these were clear," explained one senior British officer. "We knew that the Lampens had contact with the IRA, and the IRA presumably knew that they were in contact with us. There was an understanding certainly on our part, and I suspect on theirs too, that the conduit could not be used for intelligence purposes, otherwise it would be undermined and destroyed."[31] Not everyone in the British security apparatus liked the arrangement. The RUC objected "to communication with the enemy," as one source put it, while some in the military were concerned that the army could leave itself open to IRA manipulation. However, local British commanders approved, and so did the Northern Ireland Office and its security advisers. "Their attitude," remembered the same officer, "was that this was a sensible way to move forward."[32]

By 1990–91 the British army was calling the PRG conduit "the Derry experiment," and the most senior soldier in Northern Ireland then, the British GOC, Lieutenant General Sir John Wilsey, had personally endorsed the project. During a visit to Derry he assured the PRG that from then on every regimental commander posted to the city on the regular two-year tour would be told to continue the relationship. If they did not, the PRG was authorized to complain directly to British army headquarters in Lisburn.

It was not always clear whether the PRG conduit between the IRA and the British army produced results. Nothing was ever that direct or explicit; the results of the group's mediation were often expressed indirectly or implicitly. A good example was an IRA decision not to deploy the coffee jar bomb in Derry. An invention of the IRA engineering department, the coffee jar bomb was designed to explode upon impact. Packed with Semtex explosives, nails, and pieces of metal, the devices were deadly. Once they appeared in the IRA arsenal, soldiers in the PRG seminars began to express the concern that they would not be able to distinguish between youngsters throwing bottles or glass jars and those tossing coffee jar bombs, and that an innocent teenage rioter could be shot dead, something that would intensify hostility between the military and the Catholic population.

The bombs were so dangerous that army patrols in Derry would have to resume wearing helmets, and that would be an inflammatory act, a reversal of the GRIT strategy. Lampen and a PRG colleague went to the IRA and were told that this situation could not arise; IRA Volunteers had to be eighteen before they would be allowed to throw any bombs, while IRA standing orders "forbade the use of members of the public as cover for operations." They passed this reply back to the army, and that was the end of the exchange—or so it seemed. The devices continued to be used by the IRA in Belfast, but after that PRG-mediated conversation between the British army and the IRA, there were no more coffee jar bomb attacks in Derry.[33] No formal agreements had been entered into, not even a hint of what would happen. But the results were there for all to see.

The Lampens had become friendly with two Derry republicans in particular: Martin McGuinness, the IRA's Northern commander at this time, and Mitchel McLaughlin, the chairperson of Sinn Fein in Northern Ireland and a member of Derry City Council. The Lampens had sometimes slept over in McGuinness's Bogside home when visiting Derry prior to their permanent move to the city; and they occasionally took the McGuinness children away on PRG-sponsored cross-community trips. John Lampen met McLaughlin and McGuinness regularly, and in between there were informal contacts with either or both men. Later the two Provisional leaders tried to minimize the extent and significance of the arrangement, but the truth was that communication between them and the PRG was substantial, sustained, and significant.

The PRG was interested in making the GRIT strategy a vehicle for reducing IRA violence in Derry, something that could pave the way for more ambitious moves elsewhere. While it was easy to see what the IRA could do in terms of unilateral de-escalatory measures, it was more difficult to envisage the measures that the British army might contemplate. So in the autumn of 1990, in the weeks before the Coshquin "human bomb" attack, the PRG compiled a list of de-escalatory moves that the Provisional IRA and the British army and RUC could make in sequence. By this stage the PRG was in regular touch with the Northern Ireland Office, and the list was compiled after discussions with an NIO representative, the British army's Western Brigade commander, the RUC divisional commander, and Sinn Fein. Built on contributions from all these sources, the list was submitted to the RUC, the British army, and, via a trusted intermediary, to the IRA Army Council, or so the PRG believed.

The list contained eleven moves that the British army or RUC could make and ten that the IRA could make. The measures would be confined to the Derry city area and could be introduced one or two at a time without publicity and further moves made dependent on the response from the other side. If the process succeeded in Derry, then the resulting trust could be used as a basis for a full-fledged IRA cease-fire. The fact that the British government, its security chiefs, and the IRA leadership were all involved in the initiative made it full of significance for the unfolding peace process.

The document suggested the following possible moves toward a more relaxed security situation in the Derry area:

Moves the Security Forces could make immediately:

1. *Declare a moratorium on any decision about a [new] police station in Bishop Street;*
2. *Set up a Lay Visiting Scheme to police stations in Derry;*
3. *Improve response to complaints against police and army.*

Moves if there was a reduction of IRA activity in Derry:

1. *End blanket area searches;*
2. *Remove security barricades etc. from city wall—[to encourage] tourism;*
3. *Stop trying to recruit teenagers as informers.*

Moves if there was an end to attacks etc:

1. *Remove Strand Road/Spencer Road (RUC station) barriers;*
2. *Progressively withdraw Army from streets;*
3. *Reduce street patrols, road checks and personal searches;*
4. *Decide against Bishop Street police station;*
5. *Open a "walk-in" police office in the Richmond (shopping) centre— unarmed and possibly civilian staff—to provide a genuine service re insurance claims, lost property etc—not likely to be used by informers due to public location.*

Moves the IRA could make immediately:

1. *No street attacks—risk of civilian injuries;*
2. *No bombings likely to cause fear in Protestant area—especially the Fountain;*
3. *No attacks on police going to the assistance of the public;*
4. *Reduction of home takeovers.*

Moves if there was a security force response:

1. *No attacks on "off-duty" forces;*
2. *Attempt to avoid targetting Ulster Protestants even in security forces—i.e. a more positive move in the interests of Irish unity;*
3. *End of house takeovers.*

Moves if army was taken off the streets and there was a strong [and] positive RUC response:

1. *End attacks on security force installations;*
2. *Remove arms and explosives stores from the city;*
3. *Recognise public right to use the police provided the police provide only a genuine service [i.e. do not try to recruit informers].*[34]

Officially the PRG heard nothing more from the IRA leadership about these proposals, although there were private indications that the organization was ready to respond positively to some of the measures, including ending house takeovers, ending bombings that intimidated Protestants, stopping attacks on RUC officers going to the assistance of the public, and removing IRA arms dumps from the city.

The mini–peace process in Derry remained a closely guarded secret, every bit as hidden and furtive as the Reid-Adams diplomacy, which it clearly complemented. But in 1993 the Opsahl report, the product of an independent investigation into the possibilities for political progress in Northern Ireland, was published and inadvertently revealed the PRG's role as a conduit between the IRA in Derry and the British security authorities.

Not long after the Opsahl report made public the PRG's role, the author traveled to Derry to interview Martin McGuinness and Mitchel McLaughlin about the claim. In an upstairs room of Sinn Fein's office in Cable Street in Derry, the two men angrily denied reports of secret mediation moves between the IRA and the British.

Of John Lampen's role, McGuinness said, "There is just no basis for the claims made. He came to us once with the idea of making Derry a shining light, to make it a bomb-free zone. We told him to go away. There was no way the IRA would free British resources for use elsewhere. He's either very flaky, has misinterpreted conversations with our people, or something more sinister has been going on." The PRG, he went on, had been told that Lampen was "virtually persona non grata" with Derry Provisionals.[35] In March of the following year family reasons obliged John and Diana Lampen to leave Derry for good, their value as peace workers undermined by Martin McGuinness's angry public response to the Opsahl revelations.

Despite McGuinness's and Mitchel McLaughlin's denials, there was little doubt that the IRA and the British authorities did engage in a mutual de-escalation process in the early 1990s and that the process had been facilitated in no small measure by the PRG and its proposed set of sequenced measures.

The record shows that many of the proposals on the list were implemented, some earlier than others. The planned RUC station in Bishop Street in the heart of the walled city, actually a small post, was never built, for example. Had it been, it would have brought the police presence to within yards of the Bogside, the closest of any RUC base, and have required substantial military protection in order to function, something that would have antagonized Derry's nationalists. By not building it, the British sent an important signal to the IRA. Blanket army house searches also ended, and the military presence in Derry, in accordance with the PRG-inspired strategy, continued to soften. The British government also set up a lay visiting scheme to check that detainees in police cells, including IRA suspects, were being properly treated throughout Northern Ireland. In Derry the PRG members Margaret O'Donnell and Diana Lampen were appointed to the local team.

An analysis, by the author, of operations carried out by the Derry Brigade shows that the IRA also responded to the PRG paper. Figures supplied by the IRA itself in the weekly columns of *An Phoblacht–Republican News,* reveal a dramatic falloff in activity in the months and years after the PRG de-escalation proposals were submitted. Between 1986 and 1989 the Derry IRA accounted for an annual average of 13 percent of all IRA operations, whereas between 1990 and 1993, after the PRG initiative had been launched, the average fell to just under 5 percent, a reduction of more than 60 percent.[36] British military sources also confirm that the process had gotten under way: "The upshot was that when we started discussing various de-escalatory measures [throughout Northern Ireland], it was possible to say that we have already done that in Derry," recalled one senior officer.[37]

The PRG never heard back officially from the IRA leadership regarding the proposed de-escalation measures, but the group did eventually get confirmation that the GRIT strategy had been adopted by the republican leadership in the city. "A couple of years later," remembered a source familiar with the episode, "maybe at the end of 1992 or the beginning of 1993, John Lampen asked Mitchel McLaughlin if there was a chance that this agenda could be implemented, and McLaughlin replied, 'What do you think we have been doing for the last two years?'"[38] The British army, McLaughlin added, had been responding in kind. Derry had become the principal laboratory for the peace process.

The problem that figures like Martin McGuinness had with the revelations in the Opsahl report, the reason they had so angrily and brusquely disavowed the Lampens, was that the truth about the contacts between the IRA, the PRG, and the British and the proposals to run down the war in the city were kept a secret not just from the IRA rank and file, as would be expected, but from the Army Council as well. The Derry experiment was never sanctioned by the IRA leadership, nor was it ever told that it was happening.[39]

To the public and to their grassroots supporters, the message from the Provisional leaders at this time was a very different one from that communicated privately to the British from Derry. The war, they regularly assured their people, would continue until victory. At almost exactly the moment when the PRG was compiling its de-escalation proposals and preparing to submit them to the Northern Ireland Office and, so it thought, to the Provo leadership, an IRA spokesperson gave a lengthy interview to the *Independent* newspaper in London. Asked about cease-fire speculation, the spokesperson was blunt: "It's a tired old subject and it's one that comes up with predictable regularity. But the only debate within the IRA is on how best to prosecute the war against the British. We can state absolutely, on the record, that there will be no ceasefire, no truce, no cessation of violence short of a British withdrawal. That, as blunt as that, is our position."[40]

PART FOUR

Ending the War

President Bill Clinton underlines his support for the peace process by greeting Gerry Adams on the Falls Road in West Belfast during his first visit to Northern Ireland, in November 1995. *(Sygma-Corbis)*

FOURTEEN

Seven Men in a Room

When Gerry Adams embarked upon the journey that eventually led to the end of the IRA's violent armed struggle against Britain, he enjoyed one huge advantage. For all practical purposes supreme power over the IRA lay in the hands of one small body, the seven-man Army Council, which was perched at the top of the organization's pyramidal structure. It was the one part of the IRA where Adams's idea of permanent leadership found its clearest expression, and during the key decade of the peace process, from 1984 until 1994, the same men, with only one or two exceptions, sat around the IRA's boardroom table and decided the direction and policy that the organization should take. Adams could count on the absolute loyalty of three of his six colleagues, and while that, combined with his own vote, gave him a simple numerical majority, practical politics dictated that to get vital and controversial decisions, such as calling a cease-fire safely through, he would need the support of at least one and preferably two more Army Council members. The story of how he did that can now be told.

The structure of the IRA's government gave considerable leverage to those at its pinnacle, and the reason for that was not just that the IRA was a disciplined body whose members, although volunteer soldiers, readily obeyed orders. In their eyes the Army Council was not merely a military politburo that issued orders but the only rightful government of the still-born Irish Republic, which, according to republican dogma, had been betrayed first by the followers of Michael Collins, who signed the Treaty in 1921, and then by Eamon de Valera, who abandoned the republican struggle in 1926 to enter constitutional politics. The Army Council may not have had the powers and control over society exercised by conventional governments, but its right came from a higher authority; it was spiritual, conferred by the blood sacrifice of those who had fought and died to attain the Irish Republic and by the will of the whole Irish people who had voted for it back in 1919. The status of government was bestowed upon the Army Council in 1938 when the handful of surviving anti-Treaty members of the Second Dail, the last all-Ireland and independent parliament, agreed to pass on their authority to its seven members for safeguarding, lest it disappear with their deaths. Thereafter when Volunteers of the IRA—known properly as Oglaigh na hEireann, or ONH in republican shorthand—swore their allegiance to the Army Council, it was really to this almost mystical administration that they pledged their loyalty. Under the guidance, pressure, and cajoling of Gerry Adams and his allies, it was this "government of Ireland" that would bring the IRA to peace. And it was because of the Army Council's special, almost sacred status that so many of the IRA's rank and file went along with a process that caused within many of them the greatest doubts and anxiety.

THERE WERE NO WOMEN on the Army Council, and there never had been. The Provisional's Army Council had always been a decidedly male preserve, a not surprising feature of the IRA of the 1920s through to the 1960s, given the secondary role played by women in society at large in those days. But under the Adams leadership republicans had championed the concept of gender equality, and this was reflected in the IRA itself, where women were encouraged both to join the male organization and to regard themselves as being on a par with their male colleagues. At the 1986 Convention the IRA's constitution had even been rewritten to excise sexist language. In the meantime women had become brigade commanders and had even made it to the staff of Northern Command but, curiously, never to the supreme decision-making body.

Although the Army Council determined IRA policy, operational control was in the hands of the chief of staff, who had at his disposal the service of a GHQ staff and a Northern Command whose task was to conduct the day-to-day campaign of violence against the British. In the years before the 1994 cease-fire, GHQ consisted of nine departments, each headed by a director who reported to the chief of staff. Each department carried out specialized functions and had its own identity, traditions, and culture. When it came to gauging sentiment in the IRA about political matters, such as whether or not a cease-fire should be called, departmental loyalties and differences mattered as much as, if not more than, geographical ones. Whether an IRA member was in the engineering or the finance department influenced his or her views as much as whether he or she came from West Belfast or East Tyrone.

The largest department in GHQ, accounting for perhaps 20 percent of the IRA's manpower, was the quartermaster's department. This department was responsible for acquiring and smuggling weapons into Ireland and then for finding secure dumps in which to hide the organization's stores of arms and munitions. It also had the job of building arms and explosives supply lines to the ASUs in the North and to units operating in England and Europe.

The engineering department was possibly the next most important. It was responsible for mixing and manufacturing the huge amounts of homemade explosives that the IRA used each year. In secret locations, mostly in the Republic, the engineering department also invented, manufactured, and adapted the organization's impressive array of detonating devices and improvised weapons, including a formidable range of mortar bombs. Since most of the engineering department's product would be handled by the QM's department, it was inevitable that these two sections would come to share a common view of the world and that their respective heads, the quartermaster general (QMG) and the director of engineering, would form an alliance.

Next in line came the operations department, which was responsible for overseeing IRA activity, in England and Europe in particular; two sub-departments handled operations in these two theaters, and their heads reported to the director of operations on GHQ. The six remaining departments were self-explanatory: intelligence, finance, training, political education, internal security, and publicity. Assisting the chief of staff was the adjutant general (AG), effectively his second in command, whose duties included ensuring that the chief of staff's instructions were carried out, overseeing internal discipline, and making certain that the rank and file understood and implemented Army policy. The AG had more day-to-day contact with the rank and file than anyone else at leadership level and was often charged with assessing grassroots feelings, especially during the cease-fires.

Underneath GHQ, the IRA in Ireland was divided into two operational areas. Northern Command included not just the six counties of Northern Ireland but the five Border counties of Leitrim, Cavan, Louth, Monaghan, and Donegal as well. Beneath them were the various brigade areas and active-service units (ASUs). Only South Armagh retained the old battalion structure, the First Battalion around the Forkhill and Jonesboro areas and the Second based in Crossmaglen. The remaining twenty-one counties of

Ireland were grouped under Southern Command, with a similar but much smaller brigade and ASU substructure. The QM's department and the engineering department made up the strongest elements of Southern Command, since it was here that the bulk of weapons dumps and arms and explosives factories were to be found.

AT THE TOP of this structure sat the seven members of the Army Council, whose role and powers were strictly defined by the IRA's constitution. The Council's prime function was to "conclude peace or declare war," and it could do so by a simple majority vote.[1]

The Council's other important task was to choose the chief of staff and to ratify his appointments to GHQ and other key posts. It also drew up the IRA's general orders, which governed the rules of engagement, and formulated membership regulations, a disciplinary code, and the procedures and penalties for courts-martial. Crucially the Army Council, by dint of its ability to "conclude peace," was charged with negotiating with the British government if the need arose, although as far as face-to-face contact with the British was concerned, this task was left to the chairman of the Army Council, one of the seven members whose other task was to preside over the monthly Council meeting. Throughout the peace process this was a role performed by Martin McGuinness, chairman since 1982. His mandate for negotiations, however, was determined by the full Army Council, to which he had to report back regularly.

The Army Council was not, however, the supreme authority in the IRA. That was a status reserved for the General Army Convention (GAC), a delegate gathering of the IRA rank and file that was supposed to meet every two years. In practice it usually met only when the IRA was at peace or, if the IRA was at war, when the leadership so needed the endorsement of the rank and file for political changes that it was prepared to take the risk of assembling the IRA delegates. The 1986 convention, which endorsed the dropping of abstentionism, fell into this category. During those periods when the IRA was at war, and it was considered too dangerous to convene such a large meeting, the Army Council held all power in its hands. It was the Convention, theoretically representative of IRA structures and membership throughout Ireland, that alone and by the required two-thirds majority had the power to change the IRA's constitution. But that was the least of its functions. By a complex but indirect process the GAC was also supposed to choose the Army Council, to which it technically lent its powers between Conventions. It did this by electing the twelve-member IRA Executive, whose first task was to choose, usually from its own number, the seven members of the Army Council. Once the Executive had voted for the Army Council, the seven vacated seats would then be taken by substitutes previously elected by the GAC. The selection of the Executive was thus the Convention's most crucial act since the choice of Executive by the delegates would determine the leadership and therefore the direction of the IRA. It followed that the disposition of the delegates selected to attend the Convention was in turn vital to the process of shaping the political character of the IRA. This factor could and did determine whether the IRA opted for peace or for war, for abstentionism or against, for or against federalism, and so on. The selection of delegates and whether they actually managed to complete the often difficult and lengthy journey to the Convention were issues that assumed critical importance.

These two structures—an Army Council of seven members, and an Executive with twelve—were balanced, sometimes uneasily, at the very top of the IRA. This elaborate and often difficult relationship was the result of the IRA's early history when the Executive was the much more important of the two bodies. The Army Council in the early days of the IRA was a subcommittee of senior military staff answerable to the policy-making Executive, whose membership was largely drawn from Sinn Fein's ranks, but by 1938, when governmental authority was bestowed upon it by the remnants of the Second Dail, power and influence became concentrated in the Army Council's hands, not least because it was the body running the day-to-day IRA campaign. As far as the modern IRA is concerned, the relationship between the Executive, which regarded itself as the repository of the republican conscience, and the Army Council, which jealously guarded its power and authority, has traditionally been a fraught one, and the last three splits in the IRA all came about because of friction between them.

The Army Council became even more powerful during the Provisionals' campaign because it was often too dangerous to convene a Convention. The security risks attached to such an enterprise, which involved assembling between seventy and a hundred men and women, many of them "on the run" and wanted by the security forces North and South, meant that between 1969 and 1996 only four Conventions were held. Since elections to the Executive were few and far between, the Army Council became a self-replicating body. This in turn reinforced an antidemocratic and authoritarian tendency in the IRA leadership.

Gatherings of the Army Council were of necessity not easy to arrange. The logistical and security problems involved in bringing together some of the most wanted and watched fugitives in Europe were formidable. Meetings often had to be held in the most remote and least accessible spots in Ireland. The intricate journeys imposed on Council members meant that they would invariably arrive late at night at some damp farmhouse in the middle of a mountainous or isolated countryside with only a plate of cold ham sandwiches and a pot of tea to refresh them as they plowed through reams of documents in preparation for the following day's meeting. This was a feature of Council meetings that was to prove crucial during the peace process. Not least it meant that those members who arrived fresh and already familiar with the stacks of documents dealing with the complex turns and twists of the peace process had a huge advantage over their other, less *au fait* colleagues.

Although Army Council membership was limited to seven, as many as ten people could sit around the table, all of whom could influence the Council's decisions even if not all of them could vote. The chief of staff did not have to be a member of the Army Council, although the pre-1994 chief of staff was. IRA rules said that two other senior figures, the quartermaster general and the adjutant general, were entitled, if not already members of the Council, to sit in and contribute to its deliberations. That was the case before and after the 1994 cessation. An eleventh person, a secretary who minuted the meetings, would also be present. The record of Army Council meetings was possibly the most delicate and secret document in the IRA's archive, and great care would be taken in storing and hiding it. The monthly meeting usually took up the best part of a day and would be dominated by two reports, one by the chief of staff who reported on military matters and another on political affairs given by the senior Sinn Fein figure, who during the peace process was usually Gerry Adams. Meetings were opened and closed by the Council chairman.

WITH THE EXCEPTION of the short period when he was held in jail after the La Mon bombing, Gerry Adams had been on the Army Council since 1977 and was one of its longest-serving members. Since his election first as an Assembly member for West Belfast in 1982 and then the following year as Westminster MP, Adams had held no military position in the IRA, making him the only Council member in this category. This decision was taken deliberately to ensure that he could never be put at risk of being jailed again. Of all the Army Council members, he was destined to be the most permanent.

Another figure who by the mid-1980s was working exclusively for Sinn Fein was the party's Southern organizer, Pat Doherty, a close ally of Adams and identified as a senior Army Council figure by the IRA informer Sean O'Callaghan, a key witness in a celebrated libel action taken unsuccessfully in 1998 against the *Sunday Times* by Slab Murphy. Doherty's rise to the heights of the IRA is the most difficult to explain. A Scot born in Glasgow in 1945, whose family hailed from County Donegal, Doherty, known to IRA colleagues as "Smiler," is not known to have had any operational background, although a brother, Hugh, was a key member of the notorious Balcombe Street gang, which bombed and shot its way through London and southern England in the mid-1970s. A close friend of Martin McGuinness, Doherty, who was a civil engineer by profession, was famed for his ability to locate safe meeting places for IRA commanders and isolated localities for training camps in the wilds of Donegal. He also had the task of occasionally finding discreet and secure vacation homes for Gerry Adams and other figures from Belfast. Such is his knowledge of the more remote spots of Donegal that in the latter years of the peace process he was on more than one occasion made GAC convenor, charged with finding the appropriate premises for the delegates to meet.

After Ivor Bell's fall, Doherty took on the task of building up Sinn Fein's organization in the South, while the job of adjutant general was eventually filled in 1989, on Gerry Adams's recommendation, by Gerry Kelly, a former London bomber and Ballymurphy associate of the Sinn Fein president from the days when Adams was Belfast IRA commander. Adams recommended Kelly largely because of his fearsome reputation in the IRA. Known as a ruthless and fearless IRA operative, Kelly had survived regular bouts of forced feeding in Brixton jail during a lengthy hunger strike. In 1983 he took part in a mass breakout of IRA prisoners from the Maze prison on the outskirts of Belfast. Those who made it to the Republic were given the traditional options: they could either return to active service or be smuggled out to the United States to a job and a new identity. Kelly unhesitatingly chose the former and went back on active service, although he was recaptured three years later in Holland, where he was involved in an elaborate plan to smuggle weapons and explosives to Ireland. Intensely loyal to Gerry Adams, few republicans could doubt his commitment to the struggle. When the cease-fire came, Kelly's support for it was crucial in winning over the unsure and anxious.

Doherty could be depended upon to support Adams—as could Kelly, although he had no vote at Army Council meetings—and so, by and large, could a third member of the pre-1994 Army Council. Joe Cahill, a former Belfast commander and chief of staff who could trace his republican career back to the 1940s, was easily the oldest figure on the Council. A Ballymurphy-based contemporary of Adams's father, Gerry Sr., he had been close to Gerry Adams from not long after the Provisionals were founded. Credited with forging the links with Qaddafi's Libya in the mid-1970s, Cahill had, by the time the peace process picked up speed, effectively ended his operational IRA career and was in charge of Sinn Fein's often parlous finances. His value to Adams and his colleagues was the continuity he represented. A founding member of the Provisionals, Cahill had credentials going way back to the famous Easter 1942 Milltown diversionary ambush. He had been sentenced to hang along with Tom Williams for the murder of Constable Murphy during that abortive operation but had been reprieved. Cahill's emotional "I stood at the foot of the gallows for Ireland" speeches, usually in support of Adams's latest ideological shift, were a regular feature of Sinn Fein Ard Fheiseanna and IRA Conventions.

Tom Murphy from Ballybinaby in South Armagh was without doubt the wealthiest member of the Army Council. By some accounts a millionaire several times over, thanks to his business activities in the lucrative cross-Border pig and fuel trade, Slab, as he was known by everyone in the IRA, was not and never had been a member of Sinn Fein. Until 1984 Slab had been Northern commander, but with the Libyan shipments due to arrive and the "Tet offensive" to put together, he was made director of operations. He was one of a breed of republicans without whom the peace process would have been impossible, the activist who despised politics and took no interest in it. Slab personified one of the major fault lines in the Provisionals, one that divided those who saw the future in terms of Sinn Fein's electoral strategy and those who saw themselves exclusively as IRA "soldiers." The story of the peace process is as much about the triumph of the former group over the latter as it is about anything else.

Martin McGuinness was the second-longest-serving member of the Council. He had taken over as Northern commander from Slab Murphy, and held the post along with the chairmanship of the Army Council. The move was actually a demotion for McGuinness since, after Ivor Bell's removal as chief of staff, McGuinness had been made adjutant general. It was no secret in the IRA that he deeply resented having to give up the post of chief of staff when he ran for Sinn Fein in the 1982 Assembly elections, and promotion to adjutant general suggested he could be on the way back. To then be given the job of heading Northern Command looked to the untutored eye as if the Derry man was slipping down the IRA ladder. But the move made sense in terms of strengthening the forces in the leadership that were to shape the peace process. Control of Northern Command meant McGuinness decided which commanders got and which did not get supplies of the precious new Libyan weaponry, the IRA's equivalent of pork barrel politics. As a way of rewarding allies and punishing opponents, it could hardly be bettered. Under his command, central control over the ASUs tightened. Before his appointment the local units were allowed to select their own commanders; under his direction, though, the ASUs could suggest candidates, but the final decision would be his. This brought predictable complaints, as one senior IRA source recalled: "From the late 1980s onward people were maneuvered into position who were loyal to Adams and McGuinness."[2] McGuinness's appointment as Northern commander had another advantage. Since he was the man in charge of the day-to-day war against the British, his commitment to armed struggle seemed beyond doubt. So when McGuinness backed the peace process, many of the rank and file were prepared to follow.

There was a belief that for a long time Adams and McGuinness disagreed sharply about the peace process and that it was not until later on that the Derry man backed the Adams strategy. But those who observed both men close up say that was never the case. "He nearly always agreed with Adams except on small things, on details," remembered one.[3] Another recalls a figure who as far back as the early 1980s had admired and looked up to the Belfast man. "I remember Martin once saying that Adams articulates what he couldn't put into words himself," he said.[4]

McGuinness was respected by the rank and file and was popular in a way that Adams never could be. Not least there was the fact that McGuinness had an operational record, and his personal bravery had never come under question. Adams, by contrast, had no name at all as an "operator," and while he was widely respected for his strategic and political prowess, nothing mattered more in the IRA than a person's military record. Adams rarely socialized beyond a small group of confidants and was regarded widely as a somewhat distant and occasionally arrogant figure. His bad temper, which he could release on underlings without warning, was legendary.

A story told by one IRA veteran illustrates why McGuinness struck a chord with the rank-and-file Volunteer and Adams did not.

Dominic McGlinchey, Frank Hughes, and their gang were in Donegal hiding out for a while. They looked like mujahideen, longhaired, scruffy, heavily armed, driving wrecks of cars. They were fed up staying in cow barns when they heard Adams and McGuinness were on holiday in the area. They found out where Adams was staying and turned up at his chalet, where they were sniffily shown the door. There was no way Gerry and Colette would let that crowd darken their door. So then they went to where McGuinness was staying. He was annoyed and cursed them up and down, but he let them in and allowed them to stay.[5]

McGuinness's second in command, the Northern adjutant, a well-known activist from South Armagh, was the sixth member of the Army Council. He had been promoted in January 1990 when the IRA's director of publicity, Danny Morrison, was arrested in West Belfast while witnessing the interrogation of the IRA informer Sandy Lynch. Under IRA rules Morrison automatically lost his seat on the Army Council when he went to jail. The Northern adjutant's presence on the Army Council meant that during much of the time that Gerry Adams and others like him were criticizing botched military operations and urging caution and prudence on the organization, two of the key figures on Northern Command in whose area of responsibility most of those "bad" operations took place regularly shared Army Council meetings with him. There was no need for Adams to make public speeches or give media interviews criticizing the IRA; all he had to do was to take McGuinness and the Northern adjutant aside and have a quiet but firm word with them.

The eighth person around the Army Council table was the quartermaster general, Michael "Micky" McKevitt, another South Armagh figure, who until 1984 had been quartermaster of Northern Command. The Libyan arms deal was the spur for his elevation. The QMG at the time the deal was negotiated, Kevin Hannaway, Gerry Adams's cousin, had never recovered from the interrogation methods used on him by soldiers and policemen during the 1971 internment operation. Hannaway was judged too ill to handle such an ambitious enterprise and was quietly moved sideways and then eventually he was retired. Responsibility for getting the Libyan armaments safely to Ireland was given instead to McKevitt and Slab Murphy. McKevitt sat in on the Army Council's deliberations and, like Gerry Kelly, could have a say but not a vote. His real influence was felt on the IRA Executive, of which he was a leading member. Like Murphy and the other South Armagh member of the Council, the Northern adjutant, McKevitt, had spent his entire republican career in the IRA and had never been in Sinn Fein, although as the peace process moved forward he was to play an increasingly political role.

The IRA's military commander at the time of the 1994 cease-fire was the Tyrone man Kevin McKenna. Appointed chief of staff after the fall of Ivor Bell, McKenna became the longest-serving of all the IRA's chiefs of staff, and his period at the top of the IRA encompassed the crucial transition from war to peace. Born on the family farm near Aughnacloy on the Tyrone-Monaghan Border in 1945, McKenna had been in the IRA briefly before the Troubles erupted in 1969 but had emigrated to Canada and missed key moments, such as the split between the Officials and the Provisionals. The introduction of internment in 1971 brought him back to Ireland and to the IRA, as it did scores of other young Northerners made angry at the turn of events and eager to help strike back. McKenna quickly made his mark and was soon a leading figure in the Tyrone organization, as a contemporary recalled:

> His rise in the IRA was accounted for by the fact that back in those days there would have been three types of IRA men, the bulk were eighteen- to nineteen-year-olds, some in their fifties and sixties who were veterans of the '56–'62 campaign and a small number like Kevin in their mid-twenties who were the right age to take the lead. He had come back from Canada with a bit of money, enough to buy a car. He was mobile, the right age, single and willing to work, and away he went.[6]

McKenna helped form an IRA unit around the Eglish-Aughnacloy area of Tyrone and afterward rose through the Tyrone Brigade. Kevin Mallon, the first OC of Tyrone, was succeeded by another figure known for his operational daring, Brendan Hughes, who was no relation to the Belfast figure of the same name. At the end of 1972, after Hughes's departure, McKenna became commander of Tyrone but within eighteen months had been arrested and interned. Released in early 1975, he again assumed command of Tyrone, this time running the brigade from the distance of Monaghan, where he has lived ever since. The Northern commander immediately prior to Slab Murphy, McKenna was eventually elevated to the Army Council, and there was little doubt that, whatever his military skills, he was also put there to placate a Tyrone IRA made uneasy by Adams's routing of Kevin Mallon in the wake of the disastrous Tidey kidnapping.

"McKenna would have been seen as keeping Tyrone out of politicking and troublemaking," said one IRA veteran. "He'd be there to keep Tyrone happy, so they could say that their man was chief of staff. He would also empathize with the South Armagh men; he knew the price of cows and was happy wearing wellies."[7]

The chief of staff was liked by his men even if his political analysis, like that of the other "soldiers" on the Army Council, was less than sophisticated, as the same IRA source recalled:

He is a very pleasant man to talk to, thoughtful, hospitable, and affable. He wasn't a superior type nor stern, more an avuncular figure. While Twomey would be full of rage and almost physical retribution if you failed to carry out a mission, McKenna was more tolerant and understanding. If a unit was operating well, he would make sure it was well equipped. The fighting men had time for him; he was always there for them.

He had no well-defined politics as far as I could remember, and he was confused about the movement's support for socialism. I remember at the time of the 1972 cease-fire him saying to me that he wanted the Brits out but he was not sure whether we needed socialism. I then saw him at a Sinn Fein Ard Fheis in the mid-seventies wandering around. A Portuguese army colonel had just spoken, and McKenna was in a daze saying this really is a revolutionary party. He was lost in terms of economics. He knew how to buy and sell cattle and would have made a good small businessman, but the macro stuff left him trailing.[8]

The Army Council was never an entirely united body, and personality clashes often soured its meetings. The squabbling between McGuinness and McKenna, a product of deep personal rivalry, was particularly serious. McKenna, who managed to be a most secretive and publicity-shy commander, resented constant media reports that McGuinness was the real chief of staff, and he suspected that the Derry man had done little to discourage them. There was a widespread suspicion that McGuinness desperately wanted his old job back and in particular to be chief of staff when the Libyan-resourced "Tet offensive" began. Before the Libyan weapons arrived, he launched a torrent of criticism at McKenna's handling of the IRA's campaign and, but for the support of Slab Murphy, the chief of staff might have succumbed. "Everything was thrown at him except a vote of no confidence," recalled one source.[9] Adams, by contrast, generally stayed above their conflict and refused to take sides, waiting to see who emerged victorious.

After the Libyan weaponry started to arrive, the rows between the two men worsened. As Northern commander, McGuinness and his staff had the final say on which units were to receive the new weaponry. But when it was discovered that arms were being sent to areas with inactive or small IRA units, such as Lurgan in County Armagh, or where training in the new equipment had yet to be given while other well-trained areas were ignored, McKenna angrily intervened. The problem was that the weapons were being lost by inexperienced units almost as quickly as they arrived, and the drain on the Libyan stores became so great that by the early 1990s McKenna gave an order to cease replacing lost weapons and issued instructions that existing stocks in Northern Command be moved around internally, with a consequent risk that guns and equipment would be bugged by the British. There were accusations that McGuinness was either attempting to curry favor with the rank and file or was just incompetent; relations between the pair became icy.

McGuinness and McKenna clashed again when more precious Libyan weapons were lost. This time the trouble broke out after Gardai discovered two plastic tanks full of automatic rifles, Semtex explosives, and ammunition hastily buried in the beach at Five Fingers Strand near Malin Head in north Donegal in January 1988. The weapons had been moved to Donegal on the basis of assurances from McGuinness's right-hand man, an activist from the Inishowen peninsula, that the appropriate dumps had been located and readied. The assurance was bogus, and the arms had to be quickly buried on the nearest available beach as soon as they arrived. The van carrying the load was stopped by alert Gardai, who realized that the driver and passenger had republican records. The van was empty but there were traces of sand inside. On a hunch, a search of beaches near the driver's home on Malin Head was ordered, and the weapons were duly uncovered. The Inishowen activist was sacked from the IRA at McKenna's insistence, the episode being recorded as another black eye for McGuinness.

The biggest row between the pair, however, was over the activities of a well-placed IRA informer in the Derry Brigade, Frank Hegarty, who was attached to the quartermaster's department. Hegarty had been seconded to work with Northern Command staff to help move part of the first Libyan shipment to dumps in the west of Ireland. The consignment, some eighty AK-47s that had come to Ireland as part of the *Kula*'s cargo in August 1985, was being moved by stages when in January 1986 the Gardai swooped. Two transitional dumps, one in Roscommon and one in Sligo, were raided and the weapons seized. The next day Hegarty disappeared from Derry, and it soon became clear not only that he had given the dumps away but that he had been working for MI5, the British Security Service, which had spirited him away, and that he was being kept in a safe house somewhere in the north of England.

Hegarty's forced flight was a disaster for the intelligence community. An IRA member from the 1970s, Hegarty was Northern Command QM in 1982, when it was discovered that he was having an affair with the wife of a soldier in the Ulster Defence Regiment. His case went as high as the then chief of staff, Ivor Bell, who dismissed him from the IRA. Not long after-ward Hegarty was approached by an arm of British military intelligence called the Force Research Unit who persuaded him to return to the IRA and work as a double agent. Inexplicably, Hegarty was allowed back into the IRA in Derry and made his way once again into the QM's department with a brief from British intelligence to rise as far as he could, even as high as QMG. His handlers assured him that his IRA bosses would be removed one by one to smooth his way. British intelligence's ambitious plans for Hegarty were, however, frustrated by the Special Branch in the Republic's police, who insisted on moving in on the IRA dumps in Roscommon and Sligo as soon as the weapons arrived. Eager to strike a damaging propaganda blow against the IRA, the Gardai vetoed a British plan to bug and follow the weapons, and they moved to seize them. Fortunately for the IRA, Hegarty had been given a false story about where the weapons had come from; he was told that they had originated in Europe, and this, together with the fact that some Belgian FN rifles had been mixed in with the AK-47s, satisfied British intelligence. Nevertheless, the British had lost a potentially priceless agent as well as an opportunity to track the progress of the weapons.

The British had, though, come perilously close to discovering the Libyan link. Since most of the remaining Libyan shipments were still being awaited, including the *Eksund*'s 120 tons, the episode gave the IRA leadership a bad fright, and a high-level investigation was ordered. The first question to be resolved was how Hegarty had been allowed back into the IRA. Since McGuinness was Northern commander, it stood to reason that he must have known of Hegarty's return, but he denied this and argued that the real informer had to be someone other than Hegarty.

During Hegarty's period in hiding in England he was in regular contact by phone with his family in Derry. A month after his sudden disappearance Hegarty just as unexpectedly returned to Ireland, and so began one of the most controversial chapters in McGuinness's republican career. Hegarty's family would later insist that he had agreed to come back only after they passed on to him an assurance from McGuinness that he would not be touched. McGuinness has always denied this, but sources familiar with Hegarty's subsequent interrogation at the hands of the IRA say that the informer repeated the claim while in the organization's custody.

Hegarty also told his questioners that McGuinness had known and approved of his return to the IRA's ranks, an admission that sparked a blaz-ing row between the Northern commander and the chief of staff. Behind the row lay an unanswered question: why had McGuinness advanced Hegarty's second career in the IRA's quartermaster's department when there had been so much doubt about his loyalty that he had previously been thrown out of the organization? In May 1986, just four months after the Gardai seized the Roscommon and Sligo arms dumps, Hegarty's body was found on the outskirts of Castlederg near the Tyrone–Donegal Border. His eyes had been taped over, his hands tied behind his back, and a bullet wound to the back of his head indicated that he had received the punishment customary for those judged guilty of informing. The rivalry between McGuinness and McKenna would simmer on for years to come, but Hegarty's death effectively marked the end of the Derry man's ambitions to take over the chief of staff's job.

THE QUARREL between McKenna and McGuinness was an important feature of the IRA leadership in those days, but it paled into insignificance compared with the much deeper division in the IRA leadership. That was the one that separated the Army Council into the complex political operators of the Adams and Doherty variety and the simple "soldiers," like Slab Murphy, McKenna, and the Northern adjutant, all figures who never had and never would have any dealings with Sinn Fein. An understanding of how this affected the way the IRA Army Council did its business during the years of the peace process is vital to understanding how the Provisionals were brought to a cease-fire.

Contemptuous of politics, the "soldiers" paid little heed to the unfolding peace process until the cease-fire was almost upon them, and for a simple reason. They, along with much of the republican grassroots, proved to be exceptionally receptive to a steady diet of assurances from their political colleagues that Gerry Adams was only playing "word games,"[10] as the phrase had it, with John Hume and the British, Irish, and American governments and that what was said to them by the Sinn Fein leader was not meant to represent the reality of the Provisionals' politics. The strategy was disarmingly simple. The name of the game, they were told, was to forge a pan-nationalist alliance with the SDLP and Dublin that would put the British under pressure. This would supplement the IRA's military campaign, and the combined pressure would force the British to move. But securing that nationalist alliance required two things. First the IRA's military strategy had to be tailored so that it would not offend the rest of nationalist Ireland. That meant the IRA had to concentrate on hitting targets in England and military targets in the North while avoiding civilian casualties of any sort in Ireland. Meanwhile on the political front it was necessary to create the impression that republicans wanted to abandon military methods in favor of politics. The line given to the "soldiers" went something like this: to build that nationalist alliance, it would sometimes be necessary to say or do things that neither the IRA nor Sinn Fein really meant, including that a cease-fire might be possible, otherwise Dublin and the SDLP might balk at the relationship. Lies would have to be told, but the Army Council and the republican base could be sure that they were being told the truth, that the struggle was still what it had always been about, that is, securing British withdrawal. "All the time," recalled one senior source, "Adams and Co. were telling people that the IRA didn't mean it but that they had to say the sort of things they were saying. They kept assuring our people to ignore the public statements, that nothing short of British withdrawal would be acceptable."[11]

DISSEMBLING had become part of the republican political arsenal long before the peace process assumed such an important part in Provisional politics. It began not long after the 1986 victory on abstentionism. "After the 1986 convention everything was sold as a tactic," recalled one veteran IRA commander. "The use of language became a tactic, words didn't matter, they were a means to an end."[12] The roots of all this actually reach back much farther, to 1982, when Sinn Fein first contested elections.

One of the difficulties presented by the electoral strategy was that it exposed Sinn Fein's relationship with the IRA to a harsh and potentially dangerous spotlight. One election candidate after another would be quizzed by journalists about their association with the IRA, and each would have to deny it, even those like Adams and McGuinness whose role representing the IRA in talks with the British, for example, was well known and publicly recorded. Otherwise they could face charges of IRA membership, an offense that could mean up to five years in jail. To get around the problem, IRA members involved in Sinn Fein politics had been given a dispensation to deny their links. The rank and file knew what the truth was but accepted the need to deceive. It began at this level and the practice grew. Not meaning what was said increasingly became a defining and acceptable feature of republican political culture. It was to occupy a central place in the peace process strategy.

As Sinn Fein leaders moved rhetorically closer to accepting the ideas and principles of constitutional nationalism, their edgy, nervous supporters were constantly reassured. "They would keep on saying that these were tactical talks that meant nothing," recalled the same source. "They would say don't worry, what is being said is not meant, we have to say these things in order to talk to these people."[13] This message would be transmitted to rank-and-file Sinn Fein supporters and IRA activists alike and be repeated all the way up the ladder to the very top. Many, especially those who were fighting the IRA's war, believed what they were told because they wanted to. The alternative opened up an appalling vista. Others believed because they had always believed. At the same time, the Irish, British, and American governments would be assured that Sinn Fein and the IRA were genuine and sincere but needed to manage carefully their difficult constituency. In this way the Sinn Fein leadership moved the peace process forward, entrusted by their supporters to take it to the next stage, while the governments waited patiently for results, secure in the knowledge that the farther the Provisionals traveled on this journey, the more difficult it would be to go back. Even so, it was often difficult to tell who was being lied to.

Occasionally, when their guard dropped, leadership figures would admit to the tactic. In September 1995, a year or so after the first cease-fire, the author had a lengthy session with one of Gerry Adams's closest advisers, a figure who not long before had been released from prison. At the time, Adams was under enormous pressure from the Army Council's "soldiers" to break the cease-fire, but he had a problem. Bill Clinton was coming to Belfast in a few weeks and he had just visited the White House to reassure the administration that, despite the difficulties, his commitment to peace was absolute. A detailed note of the conversation records the following: "[H]e admitted/claimed that they were lying to their new friends in the U.S. [i.e. Clinton] and elsewhere and that they could go back to war even though there would be, he admitted, a high price to pay . . . At one stage he said, 'Your problem is that you mind too much about the lies'—he defended the tactic utterly, even though I said it only gets you into a wilderness of mirrors."[14]

FIFTEEN

Cease-Fire

The Army Council made a secret decision in 1988 that was to have enormous consequences for the peace process. It abandoned the traditional IRA demand that if the British ever did withdraw from Ireland they must do so within the lifetime of a British parliament. Instead, it decreed that from that moment onward the IRA would be more flexible and could settle for a much longer time line for British disengagement. No new deadlines were set, but there was a consensus that if Britain was prepared to leave Northern Ireland and signaled this to the IRA, the process could take as long as fifteen or twenty years to be completed and the Army Council would be content.

The decision was kept a tightly guarded secret, especially from the IRA rank and file, and for a very good reason. Had they known that this key, almost defining, policy had been diluted, most IRA Volunteers would have been alarmed or at the very least deeply unsettled. The demand for a speedy British withdrawal had been a Provisional policy since 1972 when, during the cease-fire of that year, Chief of Staff Sean MacStiofain told British ministers that he wanted their political and military withdrawal to be completed within two and a half years. Early IRA leaders took a tough line on this issue, partly because they did not trust the British to keep their word and partly because they feared that if the process of withdrawal was dragged out, loyalists would have enough time to sabotage it. Under the leadership of O Bradaigh and O Conaill, the Army Council realized how inflexible the demand was and instead called for "planned, phased and orderly" British disengagement, but Adams and the Young Turks of the IRA seized upon this as yet another sign of the old guard's weakness. When he and his allies secured control of the Army Council, the official policy was toughened up. Britain, if Adams and his allies got their way, would have the lifetime of a parliament, a mere four to five years, to complete its departure from Ireland. The sharp contrast with the earlier inflexible and tough approach meant that opting instead, as the 1988 policy change indicated, for a lengthy and leisurely withdrawal would set the alarm bells ringing loudly at grassroots level, especially if the change was set beside other developments, such as the talks with the SDLP. For that reason the grassroots were simply not told about it.

At the Army Council meeting that changed IRA policy, most of the talking was done by Gerry Adams and Martin McGuinness. They argued, persuasively by all accounts, that the old policy was a handicap at a time when the IRA's strategy was to forge an alliance with constitutional nationalists. If people like the SDLP leader John Hume or Fianna Fail's Charles Haughey were to be won over to a joint strategy, the IRA's adherence to such a rigid and unreasonable demand would be an obstacle. Not only that, but the British themselves would, if serious withdrawal talks ever started, regard the four- to five-year time line as simply undeliverable, and it would have to be softened anyway. And there was another argument. The unionists would be bound to resist any attempt by Britain to disengage from Northern Ireland, but that resistance was likely to be fiercer if the deadline was short. A protracted process could draw the sting out of the situation and give unionists enough time to get used to the new circumstances and provide republicans with the space within which to persuade them of the benefits of change. The Army Council, partly on the basis that the talks with the SDLP and the government in Dublin were only tactical, secretly endorsed the arguments.

The change was accepted by the Army Council for two very important reasons, and in theory these made the change less significant than it had first appeared. Although Britain could take up to twenty years to quit the North, the Army Council nonetheless agreed—with Adams and McGuinness assenting—that the IRA would still not end its military campaign unless and until the British gave a public commitment that they were actually going to leave. The IRA would still bomb and shoot the British to the negotiating table, in other words. Nor could the time frame for withdrawal be left vague or open-ended. The British would have to specify a date by which their political and military presence would be ended. Those bottom lines remained IRA policy after 1988 despite the new policy, or so the Army Council believed.

It is no exaggeration to say that the policy change made the peace process internally viable for the Adams leadership, because it created a framework for ambiguity without which the real peace process would have foundered. Thanks to the change, traditional, uncompromising republicans on the Army Council could look at the negotiations that made up the peace process and believe that they were entirely consistent with the long-held goal of forcing Britain to leave Northern Ireland. But the same policy was also perfectly compatible with the other, more secret process going on behind the backs of the Army Council and based on the secret redefinition of withdrawal that Adams and Reid had secured from the British in 1987, a withdrawal that was confined to a promise not to interfere politically in all-party talks and which would pave the way to a settlement based on the constitutional integrity of the Northern Ireland state. It is the genius of the Reid-Adams enterprise that from the outside the two scenarios looked the same and could coexist quite happily. They looked the same but in fact were very different. One was about getting the British out of Ireland; the other was about getting Sinn Fein into constitutional politics.

This latter formulation was kept secret from the Army Council, for the very simple reason that it would have been rejected out of hand had it been placed in front of its members in that form. The Reid-Adams restatement offended two key principles that had underscored the IRA's long war with the British. One was that the unionists did not have and could not have a veto on Irish unity. The principle of national self-determination in its customary form stated, as the document prepared by MacStiofain for the 1972 cease-fire talks put it, "that it is the people of Ireland acting as a unit that should decide the future of Ireland."[1] The fact that the principle had been breached in the 1921 Treaty was the reason for the IRA's existence. The other principle stipulated that the British would have to make a public declaration of intent to withdraw within a specified period of time. The Army Council after 1988 was prepared to be more open-minded about how long that period could be but would not budge from the view that it must be specific and stated. To do otherwise would open the door to Britain's backing out of the deal. The Reid-Adams formula explicitly accepted the principle of consent and, because of that, precluded any move by Britain to withdraw against the unionists' wishes, no matter what the time frame.

Not only was the Reid-Adams formula kept secret from the Army Council, but so too was the early diplomacy with Britain and the Haughey government. Senior figures were not told of Gerry Adams's correspondence with Tom King or of Father Reid's mediation with both King and his successor, Peter Brooke. The Army Council was never officially informed about the first meetings Reid had with the Fianna Fail leader on behalf of

Adams, and Reid's lengthy message to Haughey in May 1987 containing the secret offer of an IRA cease-fire was also kept hidden. It was not until 1988, when Adams told the council of an offer of talks with Fianna Fail and the SDLP, that the Army Council obtained as much as a glimpse of what had been happening.

Even then the affair was treated casually. Adams told the council that the initiative for the approach had come not from him but from Haughey, who had used Father Reid, a figure he described as an old friend of Adams, to make the connection. At the start the talks were classified as merely exploratory and were considered so insignificant that Adams was obliged to give the Army Council only oral reports on what had taken place. Had the talks been seen as at all consequential, there would have been written reports, and very possibly a subcommittee would have been established to control the contacts. But there was none of that. Sinn Fein was authorized to send along representatives to the meetings, but the Army Council was somewhat blasé about the dialogue. Over the years it had received hundreds of requests to meet and talk to all sorts of people and had long since adopted an open attitude to such overtures. All requests for dialogue were granted, but only a very few produced anything of interest. The talks with the SDLP and Fianna Fail were put into that category.

THE RESULT of all this was that there were really two peace processes running in the years leading up to the 1994 IRA cease-fire. One process was that which the Army Council believed was under way. Its aim was to secure a British commitment to withdraw from Northern Ireland, after which there could be negotiations about the time line within which that was to happen and the arrangements deemed necessary to satisfy the requirements of unionists. The other peace process was founded on a fundamental redefinition of British withdrawal, one that would allow Sinn Fein to accept the principle of consent and to negotiate a deal with unionists that fell short of what most republicans would traditionally regard as Irish unity. Both peace processes were able to shelter under the same rhetorical umbrella, but inevitably the conflict between them would from time to time burst to the surface. They were fundamentally and mutually inconsistent, and on occasion this problem became public, confusing those who were not privy to internal Provisional politics and Adams's need for careful management.

There was no shortage of examples of this. Cease-fire speculation, for example, reached fever pitch in the weeks and months following Peter Brooke's 100-day interview, in which he made a guarded offer of talks with

Sinn Fein in the event of an IRA cease-fire. Brooke, as he revealed to the author many years later, had been motivated by the secret contacts with Father Reid and was deliberately probing for a response from Adams. The media, understandably, smelled a story. A claim that the Army Council was considering a cease-fire was duly published in February 1991 in the *Irish Press,* whose editor Tim Pat Coogan had played a role in the Adams-Reid diplomacy. The speculation was not entirely ill-founded. Adams was working toward a cease-fire but his organization did not know it. All this alarmed the Sinn Fein leadership, and the party's press officers worked feverishly to deny it. Typical was the briefing given to the author at the time. "There are no grounds," insisted an IRA spokesperson, "for believing that the IRA is contemplating any kind of ceasefire or that there is a debate on the role of armed struggle . . . the next time there would be a cessation of hostilities would be when the Brits declared for withdrawal."[2] That was the official Army Council line, and it was echoed a few weeks later at the Sinn Fein Ard Fheis. In March, Sinn Fein held a private conference in West Belfast, and the media were allowed in for Gerry Adams's opening remarks. Reports of a radical change in republican policy were "mischief-making," he declared.

The secret diplomacy with the British and Irish governments demanded, however, that from time to time Adams send an entirely conflicting signal, to reassure those with whom he was dealing that he was serious about the peace project. Within days of his angry dismissal of cease-fire speculation as "mischief-making," Adams sat down in front of a British Channel Four television crew and, with his spoken words dubbed by an actor because of broadcasting restrictions, said the complete opposite. Interviewed by the *Irish Times* journalist Mary Holland, he was asked if the IRA would suspend its campaign in order to get talks with the British off the ground even if there was no public declaration of a cease-fire. Adams's reply was unequivocal. Republicans, he said, "would not be found wanting" if faced with such a possibility. "I am saying that if talks such as you . . . outlined were on the cards that no intransigence or obstacles would be placed in the way of such talks. . . . [T]here is a need for people to be pragmatic. . . ."[3] It was as close as he could come without actually using the words that an IRA cease-fire was on the table for negotiation.

The Channel Four interview, which was broadcast in April, caused an uproar in the IRA's upper reaches. Adams had not cleared his remarks with the Army Council, and Chief of Staff Kevin McKenna was obliged to send the message out to the grassrooots that this was Adams playing word games. Nothing had been seriously meant, he told the rank and file. A few days later the Easter Rising commemorations were held, and a hard-line military message was relayed by the Army Council. The message was amplified by Adams, who told the crowds that the struggle would continue as long as there was a British presence in the North.

UNDER THE ADAMS LEADERSHIP of the IRA, the word "cease-fire" had become so discredited that it was never used in republican exchanges except when assurances were needed that one would never happen again, at least not until the British had left Ireland. "Cease-fire" was associated with the leadership of O Bradaigh and O Conaill and the disastrous 1975 cessation when the IRA was brought to the brink of defeat. Not even at Christmastime, when the IRA active-service units took a few days' break to spend the holiday with their families, was the word used. The festive cease-fire was always an unofficial, undeclared affair. No one called it a cease-fire, because to do so was regarded as a sign of weakness, something that called into question the leadership's commitment to armed struggle.

When Martin McGuinness spoke up at an Army Council meeting in the winter of 1990, and proposed that there be a three-day publicly declared cease-fire starting on December 24 and ending on December 26, it was therefore an event of major significance, the first crack in the iceberg and a signal whose significance would not be lost on the British or the Irish governments.

McGuinness's proposal caused consternation in the Army Council. Three members, Chief of Staff Kevin McKenna, Slab Murphy, and Joe Cahill, along with QMG Micky McKevitt, immediately denounced the proposal as unconstitutional. They claimed that the 1986 Army Convention had passed a motion saying that the next time there was a cease-fire, no matter how short or long, it would have to be approved by a special or extraordinary IRA Convention. McGuinness, they insisted, had no constitutional authority for the move. That was the signal for a major row. Adams insisted they were wrong. The 1986 Convention had passed no such motion, he insisted, and Pat Doherty was dispatched to unearth the minutes from the relevant documents dump. When these were retrieved, they showed that Adams appeared to be right, but the minutes were not the original handwritten notes taken at the meeting but the typed-up version prepared afterward. The row rumbled on amid muttered allegations that the record of the 1986 Convention had been doctored, while other delegates to the Convention were consulted about their memory of the event. In the face of the record produced by Doherty, however, most Army Council members relented, and the cease-fire went ahead, announced to the media in a way that generated even more speculation about the IRA's intentions.

The row over the Christmas cease-fire of 1990 demonstrated in compelling fashion that the bulk of the Army Council knew nothing about the secret Reid-Adams enterprise. Adams may well have confided in individual members of the Council, figures like McGuinness and Doherty in particular, but had it been formally aware of what was going on and had endorsed the strategy, there would have been no row that Christmas. The Council would immediately have seen the sense in sending just this type of message to Peter Brooke. After all, the Northern Ireland secretary had just satisfied a crucial demand of the Reid-Adams dipomacy with a public declaration in London of Britain's neutrality in Ireland and its indifference as to the shape of final settlement. If ever there was a time for the IRA Army Council to send a message signaling flexibility, this was it. And if the Council had been aware of and agreed with the Adams peace strategy, it surely would have done so.

That was not, however, how the Christmas 1990 cease-fire was justified internally. McGuinness's main argument was that it would be a popular move with the nationalist public in the North and with Sinn Fein's potential pan-nationalist allies in the South. In briefings to the press, by contrast, out of the earshot of the Army Council and deniable as always, a clear link to the peace process was made. The Belfast nationalist daily *Irish News* reported a republican source as saying that the cease-fire was "a temporary respite to demonstrate the willingness of the IRA to respond to any genuine appeal for peace."[4] The following month Gerry Adams told the author, "What the IRA has demonstrated is that when it has the will it can stop," adding that he personally was prepared to try "for the very, very big prize." Both statements were clear hints that he meant the three-day cessation as a signal to the British.[5] But two days later he was giving the Sinn Fein faithful at their annual Ard Fheis in Dublin the opposite message: "In recent months the print media, especially sections of the British print media, have carried stories of my alleged involvement in the preparation of ceasefire proposals for Oglaigh na hEireann," he told them. "If the issue were not so serious, these fictitious accounts could be ignored. Indeed they might even be the source of some amusement."[6]

THE ROAD to the IRA cease-fire of 1994 was littered with paper, in particular policy documents prepared by the Sinn Fein leadership that slowly, carefully, and formally edged the Provisionals toward a position that Gerry

Adams and his confidants had reached privately long before. One of the most important and revealingly ambiguous of these pieces of paper was the Sinn Fein policy document "Towards a Lasting Peace in Ireland," published in mid-February 1992, only days after Albert Reynolds had succeeded Charles Haughey as taoiseach of Ireland and agreed to take up his peace torch. Hailed in most accounts of the peace process as a seminal stage in the IRA's journey toward a cease-fire, "Towards a Lasting Peace" was constructed and worded in such a way that both versions of the peace process could shelter comfortably underneath its ample roof.

The "soldiers" on the Army Council would have had no problems with the document when they read it. Much of it repeated traditional republican dogma, updated to accord with the pan-nationalism that now imbued public IRA policy. None of them could have argued, for instance, with the document's call on the British to withdraw from Northern Ireland "within a specified period."[7] That was Army Council policy, after all.

But buried in the paper's text was a crucial concession. Unionists, it said, could not impede the right of the Irish people to "national self-determination," but their consent would nevertheless be needed for the "constitutional, political and financial arrangements" in a united Ireland. In other words, the unionists could not stop the British from leaving Ireland, but they had a veto on what replaced them. Unnoticed by most observers, "Towards a Lasting Peace" had opened up an ideological can of worms. The document was conceding the unionists' right to consent in some circumstances but not in others. The point was that the right to consent is absolute, and the document came close to acknowledging that, if only implicitly. Nevertheless, by introducing the concept into public Sinn Fein discourse, Adams and his colleagues had edged the organization toward a more explicit acceptance of the principle of consent per se, and that was a central plank in the Father Reid strategy.

JIM GIBNEY had been a close friend and ally of Gerry Adams since they first met in the Long Kesh internment camp in the mid-1970s, and after his release he had become a key member of the small group of mostly Belfast republicans who acted as Adams's advisers. Like others in the group, Gibney, who hailed from the small Catholic enclave of Short Strand in East Belfast, often floated controversial ideas on behalf of Adams to see how the IRA and Sinn Fein rank and file would react. It was a ploy that kept Adams himself comfortably distant from controversy.

It fell to Gibney in the summer of 1992 to make public the real agenda of the Reid-Adams diplomacy in a move that once again served to highlight both the Army Council's ignorance of what was happening behind the scenes and the extent of potential division at the top and, by extension, the remainder of the IRA over the real peace process. The logic of the Reid-Adams enterprise, the logic of "stepping stones" and the hidden logic of "Towards a Lasting Peace," was that British withdrawal as republicans normally envisaged it had been recognized as unrealistic and unrealizable by Adams. If there was going to be political settlement at the end of the peace process, it would necessarily be based on the existing constitutional status quo, albeit with sufficient concessions to Irish nationalism to enable the Sinn Fein leadership to present the settlement as a "transitional" stage to Irish unity—although most IRA activists were still ignorant of all this. Michael Collins had presented the 1921 Treaty in the same way. There were no surprise stops on the journey undertaken by Adams.

Gibney gave the annual Bodenstown address at the grave of Wolfe Tone in June 1992 and sparked an unprecedented flurry of cease-fire speculation in the media. The fuss was caused by one sentence in his address. "We know and accept," he said, "that the British government's departure must be preceded by a sustained period of peace and will arise out of negotiations involving the different shades of Irish Nationalism and Unionism."[8] The crucial phrase was "will arise out of negotiations," a formulation suggesting that an IRA cease-fire would precede a British commitment to leave Ireland, a reversal of the sequence that was Army Council policy. Gibney's version set the stage for a transitional settlement and it was totally consistent with the Reid-Adams diplomacy. It was also the outcome of accepting, in practice, the principle of consent. These concepts were, however, both foreign and heretical to the assembled republican faithful at Tone's graveside.

Normally Bodenstown speeches were cleared beforehand by the Army Council to ensure that they conformed to IRA policy, but Gibney's had not been. There was another row, this time between Adams and McKenna, and Gibney ended up carrying the blame. Adams said his speech had been drafted at the last minute, written partially during Gibney's journey to Bodenstown, with the result that the crucial sentence had been clumsily worded. But journalists had received a neatly typed advance copy of the speech faxed to their offices before the speech. Adams also gave a sympathetic response to Gibney's remarks, as the *Irish Times* reported: "The Sinn Fein president, Mr Gerry Adams, said that Mr Gibney's speech did not signal a shift in policy but 'an elaboration of themes democratically agreed by the party over the past number of years.' He also said that . . . the points about British withdrawal and the need for negotiations should not be dismissed."[9] The affair hardly looked like a mishap. A very important cat had been let out of the bag, and the governments in London and Dublin took due notice.

TO IMAGINE that Gerry Adams constructed the peace process with all its complexities and subtle strategies by himself or at most in concert with Father Reid would be to bestow upon him talents and powers that not even his closest and most admiring friends would claim for him. Adams had gathered around him over the years a small group of trusted confidants and advisers who had helped him navigate his way first to the top of the IRA and then to the leadership of Sinn Fein. Born in the confines of Cage 11, the Adams "think tank" would perform a similar task with the peace process.

The role and influence of the think tank had contributed in no small measure to the row between McKenna and Adams. Within the group of "soldiers" on the Army Council, resentment at the growing power of the group had been festering away, and Gibney's Bodenstown speech was another example of this.

Not surprisingly, Adams had placed like-minded people into the think tank, people who were not only reliable but talented and inevitably, given the demands of the task, more likely either to have been ex-IRA or in some cases never in the IRA. The most important figure in the think tank, aside from Adams himself, was a man virtually unknown outside the closed world of republicanism. A former Second Belfast Battalion commander like Adams himself, Ted Howell was a reclusive figure who for many years used a pseudonym in public, the legacy, it was said, of years spent on the European continent liaising with foreign groups on behalf of the IRA leadership, during which he had managed to avoid the attentions of various intelligence agencies, not least of the British Secret Service, MI6. Adams made a reference to Howell, using his nom de guerre, in the acknowledgments to his book *A Pathway to Peace,* published in 1988. "This essay could not have been written without the co-operation and encouragement of the 'Kitchen Cabinet,' " he wrote. "I thank them. Thanks also to . . . Eamonn 'Ted' McCrory for access to [his] material. . . ."[10] "Kitchen Cabinet" was Adams's term for the think tank.

Ted Howell, alias Eamonn McCrory, was arguably one of the most influential figures in the Provisional movement. While he was chairman of the think tank in the years leading up to the 1994 cease-fire, hardly a document was submitted to the British and Irish governments or to the SDLP by the republican movement that was not either written or vetted by him, or whose contents he had not influenced. By the time of the 1998 negotiations that led to the Good Friday Agreement, he was indispensable to the Sinn Fein leadership, as one story told about the talks illustrated. "During the 1998 talks Adams came into the room," recalled one source, "and somebody asked him, 'What's going on?' His reply was 'I don't know but Ted Howell does, and he's the only one who does.'"[11] Howell had another brief that was every bit as important. He was the link between Adams and the Provisional support groups in North America, initially Noraid and Clann na Gael, but later he would set up communication channels with the figures in corporate Irish-America, Congress, and the White House who would smooth Adams's passage to the corridors of power in Washington.

There were six or seven other members of the think tank in the years prior to the 1994 cessation. Jim Gibney, whose republican nickname was "God's little helper," God being Gerry Adams, was a personable and friendly character who spent a great deal of time briefing the press, whose company he evidently enjoyed. He had been on the think tank since the late 1970s, as had Tom Hartley, another former press officer for Sinn Fein, who went to some trouble to cultivate the view that he had no IRA history at all. A grumpy and often imperious disposition disguised a sincere if somewhat insecure personality, but it was those negative qualities that made him less than popular with many republican activists and therefore vulnerable. Like other members of the think tank, Hartley would often float controversial ideas on behalf of Adams. If they went down well, Adams would eventually adopt them; if not, Hartley would carry the can. Once a rising star in the Sinn Fein firmament, Hartley was made a sacrificial lamb in 1995 to deflect criticism from the leadership when the peace strategy ran into difficulties. While other, less talented figures went on to become Assembly members in the new power-sharing arrangement, Hartley has languished in Belfast City Council.

Aidan McAteer was Adams's personal assistant and a son of a former chief of staff, Hugh McAteer, and nephew of the former Nationalist Party leader Eddie McAteer. Once on the staff of Belfast Brigade, McAteer had left under a cloud in the 1970s not long after his arrest, but he was brought back by Adams despite reservations at some levels of the IRA. Danny Morrison had been a founder member of the think tank, but after his arrest and imprisonment in 1990 his influence dwindled. Even so it appears he was still in the loop. He would receive regular prison visits from Father Alec Reid during his incarceration, and it was Morrison who gave the first hint of the coming cease-fire during a pre-release break from jail in the summer of 1994. Gerry Kelly, the adjutant general, was another member, and in the period leading up to 1994 so was Martin McGuinness.

By far the most unpopular and controversial member of the think tank, as far the Army Council "soldiers" were concerned, was Mitchel McLaughlin, not least because he had joined the republican movement in 1966, yet had never been in the IRA. Once famously dubbed "the draft dodger" by an unkind unionist during a debate in the post-1998 Northern Ireland Assembly, McLaughlin was a refrigeration engineer by trade who had spent much of the early part of the Troubles working in the Middle East. McLaughlin's principal role in the late 1980s and early 1990s was to take the IRA to task for botched and bungled operations, and he later became the acceptable public face of republicanism, the first to shake hands with British ministers, for example. His lack of any association with the IRA was made an asset.

When Adams revived the Revolutionary Council, McLaughlin was brought along to expose IRA commanders to criticism, and this drove the activists wild, especially when, on occasion, he repeated the censure publicly. IRA activists could take reprimands from one of their own but not from someone who had never fired a shot in anger. At one stage the Army Council, on the insistence of Kevin McKenna, ordered McLaughlin to be gagged, saying that he would have to clear all his public statements with the IRA. There were even calls from figures on Northern Command for his expulsion from the movement. At another point senior figures recommended McLaughlin's exclusion from important decision making, but Adams ignored them. His continued presence at Revolutionary Council meetings led some figures to stay away and contributed to its eventual demise.

THE THINK TANK acted in an advisory capacity to the Army Council, mostly on political matters but occasionally on military strategy as well. During the preparation of the blueprint for the "Tet offensive," for instance, it strongly advised against plans to launch rocket attacks on British embassies in Europe, on the grounds that this would almost certainly alienate potentially friendly or neutral governments. It was during the peace process, however, that the think tank came into its own.

The sheer volume of work involved in administering the process meant that the Army Council was forced to look outside its ranks for assistance. The Council was particularly ill-suited to the task. It met only once a month, and most of its meetings were spent discussing detailed IRA matters, while nearly all its members had other jobs either in the IRA structures or in Sinn Fein. The peace process required specialized skills and the undivided and virtually full-time attention of a secretariat. Since the Army Council could not do it, the task was taken on by the think tank.

During the years after Reynolds's elevation to taoiseach through to the first and second IRA cease-fires and beyond, nearly every position paper presented by the IRA in its own name or through Sinn Fein to the British and Irish governments and to the SDLP was meticulously prepared by the think tank. The process was exhaustive. If a document came into the IRA from, say, the Dublin government, the think tank, or more often a subcommittee of the group headed by Howell or Gibney, would typically draft several papers in response. One would be an analysis of the Dublin paper, another a draft reply, and a third an attempt to anticipate what Dublin's response to that might be. The Army Council would have to give an opinion on the draft response, which would go back in skeleton or outline form to the think tank, which would prepare a final draft. That would then have to go back to the Army Council for final approval before being sent on to Dublin. The same process would be repeated for communications with the British, the SDLP, and anyone else involved in the process, sometimes all at the same time. This complicated bureaucracy helps explain the at times laboriously slow pace of the peace process, an aspect of the negotiations that often perplexed and frustrated the two governments.

The role played by the think tank gave Adams an important edge over other members of the Army Council. The body was, to begin with, his creation, and he alone decided who would sit on it. By definition it was loyal to him before anyone else. It also generated a huge amount of paperwork for the Army Council to read on top of the usual workload that greeted its members at their monthly meeting, and that too worked in Adams's favor. While Adams, McGuinness, and Kelly would already be familiar with the material, having generated or helped to generate much of it, the rest of the Army Council, especially the "soldiers," would come to it new.

Some of the paperwork could be mind-boggling in its complexity. It would not be unusual for analytical documents to be written in three different typefaces—bold, roman, and italics. To read the document required constant reference to a key that explained, for example, that bold type represented the republican position, italics the Dublin or British government position, and a normal Roman typeface what republicans might end up negotiating. Since Army Council members were not allowed, at least in the early years of the process, to hold on to the documentation—whereas think tank members could have regular access—it was hardly surprising if much of it went unread or was only partially digested. The volume of paperwork became so great that the Army Council gave Adams and McGuinness, and occasionally Kelly, the authority to approve think tank final drafts without their going back to the Council. Some of the most important communications from the IRA went to the taoiseach in Dublin or to the British, unread by the IRA leadership. The think tank effectively developed into a shadow republican leadership; some came to believe that in the end it was more powerful than the Army Council.

THE THINK TANK also played a crucial role in one of the most intriguing and puzzling episodes of the peace process, the nearly three years of secret dialogue between the Army Council and the British government in the period 1990–93. A conduit that had come into existence, almost casually, just after the 1972 cease-fire facilitated the talks. The inspiration came from the Derry businessman Brendan Duddy, who has since gone on to become something of a player on the international peace circuit. After the 1972 cease-fire collapsed, he approached Ruairi O Bradaigh with a suggestion. SDLP figures such as John Hume and Paddy Devlin had helped mediate the truce terms, but the effect of that was that the republicans had lost control of the direction of events. The IRA, Duddy had said, should use another way of communicating with the British in the future.

A source familiar with the episode described what happened next:

> Later he came back and said, "If you ever want a way of communicating with the British, then I can do it for you." The opportunity came when the Anglo-Irish aristocrats the Earl and Countess of Donoughmore (who lived part of the year in Ireland) were kidnapped in Dublin in June 1974 in an attempt to force the transfer of the 1973 London bombing team, including the Price sisters, from Brixton jail back to the North. The prison dispute was settled, and so O Bradaigh contacted the conduit, who passed the message on to the British that the Donoughmores would be released. Another opportunity arose when a British officer wandered into Donegal. He was captured by the IRA and then released, and again the pipeline was utilized. Later the conduit was involved in the 1975 cease-fire passing messages to and from us and the Brits.[12]

Over the years the conduit expanded to include two other figures, only one of whom, Denis Bradley, a former Derry priest turned community worker, has ever publicly admitted his role. The third figure, who played the more prominent role in the 1990–93 dialogue, was another Derry businessman, one involved in the energy industry. Contact between the British and the Army Council had been intermittent over the years and from the IRA's point of view largely unsatisfactory.

According to well-informed republican sources, efforts to resume contact between the IRA and the British, as distinct from the Adams-Reid pipeline, began in the late 1980s when Michael Oatley of MI6 attempted to make contact with Martin McGuinness. The trigger for the contact was the capture of the *Eksund* and British intelligence's realization that many more tons of weaponry had been successfully smuggled into Ireland. The contact was made at around the time when the IRA began moving the Libyan weaponry northwards in preparation for the "Tet offensive," and the Army Council concluded that Oatley was on a fishing expedition to tease out the IRA's intentions. It responded warily to his advances, and nothing came of the approach.[13]

More substantive, if desultory and largely one-sided, contact with the Army Council was reopened on the initiative of the British in early 1990. From the pace and content of the messages between them, it seemed the British were keen to test the IRA's mind. Thanks to the secret dialogue facilitated by Father Reid, which stretched way back to Tom King's day, they had been given an insight into the sort of settlement that might be acceptable to Gerry Adams. But what they could not know for certain was whether Adams was speaking for the Army Council, or what the Council's bottom line in negotiations might be. When these talks became public in 1993, the news caused a sensation. While most attention was directed at a clumsy attempt by the then Northern Ireland secretary, Sir Patrick Mayhew, to minimize the contacts, especially a British offer to hold talks in the event of an undeclared IRA cessation, a much more significant chapter was largely overlooked. Details of this emerged in two documents published when Sinn Fein released a partial account of the dialogue in late 1993. Seen against the now revealed but then secret Adams-Reid diplomacy, they take on greater significance.

The first document had been sent to the IRA by the British side on March 19, 1993. Known as the "Nine Pointer," it set out the parameters of the British negotiating position, parameters that echoed the secret diplomacy facilitated by Father Reid. Like a fisherman casting for trout, the British had landed a large, enticing fly over the IRA's nose to see if it would bring a rise.

The kernel of the "Nine Pointer" was in paragraph 7. "[The British government] has no blueprint," it read. "It wants an agreed accommodation, not an imposed settlement, arrived at through an inclusive process in which the parties are free agents. . . . The British Government cannot enter a talks process, or expect others to do so, with the purpose of achieving a predetermined outcome. . . ." If talks went ahead on that basis and reached agreement, it continued, "the British Government would bring forward legislation to implement the will of the people."[14] Although framed in blunter language, paragraph 7 represented a repetition of the core sentiments contained in the secret British reply to Adams in 1987, in particular the key redefinition of British withdrawal. The British had secretly offered the deal to Adams in 1987, and now, it seemed, they wanted to see whether or not he was genuine.

Unaware of the secret Reid-Adams diplomacy, the Army Council rejected the "Nine Pointer" out of hand, with the "soldiers" dismissing it as falling far short of the 1988 Council policy on British withdrawal. There was no indication in the document, for instance, that the British were prepared to commit to withdraw; there was certainly no timetable for withdrawal in the document nor any indication that the British would override the unionist veto. At this point the Army Council "soldiers" urged that the dialogue be halted; if the British were not prepared to budge on such fundamental issues, there seemed little point in continuing. But Adams argued otherwise: the British should be tested all the way. To walk away at this point would be to abandon the moral high ground to the enemy; the contact should not be broken off, he urged. He got his way. Not for the first time Adams succeeded in keeping the process on the rails and by so doing limited the Army Council's ability to retrace its steps.

Eventually on May 10, 1993, nearly two months later, the IRA sent a reply, an eleven-point document. It was delicately worded, testament to the lengthy wrangling that had gone on inside the Army Council. The IRA was, as the British hoped, ready to respond positively to an offer of talks in return for a short, two-week cease-fire and would also set up a secretariat headed by Martin McGuinness which could help organize the subsequent face-to-face contact. That was the good news for the British. The bad news was that the document repeated, in strong language, the Army Council's 1988 bottom lines. The British would have to leave Ireland, said the document. The free exercise of national self-determination, it went on, required a process that "culminates . . . in the end of [British] jurisdiction."[15] The unionist veto was a major obstacle. If the British were not prepared to override the veto, as the "Nine Pointer" suggested, it meant that the British had predetermined the outcome of the process in favor of the unionists. The veto had to go.

The republican document attempted to perform a balancing act between a yes and a no, between wishing to signal a willingness to keep the process going—as Adams clearly wanted—and a need to draw lines in the sand—as the Army Council "soldiers" insisted upon. But notwithstanding the IRA document's use of subtle language, it had failed to disguise a fundamental reality; the Army Council's position fell far short of what the British had been hearing in private about what figures such as Adams would accept. The talks went downhill afterward and that fall eventually deteriorated into bickering and mutual recrimination. If the British had set out to test the IRA waters, they had found them as chilly and inhospitable as ever. The peace process had once again fallen victim to the ambiguity that Adams had built into it.

IF THERE WAS one ploy that Adams and his allies on the Army Council used with great effect to keep the peace process on the rails, until finally a cease-fire was within reach, it was the ability to persuade the "soldiers" not to walk away from the enterprise even when it seemed there was no point in doing otherwise. The gap between the secret peace process and the process the Army Council thought it had endorsed was at times so great that, with hindsight, it was Adams's greatest achievement that he managed so skillfully to stop his more military-minded colleagues from pulling the plug. That he was able to do so created the time and space for the hidden agenda to finally triumph.

There was no better example of this in practice than the talks between Adams and the SDLP leader, John Hume, which had continued in secret after 1988, even though to the public mind they had ended in sharp disagreement. Hume was acting as the de facto representative of the Irish government at the suggestion of Charles Haughey, and although the discussions had mired, they were revived when Albert Reynolds succeeded Haughey as Ireland's prime minister in early 1992. By this point the aim of the exercise was to compose a joint British-Irish declaration outlining Britain's attitude and intentions toward Northern Ireland. The Army Council had authorized the talks on the basis that somewhere in the declaration the British would indicate their desire to withdraw and, crucially, give a date by which this would be completed, even a date twenty years hence.

On the face of it this was a daunting and even an impossible task. A huge ideological rift separated the Provisionals from Fianna Fail and the SDLP. The republicans officially rejected the consent principle, whereas for the constitutional nationalist parties, securing unionist assent to a united Ireland was a defining point of principle.

Such was the magnitude of this gulf that in practice the only way in which an agreed position between republicans and nationalists could be reached was for one or the other to compromise fundamental beliefs. Neither the Irish government nor the SDLP was prepared to do that. Dublin in particular made it clear to the republican negotiators, as one authoritative account described it, that "any formula to do with Irish unity must involve consent of a majority within Northern Ireland."[16] To have done otherwise would have caused a rupture with Britain and serious internal political instability.

On the other hand the secret diplomacy begun by Adams and Reid had already demonstrated the Sinn Fein leader's readiness to make that fundamental compromise, although as far as the Army Council and most of their senior IRA and Sinn Fein colleagues were concerned, the rejection of the unionist veto, as the consent principle was termed by the IRA, remained a cornerstone of their beliefs and officially guided the talks between Adams and Hume.

The Army Council brief for the Hume-Adams dialogue was based upon the 1988 policy change on British withdrawal. While it was prepared to be flexible about the time-scale for British disengagement and would even accept a secret rather than a public pledge from the British to leave Ireland, the Council's view was that it would not compromise on the demand for a specific time line by which the process of disengagement had to be completed. Nor would the IRA leadership bend on the issue of the unionist veto. While it was prepared to give unionists the final say on the options to partition, they would not be allowed to prevent British withdrawal. That was the official Army Council line, and as such it threatened to throttle the Reid-Adams diplomacy. The task facing the Sinn Fein leader was to keep that from happening. The story of the Hume-Adams dialogue is the story of how that was done.

WORK ON DRAFTING the joint British-Irish declaration began in late 1991, during the dying months of the Haughey administration, and when Albert Reynolds succeeded Haughey the pace of events quickened. So did the traffic of paper between Hume and Adams. The number of drafts of the joint declaration multiplied. In June 1992 the Adams think tank drafted, for Army Council approval, a version of the joint declaration that eventually became known as the Hume-Adams document. Cleverly and carefully enough worded to allow for ambiguity, one paragraph—number 4—encapsulated the IRA's 1988 policy position. It reads as follows:

> The British Prime Minister reiterates, on behalf of the British Government, that they have no selfish, strategic, political or economic interest in Northern Ireland, and that their sole interest is to see peace, stability and reconciliation established by agreement among the people who inhabit the island. The British Government accepts the principle that the Irish people have the right collectively to self-determination, and that the exercise of this right could take the form of agreed independent structures for the island as a whole. They affirm their readiness to introduce the measures to give legislative effect on their side to this right (within a specified period to be agreed) and allowing sufficient time for the building of consent and the beginning of a process of national reconciliation. The British Government will use all its influence and energy to win the consent of a majority in Northern Ireland for these measures. They acknowledge that it is the wish of the people of Britain to see the people of Ireland live together in unity and harmony, with respect for their diverse traditions, independent, but with full recognition of the special links and the unique relationship which exists between the peoples of Britain and Ireland.[17]

That part of June 1992 Hume-Adams document echoed the 1988 Army Council policy almost exactly. All that needed to be done was to fill in the blank space after the commitment to withdraw to indicate how long it would be before the British left Northern Ireland. But the paragraph flagrantly offended the consent principle and flew in the face of established policy on Northern Ireland. The notion that the British or the Irish government or the SDLP could accept such a formulation was approaching fantasy.

On the other hand the Army Council seemed to be unalterably committed to its view on British withdrawal, as a message sent to Reynolds in April 1993, and unearthed by the writers Eamonn Mallie and David McKittrick, revealed. While the leadership was ready to consider alternative ways in which the British could make this announcement—a private agreement underwritten by international figures and released some months after the joint declaration was one suggestion—the message unequivocally declared that the IRA preference "is for a joint declaration which embodies a clear and specified time" for achieving national self-determination.[18] The gulf between the constitutional forces and the Provisionals seemed to be as wide and unbridgeable as ever.

It was at this point, in April 1993, that the SDLP leader, John Hume, saved the process. He put his name to the June 1992 draft in all respects save one, the part of paragraph 4 that referred to the yet to be agreed time-scale for British withdrawal from Northern Ireland. This was, of course, the defining section of the Hume-Adams document, and unless there was agreement on it the paper would remain largely an academic exercise. Nevertheless, Hume's act allowed Adams to go to the Army Council and argue to keep the initiative alive, not least on the grounds that the Hume-Adams double act was irritating the unionists and annoying other anti-Provisional forces in the Republic, as was demonstrated by the barrage of criticism directed at Hume when his secret dialogue with Adams was revealed, also in April 1993. It intensified when Hume and Adams jointly called for "national self-determination" in Ireland, although the critics could not have known that the term had been fundamentally redefined by the Sinn Fein leader and his Redemptorist helper.

Hume's move strengthened Adams's hand in another way, one that began to affect the IRA's military strategy and push the organization toward a cease-fire. On the same day in April 1993 that Hume and Adams called for "national self-determination," a ton of fertilizer-based explosives packed into a truck exploded right in the heart of the City of London, killing one man, injuring over thirty, and devastating Britain's financial center. One estimate of the damage put the cost at $1.45 billion. It was a massively destructive blow, the latest in a series of blockbuster attacks in England masterminded by the South Armagh IRA.

The explosion of April 1993 was, however, the last big IRA bomb in London during this part of the peace process. On the urging of Adams and his allies, the Army Council was persuaded "to hold back" on the English bombing campaign, as one of Adams's think tank advisers later told the author. "It was held back because it threatened to clash with the Hume-Adams process and because there were signs that Reynolds was beginning to move back into the British camp," he explained. "The risk was that we would be marginalized."[19] The IRA had stumbled on what was possibly the most successful military tactic since the start of the Troubles, yet agreed to suspend it in order to preserve a political strategy whose ambiguity they were unaware of and whose effectiveness had not been tested.

Albert Reynolds had handed over the June 1992 draft, the so-called Hume-Adams document, to John Major in June 1993, but, as he told Mallie and McKittrick, he believed there was no way he could sell it to the British prime minister, and he told the Provisionals so via the doughty Father Reid.

"I said, 'If you're talking about a time frame, forget it. I can't sell that. . . . There is no way we are going to adopt that role, and if you persist in that argument then forget that side of the discussion because we simply are not going to persuade the Unionists to do anything. . . .' My feeling was telling me that the British wouldn't run with what was in the document."[20] Reynolds was right. The British were distinctly cool about the paper, objecting in particular to what the document had to say about consent and a timescale for withdrawal. In October 1993 Major formally rejected the Hume-Adams document—his government would or could in no way impose Irish reunification on the unionists. After a series of often difficult meetings with Reynolds, the two leaders decided to start drafting their own declaration, which would incorporate the principle of consent, yet offer enough to the Provisionals to ensure that rejection of the declaration by them would attract opprobrium and blame. It would also contain all the essential elements of the Reid-Adams diplomacy—although only a very few would know that.

THE RESULT of Reynolds's and Major's work was unveiled in mid-December 1993 at a press conference in Downing Street, London, and the event was staged in such a way as to emphasize its historic importance. The world's press was invited to witness the signing ceremony, and the Irish government sent along a large political and diplomatic delegation headed by Reynolds and his tanaiste, or deputy, the Labour Party leader Dick Spring. The Irish group posed for the TV cameras and press photographers beside a large Christmas tree outside the doorway of number 10. The spectacle of the British and Irish governments making common cause on the seemingly intractable Northern Ireland problem was welcomed around the globe and added enormously to the pressure on the Provos to accept the shared analysis.

The Downing Street Declaration (DSD), as the joint British-Irish statement was called, conceded the principle of self-determination but in such a way as to weave the principle of consent through it. The relevant section of the new paragraph 4 read:

The British Government agree that it is for the people of the island of Ireland alone, by agreement between the two parts respectively, to exercise their right of self-determination on the basis of consent, freely and concurrently given, North and South, to bring about a united Ireland, if that is their wish. They reaffirm, as a binding obligation, that they will for their part, introduce the necessary legislation to give effect to this, or equally to any measure of agreement on future relationships in Ireland which the people of Ireland may themselves freely so determine without external impediment.[21]

The Downing Street Declaration conflicted fundamentally with the Army Council's 1988 policy position. There was no commitment by the British to withdraw, no time-scale for withdrawal, and no rejection by the British of the unionist veto. But the declaration was fully consistent with the secret Reid-Adams diplomacy and encapsulated perfectly the two men's redefinition of British withdrawal.

Unsurprisingly the formulation on national self-determination in the declaration had ruffled no unionist feathers; in fact many unionists were pleasantly surprised by what it said. The declaration's acceptance of the consent principle, on the other hand, dismayed the Provo grassroots; there were mutterings against Reynolds and Hume. Three days before the DSD was published, Adams anticipated his supporters' mood and echoed the official Army Council line. In an interview with the *Sunday Tribune*, he said, "The Six Counties cannot have a right to self-determination, that is a matter for the Irish people as a whole to be exercised without impediment. However the shape of a future Ireland is a matter to be determined by all groups in Ireland obviously including the Unionists."[22] One senior Belfast republican summed up the general mood of IRA despondency in the wake of the Downing Street summit: "What we're talking about here is that if we accept this we accept that everything we stood for in the last 25 years is for nothing, that's what we're talking about."[23] Neither he nor most other IRA supporters knew that the principle had actually been conceded by their leadership years before.

A KEY FACTOR in shaping events in the aftermath of the Downing Street Declaration was a growing public expectation that a peaceful settlement to the Troubles was now possible. Hopes for peace had risen following the disclosure of the secret Hume-Adams talks back in April, and they soared in September 1993 when Hume and Adams issued another statement claiming that they had forwarded a report on their deliberations to the Reynolds government in Dublin for consideration. No such report existed. The statement was merely a ploy to force movement from Reynolds, but it had the effect of raising nationalist hopes and unsettling the unionists.

Northern Ireland's one million Protestant and largely unionist population had been watching the developing Hume-Adams dialogue with growing alarm and anxiety. The sight of their two enemies—one supposedly committed to nonviolence, the other unashamedly a supporter of armed struggle—sitting down and finding common cause filled them with dismay. This turned to anger when the British began negotiating directly with Hume as, on the sidelines, the Irish government urged them on. Ever distrustful of the British, the unionists suspected the worst and concluded that a deal was being hatched to throw them out of the union with Britain.

Unionism's extremists, the loyalist paramilitary groups, had a history of turning to violence when they believed their constitutional position was threatened, and the September 1993 Hume-Adams statement was the trigger for a burst of bloody savagery that claimed the lives of three Catholics and injured dozens more. The loyalists mounted an average of one attack a day throughout the ensuing month, October 1993.

The loyalist onslaught directly challenged the IRA's raison d'être, and the pressures on the organization in Belfast to respond were enormous. After all, the Provisionals had come into existence to defend the city's vulnerable Catholic communities, and any failure to hit back at those behind the attacks could provoke uncontrollable freelance operations by IRA units. In a worst-case scenario these could even precipitate a split in the organization. The Ulster Defence Asociation, the largest loyalist grouping, was behind a majority of the attacks, in particular the so-called C Coy of the organization's Second Battalion on the Shankill Road, a tough loyalist district of North Belfast. Led by a notorious, muscled gunman called Johnny Adair, the UDA was causing mayhem in the IRA's strongest areas. In the face of all this the IRA decided to hit back. Plans were put forward by the IRA in Belfast to assassinate Adair and to wipe out the bulk of the UDA leadership.

The proposal to remove the UDA leadership was endorsed at the highest level in the IRA. The demands of the peace process meant that the Army Council had already moved to tighten its control over the organization when, in September 1993, it issued an order saying that in the future all IRA operations had to be approved by Chief of Staff Kevin McKenna. Northern Command had long had a veto on IRA operations, and now that power was extended to the Army Council. On the urging of Adams and his allies, the Council had taken this action for fear that a "bad" operation might endanger the fragile relationship with Hume. Accordingly the proposal to attack the UDA leadership was placed in front of the Council, and eventually one plan was given the go-ahead.

So it was that a car carrying three IRA men from the Ardoyne area of North Belfast drew up outside Frizzell's fishmonger's shop on the afternoon of Saturday, October 13, 1993, and set in motion one of the worst atrocities in the history of the Irish Troubles. Situated halfway along the Shankill Road, in the middle of the city's toughest loyalist district, Frizzell's was packed with shoppers that Saturday afternoon when two of the IRA men, both sporting white coats of the sort worn by delivery men, carried a bomb inside the shop. As one held up the customers and staff with a handgun, the other, a twenty-three-year-old single man, Thomas Begley, suspended the device from the ceiling and lit the fuse with a cigarette lighter. Above the shop was the local headquarters of the UDA, and usually on Saturdays the group's commanders, including Adair, gathered there for a meeting. That particular Saturday, however, the UDA leaders had left early, and the IRA operation went disastrously wrong. The fuse lit by Begley had been cropped short to give the customers in the shop just enough time to get out but not enough for the UDA men to escape downstairs. But the fuse had been cut too short and the bomb exploded almost instantly, killing Begley and causing the ancient, Victorian brick building to collapse on top of the early afternoon shoppers. Nine other people died in the explosion, four of them women shoppers and two schoolgirls, one seven years old, the other thirteen. All the victims aside from Begley were Protestants. At Begley's funeral a few days later Gerry Adams helped carry the coffin, a decision that brought expressions of outrage and condemnation from mainstream politicians and the media. What none of them knew was that as a member of the Army Council, which had approved the bombing, Adams had little choice.

The Shankill bomb ushered in a period of unprecedented terror in Northern Ireland. Following the Shankill disaster the UDA issued an ominous statement. "John Hume, Gerry Adams and the nationalist electorate," it warned, "will pay a heavy, heavy price for today's atrocity."[24] Over the next six weeks loyalists killed sixteen people, all but one of them Catholics. The UDA was responsible for thirteen of the deaths. The worst single incident was in the small County Derry village of Greysteel, where two UDA gunmen opened fire indiscriminately on a crowd of two hundred people celebrating the Halloween holiday in the Rising Sun restaurant and lounge bar. Eight people died in the hail of bullets, and nineteen were wounded. One of the gunmen shouted "Trick or Treat?" before pulling the trigger.

THE WEEKS between all this slaughter and the publication of the Downing Street Declaration in December 1993 rank among the most tense and dreadful that veterans of the Troubles could remember. Belfast became a ghost town in the evenings as workplaces and shops closed early. Most pubs and restaurants were deserted or didn't bother opening. Catholic areas braced themselves for further slaughter, while the nightly television news programs were dominated by emotional scenes of grieving relatives and friends as one funeral followed another.

It was in these circumstances that the IRA was presented with the Downing Street Declaration, a document which held out a fragile hope for peace but whose rejection by the IRA would surely have brought censure and denunciation raining down on its head. The effect of the terrible violence was profound. Most people, not least Catholics on the receiving end of the loyalist violence, yearned for an end to the killing and were prepared to give the Downing Street Declaration a chance. There were also hints of tough security reprisals if the IRA rejected the document. Albert Reynolds said the Irish public would expect "a strong security response" if violence resumed its past levels, while the British press reported accounts of cabinet briefings in London suggesting that there would be an all-out offensive against the IRA if the declaration was not accepted.

The Adams leadership had one option that, according to his advisers, was only briefly considered and then discarded. This was to publish the original Hume-Adams document of June 1992 and embarrass Reynolds and Hume by revealing that they had initially accepted the proposition that Britain should withdraw from Northern Ireland, a position very different from that promoted in the Downing Street Declaration.

Putting the June 1992 document into the public arena would certainly have disconcerted both Reynolds and Hume and would have gone a long way to reassure a republican grassroots increasingly unsettled by the concession contained in the Downing Street Declaration. But doing that would have had two irrevocable consequences. It would, in the words of one of the think tank advisers, "have destroyed the pan-nationalist alliance"[25] and demolished the relationship between Adams and his putative partners, Albert Reynolds and John Hume. More important, publicizing the document would have set limits to his flexibility beyond which Adams could not have retreated without incurring criticism from his grassroots activists and showing weakness to his political opponents. The Army Council had walked, or been steered, into a cul-de-sac from which there was no prospect of retreat.

One other consideration would figure more and more in the calculations of Adams and the think tank as the peace process progressed. The process was beginning to bring to Sinn Fein benefits of a sort the party had not seen in years. A month or so after the disclosure of the Hume-Adams meeting in

Derry, in May 1993, elections were held to the North's local councils, and for the first time in a decade Sinn Fein's share of the vote rose, and the number of seats secured by the party increased by 20 percent. In October there was an even more dramatic example of this electoral bonus when Sinn Fein won a council by-election in Derry, transforming a previous 60-to-40 vote for the rival SDLP into a 55-to-45 victory for the republican candidate. Nationalist voters, it seemed, were ready to reward Sinn Fein every time the party edged toward a cease-fire, and the lesson was not lost on Adams and his allies.

ELECTORAL CONSIDERATIONS, however, were not foremost in the mind of the Army Council, at least not as far as its "soldier" members were concerned. The Downing Street Declaration was simply unacceptable—it made no mention of British withdrawal and set the principle of unionist consent in textual stone. The Council voted in January 1994 to reject it, with Slab Murphy, Kevin McKenna, and Micky McKevitt openly contemptuous of its contents.

No one spoke up for the declaration, but once again Adams was able to persuade the Council not to take precipitate action and he argued, successfully, that the Council should keep its rejection of the document secret from the outside world and pretend that it was still being considered. Play for time, Adams urged. History may well judge this to be one of the most crucial moves, if not the most crucial move, of the entire process, one that made an IRA cease-fire inevitable and merely a matter of time and management. Having refused to say no, openly and publicly, the IRA was really saying yes.

Once again the argument that won the day was the same—keeping the game with Reynolds and Hume alive was paramount. Two delaying mechanisms were set in place. One, a peace commission was established under Pat Doherty with the brief of traveling around Ireland to hold hearings. It was supposed to report by the end of January 1994, but did not conclude its deliberations until June when, not surprisingly, it revealed that half the submissions received had opted for an IRA cease-fire. What started off as a delaying ploy ended by mobilizing pressure to end the war. The other delaying tactic was a Sinn Fein demand for clarification of the declaration. An elaborate game was played in which senior republicans suggested that buried somewhere in the text of the document might be a hidden message that the British could be teased into revealing.

While these moves clearly kept open the possibility of a cease-fire, the Army Council chairman, Martin McGuinness, was dispatched in early

January 1994 to give the Provisional grassroots a reassuring message, a role he would play again and again both publicly and privately before the cease-fire was declared. In a lengthy interview with the *Sunday Business Post* in Dublin, McGuinness warned that unless the British had a private position that was different from the one expressed publicly by John Major, then the Downing Street Declaration was "worthless," adding that "anything short of a British government decision that they are leaving this country is unacceptable."

Hinting at the 1988 Army Council decision, McGuinness went on to say that the timetable for British withdrawal was nevertheless negotiable and that the IRA might be prepared to negotiate terms that went beyond the lifetime of a British parliament, but on the issue of an IRA cease-fire he was unequivocally hard-line, as the IRA Volunteers expected their Northern commander to be. A cessation, he warned, would require an Army Convention, but as things stood republicans would regard even a three-month cease-fire as "particularly long."[26] But hidden behind this hard-line message was another signal, that the Army Council was not yet prepared to dismiss the Downing Street Declaration. Republicans needed clarification, McGuinness said, and in the meantime the leadership would continue to consult with its grassroots. Not for the first or last time tough language masked private flexibility.

THE PERIOD FOLLOWING the Downing Street Declaration was a bizarre, Alice-in-Wonderland time for rank-and-file republicans as they tried to work out why their leaders had not immediately rejected the declaration. In the ensuing weeks the Sinn Fein leadership hosted "family meetings" around Northern Ireland for republican activists which were addressed by leading members of the think tank, particularly Gibney and Hartley, whose unenviable task it was to act as lightning rods for grassroots confusion and anxiety. Hundreds of rank-and-file republicans would turn up at drinking clubs and community halls expecting or hoping to hear that Adams and McGuinness had a secret trick up their sleeves, only to be disappointed.

Instead they would be reassured not to worry and counseled to have faith and trust in a leadership they knew would never sell out; there would be no cease-fires, no dilution of the struggle. As soon as they went home, they would switch on the TV news to hear the same figures sending out completely opposite signals. One West Belfast republican described the internal turmoil in the opening weeks of 1994: "We go to meetings, and there seems to be a consensus that everyone agrees on, but every time you look at them on television or read something in the paper it seems to be taking a different direction. . . . There is confusion. I don't know whether they know what the base thinks. I don't think they're out of touch; they've had so many meetings. And they're getting the same message from the meetings. So what's the name of the game?"[27] Another rural activist put it more bluntly, although this judgment was made with the benefit of hindsight: "They told their people lies. I was at [our local] meeting . . . and their interpretation of it all was that they would run it to its natural conclusion; they would expose the Brits, the SDLP, and the Free State government, and then it would be back to the war. There would be no cease-fire and certainly no return to Stormont."[28]

Eventually Sinn Fein submitted a series of inconsequential questions about the Downing Street Declaration to the British via Albert Reynolds in May 1994, and the British sent a formalistic reply. Those republicans who were expecting sensational admissions from the British were disappointed. A few days later Suzanne Breen, a reporter in the Belfast office of the *Irish Times*, filed a story quoting republican sources explaining why the IRA had refused to reject the declaration out of hand. The anonymous interview infuriated Adams's press handlers, who denied it and privately blamed a leading Sinn Fein councillor for the leak. But the story had the touch of authenticity. "We don't want to be written off as being negative," the paper quoted the republican source as saying. "We don't want to be portrayed as the people who have rejected peace. Our reply when it comes, will be a balancing act. Sure we're playing games but what do you think the British are doing? They know damn well that we won't accept what's on offer. They would love us to be hot-headed but we've no intention of doing that."[29] It was back to playing word games.

The reality was that once the Army Council had refused to reject the Downing Street Declaration, the die was cast. It was only a matter of time, management, and negotiation before the IRA was obliged to call a cease-fire. Albert Reynolds's congenial press secretary, Sean Duignan, later wrote that the taoiseach constantly used the analogy of a hooked trout to describe the Provos in the wake of the declaration.[30] It was just a matter of keeping a tight line and reeling them in. In January 1994 the hook was driven deeper. A promise given by Reynolds to Adams during 1993 to scrap the eighteen-year-old ban on radio and television interviews with Sinn Fein in the Republic as soon as there was a cease-fire was fast-forwarded. With Sinn Fein measurably closer to being treated like a normal, respectable political party, outright rejection of the Downing Street Declaration became more and more difficult to envisage.

IT WAS TIME to play the American card or, to be more accurate, the Clinton card. The American president had been assiduously wooed by Adams's allies in the United States and in April 1992, when Clinton was seeking the Democratic nomination for the upcoming presidential election, he promised that, if elected, he would grant Gerry Adams a visa to visit the United States. Clinton had astutely realized that there were votes, Irish-American votes, to be won, and at a relatively low cost. Once Clinton arrived in the White House, however, it was a different matter. Both the State Department and the British embassy lobbied heavily against giving Adams a visa. The Provisional leader had been barred from entering the United States for twenty years, and if they had their way, that was how it would stay.

For the best part of two years Clinton refused to defy the mandarins in Foggy Bottom, but a combination of Irish government diplomacy, lobbying by John Hume, and the secret blandishments of the think tank chairman, Ted Howell, paved the way in February 1994 for a dramatic initiative. Much to the public fury of the British, Adams was granted a forty-eight-hour visa to visit New York to attend a conference on Northern Ireland hosted by the deeply establishment National Committee on American Foreign Policy, whose members included such luminaries as Henry Kissinger, Jeane Kirkpatrick, George Shultz, David Rockefeller, and, later, Margaret Thatcher. For years Sinn Fein had championed the cause of many of America's ideological foes in countries like Nicaragua, El Salvador, and Cuba. Now, in the interests of the peace process, the Sinn Fein leader was supping at their enemy's table.

The visit was a public relations triumph for Adams. The time-limited nature of his visa and the whiff of gunsmoke that trailed after him ensured that his visit became a matter of intense media interest. He was a guest on CNN's *Larry King Live* and appeared on other TV talk shows. The Irish writer Edna O'Brien was clearly bewitched by Adams's charm and composed the sort of profile in the *New York Times* that publicists only dream of. "Given a different incarnation in a different century, one could imagine him as one of those monks transcribing the Gospels into Gaelic," she wrote.[31] The American media treated Adams like a cross between Emiliano Zapata and Michael Collins. An intoxicated Irish-America, made drunk by Britain's anger at the Adams visa, responded as though the Easter Rising were being refought in front of their eyes. Wealthy supporters paid for Adams to stay in a suite at the Waldorf-Astoria where de Valera had lived during his lengthy American exile during the Anglo-Irish war. Meanwhile back in Ireland, Adams's colleagues in the IRA predicted ruefully that after tasting life on Park Avenue, Adams would find it difficult to return to the diet of cold ham sandwiches, lukewarm tea, and damp country beds that life on the Army Council offered.

The Adams trip to New York gave the Sinn Fein leader an opportunity to send some highly significant political messages. The invitation had come from a group of figures from corporate Irish-America, people like the billionaire businessman Charles "Chuck" Feeney and the insurance magnate Bill Flynn, recruited to Adams's cause by allies of Ted Howell, such as the New York publisher Niall O'Dowd. They had invested heavily in the Sinn Fein leader and expected him to deliver peace. The same people had access to the wealthiest political benefactors in America, and, if the Provisionals played their cards right, Sinn Fein could expect access to considerable political funds. The IRA leadership had already declared one unofficial cease-fire for American mediators, during a visit by the Flynn-Feeney group, but they expected more. Adams hinted they would get it. At one function he promised not to disappoint those "who had stuck their neck out for him" and noted privately that he knew there was no such thing as a free lunch. As the *Irish Times* Washington correspondent Conor O'Clery later wrote, he was quite specific about his plans: "In the limousine on the way to JFK airport, according to George Schwab (president of The National Committee on American Foreign Policy), Adams said, 'George, I promise you we'll never return to the old ways.'"[32]

Adams scrupulously honored the terms of the Clinton visa. There were no efforts to fund-raise for the republican cause during his two-day trip and no public references to the armed struggle, much to the disappointment of some of the hundreds of IRA supporters who had turned up to hear him speak. "I come here with a message of peace," he told the crowds gathered at the Sheraton Hotel for his only speech. Just two public figures were permitted to join him on the platform, the former congressman Bruce Morrison and the aged and ailing Irish-American lawyer Paul O'Dwyer. No one from Noraid was allowed on the stage, least of all the group's longtime spokesman Martin Galvin. This was perhaps the most profound of all the signals sent during Adams's two-day sojourn. Noraid had been the backbone of Provisional support in the United States during the war. Unpaid Noraid activists had spent countless hours fund-raising for IRA prisoners, organizing petitions, mounting protests against British policy, and finding jobs and new identities for IRA fugitives in cities along the east coast for the best part of twenty-five years. More secretly, Noraid sympathizers had funneled guns, equipment, and cash to the IRA. Some had gone to jail for their activities. Now they could be forgiven for thinking that Adams had turned his back on them.

POLITICAL CIRCUMSTANCES had by mid-1994 been managed and contrived in such a way that the Army Council found it more and more difficult to avoid talking about the terms for a cease-fire. Rejecting the Downing Street Declaration was by this point not an option, while establishment expectation of an IRA cessation in Washington and Dublin had been heightened and, via the Adams visa and the scrapping of section 31, already been partly paid for.

Adams introduced the idea cautiously, suggesting a short exploratory cessation. This would test the water, he argued, and determine if Dublin was serious about supporting Sinn Fein's pan-nationalist agenda and also whether or not the British were really prepared to discuss withdrawal. If it failed, if the Irish and British governments were found wanting, the IRA could return to war and nothing would have been lost—in fact the two governments could be blamed for the breakdown. That, at least, was the way the case was put.

Adams won approval to explore possibilities with Reynolds, and the shuttle diplomacy between Reid, Mansergh, who was still the Irish government's principal point man on Northern Ireland, and members of the think tank intensified. The manner of these talks signaled another huge shift. The collapse of the talks with the British meant that these negotiations were premised not on the possibility of negotiating British withdrawal, as they traditionally had been, but on the construction of a pan-nationalist alliance with the Dublin government and the SDLP leader, John Hume. This was the core proposal in the lengthy message Father Alec Reid had brought from Gerry Adams to Charles Haughey way back in 1987; it had taken seven years of patient management by Adams and his allies to reach the point where the proposal could become reality.

Not long after Adams's return from New York, in February 1994, the think tank began work on producing the strategy paper that would underpin the cease-fire while McGuinness and Kelly, who had both joined the think tank by this stage, negotiated detailed terms with the Reynolds government on behalf of the Army Council, mostly using Father Reid, by now assisted by another Redemptorist, Father Gerry Reynolds, to ferry messages to and from Martin Mansergh. The think tank was now in almost total control of IRA strategy.

The think tank came up with an acronym for the cease-fire strategy that illustrated better than any other feature of the peace process the ambiguity that underlay the Adams approach. It was called TUAS, but think tank strategists were careful never to spell out in the policy document what the word actually meant. When the strategy document was eventually circulated to the IRA rank and file in the late summer of 1994, activists were told that TUAS stood for Tactical Use of Armed Struggle, and that fitted in perfectly with the assurances given by the leadership that armed struggle was not being abandoned, merely refined so that it could be switched on and off, as circumstances demanded. The explanation given to the grassroots implied that if the cease-fire tactic failed, then armed struggle would resume.

The other players in the peace process, principally Sinn Fein's putative nationalist allies, were given the opposite spin. They were told that TUAS stood for Totally UnArmed Strategy and that conveyed the message that Adams and his colleagues on the Army Council were sincere about seeking a cease-fire and really did want to find a way to end the war and enter normal parliamentary politics.

TUAS was constructed around the notion that a sufficiently strong and effective political consensus could be reached embracing the Dublin government, the SDLP, and Sinn Fein, who would agree on a set of principles and a common negotiating position to take to the British and the unionists. In fact the think tank had to admit that this objective was beyond reach. Neither Dublin nor the SDLP would agree that British sovereignty over Northern Ireland breached the principle of national self-determination or that the wishes of the unionists could be overridden. Nonetheless, the think tank recommended that TUAS be accepted on the grounds that the pan-nationalist bloc could, if expertly controlled, drive a wedge between Britain and the unionists.

In place of IRA violence, according to the TUAS blueprint, leverage on the British would be applied by the Irish nationalist parties in concert: Sinn Fein, the SDLP, and the Reynolds government. This pressure, said the TUAS strategy, would be augmented by the Irish-American lobby, led by the Clinton White House and supported by corporate and congressional allies. On paper it looked like a formidable combination, but it failed to disguise that the constituent parties had conflicting strategic goals. While the republican side said it sought Irish unity, and British withdrawal, the priority of constitutional nationalists was to see IRA violence ended and stability restored to the island. In that sense their agenda was shared by the British.

The Clinton White House had its own reasons to get involved in the Northern Ireland peace process. It was popular with Irish-American voters, a not inconsiderable factor, given that Clinton would run for the presidency again in 1996. Northern Ireland also offered Clinton the prospect of at least one foreign policy success during his time in the White House. But the underlying interests of the United States, to achieve stability, were the same as those of the Irish and British governments, as Clinton's national security adviser Nancy Soderberg told Conor O'Clery: "The truth is we don't and I don't know whether there'll ever be a united Ireland or not. I don't really care whether there is a united Ireland or not. All I care about is that there not be violence and that the North gets developed economically and politically so that it's a functioning society."[33]

The pace of activity accelerated during the late spring and early summer of 1994. At Eastertime the Army Council was persuaded to call a three-day cease-fire to mollify Reynolds, who was pressing for more fundamental decisions from the IRA. But the countervailing need to reassure the IRA rank and file led to a series of mortar attacks on Heathrow Airport in March. These were popular with IRA activists but angered Irish-Americans who had argued for the Adams visa. The Heathrow mortars were puzzling. The Army Council was told they had malfunctioned, but republican sources in Belfast suggested to the author at the time that the devices had been doctored to ensure they would not explode. The forensic evidence later supported that explanation.

Despite the airport attack the negotiations between Reynolds and the McGuinness-Kelly team intensified, and Army Council meetings happened with increasing frequency until at the end they were weekly events. Eventually a fourteen-point proposal was put together by the Irish government and think tank teams and placed in front of the Army Council. If there was a cease-fire, Reynolds said, his government would implement the following initiatives immediately, the details of which can now be revealed for the first time:

1. Sinn Fein would be treated like any other political party and would not be subjected to harassment or marginalization. To demonstrate the Dublin government's bona fides, a meeting would be held within days of the cease-fire announcement between Reynolds, Adams, and Hume;

2. Within two weeks of the cease-fire Reynolds would meet privately with Adams;

3. Adams and Reynolds would consult as regularly as required thereafter;

4. There would be regular consultations between Sinn Fein and the Irish government at all levels as required by events;

5. There would be regular consultation between the government and Sinn Fein on wider issues, including briefings of Irish government ministers as regularly as required by Sinn Fein representatives on the full spectrum of issues affecting the peace process and Sinn Fein's constituents;

6. Arrangements to set up a Forum on Peace and Reconciliation proposed by Reynolds in the Downing Street Declaration would go ahead with immediate discussions on the matter between Sinn Fein and the government;

7. Sinn Fein would be guaranteed full participation in the Forum;

8. The ending of all measures aimed at the isolation and marginalization of Sinn Fein and all republicans in general;

9. Reynolds would set out to persuade the British to scrap all their measures which isolate and marginalize Sinn Fein, including dropping their broadcasting ban;

10. Reynolds would also set out to persuade the Clinton White House to allow an Army Council representative to visit and win over supporters in the U.S. before news of the cease-fire broke;

11. Reynolds would set out to persuade the Clinton administration to lift the general visa ban on Sinn Fein members;

12. Reynolds committed the government to repeal repressive legislation and agree to the speedy release of IRA prisoners;

13. Reynolds and Hume would press the British to open cross-Border roads, scrap repressive legislation and deal speedily with the question of IRA prisoners in Northern Ireland and British jails;

14. Reynolds would commit the Department of Foreign Affairs to seek foreign support for the peace strategy especially in the United States and friendly states with ethnic Irish communities.[34]

THE POLITICAL TERMS for the cease-fire were being worked out in some detail, and so too were the military provisions. If a cease-fire was called, according to secret terms agreed to by the Army Council, the IRA would stop recruiting, cease all military training, and end targeting activity, that is, halt all actions aimed at gathering intelligence for operational purposes in the South. The same commitments were made in regard to IRA activity in the North. In return, surveillance, arrests, and harassment of IRA members by the security forces, North and South, would cease. The British were well aware of the impending cease-fire and had been party, via various intermediaries, to the negotiations. The notion that the 1994 cease-fire was an affair whose arrangement was confined to the IRA and the Reynolds government, as was claimed afterward, was not strictly true.

Army Council meetings were characterized not just by endless discussion of these terms but also by growing pressure from Adams on his colleagues to call a cease-fire. As the summer of 1994 advanced, he put forward two major arguments in favor of a cessation. The first was that Reynolds was threatening to remove everything from the table if there was not a cease-fire and, if that happened, republicans would be more isolated and friendless than ever. The second was that Dublin was hinting broadly that the pan-nationalist alliance could be employed to force the British to talk about withdrawal. The IRA, he would say, had little to lose by seeing what might be on the table. If Dublin was wrong, then war could be resumed in more favorable circumstances. Seen from another angle, however, it was clear that the Army Council's options were being cut off, one by one. It had reached the point where wiggle room on the question of a cease-fire was virtually nonexistent.

TOWARD THE END of the third week in August 1994, the Army Council gathered at a location in south Donegal to decide whether or not to call the cease-fire. The weeks of debate had ended, and now it was time to make up minds. The proposal—for a four-month, exploratory cessation—was formally put by Gerry Adams and seconded by the Army Council chairman, Martin McGuinness. The debate and argument did not last that long, and soon the vote was taken. Five men were in favor—Adams, McGuinness, Pat Doherty, Joe Cahill, and the South Armagh adjutant of Northern Command—while only Kevin McKenna, the chief of staff, voted against. Slab Murphy abstained. Micky McKevitt and Gerry Kelly, QMG and adjutant general respectively, spoke—McKevitt against the cease-fire, Kelly for it—but neither man could vote.

Slab had been thrown into confusion by the way the meeting had gone, in particular by Joe Cahill's behavior. Cahill had given IRA colleagues the impression that he was against a cease-fire. If Cahill voted no, then Slab would follow suit. That would mean the best vote that Adams could get for the cease-fire would be four to three, too narrow a majority to risk going ahead. But during the meeting Cahill suddenly announced his support for the cease-fire proposal; unsure how to respond, Slab decided to sit on the fence and abstain. A five-to-one majority for the cease-fire gave Adams and his allies a comfortable margin.

Within days Cahill was flying to New York's JFK Airport in fulfillment of Reynolds's pledge that a republican figure would be allowed into the United States before the cease-fire became public to settle the fears of IRA activists and supporters on the east coast. His trip was later extended by fifteen days, and he was permitted to visit California and other western states.

The question of getting a visa for Cahill had been the focus of intense diplomacy for a week or ten days before the Army Council meeting. It had involved the U.S. ambassador to Dublin, Jean Kennedy Smith, Albert Reynolds, the National Security Council, and eventually Clinton himself. The affair puzzled some in the IRA. It was not so crucial that nerves in the United States had to be calmed. The IRA in America had been loyal to the Adams leadership up to then, and it was likely that it would remain so, especially if it became clear that the organization in Ireland stayed united. It had been years since Cahill had visited the United States, and it was unlikely the IRA there would know him that well. There were others who would have carried as much, if not greater, weight with the IRA there. But it was decided that without an assurance that Cahill would get to New York the cease-fire vote in the Army Council might be lost. Inevitably the suspicion took hold in the IRA's highest reaches that Cahill, who died in July 2004, had been prompted to change his mind with the offer of a lengthy vacation trip to America, a bribe that necessitated frantic diplomacy to obtain him a visa.

A few days later, on August 31, the formal announcement came. The IRA declared a complete cessation of military operations, starting at midnight that day. There was no time limit attached to the declaration; the four-month limit was kept a tightly guarded secret. Eight months earlier the Army Council chairman, McGuinness, had told the IRA faithful that there would have to be an IRA Convention before a cease-fire could be called and that anything short of a British declaration to withdraw would be unacceptable to the IRA leadership. The IRA had ended its violence, at least for the time being, without either.

It was without doubt a historic moment in Ireland's history and was greeted accordingly by the media and political world alike. The long, slow, and complex journey to the cessation had been watched with a mixture of fascination and hope by millions in Ireland and abroad. Few of them could have realized just how long, slow, and complex the odyssey had really been.

SIXTEEN

The *Sos*

Under the guiding and skilled hand of Gerry Adams, the think tank, and others, the IRA had been ushered into a cease-fire, the first in twenty years, and for Father Reid and the Sinn Fein leader, this culmination of their secret diplomacy was a truly remarkable achievement. A dialogue begun with the kidnapping and killing of UDR Sergeant Thomas Cochrane in 1982 had borne sweet fruit some twelve, patient years later, and the architects of the enterprise could afford to congratulate themselves on what they had done. This cease-fire was qualitatively different from any that preceded it, for it was predicated on a secret set of agreements that, if implemented, would end not just the Troubles but possibly bring to a conclusion the age-old tradition of armed-struggle republicanism in Ireland. A breakthrough had surely been made, even if there was still a long way to go.

None of this was at all clear in the heady days of September 1994 as Northern Ireland began to get used to a new way of living. The precise terms of the cease-fire were kept secret, and consequently there was not even agreement on what the IRA cease-fire meant or whether it was supposed to be permanent or short-lived. Irish politicians like Albert Reynolds had been pressing for a permanent cease-fire; otherwise, he said, Sinn Fein would not have a chance of getting into serious political dialogue. And so the language of the IRA cease-fire statement and comments made by senior republican figures like Adams and McGuinness in the ensuing days were anxiously scanned for clues as to the IRA's real intentions. Republican leaders did their best to reassure the British, Irish, and American political leadership that the cessation was indeed permanent, but it was a difficult exercise, primarily because their rank and file needed to hear quite the opposite message—that the cease-fire was a tentative and tactical move that would be quickly abandoned if it failed to produce results.

In order to describe the 1994 cease-fire in terms that would set grassroots' minds at rest, the think tank had come up with an Irish word designed to convey the temporary and probationary nature of the cease-fire. The word was *sos*, which translates into English as a pause, a cessation, an interval, and a rest. The word, which in everyday IRA usage became simply "the suss," succeeded in suggesting the IRA leadership's determination not to be sucked into a long and fruitless cease-fire. Other reassuring signals were sent to the base. The first IRA "War News" column in *An Phoblacht–Republican News* published immediately after the August 31 announcement, for example, repeatedly called the cease-fire a "suspension."[1] The message that the cessation would be temporary, if necessary, was reinforced by senior republican figures at private republican "family" meetings attended by IRA and Sinn Fein supporters in the days and weeks after the declaration.[2] By the end of September 1994, more comforting messages to the republican base were dispatched, Adams saying in Boston that if the causes of the conflict were not removed, no one could say that another IRA leadership would not come along, while McGuinness insisted that there was no such word as "permanent" in the republican dictionary. Both were fairly broad hints that the IRA would, if needed, resume its violence.

The truth was that a permanent cease-fire was just not in Adams's gift, at least in such explicit terms. The IRA simply would not have tolerated it, and the Army Council would have resisted it. If the cessation was to become enduring, it would have to evolve and develop naturally as political circumstances allowed. The sort of cease-fire demanded by Reynolds and others was not what Adams had been able to persuade the Army Council to back.

Far from being permanent, the cease-fire the Army Council voted for in August 1994 had to be reviewed after just four months, a time frame chosen by chance. In theory the Army Council had endorsed the short, speculative cessation that had been predicted in the media, but it was cleverly disguised. The weeks leading up to August 31, 1994 had seen numerous conjectural reports about a three-month cease-fire, much of it encouraged by think tank briefings to the media, the author included. Other reports said the cease-fire would last for six months. By choosing a four-month cease-fire, Sinn Fein leaders could honestly and credibly deny media speculation about a three- or six-month-long cessation and this served to reassure the British, Irish, and Americans that it was indeed meant to be permanent.

There were echoes of the ambiguity inherent in the TUAS strategy document in all this, another compelling clue that the Sinn Fein peace strategy

derived its dynamic from the ability of the party's leadership to send out differing messages to different constituencies. It also spoke to the readiness of
recipients, especially Sinn Fein's own supporters, to believe them. Otherwise the peace process could never have moved forward.

These conflicting messages plagued the cease-fire in its early months and
contributed in no small way to British skepticism about the bona fides of
the Sinn Fein leadership. Part of the problem derived from the fact that the
bulk of agents run by British intelligence inside the IRA knew nothing of
this subtle dissembling. While the Sinn Fein leaders might say one thing to
the British and Irish governments in public or even private, the intelligence
briefings from MI5, the military, and particularly the RUC Special Branch
reflected the quite different story being told to the IRA grassroots.

There were also pieces of hard evidence that could not be ignored by the
British. The IRA had broken the secret agreement not to recruit or train its
members during the cease-fire. It had also engaged in some targeting and
continued to produce explosives. Much to the discomfort of the Adams faction, the Army Council "soldiers" had interpreted literally an obligation in
the IRA constitution to keep the IRA "as efficient as possible" and insisted
that it be honored, despite the secret undertakings given to the British and
Irish governments.[3] In response, the British resumed surveillance of IRA
leaders. The British could not be sure whether all this meant that the Army
Council wanted to keep the IRA in fighting trim so that it could slip back
into war or whether it was merely trying to reassure the rank and file.
In this state of uncertainty, they opted for a cautious, slow-moving, and
often suspicious approach to the cease-fire, and it was this that proved its
undoing.

IT WAS NOT UNTIL eight months into the cessation that the British secretary of state, Sir Patrick Mayhew, began to think that the Provisionals
probably were genuine, and by that time it was very likely too late.[4] The
British were used to thinking the worst about the Provos, and for good reason, but evidence that has emerged from inside the republican world suggests they were wrong. From accounts given by key IRA personnel, it
appears that not only was the cease-fire called in defiance of the wishes of
most rank-and-file IRA members but that it had been structured in such a
way that, surreptitiously, the cessation could be extended again and again
no matter what the grassroots thought.

IRA activists had strongly registered their opposition to a cease-fire not
long after the Downing Street Declaration had been published. In February

1994, six months before the cessation was called, a mini-Convention was held in Donegal and came out strongly against stopping the campaign. The meeting brought together the Army Council, GHQ, Northern Command staff, brigade commanders, and operations officers, a total of nearly forty of the IRA's most senior and important personnel. Three-quarters of them, according to one estimate, rejected the cease-fire option.[5] Voicing their opposition did not halt the process, but the Donegal meeting did give the leadership a good idea of who was for and who was against their strategy.

The movement toward the cease-fire was kept a closely guarded secret, its detail known only to the Army Council and the Adams think tank. IRA activists were given private assurances that the media speculation—which by the summer of 1994 was intense—was groundless, and this continued right up to the eve of the cease-fire announcement. Even Gerry Adams joined in. Ten days before the declaration, just a day or two before he would formally propose the cease-fire motion at the Army Council meeting in County Donegal, he issued a public statement describing the media speculation as "news to me."[6]

The IRA rank and file was not consulted or briefed about the decision, and preparation for military operations continued until a few days beforehand, as one activist recalled. "A week before there was no word of a cease-fire," he said. "I had just delivered a van to ——— for a big bomb they were planning. I was being pushed to get jobs done, targets were being readied, and then four days before we heard what was coming. It hit me like a thunderbolt."[7] IRA prisoners likewise were kept in the dark. The Northern IRA was given some notice, but the IRA in Southern Command got none at all. Most IRA members in Dublin, Cork, Limerick, Kerry, and Galway first heard of the cease-fire on the day it was declared, and they heard it first on television or radio news broadcasts, not from their leaders. Even in the North not all areas were briefed about the cease-fire; Tyrone, where support for the Adams strategy was at its most lukewarm, was kept in the dark almost to the end.

The non-IRA republican base, people who would vote for Sinn Fein and work for the party during elections, knew even less about the impending events and were stunned when the cease-fire came, as one vivid account of a republican meeting in Derry held just after the declaration became public, described: "It was an extraordinary meeting because it soon became clear that a significant number of those present were in open disagreement with the decision of the IRA leadership to call the ceasefire. As for those who did support the ceasefire it was not so much because they knew why. Indeed they seemed to be as surprised by the totality of the decision as everyone else."[8] In West Belfast, Sinn Fein stage-managed a celebratory cavalcade of cars that toured the area, its occupants waving large Irish flags and honking horns. At a rally in Andersonstown, Gerry Adams was presented with a bouquet of flowers and surrounded by smiling Sinn Fein politicians. The crowd, however, was largely subdued and puzzled.

In the face of such anxiety, the Army Council used two arguments to calm its supporters. One was to urge the rank and file to keep faith and trust in the leadership, and here the record—and thus trustworthiness—of a leadership that had smuggled tons of weapons from Libya was constantly and relentlessly invoked. The other argument, possibly the most powerful of all during these days, said that only the British stood to gain by division and discord within the IRA. Those who stirred dissent and criticism were, in effect, doing the British a huge favor, and they should therefore keep silent or risk being accused of helping the enemy, IRA leaders said. This appeal for unity by and large worked, but it was not an inexhaustible argument.

The decision to review the cease-fire after four months may have enabled Sinn Fein leaders to field awkward questions from the media, but its effect was to position the review at times that made it more difficult to argue for going back to war. The first four-month review, for instance, was scheduled to take place in the month of December. That meant that if the cease-fire was ended, it would happen around the festive period, a bad time in public relations terms to go back to bombing and shooting. Although the cease-fire was going badly for the leadership at this time and would continue to worsen, the Army Council, predictably, decided against a resumption and put the decision off for another four months.

That meant the next review would be around Easter 1995, a predictable time of the year for republicans to resume war, given the association with the Easter Rising of 1916. The British would surely be waiting for the IRA to do just that. So again the Council opted to preserve the cease-fire and told the volunteers that it would end after Easter and to get ready to return to active service then. But again another review was ordered. As the weeks ran into months and the cease-fire ran into more and more trouble, IRA activists were repeatedly told to prepare for a resumption of hostilities, which never quite happened. "They were told forty times they were going back," remembered one commander.[9] Adams's approach to the cease-fire, the reassurance contained in TUAS in particular, may have persuaded the rank and file that the military option was still viable, but every month without violence made it more difficult for the IRA to launch a sustainable campaign of armed struggle. Not only was the IRA itself getting rusty with inactivity, but the longer the cease-fire lasted, the more popular it became, especially in the IRA's strongest areas, where the communities had borne the brunt of nearly two decades of violence and were now tasting peace and relative serenity for the first time.

THE CEASE-FIRE ran into trouble fairly quickly. The British response was slow and cautious, and not until mid-October 1994 did John Major make what he called "a working assumption" that the IRA cease-fire was permanent. Even so, talks between Sinn Fein and NIO officials, only talks about talks, would not commence until December 1994, when technically the IRA leadership was supposed to review the entire enterprise. There was no sign yet of Sinn Fein's sitting down with British ministers, much less of a British readiness to discuss their withdrawal from Northern Ireland. By this stage full-blooded negotiations with the British should have begun. Not that there was no movement at all by the Major government. Blocked Border roads were gradually reopened in October 1994, the broadcasting ban on Sinn Fein that prevented Gerry Adams's voice from being heard on the BBC had been lifted, and British soldiers were wearing soft hats instead of battle helmets as they patrolled the streets and fields, signaling the start of a military de-escalation. But the British ambassador to Ireland was still under instructions to boycott the opening session of the Forum for Peace and Reconciliation in Dublin Castle because of the presence of Sinn Fein delegates. By the end of November, Adams and Hume were obliged to issue a strongly worded statement calling for demilitarization to be speeded up. Talks should commence "without further delay," they said.[10]

The British instinct for caution was reinforced significantly when the IRA shot dead a postal worker in the course of a robbery in the Border town of Newry in mid-November. The victim, Frank Kerr, a fifty-three-year-old single Catholic from South Armagh, died when three armed raiders dressed as postal workers held up staff in the main sorting office and tied them up. Kerr resisted, struggled with the robbers, and was gunned down. The robbery had been carried out by the South Armagh IRA but it was very quickly disowned by the Army Council, which claimed that the operation, while the work of its members, had not been sanctioned by the leadership. Publicly Adams expressed shock at the killing, and Father Reid traveled to Dublin to assure officials that this was indeed the case. Reid had however been misinformed. According to IRA sources the robbery had been given a broad sanction by the Army Council, inasmuch as a general permission had been granted to continue "fund-raising" activity, cease-fire or no cease-fire. It was a necessary part of the job of keeping the IRA "as efficient as possible," as the Army Council "soldiers" had insisted must happen, and anyway the IRA always needed money.

The Kerr killing had an immediately negative impact on the cease-fire, in that the Major government stiffened the demand for IRA decommissioning as a precondition for Sinn Fein's entry to the political talks. It brought to the top of the agenda an item that was to haunt the peace process for years to come. Decommissioning of IRA weaponry had been simmering away on the back burner for much of the period leading up to the cease-fire. The Northern Ireland secretary, Sir Patrick Mayhew, had mentioned it as something that would have to happen eventually, as had the Irish deputy prime minister, Dick Spring—but it was not yet the dominating issue it would become. Major had merely said that IRA disarmament would have to figure in any overall deal, but by the end of the year, as a result of the Kerr killing, he was much more specific and demanding. A Sinn Fein promise on guns would not be enough, he said, and there would have to be "significant progress" on the matter before Sinn Fein could sit at the negotiating table. Mayhew was making the demand detailed by January 1995, saying that Semtex and heavy machine guns would have to be put out of commission. During a trip to the United States to coincide with the Saint Patrick's Day festivities in March, Mayhew introduced the Washington Three test, a series of decommissioning hurdles the IRA would have to jump before Sinn Fein could join negotiations. First, said Mayhew, there must be a willingness in principle to disarm progressively; next, agreement on the method of decommissioning; and third, a start to the process. Otherwise Sinn Fein would stay outside the negotiating chamber.

The caution of the British meant that they moved very slowly toward the release of IRA prisoners, one of the goals of the Adams strategy. The cease-fire had been made possible in no small measure because of an Irish government promise to press London for prison reform, but it was not until August 1995, a year into the cessation, that the British moved, when Mayhew restored 50 percent remission for sentenced prisoners. This concession had first been given to the IRA in 1976, when special-category or political status was removed, but taken away by the Thatcher government in 1988 in punitive response to the post-*Eksund* offensive. In IRA eyes it was hardly a concession at all, merely a return to what had been.

Events south of the Border intervened to complicate a rapidly deteriorating situation for the Adams leadership. In mid-November, Albert Reynolds was forced to resign as taoiseach after his party was embroiled in a sordid scandal centered on his government's failure to prosecute a pedophile Catholic priest. Reynolds's partners in government, Labour, refused to deal with his successor, Bertie Ahern, and joined instead with Fine Gael, whose leader, John Bruton, became the new taoiseach. It was a devastating blow for the Adams cease-fire strategy. TUAS derived its credibility from the creation of a pan-nationalist alliance, and while Fianna Fail was clearly a nationalist party, and a fit partner for Sinn Fein, Fine Gael certainly was not, at least in the eyes of Provo supporters.

The political successors of Michael Collins, the man who had negotiated the hated Treaty of 1921, Fine Gael had a controversial history, and at one stage in the 1930s was linked to Ireland's version of the fascist movement. The party took a traditionally tough attitude toward the IRA, and a Fine Gael–Labour coalition government in the mid-1970s pursued the IRA relentlessly. Under the leadership of Garret FitzGerald, Fine Gael developed a name for being more friendly toward unionists than toward nationalists, although political self-interest drove the party into an alliance with the SDLP in the mid-1980s when Sinn Fein first started to win electoral support. FitzGerald himself bitterly opposed the notion of talking to the Provos and had quarreled with the British over the issue. His successor, John Bruton, would have been regarded by Adams's followers as even more sympathetic to the unionist case, so much so that few would quarrel with the sobriquet "John Unionist" bestowed upon him by Albert Reynolds.

To say the least, Bruton's elevation made it difficult for Adams to convince anyone in the republican movement that the pan-nationalist alliance still had meaning. Bruton had no appetite for the strategy and signaled this in an unmistakable fashion in October 1995, when he pointedly refused to meet jointly with Adams and Hume in their capacity as leaders of Northern nationalism. It was a terrible blow to the TUAS strategy, and to Adams's credibility.

The change of government brought important changes in the personnel handling the peace process, and the dismay of the Provos grew. Out went the trusted Martin Mansergh, who had been the Southern link with Adams via Father Reid since 1987, and in came a new adviser to the taoiseach, the former head of the Department of Foreign Affairs, Sean Donlon, whose credentials were very different from Mansergh's. Whereas Mansergh was a thinking republican, Donlon was seen, by the IRA at least, as someone who sympathized with FitzGerald's tough antirepublicanism while he was minister for foreign affairs. To make matters worse for Adams, Bruton put together a coalition cabinet and included as ministers members of the Democratic Left, the latest manifestation of the Workers Party, the successors to the hated Goulding IRA. It was called the Rainbow Coalition, but it created a black nightmare for Adams.

Under Bruton's leadership the Irish government moved closer to the British on the key issue of IRA decommissioning. Both governments believed that there had to be some progress on the issue, some signal that it would happen at least, before Sinn Fein could be safely let into talks. That alone was sufficient to set alarm bells ringing in the IRA. It all confirmed the worst fears of activists that once again the real aim of the British, the Irish, and their allies was to weaken and divide the movement, much as they had done in 1974 and 1975. Adams's cease-fire strategy was supposed to create pressure on the British to quit Northern Ireland, not the weakening and emasculation of the IRA. The state of the cease-fire by the end of 1995 raised dark questions about the wisdom of the Adams leadership in going down this dangerous road. Far from showing any inclination to talk to the Provisionals, the British were as determined as ever to defeat them, or so it seemed.

TO ADD TO the leadership's problems, discontent at rank-and-file level became increasingly visible. When, for instance, it was revealed in November 1994 that Sinn Fein had secretly agreed to accept political training, in such basic skills as fund-raising and fighting elections, from the National Democratic Institute in Washington, a body it had once accused of being a CIA front when it gave the SDLP training in the mid-1980s, there was a revolt. At the party's Ard Fheis in February 1995 the leadership could only watch in embarrassment as delegates overwhelmingly passed a motion condemning as "undemocratic" the notion that Sinn Fein should accept aid or training from the Americans.

When the British prime minister, John Major, visited Derry in May 1995, local republicans rioted, venting their frustration at the British stalling tactics. The incident seriously embarrassed the Sinn Fein leadership. The occasion had been arranged so that Mitchel McLaughlin, whose non-IRA credentials were impeccable, could publicly shake hands with the British prime minister, thus signaling another stage in Sinn Fein's journey out of isolation. Instead McLaughlin could only watch helplessly as the rioters got stuck into the RUC and Major's travel plans were quickly changed. The handshake was abandoned.

In the same month Sinn Fein accepted an invitation to attend a ceremony at Islandbridge in Dublin to commemorate Irish people who had died while serving in the British forces during the Second World War. Tom Hartley was sent along—colleagues later said he had to be dragged there—and pointedly remarked to the media that he was there because Gerry Adams could not accept the taoiseach's invitation. The downward spiral in Hartley's Sinn Fein career probably began at that moment. The incident deeply unsettled the Provo base. No Irish republican had ever honored Irishmen who had donned British uniforms.

It was not all bad news for Sinn Fein. Adams was granted a fund-raising visa by Clinton, which allowed him to raise money for Sinn Fein—eventually millions of dollars—while the British slowly began troop withdrawals and then agreed to transfer selected IRA prisoners from British to Northern Ireland jails. Meanwhile the Boundary Commission redrew the West Belfast Westminster consituency in such a way that Adams was bound to regain the seat he had lost to the SDLP in 1992. The framework documents were also published by the British and Irish governments in early 1995, offering a power-sharing administration in Belfast and cross-Border bodies linking government reponsibilities in Belfast and Dublin. The idea was to enhance cooperation and even gradual integration in some economic and social matters between the two states. This was not British withdrawal, but at least it was some movement.

Even so the balance sheet showed more red ink than black, and in the face of rank-and-file unease the leadership was forced to toughen its profile. At Eastertime in 1995 Adams made an thinly veiled threat to take his supporters onto the streets and warned the British they would soon be faced with "the sound of angry voices and stamping feet" unless there was progress.

There were more ominous signs of discontent. Not long after Adams's Easter address the IRA shot dead a notorious drug dealer, Micky Mooney, in Belfast. It used a new cover name, Direct Action Against Drugs (DAAD), to disguise its role, but this fooled few people, least of all the IRA rank and file, who gained some reassurance from this brief return to the use of firearms. DAAD was back in action in September 1995 when a second drug dealer was killed. Again this was the IRA leadership sending out the signal to its own people that it was not afraid to go back to the gun. Adams had personal experience of the unrest in the ranks a few days earlier when he was faced with a restless crowd that had marched to Belfast City Hall to commemorate the August 1971 internment operation, an annual high point of the republican calendar. When a voice from the crowd shouted, "Bring back the IRA!" Adams, in a memorable phrase, replied, "They haven't gone away, you know!"[11]

Sentiment within the IRA was running strongly against the cease-fire and the TUAS strategy by mid-1995. It was inevitable that opposition to the Adams policy would become more organized and structured and that moves would be made to return the IRA to war. As in every other period of republican turbulence, the twelve-person IRA Executive became the focus of unrest and the vehicle for rebellion. IRA Executives had historically regarded themselves as the conscience of the rank and file and believed they had a brief to ensure that the Army Council never stepped too far out of line with grassroots feeling. It would be no different this time.

The IRA Executive of 1994–96 had a grievance with the Army Council and Adams so serious that the rift between them was particularly bitter. During the tortuous negotiations leading to the Downing Street Declaration and then to the cease-fire, the Executive had been excluded, on security grounds, from the information loop. Only the Army Council and the think tank knew what was going on, and the fact that the latter was a body that had no constitutional status at all served to deepen the resentment on the Executive. The Council refused to share information about the peace process with the Executive for fear of a leak to the British, and the memory that no such consideration had kept the chairman of the Army Council from hinting at the *Eksund* shipment deeply rankled. When the Army Council declared the August 1994 cease-fire, the Executive was treated just like the rest of the IRA, despite its elevated status. A few days beforehand two Executive members were briefed and told to inform the other ten. The lack of consultation and this offhand treatment served to further alienate the Executive.

The 1995 Executive was a body that the Army Council could ill afford to ignore for long. Its members included key GHQ staff and members of both Southern and Northern Command. It met formally every six months or so, but informally its members were in more regular contact. In the absence of any sign that the British were contemplating negotiations about withdrawal, the number of Executive members ranged against the Adams strategy grew. By the summer of 1995 it stood at ten out of twelve, an overwhelming majority. The Executive's complaint was straightforward. With the British barring Sinn Fein from talks and the Dublin government seemingly unable to influence them otherwise, the IRA was in trouble. The longer the *sos* lasted, the weaker the IRA would become, both politically and militarily, the Executive argued. If the *sos* did not end soon, its members complained, the game would be up.

THREE MEN EMERGED as the sharpest critics of the Adams strategy. One was Micky McKevitt, the quartermaster general who, along with Slab Murphy, had masterminded the Libyan arms shipments. The second was the IRA's director of engineering, Frank McGuinness, a young Dubliner whose department kept the organization supplied with explosives and improvised weaponry. The third was the Belfast commander, Brian Gillen, who headed the IRA's largest brigade area. Between them they encompassed the bulk of Southern Command and the most politically important section of the organization in the North. Their internal political clout was enhanced by the fact that McKevitt's partner, Bernadette Sands, was a sister of the dead hunger striker and Provisional icon Bobby Sands. They later married. As a group they presented a formidable opposition to Gerry Adams and his allies.

The British ensured that the tide moved ever more strongly in the Executive's direction. Earlier in 1995 the Army Council had ordered a canvass of rank-and-file views, and Adjutant General Gerry Kelly was given the task of testing the waters. He toured Ireland talking to the activists, and his report to the Council made depressing reading for the peace party. Virtually every brigade area was unhappy and anxious, worried that its leaders had been tricked by the British and the Irish governments into adopting a strategy in which both advance and retreat seemed likely to weaken the IRA. Feelings against the strategy were particularly strong in Belfast, Tyrone, Derry, Monaghan, and South Armagh, and IRA leaders would have had to be deaf and blind not to have known that the level of discontent was sufficiently high that it was only a matter of time before the opposition took a more tangible and even dangerous form.

Activists of this period paint a picture of an IRA that was in considerable turmoil. "A number of people at leadership level promised all sorts of things about going back to war," recalled one. "The volunteers were led up the hill so many times only to be led down again that it was embarrassing. The state of the IRA was causing great concern, morale was at an all-time low, and there were very heated meetings where people would shout that they had been misled."[12]

The Executive met in August 1995 to consider a situation that was visibly deteriorating. The Army Council sent along McGuinness and McKenna to give a briefing. The message they brought was a depressing one: Sinn Fein's efforts to get into talks were running into the sand, and the Army Council members did not see the cease-fire lasting much longer. In fact they went as far as giving the Executive an assurance that it would be called off soon. Reassured, the Executive eased the pressure.

But the cease-fire survived, and the Army Council made no move to end it. Politically the autumn and winter of 1995 brought some softening of the British line on decommissioning, and this had the effect of forcing republicans to respond positively. At the end of November, on the eve of a historic visit to Northern Ireland by Bill Clinton, the British and Irish governments announced agreement on the so-called twin track approach to political negotiations. While preparatory talks involving the two governments and the political parties got under way, an international commission chaired by the former U.S. Senate Democratic majority leader, George Mitchell, would consider how best to address the problem of IRA decommissioning.

Sinn Fein had endorsed this approach, first formulated by John Hume, earlier that month when Martin McGuinness formally presented it to the British. The party also agreed to make a submission to the Mitchell body, but the Army Council "soldiers" blocked an attempt to include an IRA figure in the delegation, as Adams and others had urged. After meeting the Mitchell commission, Martin McGuinness said his party had proposed that armed groups dispose of their own weapons in a process that could be overseen by an independent third party, a proposal that ultimately was adopted by the British and the Irish governments. The logjam was easing, but it was too little and too late.

As 1995 drew to a close there were more ominous signs of IRA discontent, nearly all of them in Belfast, where Brian Gillen held sway. They came in the form of a burst of killings during December of alleged drug dealers, most of them small-time figures, by the IRA cover group DAAD. Starting on December 8 the IRA killed four times, and the killing continued into the New Year. A fifth drug dealer was shot dead in January 1996 in Lurgan, where the local IRA leader was also a critic of the Adams strategy. The DAAD killings were a barometer of rank-and-file unease and a measure of the current weakness of the peace camp in the IRA leadership.

The dam eventually burst. In early January 1996 the Executive met, and eleven of its twelve members supported a resolution calling for an extraordinary General Army Convention, which they demanded should be held by the end of February or beginning of March. Already suspicious about the Army Council's intentions, the Executive set out to force its hand. Knowing that a Convention would almost certainly vote to end the cease-fire—and might well also replace the Adams leadership—the Army Council met on January 31 and by a unanimous vote called off the cease-fire. After fifteen months of relative peace it seemed that the process itself, not merely the cease-fire, might be over.

Preparations for the breakdown had actually begun two months earlier when, under the cover of the autumn's dark evenings, South Armagh IRA members, directed by Slab Murphy, began preparing a huge truck bomb. Slab had correctly anticipated events. After the Army Council decision, the go-ahead for the bomb was given, and the device was smuggled over to England, where it was left in the underground car park of a six-story office building near Canary Wharf Tower in South London. At seven in the evening on February 9, it exploded, destroying the office building, killing two men, and, at a cost of around £100 million, devastating some of London's most expensive commercial property.

SHORTLY BEFORE the explosion Gerry Adams phoned the National Security Council at the White House to say that he was "hearing some very disturbing news" about the cease-fire and would call back later with more details. Before he could get back the bomb exploded. The Army Council had sanctioned Adams's phone call at his request. The Sinn Fein leader had argued that otherwise he would lose all credibility with Clinton and his people. The episode was a piece of description that helped cast Adams in the role of the frustrated peacemaker, squeezed between his own hard-liners and an inflexible British government. It was a convenient cover story, but it was not too far from the truth.

As far as official IRA policy was concerned, not only was the cease-fire over but so was the Adams strategy. The new military and political policy that replaced TUAS was straightforward, simple, and direct. The IRA would once more send huge blockbuster bombs to London and other English cities, having suspended this tactic in the midst of the Hume-Adams talks in 1993, and would not stop doing this until the British agreed to enter meaningful talks encompassing withdrawal. Only then would the IRA contemplate another cease-fire. It was back to the trenches, or so it seemed; back to comforting political certitudes. The "soldiers" on the Army Council were again in the ascendancy—at least for the time being.

At its January meeting the Executive had called for an extraordinary Convention to take place by the beginning of March, but by Easter there was still no sign of one. The Army Council had asked Pat Doherty to convene the meeting, but despite his usually excellent contacts and knowledge of County Donegal, he reported back to the Council in May that he had been unable to locate a suitable venue. Amid suspicions that the delay had been contrived, the Executive complained directly to Chief of Staff Kevin McKenna, who relieved Doherty of the task and handed it over to Micky

McKevitt. By that point the evenings were getting brighter, and the IRA was again under intense surveillance on both sides of the Border. For security reasons the Convention was postponed until the end of October, when darker evenings would give the IRA cover for its gathering.

Doherty's inability to find a meeting place for the Convention bought Adams and his allies a precious nine months during which events were to give them a fighting chance to survive the special IRA Convention. With the British starting to regret their earlier intransigence on decommissioning, elections were held to a new Northern Ireland Forum, from which negotiating teams for planned interparty talks were to be chosen. Sinn Fein scored its best-ever election result, winning over 116,000 votes, some 15.5 percent of the vote, and seventeen seats. Much of Sinn Fein's success was ascribed to moderate nationalists' switching from the SDLP to Sinn Fein so as to strengthen the Adams faction in what everyone instinctively knew was a struggle with hard-liners. It was encouraging evidence for the peace camp in Sinn Fein and their supporters in the Army Council that if the cease-fire was renewed, there could be even greater electoral dividends to be won.

The huge bomb at Canary Wharf may have devastated one of London's smartest new commercial districts, as well as demonstrating the threat still posed by the IRA, but it also had serious negative consequences for Sinn Fein, not least dismaying and weakening those establishment figures in Ireland, Britain, and the United States who had heavily invested in Gerry Adams. Probing questions began to be asked about whether or not the Sinn Fein president had lied to the president of the United States about his peaceful intentions, for example, or if he had not, how much control he really did exercise over the IRA. And if he was a broken reed, as some in the three governments believed, then there was a strong argument against having any further dealings with him.

THE IMPACT OF the Canary Wharf bombing disguised a troubling reality for the IRA, and this was that the manner of its execution was actually a sign of military weakness. The bomb had been made up and delivered by the IRA in South Armagh, and this was an eloquent demonstration that by the 1990s British intelligence had well and truly gotten on top of the IRA's England department. Not only did MI5 and the RUC Special Branch have well-placed agents in Ireland and Britain feeding them information about the IRA's plans, but the routine surveillance work carried out by the British police forces—the regular checking of boardinghouses, digs and so on that occasionally brought priceless snippets of intelligence—had improved enormously since the 1970s when the IRA first began its attacks in England. The intelligence agencies had also become more sophisticated. Fifteen or twenty years earlier the police would have moved to make arrests at the first sighting of an IRA suspect; by 1995 they had learned to sit back and observe suspects for perhaps as long as a year before striking, knowing that such in-depth surveillance could yield valuable intelligence and roll up scores of IRA activists. The consequence was that IRA operations in England had become much more difficult to organize, more complex and time-consuming, and also much more expensive, a big drawback for an organization that was always teetering on the edge of penury and debt. The IRA in South Armagh was the only section of the organization its leaders could be reasonably confident had not yet been penetrated by the British, and so responsibility for important operations in England was given to it.

The problem for the IRA was that there was a limit to the number of big bombs that could be gotten out of South Armagh, and by definition these attacks were bound to be infrequent. In order to sustain the impact of the campaign, GHQ was obliged to activate existing units in England, with consequences that only highlighted the IRA's shortcomings. Ed O'Brien, a twenty-one-year-old IRA member from County Wexford who had been living quietly in London for some time awaiting orders from GHQ, was activated in February 1996, but his IRA career was destined to be short-lived. A bomb he was carrying on a London bus on February 18 exploded prematurely, killing him instantly. The circumstances of the explosion suggested that the device he was carrying might well have been tampered with, possibly by the British. Small bombs were set off outside restaurants during the next six weeks, and at the end of March two bombs placed underneath Hammersmith bridge exploded only partially, a classic sign of interference by the security forces. The most compelling evidence that the British had thoroughly penetrated the IRA's operations in England came in July there, when eight men were arrested and a bomb factory discovered in West London. Two months later the IRA member Diarmuid O'Neill was shot dead, five others arrested, and ten tons of homemade explosives, Semtex, and weapons captured by police, again in London. There were occasional IRA successes. In mid-June the commercial and shopping center of Manchester was devastated by a huge van bomb that injured two hundred people; but the circumstances suggested hasty planning and the absence of the IRA's usual caution in preparation. Overall the balance sheet painted a less than inspiring picture of success.

NONE OF THIS made good news for Adams and his allies as they waited for the extraordinary Convention to finally meet. While the IRA's failures in England strengthened the objective arguments for a cease-fire, there was every chance that the setbacks would instead be blamed on Adams and his supporters, who in an uncanny echo of the criticism leveled at the 1975 IRA leadership, would carry the can for leading the IRA down this path in the first place. As the preparations for the Convention intensified, so the need for a military success grew and, with that, so did the pressure to resume the IRA's war on the streets of Northern Ireland.

Just three weeks or so before the Convention, on October 7, two IRA car bombs exploded inside Thiepval barracks in Lisburn, the British army's headquarters in Northern Ireland. It was the first attack in Northern Ireland since August 1994, twenty-six months before. The operation was a spectacular breach of British security, deeply embarrassing to security chiefs, and as a signal that the IRA's campaign in Northern Ireland had been resumed it could not have gone better for the Adams camp. The operation had been carried out by a special unit headed by the Northern Command's intelligence officer, a West Belfast figure who had loyally policed the peace strategy in the Maze prison's IRA wings on behalf of Adams until his release two years earlier. Northern Command had set up the unit to spearhead the resumption of violence in the North, and it had spent months infiltrating unionist areas to gather intelligence on RUC and security force targets. This was its prize operation.

Although the bombs exploded deep inside the Thiepval complex, somehow major loss of life was avoided. Only thirty-two people were injured—a small toll for two large bombs—but one of them, Warrant Officer James Bradwell, a forty-three-year-old married man, died of his wounds four days later. According to the description given by his daughter, his death could only have come as a relief. "The man I saw in hospital," she said, "was a shattered human being. He had tubes attached to him and there were machines all around. He had lost all of his hair. His face was swollen up because of his burns. I stood there crying. I just could not stop myself."[13] John Major blamed what he called "this cold-blooded killing" on Gerry Adams, but the irony of Bradwell's awful death was that it had quite possibly saved both the peace process and Gerry Adams's political skin. Just two weeks after his death, on the last weekend of October, the extraordinary IRA Convention met at a venue in the Irish midlands. Thanks in no small way to Warrant Officer Bradwell's agonizing death, Gerry Adams would survive the experience.

The Convention gathered in a much more optimistic mood than would have been the case had it convened the preceding February or March, when the meeting was originally scheduled. Gerry Adams came in for a dreadful hammering at the Convention, but there is little doubt that, except for the Thiepval bombing, the weekend meeting might well have spelled disaster for him and the peace process.

It began, as Conventions always do, with a report from the chief of staff. Celebrating his twelfth year in the job, Kevin McKenna referred to the bombing in glowing terms right at the start of his address to the sixty or seventy delegates. It was a classic attack, he told them, according to an account provided to the author by one delegate, just the right type of operation to restart the war in the North. The *sos*, he assured the IRA, had been only tactical and now it was over; war was resumed. There would be more operations like Thiepval, he promised.

ORGANIZING an IRA Convention is a massive and risky undertaking. It requires a considerable portion of the IRA's manpower and resources to put together, and while great efforts are made to ensure that security is tight, the authorities North and South invariably get some inkling that it is about to happen. The most dangerous and difficult part of the exercise happens once a secure location has been chosen by the convenor and a date picked for the Convention. Around forty-eight hours beforehand a series of mini-Conventions must be held at the unit level and among battalion and brigade staffs so that delegates can be chosen and motions for debate framed.

The delegates are chosen on a basis of one for every ten IRA members, and, once the turnout at the Convention is known, that makes it possible to figure out fairly accurately the strength of the IRA. Some sixty delegates were present at the 1996 Convention, while another ten or so missed their pickups, and that suggests that the operational strength of the IRA in 1996 was around six hundred or at most seven hundred men and women.

Once the mini-Conventions have taken place, the chosen delegates are not allowed to return home but must immediately start to make their way to the larger meeting, a journey that can take over a day. Most delegates arrive exhausted and must then sit through a meeting that usually begins at midnight and may go on for five or six hours until dawn. A small number of people attend by right and do not have to have delegate authority to be there. The chief of staff, the adjutant general, the quartermaster general, and the seven members of the Army Council fall into that category, while the Executive and the GHQ are empowered to send two delegates each.

Invariably the leaders arrive in a less weary state than do the rank and file, and that gives them a special advantage.

Between drivers, internal IRA security staff, and people looking after food and drink, nearly as many people were involved in setting up the 1996 Convention as took part in it. The delegates were taken to the 1996 location via four separate stops. At each one they had to change cars and were thoroughly searched and debugged using state-of-the-art electronic detectors. The location itself was under guard by members of the IRA's security unit equipped with walkie-talkie radios and scanners. Before and during the meeting the local Garda station was kept under surveillance, and contingency escape plans had been made in case the meeting was raided. The delegates were under strict orders not to bring mobile phones or any other electronic apparatus with them, for fear that these could be detected by surveillance equipment and the meeting compromised. The rule was strictly enforced for every delegate bar one. The security searchers did not have the nerve to stop Gerry Adams from bringing in a Walkman, which he occasionally plugged into his ears, presumably to drown out speeches he would rather not hear.

Conventions go through a certain routine. First, a chairman has to be elected to lead the proceedings. At the 1996 meeting the election proved to be the opening salvo at the Adams leadership. A Sinn Fein loyalist, Pat Treanor, a councillor from Clones, County Monaghan, won but only narrowly. His opponent was a formidable adversary, none other than Brian Keenan, who had been finally released from English imprisonment in June 1993 and who had, since the 1994 cease-fire, widely advertised his criticism of the Adams strategy. A once faithful and loyal disciple of the Sinn Fein president, Keenan was now declaring himself to be a dissident. He was so strongly opposed to the TUAS strategy—or so it seemed—that he had made common cause with the rebels on the Executive, Brian Gillen, Frank McGuinness, and Micky McKevitt. Keenan lost by just two votes. The first round had gone to Adams.

After McKenna's report Gerry Adams rose to address the Convention. One delegate remembers that he looked like someone under pressure. "He was very nervous, not confident, hesitant and very mindful of saying the wrong thing. He was very nice to everybody."[14] Adams had every reason to be nervous. Under Convention rules he and his supporters did not get to see the motions presented by IRA delegates until the night before, when the Council held a special meeting. When they did, they must have blanched. Adams had had little time to digest the motions and almost no time to construct a counterstrategy when he rose to speak. It was, by all accounts, a disappointing and defensive speech. An assurance that the cease-fire was tactical, echoing Kevin McKenna, was accompanied by a plaintive plea for unity. Not all members of the Army Council had voted for his strategy, but once the vote had been taken they had supported it, he said, and he urged the delegates to act in the same spirit.

If the Sinn Fein leader ran into difficulties at the Convention, it was because some of his most determined opponents were veterans of the 1986 Convention who had learned an important lesson from that experience about how to win the argument at such events. The key to success was to make sure that the effective motions were ones that required changes to the IRA's constitution, and this is what happened at the 1996 Convention. Doing this was the only way to bind the hands of the IRA leadership. In 1986 numerous hard-line motions had been passed that their supporters believed had committed the Army Council to certain courses of action and policy positions, but because they did not alter the IRA's constitution, they had been ignored afterward.

OVER 130 MOTIONS were submitted by the IRA's rank and file to the 1996 convention, nearly 60 of which dealt with the peace strategy. All but a handful were critical of the Adams strategy either explicitly or implicitly, and it soon became clear that the dissidents had done their homework well. By far the bulk of the critical motions sought to change the IRA's constitution. Those that did not, such as one motion submitted by the East Tyrone Brigade, were blunt and to the point. The peace process, said the East Tyrone delegation, had severely damaged the IRA and the struggle against British rule. The IRA in East Tyrone, it continued, had lost all confidence in the leadership. In the interests of unity the motion was withdrawn, but the point had nevertheless been forcefully made.

Gerry Adams won the second round when a motion on IRA membership submitted by the quartermaster's department was debated. This would have barred IRA volunteers from joining any political party that recognized any of the partitionist institutions of government in Ireland or from swearing allegiance or giving recognition to them. It also forbade IRA members to make any pledge to refrain from the use of armed struggle to rid Ireland of the British presence.

The motion was a thinly veiled but full-frontal assault on Adams and the Sinn Fein members of the Army Council. It was aimed not only at stopping Sinn Fein from entering any Assembly established at Stormont as a result of talks flowing from the peace process but at preventing it from even joining negotiations with the other parties. The reason for this was that the Mitchell report had set preconditions for the entry of political parties to the talks process, one of which included a declared commitment to totally peaceful methods.

The second part of the motion, pledging IRA members to armed struggle, would have forced figures like Adams and McGuinness to choose between the IRA and Sinn Fein. Adams rose to oppose the motion in its entirety but focused on the second part. He was worried, he told the delegates, because if this motion was passed, the IRA would not be able to take back into its ranks prisoners who had been released from life sentences after signing a pledge of good behavior, something that was tantamount to recognizing the authority of British rule. Gerry Kelly asked what would happen if the IRA recruited members of the security forces or a prison guard. Would they be banned from IRA membership? Adams returned to add that if the Convention passed the motion, they could not insert any discretion. If the constitution banned some people from the IRA, no exceptions could be made. The motion was lost, largely because of objections to the bar on IRA membership, but the speed and force of the leadership's response to the threat revealed its concern that the Convention could rob it of valuable negotiating flexibility when political talks eventually got under way.

Adams's skills were unable to prevent defeat in the third battle, when the Convention turned to consider motions that were aimed at limiting the Army Council's ability and power to call a cease-fire. The constitution had historically given the Army Council sweeping powers over when and how to declare a cease-fire, bestowing upon it the authority "to conclude peace or declare war" by a simple majority. The leadership needed to refer to a Convention only when the "conclusion of peace"—that is, the settlement signaling the end of the war—had to be ratified.[15] That condition had never been tested, and no one was quite sure what it meant.

Whatever its real meaning, the mood of the Convention was clearly in favor of significantly restricting the Army Council's powers to call future cease-fires and, by definition, it also sought to limit Gerry Adams's ability to implement the peace process. This was a clear and unmistakable sign that the grassroots were deeply unhappy at the conduct of the *sos*. There were over twenty motions to this effect. All but a few either sought to time-limit any cease-fire called by the Council—three or six months appeared to be the favorite lengths—or they sought to force the Council to win approval elsewhere in the IRA if extensions were requested beyond the initial period.

Delegates favored, in descending order, the involvement of the Executive, GHQ, or a commission of IRA commanders in this decision. The very presence of such motions on the Convention agenda amounted to an unprecedented censure of the Army Council and the Adams leadership, a sign that trust in them was no longer as firm or automatic as it had once been.

Feelings on the issue ran strong. The Belfast Brigade, represented by Brian Gillen, said a time limit should have been set on the 1994 cease-fire, and he complained bitterly about the Army Council's September 1993 order tightening its control over operations and banning certain types of operations, such as the use of car bombs. This had removed all power at the local level, he complained. Moves to limit the Army Council's authority were about restoring democracy in the IRA, not about tying people's hands.

The delegate from Southern Command launched a full-frontal attack on Adams and his supporters. The *sos*, he complained, had been the work of a small, unrepresentative group of people and had succeeded only in causing widespread demoralization at the rank-and-file level. Southern Command's motion would have given the Executive and GHQ staff a veto on any future move by the Army Council to declare a cease-fire. The Munster Brigade wanted all OCs to be involved in any future cease-fire decision. Only the Derry Brigade announced its support for the peace strategy, although it too was concerned that there was no contribution from the rank and file about how long a cease-fire should be allowed to last.

An Army Executive motion was chosen as representative of these critical sentiments. It stipulated that after a cease-fire was called, a Convention had to be held within twelve months to review it and that if the Council wanted to extend the cease-fire beyond the first four months, the decision had to be ratified by the Executive and again every four months thereafter. This was not just an attempt to curb the Army Council but also a bid to shift the balance of internal power decisively in the direction of the Executive. It was a direct challenge to Adams's authority.

These assaults on his power base provoked desperate efforts by the Sinn Fein leader to deflect or dilute the challenge. Adams complained that if the British ever learned about the motion, it would give them an invaluable tactical advantage; once they knew that the cease-fire had to be reviewed after four months, they would delay and obstruct in an effort to create tension and foment a split within the IRA.

Adams entreated the Convention not to make any move that diluted the leadership's power, but he urged that if it was determined to do so, it should break up the motion and disguise it by spreading it around the IRA's constitution. That way the British might not see what had happened if or when a copy of the new constitution fell into their hands. Although he did not say so, Adams must also have known that once the British learned of the changes, they would know they were now dealing with a much weakened figure.

The Convention opted for Adams's face-saving formula, ordered the Army Council to seek a four-month ratification from the Executive, but said the first post-cease-fire Convention should be held fifteen, not twelve, months after any new cease-fire. The motion was broken up and scattered around the constitution, as Adams had urged.

Worse was to come for Adams. Under the terms of the 1986 constitution, the Army Council effectively had untrammeled control over the IRA's weapons and stores of explosives. The relevant section of the constitution approved at that meeting read, "All personnel and all armaments, equipment and other resources of Oglaigh na hEireann shall be at the disposal of and subject to the Army Authority, to be employed and utilised as the Army Authority shall direct."[16] Although there was some doubt as to whether the Convention or the Army Council constituted the "Army Authority," it was clear that on a day-to-day basis the Army Council was that "Authority" and thus held control of the IRA's weapons. McKevitt's quartermaster's department had tabled a motion that would have replaced this section and deprived the Army Council of all negotiating flexibility on the decommissioning issue.

The motive for the Executive's move was clear, a suspicion that the Sinn Fein figures on the Army Council would cut a deal on IRA weapons if they could. The suspicion was not entirely without foundation. There had been conflicting, not to say confusing, signals emanating from persons like Adams and McGuinness regarding IRA weapons. While they continued, privately and publicly, to pour scorn on any notion that the IRA would decommission its weapons, they had at the same time authorized Sinn Fein to make a submission to the Mitchell body, outlining how it envisaged that the disarming would happen. There had even been an attempt to send an Army Council member along to talk to Mitchell about it. In another sign of where Adams might lead the organization, he had announced that Sinn Fein would sign up unilaterally to the six Mitchell principles, one of which committed participants at the talks to some sort of decommissioning process.

On the face of it, McKevitt's motion removed any room for flexibility on the issue. It was unambiguously worded: "The Army Authority shall retain, maintain and ensure the safety of all armaments, equipment and other resources of Oglaigh na hEireann until such time as the sovereignty and unity of the Republic of Ireland has been attained. Once a settlement has been agreed, leading to a united Ireland, all decisions relating to decommissioning of armaments, equipment and other resources must be ratified by an Army Convention."[17] The motion was passed unanimously. Adams, McGuinness, and the peace strategy supporters on the Army Council had no choice but to vote along with everyone else. To have done otherwise would have been to vindicate the criticism and suspicion directed at them.

Once the Convention had ended and the delegates dispersed to their home areas, the Adams camp tried to retrieve the situation. For months afterward Army Council meetings were riven by disputes between the dissidents and the Adams camp over whether or not the McKevitt motion was an addition to the constitution or an amendment. The Adams supporters argued that it was an addition and that the 1986 formulation that gave the Army Council ultimate power over IRA weapons—and therefore the authority to decommission—was still in place. It was yet another clue that, with time, decommissioning would happen.

The Adams camp suffered other setbacks at the Convention. The Army Executive was given a new role by delegates and became "the custodians of the [IRA] constitution" with the right to rule and arbitrate on policy matters that infringed the constitution, while rank-and-file Volunteers were given the right to petition the Executive on such matters.[18] That meant that the Executive could take issue with moves made in the peace process by people like Adams and McGuinness. Another motion was passed ordering the Army Council to maintain "the organisational integrity and cohesion . . . the political and military strengths and capabilities" of the IRA until the organization's objectives, as defined in the constitution, had been attained.[19] There would be no running down of the IRA, in other words, by either the front or the back door.

Most significantly of all, the Army Council was deprived of the power to make decisions by a simple majority. From then on five Council members at least would have to approve critical matters such as cease-fires.[20] That came as close to a vote of no confidence in Gerry Adams and his allies as it was possible to get.

AS THE CONVENTION neared its conclusion, it also reached its climax, the point when delegates elected the new Executive. The question of who secured a majority of the Executive was a vital one, for that section could, in effect, select and choose the members of the Army Council and thus gain control of the direction and strategy of the IRA itself. The dissidents had hatched a plan to take over the Army Council in such a way, but it was entirely dependent on winning a majority of the members of the new Executive. The Convention would have to support the dissident candidates. Once they had done that, they could choose an Army Council of their liking, and Adams would be defeated.

The dissidents hoped to place Adams in a terrible dilemma. Their plan was to have their majority vote him onto the Council but then to hobble him by stacking the rest of the Council with their supporters. That way the beleaguered and isolated Sinn Fein president would then have to decide whether to stay, and be constantly outvoted, or go. The decision would be entirely his, while the dissidents could not be blamed for forcing him to go, thus losing the Provisionals their most charismatic spokesperson and leader. Either way the peace process would be dead, and so would the Adams strategy.

The last session of the Convention, in the early hours of the morning, saw the Adams loyalists on the outgoing Army Council make their pitch to delegates for election to the new Executive. Pat Doherty told delegates that the nine-month delay in holding the Convention was not his fault; it was entirely due to logistical problems. Joe Cahill assured them that he would not settle for anything less than a thirty-two-county socialist republic. He hadn't mellowed with old age, he added. If anything, his views had hardened with the years. Kevin McKenna objected to suggestions that he or anyone else in the leadership would settle for anything less than the traditional goal of unity, while Gerry Kelly admitted that TUAS had not been properly defined or explained to the membership. Apologetic, meek, defiant, they all knew what was on the line.

But the turning point, according to one authoritative account, came when the outgoing chairman of the Army Council, Martin McGuinness, rose to speak.[21] The old Army Council, he declared, had no intention of entering talks that would lead nowhere and had already decided there would not be a second cease-fire, and it would advise the incoming Council accordingly. It was as close as any leader came that night to declaring the death of the peace process, and it swung the meeting. Any question that either he and Adams would not be returned to the leadership vanished. But the dissidents were still on course for victory.

The elections were held, and Micky McKevitt topped the poll. The dissidents did well and secured a seven-to-five majority on the Executive. Joe Cahill was badly defeated and did not even make it as a substitute, one of those chosen to replace the Executive members elected onto the Army Council. Gerry Kelly was chosen as a substitute, but Adams got himself and four allies safely elected onto the Executive, including Martin McGuinness, Pat Doherty, and Martin Ferris, who replaced Joe Cahill.

The dissidents, however, quickly ran into trouble, and so did the plot to destroy Adams. One of their successful candidates, the Dubliner Frank McGuinness, had missed his pickup and failed to make it to the Convention, although he was elected to the Executive in his absence. McGuinness was supposed to have been taken to the Convention by the IRA's intelligence director, Martin "Duckser" Lynch, a West Belfast activist and Adams loyalist, but an extra leg was added to the Dubliner's journey for some unexplained reason, and Lynch never linked up with him.

Frank McGuinness's absence did not stop him from getting elected to the Executive, but it did prevent him from using his vote in the election of Army Council members. Even so it still looked as if the dissidents had the Army Council election in the bag; they had a six-to-five majority and could freely choose the new Army Council from among their own. But then Brian Keenan, who for long had played the part of a dissident, dropped a thunderbolt and announced that he was switching sides and would back Adams. With Frank McGuinness absent, a six-to-five majority for the dissidents suddenly became a one-vote advantage for Adams.

Sensing that events had turned dramatically in his favor, Adams moved for an immediate meeting of the Executive to elect the Army Council. The IRA constitution stipulated that such a gathering should take place within forty-eight hours of the Convention, but Adams was taking no chances. If Frank McGuinness was allowed to vote, then the Executive would almost certainly be deadlocked, with potentially disastrous results for the peace strategy. It was imperative from Adams's viewpoint that the Executive meet immediately. The dissidents tried to delay the Executive meeting, but to no avail. Adams won the vote, and the Executive convened straightaway. The meeting took place as dawn was breaking and voted in an Army Council that, if anything, gave Adams and his allies an even stronger grip on the IRA than they had held before the Convention.

In addition to Adams, the Council now comprised Martin McGuinness, Pat Doherty, Martin Ferris, Brian Keenan, who replaced the South Armagh–based Northern Command adjutant, Kevin McKenna, and Slab Murphy. The Army Council's "soldiers" were now in an even smaller minority. The scope for continued internal conflict was still considerable, however. The Executive that was formed after the Army Council election was substantially unchanged from that which had called the Convention. Ten of its twelve members were opposed to the Adams strategy; one was against and one unsure. The three principal dissidents, Gillen, Frank McGuinness, and McKevitt, were still in place but were now painfully aware that their putsch had not succeeded. Adams had been battered and damaged by the Convention, but he had survived to wreak revenge on his dissident enemies. And as far as the peace process was concerned, that was all that mattered.

SEVENTEEN

The Point of No Return

By one of those flukes of history, or perhaps owing to good intelligence about his enemies' intentions, Adams had emerged from the October 1996 Convention not only intact, albeit badly mauled, but with a stronger majority on the Army Council than he had enjoyed before the meeting. Because of the way the IRA worked, the dissidents had only one chance to destroy him, and although they had come very close, their effort had failed. It was unlikely they would get a second chance. Encouraged and heartened by its achievement, the Adams camp prepared for the next and most crucial part of the journey from war to peace.

The old Army Council had agreed to end the 1994 cease-fire only when it became unavoidably clear that otherwise it would be defeated at the Convention demanded by the Executive. Going back to war in February 1996 was a matter of political survival for Adams and his supporters. But with their grip on the Army Council firmer after the October 1996 Convention, they could now resume the peace process with vigor and steer the IRA toward another cessation, this time better informed about their opponents and better prepared to meet their threat. Martin McGuinness had promised the delegates at the Convention that there would be no second cease-fire, but there would be.

Even before the Convention met, Adams had been in secret negotiations with the British prime minister, John Major, using the SDLP leader, John Hume, as a mediator, and afterward that diplomacy intensified. He had told the Convention that he did not believe the British were serious about hosting talks in which Sinn Fein members involved, but within weeks of the Convention he was engaged in what clearly were businesslike discussions with Downing Street whose goal was to remove the obstacles in the way of a new cease-fire and to open the road to talks in which Sinn Fein would play a central and definitive role.

Four issues dominated the Adams-Major negotiations. To begin with, there was uncertainty about whether Sinn Fein would be allowed to enter interparty talks at all or if they did about the conditions that would be attached to this. Even if Sinn Fein was allowed into the talks, it was not clear whether or not there would be a deadline for agreements. Adams again feared being drawn into an open-ended process whose only result would be to once again enervate the IRA and unsettle the rank and file. The unresolved issue of IRA decommissioning still hung over the peace process, as did the price Sinn Fein would exact from the British: "confidence-building measures," as they were euphemistically called, in return for a new cease-fire. All these issues were on the table for discussion, and problematic though they were, the fact that Adams and his allies wanted to talk about them was a remarkable testament to their persistence.

Notwithstanding the outright hostility and doubt the IRA rank and file expressed about the peace process at the October 1996 Convention, Adams, McGuinness, and others in their camp made it abundantly clear in one public statement after another in the fall of 1996 and the early months of 1997 that a second cease-fire was not only attainable but desirable. At the end of November 1996, Martin McGuinness indicated that the IRA might be prepared to accept George Mitchell's proposal that talks and decommissioning should happen in parallel. The Derry republican had once again been appointed Army Council chairman but by this stage was no longer Northern commander, that job having gone to a Belfast veteran instead. He was later quoted as saying, at the beginning of February 1997, that there was nowhere else for republicans to go but to the negotiating table. Writing in the *Irish Times* at the end of that month, Gerry Adams promised that any new cease-fire would be "genuinely unequivocal" as long as the preconditions governing Sinn Fein's involvement were removed.[1] These were men who were confident not only about where they wanted to go but in their ability to get there. The Army Convention was already a distant memory.

Other signals pointed unmistakably in the same direction. On February 12, 1997, the IRA in South Armagh shot dead a British soldier manning a roadblock at Bessbrook. The dead soldier, Stephen Restorick, had been killed by a sniper using a formidable Barrett Light 50, the only weapon in the IRA's arsenal whose bullets could penetrate British flak jackets. This deadly weapon had killed some dozen soldiers and policemen in single-shot sniper attacks, most of them at the hands of the South Armagh men. There was an outcry at Restorick's death, prompted in part by his grieving mother's impressively moving interviews on television. A month later Gerry Adams wrote a letter of condolence to Mrs. Restorick, an unprecedented act for a member of the IRA Army Council ostensibly at war with the British. During the same month he told the *Irish News* in an interview that he could deliver an IRA cease-fire if the package was right. His Saint Patrick's Day message, now accorded the same status in the media as those from mainstream Irish and Irish-American politicians, included a statement saying that the achievement of a permanent peaceful settlement through peaceful dialogue must be everyone's goal.

AT THIS POINT events completely out of the control of Adams or anyone else in Ireland intruded—to the advantage of the peace process. A British general election was announced in mid-March, and the polls all showed a likely victory for Tony Blair's New Labour Party and defeat for the Conservatives, whose approach to the peace process had been hamstrung by doubts over Adams's bona fides and the party's own historical links to unionism. The removal of John Major would set the scene for a radical reassessment of London's policy toward Sinn Fein.

The British election also promised to strengthen the Adams camp in another very important way. The forum election of 1996, designed to jumpstart political talks, had resulted in a boost in support for Sinn Fein, and it seemed as if the 1997 election would do the same, at least as long as the IRA did not score any own goals. In the month before polling, the Army Council had secretly authorized what became known as "a tactical period of quiet" to help Sinn Fein's chances while simultaneously the party's leaders talked up the chances of peace. The party was unashamedly courting a pro-peace vote from the Catholic electorate. It was a clever tactic, not least because it created an expectation of a second cease-fire that Sinn Fein—and the IRA—could not ignore.

Blair's New Labour signaled its readiness to cater to Sinn Fein's needs in a way that had never happened when John Major led the British government. The party's new Northern Ireland spokesperson was Mo Mowlam, a down-to-earth politician whose wheeler-dealer style and sometimes coarse approach unsettled unionists but appealed enormously to nationalists. At the end of March 1997 she announced that if the IRA called a cease-fire, Sinn Fein could be in talks by the start of June, just two months afterward. Adams and other Sinn Fein leaders welcomed her remarks, not least because she omitted any reference to the need for IRA decommissioning.

Tony Blair duly romped home in Britain in May 1997, with a huge parliamentary majority—enough to give him maximum flexibility on the peace
process—while in Northern Ireland Sinn Fein made a significant electoral
breakthrough, with Adams recapturing West Belfast from the SDLP and
Martin McGuinness winning in Mid-Ulster, where the campaign was about
which nationalist party, Sinn Fein or the SDLP, was best placed to defeat the
DUP's Reverend William McCrea, a Free Presbyterian minister and out-
spoken loyalist who was hated by local nationalists. Sinn Fein's support
across Northern Ireland rose to its highest-ever level, to 127,000 votes, or
16.1 percent of the total vote in Northern Ireland. A month later its vote
rose even further, to 16.9 percent, in local council elections. The party was
within striking distance of the SDLP, and it was clear beyond doubt that
Sinn Fein's future political growth was inextricably attached to progress in
the peace process and to the declaration of another cease-fire. To the barely
disguised delight of nationalists and the anger of unionists, Mo Mowlam
was appointed the new Northern Ireland secretary.

Another piece of the jigsaw fell into place a month after the British general election, when in the Irish Republic the parties that had made up the
Rainbow Coalition were ousted and a Fianna Fail–Progressive Democrats
combination replaced them. The general election in the Republic meant that
the Fianna Fail leader, Bertie Ahern, was the new taoiseach and in charge of
Northern Ireland policy. Martin Mansergh was back in Government Buildings and soon once again serving cups of tea and plates of biscuits to Father
Reid. Gerry Adams welcomed the development; his old pan-nationalist
partners were back in place and stronger than ever. In mid-May, Blair traveled to Belfast to confirm that interparty talks would begin in June. If Sinn
Fein wanted to join the peace train, he warned, then it had better make up
its mind quickly, or the train would leave the station without it. To help it
make up its mind, he offered exploratory talks between Sinn Fein and his
officials, an offer the Provisional leadership accepted with alacrity. Soon
Martin McGuinness and Gerry Kelly were meeting the NIO's John Chilcot
and Quentin Thomas. The stage had been set for the beginning of the final
negotiations for the second IRA cease-fire.

AS ALL THESE political developments were unfolding, the IRA's campaign was falling to pieces. The special unit created by Northern
Command, which had so successfully restarted the IRA's campaign in the
North with the bombing of Thiepval barracks, was rolled up by the RUC
and its leader incarcerated within days of the Convention. It was clear from

the pattern of arrests that the British security authorities were extremely well informed about its activities and had placed some of the unit members under surveillance long before arrests were made.

Deprived of this cutting edge, the IRA leadership turned to the ordinary ASUs to deliver the goods. At the 1996 Convention, Brian Gillen, the Belfast commander, had complained about the September 1993 Army Council order banning commercial bombing. Despite that, the new Council reimposed the restriction and ordered the ASUs to concentrate instead on security force targets, particularly British soldiers. As in the late 1980s, this was a case of setting the IRA an examination it could never hope to pass—as the Army Council must have known—and it failed miserably. As one bungled or ineffective operation followed another and as more and more Volunteers were arrested, one RUC officer was prompted to describe the IRA's efforts as "a pathetic, grubby little war."[2] Even the most loyal republican would have found it difficult to disagree.

The IRA mounted dozens of attacks in the North during this period, but very few ever came near hitting their target. The IRA's killing rate dropped significantly. By mid-1997, a year or so after the cease-fire had ended, the IRA had succeeded in killing just two soldiers and two civilians. When its Lurgan, County Armagh unit killed two RUC men in June 1994, there was public outrage, and it was clear the attacks had embarrassed the Sinn Fein leadership, even though the unit was merely implementing Army Council strategy. The Clinton White House, in particular, made its anger personally known to Gerry Adams.

The overreliance on the South Armagh battalions proved to be very costly. The knowledge that the big English bombs originated there made it imperative from the British viewpoint to score some major successes against the local IRA, if only to prove that South Armagh was not unassailable. The fact that IRA activity elsewhere in the North had considerably diminished freed British intelligence resources and gave the various agencies the space to accomplish the deed. Eventually undercover soldiers and police swooped on a farm near Crossmaglen in April 1994, arrested seven men, and captured the Second Battalion's only Barrett Light 50 rifle. It was the worst blow against the South Armagh IRA that most in the area could remember, and the message was clear. If the British could hit the South Armagh IRA, then the war was as good as over.

There was another, even more compelling reason for the IRA's failures. By 1996 the organization was broke and owed money everywhere, not least to Slab Murphy, who had lent the IRA some of the proceeds from his cross-

Border business operations and had not been repaid. The IRA habitually lived in a state of penury, as Chief of Staff Kevin McKenna had reminded the Convention. The IRA managed to stay just about afloat, he said, but never got ahead. Financial shortages had worsened after the loss of the *Eksund*, when the angry Libyans had canceled the promised cash payments.

Gerry Adams's trips to the United States had briefly raised Army Council hopes that its fortunes could be improved. The prospect of thousands of dollars flowing into the IRA's coffers was indeed was one of the reasons the Council had so readily authorized his trip. But Adams, aided by Howell, had set up a new fund-raising group to supplant the long-standing American structures, centered on Noraid. Called Friends of Sinn Fein (FoSF) and based in Washington and Manhattan, New York, it was initially funded by the billionaire businessman Charles "Chuck" Feeney. FoSF was ultimately to raise vast amounts of money, primarily through $1,000-a-plate dinners in ritzy New York hotels where figures like Adams would speak, mingle, and network with figures from corporate Irish-America. Despite all this newfound wealth, the IRA's hoped-for millions of dollars never materialized. Unknown to the Army Council, FoSF agreed to a deal with the Department of Justice in Washington, which meant that every dollar raised and spent in Ireland had to be accounted for and the books audited by an accountant nominated by the federal government. The officer board of FoSF was furthermore obliged to sign an undertaking that the funds would not be used "for any unlawful purpose," which effectively meant that none of the money could legally be allowed to go to the IRA.[3]

When some officials from FoSF subsequently traveled to Ireland to meet Sinn Fein's finance officers, Adams banned the IRA's director of finance, John Deery, from attending the meeting, and when tackled by members of the Council, he blamed others for negotiating a poor deal with the U.S. government. The IRA would not get Sinn Fein's cash, by either the front door or the back.

To add to the IRA's fund-raising problems, Noraid had been considerably run down by 1996 and was in a very divided state, the result of internal disputes over the direction taken by the peace process, especially in the influential Bronx and Brooklyn chapters of the New York division. Many rank-and-file Noraid members were resentful of FoSF and saw its formation as a sign that the leadership in Ireland had decided to discard them after all their years of faithful service in favor of wealthier and more respectable friends. By 1996 traditional Irish-America was contributing negligible amounts to the IRA's coffers. In the past these contacts had enabled the IRA quite easily to raise up to $50,000–$100,000 in emergencies—for example, to fund a special operation—but not any more. One way or another the IRA's ability to run an effective military campaign in 1996 and 1997 was severely hampered by its poverty.

POLITICAL EVENTS accelerated after the changes of government in Dublin and London. The British made a crucial move in mid-June 1997, when officials gave the Provisional negotiators, Martin McGuinness and Gerry Kelly, an *aide-mémoire* setting out the terms for Sinn Fein's entry to interparty talks. The document outlined five elements to the deal. First, the IRA would have to call an unequivocal cease-fire and hold to it for at least six weeks. Second, Sinn Fein delegates to the talks would have to make clear their commitment to the Mitchell principles. Third, the British would agree to a deadline for the conclusion of the talks, and they suggested May 1998. Fourth, the republicans would have to agree that decommissioning would happen along the lines suggested by Senator George Mitchell, although it would no longer be a precondition for participation in talks. And fifth, there would be confidence-building measures on both sides. The British committed themselves to the principle of parity of esteem and equality in cultural and economic matters and to respect for human rights. They recognized the sensitivity of the prisoner issue and made a commitment to develop a police service capable of securing widespread support. The republicans in turn should bring an end to punishment attacks. If all went according to plan the interparty talks would go into recess over the summer, as these matters were working themselves out, and in September resume with Sinn Fein present. They would then have eight months to hammer out a deal.

Compared with the Conservatives, the New Labourites were bending over backward to return Sinn Fein and the IRA to the process, an indication, perhaps, that Tony Blair and his colleagues had a better understanding of what Adams and his colleagues were trying to do. After all, Blair had completed a somewhat similar journey himself after his election as Labour leader in 1994, cleansing the party of the last vestiges of its postwar socialism.

Blair was also far more flexible on the question of IRA decommissioning, the issue that had broken the 1994 cease-fire. He and Ahern announced agreement in June on a proposal that would supposedly see political talks and decommissioning happening in parallel. As the politicians hammered out a wider deal, an international body, to be headed by the Canadian general John de Chastelain, would handle IRA and other paramilitary disarmament. The deal effectively meant that issue was put on the back burner in the hope that a political settlement might create more favorable circumstances for it to actually begin. All this indicated a greater British sensitivity to Adams's internal management needs.

The British *aide-mémoire* did not mention British withdrawal or even indicate that the subject would be on the agenda for discussion once talks had started. It did, though, offer Adams and his colleagues the one element they needed to sustain the peace process and confound their critics—the prospect of speedy entry into negotiations, which they could characterize, internally, as encompassing such core isues as British withdrawal. The imperative for Adams was to get into talks quickly and to silence those who would claim that the process was about weakening the IRA with a lengthy, unproductive, and drawn-out cessation. Once Sinn Fein was in talks, as the peace camp must have known, it would be a different matter, for then the leaders could more easily control events and their own supporters.

RANK-AND-FILE IRA attitudes, however, had not changed much since the Convention, and the evidence suggested that a majority was still strongly against a new cease-fire, not because the campaign was floundering but because the British terms did not measure up to the expectations nourished by a twenty-five-year war. In June the IRA's most senior commanders met in Donegal to consider the *aide-mémoire* at an all-night meeting. Present was the Army Council, GHQ staff, and brigade, battalion, and ASU commanders, perhaps thirty of the cream of the IRA. Overwhelmingly the view from the meeting was against another *sos*, and the British *aide-mémoire* was rejected.

The meeting has entered IRA mythology not just because of this decision but because it was thoroughly compromised. Undercover Gardai Special Branch officers had the meeting place under surveillance and photographed the delegates as they arrived and left. It was one of the worst security breaches in the Provisional's history. "Everyone would have been identified, everyone had been docked," said one source with knowledge of the meeting.[4] Suspicion about the identity of the informer behind the betrayal helped to further sour internal relations.

In Dublin, Adams found another Fianna Fail wheeler-dealer sitting in the taoiseach's office. Forty-five-year-old Bertie Ahern had succeeded the unfortunate Albert Reynolds in early 1995 and headed a government in which the Progressive Democrats were a minority partner. He had perfect Fianna Fail credentials. He was born in working-class North Dublin, his mother came from a republican family in County Cork, while his father had fought with the IRA during the war of independence and then followed de Valera when he abandoned armed struggle for parliamentary methods. Long regarded as an ambitious and talented politician, he was promoted to the front bench by Charles Haughey, who became something of a mentor. With the benefit of his intimate vantage point, Haughey once said of Ahern that he was "the best, the most skilful, the most devious and the most cunning" of them all.

Once Ahern took office, contact between the Provisionals and Irish civil servants intensified as they worked out their set of cease-fire terms, separate from the British. By the end of June the officials, led by Sean O hUiginn of the Department of Foreign Affairs, Paddy Teahon of the Justice Department, and Padraig O hUiginn of the taoiseach's office, produced a 1,700-word document that was sent to the Army Council, setting out the Irish government's view of what would happen after the IRA declared a new cease-fire.

According to Irish government sources the terms were divided into two parts, those dealing with security matters and those concerning political issues. The security proposals were these:

(i)   Ten IRA prisoners would be released by Christmas 1997; the gradual early release of prisoners halted in February 1996 would be resumed; IRA prisoners serving forty-year sentences (for murdering Irish police officers) would be considered for Christmas parole.

(ii) Emergency antiterrorist legislation would be reviewed.

(iii) IRA prisoners would be moved from the old jail in Portlaoise to the new modern open jail at Castlerea, County Roscommon.

(iv) The Irish government would aim for a political settlement that included the creation of a new policing service in Northern Ireland, which could enjoy cross-community support.

(v)   The Irish government would seek to achieve paramilitary decommissioning in the manner suggested by the Mitchell report and would expect the republicans to work in good faith to achieve that objective. (However the Ahern government also gave the IRA Army Council important guarantees about decommissioning, as one key Irish source recalled. "What we told them was that we realized that it could only happen with the co-operation of the IRA and as part of a phased political process," he said. "I think the exact phrase we used went something like this: 'IRA decommissioning would only happen in the context of a benign dynamic founded on political confidence and cannot be achieved on a peremptory basis.'")[5]

The Irish government, Ahern's message continued, would oppose any effort to expel Sinn Fein from talks if any of the other participants made "a peremptory" demand for IRA disarmament. Only a breach of any of the six Mitchell principles would constitute a justified reason for such action, it added.

The political terms were these:

(i) The Irish government would take a leadership role and would give the peace process momentum.

(ii) The aim of interparty talks would be to create a new political dispensation that would address and overcome previous political failures going back to the 1921 settlement. But the principle of consent would underlie any deal; the settlement would have to command the support of both political communities in the North.

(iii) The Downing Street Declaration, the Mitchell principles, and the framework document would be the basis of the Irish government's position in talks, but the aim would be to create new power-sharing government institutions, effective North-South bodies, and parity of esteem for both communities in cultural and economic matters.

(iv) No constitutional option, including Irish unity and independence, would be excluded from the negotiations, and the Irish government would work for institutional and longer-term constitutional change in co-operation with the British.

(v) The Irish government's embassies in Washington and London would give the peace process the highest priority and remain in continuous contact with the White House, Congress, the U.S. business community, and Irish-America. Dublin would reopen the doors for Sinn Fein to establishment America, in other words.

(vi) The taoiseach's door would be open to Sinn Fein, there would be no question of refusing any joint meeting with Adams and Hume, and there could be continuous consultation between Sinn Fein and the Irish government during the coming negotiations if desired. Channels involving Adams's key advisers and government officials could be reactivated.[6]

The Irish government's terms acknowledged the dilemma that the Adams leadership found itself in over decommissioning as a result of the constitutional changes forced through, against Adams's wishes, at the 1996 Convention. It was almost as if Ahern and his advisers knew all about them. The change to the IRA constitution deprived Adams of all flexibility on the issue by insisting that only a Convention could authorize disarmament. The Executive dissidents had tied the Army Council's hands completely. Even though they had failed to overthrow Adams, the legacy of their effort was still destructive. Ahern's terms allowed for all this.

The effect of the dissidents' success on the decommissioning question was that if either the British or the unionists pushed the arms issue too hard, it would break the cease-fire and the Adams leadership. He and his supporters did attempt to argue that the Executive change was an addition to the 1986 constitution, not an amendment, and that they could, if they wished, still negotiate on IRA guns. But this was a controversial reading of the 1996 constitution, and the leadership could not be sure of the grassroots response if it went ahead on that basis. The way the Ahern government had formulated the guarantee on decommissioning cushioned the Army Council, however. It postponed the resolution of the problem of IRA guns until enough political progress had been made to give the Adams camp the room to restore the pre-1996 IRA constitution.

In essence the British and Irish political terms were nothing more than a restatement of Northern Ireland policy as it had evolved under the direction of both governments since the early 1970s. A number of characteristics defined this policy: a commitment to equality, acceptable security institutions, a power-sharing government involving nationalists and unionists, and the creation of North-South bodies, what the British had christened "the Irish dimension," were prime among them. But the principle of consent was the ideological foundation stone of the two governments' approach. There could be no constitutional change, no end to partition, unless a majority in Northern Ireland freely said so. These features, in varying proportions, had been the essential ingredients of virtually every political initiative since the fall of the Sunningdale agreement in 1974, and the political talks process that Sinn Fein was about to enter would be no different.

With the British and Irish governments' terms on the table and broadly acceptable to the Adams camp, the only question left to decide was the timing of the second cease-fire. The difficulty here was that events had conspired to produce the right conditions for a new IRA cease-fire just as the North was about to enter the worst phase of the summer Orange marching season.

THE ORANGE marching season was a nightmare period in Northern Ireland's already violence-crammed calendar. Thousands of Orange parades took place every summer, from Easter through the end of September, and each took more or less the same form. Columns of be-sashed and occasionally bowler-hatted Orangemen would march from their Orange hall to a church or a meeting place accompanied by flute-playing, drum-thumping bands, hold a prayer service, and then march back again and disperse. At one or two points in the season, the Twelfth of July being one, Orangemen from Belfast and from each of Northern Ireland's six counties would congregate for larger parades, impressive and colorful occasions that celebrated Protestant culture and history. But most parades were small, local affairs, and most passed entirely without incident. In one or two places, however, trouble could be guaranteed, usually where demographic changes meant that the Orangemen's route took them through Catholic areas. On these occasions tribal passions could easily be roused as Orangemen insisted on exercising their ancient rights, while Catholics resented what they saw as an attempt by the Orangemen to parade their supremacy.

For the preceding two years a church parade of Orangemen in Portadown, County Armagh, had pitched much of the North into serious conflict, and 1997 looked as if it would be no different. The Orangemen's route home to Portadown Orange headquarters from the picturesque Church of Ireland at Drumcree took them through a Catholic enclave around the Garvaghy Road. Population shifts meant that a once mixed area had become overwhelmingly nationalist, and for several years local residents had been campaigning to bar the Orangemen from their district. The British, under pressure from Dublin and the United States, had initially supported the residents but for two years running had buckled in the face of overwhelming Orange pressure.

On one occasion, in July 1995, some ten thousand Orangemen and their supporters had laid siege at Drumcree, and running battles broke out between them and RUC riot squads. After two nights of trouble, and confrontations on the pretty hillsides around Drumcree that uncannily resembled scenes from a seventeenth-century battle, the Orangemen were allowed to make their way through the Catholic area. In July 1996 the siege lasted five days, and this time the masses of Orange supporters at Drumcree were supported by thousands more loyalists elsewhere in the North who brought transport links and the centers of many Protestant towns to a standstill. There were riots at Drumcree and in many Protestant areas of the North. Again the authorities relented, and the Orangemen were allowed to march but in circumstances that infuriated Catholics. They were forced through the Garvaghy Road by police riot squads that batoned and physically removed nationalist protesters. This triggered several days of widespread rioting in Catholic districts, during which a youth was crushed to death by a military vehicle in Derry.

The 1997 Drumcree siege was shaping up for a repeat performance. The possibility that Protestants might once again bring Northern Ireland to a halt and that the IRA might be obliged to respond violently was right at the top of the list of problems facing the newly installed Labour secretary of state, Mo Mowlam. Her senior officials were advising her to bend once again to the Orange gale and to allow, as one of them put it, "Orange feet on the Garvaghy Road" that July. A British policy document, later leaked to the media, showed that as early as June 20, two weeks before the march was due to happen, Mowlam's advice was to try to negotiate a peaceful "controlled [Orange] parade" on the Garvaghy Road as "the least worst option."[7] This involved Mowlam in something of a ruse. Elaborate negotiations between her and the Garvaghy residents group were arranged, with a view to agreeing a compromise with the Orangemen, but it seemed that she—or at least her officials—had already decided. It did not matter that much what the residents had to say to her.

The third siege of Drumcree was due to begin on Sunday, July 6. Loyalists were threatening mayhem, Mowlam had secretly decided to give the Orangemen their way, and the disposition of the IRA in the face of all this was crucial. It was in these circumstances that four days before, on July 2, the Army Council met and by a vote of seven to nil voted secretly to renew the 1994 cease-fire and to accept British and Irish terms for Sinn Fein's entry to inter-party talks. The decision was kept well hidden, even from rank-and-file IRA members, however, until July 19, seventeen days afterward and nearly a fortnight after the Drumcree parade had once again been forced and batoned through the Garvaghy Road.

Whether the British knew anything of this decision can only be guessed at, but there can be little doubt that knowledge of the IRA leadership's move could only have strengthened Mo Mowlam's hand in dealing with Nationalist opposition to that year's Orange protest. By renewing the cease-fire on July 2, the Army Council had, in effect, given Mowlam the go-ahead to push the Orange marchers through their own district. The IRA, it was saying, was not disposed to respond violently if that happened. And even if Mowlam knew nothing of the secret IRA decision, the effect was the same. As for the IRA's volunteers, they were put on standby during the parade in case of trouble, little knowing that their leaders were unlikely to order them into action in any but the most exceptional circumstances.

In the early hours of Sunday morning, July 6, a large force of British soldiers and policemen moved into the Garvaghy area to seal it off, and violent clashes with local Catholics left seventeen residents hospitalized, according to their spokesman, Breandan MacCionnaith. After daylight there was more violence as the nationalists were penned in a car park by a large force of policemen and soldiers. At one stage an open-air Mass was held in the car park in an almost grotesque display of victimhood. After the Orangemen had marched through the area and the security forces begun to withdraw, the crowd chanted after them, "No cease-fire!"—an ironic cry in the circumstances. There were riots in some nationalist areas, and in nearby Lurgan the IRA burned a train, but in Belfast members of the organization were on the streets restraining would-be rioters and ordering off-licenses to close in case drink inflamed angry crowds. Elsewhere, at the urging of IRA commanders, the response of republicans was deliberately low-key.

THE ARMY COUNCIL'S decision set the stage for the next and last confrontation with the Executive dissidents, and once again it was over the issue of which of the two had the final say on the formulation of IRA policy.

At the 1996 Convention the Executive had secured a promise from members of the Army Council that it would, as a body, consult more regularly and closely with other sections of the IRA, in particular with the Executive, GHQ, and OCs, over matters like a second cease-fire. But the promise was honored more in the breach than in the observance. Before the May 1997 British general election, the Army Council ordered a "tactical period of quiet" to help Sinn Fein's chances, in effect declaring an unofficial if short cease-fire. But it had consulted no one else in the IRA about the move. The Executive complained about the absence of consultation, and the Army Council apologized, promising this would not happen again.

Within two months the Army Council once more acted unilaterally, this time by declaring the second cease-fire. Not only were bodies like the Executive and GHQ staff not consulted about the decision; they were not informed of it until just before the public announcement, and that rankled deeply, bringing long-held resentments once more bubbling to the surface. This time there was no apology from the Army Council. The Adams camp insisted that the Council had given no such undertaking at the Convention and that it was obliged to consult the Executive only when the first four months of a cease-fire had ended and an extension was required.

As things worked out, the only member of the Executive entitled to sit in on Army Council meetings, Micky McKevitt, had been out of circulation when the cease-fire decision had been taken, and so the Council had been able to keep the decision a closely guarded secret from all but its own members and members of the Adams think tank. It was not until two weeks later, on the eve of the public announcement, that the Executive found out what had happened. But this time Adams and his allies were better prepared to deal with their dissidents.

After a special request from the Army Council chairman, Martin McGuinness, the full Council met the full Executive on July 16 to report the July 2 cease-fire decision and agree the impending public announcement. The Army Council had met three days before and ratified the cease-fire vote, and the decision would be made public within forty-eight hours or so. McGuinness told the Executive that the Army Council had been fully consulted and informed about the background and was now united. According to a detailed account of these encounters, he gave three reasons for the renewed *sos*. There was a new government in Britain, the Sinn Fein vote was rising, and the combined pressure of the Irish government and the Clinton White House had forced the British to set a specific date, September 15, for the start of talks and a deadline for their conclusion, May 1998. The *sos*, in other words, would be time-limited and could not be extended indefinitely.

The decommissioning precondition had been dropped, he said, and went on to predict that as far as the Army Council was concerned there never would be actual decommissioning. In fact, he added, it was a good thing that the issue had been left unresolved, because this would justify a breakdown in the cease-fire later on. In the meantime Chief of Staff Kevin McKenna had been given authority to mount operations if necessary. The cease-fire would not be comprehensive and all-embracing, in other words. There would be enough leeway to calm anxious nerves in the rank and file.

Gerry Adams was then questioned by the Executive and, according to this account, like McGuinness, he justified the new *sos* on tactical grounds. The new cease-fire would not be permanent, he suggested, and the IRA would eventually return to armed struggle if its terms were not met. The Mitchell report merely demanded that Sinn Fein consider parallel decommissioning, and so the party would consider it until the cows came home but would never come to an agreement. Sinn Fein's involvement on this basis would ensure the collapse of the talks. The Army Council, Adams went on, wanted decommissioning to be left unresolved. Either the British would be broken on the issue and the unionists faced down, or the unionists would refuse to go into talks unless the IRA disarmed, and the process would collapse in circumstances in which the unionists and the British would be singled out for blame by constitutional Irish nationalism—Fianna Fail and the SDLP principally—and by the international community. Either way, taking a firm line against decommissioning would be to the IRA's advantage.

What was striking about the remarks made to the Executive by Adams and McGuinness was the extent to which both men still encouraged the view that the peace process was a just tactical ploy, designed to bring political advantage, but not intended to culminate in a political settlement of the sort that only a few months later, in April 1998, would be agreed. They similarly bolstered the view that the IRA would go back to war if its goal of achieving a promise of British withdrawal was not realized. Refusal to decommission would be the lever, Adams said, which would both cause the talks to collapse and get the IRA back to armed struggle in the most favorable of circumstances. Again actual events have demonstrated how unreliable these assurances were. Not only did Sinn Fein negotiate a deal in 1998 in which British withdrawal was never explicitly conceded or even mentioned, but in October 2001 the IRA began to destroy its caches of weapons and explosives in a bid to keep the deal from collapsing. Adams was right in one regard. The unionists did make an issue out of decommissioning, but it was not they who were faced down.

Of the two surviving "soldiers" on the Army Council, only Slab Murphy spoke up, saying that he believed the *sos* was the right way to go. But privately he and McKenna were saying that they really were opposed to the move and had gone along with the new cease-fire in order only to preserve IRA unity.

The discussion between the Army Council and the Executive got heated. The Army Council argued strongly that there really was no alternative; the IRA was having recruiting problems and needed something to boost membership and nothing boosted recruitment better than a cease-fire. Anyway, the Adams camp added, this was just a new phase of the struggle, and the IRA would eventually be back at war. Adams outlined the negotiating strategy. Sinn Fein would aim to maximize and strengthen the framework document and renegotiate the 1920 Government of Ireland Act, which had partitioned Ireland and established British authority over Northern Ireland. If things went well, he said, there might be no need for armed struggle in four or five years time, but a Convention would decide that. If the Executive failed to back the Army Council, the Irish government would get to hear of it and see it as a vote of no confidence in his leadership, and that would weaken Sinn Fein's bargaining leverage. Gerry Kelly assured the Executive that the talks were, as he put it, "shite" and would produce nothing.[8] Brian

Keenan, now completely in support of the Adams camp, said this was just a strategic decision and the Executive members should get their heads around it. Go through the tunnel, he urged.

The Executive case, put mostly by McKevitt and Gillen, basically revolved around their lack of trust in the Adams camp and the fear that, having been debilitated once by a cease-fire, the IRA could only get weaker if it went into a second one. The IRA rank and file was also distrustful, they said, and would react badly to the decision. There was the possibility of major dissension, a fear that the talks would get nowhere and a conviction that the IRA was being pushed so far into a corner that it would have no alternative but to continue with a strategy that would lead to its demise.

There were angry references to what the Executive clearly regarded as a bogus promise given to it by the Army Council chairman, Martin McGuinness. At the previous Executive meeting, in May, McGuinness had given a firm assurance that there would be no second cease-fire—the only people talking about a cease-fire, he had said, were members of the Executive—and this guarantee had been repeated at the June meeting of Army Council, GHQ staff, and OCs in Donegal. That made it twice since the 1996 Convention that McGuinness had given such a pledge, three times within nine months, if the Executive version was to be believed.

Adams eventually called a halt to the discussion and suggested that they take up a motion expressing the Executive's support for the Army Council decision. His motion failed to find a proposer or seconder, and it fell. A second proposal, to reconvene the Executive so that the whole matter could be discussed in the absence of the Army Council, was passed by eleven votes to one. The difference between the two votes measured the gulf that now separated the Army Council and the Executive. A meeting that had been testy and bad-tempered ended with McGuinness's telling the Executive that the cease-fire decision would be made public at midnight on Friday, July 18. In fact it was not publicized until the Saturday afternoon. But no matter what the Executive might think about it, the cease-fire would go ahead.

The second Executive meeting was held on July 18, with Martin McGuinness the sole representative of the Army Council present. It was a largely inconclusive event; no new decisions were made or previous ones reconsidered, but again there was a heated exchange between McGuinness and the Executive. Complaints were repeated. The first sos had lasted too long, training and the production of explosives had been for nothing, and the Army Council had not kept a promise to strengthen the Army during the period of the cease-fire. The whole struggle was going political; the IRA had no sense of direction at all and was being turned into what one Executive member complained was a "wooden spoon." The Army Council had broken a promise to improve consultation with the Executive; the Volunteers were not happy. And so on.[9]

McGuinness replied that after the joint Army Council–Executive meeting, he and Adams had held further talks in Dublin and secured a commitment from the taoiseach, Bertie Ahern, that if the unionists refused to join the talks, Dublin and London would continue negotiating without them, even if that meant they were talking only to the SDLP and Sinn Fein. That was an even stronger reason for supporting the *sos*, he said. The Executive, he added, now had only three options: to accept the cease-fire, defer a decision for four months, or say that they had no confidence in the Army Council and convene an extraordinary General Army Convention. The Army Council, he added, would happily facilitate a special Convention. That McGuinness made this offer indicated that this time the Adams camp believed it could win it. For the Executive dissidents, McGuinness's confidence was an ominous sign. As the meeting broke up, McKevitt, Frank McGuinness, and the Executive chairman, Seamus McGrane from County Louth, decided that the ASUs should be canvassed for their views about the new cease-fire. They confidently expected these would be overwhelmingly hostile, but until the mood of the IRA was gauged there would be no quick decision. The Army Council would have to wait.

WITH A SECOND CEASE-FIRE declared, there was a need for a new strategy to replace or at least augment TUAS. Not least of the reasons for this was that TUAS had been less than a spectacular success. The pan-nationalist alliance envisaged by TUAS combined with pressure from the Americans was supposed to have been strong enough to force the British to move in all sorts of directions, but the collapse of the 1994 cease-fire testified to the failure of this idea. And so the think tank came up with a new strategy to replace it, according to informed IRA sources. The problem with the idea, known as the "integrated strategy," was that no one could understand what it was supposed to mean or what it was supposed to achieve. Its critics were troubled by two features in particular. The "integrated strategy" set no goals, outlined no methods nor any timetable. There was nothing distinctive about it. The second feature—more disturbing to the IRA's "soldiers"—was the absence of any military element. The "integrated strategy" sounded like a combination of politics and violence, but it was really all about politics. There was no role for the IRA, no place for armed struggle.

Former Senate Majority Leader George Mitchell had, unwittingly or otherwise, created an ideological minefield that would eventually bring the long-simmering divisions in the IRA leadership into the open. At the request of the British and Irish governments, he had set out a number of key principles that would have to underlie paramilitary involvement in political talks, and he had included them in his report on decommissioning to the two governments in early 1996 (see appendix 6). They included a commitment to nonviolence and to the principle of decommissioning. The British and Irish governments had both insisted that if Sinn Fein wanted to attend the interparty talks, it would have to sign up to the principles. Gerry Adams had readily agreed to Sinn Fein delegates' signing, but that was not the problem. The difficulty was that some delegates, particularly the leadership figures, were also IRA members. Three of them, Adams, McGuinness, and Doherty, were Army Council members no less. On one reading of the Mitchell principles, an IRA Volunteer would be breaching the IRA constitution if he or she signed up to them and therefore would be liable for expulsion.

The Mitchell principles became the last battleground between the Executive and the Army Council. The Executive took a hard line on the principles and argued that they represented a direct infringement of the IRA's constitution. A commissioned study concluded that one consequence of acceptance would be a de facto recognition of the unionist veto, and that struck at the very heart of the reason for the IRA's existence. Accepting the Mitchell principles, the study argued, would be tantamount to abandoning the struggle to rid Ireland of the British presence.

Another joint meeting between the Army Council and the Executive was arranged, this time on the latter's initiative. It took place on August 27, 1997, and once again was a heated, fractious affair. The Executive insisted that the Mitchell principles were aimed at getting republicans to legitimize the Northern Ireland state, while the challenge they made to the IRA's right to use force and hold arms, it said, would bring about the demise of the Army. If the IRA accepted the Mitchell principles, there could be no going back, and if the Army Council subsequently did claim that it had been duped into signing up, no one would believe it. Its reputation would be in tatters.

There could be no doubt about the seriousness of the charges made by the Executive. The Army Council was being accused of dishonoring and betraying the IRA's core principles, and this battle could produce only victory and defeat; a compromise was out of the question. There might be more serious consequences. The recent history of republicanism had demonstrated how easy it was for such disputes to deteriorate into a shooting war. The conflict between the Executive and the Army Council was heading inexorably toward a split, and when splits happened and rival groups rushed to control and take over arms dumps, IRA history showed, anything could happen.

With the Belfast Brigade commander, the quartermaster general, and the director of engineering combined against them, Adams and his allies were facing the most serious challenge of their IRA careers. At the joint Army Council–Executive meeting in July, Martin McGuinness had physically tensed when he was told that signing the Mitchell principles would breach the constitution. He knew instinctively that matters were getting deadly serious.

When the dispute had first surfaced, in July, the Army Council argued that the Mitchell principles infringed no part of the constitution, but by the end of August it had reluctantly come around to accept that they did. However, at the August meeting Adams claimed that there were precedents that allowed the Council to give special dispensation to permit Sinn Fein members of the IRA to sign the principles and remain IRA members. If this dispensation was exercised again, then the Army Council could safely send delegates to the coming Stormont talks, he argued. There were two precedents for this, he said. One, in the 1980s, had allowed IRA members to recognize the Northern and the Southern courts so that they could present a defense against criminal charges; the second had allowed Sinn Fein councillors who doubled as IRA members to sign the British government's mandatory antiviolence oath. One Adams ally, Danny Morrison, signaled his contempt for the British move at the time, saying he would sign the oath with his tongue sticking so firmly in his cheek that it would come through the roof of his mouth.

Adams's argument went to the heart of his "tactical" approach to politics, in which promises would be made and pledges solemnly signed but not necessarily meant—or at least supporters told they were not meant. The Mitchell principles, Adams had said, were the same; they were just a piece of paper. In riposte McKevitt and his supporters claimed that the antiviolence oath could not be compared to the Mitchell principles. While the Mitchell principles intimately touched upon matters in the IRA's constitution, the antiviolence oath had not. And so the argument went on, back and forth.

The two sides were deadlocked. A halfhearted attempt was made by the Executive to suggest a compromise. Sinn Fein should attend the Stormont talks on September 15, but only as Sinn Fein. Before signing the Mitchell principles, Army Council and other IRA delegates would formally resign from the IRA, which would then issue a public statement explaining why it repudiated Mitchell. The Army Council would acknowledge the efforts of Sinn Fein but emphasize that until Britain gave a formal promise to quit Ireland, the IRA would reserve the right to use armed struggle. This was a nonstarter and everyone knew it. Neither the British nor the Irish government was likely to accept such a dubious arrangement, and the unionists certainly would not— after all, the whole purpose of the exercise was to corral the IRA's hard men inside a peace settlement, and the move would stymie that. Adams and the Army Council recognized the proposal for what it was—a way of unseating them or destroying their strategy—and they turned it down flat.

With debate exhausted, the Executive formally informed the Army Council that it had by a vote of ten in favor, one against—Gerry Kelly, the only firm Army Council supporter on the Executive—made a ruling that the Mitchell principles offended the IRA constitution and that if any Volunteer signed them, this would be a breach of the IRA's most sacred rules. That having been done, there was really only one thing left. An extraordinary General Army Convention had to be called to decide who was in the right, the Executive or the Council. The Army Council readily agreed.

THE TASK of organizing the Convention was again given to Pat Doherty, but this time the County Donegal man had no problems discovering a secure venue, and he did so with commendable speed. The meeting was scheduled for mid-October in the Gweedore area, one of the most picturesque parts of County Donegal, only six or seven weeks after the decision to hold the Convention had been made. The fact that Doherty got the job gave the Adams camp an enormous advantage. Those who controlled the Convention controlled its timing, location, and all the logistical aspects of setting up the meeting. That advantage had lain with the dissident camp in 1996, but now it was with their enemies.

The Adams camp had effectively had the best part of a year to prepare for the meeting. When the Convention got under way, it soon became clear that they had used the period well. Under IRA rules delegates to an extraordinary Convention must, if physically possible, be the same delegates who attended the last Convention. This was based on the reasoning that if it was necessary to call an extraordinary Convention, it was most likely because of a problem that had arisen from its original meeting. It made sense that the same delegates should attend, delegates who would already be familiar with the issues. But many of the delegates who turned up in Gweedore had not been at the 1996 Convention and knew little about its wranglings and the various constitutional changes that it had approved.

Some delegates had been replaced, the result some said of promotions and demotions made since 1996. In one or two cases troublesome delegations had been replaced altogether. The Tyrone delegation, for instance, which in 1996 had declared a total lack of confidence in the Adams leadership, was completely new; the East Tyrone commander had been replaced as well. Another factor worked in favor of the peace camp. The argument between the Army Council and the Executive had been kept very secret. Most of the delegates were unaware even that there had been a dispute between them, never mind what the arguments were on either side.

The Executive had also made a fatal mistake when, at the August joint meeting with the Army Council, it suggested that Sinn Fein members of the IRA resign and then sign the Mitchell principles. This enabled the Army Council to accuse Executive members of attempting to stage a coup, a powerful argument in an organization where loyalty to the leadership was paramount. The Executive's suggestion that Sinn Fein representatives resign from the IRA was seized on by the Army Council as evidence that the dissidents, not satisfied with their victories at the 1996 Convention, were now trying to overthrow the IRA leadership. Their real aim, said the Army Council, was not to save the IRA's soul, as was claimed, but to take power themselves. Adams protested bitterly to the delegates: "They want me— me!—to resign from the Army."[10] The Executive was put on the defensive.

The advantage that derived from the decision to give the task of organizing the arrangements for the 1997 Convention to the Adams camp was soon evident. A large number of "guests," perhaps as many as a dozen, were given special permission to attend. This was the first Convention ever that allowed nondelegates to attend, and even though they could not vote, the fact that the guests were given speaking rights—and invariably they spoke in favor of the Adams strategy—added strongly to the impression that the Convention was heavily on the leadership's side. Their number included relatives of dead IRA heroes and venerable veterans like Joe Cahill and Joe B. O'Hagan, both former IRA leaders who had spent years in jail for the cause. Emotional speeches were given, promises made that there would be no sellouts, commitments to resign if there were. Others spoke of their faith and trust in the Adams-McGuinness leadership.

According to a detailed account of the 1997 Convention given to the author by two delegates, the Army Council had choreographed the transportation arrangements cleverly. The dissidents, some twenty or thirty in all, were all picked up together as one group, long after the rest of the delegates had arrived at the Convention. As the delegates already present awaited their arrival, they were quietly briefed to prepare themselves for a possible coup attempt by the Executive supporters. When the dissidents walked in, it was to a largely cold and unfriendly reception. With the dissidents isolated and the Convention full of leadership loyalists, McKevitt and his supporters faced certain defeat.

Once more the Convention lasted the entire night. According to one delegate it was a meeting of two halves. The first half saw Adams and his allies on the defensive as McKevitt and other dissidents spoke. The outgoing chairman of the Executive, Seamus McGrane, gave a lengthy speech detailing the four reasons behind the Executive's decision to call the Convention. These were the unconstitutionality of the Mitchell principles, the Army Council's failure to ratify the July cease-fire, the poor morale of IRA Volunteers caused by conflicting assurances from Army Council members about going back to war, and the Army Council's treatment of the Executive (see appendix 4).

McGrane's last complaint brought the Convention to angry verbal exchanges. McGrane accused the Army Council of deliberately withholding key documents from the Executive, not just peace process papers such as the Hume-Adams document but the minutes of the 1996 Convention, a document that would, he claimed, reveal the hostile mood of the delegates toward the idea of calling another cease-fire.

Martin McGuinness, he went on, had given the Executive an assurance that there would be no second sos in May, but "[w]e had only to wait a few weeks to see this commitment flounder." McGuinness rose to tell the delegates that McGrane had been wrong, that all the documents he referred to had been given to the Executive. In fact the Army Council, he claimed, had done all in its power to facilitate the dissidents. At this point McKevitt intervened to call McGuinness a liar. Tempers were up, lines were drawn.

The second half of the Convention went in Adams's favor. The Convention guests started to make their pro-leadership speeches, and other delegates joined in. Adams, who had dressed down for the Convention, forsaking his politician's suit for jeans and a T-shirt, began to relax visibly, as did other leaders. A key development had swung the Convention out of the dissidents' reach, and the Army Council knew it. The Belfast commander, Brian Gillen, had sat through the first half of the meeting in total silence. In 1996 he had been one of the most vocal critics of the leadership, accusing it of running down the IRA, but not this time. As the Convention reached its climax, the reason for his silence became clear. He had switched sides, abandoning the Executive dissidents and declaring his support for Adams and the cease-fire, in return for a secret promise of a seat on the new Army Council. At that point, with the influential Belfast commander on Adams's side, the battle was effectively over.

The Executive had formulated four motions based on the points contained in McGrane's speech, and the debate on the Convention floor developed into a dispute over whether the motions should be treated separately, as the Executive wanted, or amalgamated, as the Army Council wished. The vote was taken, and the Army Council won. The four resolutions were then voted down in one go. A separate motion declaring that the Army Council had the authority to grant special dispensation to the delegates at the Stormont talks also went through, clearing the way for Adams, McGuinness, and other IRA members to attend the political talks as Sinn Fein delegates. In each case the Army Council secured a comfortable 60–70 percent majority. The Executive had been thoroughly outmaneuvered.

It was almost over but not quite. Elections were held to the Executive and then to the Army Council. Brian Gillen's *volte-face* had not gone down well with the delegates. He failed to get elected to the Executive, and when the decision came to fill the Army Council, Adams had to nominate him from outside the ranks of the Executive. The elections also saw the fall of Kevin McKenna. The chief of staff had been lucky to get reelected to the Executive in 1996. He had been given the distasteful task of assuring the IRA rank and file in 1994 that the cease-fire rumors were false, and then, when the *sos* was called, it was McKenna, among others, who constantly had to assure the grassroots that it would soon end. He was reelected at the 1996 Convention by only a few votes. By 1997 McKenna's credibility with the rank and file had evaporated, and he made it back on the Executive only as a substitute. With Adams committed to promoting the apostate dissident, Brian Gillen, there was no room for McKenna on the Army Council. The Tyrone veteran had been a faithful and loyal servant of the Adams leadership, but once his usefulness was exhausted he was discarded. When rumors circulated afterward that he had been ousted because he disagreed with the cease-fire, Sinn Fein spin doctors spread the false story in the media that McKenna had quit because he had developed cancer. The story was concocted not so much for McKenna's benefit but to scotch suggestions that such a senior figure might be opposed to the Adams strategy.

Slab Murphy was elected the new chief of staff and took pity on his old friend. He made McKenna the new quartermaster general, a position from which he later resigned. At the time of writing, the Provisional IRA's longest-serving chief of staff was still living quietly in County Monaghan in virtual retirement, unable to exercise influence at the IRA's highest levels and shunned by former dissident colleagues. The post-1997 Army Council was even more to Adams's liking. Apart from himself and Martin McGuinness, it included Slab Murphy, Brian Keenan, Martin Ferris, Pat Doherty, and the new member, Brian Gillen. Adams now enjoyed a comfortable six-to-one majority, seven-to-nil now that Slab was all by himself and unlikely to kick over the traces.

As soon as the Army Council had been chosen, the substitutes joined the Executive. Once more there was an anti–Army Council majority on the body, although this had shrunk from a ten-to-two to a seven-to-five margin. The remaining dissident leaders—Seamus McGrane, Micky McKevitt, and Frank McGuinness—had been reelected, but it was obvious that they too would eventually follow McKenna into political oblivion. Two weeks after the Convention, on October 23, the new Executive met. McKevitt was the first to resign, citing the proposed acceptance of the Mitchell principles as his main reason. Five others followed, four of them, like McKevitt, members of GHQ staff and heads of department. The quartermaster's department was next. The Belfast QM, all the Southern Command QMs, and a good number of those on the Border joined the rebellion. Much of the vital engineering department followed Frank McGuinness. A split was now a reality, and within days moves were under way to form a new IRA. Its founders would call it Oglaigh na hEireann, but the media would christen it, predictably, the Real IRA.

An IRA split had been a virtual certainty from the moment that Adams embarked on the peace process, such was the scale of the departure from traditional IRA ideology that the enterprise implied. The only questions at issue were the timing, scale, and damage that the split would cause. The fact that it took so long to occur, that the fracture came after two cease-fires had been called, irreversible changes made to republican beliefs, and the scene set for a potentially definitive settlement, not just of the Troubles in Northern Ireland but of the ancient and historic Anglo-Irish conflict, was testimony to the skill and determination of Gerry Adams and his allies. By the time the dissidents decided to move against Adams, it was already too late. And as the IRA delegates made their way home from the 1997 Convention, Adams had, after fifteen long years, finally taken the Provisionals beyond the point of no return.

EIGHTEEN

The End Begins

The four men looked grayer and heavier than in their pictures, which was not surprising since the only photographs of the IRA's notorious Balcombe Street gang had been taken twenty-three years before in a London police station shortly after their arrest, and by definition such photographs are never flattering and rarely faithful. The four, Harry Duggan, Hugh Doherty, Eddie Butler, and Joe O'Connell, then all in their twenties, had orchestrated a wave of terror in London and the southeast of England in the mid-1970s, shooting and bombing their way around the country in a campaign that claimed sixteen lives, many of them the lives of uninvolved civilians. They were eventually arrested in 1975, after a house siege in a central London street that gave the gang its name, and after their trial, which in the circumstances was a mere formality, had spent the bulk of the subsequent quarter of a century in some of England's toughest and most impregnable prisons.

The crowd in the Library of the Royal Dublin Society's vast complex in that most Anglo-Irish section of the city, Ballsbridge, on Sunday, May 10, 1998, had little difficulty, however, in recognizing the men. Encouraged by the Sinn Fein leadership on the platform in front of them, they rose as one to give a rousing ovation as the four men struggled to make their way to the podium through the shoulder-slapping throng. The cheering, shouting, and clapping lasted for a full ten minutes. A wave of emotion swept the delegates to this special Sinn Fein Ard Fheis as the party's leaders, led by Gerry Adams, queued to embrace the IRA men. The rest of the world may have regarded the Balcombe Street gang as ruthless killers who had claimed their victims indiscriminately, but to the Provisionals these men were their own, "our Nelson Mandelas," said Adams later with no sense of impropriety or exaggeration.[1]

When finally the noise subsided, Adams and his colleagues knew that their problems were over. The special Ard Fheis would vote as they wanted it to and endorse the 1998 Good Friday Agreement, for to do so meant that the prison ordeal suffered by these men would be ended at last. To reject it would be to send them back to jail, possibly for many more years. The reason for this was a clause in the Good Friday Agreement that allowed for the release of all paramilitary prisoners within two years, but only if the deal was endorsed. Less than two hours later the debate was all over. By an overwhelming 94.6 percent majority—331 out of the 350 delegates—the Ard Fheis ratified the agreement and changed Sinn Fein's constitution to allow the party's members to take seats in a Northern Ireland parliament. Abstentionism in the Republic had been abandoned in 1986, and now, twelve years later, it was gone in the North. The unthinkable had become reality.

But appearances were deceptive. Adams had secured a majority, the scale of which would have done the Soviet dictator Joseph Stalin proud, but the Good Friday Agreement, which Sinn Fein had helped negotiate and was now recommending to its membership, had caught the Provisionals' grassroots by surprise, and hostility to it was deep and widespread. The cause of this anguish was the agreement's centerpiece, a new Assembly at Stormont outside Belfast, which would have the task of governing Northern Ireland's one and a half million divided people. The realization that their leaders had put their names to such a proposal confused and dismayed many in the IRA and Sinn Fein. These were, after all, organizations in which antagonism toward any parliament at Stormont was so deeply embedded that it was almost in the genes. The parliament in Belfast was the preeminent symbol of unionist bigotry in their eyes, and even though the Good Friday Agreement had stipulated that the new government would have to be a power-sharing one, in which Sinn Fein would have a place as of right, the idea still stuck in many republican throats. A similar power-sharing administration had been set up in 1974, yet the Provisionals had opposed that, arguing that it only reformed and put an acceptable face on partition, and here were some of the same leaders who had resisted that arrangement then, asking them now to back something very similar.

Not for the first time in recent republican history, it was Sinn Fein, not the IRA, that threatened to cause the leadership the greatest problems. An IRA Convention, held a few days beforehand, had comfortably backed Adams's strategy, but in the context of the convincing defeat of the dissidents at the previous fall's convention, that was not surprising. The leadership's control over the IRA was by now complete and dissent virtually nonexistent. Sinn Fein, though, was a different matter. It was supposed to be a democratic body in which debate, argument, and dissent were encouraged, and for some IRA members unwilling to challenge military authority, the party's forums provided an opportunity to challenge orthodoxies more safely while wearing a different hat.

Ever conscious of the need to step onto firm rocks and not lily pads, Adams had arranged a first, special Ard Fheis some ten days or so after the agreement on April 10, Good Friday, had been finalized. It provided a valuable opportunity to test the waters. No decision was reached at the Ard Fheis about the agreement, no attempt made by the Sinn Fein leadership to force through an endorsement of the pact. The conference became a listening exercise. It was a wise move. At the suggestion of the author, the *Sunday Tribune* conducted a survey of opinion among the conference audience, and the result made dispiriting reading for the party's chiefs for it showed that they were well short of the support needed to endorse the settlement. Some 140 of the 1,000 people attending the conference, delegates and sympathizers, agreed to answer questions, and a total of 56 percent of them were evenly divided between outright rejection of the Good Friday Agreement and an unwillingness to express an opinion. These don't knows in all probability disguised many who were really opposed but who could not bring themselves to admit as much to the media and risk being identified. Only 44 percent backed the deal, a figure that was well short of the two-thirds majority Adams needed to enter the new Stormont Assembly. Some 58 percent objected to taking seats at Stormont or again would not reveal their views, while only 42 percent said they were prepared to enter the North's new parliament. A similar proportion, 42 percent, said the agreement was not worth the IRA's thirty years of armed struggle, and 20 percent refused to tell the newspaper's pollsters what they thought about that issue.[2] This cross-section of Sinn Fein opinion was, at best, unenthusiastic about the deal their leaders had brought home. Defeat, or at least a damaging split, was staring Adams and his colleagues in the face.

So it was that when the special Ard Fheis reconvened three weeks later, on May 10, the British and Irish governments had arranged for the wholesale temporary release of IRA prisoners especially for the occasion. Twenty-seven prisoners were set free for the day, given special parole to attend the conference in a bid to buttress the Adams leadership. The Balcombe Street gang had been transferred from England to Portlaoise prison southwest of Dublin some months before, in a move designed to strengthen the Sinn Fein leadership, and were set free for that day by order of Bertie Ahern's office. Tony Blair played his part as well. The IRA's officer commanding in the Maze prison, Padraig Wilson, was let out, as was Martina Anderson, convicted of conspiring to bomb England and since sent to join women IRA prisoners in Maghaberry jail, on the outskirts of Belfast. Both spoke up strongly for the Adams strategy. So did others held in British jails, including activists who had been recently convicted of IRA attacks in England and sentenced to brutally long terms, some for as much as thirty-five or forty years. The presence of so many IRA felons at the Ard Fheis served to remind the delegates that if they failed to support the deal in sufficient numbers, as the *Sunday Tribune* poll indicated was a real possibility, they would effectively be sending their comrades back to jail. If they voted for it, people who had already given so much for the IRA's cause would once again taste freedom. It was an exquisitely crafted piece of political management, and it worked wonderfully well.

THE SCENE was one most observers of the Troubles in Northern Ireland thought they would never see. It was the late afternoon of April 10, 1998, a month before the historic Ard-Fheis gathering in Dublin, and the party delegations involved in the months of talks had gathered in the main chamber of the stuffy, overheated office block in Belfast known as Stormont Buildings, where the negotiations had been based, to hear the talks chairman, the former U.S. Senate leader George Mitchell, offer his congratulations. The core of what would soon be christened the Good Friday Agreement had been fashioned in the early hours of the morning, with Bill Clinton working the phone from Washington, urging everyone to go the final mile. But daytime had been punctuated by crises, mostly caused by unionists unhappy at the loose language on IRA decommissioning. A leading unionist had walked out, but an intervention from Tony Blair put the show back on the road. Now the party leaders and their delegations sat side by side, Adams and McGuinness a few feet away from the unionist leader, David Trimble, with John Hume and the SDLP delegation sandwiched between them. The idea that such people could share a room would once have been dismissed with a laugh; the thought that they could all agree on a settlement, not even deemed worthy of consideration.

It took only six months, from the IRA Convention of October 1997 to April 10, 1998, to negotiate the Good Friday Agreement. By the standards of Ireland's long and troubled history, that was a remarkably short period in which to complete such a complex set of negotiations, and by the standards of the Northern Ireland Troubles, which by that time had claimed 3,588 lives,[3] seen tens of thousands of people wounded and injured, and lasted longer than any other post–Second World War conflict except that in the Middle East, the achievement was nothing short of miraculous. The agreement was testimony both to the skill with which the Adams leadership had seen off opponents within the IRA and to the determination to finish the journey started so many years earlier by Adams and Father Reid. It quite simply could not have happened at all, never mind in such a short period of time, without the proactive cooperation of the Sinn Fein and IRA leadership.

The fact that at the core of the Adams-Reid enterprise lay an acceptance by the republican leadership of the consent principle predetermined the nature and shape of the political settlement. When Gerry Adams and Martin McGuinness signed the Mitchell principles and then led the Sinn Fein delegation into all-party negotiations in Belfast on September 9, 1997, their rhetoric reverberated with pledges "to smash the Union." [4] The reality was very different. The process begun by Gerry Adams and Father Reid meant recognizing the existence of the Northern Ireland state, and the Sinn Fein leadership knew that. The deep hostility of their supporters to this meant, however, that the leaders were obliged to carefully manage their base in regard to the talks in the same way that they had managed the process at other crucial points, not least in the matter of IRA cease-fires. They devised two positions—one for the consumption of the IRA and Sinn Fein base and one for the rest of the world. Once again, it would be the version prepared for those outside their ranks which would prevail.

The British and Irish governments also knew what the parameters of any settlement would have to be, and so in January 1998, four months before the deadline for a deal, they published a "Heads of Agreement" document, outlining the necessary ingredients of the settlement and the principles that would underlie it.

The principle of consent ran through the proposals like a golden thread. The principle was the cornerstone of the sixteen-year-long Reid-Adams diplomacy, and now it was given pride of place in the new proposed settlement. Other elements of that secret process were present. The 1920 Government of Ireland Act would be repealed in accordance with the secret British offer made to Reid and Adams which redefined British withdrawal. Instead of decamping from Northern Ireland physically, Britain would agree not to interfere or dictate the shape of any settlement. Scrapping the 1920 legislation, which had given the British parliament a veto over Northern Ireland's affairs, gave practical effect to that pledge.

The centerpiece of the proposal was a new Assembly at Stormont outside Belfast, the site of the old unionist-dominated parliament. Elected by proportional representation, the Assembly would choose a power-sharing government, its members drawn from the major parties, and there would be a new North-South ministerial council to foster cooperation between Northern Ireland and the Republic. The proposal seemed moderate and reasonable to the rest of the world, and indeed very similar ideas had formed the basis of the cease-fire agreement between the Adams camp and Bertie Ahern's government in Dublin in the summer of 1997. It shocked grassroots republicans, forcing Sinn Fein leaders into hard-line rhetoric. The reason was simple. In the eyes of IRA and Sinn Fein supporters, the existence of a parliament in Belfast was anathema and symbolized British rule; the notion that their leaders in Sinn Fein could actually participate in such a body was simply too fantastic to be taken seriously. With their supporters thoroughly alarmed, Adams, McGuinness, and the Army Council all issued statements condemning the proposals, terming them a sop to unionists. Sinn Fein published its own counterproposal, which echoed traditional republican demands for an all-Ireland government. This was familiar and comforting to the grassroots but as unlikely a basis for a deal as could be imagined. The barrage of rhetorical opposition to the "Heads of Agreement" paper continued through February and March 1998, reaching such a pitch that many republicans, and a large section of the Irish media, were convinced that the interparty talks were doomed to fail.

In reality Sinn Fein did negotiate on the basis of the "Heads of Agreement" document, as it was always going to, and when, on April 10, 1998— Good Friday—agreement was announced on the shape of the settlement, the only people genuinely surprised at the similarity between the Good Friday Agreement and the document so resolutely rejected by Sinn Fein in January were the republican grassroots. They had been presented with a fait accompli, in much the same way as they had been presented with two IRA cease-fires, and there was little they could do about it.

Implementing the Good Friday settlement was a slow and tortuous business, punctuated by crises that never seemed to get so serious as to threaten the agreement itself but that happened with sufficient regularity that the demise of the deal was routinely predicted and often expected. That it never did collapse was, once again, due in no small measure to the determination of the Adams leadership in Sinn Fein that this should not happen. Bit by bit, the pieces of the agreement were assembled, each one haggled over and occasionally the cause of a brief outburst of violence or political instability that it seemed might topple the entire deal but never did. Eventually, by November 1999, eighteen months after the Good Friday Agreement had been reached, the power-sharing executive had been set up, the ministers selected, and the North–South ministerial council put in place.

The choice of two of those ministers was a measurement of just how far the IRA and Sinn Fein had traveled since that fall day in 1982 when Father Alec Reid had visited Gerry Adams. The new minister of education, charged with ensuring the proper and efficient schooling of Northern Ireland's young people, was Martin McGuinness, the chairman of the Army Council and, until a few months before, the IRA's Northern commander. The minister of health was Bairbre de Brun, a Dublin-born activist who had joined Sinn Fein because of sympathy for the H Block protest. Once pledged to destroy the Northern Ireland state by violence, the two republicans now sat at the cabinet table, technically ministers of the British crown, an elbow's length away from the leader of unionism and the new first minister, David Trimble. Within months plans for a new policing service, to be called the Police Service of Northern Ireland (PSNI), were unveiled. Sinn Fein had initially demanded the disbandment of the hated RUC but now called for the full implementation of the new policing scheme, effectively the old force in a new, reformed, and fairer guise. It was an intimation that the day might not be long off when republicans would join the new service and give more tangible expression to the meaning behind their participation in the institutions of Northern Ireland. The Provisionals' long journey from war to peace, from revolution to constitutionalism, from odium to respectabilty, was almost complete. Only one issue was left to resolve.

BY ONE ACCOUNT, 150 Colombian policemen and soldiers were waiting at the Bogotá airport for the three republicans to arrive and take connecting flights to Europe[5] that day, August 12, 2001, and it was clear they were acting on excellent intelligence.[6] When the men got off their flight from the southern lowland town of San Vicente del Caguan, their pale skins marked them out as foreigners and the police moved in quickly to arrest them. The eldest of the trio, James Monaghan, had just been named in the British parliament as a member of the IRA's GHQ staff. Martin McAuley had been shot and wounded by the RUC in a 1982 undercover operation aimed at catching a bombing team in County Armagh. The third member of the group was Niall Connolly, a Dubliner with no direct links to the IRA but who was later named as Sinn Fein's man in Havana, the party's unofficial ambassador to the Fidel Castro regime.

The arrests set off a flurry of speculation about the reasons for their presence in this part of Central America, and before long they were being linked to the FARC (Revolutionary Armed Forces of Colombia) rebels of southern Colombia, an armed Marxist movement with ties, so its enemies alleged, to the lucrative cocaine trade. Soon stories appeared in the British and Irish media claiming the three had been on an expedition to trade IRA military know-how for Colombian cash. The IRA had never been shy of fostering relations with fellow revolutionary groups around the world. The long liaison with Colonel Qaddafi in Libya, culminating in the ill-fated *Eksund* expedition, was undoubtedly the most notorious of these foreign adventures, but over the years the IRA had forged links with various groups in Europe, notably the Basque separatists, Palestinians of one hue or another, the ANC in South Africa, and groups in South and Central America, particularly in El Salvador, whose own peace process the Provisionals had observed with interest. There was nothing unusual about having a relationship with FARC.

The real reason for the expedition to FARC's stronghold may never be known, but the effect on the peace process of the Colombian "caper," as one American diplomat called the affair, was dramatic, compounded a month later by the rage against all forms of terrorism that swept the United States in the wake of Osama bin Laden's onslaught against New York and Washington. Within weeks, pressure from the Bush White House and Adams's powerful friends in corporate and congressional Irish-America were to succeed where the British and Irish had failed. Over three years had passed since Sinn Fein had agreed to "influence" the IRA in the direction of disarmament, but no weapons had been destroyed. The British and Irish governments had demanded decommissioning as a rite of passage into constitutional politics, and so had the unionists, increasingly angered that the release of republican prisoners and the renaming of their beloved RUC had brought no balancing concession from the IRA. Now, finally and ironically, it was the United States—once the key part of Adams's pan-nationalist strategy—that forced the issue to a conclusion.

The republican leadership had been sending conflicting and confusing signals about decommissioning for at least the previous five years. The Army Council chairman Martin McGuinness had, for example, suggested to the decommissioning inquiry headed by George Mitchell as far back as late 1996 that disarmament could be done voluntarily and by the paramilitary groups themselves. Two years later, Padraig Wilson, the OC of IRA prisoners in the Maze, gave an interview to the *Financial Times* expanding on this, saying that moves could be made by the IRA in parallel with the implementation of the Good Friday Agreement—as long as it was done voluntarily.[7] At an IRA Convention held two months later, in December 1998, the Adams leadership succeeded in scrapping changes to the IRA's constitution introduced by the dissidents at the 1996 Convention, including the vital amendment that took away the Army Council's powers to negotiate on weapons. Adams and his allies argued for the wholesale elimination of the amended constitution, on the grounds that it had been contrived by people who had now left the IRA, and the effect of this, possibly unnoticed by the delegates, was to free the leadership's hands on weapons.[8] During the Good Friday Agreement talks, a senior Sinn Fein delegate had assured the British and Irish governments that decommissioning would happen,[9] and much of the latter part of those talks was taken up by a dispute over how long it would take, with Sinn Fein holding out for five years and the unionists demanding immediate decommissioning. The two-year figure eventually agreed on was a compromise. As the Good Friday deal was gradually implemented, an independent arms body was set up, headed by a Canadian general. The IRA agreed to nominate members to this body and sent along Brian Keenan as its interlocutor.

Taken together, all these moves indicated a willingness to eventually destroy weapons, but the Adams leadership had an internal constituency to address and reassure, and so a completely different message was relayed to it. In this regard the pledge from the IRA leadership never to decommission, given repeatedly to military activists and Sinn Fein members, played a vital role in selling the peace process as a whole, just as sending republicans to Colombia sent the same message. As long as the IRA held on to its weapons, the leadership's claim that the process was merely tactical, and that armed struggle could and would be resumed if necessary, was invested with credibility. Going back on that pledge meant not only that the grassroots had been misled about the inviolability of IRA weapons but that they had been sold a bill of goods in regard to the entire peace process. Some figures like Gerry Adams had gone further, assuring colleagues in the IRA leadership in the summer of 1997 that decommissioning would not occur, because it would be the issue that would cause the unionists or the British to break the process and leave the IRA free to resume armed struggle in politically advantageous circumstances. To strengthen this perception, the IRA issued a series of statements, carefully and ambiguously worded to be sure, but which nonetheless ruled out decommissioning. Senior figures like Martin McGuinness, meanwhile, gave briefings to selected journalists to drive home this message.

The Adams leadership had another reason not to decommission with any speed, and that was the leverage that possession of its still substantial arsenals gave the IRA during the negotiations and implementation of the Good Friday Agreement. Whoever had betrayed the *Eksund* in November 1987 lost the IRA some 150 tons of heavy weaponry and forced the organization to effectively abandon the planned "Tet offensive." But another 150 tons of guns and explosives had already been successfully smuggled into Ireland by that point; 105 tons had come in on the *Villa* alone in October 1986. When the peace process was properly launched, Adams and his colleagues still had plenty of weaponry to negotiate away, especially large quantities of the powerful explosive Semtex, which the British were particularly eager to see put out of harm's way. A traitor somewhere in the IRA's upper reaches saw to it that the Libyan connection did not give the organization the military edge its leaders had once hoped for, but it strengthened Adams's negotiating hand nevertheless during the peace process.

In the months following the setting up of the Executive in the winter of 1999, one attempt after another to achieve decommissioning faltered, although each time the IRA edged appreciably closer to the point of no return. The issue was enfeebling the agreement, however. The Executive had to be suspended again and again, while David Trimble's authority as Ulster unionist leader was steadily undermined. More critically, his support was leaching to the extreme and wilder anti-agreement sections of unionism, notably to the Reverend Ian Paisley's Democratic Unionist Party, which wrested seats at Westminster away from Trimble's party. The center ground upon which the agreement was built was crumbling. The two governments meanwhile could not decide whether Adams was trying to use the unionists to break the agreement, whether his private pleas that the IRA was just not ready to decommission were true, or whether he was just extracting as many concessions as he could before finally delivering. By the late summer of 2001, the matter was becoming critical. Once again the Good Friday Agreement was in suspension and needed but a nudge to send it over the precipice.

So when the Colombia Three, as Sinn Fein dubbed them, were arrested, the pressure to decommission intensified, applied primarily by key figures in the United States. The discovery of the republican trio in one of America's strategic backyards angered and embarrassed many of Gerry Adams's American allies and influential friends, few of whom were impressed by the Provisionals' efforts in Ireland to disown the men or to claim that the trio were eco-tourists. Once again there was a suspicion that they might have been hoodwinked by the Sinn Fein leader. Typical was Bill Flynn, chairman of the National Committee on American Foreign Policy, who had organized

Adams's first trip to New York in 1994 and taken huge risks fostering the peace process at a time when many others were deeply skeptical of Adams. Flynn, the chairman of Mutual of America, one of the world's largest insurance corporations, issued a testily worded statement making clear his disapproval of what had happened. "The Colombia situation is the greatest puzzle that I have seen in the entire 10 or 15 years that I have been involved in the north of Ireland," he said. "I don't understand it. I disassociate myself from it. It frightens Americans of Irish heritage that there should be any connection."[10] The only way the IRA could salvage the situation was to decommission, he added.

Pressure came from another direction, one which in the past had usually been a source of comfort and support to republicans when Bill Clinton was the tenant. But the White House now had a new occupant, and George W. Bush had none of Clinton's sentimental attachment to the Irish peace process and no obligation to Irish-American voters. Bush quickly signaled a change of tack toward Ireland, and in a meaningful way. Clinton had kept the Irish peace process very close to him. Day-to-day management was handled by the National Security Council (NSC), based in the White House. The NSC's top officials, people like Anthony Lake and Nancy Soderberg, would meet regularly with Adams and other Sinn Fein people, and Clinton often intervened personally, particularly at times of crisis like the Good Friday talks, when he repeatedly phoned the key party leaders to charm them or twist their arms. Clinton had also infuriated the British and the unionists by granting Adams a visitor's visa in 1994 when the Sinn Fein leader was still a pariah.

Bush swung back the pendulum. Responsibility for the peace process was returned to the State Department, where it had been before Clinton took office, and a signal sent out that Washington would henceforth be much more evenhanded in its dealings with the Northern Ireland parties. The unionists could no longer say that they were denied a hearing on Pennsylvania Avenue. Furthermore the Colombian episode had raised hackles in the White House, and hostility toward the IRA for meddling in matters that deeply concerned America's foreign policymakers was palpable. The United States sought the extinction of FARC, suspecting it of fueling much of Colombia's cocaine trade to America, and here was an outrageous example of the IRA's seemingly giving FARC aid and assistance. The September 11 attacks on the World Trade Center and Pentagon had meanwhile given a new, uncompromising edge to Bush's war against foreign terrorism. The mood in the White House was such that few distinctions were being drawn between one terrorist grouping and another. If the IRA did not move on decommissioning, it risked angering this new president.

Bush's point man on Northern Ireland, Ambassador Richard Haass, was in Dublin when the news came in that Osama bin Laden's deadlier version of human bombs had toppled the twin towers of the World Trade Center in a cascade of death and dust. By midafternoon, as the full scale of the Al Qaeda assault on the United States was becoming clear, Haass was being driven across the border to Belfast, where he was due to sit down with Gerry Adams to discuss the Colombian escapade. A former director of Foreign Policy Studies at the Brookings Institution and a prolific writer on American diplomacy, Haass had been drafted into the State Department by the Bush administration to give foreign policy a conservative, less interventionist bent. He had already signaled that, as far as Ireland was concerned, the laxity and tolerance toward the IRA of the Clinton days had ended. On that September 11 afternoon he was in no mood to mince his words. It was by all accounts a tough and direct encounter between the American diplomat and the Provisional leadership. It ended with Gerry Adams and his colleagues in no doubt about what the White House wanted to happen. The only way to dispel doubts about the IRA's bona fides, doubts that had deepened because of Colombia, was to decommission. For the IRA, as for many others, it was time to choose sides.

The move finally came six weeks later, on October 28, 2001, in a statement from the Army Council confirming that weapons had been put "beyond use." If Adams had meant the decommissioning issue to bring down the peace process and to give the IRA the excuse to resume its war, as he had once told the IRA Executive, there was no sign of it in the statement. Quite the reverse. "This unprecedented move," explained the IRA statement, "is to save the peace process and to persuade others of our genuine intentions."[11]

It was a historic moment, recognized and welcomed as such by George Bush, Tony Blair, and Bertie Ahern and lauded in scores of newspaper editorials around the world in the following days. The *Washington Post* called the act of decommissioning "a brave gesture,"[12] while the *New York Times* suggested that now "an enduring peace may be possible."[13] The *Irish Times* described the IRA's move as "far-reaching" and "profoundly symbolic,"[14] while the *Times* of London said it was "the most decisive step in a lengthy journey" taken by the republicans.[15]

Never before in the long and bloody history of Anglo-Irish conflict had an Irish insurgent group voluntarily given up its weapons for destruction, even self-destruction, at the behest of its opponents. When de Valera recognized the inevitability of defeat in the terrible Irish civil war and called a halt to the IRA's campaign in May 1923, the organization was ordered to bury its arms, not to destroy them. Similarly when the 1956–62 Border Campaign ended, Ruairi O Bradaigh's last order to the IRA units as chief of staff was to "dump arms." The unspoken message was clear. The guns were being put away but only for the time being; the war against Britain would be resumed when the conditions improved. That was the significance of the Provisional IRA's action on October 23, 2001. It said the opposite: not just that this campaign had been brought to an end but that the age-old conflict between Irish republicanism and Britain was over. The need for guns, in other words, had disappeared.

After nineteen years of difficult, secret, and often dangerous diplomacy, Northern Ireland had finally arrived at a sort of peace. A new government, fairer than anything that had preceded it, was striving to make its roots grow, and Northern Ireland's deeply divided population was struggling to come to terms with a new political order, one in which each side had been obliged to abandon some strongly held beliefs in return for a chance at building stability. The debate about who had won the peace – whether in particular Gerry Adams had led his supporters to a spectacular political and electoral triumph or whether the IRA's war had been sold out – was only beginning. Although distrust and violence, albeit on a smaller scale, still stalked Northern Ireland, there could be little doubt that with its first act of decommissioning, the IRA had signaled the winding down of its long and bloody war against Britain.

NINETEEN

The Midas Touch

It is one of the great unknowable unknowns of modern Irish history. If the arrests in Colombia and the devastation of the September 11 attacks in America had not come together to make any other course of action unthinkable, would the IRA have begun to decommission its weapons as early as it did, in October 2001, just a few weeks after the twin towers of the World Trade Center collapsed in clouds of dust and death? Or would it have waited for a more opportune moment, one that would perhaps have brought the greatest political or electoral windfall to the IRA's political partners, Sinn Fein?

That the IRA would have had to begin disarming at some point had been the *sine qua non* of the peace process since at least the autumn of 1994 and the immediate effect of the September 11 attacks was to bring a sudden end to some five years of quibbling and prevarication. But it hadn't always been such a dominating or difficult issue. The surprising aspect of the early, pre-cease-fire years of the peace process was the extent to which disarming the IRA did not figure, or figured so slightly in the various debates and negotiations. And when the cease-fire did come in August 1994 it was clearly Gerry Adams's hope and expectation, at least as expressed to this writer,[1] that the British and Irish governments, if not the unionists, would recognize that the demand for decommissioning was so potentially destabilizing to his project that they would shelve it, at least to a point far off in the future when it could cause the least internal disquiet. But IRA actions in the weeks after the declaration of the 1994 cease-fire forced the question to the fore and transformed decommissioning into an unavoidable and, for some, a mandatory test of the IRA's bona fides.

Had the IRA kept to the letter and spirit of its cease-fire, it is possible that decommissioning could have been put off almost indefinitely, but the way the peace process strategy was constructed and sold to their IRA leadership colleagues by Adams and his allies determined otherwise. Unable and unwilling to spell out the huge ideological compromises waiting for the IRA and Sinn Fein down the road and obliged to clothe the process instead in hardline, republican garments, the ever-cautious Adams leadership had been forced to concede ground to Army Council colleagues, who insisted that the IRA be allowed to keep its war machinery in working order after the cessation began. The combined and particular effect of subsequent IRA activity undermined faith and trust in the cease-fire outside republican ranks and so the willingness of the IRA to put away its weapons for good became for many people a much more reliable and palpable index of its intentions than the IRA's words or those of its political leaders, however seductive and enticing they might have sounded.

While the British and Irish governments led by Tony Blair and Bertie Ahern did not ever, for their own reasons, regard decommissioning in quite this light, it was a vital test for unionists who would be asked, and were expected, to share power with the IRA's political wing, Sinn Fein. It was clear, especially after the Good Friday Agreement had been negotiated and Sinn Fein had signaled that it would indeed take seats in government, that no unionist leader could or would agree to sit at the same cabinet table as Sinn Fein unless the most tangible expression of the threat of renewed violence, the IRA's stocks of explosives and weapons, was being removed from the equation. But once decommissioning had been pushed to the top of the agenda and linked to Sinn Fein's participation in the power-sharing Executive, the issue assumed the potential either to destroy or secure the peace process. From thereon the question of whether or not the IRA would decommission its weapons and, if so, when the process would be completed and how convincingly it would be done, dominated Northern Ireland and Anglo-Irish politics for over a decade, and in a way no other issue had.

On the surface a debate raged over whether the Adams leadership would or would not be destabilized—and the peace lost or strengthened—if the demand was pressed too hard. It was a sharply divisive debate, in the media, in government and, most damagingly, in Northern Ireland society where it helped widen sectarian faultlines. The Sinn Fein and IRA spinmachine fed furiously into this debate, skilfully recruiting many in the media and government to the view that for Adams and his allies, IRA decommissioning was a bridge too far. But the available evidence strongly suggests that all this was a canard, constructed for strategic reasons. The truth was that very soon after the Good Friday Agreement was ratified, the principal obstacle in the way of the Adams leadership undertaking decommissioning was removed with minimal internal dissent and from thereon the Army Council, which Adams utterly dominated, could have started to disarm whenever it wished. But instead of starting the process and shoring up the power-sharing agreement and their unionist partners in government, the Provo leadership decided to use decommissioning to their advantage. By employing delays in delivering disarmament and withholding transparency from the process—and justifying this on the grounds of internal opposition—the Adams leadership divided and destabilized mainstream unionism, rendered their SDLP rivals almost irrelevant, and polarized Northern Ireland politics to the advantage of the extremes. But most important of all, the way decommissioning was manipulated enormously assisted Sinn Fein's bid to become the master of the Northern nationalist house and a new, rising electoral power in Southern politics.

GERRY ADAMS and his colleagues in the leaderships of the IRA and Sinn Fein did not achieve these electoral goals unaided. Elections in Britain and the south of Ireland in the summer of 1997, a year or so before the Good Friday Agreement, had brought new governments to both countries and with them significantly positive consequences for Sinn Fein's peace process strategy, not least in the way the republican leadership was thereafter able to handle decommissioning.

In the Irish Republic, the Fianna Fail party, whose roots lay in the anti-treaty IRA of 1921, combined with the Progressive Democrats to replace the so-called Rainbow Coalition of Fine Gael, Labour, and Democratic Left. The Fine Gael party, whose leader John Bruton was taoiseach, was historically ill disposed to physical-force republicanism and both Bruton and the leaders of Democratic Left, who could trace the lineage of their party back to the Official IRA and the often violent and bloody split with the Provisionals in 1969–70, viewed Sinn Fein's leaders with a baleful eye and their conversion to peaceful politics with barely disguised skepticism. Under the controlling hand of the Rainbow Coalition, the peace process, from Sinn Fein's point of view, had experienced near-fatal turbulence. The new Fianna Fail-dominated government led by Bertie Ahern was, however, a horse of an entirely different color. Fianna Fail was ideally positioned to assist the Provisional leadership to lead their people out of warfare. Not only was Ahern's party on the same ideological waveband as Sinn Fein but some seventy years earlier Fianna Fail had made a very similar journey away from violence. Ahern and his colleagues could recognize something of themselves—or at least their predecessors—in Adams and his supporters. But there was another compelling reason to indulge the Provisional leaders. The peace process was hugely popular in the Irish Republic and Gerry Adams was its charismatic architect. As Adams's approval ratings in the Republic soared, electoral support for Sinn Fein began to swell dramatically and Fianna Fail would increasingly find itself in competition with Sinn Fein for the same constitutional and populist republican vote. While some foresaw the day when the two parties would merge, for the time being they were both rivals and putative coalition government partners. Ahern would need to tread carefully in his dealings with Sinn Fein, especially over decommissioning, for fear of alienating their common electoral base to the Provos' advantage.

But the more significant political change was in London, where Tony Blair had led New Labour to a stunning landslide victory over John Major's Conservatives. Whereas the Major government's instinctive distaste for dealing with the Provisionals was reinforced by its slim parliamentary majority and consequent dependence on the support of unionist MPs, Blair had a huge 180-seat majority in the House of Commons and the freedom to act as he wished. It soon became clear that, despite maternal roots in the planter, Protestant community of County Donegal and his embrace of the "Irish unity only with consent" principle, Blair's sympathies lay more with Irish nationalists, as did many of his generation in Britain who had grown up with the "Troubles" and watched events across the Irish Sea with a mixture of guilt and horror. A speech he gave in Belfast at a critical moment in the peace process offered a revealing insight into his mindset: "For years", he told his audience, "nationalist [Northern] Ireland felt treated as second-class citizens. Let me cross out the word "felt". They were treated as second-class citizens."[2] Later he would compare Muslim terrorists who had bombed London in July 2005 not to the IRA bombers who had twice devastated the City of London and slaughtered innocent revellers in bars in Birmingham and Guildford but to "the Protestant bigot who murders a Catholic in Northern Ireland".[3] No other British prime minister had pinned colors to the mast in such a way, but then no other prime minister spent as much of his tenure in Downing Street dealing with Northern Ireland as Blair would.

While the approach of the Major government to the Provos was characterized by caution, suspicion and grudgingly slow recognition of the IRA's and Sinn Fein's bona fides, Blair, aided by his chief of staff, Jonathan Powell, took a different tack. If the Major government could be accused of overusing the stick in its dealings with the Provisionals, then Blair and Powell faced the charge of proffering the carrot too often and too easily. In particular Blair appeared to have accepted almost uncritically the view that the project crafted by Gerry Adams was a delicately balanced, vulnerable creation that could be thrown out of kilter in an instant if the IRA's hard men wished. Integral to this approach was the belief that the IRA could sustain a return to war, notwithstanding all the radically altered circumstances on the ground. While other observers concluded that between them the ravages of time on IRA capabilities, the impact of the Al Qaeda attacks on September 11, the complete control over the IRA exercised by the Adams leadership, the weakness of his opponents and the likelihood that renewed violence would exact punishment from the Catholic electorate suggested otherwise, the Blair government seemed to differ. One American participant in the peace process offered the view that Blair's priority in dealing with the IRA was to eradicate even the smallest risk that the IRA might again devastate London with huge Canary Wharf-size bombs, especially when Britain also faced a threat from Islamic jihadists. Indulging Adams and sacrificing politicians like Unionist leader David Trimble, he added, was in Downing Street's view a small price to pay for Blair's peace of mind.[4] Despite accumulating evidence that the IRA neither had the ability to deliver Canary Wharf-type bombs nor wished to resume armed struggle, Blair and Powell persevered in the view that if Adams's leadership and the peace process were to be preserved, then movement could not be much faster than that judged prudent by the Provisionals' own chiefs, and was best achieved through inducements and concessions, even by quos often given in the absence of any quids. Side deals with the Provisional leadership, extra sweeteners to seal agreement, became a permanent feature of all-party negotiations under Blair's watch. In one sense the British prime minister's approach recognized that Adams was selling the IRA short and that he needed cover to complete the task of ending its war, but in another way the Blair–Powell doctrine was tailor-made for the Provisionals' post-September 11 strategy of manipulating decommissioning for political and electoral gain.

WITHOUT A doubt the peace process journey would have been much less problematic and arduous for the IRA, the risk of internal schism minimized dramatically, if all the other parties to the process had accepted that the best way of obtaining decommissioning was not to make it an issue but to regard it as something that would evolve naturally with the implementation of the Good Friday Agreement and the passage of time. At one level the Provos had reason to hope—if not expect—that something like this might have been possible. In the long history of Ireland's often violent quest for independence and self-determination, republicans had never been obliged to give up their weapons before being allowed to enjoy the fruits of peace. To the contrary, the precedents, especially recent ones, showed that governments in both parts of Ireland had either not made or pressed the demand or had tolerated the IRA merely burying or dumping its arms after a campaign had ended. In 1921 the British government of Lloyd George agreed the terms of a cease-fire and began settlement talks with republicans without decommissioning. This is also what had happened at the conclusion of the Irish civil war in May 1923 when the IRA's Chief of Staff, Frank Aiken, had called a cease-fire and ordered volunteers to "dump arms." Three years later de Valera broke with Sinn Fein and set up Fianna Fail, bringing the bulk of IRA units, along with their "dumped" weapons, with him, and when he took his new party into the Dail a year later the absence of decommissioning was no bar to their entry. Likewise, when the IRA campaign of 1956–62 ended, the organization's weapons were dumped and within a short time the hard-line unionist government led by Lord Brookeborough agreed to release IRA internees and prisoners. The fact that the IRA held on to its weapons was no impediment to this. In practice the IRA's opponents were happy to accept the organization's defeat and declined to insist upon its humiliation.

It was the acrid whiff of surrender accompanying the concept of decommissioning that gave the Provisionals another reason to hope that the peace process parties, particularly the governments, would soft-pedal the issue. The word itself conjured up the image of defeated soldiers laying their guns at the feet of a gloating, victorious enemy before being marched off to a prison camp, and that was the last impression that the Sinn Fein leadership wished to promote. The governments shared the view that a disarming process that implied surrender could be fatal to the Adams project and it is one reason why they and the IRA preferred the phrase "putting arms beyond use" to describe the process. The success of Adams's years of manoeuvering and edging his movement into the peace process was vitally dependent on his followers accepting the notion that what was happening was a tactical ploy consistent with the IRA's traditional goals and not a strategic shift that meant accepting all that they had been pledged to destroy. Ideally, being allowed to keep their weapons and letting them rot away in dumps—"trust in rust" as the phrase had it—was the best way of ensuring the fealty of the IRA rank and file. Accusations that Adams and his allies had engineered a sell-out would be considerably strengthened if the IRA gave up its weapons.

While the Sinn Fein leadership hoped that the governments would not press the disarmament issue too forcefully, decommissioning was fated to take center-stage by virtue of the less than straightforward way that the Adams leadership had brought their more hard-line IRA colleagues into the peace process. The hard-liners had been persuaded to call a cease-fire in 1994 and give the political process a chance on the foot of assurances that the move was merely tactical—the cease-fire would be time-limited, would be dependent on the British giving Sinn Fein a speedy entry into talks, and if it all failed then war would be resumed. Indeed, at this stage the demand for decommissioning was portrayed during IRA leadership discussions as a *casus belli* that would justify breaking the cease-fire and was once described in such terms by Adams's closest ally, Martin McGuinness, during a high-level internal IRA meeting.[5] So when the cease-fire was called, Adams and his allies on the Army Council were in no position to deny demands from others in the leadership that the IRA be kept in fighting trim through continuing recruitment, training, production of explosives, intelligence gathering and "fund-raising", a euphemism for robberies.

The members of the South Armagh IRA unit that raided Newry post office in November 1994, less than three months into the cease-fire, were acting under this type of Army Council dispensation and had it not been for the fact that in the course of the robbery a postal worker, Frank Kerr, resisted the robbers and was shot dead, the event might not have had the reverberations it did. A huge political row followed the Kerr killing. While the Army Council denied that it had been an authorized operation, not many people believed them and the effect of the killing was to destroy any credibility attached to the Adams leadership's already ambiguous assurances that the cease-fire was permanent. If it was not possible to put trust in the IRA's words, the skeptics concluded, then actions would be needed instead and they turned to decommissioning as a more tangible way of establishing republican credentials. The Major government in London began by hardening its language on decommissioning and in March the following year outlined a new policy that became known as Washington Three, after the preconditions set for Sinn Fein's entry into negotiations. Enunciated by then Secretary of State in Northern Ireland Sir Patrick Mayhew during the Saint Patrick's Day celebrations in America, the conditions barred Sinn Fein from political talks until the IRA publicly agreed three things: its willingness to decommission, its agreement on the modalities of decommissioning, and finally to actually make a start to decommissioning its arms. Prior to the killing of Frank Kerr, decommissioning had largely been a side issue, as much an aspiration as anything else, but afterwards it was propelled to the top of the political agenda and stayed there.

Washington Three was the high mark in hard-line attitudes towards decommissioning, both on the part of the British government and, notwithstanding an image very much to the contrary in nationalist eyes, David Trimble, whose decade-long leadership of the Ulster Unionist Party and brief reign as Northern Ireland's first minister ultimately came to an end because of his perceived weakness on the issue. In January 1996, ten months after the Washington Three conditions were announced and only a few weeks before the breakdown in the IRA cease-fire which Mayhew's intervention had helped to precipitate, an international commission headed by former US Senate leader George Mitchell weakened Washington Three and thus set in motion a lengthy process of diluting the terms under which IRA disarmament would happen. Mitchell concluded that decommissioning prior to all-party talks was just not attainable and he recommended a number of adjustments in the way it should be approached thereafter. Rather than happening as a precondition to talks, it could take place during negotiations and should be governed by a number of guidelines: the process should suggest neither victory nor defeat; it should be overseen by an independent body; it should result in the complete destruction of armaments; paramilitary groups should be allowed to destroy their own weapons and the process should be verifiable. In other words, IRA decommissioning should not be cast as a precondition but instead be done voluntarily and on terms acceptable to the IRA leadership, albeit overseen and agreed by an outside body, the Independent International Commission on Decommissioning (IICD), which was established in 1997. The Mitchell Report shifted the decommissioning debate decisively in the republicans' direction and towards the view that it would be a mistake to hard-pedal the issue, a view that was reinforced by the breakdown of the cease-fire just days after it was published.

The Good Friday Agreement of April 10, 1998, agreed only eight months after the IRA had restored its cease-fire, balanced the Provisionals' acceptance of the consent principle against a guaranteed place in government for Sinn Fein, the release of IRA prisoners, an equality agenda, cross-Border cooperation and reform of the RUC. But decommissioning was left hanging, largely unresolved. The parties to the agreement, Sinn Fein included, merely confirmed their intention "to work constructively and in good faith with the Independent Commission, and to use any influence they may have, to achieve the decommissioning of all paramilitary arms within two years" of planned referenda on both sides of the Border that would endorse the agreement—in other words by the end of May 2006.[6] One extraordinary feature of the tortuous negotiations that had led to the agreement was the minimal degree to which IRA disarming had featured in them. According to Dean Godson's seminal and hugely detailed account of David Trimble's stewardship of the Ulster Unionists during the peace process, Trimble, who became first minister of the power-sharing Executive, the Northern Irish version of prime minister, claimed he had not made an issue of IRA arms because he, like many others, did not foresee that Sinn Fein would take its seats in the planned new power-sharing Executive.[7] Whatever the truth of that, the loosely worded terms of the Good Friday Agreement gave the Provos huge latitude to dodge and weave around the issue.

Once Sinn Fein's delegation agreed to recommend the deal to a wider party conference, it was clear that the republicans intended to take their place in government and decommissioning immediately resumed its prior centrality and importance. Trimble's ally and fellow negotiator, Jeffrey Donaldson, had already signalled his uneasiness by walking out of the unionist delegation at the end of the negotiations in protest at the terms for decommissioning. Two of Donaldson's cousins were RUC officers killed by the Provisional IRA and his stand reflected the feelings of many Northern Protestants. The prospect of Sinn Fein leaders becoming government ministers was a shock whose tremors were felt along the length of Ireland's political spectrum, but the idea that this could happen while the same leaders ran a still well-armed private army was especially noxious to unionists.

In a bid to shore up Trimble and win unionist support in the upcoming referendum, Tony Blair gave Trimble a side letter within hours of the conclusion of the Good Friday Agreement negotiations, confirming the British view that IRA decommissioning should start by June 1998, less than two months after the successful April negotiations. The letter had no legal status, and its terms could never be imposed, but the incident was revealing. Whereas Trimble and other unionists might be forgiven for not realizing that the peace process strategy crafted by Adams meant that Sinn Fein would participate in government, the British and Irish governments had no such excuse. Both governments had engaged in years of secret diplomacy with Adams and it would be extraordinary if they had not realized that being in government was the logical end of the path Adams had taken, in fact the *raison d'être* of his strategy. Decommissioning was thus always very likely to become an issue, at least for unionists, but the fact that neither government, especially the British, wanted to tie the IRA's disarming to any of the concessions in the Good Friday Agreement—such as the release of prisoners—indicated their preference to soft-pedal the issue. In this context Blair's side letter can be seen as a hastily contrived and even desperate effort to cover Trimble's exposed flank, but it gave republican leaders cause to believe that in Tony Blair they had a British leader who would be reluctant to jeopardize the peace for the sake of destroying already silent IRA weapons.

Although it was not the only issue that figured in post-Good Friday Agreement negotiations to set up the power-sharing Executive and cross-Border bodies, IRA decommissioning dominated them in the same way they would dominate the politics of the peace process for the next six years. The first post-Good Friday Agreement talks on decommissioning began in March 1999 at the Saint Patrick Day's celebrations in Washington, when David Trimble abandoned the demand that disarming should be a precondition to Sinn Fein entry to government, and at a meeting with Adams agreed the principle of "jumping together", the sequencing approach implicitly endorsed by George Mitchell back in 1996. But after a conference at Hillsborough Castle failed to get the IRA to deliver, Trimble tacked again and let it be known that he would now accept decommissioning "days" after the Executive was formed. (Gatherings at Hillsborough Castle, the British monarch's official residence in Northern Ireland during royal visits but used as a home by the serving British Secretary of State, became a permanent feature of political life after 1998, usually to deal with crises or to broker deals. Although their delegates were surrounded by the symbols and trappings of British royalty, including a Throne Room where the visiting monarch would receive VIPs and there was a strong possibility their conversations were being electronically monitored by British intelligence, Sinn Fein, interestingly, never objected to the venue.) In July 1999, Blair declared that he had detected a "seismic shift" in the IRA's attitude to decommissioning and agreed with Irish taoiseach Bertie Ahern on an approach that implicitly killed off the idea of simultaneous decommissioning.[8] The IRA would only have to indicate a willingness to decommission for devolution to be triggered. But a bad reaction from his party obliged Trimble to harden his position, notwithstanding any signals he may have given to the contrary, and the proposal stalled.

23. The Fianna Fail leader and Irish prime minister Charles Haughey with his British counterpart, Margaret Thatcher. *(Derek Speirs/Report, Dublin)*

24-A. INSET: Jim Lynagh, the commander of the ill-fated East Tyrone Brigade. *(Kelvin Boyes, Belfast)*

24. BELOW: As Gerry Adams attended Lynagh's funeral in May 1987, his secret cease-fire offer was en route to Charles Haughey. *(Derek Speirs/ Report, Dublin)*

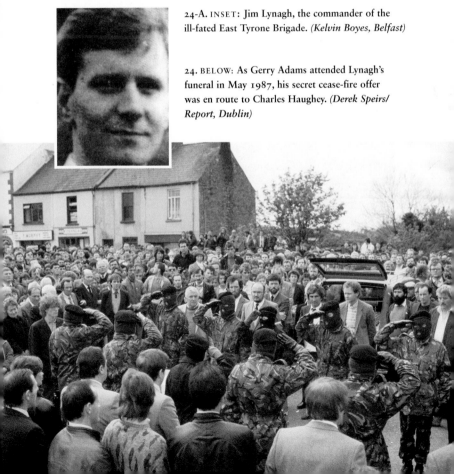

25. Bloody Sunday, January 1972. Father Edward Daly, later bishop of Derry, shepherds one of the fourteen fatally wounded victims.
(Pacemaker Press, Belfast)

26. Ferocious rioting in Derry followed the deaths on Bloody Sunday.
(P. Michael O'Sullivan)

27. The aftermath of the IRA's first "human bomb" attack, in Derry in October 1990. *(Pacemaker Press, Belfast)*

27-A. INSET: Patsy Gillespie, forced to deliver the bomb, died alongside five soldiers in the attack. *(Pacemaker Press, Belfast)*

28. John and Diana Lampen, with Traveler children in 1992. The Quaker peace workers were regarded by the British government as "the Father Reids of Derry."

29. Tom "Slab" Murphy, South Armagh IRA leader and chief of staff from 1997 on. *(John Cogill, Dublin)*

30. Micky McKevitt, who masterminded the Libyan arms shipments with Slab Murphy and later led the opposition to Adams's peace strategy. *(John Cogill, Dublin)*

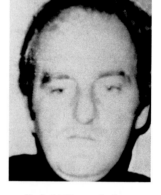

31. Kevin McKenna, the longest-serving IRA chief of staff.

32. The key think tank member and skilled IRA propagandist Danny Morrison leaves the Maze prison in 1995. *(Pacemaker Press, Belfast)*

33 A-B. Jim Gibney, a think tank member whose role was to fly controversial kites for Adams. Pictured in 1980 before the peace process began (*above*) (*Pacemaker Press, Belfast*) and (*right*) after, in 1996. (*Derek Speirs/Report, Dublin*)

34. A rare photograph of the think tank chairman, Ted Howell (*left*), pictured with Gerry Adams during the Good Friday Agreement negotiations. (*Alan O'Connor, Dublin*)

35. Mitchel McLaughlin, the Derry-based think tank member who was loathed by IRA activists. *(Kelvin Boyes)*

36. Gerry Adams, the Irish prime minister, Albert Reynolds, and the SDLP leader, John Hume, in a show of Irish nationalist unity after the August 1994 IRA cease-fire declaration. *(Derek Speirs/Report, Dublin)*

37. The Belfast IRA commander Brian Gillen. Initially opposed to Adams's peace strategy, he switched sides at the 1997 IRA Convention and was rewarded with a seat on the Army Council. *(Pacemaker Press, Belfast)*

38. Brian Keenan had the image of an IRA hawk but his record showed unswerving support for Adams. Pictured here carrying the coffin of the IRA veteran Jimmy Drumm in 2001. *(Pacemaker Press, Belfast)*

39. On the eve of the 1996 IRA Convention, the British army HQ at Thiepval barracks in Lisburn, County Antrim, is bombed. *(Pacemaker Press, Belfast)*

39-A. INSET: Warrant Officer James Bradwell later died of horrific injuries, but his death helped to save the Adams leadership. *(PA)*

40. The strangest of partners? Ian Paisley and Gerry Adams announce a power-sharing deal at Stormont in March, 2007. Sinn Fein's support for the new Police Service of Northern Ireland made the deal possible.

41. As Gerry Adams languishes outside, President George W. Bush meets the sisters and partner of Robert McCartney in the White House, St Patrick's Day, 2005. The Provisional leadership's clumsy cover up of McCartney's brutal murder alienated powerful American allies and forced the IRA to complete decommissioning and end its war with Britain.

These negotiations were to set a pattern for dealing with IRA arms that could best be compared to a ritualistic, but very tedious slow waltz in which, every few months, Sinn Fein and the unionists would take to the floor to the same tune. While the dance would invariably begin full of hope and promise it would always conclude in the same unhappy way, usually with David Trimble tripping over Gerry Adams's feet and landing on his face. No less than five British Secretaries of State tried their hand at leading the orchestra during these years—Mo Mowlam, Peter Mandelson, John Reid, Paul Murphy and Peter Hain—while the events' virtuoso, Tony Blair, supported by Irish premier Bertie Ahern, chalked up thousands of man-hours, perhaps 40 percent of his time in Downing Street, according to some estimates, trying to get Adams and Trimble to complete the waltz in step and unmarred by tumbles.

After the debacle of July 1999, when the "seismic shift" in the IRA's decommissioning policy detected by Blair turned out to be not much more than a slight tremor, George Mitchell was once again prevailed upon to return to Ireland in an effort to get Sinn Fein and the unionists to agree a way forward. The significance of the deal he put together in November 1999 was that it formally ditched decommissioning as a precondition for Sinn Fein's entry to government. Devolution would happen on December 1, 1999, but while the IRA agreed to nominate Brian Keenan as its interlocutor to the IICD, it would not have to actually come up with the "product" i.e. weapons to be decommissioned, until the end of January 2000. Trimble got the deal approved by his party only by lodging a post-dated resignation letter, due to come into effect on February 1 if the IRA had failed to keep its side of the deal. Despite Sinn Fein signing up to the Mitchell deal, January 31 came and went without the IRA delivering any product—merely a promise from Keenan that the IRA would take the most minimal step forward and begin examining the modalities of decommissioning.

With the Good Friday Agreement slipping into irreversible meltdown, British Secretary of State Peter Mandelson stepped in to suspend the Assembly and the Executive and thereby preserve them for a better day. In retaliation, the IRA withdrew Brian Keenan from his dialogue, such as it was, with the decommissioning body. There it rested until Blair and Ahern returned to Belfast in May and another deal was struck in which the IRA agreed in principle to decommission an unspecified amount of arms and, until that happened, to allow two international luminaries, a former president of Finland, Martti Ahtisaari, and the ANC trade unionist-turned-millionaire businessman, Cyril Ramaphosa, to inspect IRA weapons in arms dumps on a regular basis to ensure they had not been moved and therefore used. This so-called Confidence Building Measure (CBM) was sufficient to restore the power-sharing institutions but, crucially, Sinn Fein had got back into government without any indication that the IRA might actually start to physically disarm. In fact the arms inspectors visited IRA dumps three times on behalf of the IICD, the last occasion in May 2001, and not only was there no decommissioning during this time but there was not even a single meeting between the IRA and the decommissioning body from June 2000 until March 2001. It wasn't until August 2001 that Brian Keenan and the IICD even agreed upon the method by which the IRA would put its weapons beyond use. In a matter of six years the terms for IRA decommissioning had slipped dramatically in favor of the republicans, from being a precondition to Sinn Fein's participation in talks about a settlement to the point where Sinn Fein ministers had been in government for over a year without the IRA giving up a single gun or bullet.

Another tedious and especially convoluted waltz began in July 2001 when the parties were shipped off to a country house in Shropshire, England, for inconclusive talks which were followed, in the ensuing weeks, by a dizzy series of events. Trimble and his ministers in the Executive first resigned and the Assembly was then suspended twice (with foresight, the architects of the 1998 deal had anticipated a troubled journey and wrote a one-day, repeatable suspension power into the GFA legislation which could bestow six-week breathing spaces during a crisis indefinitely). Then the IRA agreed on the modalities of disarming, then it withdrew from the IICD, only to return to decommission for the first time when the combined impact of the Colombia arrests and the Al Qaeda attacks in New York and Washington shamed and pushed it into action. It was noteworthy that when decommissioning did take place for the first time, it was due not to the diplomatic skills of Tony Blair or Bertie Ahern but because of hubris on the part of the IRA in the jungles of South America and bloodthirsty daring by Osama bin Laden and his jihadist warriors.

SO WHY did it take so long for the Provos to begin disarming? And why were the governments so reluctant to put pressure on the Provos to move more speedily and convincingly in the direction of decommissioning? After all, the peace process was essentially a covenant between the Provos and constitutional democrats in Britain and Ireland in which the latter agreed to bring Sinn Fein in from the cold and to treat them in the same way as other democrats as long as the IRA left all its violent ways behind, including its guns. One part of the bargain, power-sharing, had been implemented, or was at least irreversibly on the way to being so, yet despite an implied promise or understanding that decommissioning would take place within two years of the Good Friday Agreement, the IRA had still not agreed how or when it would destroy its arsenals three years after the deal had been struck. Not only that, but as incidents like Colombia illustrated, the IRA's propensity to mount operations that threatened the integrity of the cease-fire was undiminished. The IRA's part of the bargain was not being honored. The governments would have been entitled to respond accordingly but they always baulked.

The reason, of course, was that both governments had bought heavily into the argument that Gerry Adams and his colleagues had limited freedom of movement and could not move much faster than their slowest and most recalcitrant colleagues. Given the IRA's turbulent history between 1995 and 1997, this was a reasonable view but it was also one that was unique to its time and circumstances. As the years passed and the realities on the ground changed in their favor, the IRA leadership's hand strengthened and so did its leeway on the issue of weapons. The question is not whether Tony Blair, Bertie Ahern and their various advisers were wrong in 1998 to think there was a limit to how fast or far Gerry Adams could move his IRA colleagues, but whether they were naive, not to mention foolish, to believe or to behave as if this was still the case by late 2001 and during the next four long years.

In theory there were two areas in which an external threat existed to the Adams leadership that was sufficiently strong to limit their freedom to move. The first was the threat posed by its most recent home-grown dissident group, the Real IRA, and the second was the possibility that the Real IRA would link up with the other two dissident republican groups, the Continuity IRA, associated with Ruairi O Bradaigh's republican Sinn Fein, which came into being after the 1986 split in the Provisionals, and the INLA, the left-wing, violent but feud-prone breakaway group from the Official IRA. Pledged to reverse the Adams sell-out, this coalition would be a formidable opponent and a natural magnet for disgruntled members of the Provisionals.

The fear of a split was one reason Gerry Adams moved so cautiously and slowly when he and Father Reid began developing the peace process after 1982. Adams had experienced at first hand the bitter and often bloody fracture between the Provisionals and the Officials in the 1970s and knew how physically dangerous and politically damaging such schisms could be. That split had been due in no small measure to Cathal Goulding's confrontational style and because his political goals had been so transparent as to forewarn his enemies and rivals. Adams knew that if he was to deliver the Provisionals into the peace process intact and undivided, he had to avoid the most egregious of Goulding's errors, as he told Irish government officials many years later.[9] By moving slowly and carefully and keeping his cards close to his chest, Adams hoped to avoid the sort of split Goulding had created.

In fact a split turned out to be unavoidable and given that Adams's ambitions for the Provisionals dwarfed Goulding's agenda, this was to be expected. But Adams's caution meant that when the break with Micky McKevitt and his supporters came it was probably too late for the dissidents to make a significant enough impact on the Adams strategy. It is arguable that the dissidents stayed their hand for too long, faltered at the prospect of unseating Adams and delayed delivering the fatal blow while they themselves turned out to be vulnerable to infiltration by Adams's loyalists posing as fellow rebels. The very fact that the McKevitt group was ultimately obliged to leave the IRA was itself a convincing sign that they would never get off the back foot. They had failed to topple Adams at the 1996 Army Convention and had been trounced at the 1997 Convention. They could either stay in the Provisionals and face humiliation, marginalization and ultimately ejection, or they could leave. They chose the latter but by so doing they ensured that Adams and his allies remained in control of the bulk of IRA weapons and of most of its structures, and in possession of an undiminished claim to republican legitimacy.

McKevitt and his allies had chosen a piece of ideological high ground for the battleground with Adams. They fought their battle in opposition to the Mitchell Principles which committed the IRA to peaceful methods and to decommissioning. These were concessions that were like fingers dabbling in the IRA's soul, but McKevitt's critique had not cut much ice with the IRA rank and file in the place where it mattered—the Northern war zone. The failure of the McKevitt rebellion was testament to two defining features of the Provisional movement. The response of the Adams camp to McKevitt's attack was to say, effectively, "We'll accept the Mitchell principles but not mean it." This was evidence of the extent to which Adams had successfully reduced every cherished republican belief to a tactic that could be bent and twisted to suit requirements. He was able to do so because he had a compliant membership who had been motivated to join and fight with the Provisionals not because they believed in the values of traditional Irish republicanism but by an atavistic need to confront and strike back at unionism and loyalism, in and out of uniform. So it was that the Adams leadership had much less difficulty jettisoning the IRA's most defining beliefs, like opposition to the consent principle, than it did with decommissioning weapons, the instruments of defence and confrontation.

There were other factors. Adams and McGuinness were Northerners with a trusted track record, republican superstars in the eyes of the grassroots, who had rescued the IRA from near defeat in the 1970s and brought undreamed-of electoral success, whereas McKevitt and his supporters were Southerners with whom IRA and Sinn Fein activists in Belfast, Derry and elsewhere in the North had had little direct contact or knowledge. And so it was that, thanks to such factors, the bulk of the Provisionals' Northern Command stayed loyal to the Adams leadership in the end, while the dissident group, called Oglaigh na hEireann (Army of Ireland) by its founders but soon to be dubbed the Real IRA by the media, got most of its support from the IRA in Southern Command, especially in McKevitt's quartermaster's department, in the engineering department led by Dubliner Frank McGuinness or along the Border. The split was a seminal moment in the evolution of the peace process because it revealed how shallow the Provisionals' political ideology really was and how easily the movement could be led into greater and wider ideological compromise. From the moment the McKevitt rebellion failed to topple Adams, the IRA leadership could be confident that if disaffected members left, they would leave as individuals or in small groups and that the threat of an organized, coherent opposition had faded.

The Real IRA's leaders were aware of their weaknesses and so contact was made with the Continuity IRA and the INLA and their political leaders in an effort to forge a common military and political strategy against the peace process and the Provos. On the military front, the three groups cooperated and pooled resources to launch a bombing campaign which began with a van bomb attack on the RUC station at Markethill, County Armagh, in September 1997 and continued throughout 1998 with a series of car bomb and mortar attacks, mostly in County Armagh. The attempt to write an agreed political manifesto proved to be much more problematic. The difficulty was that Ruairi O Bradaigh, the president of republican Sinn Fein, Continuity IRA's political wing, and Micky McKevitt, whose 32-County Sovereignty Movement represented the Real IRA, had taken opposing positions during the bitter 1986 split over recognizing the Dail. O Bradaigh had walked out of the Provisional Sinn Fein Ard Fheis with his supporters when Adams won the abstention vote, whereas McKevitt had not only stayed within the fold but had stood alongside Adams during the angry lunchtime confrontation with O Bradaigh and his people on the Sunday the vote was taken. The Real IRA people still didn't care about abstentionism and believed holding on to it would mean political isolation, while for O Bradaigh it remained a defining matter of political principle. Dividing them was both an ideological gulf and the memory of an angry confrontation that still rankled; the combination of political and personality differences meant achieving an agreed political programme was nigh impossible.[10]

Any remaining chance that the three dissident groups could make common cause was literally evaporated on August 15, 1998, when a car bomb exploded in the County Tyrone market town of Omagh, killing twenty-nine people. The death toll was the worst for any single incident of the Troubles, the result of an inaccurate telephone-warning which actually drove people into the path of the bomb rather than away from it. The bombing had been the work of all three dissident groups. Continuity IRA provided the target and the intelligence, the Real IRA the code word, materiel and manpower, while the INLA provided the car used to ferry the bomb. The fact that a Real IRA code word was used meant that it got the blame. Neither the INLA nor Continuity IRA volunteered their role in the blast, leaving the Real IRA to carry the can alone, an aspect of the incident that further soured relations between them. Within three weeks both the INLA and the Real IRA had called cease-fires, although in the latter's case it was not to be a permanent cessation.

Dissident unity had been smashed within a year of the Real IRA's break with the Provisionals and none of the three groups was thereafter able to mount any sort of serious challenge to the Provisionals, who took to terming them, contemptuously, "micro groups." Further evidence that the Provos regarded the Real IRA as a minimal threat came in October 2000 when, in broad daylight and with little attempt to disguise their identity, Provo gunmen in Ballymurphy shot dead twenty-six-year-old Real IRA member Joe O'Connor, pumping seven shots into his head as he sat in a car outside his mother's house. There had been a recent history of friction between the Real and Provisional IRA in the area and O'Connor's death was meant to send a message to the dissident group's leadership. Had the Provos believed that there was any chance the Real IRA would have retaliated or that the group posed a real threat to Provo hegemony, O'Connor's killing would never have been sanctioned. In the same year the Real IRA abandoned its cease-fire and carried out a series of bomb attacks in England, including an anti-tank missile fired at MI6's headquarters, but these were few in number and never even remotely approached the scale of the threat that had been presented by the Provisional IRA. If anything, the attacks underlined the group's marginal influence on republican politics.

In March 2001, the Real IRA was dealt a huge blow when Micky McKevitt was arrested and subsequently tried, convicted and given a twenty-year prison term on the basis of evidence provided by a US sympathizer who had infiltrated the group's inner sanctums at the behest of the FBI and MI5. The agent, David Rupert, a German-American and part Mohawk Indian with no direct links to Ireland, was a serial bankrupt, tax defaulter and failed businessman from upstate New York who had been expelled by Continuity IRA's American support group and then, at the urging of the FBI and MI5, turned his attention to the Real IRA. The fact that such a disreputable character was able to get so close to the Real IRA leadership was hugely embarrassing but it also confirmed a widespread perception in the republican community that the dissident group had been widely infiltrated and that those who joined it were only risking imprisonment or worse. The revelations about Rupert were a deterrent to seasoned Provisionals tempted to jump ship and increasingly the group turned to inexperienced and poorly motivated teenagers for recruits. The Real IRA also succumbed to an affliction common to Irish revolutionaries when in October 2002 it split after one faction, based in Portlaoise prison, accused the leadership outside the jail of corruption. By the time the Provisionals decommissioned for the first time, the dissident threat had been reduced almost to the level of a minor nuisance.

WHATEVER JUDGMENT British and Irish intelligence made on the dissident threat, it is clear that Tony Blair and Bertie Ahern continued to view the Adams leadership as vulnerable to internal criticism. The conviction took hold that if the IRA was compelled to move too fast or too far, the Provisionals' unity could be threatened and there would be unthinkable consequences for the peace process. This produced an extraordinarily conflicting mindset about the leaders of the IRA in government circles in Britain and Ireland.

At one level the governments behaved as if Gerry Adams and Martin McGuinness were telling the truth when they claimed they had never had any links to the IRA, or in McGuinness's case that he had severed them in 1972, and that the IRA leadership was separate from them and took decisions by itself, heeding the advice of Adams and McGuinness only when it suited. Given their access to intelligence briefings, both premiers certainly knew otherwise, particularly that Adams and McGuinness were not just senior members of the Army Council but that they were the IRA's senior strategists and that no decisions would ever be made without their knowledge and approval. A former colleague of the two leaders, John Kelly, a founding member of the Provisional IRA and a scion of one of Belfast's best-known republican families, put it well when asked whether figures like Gerry Adams would be aware of IRA operations: "I go back to what the Bible said, that not a sparrow falls from the sky but that the man above does not know about it and Gerry Adams in terms of the republican movement is the man above. He is God, so he knows and would want to know and would be disappointed if he didn't know everything that happens within the republican movement and nothing will be hidden from him."[11] For reasons that defy understanding, both governments acted as if they believed otherwise.

A bizarre example of how this sort of fantasy infected government thinking occurred after the Colombia arrests and was described in detail by Dean Godson: "When the three [IRA members] were arrested, however, there was a level of disbelief in the highest reaches of Government: [John] Reid [Northern Ireland Secretary], for one, told Sir Ronnie Flanagan [RUC Chief Constable] that he believed that the three men may have been in Colombia without the knowledge of Adams and McGuinness. Furthermore, Jonathan Powell [Blair's Chief of Staff] told Trimble on 29 August 2001 that he thought that Adams and McGuinness had lost an internal battle inside the movement."[12] Just before the Colombia arrests, during the July 2001 Shropshire conference, Tony Blair approved a package of concessions dealing with policing and demilitarization for Adams to present to his colleagues, even though intelligence officials had told him that the IRA was active in the central American country.[13] Blair would have known that Adams was aware of what was happening in Colombia and the only explanation for his behaviour in Shropshire is that he believed Adams was an unwilling participant and that he needed to be strengthened to withstand his hard men. In fact the British prime minister continued indulging Adams in this way for years afterwards, even though intelligence officers had told him that at one meeting senior republicans had half-jokingly suggested sending a list of especially extravagant demands to Downing Street to show that Tony Blair would concede virtually anything that was asked of him to ensure the survival of the Adams leadership.[14] And an intriguing clue as to how the IRA leadership really regarded Blair emerged from a pile of IRA documents seized by police investigating a spy ring based at the British government complex at Stormont in the autumn of 2002. One document referred to the British prime minister by his IRA code-name: "The Naive Idiot".[15]

In fact the expedition to Colombia had been authorized by the Army Council, upon which both Adams and McGuinness sat. In overall charge was their fellow Army Council member Brian Keenan, who also played a part in setting up the affair, traveling to and from Colombia and exploiting family links in New York to put the arrangement together.[16] According to Irish Justice Minister Michael McDowell, if the deal had not been intercepted the IRA would have been paid as much as $35 million by the Colombian FARC guerrillas for training in explosives and mortar production.[17] FARC could well afford such generous payments. A left-wing liberation guerilla group with ties to Venezuela's Hugo Chavez and Fidel Castro's Cuba, FARC held unchallenged sway over much of Colombia's eastern region where the bulk of the country's coca and poppy crop is grown, harvested and turned into drugs that are destined for the US market. One estimate put the region's drug trade turnover in 2001—of which FARC held a majority share—at $300 million.

If evidence given at a 2002 hearing of the US Congressional House International Relations Committee is correct, then the IRA team in Colombia was of such a calibre that the suggestion that it was a freelance or unauthorized operation appears so far-fetched it approaches fantasy. As for Sinn Fein's claims that those arrested in Bogotá were interested in eco-tourism or had come to study the Colombian peace process, Committee chairman Rep. Henry Hyde dismissed these as "an insult to our intelligence."[18]

The team, all of whom traveled on false identities, consisted of some of the organization's most experienced and senior explosives engineers, whose republican curricula vitae had also included trusted, senior roles in Sinn Fein. The head of the training team, according to testimony provided by the chairman of the Colombian armed forces general staff, General Fernando Tapias, was Niall Connolly, who doubled as Sinn Fein's representative in Havana, Cuba, and had lived there since 1996. He had also worked as a volunteer for the Irish Foreign Service for ten years before that and was named by General Tapias as the man who was first introduced to FARC by the Basque paramilitary group, ETA, around the time he moved to Cuba. He traveled under the alias David Bracken, a Dublin boy who was accidentally killed in 1965. Tapias claimed that Connolly, whose brother Frank, a Dublin journalist, had also allegedly traveled to Colombia on false identity papers, was "well known for his expertise in firearms and explosives."[19] The second key figure was James Monaghan, who had joined the Provisionals' engineering department way back in 1970, rapidly becoming one of the IRA's foremost bomb-making experts, and was, at the time of his arrest, the IRA's director of engineering, in charge of the department that produced all the IRA's home-made explosive mixes, detonating devices, mortars and other improvized weaponry.[20] Monaghan's post meant that he automatically sat on the IRA's GHQ, near the very pinnacle of the organization, only a bracket or two on the organizational chart away from Adams and McGuinness. He had also served with the two men on Sinn Fein's ruling executive, the Ard Comhairle. The deputy director of the engineering department, Martin McAuley, from County Armagh, was the third member of the team arrested. McAuley had been wounded near Portadown, County Armagh, by a crack police squad in 1982, in one of a series of so-called "shoot-to-kill" incidents that caused a bruising scandal for the RUC when they were investigated by Greater Manchester police chief John Stalker. McAuley had also been Sinn Fein's director of elections in Upper Bann. Two other suspected IRA figures, "Kevin Noel Creemley" and "Margaret Steindoughtery", were arrested at the same time as the three men but were let go for lack of evidence. Tapias said that a further two IRA members had been traced visiting the FARC area four months before, "John Francis Johnson" and "James Edward Walker". The training team's principal task, Tapias told the committee, was to show FARC how to manufacture and use mortars capable of traveling 3,000 meters.

There were claims and reports subsequently that among a total of some twelve to fifteen IRA operatives, tracked as having entered and left Colombia during this period, was Padraig Wilson, a recently released former commander of IRA prisoners at the Maze jail.[21] Wilson was a close ally and supporter of Gerry Adams and had been used by the leadership as a conduit to announce IRA concessions on decommissioning in 1988 via a newspaper interview. The overall director of the Colombian adventure, Brian Keenan, was another Adams loyalist who had backed his strategy at critical points, not least during the McKevitt-inspired revolt in 1996 when Keenan pretended to sympathize with the rebels to gather vital intelligence for the Adams camp. At the time of the Colombia arrests, Keenan was the IRA's contact man with the IICD, a mark of the trust the Adams leadership had placed in him. The second key figure in the IRA's Colombian team was Gerry Adams's cousin Davy Adams, and if all these claims are true then it would be stretching credibility to suggest that both Gerry Adams and

Martin McGuinness had been left out of the loop in an operation of such critical importance to the IRA. The idea also that all this could or would be organized behind their backs and that characters like Keenan and Wilson, not to mention Adams's own cousin, would abandon years of loyalty to Adams to undermine him was a notion whose absurdity was matched only by the naivety of those in government ready to believe it was possible. Nonetheless, as government ministers and officials reached out to excuse the Sinn Fein leadership and as Adams denied all knowledge of Connolly's role as Sinn Fein's "Man in Havana", the party's public relations machine whirred into action to separate the Adams leadership from Colombia by hinting to the media that Keenan had embarked on a solo run in South America, just as a few years earlier the same spin doctors had characterized Wilson's 1998 remarks on decommissioning as his own. A few gullible journalists had fallen for the latter piece of fiction but the best brains in the British government swallowed the former.

At another level entirely, both governments cheerfully acknowledged that Adams and McGuinness did in fact have sway over the IRA leadership and had authorized various IRA operations. But this was viewed in a very different light, one that characterized their actions as a necessary and legitimate part of the working out of the peace process. The line of thinking went something like this: Adams and McGuinness would never be able to take the IRA's hard men with them if they knew where the peace process was really heading; so to keep the hard men happy and on board, Adams et al. would have to give them their head and approve operations like robberies, gun-running and the like; but at some point down the road matters would be so far advanced that the peace process would be irreversible and at that point the hard men could be brought to heel. Until that happened the best policy was to turn a Nelson's eye to all but the most outrageous IRA operations and give Adams and McGuinness the benefit of the doubt.

In one exceptionally egregious example of this type of thinking, an official speaking on behalf of the late Northern Ireland Secretary Mo Mowlam had characterized the killing of a Belfast punishment shooting victim by the IRA in August 1999 as "internal housekeeping".[22] But the Irish authorities could be every bit as economical with the truth, as one brazen armed robbery in Dublin, also in 1999, demonstrated. On January 5, 1999, an armoured car carrying some £600,000 was travelling through Dalkey in south Dublin when its path was blocked by a large transit van. It was then rammed by a flat-bed lorry onto whose superstructure had been welded two heavy girders that stuck out like a medieval battering ram. The impact of the girders smashed open one of the armored car's rear doors. Masked men armed with AK-47 automatic rifles jumped out of the van and swarmed around the car, making off with a dozen bags of cash. These they threw into the boot of a waiting Ford Granada getaway car but the vehicle's engine stalled and wouldn't start up again. The impact of the bags of cash had triggered a safety valve in the boot designed to stop the flow of petrol to the engine, thus reducing the chances of a fire in the event of a rear-end collision. The only mistake made by the robbers, in an otherwise meticulously planned and executed operation, was their choice of escape car. Forced to abandon the money, the gang made their getaway in another car which they hijacked after firing shots at the driver, who was cut around the head and shoulders by flying glass from his shattered windscreen. The gang had switched off the safety catches on their weapons, indicating they probably would have engaged the Irish police if necessary.

Immediately afterwards there was intense speculation about the identity of those responsible. The robbery was too well planned and the robbers too heavily armed for it to have been the work of one of Dublin's many criminal gangs and the finger of suspicion at once pointed to a republican paramilitary group of some stripe. For the same reasons, common sense suggested that the well-armed and resourced Provisionals, rather than the smaller and more amateurish dissident groups, had been behind the raid, but in the following days the Dublin newspapers and media performed alarming contortions in an attempt to put dissidents in the frame. Since the stories were written mostly by the media's security correspondents, a group of reporters whose dependence upon the Garda press office for their bread and butter had been a legendary if less than distinguished feature of Irish journalism for many years, it was difficult not to conclude that their stories reflected what the Irish political and security establishment wanted to see reported—although by this stage in the peace process the media rarely needed such encouragement.

Immediately after the robbery, reporters cited Irish police sources as unequivocally blaming either the Real or Continuity IRA, but as the days passed and it became clearer that the expertise of the raid was beyond these groups, the coverage changed in a bizarre way. The reports began to concede that there were differences of opinion within the Gardai about who had planned the robbery and edged close to suggesting the Provos might have had some hand in it—but they stopped significantly short of actually saying so. Instead, reporters wrote that the robbers "had learned their trade with the Provisional IRA," that they might have acquired weapons from the Provos and might also have attracted figures to their ranks "who must have been among the Provisional IRA's most able and dangerous . . ."[23] This was as close as the Dublin media, *circa* 1999, could come to saying that one of the most audacious robberies in the city's recent history had been perpetrated by a group whose leaders were dealing with the government and its leaders on a daily basis to supposedly deliver peace to the island. The same report, which had coyly hinted at some mysterious Provisional IRA association with the raid, ended, inexplicably, by returning to safer ground: "Dalkey undermines the case that the dissidents are finished. Here was an expertly planned raid executed by terrorists who were quite prepared to kill anyone who got in their way. According to some Gardai, the raid has shown not only that these 'dissidents' are undeterred by the shame of Omagh and the so-called 'draconian' anti-terrorist laws and threats from the Provisionals, but that they appear to be determined to continue and even escalate their activities."[24] The same sort of doublespeak came from government ministers in the days after the robbery. There was an 800-pound gorilla sitting in the middle of the room but no one in the Irish State, police, press or politicians, wanted to admit it.

In fact the robbery was a Provisional IRA operation which had been authorized by the Army Council and planned by the IRA's finance department. It was remarkably similar to a bungled robbery in Limerick three years before which had gone badly wrong when a Garda Special Branch detective was shot and killed by IRA members who had also switched off their AK-47 safety catches.[25] Had Irish police arrived on the scene at Dalkey any sooner than they did, then there might well have been fatalities that day as well. Within weeks Irish government officials were admitting privately that the Garda/media spin was incorrect and that the Provisionals had indeed been responsible. But publicly no Irish government minister or official would ever blame the Provos for what had been a barefaced and flagrant breach of their cease-fire.[26] The effect of incidents like this—and there were many of them—was to tempt the IRA into more and more contumelious activity. Since the first cease-fire was called in 1994 this was the third brazen armed robbery carried out by the Provos. The first two had caused fatalities but neither had deterred the IRA from proceeding with the Dalkey robbery, and that was compelling evidence both of the contempt the IRA had for the Irish and British governments and its leaders' confidence that neither administration would respond in anything like a punitive way. Given the timidity of the reaction to events like Dalkey, the IRA could hardly be blamed for pushing the envelope to its limit. The nature of government response also helped create an ideal set of circumstances for the Adams leadership in which no matter what the outcome of IRA activity, they, the leadership, would always come out ahead: if the IRA did something and neither London nor Dublin responded, then, to the great satisfaction of the IRA rank and file, their weakness would be evident for all to see, while the IRA would be able to pocket the proceeds of their operations. But if they reacted badly, which eventually they would have to, Adams and his allies would then be able to use this as a lever to push the IRA into making concessions necessary to keep the peace process alive.

The degree of unease within the Provisionals' grassroots during the years between the departure of the Real IRA rebels and the first act of decommissioning is by definition impossible to measure accurately. Certainly the Adams leadership continued to behave as before, disguising and misrepresenting their moves to their grassroots as they had done since the peace process began. The way decommissioning was presented internally was a classic example of this. While the world hailed the decommissioning act of October 21, 2001 as a breakthrough and a brave initiative by the IRA leadership, the Provos' rank and file were assured that it was a meaningless piece of theatre. The arms dump that had been decommissioned, the IRA told its volunteers, had already been discovered by the security forces and was under surveillance by them. The IRA had given up no arms that had not already been lost or compromised. A similar approach was taken to the next two acts of decommissioning, in April 2002 and October 2003. In one instance, the IRA told its members that the engineering department had been busy manufacturing bogus armaments, such as electronic fuses, and had fooled the head of the IICD, General John de Chastelain, into accepting *faux* weaponry. In another manifestly false claim, the grassroots were told that a senior member of the IICD had been caught by the IRA with another woman and was being blackmailed to lie to the world about the decommissioning process. Far-fetched though all this may sound now, it was actually believed at IRA grassroots level by enough people to matter, as one former IRA prisoner, Michael Benson, found out. Writing on *The Blanket* website he recalled: "One honest and sincere young man for whom I have the greatest respect and who unlike so many recent Republican converts actually found himself in Long Kesh told me that the Republican Movement had NEVER [*writer's emphasis*] decommissioned anything and that de Chastelain had been conned. Conning there may well have been but I don't think it was the Canadian General who was conned. And no doubt if there is another act of decommissioning that the foot soldiers will be again told some outlandish story."[27]

Whether the Adams leadership really needed to resort to such dissembling, or did so in the knowledge that the intelligence feedback to the British and Irish would strengthen the view that Adams's freedom of movement was indeed limited, or even that this was another example of Adams indulging his own legendary caution, the reality was clear. In various ways and for various reasons, the Adams leadership was altogether much stronger by 1999 than at any time since the failed putsch carried out by Michael McKevitt and his allies in 1996–97, and arguably more in control of the republican movement than at any other point in the peace process.

To begin with, the malcontents on the Army Executive who had led the revolt against the Adams leadership had been soundly defeated. The 1997 Convention had put them in a minority and when the McKevitt rebels left weeks later so did they, and the new IRA Executive that took over was much more to the leadership's liking. There was little likelihood of trouble from this traditional source of internal unrest. In addition, the Army Council was, by a very comfortable margin, solidly in the Adams camp. The former chief of staff, Kevin McKenna, who had never liked the peace process, had departed, replaced by Tom "Slab" Murphy of the South Armagh IRA. "Slab" was a much less self-confident figure than his predecessor, as was evident by his demeanour during the 1994 Army Council meeting that declared the first cease-fire. Committed beforehand to voting against the cessation, he elected to sit on the fence when Joe Cahill suddenly switched sides to back Adams and give him victory. McKenna, by contrast, stuck to his guns and voted against, the only Army Council member to do so. A year after his appointment as chief of staff, Slab sued the *Sunday Times* for libel and lost badly after a less than spectacular performance in the witness box which did neither his image nor his authority on the Army Council much good. Aside from Adams and McGuinness, there were two other Sinn Fein stalwarts on the Council, Pat Doherty and Martin Ferris, the Kerry-based activist who had been jailed for his part in an arms-smuggling venture (betrayed by the spy Sean O'Callaghan). Both men were strong supporters of Gerry Adams. The remaining Council members were also on Adams's side: Brian Keenan and Brian Gillen, the latter the former Belfast commander who had come over to Adams's side during the 1997 Convention and had been elevated to the Army Council as a reward. On a bad day Adams could count on a six-to-one majority in his favor; on a good day all the Army Council members would vote for his proposals.

But the most significant improvement in Adams's fortunes was that the changes in the IRA's constitution pushed through at the 1996 Convention, notably the restrictions placed on the IRA leadership's ability to decommission weaponry, were reversed at a Convention held in early 1999, the second since the eclipse of the McKevitt dissidents in 1997. The first, in 1998, had approved IRA members of Sinn Fein taking seats in the new power-sharing Assembly, a move that completed the ending of abstentionism begun in 1986. At the 1999 meeting, the Army Council had restored to it total control over the IRA's "equipment and other resources" in between Conventions. The McKevitt constitutional changes had taken away control of IRA weaponry, specifically if they were to be decommissioned, and given it to the Convention, which became the only body with such authority. But this power had been handed back to an Army Council now fully under the control of Adams and his peace process allies and unthreatened by dissidents. There was only one caveat, and a minor one at that. The Army Council's authority to dispose of IRA weapons was linked to Sinn Fein's entry into the yet-to-be established power-sharing Executive.[28] That restriction probably suited the Adams leadership since it buttressed the republican insistence that devolution must precede IRA disarming, an essential condition if the strategy of destabilizing Trimble and the SDLP was to succeed. The important point was that the leadership now had the authority to begin decommissioning whenever it wished and didn't need to call a special Convention to win approval.

None of this deterred the Sinn Fein leadership from pretending otherwise. In 2000 the SDLP was told, for example, that decommissioning was unlikely because Sinn Fein "no longer" had much influence with the IRA, even though this was more than a year after the 1999 Convention.[29] The Irish government accepted, seemingly without hesitation, the claim from Sinn Fein that "Adams did not have the votes" at a Convention to move on arms, a belief that cannot have been grounded in anything remotely resembling accurate intelligence.[30] The Irish government flip-flopped alarmingly during these years, a sign that its understanding and analysis of the Provos was less than perfect. In February 1999, for instance, Irish prime minister Bertie Ahern gave an interview to the *Sunday Times* in which he said that Sinn Fein would not get into government until and unless a start was made on decommissioning. Yet only four months later he performed a U-turn, saying decommissioning could begin only after Sinn Fein ministers were seated around the cabinet table. When another decommissioning deadline was missed, this time at the end of January

2000, the Irish government's explanation was that Gerry Adams had tried to sell the idea "on a tour of IRA units around the country" but had given up, presumably because of the bad reaction.[31] The truth, of course, was that the heavy lifting on decommissioning, such as it was, had already been done.

That the Irish government believed that before Gerry Adams or his colleagues could take risky and important decisions they needed to consult with and win the approval of the IRA rank and file seemed sensible—or at least it would have been if one was talking about any other organization, even one like Fianna Fail, but not the Provisional IRA. The whole point about the Adams peace strategy, the characteristic that made it really special, was that the entire expedition had been undertaken without the say-so or knowledge of the IRA's rank and file and that if they had been given a real veto over the process it probably would never have got off the ground. The priority of the Adams leadership was never to seek and win the consent of the grassroots for what it wanted to do, but to side-step, identify, undermine or subvert opposition and then manoeuvre the IRA or Sinn Fein into the desired place.

Two key events that took place before IRA decommissioning was an issue stand out as examples of how, eventually, the question of IRA guns would be dealt with. The 1986 Ard Fheis, which approved dropping abstentionism in the Dail, gave the leadership the result it wanted not because Adams or any of his colleagues toured the rank and file and won them over by argument but as a result of a piece of political trickery that Tammany Hall would have been proud of. Fictitious Sinn Fein cumainn were invented and registered with head office and when the Ard Fheis came around, dozens of delegates, invariably IRA men loyal to the military leadership, were sent to vote to drop abstentionism on behalf of a non-existent membership. That's how the leadership won the debate. Had they not done that, the proposal would probably have been comfortably defeated. In the run-up to the 1994 cease-fire, then Northern Commander Martin McGuinness publicly assured the republican grassroots that there would have to be an Army Convention before any cessation proposal was approved and the effect was to calm the ranks. But there never was a Convention because the Adams leadership knew they would probably lose the vote if there had been one. The first rule of IRA politics, as was very evident to the Adams camp in 1996, is never to call a Convention unless you know you can win it, preferably because your people are in charge of organizing it. No Convention was called before the 1994 cessation and, instead, the decision was left in the hands of the much more easily managed and manipulated Army Council. And it was the same story with decommissioning, once Adams had won the 1999 Convention.

Sleight of hand was, as always, employed by the leadership to ensure that the decommissioning issue was handled in the way it wished, notwithstanding opposition at grassroots IRA levels. One long-time and now former republican activist described how this process worked: "There is widespread consultation, but it's not that simple. Command or Departmental OCs call meetings and there is the opportunity to put your case but then the leadership goes ahead and does what it wants. When asked, the leadership says, 'We have consulted' but the grassroots never find out what the overall result was because they only know about what took place at their own meeting. And if you say to them [the leadership] 'We were against this or that' the answer is that 'well you don't know how others we consulted felt'. The logic is that the leadership does what it wishes."[32]

Irish government policy on decommissioning may have become what it was, due—at least in part—to the fact that policy-makers relied in large measure on the Sinn Fein leadership for their insight into IRA affairs, a dependence that had its origin in the Adams—Father Reid—Martin Mansergh chain established in the late 1980s. According to one senior Irish political source, policy formulation by the Dublin government in regard to the peace process, which was largely in the hands of the Department of Foreign Affairs (DFA), happened with little or no reference to the Garda Special Branch or the Department of Justice during these years. The Irish Special Branch had agents inside the IRA who gave accounts of internal matters that could have assisted policy-making, but their information was ignored. "They [DFA] had been co-opted by the Provos," asserted the source. "They ended up having a sort of Stockholm Syndrome relationship with them in which the rule was 'Gerry's problems are our problems'." It wasn't until 2005 that Garda intelligence was fed regularly into the process and by then it was far too late to influence the decommissioning process.[33]

The 1999 Convention imposed two other restrictions on IRA involvement in the institutions of the Good Friday Agreement. One prevented ranking IRA members from taking seats in the new Assembly, and as a result Gerry Kelly, an Assembly member for North Belfast, coud not be reappointed as adjutant-general. Another said that no IRA member could hold office in the new Executive, a restriction that possibly puts Adams's own reluctance to take government office in a new light. This also had implications for Martin McGuinness, slated to be minister of education, when in December 1999 the deal brokered by George Mitchell paved the way for the Executive to be established. As Dean Godson noted, the Irish government became aware that Martin McGuinness "stopped going to IRA meetings" when he was appointed to the Executive, although it is not clear if Dublin fully understood why. Godson was told this was happening "so as to keep a clear division between ministers and 'the movement'," whereas it was in fact a condition that had been imposed by the 1999 Convention.[34] These limits to the leadership's freedom of movement were pretty mild and fell way short of the sort of hobbling measures that an unhappy and assertive IRA grassroots would have demanded, the sort of grassroots that the Sinn Fein leadership would afterwards maintain prevented greater or faster movement towards IRA disarming. The Adams leadership could be well satisfied at the outcome of the 1999 IRA Convention. It had restored the Army Council's tactical flexibility and had encountered no real, organized opposition, while the Irish and British governments continued to believe, or acted as if they believed, that the opposite was the case.

MEANWHILE the destabilizing impact on unionism of the IRA's dodging and weaving around the decommissioning issue was becoming more evident as well as threatening to the Ulster Unionist leader, David Trimble. He had significantly moderated his decommissioning stance since the Good Friday Agreement was signed and had dropped the demand that it be a precondition for Sinn Fein's presence in government. Instead he accepted that it could happen after devolution was underway, although the deadline for this kept being extended further and further into the future. As this happened, unionist unrest intensified. Even when the IRA agreed to its first act of decommissioning in October 2001, Trimble won no relief from internal criticism. The IRA had moved, after all, not out of consideration for unionists' susceptibilities but in self-interest, lest by not decommissioning the White House would place it in the same camp as Al Qaeda. Furthermore, Trimble had lost some of his Assembly members to anti-GFA unionist dissidents and was only re-elected as first minister when members of the Alliance Party and the Women's Coalition temporarily redesignated themselves as unionists, a device that Trimble's critics roundly condemned as shabby and demeaning. In some telling ways the first act of IRA decommissioning actually weakened Trimble.

Even though the IRA had begun decommissioning, it soon became clear that another difficulty had emerged. The IICD, which oversaw and verified the process, gave no details at all about what had happened. A 144-word statement outlining the first decommissioning act of October 2001 said merely that the IICD's members had witnessed "an event" in which "arms, ammunition and explosives" were put beyond use. How much weaponry was decommissioned or precisely what type was not revealed and neither was the method of decommissioning. The IICD would not even say where the event had taken place, whether it was North or South of the Border or even in Ireland. The IICD's statement after the second act of IRA decommissioning in April 2002 was even shorter, at 112 words, and again no details at all were given about what had happened.

The IICD was led by three members: Tauno Nieminen, a Finnish Brigadier-General, Andrew Sens, a former US diplomat and John de Chastelain, a retired General in the Canadian Army, who was the IICD's chairman. Ironically, in view of subsequent events, de Chastelain's appointment had been resisted by Sinn Fein since both his parents had links to British intelligence, his father as an MI6 officer in the Balkans during the Second World War, and his mother who was on the staff of Churchill's legendary US-based spymaster, Sir William Stephenson. De Chastelain had sat on the Mitchell International Body, whose report in 1996 had established the need to avoid the appearance of surrender or defeat as a central principle in any disarming process. In line with that thinking, de Chastelain and his colleagues agreed an arrangement with Brian Keenan in which no detail pertaining to the decommissioning process would be made public.

"It became clear to us," the IICD chairman explained, "in our continuing discussions with the IRA representative that they would only agree to decommission on that basis." De Chastelain went to the two governments with that proposal and Tony Blair and Bertie Ahern agreed. "Now the IRA representative didn't tell us this but I think they also had to do a selling job to their own rank and file about how things would be done," he recalled, "... they didn't want to be humiliated."[35] The confidentiality deal was negotiated, de Chastelain believes, by either late 1999 or early 2000, by which time the Army Council had recovered its authority over IRA weapons. Significantly de Chastelain now admits he knew nothing about the 1999 IRA Convention. Out of a wish not to be compromised, the IICD had eschewed links to the British or Irish intelligence network and therefore had no way of knowing about it.

The IRA's confidentiality agreement with the IICD meant that no evidence that decommissioning had even happened could be made public and it was this that allowed the leadership to tell rank-and-file volunteers that de Chastelain had been conned. But it also unsettled an already uneasy unionist community, many of whose members assumed that the real purpose of the secrecy was to hide the fact that no weapons or a very insignificant number of them had been destroyed. One consequence was that an already weakened faith and trust in the IRA's bona fides, Tony Blair's veracity and David Trimble's political leadership, slipped away at an accelerating rate. By October 2000 the slim majority of Protestants, 51 percent, who had voted in favor of the Good Friday Agreement in 1998, had become a slightly larger majority, 53 percent, who would now vote against given a second chance.[36] Just under three years later, according to a Joseph Rowntree Trust/Queen's University Belfast poll, Protestant support had fallen to around a third. Trimble faced growing opposition from within his own party; at increasingly agitated meetings of his party's supreme decision-making body, the Ulster Unionist Council, he was doing well if he won the support of more than 55 percent of delegates. In September 2000 disaster struck when in a by-election for the Westminster constituency of South Antrim, the Reverend William McCrea, a Free Presbyterian minister shipped in from far-off south Derry to fight the election and one of the wilder fundamentalists in Paisley's Democratic Unionist Party, took what had been the Ulster Unionist's safest seat in Northern Ireland, beating David Burnside, who was himself something of a hard-liner and critic of Trimble. Grassroots unionist sentiment was moving away from the moderate center ground and that process would quicken in the next few years.

Any hope that the start of decommissioning would signal a change of direction by the IRA was dashed on the night of Sunday, March 17, 2002, St. Patrick's Day. Three intruders burst into a Special Branch office located deep in the Belfast headquarters of the Police Service of Northern Ireland (PSNI), the renamed Royal Ulster Constabulary, at Castlereagh in the east of city, overpowered the duty officer and made off with scores of files containing the code-names of double agents, the names of their handlers and details of the Special Branch's complete battle order, including names and phone numbers. It was a devastating strike against British intelligence, and because the raiders appeared to have intimate knowledge of the Castlereagh base the authorities at first discounted IRA responsibility and assumed that the raid had to be an inside job, possibly carried out by disgruntled intelligence officers. The PSNI Chief Constable, Sir Ronnie Flanagan, said he would be "most surprised" if paramilitaries or civilians were responsible.[37] A week later, however, the PSNI had changed its mind and began raiding and arresting leading republicans in Belfast and Derry. The Castlereagh raid was an

IRA operation, the police had concluded, carried out with the assistance of a civilian accomplice working at the base, which was under reconstruction at the time and consequently not guarded with the customary level of vigilance.

Possibly because of the initial confusion about who was responsible, the impact of the Castlereagh raid was somewhat less explosive than it could have been, but angry unionists were nonetheless soon taking aim at the Provo leadership. Republicans in turn fiercely denied any IRA hand in the raid and accused malicious security force elements of staging it to discredit Sinn Fein and the peace process. This was yet another example of a long and concerted effort by the republican leadership to blame allegedly reactionary elements in the intelligence world, whom they dubbed "securocrats", for IRA operations or other incidents that caused problems for the peace process.

As it turned out, the police investigation into the Castlereagh break-in was a slow-burning fuse. As raids and searches continued, the authorities uncovered more and more evidence that the IRA's intelligence department was running an extensive spy ring at British government offices in the Stormont complex in east Belfast. According to one security source with intimate knowledge of the affair, the IRA had as many as five spies inserted into the lower levels of the civil service, or recruited by them, who were funneling sensitive documents to the IRA and Sinn Fein.[38] Amongst these were papers listing the names and addresses of some 1,600 prison officers, and around 600 soldiers, policemen, politicians and civil servants. But the more significant material included position papers prepared by the British government for peace process talks, documents and correspondence from other parties to the Northern Ireland Office, and transcripts of phone conversations, including those between British premier Tony Blair and the US President George W. Bush. Some of the material was of value only to the IRA, but the bulk of it was potentially of enormous help to Sinn Fein's leaders as they constructed their negotiating positions for talks with the British and other parties.

On October 4, 2002, a large force of PSNI officers raided Sinn Fein's offices at the Stormont parliament and took away computer disks. Two days later, the head of administration for Sinn Fein at the Assembly, Denis Donaldson, and his son-in-law Ciaran Kearney, appeared in court charged with possessing documents likely to be of use to terrorists, and later a Stormont messenger was also charged. A bag full of British papers had been discovered at Donaldson's home and the involvement of Donaldson, an

IRA veteran and apparently loyal disciple of the Adams leadership from the Short Strand area of Belfast, would later reverberate massively within the republican movement.

Within a week the peace process was in the middle of a full-blown crisis. Faced with unionist threats to quit the power-sharing Executive, the British suspended the Good Friday Agreement institutions and direct rule was re-instituted. Once again IRA activity had collapsed the house of cards and raised dark questions in unionist minds about the wisdom of David Trimble's seemingly interminable and unsatisfactory political liaison with the Provos.

Faced with widespread criticism, and doubtless encouraged by the question marks still in the public's mind about the Castlereagh raid, the Sinn Fein leadership once again played the "securocrat" card. Party leaders alleged that the spy ring, quickly dubbed "Stormontgate" by the local media, was an invention of hostile intelligence officers who had contrived the affair to rescue David Trimble from hard-liners in his party who were moving against his leadership. The claim that "Stormontgate" had been staged to "Save Dave," combined with TV footage of a PSNI raid on Sinn Fein offices that was clearly over the top, helped the Provos retrieve some ground, at least within the nationalist constituency. For instance, Martin Mansergh, who had spent years as the Irish government's contact man with the Provos in the early days of the peace process and was by now an Irish senator, questioned the timing of the raid, which he said was reminiscent of what might happen in Robert Mugabe's Zimbabwe.

The security authorities in Northern Ireland had been aware of the spy ring for months but had been slow to act. If the testimony of one former senior intelligence officer involved in the affair is correct, then far from staging the operation to rescue Trimble at the expense of the Provos, British intelligence strove to minimize the damage that would accrue to them once it all became public. Former Chief Superintendent Bill Lowry, head of the PSNI Special Branch in Belfast who headed the operation, code-named "Torsion," later said: "I felt during the whole operation that I was running, constant pressure from the security services [MI5], that it would be better if we didn't take skulls, if we just took papers. It would leave Sinn Fein/Provisional IRA a chance of denying they were involved in it."[39] Lowry quit the PSNI weeks after "Stormontgate" was exposed and after a row with MI5 over his alleged contacts with media. This would not be the last time that republican claims of "securocrat" influence would be seriously questioned.

The other reason why the authorities stayed their hand was the hope that they would be able to ensnare the mastermind behind both the spy ring and the earlier raid on the Castlereagh Special Branch office. Both operations had been run by the IRA's director of intelligence, Bobby Storey, a West Belfast IRA veteran who by this time had become something of a republican legend. An active gunman and bomber in the 1970s who had reputedly inspired Mairead Farrell, later killed by the SAS in Gibraltar, to join the IRA, he was jailed in the 1970s and again in 1981 for eighteen years after an ambush on British soldiers during the hunger strikes. Two years later he helped lead a spectacular IRA break-out from the Maze prison, the old Long Kesh, in which thirty-eight prisoners escaped. Around half were recaptured shortly afterwards, including Storey, who had tried to hide under water in a nearby river by breathing through a reed. Back in the H Blocks, he headed IRA security inside the jail, a job that entailed, *inter alia*, policing republican prisoners for dissent against the Adams leadership. After his release around the time of the first cease-fire, Storey—at 6'4" he was known as "Big Bobby" in IRA circles—rose in the ranks and was soon deeply involved in the organization's intelligence work. Immediately after his release, Storey was appointed Northern Command intelligence officer and in that capacity he was to play an enormously significant role in saving Adams's IRA skin. He helped organize and mastermind the bombing of Thiepval barracks, the British army's headquarters in Northern Ireland, on the eve of the 1996 IRA Convention, and by so doing strengthened Adams's hand with delegates as he faced criticism orchestrated and led by Michael McKevitt.

It is Storey's close relationship with and uncritical support for Gerry Adams that adds a fascinating twist to the destabilizing events of 2002. Just as in the case of the Colombian adventure, it is inconceivable that operations on the scale of the Castlereagh raid and "Stormontgate" would have been unauthorized or unknown to members of the IRA's Army Council, which included both Gerry Adams and Martin McGuinness. Nor is it likely or at all credible that someone like Storey, ever the loyal soldier, would undertake such missions knowing that they would or could undermine Adams. The logic of all this strongly suggests that Adams, as well as McGuinness, both knew and approved of operations like Castlereagh and the spy ring before they happened and that when Bobby Storey planned and crafted them, he knew it was with their support and endorsement, as IRA leaders.

The next obvious question is why did Gerry Adams and his allies in the leadership give the go-ahead to such activities? One part of the answer is a variant on the old response, "because they could," in this case "because they could get away with them." As Bill Lowry's experience demonstrated, and the response of British and Irish ministers to previous incidents showed, there was huge reluctance on the part of officialdom to confront the republican leadership over such matters. In the cause of Adams's careful and hopefully successful management of his hard men, all things, or virtually all things, were permissible.

Nonetheless, this course of action was not without huge risk for Adams and his allies. By this stage of the Troubles security force penetration of the IRA was extensive. The PSNI Special Branch, British military intelligence and MI5 had so many agents placed at different levels of the IRA that at the time of the first cease-fire in 1994 eight out of every ten IRA operations were known to the intelligence agencies, according to one very authoritative assessment.[40] So when the Army Council authorized activity, whether it be an ambitious scheme like Stormontgate or a local shooting or abduction, the chances that it would come to light, notwithstanding the Nelson's eye of British intelligence and the indulgence of the British and Irish governments, were statistically very high indeed.

One possible explanation for this risk-taking was that the political fallout from such operations made it worthwhile. Within unionism, the impact was always to strengthen hardliners like Ian Paisley's DUP and undermine more accommodating figures like David Trimble. Destabilizing unionism was, by itself, a worthwhile prize for many nationalists. Not only that but against a background of rising unionist protest over sharing power with a Sinn Fein that was linked to a still very active and armed IRA, Trimble was obliged to toughen his language, if not his policy, on IRA decommissioning, and to deny Sinn Fein a place in government or restrict the workings of institutions like the cross-Border bodies until the matter was settled. All this had an equal if opposite effect upon nationalist opinion, which needed little encouragement to conclude that decommissioning was just an excuse invented or inflated by unionists to deny Sinn Fein, and the Catholics who supported it, the mandated right to participate in government.

To begin with, many Catholics had difficulty seeing David Trimble in anything resembling a friendly light or in accepting that he may have moderated his views over the years. His history and background had been one of association with the more hard-line, inflexible elements of unionism. He had, for instance, made political alliances with Paisley in the very recent past, most notoriously over the issue of the annual Drumcree Orange march, in Portadown, County Armagh, where each year local Orange lodges would attempt to march through a small Catholic area despite the intense opposition of its residents. For a number of years in the late 1990s the Drumcree march became an annual arm-wrestling match between unionism and nationalism and on one occasion, when the Orangemen won, Trimble danced a victory jig with Paisley through central Portadown and earned the undying hatred of many Catholics. In the 1970s he had joined the Vanguard party which had been founded by Bill Craig, the unrelenting unionist home affairs minister who had banned some of the early civil rights marches. In 1974 Trimble had sided with the loyalists opposed to the Sunningdale power-sharing deal and wrote the rule book for the Ulster Workers' Council whose general strike had combined with loyalist para-military muscle to bring down the deal. The image of Trimble as a liberal proponent of power-sharing with republicans was difficult for nationalists to swallow and so the Trimble who toughened his rhetoric on IRA decommissioning and stopped Sinn Fein from sitting at the cabinet table looked not much different from the ungenerous, inflexible Trimble of old.

Nationalists also saw Gerry Adams's stewardship of the Provisionals in much the same sympathetic light as Tony Blair and Bertie Ahern, and agreed that he would have to manage his activists carefully and delicately if he and his peace project were to survive. In particular they sympathized with him on the question of IRA decommissioning and regarded unionist demands for it as tantamount to seeking a humiliating surrender. As the battle over IRA decommissioning lengthened and became more bitter, another effect was to make the SDLP largely irrelevant and reduce it to quasi-spectator status. The political impact of all this was to drive more and more nationalists into Sinn Fein's camp and out of the SDLP's, while increasing numbers of unionists deserted David Trimble for the DUP.

The election results during the years between the resumption of the IRA cease-fire in 1997 up to the "Stormontgate" affair show a decisive swing within nationalist politics to Sinn Fein. In the 1997 Westminster general election the SDLP was still the dominant bloc, winning three seats to Sinn Fein's two and 60 percent of the nationalist vote. Four years later the situation had reversed. Sinn Fein outpolled the SDLP at the 2001 Westminster election by 51 percent to 49 percent and won four seats to the SDLP's three. It was a very similar, if not quite so dramatic, story on the unionist side. In 1997 Trimble's Ulster Unionists secured 71 percent of the Protestant vote to the DUP's 29 percent and held ten seats to the DUP's two. By 2001, how-ever, the share of the UUP vote had fallen to 54 percent, while Trimble's party now held just six seats to the DUP's five.

The battle over decommissioning and controversies surrounding IRA activity had benefited the extremes to the disadvantage of the center ground in Northern Ireland politics. The message for Sinn Fein from all this was that more of the same might help the Provos deliver the *coup de grâce* to the SDLP and hand the party complete dominion over nationalist politics. Or, put another way, conceding transparent decommissioning to Trimble might resolve the political impasse and take the heat out of politics but very possibly at the cost of re-energizing the center ground of nationalist politics and reviving the SDLP. In a very significant sense this was history repeating itself, a history whose lessons Sinn Fein had digested well. In 1981, the fact that the hunger strikes were still ongoing when Owen Carron stood in a by-election to replace Bobby Sands as MP for Fermanagh–South Tyrone meant that nationalists had a reason, almost an obligation, to turn out to vote for him. Had the hunger strikes been resolved before polling day, as they nearly were, Catholic voters would have stayed home in droves and Carron would never have won. Twenty years later, the decommissioning dispute would play a very similar motivating role on Sinn Fein's behalf throughout nation-alist communities in Northern Ireland. Like prolonging the hunger strike, Sinn Fein had everything to gain from drawing out the decommissioning dispute.

In the South the peace process, for somewhat different reasons, had also brought electoral benefits for Sinn Fein. The party had won its first Dail seat in the 1997 general election when Caoimhghin O Caolain won a seat in the Cavan–Monaghan constituency. In the 2002 election Sinn Fein's tally rose to five seats and the party fared well enough elsewhere to suggest it might triple its tally of seats at the next outing. One of those to win a seat was Martin Ferris, in Kerry North, and his victory meant that three of the seven members of the IRA's Army Council had been elected to parliaments in Ireland and Britain; if Pat Doherty had not left the Council in the interim, it would have been four. The peace process was enormously popular in the Irish Republic and the charismatic Sinn Fein leader, Gerry Adams, espe-cially so. Sinn Fein was also a new fresh face at a time when scandals about political corruption in other parties, especially Fianna Fail, abounded; the fact that the Provisionals' leaders had just emerged from armed struggle suggested they were still guided by principle and unlikely to be subverted by brown envelopes stuffed with cash, at least for a while.

There was also a good deal of pan-nationalist sympathy with Sinn Fein over the decommissioning battle with David Trimble and it was surely no coincidence that the IRA's second decommissioning event took place just weeks before the May 2002 Irish election, underlining the IRA's perceived fealty to the peace process even in the face of Trimble's unreasonableness. Indeed, some observers believe that but for the Colombia arrests and the September 11 attacks, this would have been the date for the first act of decommissioning. Adams and his allies were also aided by Trimble's own personal failings, not least an inability to resist intemperate language. He had won no friends in the South, for instance, when in March 2002 he called the Irish Republic "a pathetic, sectarian, mono-ethnic, mono-cultural State." Not surprisingly there was an indignant reaction in the Republic and Sinn Fein reaped the benefit. The message from the South, at least, was that denying transparency in the decommissioning process and continuing IRA activity while maintaining a rhetorical commitment to peace wasn't doing the party any harm.

If, as many people believed, the goal of the Adams strategy was first to become the dominant nationalist party in the North and a significant polit-ical force in the South, and second to subsequently occupy seats around cabinet tables on both sides of the Border at the same time, then it was on the way to being realized.

ACCORDING to the rules of the Good Friday Agreement, the next Assembly election, and therefore Sinn Fein's chance to deliver a knockout blow to the SDLP, was scheduled to take place in May 2003. Otherwise there wouldn't be a proper opportunity until at least 2005, when the next local council and Westminster elections would take place, and that was too far off for comfort. The problem facing Sinn Fein's strategists was that in the post-Stormontgate atmosphere there was no guarantee that there would still be an Assembly around in May 2003 to which elections would be held. The task facing them was to do just enough in terms of movement towards satisfying Trimble's demands to keep him in the game and to get a date con-firmed for the Assembly election while not doing so much that the fire under the decommissioning pot might be quenched.

And so the weary waltz recommenced, kick-started by an obliging Tony Blair who came to Belfast within days of the Assembly's suspension. He brought a message of comfort and reassurance to Trimble in the form of a warning to the IRA that it could no longer be "half in, half out" of the process and that "a fork in the road had been reached" in relation to con-tinued paramilitary activity. It was time for "acts of completion," he declared. A few days later the Sinn Fein charm offensive began with a speech from Gerry Adams in which he talked of seeing a future "without the IRA" and admitted that IRA actions had strengthened unionist inflexibility. Blair had also announced an end to endless "inch by inch" negotiations—but in fact the two speeches were the signal for another yearlong bout of precisely that sort of diplomacy.

By March 2003 talk of another deal-saving agreement was in the air and, with speculation rife that it could include both a resolution of the IRA decommissioning impasse and an indication that the IRA's war would be over for good, the parties and the two governments reassembled at Hillsborough Castle for talks that stretched into April and overlapped with the beginning of the U.S.-led invasion of Iraq. Blair and President Bush met at Hillsborough Castle just as American troops entered Baghdad. Blair hoped to talk Bush into giving the United Nations a greater role in reconstructing a post-Saddam Iraq. He also wanted the American leader to join him in giving the Irish parties a pep talk. According to one well-informed Irish political source, Sinn Fein had hinted that this summit would be the occasion to announce an IRA acceptance of the demands being made of it, something that might help cast Bush, already being castigated as a warmonger, in the role of peacemaker, or at least peace helper.[41] But as Irish officials arrived at Hillsborough, their glum faces signaled yet another disappointment and Bush, Condoleezza Rice and other White House luminaries had to settle for a tour of Hillsborough Castle and its Royal Throne Room instead of playing a supporting role in ending the Irish Troubles. As Sinn Fein leaders mixed and socialized with Bush and his entourage inside the Castle, outside a few party activists joined an anti-war rally. But the anti-war protesters were in no mood to indulge the spectacle of Provos riding two horses on this occasion and by all accounts gave them a dusty reception.

The talking stretched on for weeks and finally ended in early May 2003 in stalemate and a postponement of the Assembly elections. But before the blinds came down the IRA did just enough to ensure that the process would resume after the Orange marching season had ended and to preserve Sinn Fein hopes that the Assembly election might yet take place. The governments, through Tony Blair, were pressing the IRA to answer a number of questions: would the IRA end its activities, complete decommissioning and signal that the conflict would be over for keeps if the Good Friday Agreement was fully implemented? The IRA refused to give an explicit answer and instead Gerry Adams delivered a speech which replied "yes" to each question, albeit without stipulating a timeline. At this point events took a Kafkaesque turn. Rather than demand straight answers and honest dealing from the IRA, the governments instead asked if Adams had spoken with the IRA's authority and eventually the IRA agreed that he had. By participating in this style of diplomacy, the British and the Irish not only signaled their unwillingness to confront either Adams or the IRA but they also gave implicit credibility and legitimacy to one of the peace process's hoariest canards—that Adams had no direct ties to the IRA. Although he had been on the Army Council since the late 1970s, was a former chief of staff and adjutant-general and had been the IRA's leading political—and before that military—strategist for twenty-five years, Adams himself continued to insist that he had never even been a member, so much so that many in the media had long since abandoned attempts to probe the matter. By asking whether or not Adams's views reflected those of the IRA, Blair and Ahern gave credence to the idea that the Sinn Fein leader might not have any association with the IRA. If the way the IRA's peace process strategy was constructed under Adams's guiding hand is a reliable guide, then in much the same way that he talked to himself in the bathroom mirror each morning, Gerry Adams had probably helped to compose, and most certainly had approved, all three statements: the IRA's first statement which declined to specifically answer Tony Blair's questions, his own speech which did and finally the IRA's confirmation that Adams's affirmative answers reflected its own views. Asking if Gerry Adams spoke for the IRA was like asking George Bush if he spoke for the White House. In such ways did grown men manage the ending of one of Europe's longest post-war conflicts.

It all started up again in October 2003 but in ominous circumstances for David Trimble when three of his MPs, Jeffrey Donaldson, Martin Smyth and David Burnside, who had won back the South Antrim seat in the 2001 election, resigned the party whip. They demanded "acts of completion" before the Good Friday institutions could be restored and this added significantly to the likelihood that another failure would end Trimble's leadership. Senior Sinn Fein figures like Martin McGuinness warned, "We have no intention whatsoever of going near the IRA" unless an Assembly election date was offered and this appeared to have the desired effect.[42] Irish premier Bertie Ahern threw his weight behind the demand, even though a good result for Sinn Fein would likely strengthen the Provos' challenge to his own Fianna Fail party. Bush's ambassador to the peace process, state department official Richard Haass, also backed elections, and by the end of the first week in October, Blair's spin doctors were telling the media that an election date, November 13, 2003, had been penciled in. With an election all but confirmed, the only leverage on the IRA to do something significant had effectively been removed.

Once again speculation revolved around a deal that would involve a third and major act of IRA decommissioning, this time done in a credible and persuasive fashion, despite the confidentiality deal struck between Brian Keenan on behalf of the IRA and General de Chastelain for the decommissioning body. A statement from the IRA declaring an end to its activities and the conflict would be published and a commitment given by Sinn Fein to sign up to the new policing arrangements. Unofficially the election date was being described as a racing certainty. If the deal was anything like this, observers predicted, the Good Friday Agreement, the peace process and Trimble's leadership of unionism would all be assured.

The full story and explanation of the extraordinary events that unfolded on the day the deal was unveiled, October 21, 2003, have still to be fully established. Nor is it known whether what happened was the result of incompetence or deliberate neglect, especially on the part of the governments. What can be said with certainty is that the day was a debacle for David Trimble and led directly to his political downfall—but it was a triumph for Sinn Fein, thanks to IRA obduracy. Despite all the speculation about a breakthrough deal, the sequence of events was characterized by sloppy preparation and the absence of required detail. There was no statement ending its war by the IRA, merely a variation on the bathroom mirror diplomacy of the previous May, and no promise that the IRA would start winding down. Gerry Adams issued a statement saying merely that full implementation of the GFA would "provide full and final closure of the conflict" and while the IRA announced that Adams's statement "accurately reflects our position," the reality was that his statement was conditional, aspirational and lacking in necessary detail. Arguably the Adams–IRA statements of May 2003 were actually more compelling. Nor was there any commitment by Sinn Fein to sign up to the new policing dispensation.

What brought the edifice tumbling down was the inadequacy of the decommissioning event. Although everyone had assumed that the chairman of the IICD, General de Chastelain, had persuaded the IRA to relax its insistence on secrecy, it seems nobody, least of all David Trimble, had bothered to check whether this had happened. In fact the IRA had not budged at all and this failure was compounded by what was widely agreed to have been a dreadfully unpersuasive public performance by de Chastelain. At a press conference to announce the third decommissioning event, a weary and distracted de Chastelain, who had spent several sleep-deprived days in the field with Keenan and the IRA, could give no more details about what had happened than on the two earlier occasions. Even though a large amount of IRA weaponry had apparently been decommissioned, much bigger than on the two previous times, it was hinted, de Chastelain struggled to find the right words to get this message across and a colleague, the American member of the IICD, Andrew Sens, had to intervene in an effort to compensate. But it was too late. The fact that no details were provided, no inventory of destroyed weapons supplied, no description of how the arms had been put beyond use and no timetable for future decommissioning published meant that an event advertised as hugely significant was no more credible or compelling to unionists than the earlier decommissioning acts. The culprit was the confidentiality agreement which de Chastelain had agreed with the IRA, and without which, the General insists to this day, decommissioning would not have been possible.[43] All the non-IRA participants had failed to establish whether the confidentiality deal could be, or had been eased while Provo leaders sent out misleading signals. Martin McGuinness said that while there could be no independent witnesses to the decommissioning act the credibility problems associated with the two earlier decommissioning acts would be addressed. The third one, he told the media, "would prove more convincing for unionists."[44] That turned out to be an empty promise.

On the appointed day the IRA refused to budge from the confidentiality agreement and by so doing predetermined the day's outcome. Neither the British nor the Irish had tried to ensure that it would do otherwise; in fact the effect of their conceding the Assembly election date to Sinn Fein some time beforehand was to virtually guarantee that outcome. Having himself failed to compensate for the governments' shortcomings and with next to nothing to show for the day's work, Trimble halted the day's sequenced announcements, which were to have culminated in his agreement to restore the Assembly and Executive. By so doing he saved his leadership, at least for the time being. Sinn Fein had pocketed its election date, however—the announcement that an Assembly election would be held some five weeks later, on November 26, was the first act in the day's sequenced events, announced at 7 a.m., long before de Chastelain's disastrous performance in front of the media. As Sinn Fein prepared to go to the hustings it could argue to nationalist voters that the IRA had decommissioned more of its arsenal and indicated an intention to end the conflict, yet David Trimble and his unionist allies were still not satisfied and would not share power with republicans. If nationalists wanted to register their feelings about this they knew exactly how to mark their ballot papers on November 26.

No one was or could be surprised at the result of the Assembly election. Sinn Fein comprehensively hammered the SDLP, winning 58 percent of the nationalist vote, compared to the 44.5 percent it had secured in 1998. Its tally of seats in the 108-member Assembly rose from eighteen to twenty-four while the SDLP's fell from twenty-four to eighteen. The fortunes of the two parties had been reversed exactly and as the largest nationalist party in the parliament, Sinn Fein's likely nominee, former IRA chief of staff, Northern Commander and Army Council chairman, Martin McGuinness, would now become deputy first minister of Northern Ireland if the power-sharing Executive was ever restored. On the unionist side, Paisley's DUP triumphed, more by mopping up fringe loyalist support than by making a huge inroad into Trimble's Ulster Unionists. With thirty seats in the Assembly for the DUP, it would be Ian Paisley, not David Trimble, who would become first minister in a new government. By any stretch of the imagination it was an extraordinary result. As for Sinn Fein, the party's leaders and strategists surveying the landscape afterwards could be forgiven for believing that everything they touched turned to political gold. The Midas touch had been with them for the better part of two decades. The only question was—would it last?

TWENTY

The Last Kalashnikov

Belfast is one of those Victorian cities that looks its best in winter, during the dark, gloomy and wet months of the year; in summertime it is a city to vacate, if one can. This has something to do, perhaps, with the predominance of red brick in the city's buildings and the unsettling effect of bright sunshine reflected from rows of russet-stained houses. Overcast skies, rain streaming down the roof tiles and days when dusk begins to fall not long after lunchtime seem to suit the architecture of Belfast much better. December 2004 was a particularly dark month. Weather records show that there were less than fifty-one hours of sunshine during the entire month and Monday, December 20, was a typical day. The sun shone for just over two hours, peering fitfully through gaps in clouds that from time to time deposited a light drizzle over the city. That night, temperatures dropped below freezing, to 30 degrees Fahrenheit, a cold night for Belfast.

The dark winter months were also the season the IRA preferred. The cover of darkness allowed them greater rein and it was no accident that Army Conventions were invariably held at this time of the year or that it was in these months that the IRA had brought its Libyan weapons to Ireland. But those days had gone, or so it seemed, and the city had reason to be cheerful. Christmas was just a few days away and once again it promised to be a peaceful holiday. It had been ten years since the IRA had called its first cease-fire and while a political settlement was still beyond reach there was a growing conviction that the bad old days of bombs and bullets would never return. People were getting used to the idea that they could travel without being held up at security force roadblocks or contemplate a night's drinking or a meal in one of the city's many new restaurants without the fear that it might end in a hail of machine-gun bullets. Traders in the city centre were looking forward to a bumper holiday season. Peace and currency-related price differentials that favored the shopper were tempting thousands of newly affluent Southerners to abandon their fear of the North in favour of bargain-hunting, and there were predictions that this year's holiday business in Belfast would rise by as much as five percent. On the evening of December 20, as office workers streamed home, their journey was cheered by Christmas lights and decorations strung around the city hall and the festive, expectant melodia of carols piped into the frosty evening air.

At 11 o'clock that night, as the city centre emptied and began slipping into slumber, the phone rang in the control room of the Police Service of Northern Ireland in the Knock district of East Belfast and soon, nothing would ever be the same again. At the other end of the phone was a twenty-four-year-old bank official called Chris Ward, a Catholic from Poleglass, a rambling estate of public sector housing built in the 1980s to accommodate the overflow from West Belfast. Ward was a beneficiary of Northern Ireland's reformed work practices and held down a good, pensionable job with the Northern Bank, one of four local clearing banks that had the right to print their own distinctive notes. There were more Catholics working in the banking sector in 2004 than ever before in Northern Ireland's history. Long a preserve of the Protestant lower middle classes, fair employment laws that came into force in the late 1970s, and which were beefed up after the IRA cease-fires, obliged the banks to appoint their workforces on the basis of merit rather than background or nepotism. Ward's work was in the underground vault of the Northern Bank's Belfast cash center in Donegal Square, adjacent to city hall, which distributed notes to the bank's ninety-five branches and to hundreds of ATMs scattered around the country. It was Christmastime and there were an awful lot of notes in the vault that day.

Ward's phone call to the PSNI was to tell the police that a great number of those notes had just been stolen in an audacious, meticulously planned robbery carried out with military-style efficiency by an armed and determined gang. The night before, as he and his family watched television, armed men had tricked their way into his home and Ward had been abducted and his family held hostage, guarded in the house by armed men. He was driven to Loughinisland, near Downpatrick, County Down, to the home of Kevin McMullan, a colleague and supervisor at the cash center. Earlier, men posing as PSNI officers had called at the McMullan home and, pretending to have bad news for Kevin's wife Karen, gained entry to the house. There had been a bad car crash in County Tyrone involving her sister, they claimed, but this was a lie. The men produced handguns, tied up Kevin, blindfolded Karen and took her away. That night the gang forced the two bank officials to an upstairs bedroom and coached them in the parts they would play in what the following day would be the world's largest robbery of cash from a bank. Members of the gang were very forensically aware; they wore surgical gloves, overalls and had masks over their faces. Even their hair had been cut short so as to reduce the chance that discarded strands might provide vital DNA evidence to the police. The gang also questioned the men about procedures at the bank, but it was more a case of double-checking what they already knew. Both the bank and the PSNI would say later that the gang was very well informed about security at the cash centre. With their families held as hostage Ward and McMullan had little option but to cooperate.

The next morning the two men arrived at work as usual, armed with mobile phones supplied by the gang to communicate with them. In the afternoon, Ward took £1 million from the vault, placed it in a holdall and, following the gang's instructions, left the building. Outside he passed the bag over to a man waiting at a nearby bus shelter. This was the gang's way of testing if the police had been alerted. At the close of business the rest of the staff went home but Ward and McMullan stayed on. Eventually a white transit van pulled up in an alleyway beside the bank where Ward and McMullan were waiting with trolleys piled high with what appeared to be rubbish, shredded documents and so on. But underneath the covering of garbage lay green cardboard boxes stuffed with banknotes which the two bank officials had removed from the vault. These they rolled through a gate and into the alley where the van was loaded. A passer-by would assume that the van was carting away bank rubbish and be completely unaware that an audacious robbery was taking place. The van drove off and forty minutes later it returned, suggesting that the gang had an operational headquarters not far away. Ward and McMullan were waiting with more trolleys piled high with rubbish-covered boxes of cash. The gang could have returned for a third run but decided against it—perhaps this would have been tempting fate. The vault had not been emptied entirely but as the scale of the raid emerged that became an academic point. By the time Northern Bank's management had finished their sums the following morning it was clear that the gang had netted a huge haul: £26.5 million in all; £16.5 million in new Northern banknotes and £10 million in old notes and various currencies.[1]

It took the PSNI eighteen days to confirm publicly what the dogs in the Belfast streets had already guessed, which was that only one organization had the manpower, discipline, track record and intelligence skills to carry out such an ambitious robbery and that was the Provisional IRA. Precisely why the PSNI chief constable, Hugh Orde, held back for so long is still unknown. Unionists blamed this slowness on policing reforms introduced as part of the process of weaning the Provos into democratic politics. In particular, they claimed, the Special Branch had been vitiated; well-placed informers had been discarded in a vetting procedure designed to weed out disreputable types, leaving the Branch blind and able to learn of IRA activity only too late. It seems, however, that the PSNI knew almost immediately who was responsible. Others speculated that the delay was not the fault of any weaknesses in police intelligence but was caused by political considerations and inspired by British and Irish governments at a loss what to do in the face of such brazen criminality, knowing that their Nelson's eye approach to previous IRA activity had finally caught up with them and perhaps hoping something would happen to save them from having to confront the IRA's political leadership.

IF POLITICAL FUNK by the two governments explains the delay in responding to the Northern Bank robbery, one obvious reason was that ten days before the robbery Tony Blair and Bertie Ahern had come within an ace of announcing a comprehensive agreement between Sinn Fein and the DUP and they didn't want to lose it entirely. The scale and ambition of the putative deal were astonishing given the glacial pace of events in the previous seven years and it would have been surprising had the two prime ministers not paused before reacting to the Northern Bank heist, given the potential that this would have to destroy a deal that was still, technically, on the table. The near settlement, after all, would effectively have brought the peace process to a conclusion by completing the Provos' journey into constitutional politics. Its principal elements were:

- The completion of IRA decommissioning by the end of December 2004;
- A commitment by the IRA to permanently end all paramilitary activity;
- Verification of this by the new Independent Monitoring Commission (IMC);
- Policing and justice to be devolved to the power-sharing Executive;
- Sinn Fein commitment to win party approval for joining the North's Policing Board and recognition of the PSNI;

- Agreement by the DUP and Sinn Fein to nominate candidates for first and deputy first minister posts;
- Restoration by March 2005 of the Assembly, Executive and North–South Ministerial Council and abolition of the British government's power to suspend them.

Barely a year had passed since the decommissioning crisis that had fatally undermined David Trimble and paved the way for a new Assembly election. Suddenly all those internal difficulties and weaknesses which had allegedly prevented the Adams leadership from rapid and decisive action had melted away like snow off a ditch in springtime. There had been no dramatic changes in the IRA's internal structures or mechanics in the meantime to explain this startling transformation; the same Army Council that had refused Trimble decommissioning transparency in October 2003 and declined to explicitly state that its war was over was by December 2004 suddenly willing to approve the completion of decommissioning and declare a permanent end to all IRA activity. The willingness of the IRA to make such a commitment was compelling evidence that the protestations in the years before about the great internal obstacles in the way of such moves were self-serving. Observers with long enough memories recalled how the 1981 hunger strikes had been handled with a similar sleight of hand. Throughout the protest figures like Gerry Adams had protested that the Army Council could not order it to end, but after Sinn Fein had extracted the maximum political profit, the Army Council brought it to a halt with the stroke of a pen.[2]

What had changed was that, thanks to the Assembly election, Sinn Fein was now the dominant nationalist party and their once powerful rivals, the SDLP, reduced to a shadow of what the party had once been. Those friendly to Sinn Fein would argue that having now proved that politics worked the Provo leadership had the self-confidence to move into acts of completion. A more cynical view held that the decommissioning issue had served its purpose and, having exploited it in order to attain nationalist electoral hegemony, it was time for the Provos to seize their political prizes, including a Sinn Fein deputy first ministry, and do a final deal. Whichever version is correct, one reality is undeniable: had the Adams leadership's claim of internal resistance to decommissioning been correct—and on the scale asserted between 1998 and 2003—then the 2004 deal would never have been possible.

The other element that made the 2004 deal viable was that the DUP's dislike of the Good Friday Agreement was not so deep or strongly held that its leadership would reject the opportunity of taking power, even if the cost was having to share it with loyalism's mortal enemy. Although the DUP had boycotted the Good Friday Agreement negotiations, once the power-sharing Executive was up and running the party's leaders decided that the ministerial posts on offer by virtue of the DUP's electoral strength were too tempting to reject. And so the party's deputy leader, Peter Robinson, and the North Belfast MP Nigel Dodds became ministers in the Executive. They declined to attend full Executive meetings or to take part in the North–South institutions but otherwise they enjoyed and exercised the full benefits and powers of office. While they did this, they sniped away at David Trimble from the sidelines over issues like decommissioning and continuing IRA activity. As Trimble lifted unionism's heavy load, the DUP sat and waited for him to stumble and fall, which in the November 2003 Assembly election he finally did, allowing the DUP to do to the Ulster Unionists what Sinn Fein was doing to the SDLP. The DUP benefited electorally from the IRA's stance on decommissioning every bit as much as Sinn Fein and if some observers could see in the DUP a mirror image of the Provos' cynical opportunism, it was understandable.

The path to the deal had been reasonably smooth, at least by the standard of previous years. The IRA's attempted abduction in February 2004 of a republican dissident, Bobby Tohill, from a Belfast city-center bar, which Gerry Adams attempted to characterize as "a bar room brawl", briefly revived doubts about the IRA's intentions. But by May, following contacts with Sinn Fein and the DUP during a review of the Good Friday Agreement, Blair and Ahern declared themselves confident that a deal could be finalized by the autumn. European elections in June confirmed the electoral dominance of Sinn Fein and the DUP. The seat held since 1979 by the former SDLP leader John Hume, who had quit politics entirely in February 2004, went to Bairbre de Brun as Sinn Fein outpolled the SDLP by a margin of five to three. Ian Paisley had also retired from Europe and his seat went to a DUP barrister, Jim Allister, who more comprehensively trounced the Ulster Unionist candidate, winning two votes for every one for the UUP. In September the Northern parties and the two governments decamped to Leeds Castle in Kent for talks which later resumed in Belfast. By the end of November all the elements of the deal had been agreed bar one.

Once again the process was being held up by the lack of transparency in the proposal for IRA decommissioning. Although the Army Council agreed that it would fully disarm within weeks and that two clerical figures, one Protestant and the other Catholic, could witness the event, it was refusing to accept the DUP's nominee. Paisley wanted to nominate the Reverend David McGaughey, a former Presbyterian moderator and a strong opponent of ecumenism. He had once called the Catholic Church's teachings "unbiblical" and often excoriated the IRA; he was, in DUP eyes, a figure likely to be more credible to Protestants than the IRA's choice.[3] Nor was the IRA prepared to allow the clerical witnesses freedom to describe in detail what they had seen. One exchange between the DUP and Tony Blair over this issue gave a revealing insight into the British prime minister's elasticity in such negotiations. The DUP pointed out that the decommissioning act barred such witnesses from speaking out unless they had been given permission to do so and since the IRA was refusing to relax this rule, the IICD could not budge either. The witnesses would have to stay silent and their contribution would thus be greatly devalued, unless a way could be found around the problem. "Blair's answer to that was 'Well, the moment these people come back they can resign [from the IICD] and speak,' recalled one DUP participant. "We pointed out that the legislation says they must stay silent 'during or after they leave the service' and Blair said 'It's up to them'. We said back, 'We're talking about Christian ministers here, they're not going to come back and break their word on these issues!'"[4]

A bigger problem was posed by a proposal that the decommissioning event be photographed and the pictures published so as to convince unionists. The republicans rejected this idea outright. Publicly and in the privacy of negotiations they maintained this was because to do so would be to allow the IRA to be to humiliated. But another effect of photographs appearing would be to remove any doubt whatsoever that when IRA and Sinn Fein leaders assured their grassroots that de Chastelain "had been conned" and no guns had been destroyed, they had been lying.

Although a settlement that would see Ian Paisley and Martin McGuinness share the top political jobs in Northern Ireland was within reach, the DUP was still refusing to have face-to-face talks with Sinn Fein and it had to rely on the British for information about the republican negotiating stance. The British kept the Provos' refusal to allow photographs to be taken from the DUP and instead directed the negotiations towards the question of when photographs would appear. The DUP wanted immediate publication but agreed to delay this until the Executive was up and running, an event planned for the following March. This idea came from the new US envoy to the peace process, Mitchell Reiss. Then Ian Paisley publicly called on the IRA to express repentance for its past violence; the republicans should be made to wear "sackcloth and ashes," he said. By the end of the first week of December the issue of photographs had stalled the negotiations but this didn't mean they had failed. Gerry Adams said that Sinn Fein should accept everything in the British—Irish proposals except the decommissioning plan and when Blair and Ahern traveled to Belfast on December 8, they published the full text of the planned and sequenced agreement. In the past the Provos had always withdrawn their proposals if negotiations broke down but this time they stayed on the table for all to see, at least for a while. Only the practicalities of final decommissioning stood in the way of a settlement; the principle had been conceded. The problem Gerry Adams and his leadership colleagues then faced was how to revive the deal without having to address the DUP's demand for photographic proof of decommissioning.

IT WAS against this background that news of the Northern Bank robbery broke and London and Dublin struggled to construct a response. The eighteen-day hiatus between the raid and the PSNI chief constable's announcement of IRA culpability had at least given the governments time to ponder what this should be. When Hugh Orde finally pointed the finger at the IRA, both Blair and Ahern were quick to back him up. It was evident that the two leaders realized that the huge scale of the robbery meant that turning a Nelson's eye to IRA activity was no longer sustainable. But what had brought this about? The governments knew that the IRA had put together a special robbery team and that it had been active throughout 2004. In May the IRA had staged a multimillion-pound theft of white goods, freezers, washing machines and the like, from a wholesale supermarket in Dunmurry, on the edge of West Belfast. In September, several hundred thousand pounds' worth of produce were stolen from the Strabane, County Tyrone, branch of the supermarket chain Iceland. In October, cigarettes with a retail value of over £2 million were stolen from a bonded warehouse in Belfast docks. Both this robbery and the raid in Strabane involved abductions and hostage-taking and may have been practice runs for the much bigger Northern Bank heist.[5] Yet neither London nor Dublin had protested to the republican leadership. What made the difference, clearly, was the scale of the Northern Bank robbery. That made a tough response obligatory.

The governments played the role of outraged and betrayed partners. While Tony Blair called on republicans to end all criminal activity and said unionists would be justified in spurning Sinn Fein as a government partner until that happened, Bertie Ahern took the offensive, presumably on the grounds that a fellow nationalist could get away with saying things to the

Provos that a British leader could not. Immediately after Hugh Orde's announcement, the taoiseach implicated the Sinn Fein leadership in the crime. The robbery, he said, was "obviously being planned at a stage when I was in negotiations with those that would know the leadership of the Provisional movement." Ahern didn't quite name Gerry Adams and Martin McGuinness but everyone knew what he meant. A few days later he gave an RTE radio interview and went a step further. "This was an IRA job. This was a Provisional IRA job. This was a job that would have been known to the leadership. This was a job that would have been known to the political leadership. That is my understanding. I am upset, quite frankly, that in the period when we were in intensive talks trying to get a comprehensive agreement that my information is now that people in very senior positions would have known what was going on."[6] The following month the Republic's justice minister, Michael McDowell, filled in the blank spaces, naming Adams, McGuinness and Martin Ferris as members of the Army Council and alleging that the Provisional movement was "engaged in massive criminality," earning millions of pounds which was laundered through a network of solicitors and accountants.[7] In the coming months McDowell, a leading member of the Progressive Democrats, would emerge as the Provisionals' most acerbic critic, given free rein by government colleagues to vent his deep dislike of the IRA and Sinn Fein. As much as anything else, this was a reflection of the newly enhanced role the Northern Bank robbery had given to Garda intelligence and McDowell's Department of Justice in formulating Irish policy on the peace process.

Bertie Ahern's and Michael McDowell's logic was that if Adams and McGuinness had, as Army Council members, given the go-ahead for the Northern Bank raid, then it surely followed that they had foreknowledge of other major IRA operations, like the Colombian adventure, the Castlereagh raid and "Stormontgate". The notion that the IRA organized operations behind their backs was therefore a fiction—and the governments knew this. And if this was the case, then it was possible also that the parallel presentation of Adams and McGuinness as moderates battling against hard-liners and obliged to move slowly and carefully was also a fabrication which the two governments had either fallen for or decided to indulge. The Northern Bank robbery did nothing less than raise large question marks against British and Irish policy towards the IRA in the post-Good Friday Agreement years.

The Provisionals' response to all this was predictable. The Sinn Fein denial featured the now-familiar assertion of pot-stirring by British securocrats who had staged the robbery, as they had the Castlereagh break-in and the "Stormontgate" spy ring, in order to damage the peace process and blacken Sinn Fein. Only Sinn Fein's most uncritical supporters in Irish America fell for this. The IRA also issued a terse, two-line statement denying responsibility and then in early February took the December 2004 proposals off the table. When that failed to impress the governments, the IRA warned London and Dublin not to "underestimate the seriousness of the situation," an implied threat that the cease-fire could break down.[8] If the statement was meant to spread alarm in London and Dublin, it signally failed; the days of pretending the IRA could go back to war had ended as comprehensively as had tolerance of its excesses.

So why had the IRA authorized the Northern Bank robbery? One obvious answer was the £26.5 million in proceeds, a sum that could be invested in lucrative, money-making ventures. In February, the Gardai recovered £60,000 in raids in Cork and Dublin that was subsequently traced to the Northern Bank cash center and arrested several people, including one man who was found trying to burn sterling banknotes in his back garden. Meanwhile the investigation of a County Cork-based finance company, Chesterton Finance, which had been tied to the discovery of £2.3 million in Northern Bank-linked cash, forced the resignation of Phil Flynn, a nonexecutive director of Chesterton, as chairman of the Irish branch of the Bank of Scotland. Flynn, an associate of Bertie Ahern, was a former vicepresident of Sinn Fein and a leading trade unionist who had, in the public eye at least, dropped out of republican politics. Subsequent police inquiries led to Bulgaria where intermediaries for the IRA were said to have been interested in buying a £15 million apartment block, a hotel and a shopping centre as well as a small bank, which police suspected would be used to launder this [Bulgarian] and other investments.[9] The Northern Bank raid had lifted a small corner on the IRA's burgeoning financial empire. Always broke and casting around for money when the war was raging, in peacetime the IRA had little on which to spend its revenues and had amassed a small fortune. According to one authoritative claim, by 2006 it had built up an investment portfolio worth some £200 million in hotels, discos, bars and apartments in the Caribbean, Portugal, Turkey and of course both parts of Ireland.[10]

But the IRA's political leaders, who were as astute a group of strategists as could be found in any political organization, must have known that the Northern Bank raid would be a robbery too far. The robbery took place just a week before Christmas, days before the peak of the seasonal shopping spree, when demand at outlying branches of the bank for notes would be at its height and stocks at the cash center consequently large. A Northern Bank spokesman confirmed that it would not have been unusual for the cash center to be holding as much as £26.5 million, given the time of the year,[11] while other banking sources said there was perhaps twice as much cash in stock on the night of the raid, more than £50 million. Suggestions that the IRA was taken by surprise by the amount of cash available sit uneasily beside the evidently high level of inside information about the bank's affairs and procedures in the IRA's possession. The gang's questioning of Chris Ward and Kevin McMullen alone pointed strongly in that direction, as did the timing of the robbery. It seems very likely that the IRA would have been fully aware beforehand that the haul would be very large and that the political consequences would therefore be profound and wide-ranging. If the IRA had taken £2.6 million they might have got away with it and the governments enabled to turn a blind eye once more. But knowingly stealing £26.5 million was an entirely different matter, something no one could ignore. If Adams and McGuinness had known about the robbery before it took place, as the Irish prime minister alleged, then they would surely have known this too.

Claims by Bertie Ahern that Sinn Fein leaders like Gerry Adams and Martin McGuinness knew the raid was imminent as they negotiated the December 2004 peace deal with him are credible for two reasons. One is that, once again, the mastermind behind the raid was the IRA's director of intelligence, Bobby Storey, the loyal disciple of the Adams leadership who had organized the Castlereagh and Stormontgate operations on behalf of the Army Council.[12] Another compelling clue was provided by the Independent Monitoring Commission in a report of May 2005. This pointed out that in the draft peace agreement published by London and Dublin in early December 2004, a statement to be issued by the IRA was to have included a commitment "not to endanger anyone's personal rights and safety." Yet when the IRA issued its own version of this statement on December 9, eleven days before the robbery, these words had been excised from the text, which otherwise read exactly as anticipated by the two governments.[13] Participants in the negotiations also say that during the talks, the Sinn Fein delegation fiercely resisted the wording about "personal rights and safety." Since the Northern Bank robbery most assuredly did lead to the endangerment of "personal rights and safety," the obvious explanation for Sinn Fein's negotiating stance and the December 9 IRA statement was that they were well aware of the planned robbery and the abductions and hostage-taking that it would entail. It also suggests that the robbery might well have gone ahead even if there had been a deal with the DUP.

In the days and weeks that followed the robbery the damage caused to the Provisionals mounted. IRA criminality became an issue and was fueled when on a popular RTE television programme, Derry Sinn Fein leader Mitchel McLaughlin refused to describe Jean McConville's murder and disappearance in 1972 (when Gerry Adams was Belfast Brigade commander) as "a crime." The spotlight then turned on the IRA's chief of staff, Slab Murphy, in South Armagh and to the IRA's involvement in cross-Border smuggling, counterfeiting and other forms of criminality. Michael McDowell then named Gerry Adams as an IRA leader, the first time his claim to have no links to the IRA had been challenged in such a public and damaging way by the Irish government. Bertie Ahern then ended any possibility that the killers of a Garda Special Branch detective, Jerry McCabe, shot dead during a Post Office robbery in County Limerick in June 1996, would be released. Four members of the IRA unit responsible were convicted and sentenced to between eleven and fourteen years in jail, but the Irish government, ever sensitive to the feelings of Garda rank and file, refused to release them along with other IRA prisoners under the terms of the Good Friday Agreement. The IRA Army Council and Sinn Fein had denied the robbery was an authorized operation, but a subsequent internal inquiry found that the robbery had been approved but that Garda McCabe had been accidentally shot by a member of the gang. They went on the run and were eventually arrested in circumstances that caused controversy inside the IRA following allegations that their apprehension had been contrived to end Sinn Fein's embarrassment over the affair.[15] Sinn Fein leaders then took up their case and their release was, until the Northern Bank robbery, a side deal to the final settlement agreed with Dublin. The days of indulging the Provisional leadership had come to an end, at least for now. As one *Irish Times* political reporter put it: :"The [governments] new stance marks nothing less than a fundamental break with the tolerance of fudge and ambiguity, qualities deliberately deployed for 10 years to help the process along."[16]

As the damage intensified, the language used by Sinn Fein's leaders underwent subtle changes. Former IRA adjutant-general Gerry Kelly called the robbery "wrong." Along with Adams and McGuinness, Kelly had held face-to-face talks with Bertie Ahern before the raid and was presumably one of those in the "political leadership" the taoiseach had classed as having foreknowledge. Martin McGuinness, who initially had strongly supported the IRA denials, modified his line, saying: "Whoever carried out the robbery are also hostile to the Sinn Fein agenda and the peace process, and under no circumstances should any of these people get their way in the ongoing discussions which will have to take place if we are to resolve our political difficulties."[17] A few days later he went further: "If the IRA had been involved ... there would have been a defining moment in Sinn Fein's leadership's work with the IRA. It would have been totally and absolutely unacceptable to me."[18]

It was clear that by robbing the Northern Bank, the IRA had shot itself badly in the foot and the organization's political leaders needed to prepare their supporters for the radical corrective action that would be needed if lost ground was to be recaptured. The only credible way to do that would be if the IRA disposed finally of its remaining weapons. Whether or not figures like Adams and McGuinness had guessed that the robbery would cause huge political fallout or had endorsed it in the hope that it would, a resolution of the decommissioning impasse had nonetheless been opened up. But the story was only beginning.

EVER SINCE BRITISH paratroopers had gunned down fourteen men during a civil rights march and demonstration in Derry against the use of internment without trial in January 1972, the events of "Bloody Sunday" had assumed iconic importance in the Northern nationalist psyche. What the bulk of nationalists viewed as the outrageous cover-up of the day's bloodshed was orchestrated by the Lord Chief Justice of England and Wales, Lord Widgery, at the tribunal of inquiry named after him. The Widgery tribunal had, for many, become a metaphor for British misrule in Northern Ireland, and its conclusions, which were published just eleven weeks after the killings and essentially took the British army's version of events at face value, saying that the shooting spree had been justified when soldiers had been fired upon. Lord Widgery's strongest criticism of the paratroopers' action was to say that their firing had at times "bordered on the reckless". By the 1990s there was a consensus stretching way beyond Irish nationalism that the Widgery tribunal had been deeply flawed. As new evidence emerged about the events, a campaign to reopen the inquiry won the support of the Irish government and in January 1998, British premier Tony Blair announced that a new inquiry would be held. Headed by Lord Saville of Newdigate, assisted by Canadian judge William Hoyt and Australian judge John L. Toohey, the new tribunal was to last six years and cost a staggering £400 million,[19] a boon to Northern Ireland's already Troubles-enriched legal profession, but setting up the new inquiry was a move that the British doubtless regarded as a preparatory soothing balm for the Provisional movement as the Good Friday Agreement negotiations moved towards a conclusion.

Every year the deaths of Bloody Sunday were commemorated by the people of Derry in a march that traced the same route as on that fateful day and the nearest weekend to the anniversary would be taken up with talks, films and music organized by and for the community still affected by the tragedy and for republicans throughout Ireland. By January 2005 the Bloody Sunday commemoration ranked alongside June's trip to Bodenstown, August's West Belfast festival and the annual Sinn Fein Ard Fheis as occasions for pilgrimage when Provisional supporters from all over the country would gather to reaffirm their political faith, renew acquaintances and enjoy the *craic*.

On Sunday, January 31, 2005, Belfast republicans had as usual traveled to Derry to take part in the march and then returned to Belfast by bus. In Magennis's Bar in central Belfast that evening a crowd of perhaps two dozen republicans, most of them Sinn Fein members or supporters but some who were senior figures in the Belfast IRA, gathered for a drinking session after the journey. Magennis's Bar is situated in May Street, behind Belfast's Law Courts and was a popular lunchtime haunt for barristers, solicitors and their clients. At night time and at the weekend, however, Magennis's clientele was very different—much of the bar's trade came from the adjacent Markets area and nearby Short Strand across the River Lagan, two small nationalist enclaves well known for their republican activism. Amongst the drinkers in the bar that night were two friends, Brendan Devine and Robert McCartney, a thirty-four-year-old father of two small boys from Short Strand who was engaged to be married later that year to his long-time partner Bridgeen Hagans.

The pair hadn't been to Derry but they knew many of the republicans in the bar and had cause to be wary of them; there was a history of bad blood between some of the IRA men and Brendan Devine. A row began when one of the IRA men challenged them over rude gestures they were making to each other, which were seen as being directed at a woman in their company. The matter was quickly settled but one IRA man was not satisfied and began an argument with Devine. He was the senior IRA man present, Gerard "Jock" Davison, a former Belfast Brigade commander.[20] Davison had once been associated with anti-Adams elements on the Brigade staff, and was even considered by them at one point as a potential new chief of staff if their conspiracy against the pro-peace strategy leadership had succeeded. But Davison had since defected to the peace process camp. The events in Magennis's Bar that night were later painstakingly reconstructed by the family of Robert McCartney, the PSNI and the local media and, although elements were denied by Davison, no independent evidence has emerged to disprove their account. During the brawl, Davison was reported as having "glanced at some of his IRA associates and to have drawn his finger across his throat, a signal as to what he wanted done to Mr. McCartney and his friend Brendan Devine.[21] The row between Davison, his IRA associates and Devine ended when Devine's throat was slashed open and a bottle smashed over his head; blood spilled everywhere, mixing with shards of glass on the bar floor. There was a lull, significantly, between that violence and what followed a few minutes later. According to one informed source, a gun was sent for but, before it arrived, the IRA men had managed to obtain other weapons, including knives.[22] As that was happening, Robert McCartney half-carried his friend Brendan Devine out of the bar but as they staggered into a nearby alleyway, the IRA gang, up to eight-strong according to eye-witness testimony given later to the PSNI, pursued them, kicking and punching them and fatally stabbing McCartney and leaving Devine badly injured.[23] McCartney was left to lie bleeding profusely as the IRA gang returned to the bar where, led by Davison, they ordered customers not to talk about what had happened while an IRA team was dispatched to clean up the bar to destroy any forensic evidence of the fight and to remove CCTV security footage. No attempt was made to help McCartney nor even to send for an ambulance. A passing PSNI patrol discovered him and he was taken to hospital where he died the next day. It was later established that Robert McCartney's murder was not the result of a bar brawl that had got out of hand but was premeditated and planned.

If it hadn't been for Robert McCartney's five sisters, Gemma, Paula, Claire, Catherine and Donna, and his partner Bridgeen Hagans, it is possible that his murder would have been quickly forgotten, filed away as just another manifestation of the knife culture then spreading throughout Belfast. The murder of Robert McCartney was not an authorized IRA operation but it had been carried out by IRA members and, his family insisted, was then covered up and witnesses silenced by the IRA. "Their cover-up and their clean-up operation afterwards was meticulous," said Paula McCartney.[24] The campaign the McCartney family launched to bring the killers of their brother to justice would have implications for the peace process that at the time no one could have anticipated.

The most puzzling aspect of the events that followed concerns the way the Provisional leadership, Sinn Fein and the IRA, handled calls for the killers of Robert McCartney to be dealt with. There was no nationalist sympathy at all for the IRA gang responsible and seasoned strategists like Gerry Adams would very quickly have known that. What had happened to Robert McCartney was in no way political and couldn't remotely be associated with the IRA's struggle or Sinn Fein's political agenda. In fact the killers had abused and misused IRA resources by employing a forensic team to destroy evidence of an indisputably criminal act. A vigil in the Short Strand a few days afterwards demonstrated the depth of grassroots feeling in a district whose fierce loyalty to the Provisional IRA had been sealed thirty-five years earlier when Belfast IRA commander Billy McKee and two other men had fought off an armed loyalist assault on the area at the cost of one of their lives and severe bullet wounds to McKee. Some 1,500 people turned out, a significant proportion of the area's population—most of them, like some in the McCartney clan, Sinn Fein supporters and voters. One account of the vigil posted on the internet described members of the crowd openly using terms like "scum of the earth" and "animals" to describe the killers.[25] These were the Provisionals' own grassroots excoriating members of the IRA.

The cost to the IRA leadership associated with bringing the affair to a speedy and satisfactory conclusion by obliging the killers to turn themselves in, as the IRA arguably could have done, or by assisting the collection of eyewitness evidence against them, was very low and the benefits potentially very high. The murder of Robert McCartney had after all happened in the wake of a bank robbery that had stained the IRA with the charge of gangsterism and criminality. Bringing the killers to justice or to distance the IRA from them convincingly would have gone a long way to repair the damage and the move would surely have been popular with nationalists. Just over a year later both Gerry Adams and Martin McGuinness would publicly urge the alleged abductors of Bobby Tohill to turn themselves in for trial after the men had absconded. Yet they and their associates would dodge and weave to avoid taking an equally resolute position against Robert McCartney's murderers.

Towards the end of February the IRA announced that it had courtmartialled and dismissed three of its volunteers involved in the events. One of these was "Jock" Davison. But within days the IRA sent a very different message about Davison's status in the organization when he walked through the Short Strand area beside Bobby Storey, the IRA's director of intelligence and one of Gerry Adams's most fervent supporters. It was a brazenly defiant gesture, meant to signify that he was still in the fold and able to enjoy the protection of the IRA. A few weeks later Davison was seen canvassing for Sinn Fein candidates in local elections. The implied leniency towards Davison was later confirmed by the IRA which told the McCartneys that Davison was expelled because he had been involved in a bar brawl but would be allowed to reapply for IRA membership after six months. Davison had been charged by the IRA with a minor offence; he could have been court-martialled with the far graver crime of misusing IRA resources—employing IRA members to forensically cleanse a non-IRA operational scene. Other IRA members convicted of similar activity in the past had been shot dead by the organization.

Robert McCartney's sisters had compiled a list of Sinn Fein members who were in the bar at the time of the attack, all of them potential eyewitnesses, which they passed on to Gerry Adams. The Sinn Fein president then announced that a number of party members had been suspended until the legal process was completed, adding that he had urged them to make statements to the police, either via a lawyer or to the police ombudsman, about what they had seen. But those suspended—allegedly some twelve party members—were, according to Sinn Fein, not on the list supplied by the McCartneys and the party refused to name them.[26] Nothing happened to those named by the family. Catherine McCartney is in little doubt what this meant: "They're telling lies, they didn't suspend anyone. They didn't name them for that reason."[27] The witness statements turned over to the police turned out to be useless. Some were unsigned, others maintained they had seen nothing, an unlikely claim given the violence of the affray, or that they had been in the toilet at the time of the incident, an assertion that led some to suggest wryly that Magennis's Bar must have had the largest toilet of any pub in Ireland. When one witness did agree to be interviewed by PSNI detectives, the detectives' questions were so lengthy and probing that afterwards no other Sinn Fein member would come forward.[28] When two men were eventually charged in connection with the McCartney murder, they were housed in a remand wing of a local jail reserved for republicans, something that couldn't happen without the say-so of the IRA Command structure.

At one point the McCartney family met with the IRA, which afterwards issued a statement saying that an offer had been made to shoot the men responsible. But according to Catherine McCartney this never happened: "One of them said these people [the killers] meant nothing to him and he would shoot them in the morning. That was just an expression. The only thing they offered was to make it impossible for them to abscond. Some said it was for the benefit of their grassroots, so that they could say, 'We offered to shoot them but they refused. What more do they want?' But I don't know why they did it."[29] Whatever the reason, the incident put the IRA in an even worse light, especially across the Atlantic.

In March, the White House announced that President Bush had invited the McCartney sisters to the annual St. Patrick's Day bash, an event that since Bill Clinton's time had given Gerry Adams the opportunity to revel amid the powerful friends that the peace strategy had won Sinn Fein. But this year, on the advice of the new U.S. peace process ambassador Mitchell Reiss, no Northern politicians would be invited. This was the Bush administration's way of signaling its displeasure over the Northern Bank robbery and Sinn Fein's part in it. It was also a sign that the Americans were ready to take a tougher line with the Provos than either Tony Blair or Bertie Ahern would ever contemplate. Disinviting Sinn Fein alone would have allowed Gerry Adams to don the mantle of victimhood, and it might have prompted the SDLP to side with him, so it was decided to bar all politicians from the celebrations. While all the North's political parties lost out, Sinn Fein would be hurt most of all. The prospect of the McCartney sisters supping inside the White House while Gerry Adams languished outside enraged Sinn Fein's supporters and prompted Martin McGuinness to warn the McCartneys, just as they arrived in Washington, to "be careful" not to stray into party politics. The menace in McGuinness's words again made things worse for the Provos with Irish America.

The trip to Washington by the McCartney sisters signaled the most serious and sustained assault by the Irish-American political establishment on the Provos since the start of the peace process. It began when Sinn Fein's most valuable friend in Irish America, Senator Ted Kennedy, abruptly cancelled a planned meeting with Gerry Adams, an unmistakable snub which was underlined when Kennedy later squired the McCartney sisters and Bridgeen Hagans around the Capitol building. The presence of the McCartney sisters, Kennedy said, sent "a very powerful signal that it's time for the IRA to fully decommission, end all criminal activity and cease to exist as a paramilitary organisation."[30]

As a huge media pack struggled in the corridor, the McCartneys met Kennedy, Senators John McCain, Christopher Dodd and Hillary Clinton, the last two long-time allies of Adams, in a congressional office to tell them about their brother's murder and the Provos' inadequate response. Dodd and Clinton joined the chorus calling for the IRA to end all its activities and later sponsored a Senate resolution that condemned IRA violence and criminality, supported the McCartney family and described as "outrageous" the IRA offer to shoot the killers of Robert McCartney. Another long-time IRA supporter, Congressman Peter King of Long Island, who had backed the Provos since the hunger strikes when it was not fashionable to do so, called on the organization to disband. New York Representative Jim Walsh, head of the Friends of Ireland group in Congress, openly criticized Sinn Fein's handling of the McCartney murder: "I get the sense that the IRA has lost its discipline … They [Sinn Fein] have not handled it well. I do think they have handled it very poorly … They should have been far more aggressive about getting to the bottom of this murder."[31]

In New York, Richard Haass, Bush's first Irish peace process envoy and now president of the Council on Foreign Relations, hosted a breakfast speaking event for Gerry Adams and delivered a blunt lecture to the Sinn Fein president: "The risk is that over time they [the Sinn Fein leaders] will suffer the fate of people such as Yasser Arafat of being ostracized. Gerry Adams does not want to become someone who's unwilling to choose [as] in Mr. Arafat's case between the olive branch and the gun. Mr. Adams and, more broadly, the republican movement, has to make the choice 100% to play by democratic rules, to play a political game only."[32]

On the eve of Saint Patrick's Day, Senator John McCain addressed the American-Ireland Fund dinner and, with Adams sitting just a few yards away, launched a blistering attack on the Provos. To repeated bursts of applause from the mostly Irish-American audience, McCain said no one could now describe the IRA as "anything better than a criminal syndicate that steals and murders to serve members' personal interests."[33] One U.S. official commented: "He just peeled the paint of the walls in that building that night."[34] Donna McCartney noted in her diary: "[I] … just watched Adams during the Senator's speech. He stared ahead and looked really grim. I didn't expect him to clap when there was criticism of Sinn Fein, but he didn't even put his hands together when McCain praised our courage. That speaks volumes. I realize now how badly this is going for Adams."[35] The next day Bush greeted the McCartneys in the Oval office and the Provos' misery was complete.

Later that day, Bertie Ahern told Irish media correspondents that Sinn Fein faced "total exclusion" in the United States unless the IRA disbanded and ended criminality. Every leading U.S. figure he had spoken to, he said, wanted to "see action now"; patience in Washington was wearing thin.[36] Ahern was quick to spot that the U.S. action had shifted the advantage away from Sinn Fein but the irony here is that prior to all this both his government's officials and the British had been criticizing Mitchell Reiss for the decision to bar Adams from the White House. This was not the first or last time they would clash with the Bush envoy over his more muscular approach to the Provos. Nor had either the Irish or the British offered sympathy or support to the McCartney girls and neither government had attempted to pressurize the Sinn Fein leadership to turn over his killers. Only the Americans had helped the family.

Unknown to the public, the Americans had actually been much tougher on Adams. The U.S. administration had told Sinn Fein that any fund-raising by Gerry Adams or other figures during the St. Patrick's Day festivities would be unwelcome and that if Adams persisted in his application for a fund-raising visa to cover the trip it would be rejected, with consequent embarrassment that would be impossible to hide. The Provos got the message and Adams quietly abandoned the bid, settling instead just for a visitor's visa. When the Sinn Fein leader addressed hundreds of supporters at a trade union hall in New York, the plastic buckets that would usually have been passed around the crowd and filled with $20 and $50 notes were nowhere to be seen. The Robert McCartney murder was now hurting Sinn Fein in its most sensitive spot, its wallet.

The Provos had gone through a bruising time in America and the irony was that it all could have been avoided had Adams and his colleagues taken Jim Walsh's advice and been "more aggressive" about getting to the bottom of the McCartney murder. So why hadn't they done this?

From her close vantage point, Catherine McCartney suspects that, along with the Northern Bank robbery, Sinn Fein's disastrous handling of her brother's murder provided the IRA leadership with a route out of the decommissioning cul de sac: "If you look at it in the broader picture of Gerry Adams, the Northern Bank and then Robert's murder, the pressure he was being put under. He knew the only thing he could offer was decommissioning ... I would say that Sinn Fein manipulated Robert's murder as much as anyone did to get themselves to a point where they knew they had to go and decommission. They knew they were going to have to do it, but never on Paisley's terms."

It was also, she believes, about policing and the fact that Sinn Fein knew that republicans would sometime soon have to sign up to the PSNI. "I think the thinkers in the party who could see the vacuum that they had left, squabbling over the police, that they couldn't ride two horses for ever and couldn't leave the Nationalist community in the hands of what essentially would be gangs. At the end of the day they could have had Robert's murder solved within weeks had they wanted to and it wasn't because of their love for 'Jock' Davison and that other crowd that they didn't. It was for some other reason."[37]

This was not the first time in the long and tortuous evolution of the peace process that the Adams leadership had used the IRA's own excesses against itself, to curb the IRA and then manoeuvre, cajole and even compel the organization to take political paths that otherwise might never have been contemplated. Sometimes, as in the case of the Colombian adventure and the September 11 attacks which forced the beginning of decommissioning, the opportunity fell into their laps. At other times the matter appears more contrived. The endorsement of the IRA's "human bomb" tactic in the autumn of 1990 by both Northern Command and the Army Council was an example of this. It was sanctioned at a time when Adams and other republicans were openly criticizing the IRA for military operations that alienated nationalist public opinion by killing civilians, yet despite all this the go-ahead was given. Predictably the tactic backfired badly. The first human bomb attack in Derry involved strapping a local Catholic in the driving seat of a bomb-laden van and exploding it at a checkpoint before he could escape. The operation carried appalling PR consequences for the IRA but these validated Adams's criticisms of the conduct of the IRA's war and profoundly undermined the Provos' militarists to the advantage of those urging an alternative political course.

The murder of Robert McCartney arguably fell into the same category as Colombia and September 11, an unforeseeable event whose subsequent handling nonetheless assisted the move towards final decommissioning and the ending of all IRA activity. But was the Northern Bank raid the equivalent of the "human bomb" tactic of 1990, an operation approved by the IRA's political leadership in the knowledge that its consequences would force the organization to contemplate far-reaching measures? Alongside the identity and motives of the traitor who betrayed the *Eksund*, this is one of the more intriguing, unsolved mysteries of the Irish peace process.

BY THE TIME Gerry Adams left New York and Washington after the Saint Patrick's Day holiday he had come very close to admitting that the IRA had indeed carried out the Northern Bank robbery and that it had been a bad mistake. As he told the Council on Foreign Relations meeting during a question-and-answer session following his speech: "The Northern Bank robbery was totally and absolutely wrong, it should not have happened, and any other actions that one could conceive of, and all, all because there is now an alternative. There's now a way to move forward through entirely peaceable and democratic means."[38] Why, if the IRA had not robbed the bank, did Adams make reference to the existence of a peaceable and democratic alternative, presumably that offered by the peace process? These were words that only made sense in the context of IRA culpability for the raid.

He also used language about the Robert McCartney murder of a condemnatory quality and passion that, to say the least, was in sharp contrast to Sinn Fein and the IRA's ducking and evasion back in Belfast: "And let me tell you about the killing of Robert McCartney. Sinn Fein did not kill Robert McCartney, and neither did the IRA. And the people, apart from Robert McCartney's immediate family, who have been most angry and frustrated over this man's death are people like myself, because I have given, as have many others, our entire lives—whatever people think about us, we've given our entire lives to this struggle. And for republicans—and there are rogue republicans; there are a very, very small number—to behave like thugs, to take this man's life, to sully what we feel is our good name—and I have travelled extensively. I've been speaking from Cork to Tyrone, through Dublin, Wexford, and I can tell you the hundreds and thousands of Irish republicans feel exactly the same as I do. And the only way that the family will get justice is on their own terms: through a court, through people being held accountable for their actions ... And what I have said very, very publicly—and I'll put my reputation on the line—is that those people who did this should be man enough—should be man enough—if I had got myself, by some freak, caught up in this situation and I had been responsible for killing Robert McCartney and I had woken up the next day, I would have walked straight into whatever I thought was the appropriate body and admitted what I had done. That's what I would do. I think that those who did this are behaving in a most cowardly way and are motivated entirely by self-preservation."[39]

The message sent by Irish America and the Bush White House had hit home. "One, Sinn Fein does want to bring about an end to the IRA," he went on to tell the Council on Foreign Relations. "Two, Sinn Fein, I think with others, will be successful in achieving that; and then, three, for Irish republicans, the alternative to the IRA has to be Sinn Fein." Perhaps unwittingly, he went on to suggest that persuading the IRA rank and file would not be that difficult: "I found when we were on the cusp of last December that there was a huge, an emotional backlash against what we were trying to do, and not so much from what you would call IRA people—who seemed to be fairly, I suppose, philosophical that they, their leadership was going to move into this new phase and that they would go with it—but others who in some way maybe felt that the IRA represented them against the British, against British aggression, against the British army occupation and so on."[40]

Adams and his Sinn Fein entourage departed the United States for Ireland on or around March 18, 2005. Just nineteen days later, on April 6, almost exactly a month before another Westminster election at which Sinn Fein hoped to complete the demolition of the SDLP, only thirteen weeks after the Northern Bank raid and just nine weeks after Robert McCartney's killing, Adams began to do what he had promised at the Council on Foreign Relations conference. Flanked by elected and prospective Sinn Fein candidates gathered at Conway Mill in West Belfast and careful to use the word "we" when referring to Sinn Fein, and "you" when talking of the IRA, Adams urged the IRA leadership to fully embrace political methods. "The IRA", he said, "is being used as the excuse [by rejectionists] not to engage properly in the process of building peace with justice in Ireland."[41]

The Irish deputy prime minister, or tanaiste, Mary Harney, described the Conway Mill event as another example of Adams talking to himself, but nonetheless in due course, and to no one's surprise, on July 28 the IRA announced an end to its campaign of armed struggle, ordered its volunteers to dump arms and to pursue republican goals by only peaceful means. It also disclosed that the decommissioning of IRA weapons would be completed quickly and verified by two clerical witnesses, one Catholic, the other Protestant. The Provisionals' ever-slick publicity machine provided the electronic media with a DVD featuring long-time IRA prisoner Seanna Walsh reading the Army Council statement, an act that at an earlier time could conceivably have landed him in trouble with the police. Walsh was a former commander of IRA prisoners in the H Blocks who had shared a cell with Bobby Sands, the IRA icon, and taken part in the lengthy "blanket" and "no-wash" protests prior to the hunger strikes that claimed Sands's life. Twice convicted of explosives offences, he had spent twenty-one of his forty-eight years on earth in prison and, finally released under the terms of the Good Friday Agreement, he had become a committed supporter of the Adams leadership.

In many ways Seanna Walsh was a prototypical Provisional IRA member, a fitting choice to declare an end to its armed struggle. He had joined the IRA after loyalists intimidated his family out of a mixed area of South Belfast, forcing them to flee to the safety of Catholic Short Strand. At around the same time a friend, Patrick McCrory, was shot dead by the loyalist paramilitary group the UDA. Like so many of his colleagues, especially in Belfast, Walsh's motivation in becoming an IRA volunteer sprang as much from an obligation to protect his community and assert its rights as anything else. In its statement, the Army Council felt obliged to refer to the reason why the Provisional IRA had come into being in the first place and the fear that now there would be no one to perform that role: "The issue of the defence of nationalist and republican communities has been raised with us. There is a responsibility on society to ensure that there is no reccurrence of the pogroms of 1969 and the early 1970s." In effect, the IRA was relinquishing its *raison d'être* and handing the job to others, not least the security forces under the control of the British government. In some respects these were the most meaningful words in its valedictory.

What was otherwise striking about the IRA announcement—the most far-reaching and significant since the birth of the Provisionals in 1970—was that the decision to end the war had not been taken at an Army Convention. For years the IRA's political leaders had told all who would listen that only a Convention could declare an end to armed struggle, just as Martin McGuinness had assured republicans in early 1994 that a cease-fire would have to be ratified by a Convention. Not only was the cease-fire declared without such endorsement but the final act in the IRA's life as an army of national liberation had been taken by seven men sitting in a room, after a consultation process amongst the IRA rank and file about whose outcome only the barest details were made known to them afterwards and which at all times was firmly under the control of those seven men or others acting for them. In its way, this is as good a metaphor as any for Gerry Adams's leadership of the IRA and the way he and his colleagues brought them into war, and then out of it.

There only remained the matter of carrying out the decommissioning of the last of the IRA's weapons. The weeks before and after the IRA's statement were spent in scouring arms dumps throughout Ireland. General de Chastelain's IICD issued certificates, valid on both sides of the Border, exempting anyone carrying IRA weapons from dumps from prosecution, should they be intercepted. The weaponry was deposited at central sites, warehouses, outbuildings and even houses where the IRA's interlocutor with the IICD, Brian Keenan, oversaw the preparation of inventories to hand over to de Chastelain and his two colleagues for checking. Each IRA weapon, rocket-launcher, box of ammunition and packet of Semtex explosives was numbered with a green tag.

On or around the weekend beginning September 17 the actual decommissioning process commenced and lasted for most of the following seven days. The two clerical witnesses, both approved by the IRA leadership, arrived to join de Chastelain and his two colleagues, the Finnish Brigadier Tauno Nieminen and the American diplomat Andrew Sens. One was the Revd Harold Good, a former Methodist president, a liberal and ecumenist who had long engaged the IRA in dialogue, and had persuaded its leadership to apologize for the bombings of "Bloody Friday". Good was not the choice of most unionist politicians, who had argued that only a hard-line evangelist would be believed by their people. Nor would they have chosen the Catholic clerical witness. In some ways it was fitting that Father Alec Reid was there to witness what many regarded as the final act in the IRA's life as an army since he had been there at the beginning of the peace process, back in 1982, when his dialogue with Gerry Adams began. Unionists would have great doubts about his part in the events, arguing that he was too credulous of the IRA. When a month later he said he still believed IRA denials of involvement in the Northern Bank robbery many of them felt their doubts had been well justified.

Although these two clerics would be witnesses, the same confidentiality restriction that had bedevilled earlier phases of the decommissioning process applied to what they could say now and what the IICD could reveal. For much of the next week, the IICD members and the witnesses were ferried from one location to another in a blacked-out van. "I spent a lot of the time on the road asleep," Father Reid said later. "We could not see where we were going. We did not know where we were going. And we didn't want to know."[42] The Redemptorist priest would later reveal that decommissioning took place at nine locations altogether.[43] As for the process itself, de Chastelain was guarded: "I can only tell you that we worked a number of days, and long hours. I am not looking for sympathy, but it was six in the morning, until late at night, with the three of us involved at each event. Brigadier Nieminen and I have handled every weapon that was put beyond use, to examine it, to identify it ... counting, weighing."[44]

According to the later account provided by Father Reid to the *Irish Times*, the process was at times even convivial: "We were very well looked after, I can tell you that ... We had two or three picnics. We would be working away and one of the IRA people would shout, 'Come on, we'll get a few sandwiches'. They had sandwiches, flasks of hot water, coffee and all kinds of bits and pieces, cups of soup ... we would chat."[45]

But when it came to the sort of detail that could overcome deep unionist skepticism about the process, none of the salient facts were made public by de Chastelain or the two witnesses. Key questions such as where decommissioning took place, how many events there were during that week, what weaponry and how much of the IRA's arsenal was put beyond use went unanswered. The most important aspect of all, *how* the weapons were decommissioned, has never been revealed and is still a matter of intense speculation. The IICD will only say that the decommissioning was done in a way consistent with its legal obligation to put weapons "permanently inaccessible or beyond use." Two of the most obvious ways of destroying weapons, blowing them up or cutting them into pieces with heavy industrial saws, as happened to some of the Loyalist Volunteer Force's weapons in December 1998, can presumably be eliminated, the first on the grounds that it would have been hard to keep such events from public notice, and the second because it would have been just too impractical. Nor is it likely that weapons were dumped at sea since the limited accounts suggest land-based activity.

Security sources suggest that guns, bullets, rocket-launchers and the like may have been plunged into fast-setting concrete while explosives like Semtex were boiled away in water.[46] But this possibility raises as many questions as it answers. Where was the concrete, in holes in the ground or in containers, and if the latter, what happened to them, where are they now? Would it be possible to separate the weapons from the concrete after the IICD had departed? Did the IICD stay around to ensure the concrete had set solidly? Where are the sites and are they secure? And so on.

The same lack of clarity surrounds the amount of weaponry decommissioned and the question of whether or not the IRA had given up all its weaponry. The IICD's remit said that records of what had been decommissioned could be publicly released only when the entire process had ended and since neither of the two largest loyalist groups have, at the time of writing, even started to give up their weapons it may be a very long time before that happens. De Chastelain maintained that the weapons put beyond use related to the inventories of IRA weaponry provided by security force intelligence on both sides of the Border. But these inventories described ranges of quantities, not precise quantities. Only in the case of the Libyan weaponry could the authorities be confident that they knew more or less exactly what was in the IRA's arsenals. In the 1990s, the Libyan leader Colonel Qaddafi had handed over to the British Foreign Office manifests of weapons he had supplied to the IRA as part of his effort to rehabilitate himself with the West, and the authorities needed only to subtract from this the weaponry used up or captured to work out what was left. But how could it be known how much the IRA had in its dumps before this or what weapons were smuggled in afterwards?

It came down to accepting de Chastelain's assurances that he believed the IRA had told him the truth. "We are talking about flame-throwers, surface-to-air missiles, we are talking about rocket-propelled grenades, both commercial and home-made; heavy machine guns, all of the things you have seen in the papers. Of course, we have no way of knowing for certain that the IRA hasn't retained arms. But it is our understanding from discussing with them and our belief in what we had done that they were sincere when they said that. This time, when we said, 'Is this everything?', they said, 'Yes, this is everything'. That certainly wasn't the case two years ago."[47] Although skeptical unionists were unconvinced, there could be little doubt that an awful lot of weaponry had been put out of commission and with it the IRA's ability to resume war.

Two weeks later, at a public meeting in South Belfast jointly hosted by the Reverend Good, Father Alec Reid described one incident at the end of the week they had spent with the IRA and the IICD which did more than anything else said or written to convince the outside world that something of significance had indeed happened: "I was surprised, you know, we used to go to these sites and you have all this war material, if you like, guns and explosives and bullets and all this kind of thing, all very carefully prepared, most of it with tags, all numbered by the IRA people so that the three people, the three commissioners then were given an inventory of everything that was there with a number and all that.

"It was very, very well prepared. But one of the first things I saw was this man carrying a Kalashnikov and as far as I could see it was loaded and I was wondering, 'In the name of God', you know? I noticed that he was kind of the lookout as well, and he had this thing either over his shoulder or carrying it in his hand. And everywhere we went, there was a man out there with, this Kalashnikov was there and you could see it was loaded.

"So, I began to wonder, were they afraid the dissidents would come in and try and rob the guns? In the end, I picked up that they were defending the site but particularly defending the three commissioners. They were providing a bodyguard if you like. But then at the end of the, the very last act, this gun, the bullets were taken out of it and it was handed over to General de Chastelain by the senior IRA person, the person who was in charge of the whole operation of the decommissioning.

"And it was kind of a significant moment, that this was the last gun, and the man handing it over was quite emotional. He was aware, I think, that this was the last gun."[48]

TO CLAIM THAT that the IRA's July statement or the final decommissioning carried out in September 2005 were greeted with universal acclaim would be something of an exaggeration. Many unionists, for one, were still inclined to cast a deeply skeptical eye on anything and everything the Provos said or did. By this stage it was also apparent that the Northern Bank raid, the murder of Robert McCartney and its subsequent cover-up, added to all the IRA's previous escapades, had had a cumulatively corrosive impact on a wider section of opinion, on both sides of the Border. While the IRA's words were welcome and de Chastelain's assurances widely accepted, experience had taught many the foolishness of immediately accepting that the IRA was for real. Not only that but the IRA's and Sinn Fein's lies over the bank robbery had been pretty transparent. While there were understandable doubts over the identity of the culprits behind Castlereagh and a possibility that "Stormontgate" may have been contrived or exaggerated by the British, robbing banks was something the IRA did. Sinn Fein and the IRA were also badly affected by their handling of the McCartney murder. The brutality and cold-blooded nature of the killers contrasted starkly with the dignity of the dead man's sisters as they campaigned for justice in Ireland, America and Europe, winning plaudits for their courage and persistence. By not taking assertive action against McCartney's killers, Gerry Adams and others in the Provo leadership were widely perceived to be shielding the worst sort of thugs. What that did was to raise up again an image of the republican movement that had been seemingly banished years before. If the Northern Bank and the McCartney murder had helped the Adams leadership throw the IRA monkey off their backs, the events were also the first in a long catalogue of woes for the republican movement that would stretch over the next two years and prick the image of invincibility.

Gerry Adams had timed his call to the IRA to step down a month before the May 2005 Westminster election and while he denied this was deliberately done with an eye to the polls, it was obvious that Sinn Fein hoped his speech would give the party a boost and even help it finish off the SDLP. The Provos were casting a hungry eye on two of the SDLP's three House of Commons seats: Newry and Armagh, whose incumbent, the former SDLP deputy leader Seamus Mallon, had retired from politics, and Foyle, the seat held by John Hume for decades and now being defended by the new, less than charismatic SDLP leader Mark Durkan, against Sinn Fein's Mitchel

McLaughlin. Of the two seats it was Foyle that the Provos coveted most of all. The third SDLP seat, South Down, held by Eddie McGrady, was thought unwinnable this time round, but in four or five years' time, when McGrady had retired and if Sinn Fein worked hard, it might fall into the party's lap. If everything went well Sinn Fein could end up with six seats at Westminster to the SDLP's one. But it didn't work out like that at all. Newry and Armagh fell to Sinn Fein as expected, but in Foyle, Durkan easily beat McLaughlin, much to the consternation of the Provos, who managed to secure only two votes for every three cast for Durkan. In addition, the SDLP was a surprise victor in the usually safe Ulster Unionist seat of South Belfast, where Alastair McDonnell, the new SDLP deputy leader, was the benefici- ary of a split unionist vote and some tactical voting against the Sinn Fein candidate, Alex Maskey, who had distanced the IRA from the McCartney killing by attempting to describe it as the result of knife culture as opposed to IRA thuggery. The election ended with Sinn Fein holding five seats at Westminster to the SDLP's three, a result that consolidated Provo support but which was far from the romp their strategists had anticipated.

There was compelling evidence that the bank robbery and the McCartney killing had also tarnished some of the lustre on Sinn Fein in the South, where a general election was to be held in May 2007. Sinn Fein had targeted the Republic for significant electoral growth and if that worked out and the party polled as well as its leaders hoped, then Sinn Fein might even be in line for cabinet seats as part of a coalition government before the decade was out. In October 2004 an opinion poll carried out for the *Irish Times* by TNS MRBI showed Sinn Fein winning the support of 12 percent of the electorate, making it the fourth largest party in the state, and Gerry Adams scoring a 51-point leadership approval rating with voters, only 2 percent behind that of the prime minister, Bertie Ahern.[49] At that point the party could be confident that it was well on target. Events in the North then intervened, but self-inflicted disaster in the South also hit the Provisionals. In early February, just as the McCartney scandal was building up steam, five Dublin men were convicted of IRA membership after they were found in a van used for Sinn Fein electioneering in possession of a sledgehammer, a stun gun, pickaxe handles and CS gas spray, along with election posters for Aengus O Snodaigh, the Sinn Fein TD for Dublin South, Central.[50] The previous November, Niall Binead, also an election worker for O Snodaigh, was convicted of IRA membership and his trial was told he was running a spying operation targeted at government ministers and TDs.[51]

The impact of all this was soon evident in the opinion polls. By March

2005, Sinn Fein's support had plummeted by a quarter down to 9 percent, while Adams had suffered a catastrophic fall in his approval rating to 30 points, the lowest since it was first measured.[52] If the Provos were hoping that ending its war and then completing the decommissioning process, would help Sinn Fein retrieve all this lost ground, they were to be disappointed. By May 2006, nearly eighteen months after the Northern Bank robbery, Sinn Fein's support was still at 9 percent, while Adams's rating had risen only to 39 points.[53] Towards the end of September, a *Sunday Business Post* poll put Sinn Fein at 8 percent, while an *Irish Examiner* survey conducted at around the same time showed an alarming drop in Sinn Fein's support in Dublin, where the party would have to do well in order to grow to just 5 percent.

THE NORTHERN BANK raid and the McCartney killing had tarnished the Provos with a criminal image and their enemies in the South, in particular the combative justice minister, Michael McDowell, rarely missed a chance to remind voters of the Provos' criminality and supposed links to cross-Border smuggling, money-laundering and counterfeiting. Nobody in the Provisional movement was more associated with the label of criminality than its chief of staff, South Armagh IRA veteran Tom "Slab" Murphy, whom the British and Irish authorities had long believed ran a fuel-smuggling empire from the family farm in Ballybinaby, which literally straddles the Border. In May 2004 the BBC named him as the UK's richest smuggler, with a fortune estimated at between £35 and £40 million.[54] Throughout the years of the IRA cease-fire the British and Irish governments had resisted pressure, especially from the Bush White House, to pursue "Slab" Murphy on the grounds that to do so would alienate a key figure on the Army Council and possibly set the IRA in South Armagh against the Adams peace project. In early October 2005, just days after the IRA had decommissioned the last of its weapons, officers from the British Assets Recovery Agency (ARA) raided businesses in Manchester while their Irish counterparts, the Criminal Assets Bureau (CAB), raided premises in Dundalk, just south of the Border. Briefings from CAB sources suggested that they suspected that "Slab" Murphy had built up a significant property portfolio in Britain to launder the proceeds of cross-Border smuggling and the raids were aimed at discovering evidence against him.[55] In November 2006, nine Manchester properties worth £1.25 million owned by Slab Murphy's brother, Francis, were frozen by a court order sought by the ARA.

Six months later, in March 2006, some 300 police officers, backed by

British and Irish troops, raided Slab Murphy's farm in South Armagh. The IRA's chief of staff was given a few minutes' notice of the raid and slipped through the security cordon, leaving behind a half-eaten breakfast on the kitchen table. The police seized nearly £700,000 in cash and cheques, twelve vehicles, some 30,000 cigarettes and fuel from the farm. During the raid, a preliminary income tax assessment of £3.5 million, based on his estimated smuggling income over the years, was left beside Murphy's breakfast plate.[56] This would have to be paid unless Slab could prove that his income was less than the estimate and that would necessitate airing the smuggling allegations in court, possibly opening the way to criminal proceedings. Following the raid Gerry Adams publicly threw his weight behind the IRA's chief of staff: "Tom Murphy is not a criminal. He's a good republican ... and very importantly he is a key supporter of Sinn Fein's peace strategy and has been for a very long time." Slab also denied the allegations, but as he fled his breakfast table that March morning it would be surprising if the thought had not crossed his mind that no one, least of all Gerry Adams or Martin McGuinness, had told him that losing his fortune was part of the peace process script.

What the moves against Slab Murphy signified in unequivocal fashion was that when the IRA decommissioned the last of its weapons, the consideration and protection they had afforded its leaders had evaporated, along with the implied threat they represented of renewed armed struggle. Also gone, but only if the British and Irish governments had the necessary political will, was Sinn Fein's excessively generous leverage in the political process. For years the republican party's unionist and nationalist opponents had complained that when Sinn Fein came to the negotiating table there was a metaphorical gun hidden under their seats and stacks of real ones piled outside the door. Not any more.

MARCH 1, 2005, was the twenty-fourth anniversary of the day that Bobby Sands began his sixty-six-day-long hunger strike to the death, and the Sinn Fein leadership—as they did every year at this time—were making ready to remember his sacrifice and that of his nine comrades in speeches, rallies and marches around Ireland that would last until August. They were also gearing up to make the next year, the twenty-fifth anniversary of the 1981 hunger strikes, one of constant commemoration and celebration of the ten dead hunger strikers who had perished during that never-to-be-forgotten year. It was also the day of publication of a book, written by one of Bobby Sands's prison colleagues, that would challenge the most cherished assumption of the hunger strikes and shake the Sinn Fein leadership, Gerry Adams in particular, to its core. Remembering the hunger strikers would never be the same again for many republicans who had lived through it.

The ten dead hunger strikers were the Provisional IRA's icons, the equivalent for the modern-day IRA of the leaders of the 1916 Easter Rebellion executed by the British in the wake of their failed rising. Just as the martyrs of 1916 were venerated for having inspired the war of independence of 1919–21 that followed, so the hunger strikers were presented by the Sinn Fein leadership as the forerunners of the peace process strategy, their names and memories invoked in support of the Adams leadership at every occasion. The hunger strikers had been protesting at the British government's determination to treat them as criminals and their campaign for political status—especially their willingness to starve themselves to death to achieve it—had helped validate the IRA in the eyes of its supporters and had reverberated around the world. The protest had five demands: the right to wear civilian clothes, the right not to do prison work, the right of free association, the right to receive weekly parcels and visits and unlimited letters and the return of remission lost during a five-year protest during which IRA prisoners would wear only a blanket and refused to slop out, instead smearing the walls of their cells with excreta. In 2005, as in every year since the 1994 cease-fire, the memory of the hunger strikers was employed to legitimize the IRA's modern, non-military methods and strategy.

In a very real sense the Sinn Fein leadership was right to make the claim, for a straight line can be drawn between the events of 1981, the Good Friday Agreement and everything else that happened during the peace process. Bobby Sands's chance election as the MP for Fermanagh–South Tyrone in a Westminster by-election had enabled the Provisional leadership to fast-forward what before the hunger strikes had been modest and long-term plans for Sinn Fein to become an electoral party. At a later stage in the protest, two other prisoners were elected to Dail Eireann at an Irish general election, and after Bobby Sands's death another by-election was held in Fermanagh–South Tyrone, which was won by Sands's polling agent, former teacher and Sinn Fein activist Owen Carron. That winter, after the hunger strikes had ended, Gerry Adams was able to go to the annual Sinn Fein Ard Fheis and, with Owen Carron on the platform as living proof of the viability of the tactic, win party support for the strategy of fighting elections while waging a violent war of national liberation. The so-called ballot box and Armalite strategy was born. A year later, Sinn Fein won seats to a new Northern Assembly and, with a political alternative to violence now available, shortly afterwards Gerry Adams began his talks with Father Alec Reid and the peace process was underway. The rest, as they say, is history—but none of it could have happened without the hunger strikes.

The deaths inside the H Blocks of the Maze prison in 1981, as well as outside, were relentless. An immovable British prime minister, Margaret Thatcher, faced an irresistible force of republican hunger strikers and after Sands died, one by one, they went to their graves. The hunger strike was organized in such a way that it became a drip-feed of death, each hunger striker beginning his protest a week or so after the one before him. After Sands, the Tyrone IRA legend Francis Hughes died, and then on May 21 the third and fourth hunger strikers, South Armagh IRA man Raymond McCreesh and Derry INLA man Patsy O'Hara, who began their protest at the same time, died. After the fourth death a large gap, potentially six weeks long, opened up before the next likely death, slated to be Belfast IRA man Joe McDonnell. During this time the prisoners' public relations officer, Richard O'Rawe, drafted a statement moderating the rhetoric of the prisoners' demands, in particular dropping language about "political status," a neuralgic term as far as the Thatcher government was concerned, and it was published on July 4. As he later wrote in his 2005 book *Blanketmen*, the effect of the statement was immediately to encourage the British to open negotiations. It is his account of what he knows of those negotiations that has proved to be so explosive for the Adams leadership.

According to his account, the day after the statement was made public, July 5, the commander of the IRA prisoners, Brendan "Bik" McFarlane was called out for a visit with Danny Morrison, the former Sinn Fein and IRA publicity director and a long-time member of the Adams think tank. McFarlane came back and in a "comm", a message written on a cigarette paper sent down to his cell, he told O'Rawe that the British had begun confidential contact with the IRA leadership and had made an offer to end the hunger strike. Four of the prisoners' five demands, including the crucial insistence that IRA prisoners be allowed to wear their own clothes instead of a prison uniform, could be granted if the protest ended. O'Rawe wrote that Morrison had said that a British intermediary, code-named "Mountain Climber", who was believed to be an officer in British intelligence, had passed on the offer. O'Rawe and McFarlane, conversing in Irish for security reasons, discussed the offer for several hours and, concluding that 80 percent of the protesters demands had been met, they wrote a "comm" out to the IRA leadership saying that the prison leadership wanted to accept the British offer.

The response was a "comm" sent back from an IRA leader, code-named "Brownie", saying that the British offer was regarded as inadequate, that four hunger strikers had died for much more and not for this offer.[57] The Mountain Climber offer shriveled on the vine and three days after O'Rawe had learned of the British approach, Joe McDonnell died. The offer was briefly revived later in August, just before, at the request of hunger striker relatives, Gerry Adams visited the protesters in the hospital wing of the Maze prison. Adams outlined the renewed offer but declined to say that it was good enough for the protest to end or, on behalf of the Army Council, to order the men to end it as some relatives had wanted, and he left it to the prisoners to decide. Weighed down by the deaths of their comrades and the fear that ending the protest in such circumstances would amount to betrayal, they decided to carry on. By this stage six prisoners had died—Joe McDonnell and Martin Hurson had succumbed since the first Mountain Climber initiative, and a further four would die before the protest finally ended in early October.

The effect of the failure of the Mountain Climber initiative, both in early July and then in August, was that the hunger strike was still ongoing when on August 20, 1981, the second Fermanagh–South Tyrone by-election was held. Sands had won the first by-election but on his death the seat became vacant. Since the Thatcher government had rushed through a law barring convicts from standing for parliament, Owen Carron, Sands's Sinn Fein election agent, was put forward instead. The fact that the prison protest was still underway when election day dawned had enormous implications for the outcome. Sands and later Carron both contested the Fermanagh–South Tyrone seat on the basis of an informal understanding that as long as IRA men were on hunger strike, other nationalists, principally the SDLP, would agree to allow them a free run. In this way the seat was being "borrowed" by the H Block prisoners and once their protest was over normal politics in the constituency would resume. The fact that IRA men were starving to death and dying in defiance of Margaret Thatcher, a politician who was particularly disliked by all shades of Irish nationalist opinion, meant that there was a huge incentive on the part of the Catholic electorate of Fermanagh–South Tyrone to vote for Carron. The IRA leadership's rejection of the Mountain Climber offer in July had ensured not just that the hunger strike would still be underway but that the by-election would be governed by the same local understanding that had applied during Sands's election. On election day Owen Carron was not only the sole nationalist candidate standing, but the continuing threat of hunger-strike deaths brought thousands of nationalists out to vote for him. Had the hunger strike ended after nominations had closed, for instance when Adams had visited the prison hospital, the heat would have gone out of the situation and many nationalists, especially those in the constituency who usually voted for the SDLP, would not have felt the same pressure to support Carron. The result would almost certainly have been his defeat. But instead Carron was easily elected. One especially significant consequence of this was that Adams's bid to win his party over to an electoral strategy was considerably strengthened. The import of O'Rawe's assertion is that the hunger strikes were kept going longer than necessary, and six of the ten dead hunger strikers sacrificed so that Gerry Adams could lead Sinn Fein into electoral politics.

"Brownie", the IRA leader who in O'Rawe's account had advised the prisoners' leaders not to accept the Mountain Climber proposal, was none other than Gerry Adams, using the same pen-name he had invented when imprisoned in the 1970s so that he could write pseudonymously articles for *Republican News*. At the time O'Rawe believed that Adams was writing to McFarlane on behalf of the Army Council but he now believes that Adams ran the protest on the Council's behalf: "I have since learned that a subcommittee [of the Army Council] was designated to manage and monitor the hunger strike. Given that 'comms' were coming in two or three times a day it is simply not possible to believe that the Council could have been kept informed of all the developments. Could the Council even have met regularly during that turbulent period? Adams ran the whole show. He sent the 'comms' in. He read the 'comms' that came out. He talked to the 'Mountain Climber'. He ran everything from A to Z. Nobody knows the hunger strike like he knows it."[58]

In 1985, O'Rawe was asked by Adams, along with two other republicans, to sift through the IRA's archive of "comms" from the 1981 hunger strikes and to remove any letter that made reference to the "Mountain Climber" and the role he had played. He was then to make the sanitized collection available to the *Guardian* reporter David Beresford, who was researching and writing what became his seminal book on the protest, *Ten Men Dead*. By mistake, one comm mentioning the secret British official was overlooked and in this way Beresford and the world learned of the Mountain Climber. Gerry Adams's intention, according to O'Rawe, was to keep Mountain Climber's role completely hidden. In the course of this task, O'Rawe also searched for the comm he and McFarlane had sent out accepting the British offer, only to find that it was not in the archive. Its absence, he wrote, "was surely significant."[59]

The impact of O'Rawe's book on the Provisionals was strengthened by the fact that he had street credibility with rank-and-file supporters. He was not one of the republican movement's political enemies but a fellow former IRA man with a long family history of involvement in IRA politics. He had also been on the H Blocks' "blanket" and "no wash" protests alongside those who had died and was sufficiently highly regarded to be appointed to the IRA's prison staff. After his release from jail, he worked for a while in the Sinn Fein press office in Belfast and later supported the Adams peace process strategy. He decided, he said, to speak out about events that had weighed heavily with him for so long only when it had become clear that the IRA's violence was over and no damage could be done to its war effort. At the time of the 1981 protest many republicans had been greatly troubled that the IRA leadership had allowed the hunger strike to last so long and that many prisoner deaths had been pointless. O'Rawe's explanation of this period made a great deal of sense to them.

Publishing his account was certainly not cost-free. Some, including this writer, had advised him not to publish his book because of the personal vilification that he would suffer, but he persevered. And the vilification was intense, as he later described: "All of a sudden I was persona non grata, someone who was to be ostracized. The smears started. People who I had been friends with avoided me. One person who I shared a cell with on the blanket refused to speak to me. Friends I had all my life blanked me out and made it clear when I went in to a pub that I was not welcome in their company. The leadership apologists 'cut the tripe out of me' on television, radio, newspapers—anywhere they had the chance. They tried to attribute false motives to me. They said it was about money. All of this was bullshit."[60]

Sinn Fein's usually slick and well-coordinated publicity machine reacted clumsily to O'Rawe's account. While Gerry Adams initially opted for silence, other aides contradicted and tripped over themselves. Bik McFarlane flatly denied there had been any offer from Mountain Climber or that the exchanges with O'Rawe described in *Blanketmen* had happened: "There was no concrete proposals whatsoever in relation to a deal," he said.[61] All that Morrison had told him, he maintained, was that the British had opened up a line of communication, but he, McFarlane, shouldn't get his hopes up too high.

Morrison's own account was very different. Mountain Climber had indeed made an offer, he said, which he had outlined to McFarlane, but the deal had stalled when a request from the prisoners that the British verify and confirm the offer was turned down.[62] McFarlane insisted there was no deal, while Morrison said there was one but it was killed off by the British, not the Adams leadership. Later, on an RTE television documentary, Gerry Adams claimed, to general astonishment, that he hadn't known or heard of Mountain Climber until after the hunger strikes. [63] O'Rawe has since let it be known that he has independent verification of his exchange with McFarlane and will release it if necessary. As the battle between them continued, the hugely damaging accusation that the peace process strategy was constructed on a foundation consisting of the graves of six republican hunger strikers who needn't and shouldn't have died was fated to hang forever over Gerry Adams's head.

AT MOMENTS OF crisis during the years of the peace process and especially when the IRA was singled out for blame, the Sinn Fein leadership was fond of shifting responsibility instead on to British "securocrats," so-called bureaucratic elements in the security establishment who, supposedly because of self-interest and hatred of the Provisionals, had set out to sabotage the process. The term began to appear in the Provo lexicon in 1995, around the time that the Washington Three decommissioning conditions were promulgated by the then Northern Ireland secretary, Sir Patrick Mayhew. It was apparently borrowed from South Africa where the ANC, long-time allies and friends of the IRA, had coined the term to describe elements in the apartheid system who were resisting change.[64] As the peace process continued and its problems multiplied so did the frequency of the word in Sinn Fein speeches and statements. The securocrats were blamed for the Castlereagh break-in and for Stormontgate in particular. Way back in 1997, Gerry Adams even blamed them for suggesting he was on the IRA's Army Council. Asked who these securocrats were, he replied: "Whether it's the London civil servant who coordinates security, or the head of the RUC or the British generals, or whether it's the people in MI5 or MI6 who don't have another pot to stir, there are people who want to stick with the old security agenda rather than move to a new political agenda."[65] Blaming "securocrats" served a double purpose for the IRA and Sinn Fein: it conveyed the impression that republicans were still in struggle with the British while suggesting that if the British security establishment wished to destroy the peace process, then the strategy had to be injurious to British interests.

The existence of often compelling evidence to the contrary was never a deterrent to the claim being trotted out by Sinn Fein figures. For example, the "head of the RUC," or at least the RUC's assistant chief constable at the time Gerry Adams offered his definition of a securocrat, was Sir Ronnie

Flanagan who, in 1995, publicly expressed the very un-securocrat thought that the best possiblity of ensuring peace was if organizations like the IRA remained intact and under the control of their leaderships. When the issue of IRA decommissioning began to assume greater importance in the wake of the Good Friday Agreement, one of the staunchest critics of those insisting the IRA had to disarm before Sinn Fein could enter government was Michael Oatley, an MI6 officer who had had many dealings over the years with senior IRA figures as far back as the mid-1970s, and who was said to have used the "Mountain Climber" code-name at one point. He wrote of the decommissioning demand: "This tactic might be described as the picador approach to introducing a terrorist organization to the attractions of the political arena. No doubt, if sufficient barbs are thrust into its flanks, the animal will eventually, with reluctance, charge. The picadors can then claim the beast was always a ravening monster."[66] As for the other branch of British intelligence, MI5, its agents had worked with the FBI to persuade David Rupert to infiltrate the Real IRA and to bring Michael McKevitt to court on terrorist charges after the Good Friday Agreement was concluded. An MI5 committed to destroying the peace process would surely have left the Real IRA and McKevitt alone. Former RUC and PSNI Special Branch commander Chief Superintendent Bill Lowry also claimed that MI5 had pressured him to minimize the scale of the Stormontgate spying operation so as not to damage the Adams leadership, and he furthermore disclosed that in 1996, at the time of the crucial IRA Convention and Adams's clash with Michael McKevitt, the Special Branch successfully stopped a number of anti-Adams delegates from getting to the meeting. As it was, Adams survived the Convention by the skin of his teeth but he might not have without the assistance of Bill Lowry and the Special Branch securocrats.[67]

Nor did it matter if, from time to time, the Sinn Fein accusations were so wide of the mark they embarrassed those making them. In the midst of the furore caused by the Northern Bank robbery, two of the Provisionals' most senior figures, Martin McGuinness and Pat Doherty, launched an assault on the Permanent Secretary at the Northern Ireland Office (NIO), Joe Pilling, for remarks he had made during a trip to the United States. Doherty said: "The NIO's top securocrat, Joe Pilling stated, at what he thought was a private meeting in the US in October, that the worst case scenario would be that Sinn Fein would become the largest party in the North and that the priority was to stop this happening. The full frontal onslaught now being rolled out against Sinn Fein is therefore no coincidence."[68] McGuinness added: "This is the NIO line of the last 30 years. It is a position of failure and it is evidence of a British system that seeks the defeat of Irish republicanism."[69] Pilling was the NIO's most senior official at the time of the Good Friday Agreement negotiations and it was largely at his urging that the issue of IRA decommissioning was decoupled from the release of IRA prisoners.[70] Thanks to him, hundreds of IRA prisoners got out of jail without their leaders having to surrender as much as a single bullet. If Pilling truly was a securocrat and was seeking the defeat of the peace process strategy, would he have done this?

Without a doubt there were elements within the security forces, especially locally raised units, whose hostility to the Provisionals would have been sufficiently deep to tempt them into acts of sabotage against the Adams project. But it hardly makes sense to suggest that at an institutional or leadership level, MI5, MI6, military intelligence or the RUC/PSNI Special Branch would share this animosity. The IRA's campaign of violence was, after all, being brought to an end on terms that in the past would have been dismissed as impossibly modest, and since it was the IRA's own leaders who were winding up the armed struggle, it was coming to an end with a certainty and finality that no amount of security successes could have guaranteed. Far from obstructing this process, it was entirely in the interests of the British security establishment that they should lend a helping hand.

FREDDIE SCAPPATICCI WAS one of the IRA's most feared and disliked members, a man whose name could send a shiver of sheer terror down the backs of fellow republicans. It was Scappaticci's work for the IRA that caused this type of reaction. Scappaticci, or "Scap" as he was known to fellow IRA men, had spent the bulk of his paramilitary career in the IRA's security department, which had the job of rooting out British double agents in the organization, IRA members who had been turned by the police or military and were betraying secrets to the enemy. Scap eventually rose to the top, becoming director of security, from which position his vantage on the IRA was unprecedentedly extensive, his knowledge of its internal affairs impressive. The security department's remit and powers were wide. Its task was to identify suspected informers, interrogate them, persuade the guilty to confess and then hand them over to others in the IRA who would court-martial them and then, if convicted, despatch them with a single shot to the back of the head. Attracting the interest of the security department was not good for an IRA member's health.

Scap was a member of five families of Italian origin which had been involved with republican paramilitaries during the Troubles, one of an esti-mated 1,800 people of Italian extraction in Northern Ireland whose ances-tors were late nineteenth-century economic migrants, mostly from the area south of Rome. They arrived in Belfast via northern England and opened fish and chip shops and ice cream parlors. Most were assimilated fully, invariably into working-class Catholic areas, and many lost their ability to speak the language and their interest in Italy. Sometimes the only link to their past was the Christian names their parents would choose. A bricklayer by trade who hailed from the Markets district of Belfast, Scap joined the IRA at the start of the Troubles and was interned in 1971; after release in 1974 he rejoined and worked in IRA intelligence. When the security depart-ment was set up, he gravitated towards it.

The idea of the IRA creating a proper counterintelligence unit had its ori-gins in Long Kesh in the mid-1970s when Gerry Adams and Ivor Bell began debriefing IRA members arriving in prison to discover what the authorities knew or wanted to know about the IRA. When the criminalization process began a few years later, and IRA volunteers started cracking under interro-gation, Belfast Brigade set up a unit to debrief anyone who had survived police questioning without confessing or being charged. This was partly to discover what the RUC knew or was interested in, but also to look for clues that would suggest a volunteer had been turned. Thus was born the secu-rity department which grew in size and scope over the years, expanding to cover Northern Command's area of operations and then all the IRA. The department was tasked with vetting recruits and investigating IRA opera-tions that had gone wrong. Those who worked in the department, and espe-cially those who led it, knew an awful lot about the IRA's business.

Not surprisingly, the British security authorities made a priority of infil-trating the security department and turning those of its members it could, and there are at least three instances where it is known or strongly suspected that they were successful. One was Brendan "Ruby" Davison, an uncle of Jock Davison of Robert McCartney infamy, who was shot dead by loyalists in the late 1980s. Another suspected traitor was the late John Joe Magee, a former British soldier who headed the department before Scap. The third was Freddie Scappaticci himself. Between them, these informers or sus-pected informers would have been able to give the British a priceless insight into the IRA.

Scap's role as an informer came to light at least in part thanks to the exer-tions of a former British soldier, a staff sergeant who had worked with mil-itary intelligence in Northern Ireland in the 1980s. He had come across

Scap by chance, was deeply troubled by what he learned and when he left the army set out to tell as much of his story as he could to the media. The soldier, a chirpy, friendly native of Manchester who used the pseudonym "Martin Ingram", worked as an agent co-handler in a special outfit called the Force Research Unit (FRU) whose headquarters were in Thiepval barracks near Belfast. One evening Ingram was serving as the duty officer in FRU's headquarters when the phone rang. It was a policeman in Derry who had a Belfast man, Freddie Scappaticci, under arrest for drunk driving. Scappaticci had asked the police to ring the FRU who would vouch for him and extract him from his difficulty. Ingram consulted the files and contacted Scap's handlers who arranged for his release.

Ingram learned that Scap's FRU code-name was "Steaknife"[71] and that an official blind eye had been turned to the many executions Scap had engineered. Scap was a "walk-in", someone who had volunteered their services rather than being blackmailed or bribed into service, as was usually the case with informers. In his case, Scap was allegedly seeking revenge for a bad beating at the hands of IRA colleagues. Ingram was appalled at the fact that, through the double agent, the British army was sanctioning murder and also by the possibility that some of Scap's victims might have been innocents set up to die to give the informer credibility while others were genuine agents sacrificed to preserve Scap's cover. Freddie Scappaticci was eventually exposed as a double agent by the media in May 2003.

The IRA had known about Scap's treachery for some years but had taken no action against him, despite the enormous damage he had done. Clearly the embarrassment would have been enormous had Scap been found, like many of his victims, dumped by the side of a road in South Armagh, his hands bound behind his back and the brains blown out of his head. Many questions would have been asked and some would have been directed at the Adams, leadership. Scap's elevation in the security department, along with that of John Joe Magee, had been engineered in the mid-1980s by Gerry Adams, who had got their predecessors thrown out.[72] The two men would be intensely loyal to Adams over the best part of the next two decades and many republicans suspected that part of their brief was to hunt down and expose internal critics of the leadership or its strategies, including of course the peace process strategy. Whatever the truth, the fact remains that the basic rule of counterintelligence, that key figures should be replaced or rotated regularly to minimize any damage caused by treachery, was not followed in their case. They stayed at or near the top of the security department for many years, causing incalculable damage to the IRA. When the

IRA finally did come to suspect Scap, he was allowed to live and he settled in Andersonstown in the heart of West Belfast. When he was exposed, Scap denied everything, threatened but then abandoned court action to clear his name and finally fled to Italy, where he now lives.

The Force Research Unit which ran Scap had agents in other Northern Ireland paramilitary groups, including the largest loyalist outfit, the Ulster Defence Association (UDA), a group responsible for many bombings and assassinations of Catholics. The key FRU agent inside the UDA was its head of intelligence, Brian Nelson, a former British soldier who had worked as a double agent in the UDA since the 1970s. By the late 1980s Nelson, who was from the fiercely loyalist Shankill Road part of Belfast, was living and working in Germany in the building trade, but in 1987 he was tracked down by MI5 and persuaded to return to Belfast to resume spying for the FRU. He became head of UDA intelligence, compiling information on republicans provided by his FRU handlers which he would hand over to the UDA's assassination squads. In theory he would also inform his FRU handlers, who were supposed to tell the RUC so that murder plots could be intercepted and gunmen arrested. In most cases the army did nothing of the sort. Part of the reason for persuading Nelson to return to Belfast was, in the words of FRU's commander, to "persuade the UDA to centralize their targeting through Nelson and to concentrate their targeting on known Provisional IRA activists," and military intelligence had little interest in obstructing the UDA.[73]

One of those set up for assassination by the UDA, courtesy of intelligence provided by Nelson, was the Belfast solicitor Pat Finucane, who was gunned down in his family home in February 1989. Nelson had told his handlers of the plot but they did nothing to stop it. Separately, the RUC Special Branch had learned that Finucane had been targeted from another UDA informer, William Stobie, the quartermaster who supplied guns to the assassination team. The police also failed to act, even afterwards when they could have caught the killers with the murder weapons. Finucane, who had been Bobby Sands's solicitor, was the principal defence lawyer for arrested IRA suspects in Belfast and his family was steeped in republican activity. A brother John was killed on IRA active service in a car crash in 1972; another brother, Dermot, was on IRA GHQ staff, and a third brother, Seamus, was on the Belfast Brigade staff, at a time when the Brigade opposed the Adams peace strategy. While the UDA asserted that Pat Finucane was also an IRA member, this was widely denied, not least by the RUC chief constable. But his work on behalf of IRA clients meant that all the branches of British security in Northern Ireland had a reason to view Finucane with hostility.

The FRU's relationship with Nelson came to light when the UDA boasted about its improved intelligence on the IRA and released video footage of military security documents and photomontages to which it had access. A police inquiry by an English team led to Nelson who was charged with murder. At his trial he cut a deal with the prosecution and pleaded guilty. In return for a ten-year jail term he spared the British army days of embarrassing and revealing court testimony. The FRU's commander, Colonel "J", as he was identified, gave mitigating evidence claiming that Nelson had saved over 200 lives.

In fact the English police inquiry had established that only two lives had been saved as a result of Nelson's work with the FRU.[74] One was Freddie Scappaticci, who was targeted by the UDA soon after Nelson became the group's intelligence chief. According to "Martin Ingram", the FRU stepped in to save their most valuable IRA agent and steered the UDA assassins away from Scap and towards another republican of Italian extraction, Francisco Notarantonio, an elderly IRA veteran from Ballymurphy who was duly shot in his bed in October 1987.[75]

The other person whose life was saved by Brian Nelson and the FRU was Gerry Adams. The UDA had tried to kill Adams once before, in 1984, when he was ambushed by UDA gunmen in Belfast city centre in a plot reportedly known beforehand to British intelligence.[76] Adams survived with remarkably light wounds. A second UDA plot to kill Adams was hatched around August 1988 when the group discovered that the Sinn Fein MP visited a public housing office in downtown Belfast on behalf of his constituents on the same day each week. At first they contemplated shooting him from nearby scaffolding but then the UDA learned that Adams's armor-plated car had one weakness – the roof had not been protected. The UDA obtained a limpet mine and planned to draw up beside Adams's car as he left the office and place the mine on the roof, as close to his head as possible, and set it to explode after five seconds.[77] Nelson told his handlers about the plan. In 1984, British intelligence agencies may have allowed the attempt on Adams's life to go ahead but this time they intervened to save him. The limpet mine was discovered in a police raid and the plot was abandoned. Nelson's FRU handlers subsequently told him, according to extracts from his diary published later, that killing Adams would have been, "totally counter productive ... Adams and his supporters were committed to following the political path."[78]

MI5 had a permanent liaison officer stationed with the FRU and would have been aware of the intelligence provided by Brian Nelson. By this stage Adams had, via Father Reid, opened a dialogue with the then Secretary of State, Tom King, in an effort to advance the peace process. Given the FRU's decision to save Adam's life, it seems reasonable to assume that British intelligence knew of these contacts and recognized the huge potential of the path Adams was taking. If the securocrats really wished to scupper the peace process, they had missed an ideal opportunity to strangle the infant at birth by turning a blind eye to the killing of its principal architect. At the very least one question remains unanswered: why did British intelligence allow Pat Finucane to die but not Gerry Adams?

ANOTHER INTRIGUING EXAMPLE of securocrat benevolence towards the peace process came towards the end of 2005 when the Stormontgate scandal of October 2002 returned with a sensational vengeance. Three men, including one senior Sinn Fein official, fifty-five-year-old Denis Donaldson, had been charged with spying offences, but suddenly on December 8, the Public Prosecution Service announced that charges against the three men were being dropped "in the public interest." Under new disclosure rules, the prosecuting authorities were obliged to reveal any relevant details to the defence and had only Donaldson been on trial no problem would have arisen. The difficulty facing the prosecution was that unless the presiding judge ruled otherwise, they would have to tell Donaldson's co-defendants, one of whom, Ciaran Kearney, was his son-in-law, that the man standing beside them in the dock had been a British spy for around two decades. The judge refused an application from the prosecution to keep the information secret and, faced with the prospect that the trial would collapse in spectacular fashion, the plug was pulled.

The detail of what happened next is far from clear but the events followed upon each other like scenes from a spy movie. On December 15, Donaldson was contacted by a Special Branch officer and shortly afterwards met Sinn Fein's Northern chairman, Declan Kearney, to confess his secret past. Two days later Gerry Adams announced that Donaldson had admitted to being a spy while Donaldson himself read a statement to RTE television in which he denied there had been a spying ring at Stormont but admitted: "I was recruited in the 1980s after compromising myself during a vulnerable time in my life. Since then I have worked for British intelligence and the RUC/PSNI Special Branch."[79] Donaldson had a notorious reputation as a womanizer but his sexual appetite apparently ranged wider.

According to a security source, the British recruited Donaldson when they found out about one of his sexual peccadilloes and blackmailed him. But for some time before Stormontgate he had "gone dead as an agent."[80] According to security sources, Donaldson was working for a GHQ intelligence unit headed by Bobby Storey, and ran the spy ring, using his post as Sinn Fein's head of administration as cover.[81] For reasons that remain unexplained, he had not told his handlers about the Stormont spying operation and a wish to punish their out-of-control agent was one reason why he was charged.[82] Gerry Adams claimed that the PSNI had warned Donaldson that he was about to be "outed" by the media and it was this that caused him to confess to republican colleagues. It may have been that forcing Donaldson into the open was the Special Branch's final revenge on their errant agent.

The revelation that Donaldson had been a long-term traitor came as a deep shock to the wider Provisional movement and set off an almost hysterical bout of speculation about which senior figure would be exposed next. Donaldson, who was from the Short Strand area of Belfast, had been in the IRA from the outset. He was interned along with figures like Bobby Sands, subsequently rose in the IRA (this writer first interviewed him as a Belfast Brigade explosives expert in the late 1970s) and later was entrusted with delicate missions, such as a trip in the late 1980s to Lebanon for talks with Hezbollah in a bid to obtain the release of the Belfast hostage Brian Keenan (no relation to the IRA leader of the same name), held by Islamic Jihad for five years. By the time of Stormontgate, he was in the outer circle just beyond the Adams think tank, often charged with ensuring that leadership decisions were fully and properly enforced. His proximity to the inner circle was the reason for the widespread shock in the IRA and Sinn Fein since this opened up the possibility that British intelligence not only knew about the Adams strategy but had helped to shape it. Those who had dealings with Donaldson in the years before he was exposed as a spy knew him as a devoted disciple of the peace process strategy who would often become angrily defensive when others questioned where the process was taking republicanism.

Donaldson's outing provoked charges from Gerry Adams of dirty tricks by "securocrats" who were trying to provoke, he said, another peace process crisis by forcing the IRA to execute him for informing. But there was evidence elsewhere to suggest that British intelligence had used Donaldson in the past to advance the peace process rather than to undermine it.

In the autumn of 1988, as the first public talks between Sinn Fein and the SDLP climaxed, Donaldson was sent to New York to be the IRA's representative in the United States. From his very first night in the Bronx, where he was to live for the next year, Donaldson set about undermining figures who would later oppose the Adams strategy. The two principal people in his sights were the U.S. commander of the IRA, Gabe Megahey, a Belfast man who had lived in New York since the 1970s, and Martin Galvin, an Irish-American lawyer who was the publicity director of Noraid, the support group for IRA prisoners, and publisher of its weekly paper, the *Irish People*. Megahey once described himself as "a hard-liner"[83] who was distinctly unenthusiastic about the republican movement's political direction while Galvin was seen as an obstacle to Sinn Fein's plans to leave its working-class Irish-American base behind and move into the American political and corporate mainstream.

The night Donaldson arrived in New York, Megahey and Galvin took him out for a drink in one of the many bars in Bainbridge Avenue in the Bronx, then a largely Irish area known for its IRA sympathies. Galvin had another appointment and after a while he left Megahey and Donaldson talking and drinking. The next morning Megahey rang Galvin in alarm to say that Donaldson had told him that the Belfast leadership wanted Galvin out and his days were numbered. Donaldson denied this, suggesting Megahey had a drink problem, while Donaldson's boss in Belfast, think tank chairman Ted Howell also denied it.[84] (Later Megahey's dislike and suspicions of Donaldson sharpened when he was seen buying drinks for FBI men in the same Bainbridge Avenue bar.) Donaldson then moved against Megahey, first introducing him to a Belfast man who had been thrown out of Ireland by the IRA as a security risk and then reporting Megahey to Belfast for consorting with him. The IRA's commander in America was stood down and nearly court-martialled. Megahey, who had a fierce shouting match with Donaldson over the matter, later recalled the IRA representative's penchant for creating dissension: "He was always saying things like: 'Oh, Ireland doesn't like this person, Ireland doesn't like that person.' These were very hardworking people in Noraid being sidelined."[85]

Donaldson drove other long-time Noraid activists to the margins of the group, people who were hard-line republicans and potential obstacles to the Adams peace process strategy. Important projects were sabotaged, like a proposed hunger strike movie starring Mickey Rourke and Sean Penn. Whenever complaints were sent to Belfast, Ted Howell would invariably leap to his defence, saying, "Denis has tremendous Army credentials, ... he was impeccable."[86] The clues that Donaldson was not what he seemed to be are evident in hindsight. He was never harassed by the FBI, was allowed to travel freely back and forth to Ireland and spoke openly about IRA matters on the telephone. He also took long trips to Cincinnati, allegedly to visit relatives but possibly to meet his handlers—but no one checked. His successor, Hugh Feeney, one of the 1973 London bombers, was by contrast arrested not long after his arrival in the United States and deported.

Megahey opposed the Adams strategy but later moved back into the leadership camp when the U.S. government threatened to deport him because of a prison term he had served for attempting to buy a surface-to-air missile from an FBI agent. Galvin quit his Noraid positions in 1994 after the first IRA cease-fire and following his departure Noraid was gradually run down and replaced by Friends of Sinn Fein (FoSF), a business-friendly, distinctly IRA-free support and fund-raising group. While Noraid had led street protests against British policy, raised money for IRA causes and sheltered IRA fugitives from Ireland, FoSF lobbied corporate Irish-America and politicians in Congress. Sinn Fein moved out of the backrooms of bars in the Bronx into the boardrooms of Park Avenue and Donaldson helped do the groundwork. Had his handlers really been out to undermine the peace process then it is more likely they would have instructed him to bolster Megahey, Galvin and other hard-liners in Noraid rather than undermine them.

BY THE TIME Denis Donaldson was revealed as a British spy, the IRA was powerless to take action against him, at least officially. To have done so, in the post-Northern Bank/Robert McCartney atmosphere, would have been such a serious breach of the cease-fire that it could have sunk Sinn Fein entirely. Although this example of IRA impotence against the work of British intelligence was a persuasive index of the changed times, the Provisionals had long employed double standards when it came to dealing with informers. While someone like Freddie Scappaticci, who had done more damage to the IRA than a dozen spies put together, had been allowed to live in order to spare the Adams leadership any embarrassment, others, like twenty-four-year-old Seamus Morgan from Dungannon, County Tyrone, were not so fortunate. Morgan's crime against the IRA was to betray an empty arms dump and he paid for it with his life. He was shot dead and his body thrown by a roadside near Forkhill, County Armagh, in March 1982, his hands tied behind his back and white tape wrapped tightly over his eyes. His captors fed him whisky and vodka while he cried over photos of his children before his life was abruptly ended.[87] The human rights group British Irish Rights Watch lists Seamus Morgan as one of Scap's many victims.[88]

Donaldson appears to have believed that the days of the IRA killing traitors had gone forever. There seems to be no other explanation for his decision not just to stay in Ireland but to move to the Glenties, in County Donegal, to an area frequented by republicans and not far from a part of the county—one of Ireland's most beautiful and remote areas—that had been dubbed "Costa del Provo" by the media. In fact the abundance of holiday homes owned by IRA and Sinn Fein leaders included a four-bedroom, £150,000 summer retreat in Gortahork built by Gerry Adams.[89]

Donaldson settled in a cottage some eight kilometers from Glenties on a remote bog road and it was there in mid-March 2006 that he was tracked down by a reporter from the Northern tabloid newspaper the *Sunday World*, who briefly interviewed him. Still denying there had been a Stormont spy ring, Donaldson opined: "All conflicts end in political solutions—it's the only way." Asked about his future, he replied, gesturing around him: "This is it."[90] The last person to see Denis Donaldson alive was sheep farmer Pat Bonner, who saw him driving his car in the midmorning of April 3, 2006. On the afternoon of the next day, Donaldson was found dead, lying near the front door of his cottage. A shotgun blast from close range had taken part of his right arm off and two spent cartridges were lying on the floor.

The IRA quickly issued a statement denying any part in his death. The authorities on both sides of the Border now believe that IRA members did kill him but that the operation was probably not authorized by the leadership. Gerry Adams issued a statement dissociating "Sinn Fein and indeed all those republicans who support the peace process" from the killing.

Even if the IRA Army Council had authorized Donaldson's killing, Gerry Adams and his closest colleagues had contrived a way to avoid any suggestion they had been involved in the decision. Around the time of the July 2005 IRA statement that formally ended the armed campaign, Adams, McGuinness and Kerry Sinn Fein TD Martin Ferris had all quit the Army Council and three veteran activists, Bernard Fox, a former hunger striker from Belfast, Brian Arthurs from County Tyrone and Martin Lynch from Belfast, had replaced them. At the same time a seriously ill Brian Keenan was replaced by Sean "Spike" Murray, a Belfast activist who had succeeded Martin McGuinness as Northern commander in 1996. This move was designed to finally cleanse the Adams–McGuinness leadership of any IRA traces and to end damaging speculation about the Sinn Fein politicians' part in future IRA actions—but it was a fiction. According to republican sources, Adams and McGuinness continued to control the Army Council, but from behind the throne. "Have you ever met [IRA chief of staff] Slab?" asked one former activist. "If you had you would know that he needs their advice and counsel, he's that type. No IRA volunteer I know of has ever met

Slab by himself. He always has someone with him to explain and guide him and it's the same with the Army Council."[91] At least one of the three replacements, Bernard Fox, eventually realized the scale of the fraud and resigned in protest, but not before harsh words were exchanged with Martin McGuinness and Brian Keenan.[92]

It had been an *annus horribilis* or two for Gerry Adams and his colleagues in the Provisional leadership, but it did not end with Donaldson's killing. In a burst of exuberance after Sinn Fein's electoral triumphs, the West Belfast-based Andersonstown News group, publishers of weekly community papers and an Irish-language paper, unveiled a new, all-Ireland daily paper in January 2005 that would aggressively promote an Irish republican view of the world. *Daily Ireland* was a barely disguised platform for Sinn Fein and its appearance invited comparisons with the now defunct Irish Press group which had been founded by Eamon de Valera and supported his Fianna Fail party. Although a formal association was denied, the fact that, for example, its managing director Mairtin O Muilleoir was a former Belfast Sinn Fein councillor strengthened the suspicion. Irish justice minister Michael McDowell openly linked the Provos with the paper and compared it to the Nazi party newspaper *Volkischer Beobachter*.

If the founders of *Daily Ireland* imagined there was a market hungry for the Sinn Fein gospel, as there had been for de Valera's *Irish Press*, they were to be sadly mistaken. The paper never managed to sell more than 10,000 copies a day, a miserable tally compared to other Irish newspapers: the *Irish Independent*'s circulation is around 160,000, the *Irish Times* has sales of 117,000 and the *Irish News*, which circulates only in Northern Ireland, sells 50,000 copies a day. *Daily Ireland* wasn't even approaching a break-even point and in September 2006, after just 475 issues, the paper folded. Mairtin O Muilleoir blamed the British for refusing to allow *Daily Ireland* to tender for public service advertisements, thus starving the paper of revenue. The British responded by saying that the paper's circulation was too low to be considered viable and pointed out that the Northern Ireland Office had given £556,000 in grants to the *Andersontown News* and £368,000 to the group's Irish publication.[93] The real reason *Daily Ireland* collapsed was because it failed to attract enough readers and that was a depressing message for Sinn Fein. It raised some troubling questions for the party's leaders: was Sinn Fein's popularity based on its ability to guide the IRA into peace rather than its politics? And once the IRA had completed that journey, would people still vote for Sinn Fein?

Three days after two shotgun barrels ended Denis Donaldson's life,

British premier Tony Blair and his Irish counterpart Bertie Ahern travelled to Armagh city to announce one more initiative. The suspended Assembly would be revived in mid-May and a deadline of November 24 set for agreement between Sinn Fein and the DUP. If there was no deal by then, the Good Friday Agreement would be shelved. On May 22, Gerry Adams stood up in the Assembly chamber and nominated Ian Paisley as first minister and Martin McGuinness as his deputy. Paisley's response was curt. "Certainly not," he replied. The circle had been closed. In 1964, riots over an Irish tricolour displayed in the window of a republican election office on the Falls Road, fomented by Ian Paisley, had persuaded a sixteen-year-old Gerry Adams to join the IRA's junior wing. Forty-two years later they would once again be joined, but in a way neither could ever have imagined or foreseen.

In the weeks that followed, the DUP and Sinn Fein jostled for advantage in the talks that everyone knew would take place in the autumn, notwithstanding Paisley's abrupt rebuff of Adams. Speculation that the Provo leaders would sign up to the new policing arrangements intensified but there could be no doubt that, like the cease-fires, the Good Friday Agreement, the principle of consent and IRA decommissioning beforehand, grassroots reservations would be skilfully managed to ensure a result already decided by the leadership.

In the late summer of 2006, republican circles in Northern Ireland were alive with stories of seasoned activists finally quitting the cause they had spent their adult lives serving. But no one expected them to flock to the dissidents or foment rebellion. It was far too late for any of that. As old comrades left, Gerry Adams and Martin McGuinness donned the mantle of international peacemakers, shrugged off the unresolved problems of Northern Ireland and strutted the global stage to offer their services—Adams in the Basque country to help broker a cease-fire between ETA and the Spanish government, and as a conduit between Israel and Hamas; while Martin McGuinness journeyed to Sri Lanka to urge the Tamil Tigers to learn the lessons of the Irish peace process and end its war.

As for the IRA, one well-placed security source offered this judgement: "They are adhering to the bargain. Their civil administration is not giving out punishment beatings, there is no major criminality, recruitment has stopped, we assume they have a handful of guns for self-protection but weapons are no longer an issue. They see the future entirely as being political.[94]

In this sense it really didn't matter whether or not there was a deal between the DUP and Sinn Fein. After thirty-five bloody years and nearly 4,000 deaths, the war was finally and undeniably over.

EPILOGUE

"Turning the *Titanic* in a Bathtub"

By the autumn of 2006 the Northern Ireland peace process had set a record for longevity which only the halting and often half-hearted attempts to end the Israeli–Palestinian conflict could come near to equalling in modern times. By the most conservative criterion, the process had lasted twelve years at this point—that is from the IRA cease-fire of 1994 onwards. But if the starting date is taken as late 1982 when Father Reid and Gerry Adams began talking then the process is much, much longer.

By this calculation it had really lasted twenty-four years, which is longer than America's involvement in Vietnam and means that almost two thirds of the thirty-six years that the Troubles in Northern Ireland had lasted were spent in an effort to bring them to an end. Even by the more orthodox metric of twelve years, it was an inordinately protracted process, three times longer than the First World War and twice that of the Second World War. There cannot have been many peace processes in history that took longer to consummate than some of the worst global conflicts.

The two prime ministers centrally involved in the process, Britain's Tony Blair and Ireland's Bertie Ahern, spent their entire period in office, from the summer of 1997 onwards, attempting to push it over the finishing line. In Blair's case he still could not be sure that the job would have been accomplished by the time he was scheduled to leave Downing Street in the summer of 2007.

The sheer scale of the task and Gerry Adams's finely honed instinct for caution and self-preservation explain the glacial pace of the process in the years up to the 1994 cease-fire and the Good Friday Agreement. The huge ideological compromises that would be involved, the decades of bloodletting, suffering and sacrifices that would have to be pushed to one side and the very real risks of a bloody split in those early years were testament to the magnitude of Adams's achievement, even if dissembling and manipulation were among the tools he used. One Protestant friend of the Sinn Fein leader, a Presbyterian minister, put it well when he compared what Adams had done to "Turning the *Titanic* in a bathtub."[1]

The years after the Good Friday Agreement are a different matter. It is difficult to examine the evidence from those years and not conclude that the slow pace of events, especially regarding IRA decommissioning, were, on the part of the Sinn Fein and IRA hierarchy, deliberately contrived to destabilize moderate unionism and secure nationalist electoral dominance for Sinn Fein. But none of this would have been possible without the goodwill of the British and Irish governments whose indulgence of the Provo leadership in these years was the direct consequence of a flawed reading of the IRA's internal politics.

Those chickens came home to roost, as one day they would have to, in the second week of October 2006 in a five-star hotel in St. Andrews, Fife, on the east coast of Scotland. The venue was chosen for yet another all-party conference on the peace process on the grounds that agreement might be easier to achieve the farther away the participants were from Belfast.

And against all the odds an agreement did emerge. The bulk of the talking was done—virtually all of it through intermediaries—between the DUP and Sinn Fein, and between them and the two governments. The result was a deal that would restore the power-sharing Executive by the end of March 2007, an event that would be preceded by another election. If, as expected, the DUP and Sinn Fein emerged as the largest two parties, then Ian Paisley would become the first minister and Martin McGuinness his deputy.

The success of the deal, that is the DUP's willingness to share power with Sinn Fein, hinged entirely upon the readiness of the Provos to accept the Police Service of Northern Ireland (PSNI), and written into the small print of the deal was a pledge of office which the first and deputy first minister would have to swear, "endorsing fully the PSNI and the criminal justice system." Recognition of the partitioned state would then be complete but in order to do that, Sinn Fein would have to stage a special Ard Fheis to approve the move.

This endgame was the logical outcome of the journey undertaken by Gerry Adams and those around him, but there were other compelling

reasons to believe that the Provo leadership saw many advantages in signing up to the PSNI. There were plans to enlarge the part-time Reserve inherited from the RUC by up to 2,500 members and the rules stipulated that
these should be recruited from areas where there were very few existing
reservists.[2] This meant that nationalist areas, especially those where the
Provos were strongest, such as West Belfast, would provide the bulk of these
new recruits. By design or default, many would be loyal to the Sinn Fein
leadership and some even members of the IRA. The Provos were also heavily involved in a number of Community Restorative Justice schemes, low-
level efforts to eradicate minor crime, and between this and the PSNI
Reserve, Provo influence on policing at grassroots level, and especially in
the communities they already controlled, would be considerable. The St.
Andrews Agreement also foresaw the day when policing and justice would
be devolved and that meant that Sinn Fein would have a chance of nominating the responsible minister—although crucially there was no agreement
on a timetable for this to happen. Gerry Kelly, a former London bomber
and one-time IRA adjutant-general, was often named as the party's candidate. Accepting the PSNI could cement Sinn Fein's long-term control of
their communities.

   Either because of the deep, atavistic hatred the Provisional grassroots had
always harbored against the police in Northern Ireland, or because accepting the PSNI would be part of a final deal which would also see Ian Paisley,
of all people, at the top of the heap, or even because such an outcome would
signal undeniably Sinn Fein's acceptance of partition, the republican base
resisted the policing issue with more vigour than any other concession made
during the peace process. There were rumors of death threats against leadership figures and reports of defections and resignations and privately,
according to leaks in the media, the Sinn Fein leadership worried about the
margin of victory they would secure at the special Ard Fheis.

   In the North the Provisionals' leverage had disappeared with the final
acts of IRA decommissioning and in the DUP they faced unionists made of
sterner stuff than David Trimble, who would walk away rather than accept
Sinn Fein in government on lesser terms. In the South there were alarming
signs for Sinn Fein that the party had settled at the bottom of a political
trough and that the Green party was now capturing the voters' imagination in the way Gerry Adams had done a few years earlier. Something had
to be done to restore Sinn Fein's support in the South and perhaps the
North could provide a way. And, when all was said and done, getting into
government on both sides of the Border remained the Provos' primary

strategic goal. Everything pointed in the same direction—it was time to cut a deal.

If it had been left to the British government, Sinn Fein would probably have been let into government without having to formally sign up to the PSNI, and again a flawed reading of the IRA's internal politics was the cause. In July 2006 Northern Ireland Secretary Peter Hain visited the United States to tell Irish-American leaders that what was needed, "as the way forward," from Sinn Fein was greater cooperation with the PSNI of the sort witnessed during the recent Orange marching season. There was no mention of the requirement to support the PSNI, merely more face-to-face get-togethers between PSNI officers and Sinn Fein leaders. At one meeting, a Sinn Fein official said that, while the leadership knew what had to be done, they had to go carefully and slowly to avoid a split. It was the same argument that had been made so successfully again and again during the decommissioning saga—and it appeared to be working once more. According to an informed source Hain described the Sinn Fein official's comments as being "full of common sense."[3]

The British were not alone in wishing to soft-pedal the policing issue with Sinn Fein. At least one of Ian Paisley's closest lieutenants was of the same view, arguing that it was an undeliverable demand for the republicans. But the DUP leader himself took a tougher line, recognizing that without Sinn Fein signing up to the PSNI, a power-sharing deal would be devoid both of moral value and any credibility within his own community. So it was that at St. Andrews Paisley dug his heels in and prevailed.

Ian Paisley's conversion to power-sharing with Sinn Fein is one of the most extraordinary and least understood features of the peace process. In one way he appears to be the most unlikely candidate for partnership government with republicans. After all he had spent his entire political life opposing any and all forms of political reconciliation, accusing fellow unionists who advocated accommodation with even moderate nationalists as traitors and "Lundies." Many even blamed Paisley for the Troubles on the grounds that his agitation against the mildly reforming unionist prime minister Capt. Terence O'Neill in 1969 which led to his downfall paved the way for the slide into conflict, violence and ultimately the birth of the Provisional IRA. Gerry Adams's own decision to join the IRA in 1964 followed riots in West Belfast stirred up by Paisley. The idea of Ian Paisley sharing a political bed with Gerry Adams seemed laughably absurd.

But there are other aspects of Paisley's politics which help to explain why a deal between them is both possible and likely. One is, quite simply, that he could argue to his own people that he had forced the IRA to decommission (even though the truth may have been much more complicated) and by obliging Sinn Fein to accept political office in an arrangement based upon the consent principle and acceptance of the policing and criminal justice system, he had achieved something that had eluded every other unionist leader: the final and certain political and military defeat of Irish republicanism and the longterm security of the union with Britain.

The other has to do with Paisley's history of conflict with, and rejection by, the major pillars of the Northern Protestant establishment. Spurned and reviled by the mainstream Protestant churches, he set up his own Free Presbyterian Church and set about poaching and winning converts from the competition. He was banned from the Orange Order and so he built up the Independent Orange Order as a rival. Politically shunned as an irritating and embarrassing nuisance by the mainstream unionist party, he set up his own party, first the Protestant Unionists and latterly the Democratic Unionists and then set about bringing his rivals down. He was always the outsider but now, in his eighty-first year, victory stared him in the face, victory over the IRA and victory over the unionist establishment that had always shunned him. Ending his political career as Northern Ireland's first minister was surely an irresistible prize. It was also evidence of another key and often overlooked—aspect of Paisley's political character: his innate pragmatism.

Paisley's judgement on the PSNI issue proved to be correct, and more accurate than Peter Hain's. On January 28, 2007 Sinn Fein met in an extraordinary Ard Fheis in Dublin's RDS and on a show of hands overwhelmingly passed a leadership motion advocating the acceptance of the PSNI and authorizing Sinn Fein's executive, or Ard Comhairle, to implement the decision upon the satisfactory establishment of the power-sharing executive. While there was no count, media estimates put the majority in favor at around 90 percent. Of the much predicted internal opposition there was no or little sign; only Sinn Fein's youth wing, Ogra Sinn Fein, opposed the motion.

There are several significant aspects about the vote. One rests on the fact that around half the votes at every Sinn Fein Ard Fheis are IRA votes and they are cast in whatever direction the Army Council decrees. Had the Adams leadership wished to signal that it could not move as fast as others wanted and required more concessions, it could have been easily arranged, and even more readily accepted in Downing Street and Dublin. But that course was resisted, surely evidence that the Provo leaders knew they had come to the end of their journey.

Another conclusion from the scale of Adams's victory is that the British and Irish governments had been completely wrong, possibly for years, in their assessment of the internal threat to his leadership and its consequent freedom to move. As one government participant noted in an email to the author: "The margin of the vote says loudly and clearly that he [Adams] could have done this years ago. Would the dissident threat have been greater then? Maybe, but the benefits of getting the business done and finished would have outweighed the small risk of having a few dozen more dead-enders joining RIRA, which is completely penetrated anyway. More toughness from Blair earlier would have done the trick."[4]

The indulgence shown to the Provo leadership by Blair and Ahern had, over the years, chipped away at the center ground of Northern Ireland politics and now, with the Sinn Fein decision on the PSNI out of the way, the stage was set to complete the process.

A fresh election to the Stormont Assembly was held on March 7 and it would be difficult to have designed an election more calculated to appeal to sectarian passions and to strengthen the most extreme parties. With inter-party talks likely to precede any formation of a power-sharing Executive, the voters were effectively being asked to send the strongest possible team from "their side" into negotiations with "the other side." The DUP at one point was quite blatant about this, warning Protestants that a vote for any other unionist party could open the way for Sinn Fein to top the poll. Sinn Fein made no comment but privately must have been gleeful, for their message, more discreetly communicated, was exactly the same. In such ways did the extremes feed off each other.

The counting, completed two days later, confirmed the virtual collapse of the center ground. Paisley's DUP won 36 seats in the 108-seat Assembly, a gain of six seats while their Ulster Unionist rivals lost nine seats and fell to 18. Sinn Fein gained four seats to win 28 seats and the SDLP lost two seats, to win a mere 16 seats. It was a sectarian head count whose outcome had questioned the *raison d'étre* for a second unionist party and raised real doubts over the longterm future of the SDLP.

A power-sharing deal between Ian Paisley and the Adams/McGuinness leadership now looked a matter of when not if. For the British and Irish governments the outcome of the March 2007 election presaged a final triumph in their long, gruelling stewardship of the peace process. For the about-to-retire Blair in particular, his record in office deeply tarnished by the Iraq war and his relationship with President George W. Bush, the success of the Northern Ireland peace process is one of the few bright spots in his legacy. He and Bertie Ahern had brought final peace to one of Europe's most troubled regions, but at the cost of handing it over to the least deserving, most adamantine elements of that society. That's one tragedy about the way the peace process has worked. The other and greater tragedy is that it needn't have ended this way.

APPENDIX 1

Special Sinn Fein Ard Comhairle Meeting, April 12, 1980

The divisions within the Provisional movement, between the Adams faction and the O Bradaigh–O Conaill supporters, over the amalgamation of *An Phoblacht* and *Republican News*, the Adams move to the left, the production of Adams's so-called grey document, and the undermining of Eire Nua were graphically illustrated by the minutes of this Sinn Fein Executive meeting held in April 1980.

Danny Morrison: Donegal refused papers—our man was arrested delivering them—didn't have the courtesy to ring up and cancel.

Ruairi O Bradaigh: If there is no confidence in Leadership, policies are no use to us. Anonymous articles and letters in AP/PN do not go down well. We must re-establish confidence by printing own names above articles.

Joe Cahill: I never believed in Federalism. This may come as a surprise to many of you.

Joe O'Neill: More harmony before amalgamation although I agreed with amalgamation. Reason for refusing papers—IRSP and other articles, disagreement with policy. Bundoran S. F. Cumann refused to sell papers—not Joe O'Neill.

Tony Ruane: If there is some little mistake in the paper don't exaggerate it. Sinn Fein was not fully acquainted before the document.

Charlie McGlade: Sinn Fein looks upon itself as back-up to Provos. We would need to watch that we don't just call ourselves socialists and not Republicans. Don't get into

	entrenched positions—we must get rid of any discontent. In rural areas there is a real fear of Communism.
Liam Haddock:	Grass roots are not aware of what is happening at top—change of direction or whatever should be passed on to members.
Matt Devlin:	People of Tyrone felt bad after what happened at Ard-Fheis—they felt there had been a split. Wrong time for change in policy. S.F. does not have the same credibility since the document.
Paddy J. Kearney:	No lack of faith in leadership. People are thinking that S.F. has been demoted. Not as significant anymore. If the original document was rejected out of hand it shows how ill informed were the people who drew it up. No stance of boycott in Connaught. We sold papers. Rejection of fisheries in newsletter.
C. Kelly:	Country areas thought document was too far to the left and that they didn't have any say in the organisation.
Niall Fagan:	Danger is that we will defeat ourselves. General consensus of opinion right around the country is that we are demoted—of no consequence. The most dissenting voices are the ones who are fully behind the "Brits Out" campaign. AP/RN leading us to extreme left—red left. Stifling veto on policies by one branch of the movement over the other. We need to have our confidence restored—custodial ownership—the key word. This drives them mad.
George Stagg:	I made my position clear and that's where I am staying. Horrified at G. Adams' statement at Ard Fheis that "without policy going through it is not worth death of one Brit or one man in prison." Hope we are not going to have witch-hunt. Are rumours about Sean MacStiofain true?
Joe Cahill:	He has been given job of distribution manager in AP/RN. He is not in Sinn Fein.
Tom Hartley:	Sinn Fein is demoting itself. If there is loss of membership that is Sinn Fein's fault and not the [IRA]. There has been a policy crisis. We are part of a mass of people who want freedom. Perhaps that is truly international.

Phil Flynn: I already had my say.

E. O Doherty: Sixth sense says that there is discontent. Since amalga-
                         mation—discontent. No editorial and withdrawal of
                         Christine [sic] Ni Elias's Eire Nua.

Paddy Bolger: There was not the same unanimity in A/C as was in
                         the military leadership. Smouldering discontent mani-
                         fested itself after Ard Fheis. Socialism and national-
                         ism are related. Confusion about general aims of the
                         Movement. Sticks betrayed the Movement. Hysterical
                         reaction to the new policy. It's a development of
                         Republicanism. Nothing sinister.

John Joe McGirl: Present policies of political parties are breaking down
                         in front of them. No point in having document unless
                         it is implemented. Fully support the document—it is in
                         the line of Republicanism. Discontent being promoted
                         from the A/C by those who do not accept document.
                         If we want unity we must have it from in here.

Sean O Bradaigh: We must move on the basis that there is trust and con-
                         fidence in the leadership. Original Eire Nua was
                         designed as a left document but to win over as wide a
                         spectrum of people as possible. There was a directive
                         from the [Army Council]—Federalism to be put in
                         cold storage. You cannot issue directives to the Ard
                         Comhairle of Sinn Fein like that. Concept of leader-
                         ship is meaningless unless you have followers.

Daithi O Conaill: Motivation of Movement has been damaged. Trust
                         damaged—air of apathy. 1) Policy Review Committee
                         was a failure 2) Air of arrogance coming from the
                         [Army Council] These statements usually unify and
                         point the way forward. You must win respect—not
                         take it for granted. Sinn Fein committed itself to
                         Federalism at last Ard Fheis, [the Army Council]
                         rejects this policy. [The Army is] committed to policy
                         of de-centralisation, nothing outlined. No alternative
                         proposed by them to Federalism. There should be
                         equal participation.

Richard Behal: Not pessimistic about outcome. Shock of this dissent
                         may set us back on the right road. Political wing
                         should make policy statements not the other way

around. Get rid of division between [the IRA] and S.F. No inquest into why we did not contest local elections in 6 counties. Should take RTE to Strasbourg over Section 31. There is Marxist influence within the Movement. G. Adams was pulling a fast one when he stated there wasn't.

Gerry Adams: Campaign of innuendo and vilification. There are nationalists within the R.M. [separatists] wrong to be only a separatist. Can anyone outline the anti-Republican essence of this document? Republicanism is composed of many elements. This struggle is a life and death struggle. Going left is not something for-eign. Failed to harness the anti-establishment feeling, successive A/C have failed. What [the Army Council] did was done with best intentions. Perhaps they did make mistakes. Need to stop backbiting. We are not a National Liberation Movement. We are a Republican Movement going through a stage of national libera-tion. Are we a radical republican Movement?

T. O. Sullivan: As a member of A/C I accept document but how to sell it to the people. [The Army Council] statement is what caused division. There is not backstabbing of leader-ship. Leadership should have seen what the reaction would be around the country when document 1. was rejected. We have a duty to tell membership where we are going.

Jimmy Drumm: Comments should be passed on to the other side. G. Stagg should not be criticised for probing worms out of the woodwork. Dissension in Donegal re AP/RN not insurmountable.

Des Long: Changes in policy—grass roots not informed. A/C was not even kept informed. Ten acre capitalists are not going to let their land go. We will not get votes from these people with this document. Unless something else is offered we must keep Federalism. Attitude of AP/RN was—we are not carrying your policy but you will sell our paper. Insensitivity of AP/RN re centre-spread. Appeared at wrong time. We need a cooling off period.

Christin Ni Elias: Primary duty of party is to lead people. Lack of consultation with members of S.F. Lifting of ban is recognition of mistake that was made. Level of political awareness is greater now then in early seventies. Custodial ownership frightened people. There must be evolution. We must re-assure people that we know what membership wants.

George Lynch: AP/RN is whipping boy. Other side also. With exception of Meath there has been no backlash. A/C members cause of there being a backlash. I abide by decision. Never favoured Federalism but as education officer I spread it. We must abide by democratic decision of majority in this organisation. Urban and rural conflict. Land should be distributed to meet the needs of the people. The social message is not being put across. No effort was put into Federalism but now we are being told how great it was. The presentation of document is bad—people have to be told what we mean. Adverts are up in the Brochure this year—that is an answer. If leadership in consultation with S.F. members want to drop Federalism I will abide with that decision.

Ruairi O Bradaigh: A few points—I did not propose something at Ard Fheis that I did not believe in.

Joe Cahill: There is a desire to resolve difficulties. Let us now have proposals.

Phil Flynn: We must stand behind decision of Ard Fheis—create structures which will bring back confidence.

These are merely the comments of all Ard Comhairle members present at the special meeting of An Ard Comhairle on 12th April, 1980. Minutes recorded in official minute book.

TUAS Document—Summer 1994

The briefing paper of April deals with Strategic Objectives and events to that date in more detail than this paper. However a brief summary is helpful.

Our goals have not changed.

A United 32 County Democratic Socialist Republic.

The main Strategic Objectives to move us forward towards that goal can be summarised thus.

To construct an Irish nationalist consensus with international support on the basis of the dynamic contained in the Irish Peace initiative.

This should aim for:

(a) The strongest possible political consensus between the Dublin govt, SF and the SDLP.

(b) A common position on practical measures moving us towards our goal.

(c) A common nationalist negotiating position.

(d) An international dimension in aid of the consensus (mostly U.S.A. and E.U. [European Union]).

The Strategic Objectives come from a prolonged debate but are based on a straightforward logic; that republicans at this time and on their own do not have the strength to achieve the end goal.

The struggle needs strengthened [sic]; most obviously from other nationalist constituencies led by SDLP, Dublin government and the emerging I.A. [Irish-American] lobby, with additional support from other parties in E.U. rowing in behind and accelerating the momentum created.

The aim of any such consensus is to create a dynamic which can:

1. Effect [sic] the domestic and international perception of the republican position, i.e. as one which is reasonable.

2. To develop a northern nationalist consensus on the basis of constitutional change.

3. To develop an Irish national consensus on the same basis.

4. To develop Irish-America as a significant player in support of the above.

5. To develop a broader and deeper Irish nationalist consensus at grass-roots level.

6. To develop and mobilise an anti-imperialist Irish peace movement.

7. To expose the British government and the Unionists as the intransigent parties.

8. To heighten the contradictions between British unionism and "Ulster Loyalism."

9. To assist the development of whatever potential exists in Britain to create a mood/climate/party/movement for peace.

10. To maintain the political cohesion and organisational integrity of Sinn Fein so as to remain an effective political force.

Present British intentions are the subject of much debate and varied opinion. However what can be said is that sometime preceding the D.S.D. [Downing Street Declaration] of December '93 a deal was done with the U.U.P. [Ulster Unionist Party] to keep the Conservatives in power.

This becomes an obstacle to movement.

The D.S.D. does not hold a solution.

Republicans are not prepared to wait around for the British to change, but as always we are prepared to force their hand.

It is nonetheless important to note that there has been no recent dialogue between the Brit government and Republican representatives since November '93.

The Republican position is that if the Brits want to talk they should do so through normal political channels.

At the end of the April briefing it states: "Our (strategic) objectives should guide all our actions. Given that these are our guidelines we must now look at what our options are and what initiatives we can undertake."

After prolonged discussion and assessment the leadership decided that if it could get agreement with the Dublin government, the SDLP and the I.A. lobby on basic republican principles which would be enough to create the dynamic that would considerably advance the struggle then it would be prepared to use the TUAS option.

We attempted to reach such a consensus on a set of principles which can be summarised briefly thus:

1. Partition has failed.
2. Structures must be changed.
3. No internal settlement within 6 Counties.
4. British rule breaches the principle of N.S.D. [National self-determination].
5. The Irish as a whole have the right to N.S.D.—without external impediment.
6. It is up to the Dublin/London governments with all parties to bring about N.S.D. in the shortest time possible.
7. The Unionists have no veto over discussions involved or their outcome.
8. A solution requires political and constitutional change.
9. An agreed united and independent Ireland is what republicans desire. However an agreed Ireland needs the allegiance of varied traditions to be viable.

Contact with the other parties involved have been in that context.

There are of course differences of opinion on how a number of these principles are interpreted or applied.

In particular:

on British rule breaching the principle of N.S.D.;

on the absolute right of the Irish to N.S.D. without external impediment;

an interpretation of what veto and consent mean;

on the issue of timescales.

Nevertheless, differences aside, the leadership believes there is enough in common to create a substantial political momentum which will considerably advance the struggle at this time.

Some substantial contributing factors which point towards now being the right time for an intiative are:

Hume is the only SDLP person on the horizon strong enough to face the challenge;

Dublin's coalition is the strongest government in 25 years or more;

Reynolds has no historical baggage to hinder him and knows how popular such a consensus would be among grassroots;

There is potentially a very powerful I[rish] American lobby *not* in hock to any particular party in Ireland or Britain;

Clinton is perhaps the first U.S. President in decades to be substantially influenced by such a lobby;

At this time the British government is the least popular in the E.U. with other E.U. members;

It is the first time in 25 years that all the major Irish nationalist parties are rowing in roughly the same direction.

These combined circumstances are unlikely to gel again in the foreseeable future.

The leadership has now decided that there is enough agreement to proceed with the TUAS option.

It has been stated from the outset that this is a risky strategy.

Its success will depend greatly on workload. All activities must be pro-active.

Those who continue their present work need to double effect.

If you find yourself idle, help in another field.

TUAS has been a part of every other struggle in the world this century.

It is vital that activists realise the struggle is *not* over.

Another Front has opened up and we should have the confidence and put in the effort to succeed on that front.

We have the ability to carry on indefinitely.

We should be trying to double the pressure on the British.

For various reasons, which include the sensitivity of discussions up to this point, communication up and down the organisation has been patchy.

Since we are now entering a more public aspect to the initiative communication should be a less encumbered matter and therefore more regular than before.

Post–1996 Convention
IRA Constitution

This is the version of the IRA constitution as amended by the 1996 General Army Convention.

Additions to the previous constitution, agreed in 1986, are in *italics*; excisions are enclosed by ( ).

The Executive and the Army Council disagreed about which sections of the constitution had been removed at the 1996 Convention. These sections are indicated by [ ], i.e., square brackets.

1. Title:

The Army shall be known as Oglaigh na hEireann.

2. Membership:

1. Enlistment in Oglaigh na hEireann shall be open to all those over the age of 17 who accept its objects as stated in the Constitution and who make the following pledge:

   "I . . . {name} . . . promise that I will promote the objects of Oglaigh na hEireann to the best of my knowledge and ability and that I will obey all orders and regulations issued to me by the Army Authority and by my superior officer."
2. Participation in Stormont or Westminster and in any other subservient parliament, if any, is strictly forbidden.
3. Enlistment shall be at the discretion of the Army Authority.

3. Objects:

1. To guard the honour and uphold the sovereignty and unity of the *Irish* Republic (of Ireland) *as declared by the First Dail.*

2. To support the establishment of an Irish Socialist Republic based on the 1916 Proclamation.

3. To support the establishment of, and uphold, a lawful government in sole and absolute control of the *32 County Irish* Republic *as constituted by the First Dail.*

4. To secure and defend civil and religious liberties and equal rights and equal opportunities for all citizens.

5. To promote the revival of the Irish language as the everyday language of the people.

4. Means:

1. To organise Oglaigh na hEireann for victory.

2. To build on a spirit of comradeship.

3. To wage revolutionary armed struggle.

4. To encourage popular resistance, political mobilisation and political action in support of these objectives.

5. To assist, as directed by the Army Authority, all organisations working for the same objectives.

5. Army Control:

1. The General Army Convention shall be the Supreme Army Authority.

2. The Army Council shall be the Supreme Authority when a General Convention is not in session.

3. The Army Council, only after Convention, shall have power to delegate its powers to a government which is actively endeavouring to function as the de facto government of the Republic.

4. When a government is functioning as the de facto government of the Republic, a General Army Convention shall be convened to give the allegiance of Oglaigh na hEireann to such a government.

[5. All personnel and all armaments, equipment and other resources of Oglaigh na hEireann shall be at the disposal of and subject to the Army Authority, to be employed and utilised as the Army Authority shall direct.]

5. *The Army Authority shall retain, maintain and ensure the safety of all armaments, equipment and other resources of Oglaigh na hEireann until such times as the sovereignty and unity of the Republic of Ireland has been attained. Once a settlement has been agreed, leading to a united Ireland, all decisions relating to decommissioning of armaments, equipment and other resources must be ratified by an Army Convention.*

6. General Army Convention:

1. (a) A General Army Convention of Delegates {selected as set out hereinafter} shall meet every *four* (two) years unless the majority of these delegates notify the Army Council that they deem it better for military purposes to postpone it. When a General Army Convention is postponed, it *must* (shall) be summoned *to meet not later than twelve months after postponement* (as soon as the majority of the delegates shall notify the Army Council that they deem it advisable).

1. (b) *A Convention must be called within 15 months of a cessation being declared.*

2. An Extraordinary General Army Convention shall be called when a majority of the Executive so decide.

3. That should it be necessary to summon an Extraordinary General Army Convention and that the urgency of the issue for the Convention does not permit of the selection of delegates as prescribed, that the delegates to the previous General Army Convention constitute the Extraordinary General Army Convention. When for any reason a delegate to the previous General Army Convention has become ineligible, or is not available, the Battalion Council shall elect a delegate in his/her stead. Every active Volunteer in the Battalion shall be eligible to stand as a delegate.

4. An Executive of twelve members shall be elected by ballot at the General Army Convention: at least eight of these members shall be delegates to the Convention: Four members may be elected from active Volunteers who are not delegates. The next six in line shall, however, be eligible as substitutes to the Executive in order of their election. The Executive shall always have six substitutes in readiness.

5. No member of the Executive may also be a member of the Army Council and members of the Executive subsequently elected to the Army Council will resign from the Executive. Vacant positions on the Executive arising in such a way shall be filled by those substitutes next in line from the Convention delegates.

6. The following shall be entitled to attend and vote at the General Army Convention:
Delegates selected by Battalion Convention.
Delegates selected by General Headquarters Staff and Staffs of Brigades, Divisions and Commands.
Two members of the Executive.
All members of the Army Council.
The Chief of Staff, the Adjutant-General and the Quartermaster-General.

7. Only Volunteers on the Active List shall be eligible as delegates to the General Army Convention.

8. A majority of the General Army Convention may invite anyone whom they wish to attend to speak.

9. The Chairperson of the General Army Convention shall be chosen by the General Convention.

7. Duties and Powers of the Executive:

1. The Chairperson of the General Army Convention or his/her representative shall, within forty-eight hours of the termination of the Convention, summon a meeting of the Army Executive over which he/she shall preside during the election of a Chairperson and Secretary. The Army Executive shall then proceed with the election of an Army Council of seven members.

2. The Army Executive shall meet *at least every three* (once every six) months. The Secretary of the Executive shall be responsible for the summoning of the members. *The Chairman of the Army Council and the Chief of Staff attend all meetings of the Executive with the right to speak but without voting rights.*

3. It shall be the duty of the Executive to advise the Army Council on all matters concerning the Army. *This includes ratifying any cessation within four months of its declaration and two further extensions of four months.*

4. The Executive shall have powers, by a majority vote, to summon an Extraordinary General Army Convention.

5. A member of the Executive who, for any reason, ceases to be an active member of Oglaigh na hEireann shall cease to be a member of the Executive.

6. Casual vacancies on the Executive shall be filled by co-option after any substitutes that [*sic*] may be elected by the General Army Convention have been exhausted. Vacancies shall be filled within a period of one month.

7. The Executive shall hold office until the following General Army Convention shall elect a new Executive.

8. An extraordinary meeting of the Executive shall be summoned by the secretary of the Executive when a majority of the Army Council or a majority of the Executive so decide.

9. Two-thirds of the available members shall constitute a quorum of the Executive, for co-option purposes only. Full Executive powers shall not be vested in less than five members.

10. *The Army Executive are the custodians of the constitution and have the right to rule and arbitrate or rule on policy matters which may infringe the constitution and Volunteers have the right to petition the Executive on such matters.*

8. Duties and Powers of the Army Council:

A

1. The Chairperson of the Army Executive or his/her representative shall, as soon as possible after the election of the Army Council, summon a meeting of the Army Council, over which he/she shall preside, until a Chairperson and Secretary have been elected.
2. The Army Council shall meet at least once a month.
3. Vacancies occuring in the Army Council shall be filled from substitutes elected by the Executive or co-opted by the Army Council in advance. Co-options by the Army Council must be ratified by the Executive at its next meeting.
4. Any active Volunteer shall be eligible for membership of the Army Council.
5. The Army Council shall:
1) *Maintain the organisational integrity and cohesion of Oglaigh na hEireann until the objectives have been achieved.*
2) *Maintain the political and military strengths and capabilities of Oglaigh na hEireann until the objectives have been achieved.*

B

1. The Army Council shall have power to conclude peace or declare war when a majority of the Council so decide. The *final* conclusion of peace must be ratified by a Convention.
2. The Army Council shall have power to appoint a Chief of Staff and ratify all appointments to the Commissioned ranks.
3. The Army Council shall have power to make regulations regarding organisation, training, discipline, equipment and operations, such as will ensure that the Army will be as efficient as possible.
4. The Army Council shall have power to take all necessary steps to secure co-ordination with other republican organisations.
5. The Army Council shall have power to keep in touch with all foreign organisations and countries which may help the Army in any way.
6. The Army Council shall have power to arrange for the care of wounded Volunteers and their dependants and the dependants of Volunteers killed, imprisoned or on active-service.
7. The Chief of Staff, Adjutant-General and Quartermaster-General shall be entitled to attend and speak at all meetings of the Army Council but not be entitled to vote unless they are members of the Army Council.

8. Four members shall constitute a quorum of the Army Council *for co-option purposes only. Full power shall not be vested in less than five members.*

9. A member of the Army Council who, for any reason, ceases to be an active Volunteer, shall cease to be a member of the Army Council.

10. *The Army Council shall appoint a commission which sits every two years to ascertain the views and opinions of Volunteers at all levels in the Army.*

9. Selection of Delegates:

Delegates to the Command Conventions shall be elected by ballot as follows:

1. At each parade called for the purpose, each unit in Command Area shall elect a delegate to attend the Command Convention.

2. One member of the Command Staff, elected by the Staff at a special meeting called for the purpose.

3. The Command OC shall be entitled to attend and vote at the Command Convention.

4. Each Command Convention shall meet when instructed by the Army Authority and elect one delegate when the total number of Volunteers who parade for Unit Conventions do not exceed twenty, and two when the number of Volunteers do not exceed fifty, and one delegate for each twenty additional Volunteers on parade at Unit Conventions.

Brigade Conventions:

Where the Independent Unit is a Brigade, a Brigade Convention may be held consisting of the delegates elected by the Units, Battalion Staffs and the Brigade Staff, with the power to pass or reject any resolution brought forward by these delegates. The delegates from each Battalion shall each elect their own delegates to the Army Convention.

Election of Brigade, Divisional and Command Staff delegates to the General Army Convention:

Two delegates shall be elected at a meeting of General Headquarters Staff officers, with the exception of the Chief of Staff, Adjutant-General and Quartermaster-General.

Resolutions to General Army Convention:

Command Conventions and the meetings of GHQ Staff for the election of delegates to General Army Convention shall have power to discuss any matter relating to the Army or to the Nation and to pass resolutions regarding such matters. These resolutions shall be forwarded to GHQ within the time specified by the Army Authority and shall appear on the agenda for the General Army Convention.

10. Changes to the Constitution:

It shall require a two-thirds majority of a General Army Convention to change articles in this Constitution.

IRA Executive Chairman Seamus McGrane's Speech at the 1997 Convention

As chairman of the outgoing Executive it is my duty to outline to Convention the reasons behind the decision made by the Executive to call an extraordinary Convention. It is our opinion that only an extraordinary Convention, recalling the delegates from the previous Convention, would be sufficient to clarify major inaccuracies on fundamental constitutional and policy decisions taken by the Convention at that time.

This decision was not taken lightly. It came about after much debate and consultation. At all times the Executive acted in good faith striving to fulfil its constitutional role as laid down in the constitution. It is our opinion that only an extraordinary Convention would be sufficient to prevent serious internal problems in ONH over the foregoing fundamental principles.

The critical issues cited for the calling of this Convention are: (1) The Mitchell Principles, (2) Non-ratification of the ceasefire, (3) Treatment of the Executive by the Army Council, (4) Morale of the Volunteers.

Although these have been cited as separate they are inextricably linked.

Mitchell Principles

The Executive ruled that the signing of the Mitchell Principles was a breach of the constitution. They alerted the Army Council to this and after a lengthy, heated debate the Army Council agreed with this but stated they could give special dispensation to allow a Volunteer to break the Constitution. This was not accepted by the Executive. We are all aware of the consequences of when past leaderships attempted to interfere with or alter the fundamental aims and constitutional status of ONH.

The Army Council was advised by the Executive of the consequences of allowing this to happen. Furthermore the Executive insisted that a public statement be released clearly stating the Army's position in relation to the Mitchell Principles. Experience on this occasion after the heroic struggle of the last 27 years means that the present leadership must be clear with the membership on these vital points so as on this occasion the great advances made will not be wasted. It must be fully recognised that great advances have been made but are we going to throw these away?

Non-ratification of the Cease-fire

The majority of the Executive were opposed to the cease-fires. They were critical of the timing of it, concerned about the weak state of the Army having just emerged from a previous lengthy "suss." It was felt that the consensus of the last Convention was against a "suss" and the subsequent Donegal meeting re-affirmed this with the rejection of the aide-memoire.

A majority of the Executive felt that a reconvening of the delegates would have been the proper thing to do to clarify this position. Furthermore there was grave concern about the implementation of the integrated strategy. The Executive agreed with the principle of an integrated strategy but were critical of the term integrated as there was no evidence of a military strategy and the political strategy contained elements that were in conflict with the Army constitution.

For almost the last year we have relayed these concerns to the leadership and as yet a strategy which could be truly described as integrated has not been forthcoming. The most recent attempt at a military strategy was cobbled together and presented no later than three days ago at an Executive meeting after it was stated at a previous Executive two weeks earlier that there hasn't been time to assemble one as people were tied up with meetings and going to talks at Stormont.

Treatment of the Executive by the Army Council

Having been a member of the previous Executive since 1986 I feel I am in a position to state that the outgoing Executive in my opinion was the first Executive I have seen which took its role seriously. This Executive was determined to carry out its function as laid down in the constitution by the last Convention.

In order to fulfil its role as advisers to the Army Council on policy matters relating to the Army it was essential for the Executive to be fully briefed. Resolutions passed at Convention help formulate future Army policy. The Executive repeatedly requested a copy of these at all meetings from after the Convention was held. These were withheld and only came into our possession a few weeks ago by mistake. It transpired that we were not to have them at all. These documents would have undoubtedly been of assistance in clarifying the consensus of the last Convention in its attitude to cease-fires being called, dual roles etcetera.

Incidentally a number of other documents were requested, one in particular, the aide-memoire, was requested and the reply was: these can be got in government buildings.

Prior to the general election in the Six Cos. the Army Council decided on a "tactical period of quiet" which lasted several weeks. The Executive was not informed of this. When it was raised at the Executive meeting in May the Army Council Chairman apologised and gave commitments that this would not happen again and that there would be better communication.

At this same meeting and as a consequence of what had already taken place members of the Executive expressed fears of a possible cease-fire being called. The Army Council chairman stated: "There was no case for a ceasefire" and he didn't understand why it was even being discussed. We had only to wait a few weeks to see this commitment flounder. At the next meeting of the Executive the Army Council joined us. We were informed of the decision to call a ceasefire. We were informed that it was to be announced within 48 hours. Pressure was brought to bear on the Executive to support the decision. We were told to "endorse it or go to a Convention."

The Executive realised the enormity of their responsibility and was reluctant to make rash decisions before discussing and consulting on this further, regardless of the criticism being directed at them. Several meetings took place where much consideration was given to the feedback from the Volunteers and the constitutional implications of the Mitchell Principles.

We were criticised for taking time to make our decision and then when we finally did we were asked to reconsider it. This is an example of the double talk and contradictions which we had become accustomed to. We were told: "If such a Convention is [held] at this time there is potential for disaster coming out of a Convention." Yet as stated earlier we were also told "endorse or go to a Convention."

The Morale of the Volunteers

In conclusion the majority of the Executive were conscious of the confusion and frustration felt by Volunteers when the decision to call a ceasefire was announced. Three months on this has not subsided, in fact it has been fuelled by conflicting assurances being given by members of the Army Council to

Volunteers that we are going back to war in a couple of months while other members have stated they are fearful the struggle would be over if we did go back. Confusion breeds fear; fear breeds disillusionment; disillusionment breeds dissent. Too many sacrifices have been made by the Volunteers of ONH; for us to allow this sort of practice to continue we would be undermining our responsibility to the Volunteers who elected us to the position of Executive.

IRA Chiefs of Staff

1. Sean MacStiofain – from December 1969 until November 1972
2. Joe Cahill – until March 1973
3. Seamus Twomey – until June 1973
4. Eamon Doherty – until June/July 1974
5. Seamus Twomey – until December 1977
6. Gerry Adams – December 1977 until February 18, 1978
7. Martin McGuinness – until autumn of 1982
8. Ivor Bell – until September 1983
9. Kevin McKenna – until October 1997
10. Tom "Slab" Murphy – from October 1997

The Mitchell Principles

Accordingly, we recommend that the parties to such negotiations affirm their total and absolute commitment:

(a) To democratic and exclusively peaceful means of resolving political issues;

(b) To the total disarmament of all paramilitary organisations;

(c) To agree that such disarmament must be verifiable to the satisfaction of an independent commission;

(d) To renounce for themselves, and to oppose any effort by others, to use force, or threaten to use force, to influence the course or the outcome of all-party negotiations;

(e) To agree to abide by the terms of any agreement reached in all-party negotiations and to resort to democratic and exclusively peaceful methods in trying to alter any aspect of that outcome with which they may disagree; and,

(f) To urge that "punishment" killings and beatings stop and to take effective steps to prevent such actions.

Letter from Father Alec Reid to Charles Haughey, May 11, 1987

11–5–87
Clonard Monastery

Dear Mr. Haughey,

I am writing to ask your advice with the following because it concerns what the Church may be able to do over the coming months to help the cause of peace. I am thinking in particular of what you may be able to do to persuade the IRA to end their military tactics and so to open the way to political dialogue and cooperation between all the nationalist parties, a development which I believe would in turn open the way to new relationships between the nationalist and unionist communities.

I am writing personally but I know that others who are associated with me including people of standing and influence in politics and the Church would agree in principle with the main points that I shall make.

To set these points in context I would like first to explain that my interest is not political but pastoral and moral. I know that a priest of the Church itself cannot get involved in party or even nationalist politics nor can he take sides in matters of political opinion and judgement. At the same time however I believe that a priest, again like the Church itself, must respond to the human and moral dimensions of the political situation especially insofar as it involves people whoever they may be in suffering and tragedy.

It is this tragic dimension of the situation in Northern Ireland that concerns me and also I know concerns those who are associated with me both inside and outside the Redemptorist community. Whatever my private opinions may be I am not as a priest either for or against any particular political form of solution to the conflict whatever that might be provided it is just and acceptable to the people as a whole. My only aim is to help those people who if the present situation continues will be killed, injured or imprisoned over the next few weeks and months and whose personal tragedies will blight not only their own lives but also the lives of those to whom they are near and dear.

I can bring this explanation of my interest into sharper focus by saying it was the death of a UDR man in South Armagh about three years ago that sparked off the efforts which my colleagues and I have been making since then to end once and for all the violent situation which is causing such tragedies.

I have been involved in the processes of peace-making since the Troubles began in 1969, sometimes at the level of political and Church leadership; sometimes in the prisons, sometimes across the political divide between loyalist and nationalist but most often at the level of the streets in nationalist areas. Because of illness I gave up this kind of involvement for a number of years and it was only when the UDR man I mentioned was killed that I felt that the Church and priests like myself could and should be playing a more active and effective role in ending these kinds of tragedies that I became involved again.

I am writing all this to explain not only my own standpoint and interest but also the standpoint and interest of my colleagues and associates. Our approach is based on two principles, one of which comes from our faith, the other from our common sense.

Our principle of faith is that whenever we are working for peace and reconciliation between people we can be certain that the Lord is with us. His presence is the sure guarantee that we shall succeed if trusting in Him and doing what we can ourselves we keep on keeping on.

The second principle which comes from our common sense is that the most human and most Christian way to achieve reconciliation and peace between people who are in conflict is the way of dialogue carried out in the spirit of respect and compassion for everyone involved. We believe that if we keep these two principles in mind and follow them out in practice we can confidently hope to succeed.

The first principle tells us that the Lord is always with us and never more than when we are working for peace. This knowledge gives us the courage we need because it assures us that in Him the power to overcome every obstacle is always available to us. Given this principle in practice means setting our minds and our hearts sincerely on the search for peace and then going forward sustained by our trust in His presence and His power, by the confidence which tells us that if we do what we tell ourselves He will, step by step, light up and open the way.

The second principle tells us that respectful and compassionate dialogue is the ideal way to settle conflicts. This knowledge gives us the basic guideline that we need in terms of the first steps we have to take when we set about the practicalities of making peace. If our experiences over the past two years or so have confirmed the need for faith and the need for dialogue they have also shown the power of these two principles when they are applied to our divisions and conflicts because as we went along we could see to our great surprise a whole scene opening up in which ways to a true and lasting peace were beginning to define themselves which if they had been followed up effectively as they appeared would by now, I believe, have led us forward to a situation in which the ending of "the armed struggle", if not actually achieved would at least be within our grasp and where the processes of healing and reconciliation within the nationalist community itself and across the political divide between nationalist and unionist could have been significantly advanced.

I am saying this in faith but also in the knowledge which has come from our experience during that time when we were dealing with hard-headed and realistic people with influence in both communities.

I shall now try to summarize the results of our peace-making efforts over the past two years and then in view of them outline some proposals which I would like to put to you for advice and comment.

We began by seeking advice of people in the nationalist and unionist communities whose judgement we knew we could trust because of their political knowledge and experience and also because of their closeness to the actual political situation in these communities. We asked them specifically how they thought the Church could help in the search for peace.

Generally speaking they told us that in their view the Church could give invaluable help because of her resources, her influence, her independence and authority and the lines of communication that were open to her. They said that for the sake of the people of both communities she should use these assets to define, organize and develop her pastoral responses to the causes and the effects of the conflict and that in keeping with her pastoral role in reconciling and peace-keeping in the community she should encourage, foster and where necessary even initiate dialogue between the various parties and groupings who are in conflict or at odds with each other especially where positive communication has broken down between them.

Since our main concern is to end the use of violent tactics on the nationalist side we spoke first to representatives of Sinn Fein including their present leader because we felt they could best advise us on this issue. They told us that in their view the Church could play a vital role not only in the general search for peace but also in the creation of ways and means for ending "the armed struggle".

Their general opinion of the situation at that time was that there would be no substantial progress towards a just and lasting peace and, especially, no hope of persuading the IRA to end their campaign unless the processes of dialogue were set up and maintained between all the parties concerned. In these they included the Church herself because as they saw the situation she was in a unique position to help.

Here they referred to Pope John Paul's speech at Drogheda and said that while everyone could recall his statement on violence few seemed to remember what he said about the responsibilities of political and community leaders in Ireland to create the peaceful and effective means for overcoming injustices so that those who were suffering from them would not be driven back on their own resources and as a result be tempted to justify resort to violence.

Taking their cue from this part of the Pope's speech they said that the only way to persuade the IRA to end their campaign was to show them that the use of force was no longer necessary to achieve justice for the nationalist community because of the availability of a peaceful strategy which in terms of the political forces involved could be reasonably regarded as a realistic alternative.

This was the gist of the advice which the Sinn Fein representatives gave the Church representatives at the various meetings which took place between them. It was clear therefore to the Church representatives that in view of this advice the only way to achieve their aim of ending "the armed struggle" and the tragedies that went with it was to create a dialogue through which a powerful political alternative could be formulated, initiated in concrete terms and then proposed to the IRA as a viable and going concern.

The representatives of the Church were naturally depressed by the implications of all this but at the same time heartened by the evident willingness of the Sinn Fein leadership to cooperate with them. Whatever our personal opinions might be we realized that to make progress we would have to work on the possibilities that the Sinn Fein leadership had presented to us.

We therefore held discussions on the questions of "an alternative method" with a number of people who we felt were in a position to advise us because of their knowledge of both the nationalist and unionist communities. As a result we decided that the following proposal for "an alternative method" should at least be explored because it was favoured by the consensus of opinion amongst those whom we consulted.

The essence of this proposal is that the nationalist parties, North and South, would agree through dialogue amongst themselves to formulate and then to cooperate in a common nationalist policy of aims and methods for resolving the conflict and establishing a just and lasting peace. This would mean that while retaining their own separate identities the nationalist parties would make an ad hoc agreement to combine their political forces and to act in unison in a common campaign for reconciliation and peace.

This is the theory of this particular proposal for "an alternative method": the creation of a powerful combined political force on the nationalist side to which the IRA would respond by ending "the armed struggle" and with which they would begin to cooperate once the first serious steps to set it up were taken.

I believe that as a theory this proposal has a lot to recommend it. It would for example end the violent and tragic dimensions of the conflict which would be a blessing beyond words and which I have said is the main concern of the Church.

The common nationalist policy envisaged in this proposal would provide the nationalist people with a powerful but peaceful basis for achieving their aims, aims which would be defined and expressed in terms of a broad nationalist consensus and which for that reason would be moderate, reasonable and just. This in turn would win respect, sympathy and support for their cause throughout the world.

Such a common nationalist policy would also be of great benefit to the unionist community because in the first place it would end the use of arms in the nationalist community, a tactic which must be a nightmare to them and which they so often see as sectarian in intent and motivation. It would also convince them of the need to develop new political attitudes because in the face of a nationalist community so powerfully and yet so peacefully united it would be clear beyond any doubt that real peace would never come until they came to terms, realistically and positively, with nationalist rights and aspirations. I also believe that such a common nationalist policy would be welcomed in the unionist community by the realists among them and also by those whose political attitudes are inspired by wisdom and compassion, people who are more numerous and at the end more influential than the "not an inch" image of their community often suggests.

I am not saying this off the top of my head but because of soundings I have made among unionists and loyalists who are sensitive to political possibilities within their own community and who responded positively and favourably to the idea of a common nationalist policy.

This then is the theory of the proposal which we decided to put forward for examination and discussion. All the time however it was clear that more important than any proposal for "an alternative method", however appealing in theory it might be, the crucial exercise in the whole enterprise would be ongoing, open-ended dialogue between all the parties concerned, that is between the representatives of the Church and the initiators and coordinators of the discussions, the representatives of constitutional nationalist parties as the holders of the main political authority in the situation, the representatives of Sinn Fein as the party directly related to "the armed struggle".

The discussions we have held to date including those with the representatives of Sinn Fein had emphasized the primacy of open-ended dialogue as the key to the whole problem and as the sine qua non of progress. Without it theories about "alternative methods" would remain forever in the air because it would be only through the processes of dialogue involving hard and realistic discussion and a compassionate willingness to give and take that "an alternative method" to the armed struggle acceptable to every party concerned could be worked out and set in motion.

Its formal structure therefore would emerge from the dialogue itself and not from any preconceived notions and theories. At the same time however the representatives of the Church decided that to get the dialogue going they should proceed on the basis of the proposal for a common nationalist policy outlined above because in theory at least this offered the best hope for progress and also because it would serve to focus the main purpose of the dialogue, the ending of "the armed struggle" through the creation of "an alternative method".

This decision however did not mean that other proposals would be excluded from discussion because from the beginning and in accordance with the principle of open-ended dialogue the actual agenda for any meeting would be a matter for all the participants to decide.

To sum up then on this part of the letter our basic concern is to do all we can to remove the tragic and violent dimensions of the conflict insofar as the nationalist community at least is involved.

Our reading of the possibilities of doing this at the present time is definitely positive provided that the Sinn Fein movement in general and the IRA in particular could be shown that a powerful political strategy is available as an alternative to the use of force. Indeed my own conviction is that if the processes of dialogue which would be necessary to create such a common policy were even initiated on a serious basis among the nationalist parties everyone concerned including the representatives of the Church, the representatives of the constitutional parties and the political leadership of Sinn Fein would be in a much stronger position than they are at the moment to influence the course of "the armed struggle" and the attitudes of those who are committed to it. I also believe that once this dialogue were under way the IRA would begin to respond to it and to cooperate with those involved especially the representatives of the Church.

I am also convinced that the opportunities for making peace were never greater than they are at the present. I say this because of close contact with the situation and also because of past experience. These opportunities relate both to the IRA and to the unionist community and to fail to recognize and grasp them would I believe be a tragedy beyond words. I am sure therefore that the resources of the Church should be mobilized to help in the creation of "an alternative method". I am also sure they can be mobilized provided the constitutional parties on the nationalist side agree to cooperate.

I should say here that the representatives of the Sinn Fein movement have consistently told me over the past two years that they will cooperate fully with the Church and her representatives in any effort they may make to promote the creation of an alternative method to "the armed struggle" and to substitute political methods for military ones. They have also said that they will give the whole matter the highest priority, devote all the necessary resources and energies to it and engage positively and constructively in discussions and negotiations with any party or group representative, nationalist or unionist and indeed with any individual from either side who is willing to cooperate with the Church and whose influence on the political scene places them in a position to help. They will do this at any time, without preconditions either officially or unofficially and in the strictest confidence.

As I have already said I do not believe that it normally belongs to the pastoral role of the Church to get directly involved in the creation of political policies although in a situation like that under consideration here where it is a case of creating policies which will serve as an alternative to the use of force I believe that she should get involved in facilitating their creation. In borderline areas between political responsibility and pastoral responsibility the nature and degree of her involvement will depend on circumstances and judgement.

Circumstances in Northern Ireland must I believe be judged in the light of the fact that since 1969 a lot of the real power to influence the course of events has been on the streets. With the breakdown of normal law and order this has also meant the breakdown in lines of trust, access and communication which normally help to hold a peaceful society together.

In this kind of situation the Church has, I believe, a pastoral responsibility to intervene where she can and where others who normally would, cannot, in order to bridge the gaps in these lines otherwise the breakdowns will continue and grow worse and only soldiers and police with guns will be able to contain the situation. This is one of the reasons why the Church has a pastoral role to play in the initiation at least of the kind of enterprise I have been discussing and also in the creation of the kind of supportive and neutral setting that would be necessary to make it viable and successful.

I also believe that in keeping with the Pope's words at Drogheda about the need to create peaceful ways for achieving justice the Church must look again at a political situation in which for the past sixteen years in spite of repeated condemnations significant numbers of her own flock have either directly or indirectly been involved in the determined, tragic and terrifying use of well-organized military tactics to achieve political aims which have been traditionally accepted as right and just by the nationalist community as a whole and therefore by the community for which the Church has pastoral responsibility.

The Church's main response to date has been to condemn these tactics as immoral but however this may have helped to contain the situation it has clearly failed to end it. In addition ... moral guidance especially when this guidance takes the form of condemnations that are not being heeded the Church must consider what further practical responses she can make to a situation which has lasted for so long and which shows every sign of lasting into the foreseeable future.

Here in support of the point I have been making I would like to give some quotations from a general comment which another Redemptorist, Father Sean O'Riordan, made on a public letter which at the beginning of last year Mr. Gerry Adams addressed to Dr. Cahal Daly, the Bishop of Down and Connor. Father O'Riordan is Professor of Moral and Pastoral Theology at the Alphonsian Academy, Lucerne University, Rome. He gave his comments on tape and so I shall quote them verbatim. They covered the whole letter in question but here I shall only give those that are relevant to the present letter.

Father O'Riordan said: "I have been asked to comment on the recent open letter addressed to Dr. Cahal Daly, Bishop of Down and Connor by Mr. Gerry Adams, Sinn Fein MP for West Belfast. I would like to begin by stating the context in which I have carefully read and studied Mr. Adams's letter. The context I refer to is that of the morality and moral dimension of politics in general. From a moral standpoint what is politics? What is political activity of any kind? What is the purpose of politics and political activity? Politics is supposed to be the search for the good of all, all the people in certain geographical and human territories, small or large as the case may be. Those engaged in politics are supposed to be concerned with just that, the common good, to use an old philosophic phrase, that is the human good of all the people who are involved in any particular form of political activity and by involvement I don't merely mean the activity of those who carry on politics in an active and professional manner. Those involved in politics are above all the people on behalf of whom and in whose name political activity is carried on. The essential point then is to keep in mind in all discussions of politics the good of all people who are in one way or another involved in political activity. It was with this context and this principle in mind that I read and reread Mr. Adams's open letter to Dr. Cahal Daly. My question all the time was to what extent is the position stated here by Mr. Adams a contribution to the common good of the Irish people, and I take the Irish people to include all those who live on this island and who look on this country in one way or another as their home. From this point of view I find some interesting and very positive things in Mr. Adams's letter. I note in particular the following points:

"1) In point (8) of his letter Mr. Adams addresses the following question to Dr. Daly, I quote, 'You call on republicans to renounce violence and to join the peaceful struggle for the rights of nationalists. What peaceful struggle?' I think that is a very reasonable question to address to Dr. Daly and looking at things in a still broader way I would say that people of Mr. Adams's political school and indeed people of all political schools have the right to address questions to those who hold responsible office in the Catholic Church. I do believe myself that our Bishops should be open to dialogue with republicans, say Mr. Gerry Adams, with Catholics who have other political points of view, with all Protestant political points of view including hardline unionists. I do believe that churchmen should be willing to listen to them all. This does not mean that they would take any one particular point of view put forward but surely it is part of the office of those who are responsible for the good of the Church to look for the good of all people. The Church is concerned for the good of all people, not for their spiritual good alone in the narrow sense but for the general good of their lives. It is in this sense that the Church has to be involved in politics, politics being part of human life. The Church would surely be falling short of the fulfilment of its mission if it were to refuse to talk to any political school or all political schools. That is why I believe that Mr. Adams is fully justified in addressing this letter to Bishop Daly and I think he comes up with a really good question, a meaningful question (No. 8 of his letter).

"2) I am also impressed by point (9) in the text of his letter and again I quote, 'Those who express moral condemnation of the tactic of armed struggle,' [the armed struggle in this case carried on by the IRA] those who condemn this tactic,' said Mr. Adams, 'have a responsibility to spell out an alternative course by which Irish independence can be secured.' While I wouldn't say that is just the business of the Church to spell out an alternative course but I do believe that the Church officially too should be involved in the search for an alternative course. I do believe that the Church should participate in trying to discover and formulate a course of politics in this part of Ireland alternatively to the armed struggle, as Mr. Adams called it, being carried on by the IRA. Mr. Adams adds, and I quote, 'I for one would be pleased to consider such an alternative.' I am very glad that he says that. The fact that he does shows him to be not a man of fixated mind. I shall have more to say of the mental fixation shortly. This shows he is prepared to consider all strategies that could be seen as making for the common good and as I said at the outset, here the moral dimension of politics comes in. From a moral point of view the thing to be looked at in any political programme is, is this programme geared to the common good of all the people? Does it make for the good of the people? In the present case does such and such programme make for the general good of the Irish people, of all those who live in this land and look upon it with whatever differences of perspectives as their home? Gerry Adams concludes this (9) of his letter, and again I quote, 'I know that many of my constituents who are also lay people in your diocese would be equally anxious to have such a strategy, that is an alternative to the armed struggle, outlined to them.' I repeat that it cannot possibly be the task of the Church only to outline or to develop an alternative strategy but certainly the Church should take part in the search for such a strategy and I am sure that Gerry Adams is quite right in saying that not only he but many of those whom he represents in the constituency of West Belfast would welcome the putting forward of an alternative or alternatives to the strategy of armed struggle."

Father O'Riordan then goes on to comment in a critical way on some of the other points that Mr. Adams makes in his letter to the Bishop. I won't give them here because they are not really relevant to this letter. He concluded his comments as follows: "These then are my comments on Gerry Adams's letter but again I would again say that if here and there language is used in his letter that tends to echo fanatical thinking, which I am sure is not Gerry Adams's thinking at all, but if that sort of language figures in his letter it is in large part due to the fact that people like Gerry Adams have not been sufficiently heard and listened to, and I would say that here again the Church owes it not only to Gerry Adams and to those whom he represents but to all political parties in this part of Ireland, the Church owes it to them that it will listen and will try as far as is possible to take part in developing an alternative, flexible strategy which as far as possible will serve the best interests of all the Irish people."

These comments of Father O'Riordan will help to emphasize the point I was making about the pastoral responsibility of the Church in the present political situation. I would be grateful then for your advice and help regarding the pastoral role which the Church might play in the search for peace and reconciliation. As I have said our crucial interest at the present time is to develop a dialogue between the nationalist parties, North and South, which on the basis of a common approach to the Northern conflict would produce a credible political alternative to "the armed struggle".

I would like in particular to have your advice on how such a dialogue could be initiated and developed between the representatives of Fianna Fail and the representatives of Sinn Fein. Here I should say that from my knowledge of their attitudes and abilities I am certain that in any dialogue about a common nationalist policy for peace the representatives of Sinn Fein would prove themselves to be positive and constructive, flexible and fair-minded provided that one very traditional and, from a nationalist point of view at least, very reasonable principle were safeguarded, namely the right of the nationalist and unionist people of Ireland to decide their own constitutional and political future through dialogue among themselves and without dictation from the British authorities.

Any democratic decisions about the form of future political institutions which might be made in this context would be acceptable to the Sinn Fein movement even if they were not in keeping with their own political ideal of a 32-county socialist republic. This, as I understand it, would be the basic position of the Sinn Fein representatives in any dialogue with other nationalist parties about the creation of a political alternative to "the armed struggle". It would also be their basic position in any dialogue they might have with the unionist parties about the political future of Ireland.

It is important to spell out the implications of this position because they indicate the principles which I believe would guide the approach of the Sinn Fein movement in any dialogue with either the nationalist or the unionist parties. These principles as I understand them may be set out as follows:

1) The aim of "the armed struggle" is to establish the right of all the Irish people to decide their own political future through dialogue among themselves. The establishment of a 32-county socialist republic is not therefore the aim of this struggle. From the Sinn Fein point of view this is a political ideal to be pursued and achieved by political strategies only.

2) The British must in some formal and credible way declare their willingness to set aside the claim enshrined in the Government of Ireland Act, 1920, that they have in their own right the power of veto of the democratic decisions of the Irish people as a whole. In practice it would be sufficient for

them to declare their willingness to set aside the Government of Ireland Act, 1920, in view of any agreements that the representatives of the people of Ireland in dialogue among themselves might make about their constitutional and political future.

Such a declaration would set the scene for a cease-fire by the IRA.

This principle relates only to the right of veto which the British authorities claim in Ireland on the basis of the 1920 Act. It should not therefore be taken to mean that Sinn Fein want the British to withdraw from Ireland at the present time. On the contrary they accept and would even insist on the need for a continuing British [presence] to facilitate the processes through which the constitutional and political structures of a just and lasting peace would be firmly and properly laid by the democratic decisions of the Irish people as a whole.

Once the representatives of all the Irish people, nationalist and unionist, could meet together in accordance with the principle of independence outlined in (2) above, all options for a settlement of the national question, for organizing the constitutional and political structures of a just and lasting peace would be open for dialogue and decision.

This principle relates specifically to the people of the unionist community because it outlines the context (the only proper one in the Sinn Fein view) where their constitutional and political position and their cultural heritage and identity could and would be democratically decided, accommodated and safeguarded in accordance with their right of consent and the right of consent of the Irish people as a whole.

I would also like to give my understanding of what would, on the basis of a common nationalist policy, constitute a credible political alternative to "the armed struggle" or at least the crucial constituent element of a policy which I believe Sinn Fein would be prepared to put forward as an alternative. It would centre on the attitude which the main nationalist parties, North and South, would be prepared to take to the Government of Ireland Act, 1920. I believe that if they were to take what is in fact the traditional attitude and agree among themselves to use every political pressure to persuade the British government to set aside this Act especially insofar as it involves their claim of veto over political developments in Ireland they would then have created a political alternative with sufficient credibility even before any progress could be reported and even if in the event the policy were not to be successful.

I would like now to list two ways in which under the auspices of the Church the dialogue I am suggesting between the leadership of Fianna Fail and the leadership of Sinn Fein could be initiated:

1) In the first way leading representatives of the Church would invite the representatives of Fianna Fail and representatives of Sinn Fein to meet under their auspices for discussions which would aim at creating a political alternative to the IRA campaign. The actual agenda for these discussions and the conditions under which they would take place, including conditions relating to confidentiality, would be matters for the political participants. The primary responsibility for holding the discussions would therefore rest with the Church.

2) In the second way representatives of the Church would invite representatives of Fianna Fail to meet them for discussions on 1) the pastoral help which the Church could give to the search for peace; 2) ways of initiating a political dialogue which would aim at creating a political alternative to the IRA campaign.

Here I would like to emphasize that the discussions I am proposing would take place with the representatives of the Sinn Fein party and not with the representatives of the IRA. I say this because of a mistake which is often made, understandably perhaps, but at the same time unfortunately, the mistake of those who believe that to talk to the Sinn Fein party is to talk to the IRA. This, as I know from my own experience, is not true because in spite of impressions and suggestions to the contrary, especially among their opponents, they are two separate organizations, separate in leadership, membership, structure and tactics. Sinn Fein, especially under its present leadership, is a political party in its own right and with its own character. Like other political parties in Ireland it has its own leadership, its own policies and structures, its own elected representatives and political supporters. It is a mistake therefore to believe that the Sinn Fein party is a puppet of the IRA or merely a front for it, that it lacks any independence of leadership or approach. I am saying this because I am convinced that the consequences of this mistake have been and may continue to be tragic in terms of the relationship between the ostracization of the Sinn Fein party and the prolongation of the conflict in Northern Ireland.

I won't develop this point any further except to say that the quality of the present Sinn Fein leadership and their freedom to initiate and organize their own policies were illustrated at their recent Ard Fheis when the long-standing policy of Dail abstentionism was reversed without significant splits or upheavals, a fundamental development which even people like Michael Collins, Eamon de Valera and others, including the leaders of Sinn Fein in 1970, could not accomplish. This fact alone indicates the ability of the present Sinn Fein leaders to take great personal and political risk, to make great changes and move forward to new political horizons.

I should be grateful then for your advice regarding the proposals I have made above and as I realize that the best and most efficient way to deal with matters like these is not through letters but through personal contacts and discussions I would welcome an early opportunity to speak to you personally about them. I am certain that, if the situation is handled properly, the IRA could be persuaded to end their campaign.

I am not saying this lightly but from long experience of dealing with the republican movement. Although I am not and have never been associated with them in a political sense, as they themselves would testify, I know that they trust me and understand any contacts I have made with them were always in the context of making peace. In this context I have, I believe, had close and more continual contact with them than any other priest and perhaps any other individual outside their own movement. I believe therefore I can sense opportunities for making peace and I know that I can sense one now in the context of the approach I have set out in this letter.

I can indeed go one further than that and say that the opportunity which now exists is the best that has presented itself since the present Troubles began in 1969 and that it is an opportunity not just for a cease-fire but for making final peace with the IRA and taking the gun out of nationalist politics forever. At the same time however it is a precarious opportunity because it depends on circumstances which can change from day to day and in the context of Northern Ireland even from hour to hour. That is why the need to seize and use it is so urgent.

I would now like to give the reasons for the pastoral role which I believe the Church can play in the search for an alternative to "the armed struggle".

The first has to do with the whole question of trust because the IRA are very wary and very suspicious of any proposal for a cease-fire and they will not enter any discussions or negotiations about one unless they know they can trust the processes and the people involved. I am certain however that the witnessing presence of the Church would be sufficient reason for them to trust and indeed to cooperate positively in any discussions or negotiations that would take place.

My second reason has to do with the whole position of the Church in Ireland, her moral authority and influence and especially the vast numbers of people who believe in her, support her and whom therefore she represents. The presence of the Church in negotiations on a political alternative to the armed struggle would therefore give these negotiations a moral and pastoral stature which would be rooted in and supported by the attitudes of the Catholic people of

Ireland as a whole. This fact alone would I believe have a powerful influence on the respect for which the Sinn Fein movement in general and the IRA in particular would have for them and especially on their willingness to cooperate with them.

I also believe that the Church could provide the kind of neutral and independent setting which would be necessary for the success of such negotiations. I realize that the main and indeed the only objections which you or the Fianna Fail party would have to discussions with the Sinn Fein party is their relationship with the IRA while the IRA are continuing their campaign. This indeed is another very cogent reason why the presence of the Church is so important to the whole dialogue because the fact that it would take place under her auspices and that Fianna Fail, Sinn Fein and the other nationalist parties would take part in it at her invitation would I trust enable you and the Fianna Fail party to overcome the problem which stems from the relationship between the Sinn Fein party and the IRA.

Finally in relation to what I have been saying I would like to give a personal opinion of the unionist community. From contacts, discussions and friendships that I have had with them over the years I believe that they are a people waiting to be redeemed from the political fears and constraints which their community has imbued in them and which have crippled their best political instincts and suppressed the development of the Irish soul which deep within their hearts and peculiar to themselves is longing to be free. This redemption cannot properly begin or develop while as individuals and as a community they feel that they are under actual physical attack from the nationalist community. Out of respect for themselves and their own traditions they can only in these circumstances close ranks and withdraw even deeper behind the emotional and political barriers they have built through the centuries against the nationalist community.

This situation will continue as long at least as the IRA campaign continues especially when so many of its targets are Ulster people. If however this campaign were to end in a political reconciliation within the nationalist community which would unite it in peaceful policies towards the unionist community then at least the way would be more open for them not only to come out from behind their barriers but also to grow politically into their best and native selves. This may seem like an impossible dream especially in the cold light of the present attitude to the Anglo-Irish Agreement. But the signs I have seen and the hints I have heard over the years suggest to me that given the right circumstances, the right opportunities, the right leadership it is well within the bounds of the possible. Only a time of peace will tell and to create that time for them must be even from the point of view of the nationalist community the most important reason of all for doing what we are trying to do.

This has been a very long letter but I trust you have been patient with me because of the importance of the matters it discusses, matters really of life and death. I also trust that you don't think it presumptuous of me to write a letter like this to you but as you will have seen from its contents what we are trying to do is to define and organize our own pastoral role in the situation. Here both you and Fianna Fail can be of immense help in terms of the advice, guidance and cooperation you can give us.

I look forward then to an opportunity to speak personally in the very near future so we can discuss the points I have set out in this letter and see how your representatives and the representatives of the Church could cooperate in the coming months in the search for peace.

Mr. Tim Pat Coogan has kindly agreed to give you this letter and explain its general background.

Alec Reid

"Concrete Proposals" and "Stepping Stones": two undated documents by Father Alec Reid

A Concrete Proposal for an Overall Political Strategy to Establish Justice and Peace in Ireland

This paper sets out:

1. The fundamental principles of the proposed strategy;
2. Suggested stepping stones towards an agreement in principle on the strategy;
3. Some comments on the background and the validity of the whole proposal.

The fundamental principles of the proposed strategy

1. **The Principle of Self-Determination.** This principle guarantees and if put into practice would implement the right of the Irish people as a whole to determine their own constitutional and political future freely, independently and democratically amongst themselves and without any interference or dictation by the British authorities. This springs from the basic human rights of the Irish people as a whole. The fundamental principle of the proposed strategy, it may be stated formally as follows: "The free, independent and democratic consent of the Irish people as a whole is the only basis for a just and lasting peace."

2. **The Principle of Definition.** The Principle of Self-Determination leads naturally to the Principle of Definition because "the Irish people as a whole" to whom the right of self-determination belongs must be defined before this right can be implemented. While the facts of geography identify the Irish people as "the people who live in the 32 counties of Ireland", the facts of history, politics, religion and culture define them as "the Irish people of the nationalist tradition and the Irish people of the unionist tradition who live in Ireland as a whole". Dictated by the realities of the situation therefore this principle may be stated formally as follows: "The Irish peo-

ple as a whole are defined by the historical, political, religious and cultural realities of the present situation as the Irish people of the nationalist tradition and the Irish people of the unionist tradition who live in Ireland taken as a whole."

3. **The Principle of Consent.** The Principle of Self-Determination and the Principle of Definition lead naturally to the Principle of Consent because the right to self-determination can only be realized through the consent of the Irish people as a whole and this consent, as the Principle of Definition implies, must be defined as twofold in its very nature because of the composition of the Irish people as a whole. This, the crucial principle of the proposed strategy, is dictated therefore by the realities of the situation and indeed by the very nature of a just and lasting peace. It may be stated formally as follows: "The free, independent and democratic consent of the Irish people as a whole, which is the only basis for a just and lasting peace, is defined by the historical, political, religious and cultural composition as the twofold consent of the Irish people of the nationalist tradition and the Irish people of the Unionist tradition who live in Ireland taken as a whole."

4. **The Principle of Dialogue.** The Principle of Consent leads naturally to the Principle of Dialogue because the consent of the Irish people as a whole, since it is twofold in nature, can only be achieved through political dialogue between the people of the nationalist tradition and the people of the unionist tradition. This principle sets out the procedure, the only procedure through which the people of both traditions can reach consensus and agreement about their constitutional and political future. It is the principle at the heart of the proposed strategy because it embodies and expresses that spirit of respect and compassion of people of all traditions which is the only spirit from which peace can really flow and live. The Principle of Dialogue springs therefore from the very nature of peace and must be seen as the life principle at the very heart of the strategy that would create it. It may be stated formally as follows: "Because it is twofold in nature the consent of the Irish people as a whole can only be achieved through political dialogue between the people of the nationalist tradition and the people of the unionist tradition."

5. **The Principle of Commitment.** An agreement between the main leaders and the main parties concerned to accept the foregoing principles as the fundamental principles of an overall political strategy for justice and peace would lead naturally to the Principle of Commitment. There is a need to formalize such an agreement to guarantee its honour and integrity. This principle therefore would secure the commitment of the people of our two traditions and of all parties concerned to the fundamental principles of the strategy and to their proper implementation. It would guarantee that in

an ongoing way the people of both traditions and all the parties concerned would abide faithfully and consistently by these principles and by their implementation until a final agreement on the constitutional and political future of Ireland had been reached. It may be stated formally as follows: "The leaderships of the main parties concerned would make a formal commitment to abide fully and faithfully by all the fundamental principles of the strategy and by their proper implementation until a final agreement about the constitutional and political future of Ireland had been reached, no matter how long or how short the time factor involved might be."

The Constitutional Conference

While the manner in which the strategy for justice and peace would be actually implemented would be a matter for discussion and decision between the main parties concerned, it is clear that a suitable framework for the necessary political dialogue between the people of the two traditions would have to be set up and, in part at least, would have to take the form of a constitutional conference which would remain in existence and continue to function until a final agreement about the future of Ireland had been reached. The membership of this conference would consist of the constitutional representatives who would have been elected by the people of both traditions to achieve the aims of the conference. The details of how these representatives would be elected by the people of both traditions and of the mandates that the people would give them would be a matter for discussion and decision by all the parties concerned. Any necessary interim constitutional and political arrangements for the time between the setting up of the conference and the time when a final agreement on the future of Ireland would have been reached would be a matter for dialogue, agreement and decision between the constitutional representatives attending the conference. This conference would be open to submissions from all significant organizations in Ireland, for example the churches, the trade union movement, the women's movement, etc.

Note: The phrase "all the parties concerned" as used above refers to 1) the leaderships of the main nationalist parties, North and South; 2) the leadership of the republican movement; 3) the leaderships of the main unionist parties; 4) the British authorities.

The attitude which the British authorities would take to such a conference

I am satisfied from expert advice on their present policies towards Ireland that the British authorities would stand aside from such a conference in the sense that they would not interfere with its deliberations or attempt to influence or much less dictate its decision. I am also certain that they would be prepared to sponsor such a conference in the sense that they would encourage it and facilitate it in every way possible to them. I am satisfied too, again on expert advice, that they would respond with the necessary legislation to any constitutional and political decisions about the future of Ireland which such a conference might make.

The British authorities and the proposed strategy

I am satisfied, from an authentic and authoritative explanation of present British policy towards Ireland, that the proposed strategy would be acceptable in principle to the British authorities provided it becomes acceptable to the main nationalist, republican and unionist parties. I am also satisfied from expert advice that the British have no longer any colonial interest in Ireland, that is, they have now no political, economic, strategic or military interests of their own for remaining in Ireland or for exercising authority there. I am satisfied too, again from expert advice, that they are willing to declare this ending of any self-interest in staying in Ireland publicly and authoritatively provided that they are convinced that such a declaration would make a significant contribution to the cause of peace in Ireland. I am convinced from expert advice and from an authentic and authoritative explanation that their reasons for refusing, the British authorities will not set aside the 1920 Government of Ireland Act or declare that they intend to withdraw from Ireland at some future date. They will not set aside the 1920 Act or declare that they intend to set it aside until alternative constitutional and governmental provisions have been worked out and agreed by the Irish people themselves. If and when this happens they will set aside the 1920 Act. We can say then in the proposed strategy that the British authorities would withdraw politically from the central forum of dialogue and decision-making which would shape the constitutional future of Ireland. They would, in effect, hand over the power of constitutional decision-making to the Irish people themselves. Their role would be to facilitate such a dialogue and decision-making and then to respond to it with the necessary legislation. We may add another principle therefore to the proposed strategy: the Principle of British Withdrawal.

6. **The Principle of British Withdrawal.** In the proposed strategy the British authorities would agree to withdraw politically from the central procedures of political dialogue and decision-making which, on the basis of the twofold consent already defined, would take place among the Irish people as a whole to work out a new constitution for Ireland. At the same time, however, these authorities would agree to facilitate this dialogue and decision-making and to respond to its results with the necessary legislation.

Suggested Stepping Stones to an Agreement in Principle on an Overall Nationalist Political Strategy for Justice and Peace

1. An agreement in principle that an overall nationalist political strategy would help the cause of justice and peace in Ireland and so benefit the Irish people as a whole.

2. An agreement in principle that the free, independent and democratic consent of the Irish people as a whole is the only basis for a just and lasting peace.

3. An agreement in principle that the overall strategy should, therefore, be designed to create a new Ireland, structured and governed under a new Constitution.

4. An agreement in principle that the Irish people as a whole should decide the form of this new Constitution on the basis of free, independent and democratic dialogue among themselves.

5. An agreement in principle that the Irish people as a whole are defined by the historical, political, religious and cultural realities of the present situation as the Irish people of the nationalist tradition and the Irish people of the unionist tradition who live in Ireland taken as a whole.

6. An agreement in principle that the free, independent and democratic consent of the Irish people as a whole, which is the only basis for a just and lasting peace, is defined by their historical, political, religious and cultural composition as the twofold consent of the Irish people of the nationalist tradition and the Irish people of the unionist tradition who live in Ireland taken as a whole.

7. And agreement in principle that because it is twofold in nature the consent of the Irish people as a whole can only be achieved through political dialogue between the people of the nationalist tradition and the people of the unionist tradition.

8. An agreement in principle on points (a),(b),(c),(d) and (e) of the following statement which relates to the setting up of a Constitutional Conference.

   (a) While the manner in which this strategy for justice and peace would be actually implemented would be a matter for discussion and decision between the main parties concerned, it is clear that a suitable framework for the necessary political dialogue between the people of the two traditions would have to be set up and, in part at least, would have to take the form of a Constitutional Conference which would remain in existence and continue to function until a final agreement about the future of Ireland had been reached.

(b) The membership of this Conference would consist of the constitutional representatives who would have been elected by the people of both traditions to achieve the aims of the Conference.

(c) The details of how these representatives would be elected by the people of both traditions and of the mandates that the people would give them would be a matter for discussion and decision by all the parties concerned.

(d) Any necessary interim constitutional and political arrangements for the time between the setting up of the Conference and the time when a final agreement on the future of Ireland would have been reached, would be a matter for dialogue, agreement and decision between the constitutional representatives attending the Conference.

(e) This Conference would also be open to submissions from all significant organizations in Ireland, for example, the churches, the trade union movement, the women's movement etc.

9. An agreement in principle that the British authorities should withdraw politically from the central procedures of political dialogue and decision-making which, on the basis of the twofold consent already defined, would take place among the Irish people as a whole to work out a new Constitution for Ireland and that, at the same time, they should agree to facilitate this dialogue and decision-making and to respond to its results with the necessary legislation.

10. An agreement in principle that the nationalist-republican parties will combine their political forces to persuade the British authorities to declare:

(i) that they will set aside the 1920 Government of Ireland Act when the Irish people themselves provide them with a viable alternative;

(ii) that, whatever the situation may have been in the past, they no longer have any self-interest in remaining in Ireland or in exercising authority here;

(iii) that they will support and facilitate the kind of constitutional Conference that would enable the Irish people to decide their own constitutional and political future through free, independent and democratic dialogue among themselves;

(iv) that they would not interfere in the deliberations of such a Conference or attempt to influence or, much less, dictate its decisions;

(v) that they would respond, with the necessary legislation, to any constitutional and political decisions about the future of Ireland which such a Conference might make.

11. An agreement in principle that, if the proposed strategy proves to be acceptable in principle, an advisory committee or conference, representative of the leaders and parties concerned, should be set up immediately to proceed with the organization of the strategy.

The function of this committee or conference, in part at least, would be:

   (i)   to consult and advise on the tactics of the strategy;

  (ii)   to consult and advise on ways and means of presenting, explaining and publicizing it;

 (iii)   to consult and advise on ways and means of winning support for it at home and abroad but especially from the main nationalist-republican parties, the main Unionist parties and the British authorities;

 (iv)   to consult and advise on the form of a new Constitution for Ireland.

12. An agreement in principle that, when those first concerned have discussed the proposed strategy between themselves, they would then approach others whom it would be necessary to approach to explain it to them, and to obtain their views on it.

Some Comments on the Background and on the Validity of this Proposal

This proposal for an overall political strategy for peace emerged from discussions and communications which took place over the past two years or so and which involved people who, from their knowledge and experience, were able to give expert advice on the present attitudes and policies of the nationalist parties, the republican movement, the unionist parties and the British authorities.

The proposed strategy is based on this advice so it may be said that it was not thought out in any abstract or a priori way but that it emerged from the heart of the conflict. This fact alone should guarantee its validity as a viable and realistic strategy for peace.

I believe that a comparative examination of the political principles of the strategy and the political principles of the main parties engaged in the conflict will show that they are in keeping with one another; that the principles of the strategy do not essentially contradict the principles of any of these parties but that, in a true sense, they respect, encourage and embody them.

I suggest therefore that this strategy is in keeping with the realities and the needs of the conflict in that it faces and meets them with a peace dynamic which is powerful enough to bridge the gaps and to reconcile the divisions that are at the heart of it.

Its inherent and enduring viability as a strategy for peace is also guaranteed by its commitment to the ongoing use of the principles of political dialogue, political persuasion and political force—the only principles through which agreement on a constitutional and political framework for a just and lasting peace can be worked out and put into effect.

Given this understanding of the strategy, there is, I believe, no reason in principle, why any of the main parties concerned should refuse to accept it as an overall political strategy for peace.

How the principles of the strategy relate to the principles of the main parties concerned

The nationalist parties: the principles of the strategy, especially its basic ones (the Principle of Self-Determination and the Principle of Consent or Co-determination) are in keeping with the traditional principles of the Nationalist parties, North and South.

The principles of the strategy are also in keeping with the principles which, from a nationalist point of view, underlie the Anglo-Irish Agreement insofar as this Agreement formulates and expresses the Irish, unionist and British dimensions of the conflict because these dimensions imply the Principles of Self-Determination and Co-determination or at least open the door to the kind of political dialogue which would develop and apply them.

I believe, therefore, that the proposed strategy should be acceptable in principle to the leadership of the main nationalist parties, North and South.

The republican movement: I am satisfied, from my knowledge of the spirit and principles of the republican movement, that this strategy should be acceptable in principle to its leadership provided they are convinced that the other parties concerned would genuinely commit themselves to it until a final agreement about the constitutional and political future of Ireland had been reached.

I say this, first of all, because the cardinal principle of the republican movement is the right of the Irish people as a whole to self-determination and this is also the cardinal principle of the peace strategy. Up to now, as the republican movement have seen it, the first step in the actual implementation of this principle of self-determination would be a declaration by the British authorities that they intend to leave Ireland at some future date or that they intend to set aside the 1920 Government of Ireland Act with a view to introducing an alternative constitutional arrangement.

One or other of these declarations would imply that the British authorities intended to give the Irish people, as a whole, the freedom and the independence to decide their own constitutional and political future. This strategy of "withdrawal" by the British authorities and its relationship to the implementation of the Principle of Self-Determination are also embodied in the proposed strategy, not in the sense in which, up to now, the republican movement has understood them but in the sense that, in keeping with a situation in which all the parties concerned had accepted the proposed strategy, the British authorities would withdraw from the central area of historical, political, religious and cultural conflict in Ireland and allow the parties to it, that is, the people of the nationalist tradition and the people of the unionist tradition, to resolve it through free, independent and democratic dialogue among some themselves.

In this definition of a "British withdrawal" the British authorities would act as the facilitators and the sponsors of the dialogue between the two traditions but they would not interfere in it, much less, dictate to it. While this definition of a withdrawal by the British authorities is not the same as the definition which, up to now, the republican movement has given it, it embodies the same principle.

It also gives the same strategic reason for such a withdrawal, namely, the creation of a situation in which the Irish people, through dialogue among themselves, could determine their own future without interference or dictation from the British authorities. Given then that the proposed strategy is in keeping with the policy of the republican movement insofar as both embody the Principle of Self-Determination and the strategy of a British withdrawal, it follows that the Principle of Consent, as defined by the proposed strategy, is also in keeping with their policy because, as this strategy notes, the people of Ireland as a whole, to whom the principle of self-Determination applies, are defined, by the realities of the situation, as the people of the nationalist tradition and the people of the unionist tradition. The Principle of Self-Determination cannot therefore be implemented without the consent of both traditions.

There is no reason of principle, therefore, why the republican movement should refuse to accept the principle of consent as defined by the proposed strategy.

It may also be said that, were they to refuse, they would be going against the whole spirit of their own movement, because, by its own definition, it exists to resist the oppression of the Irish people by what it sees as colonial interests. It would be a strange turnabout, to say the least, if such a movement were itself to become an oppressor and colonizer of Irish people by trying to coerce the consent of Irish loyalists.

The British authorities: I am satisfied, from an authentic and authoritative explanation of present British policy towards Ireland, that the proposed strategy would be acceptable, in principle, to the British authorities provided it becomes acceptable to the main nationalist, republican and unionist parties (see page 6 of the document "A Concrete Proposal for an Overall Political Strategy to Establish Justice and Peace in Ireland").

The unionist parties: I am satisfied, on expert advice, that there is no reason why the main unionist parties and the people whom they represent should refuse to accept the proposed strategy provided they are assured that the main nationalist parties and Republican movement would genuinely commit themselves to it as an overall political strategy for peace.

IRA Statement Ending its Armed Campaign against Britain, July 28, 2005

"The leadership of Oglaigh na hEireann has formally ordered an end to the armed campaign.

This will take effect from 4 p.m. [1600 BST] this afternoon [Thursday, July 28, 2005].

All IRA units have been ordered to dump arms.

All Volunteers have been instructed to assist the development of purely political and democratic programmes through exclusively peaceful means.

Volunteers must not engage in any other activities whatsoever.

The IRA leadership has also authorized our representative to engage with the IICD [Independent International Commission on Decommissioning] to complete the process to verifiably put its arms beyond use in a way which will further enhance public confidence and to conclude this as quickly as possible.

We have invited two independent witnesses, from the Protestant and Catholic Churches, to testify to this.

The Army Council took these decisions following an unprecedented internal discussion and consultation process with IRA units and Volunteers.

We appreciate the honest and forthright way in which the consultation process was carried out and the depth and content of the submissions.

We are proud of the comradely way in which this truly historic discussion was conducted. The outcome of our consultations show very strong support among IRA Volunteers for the Sinn Fein peace strategy.

There is also widespread concern about the failure of the two governments and the unionists to fully engage in the peace process.

This has created real difficulties. The overwhelming majority of people in Ireland fully support this process.

They and friends of Irish unity throughout the world want to see the full implementation of the Good Friday Agreement.

Notwithstanding these difficulties our decisions have been taken to advance our republican and democratic objectives, including our goal of a united Ireland.

We believe there is now an alternative way to achieve this and to end British rule in our country. It is the responsibility of all Volunteers to show leadership, determination and courage.

We are very mindful of the sacrifices of our patriot dead, those who went to jail, Volunteers, their families and the wider republican base.

We reiterate our view that the armed struggle was entirely legitimate. We are conscious that many people suffered in the conflict.

There is a compelling imperative on all sides to build a just and lasting peace. The issue of the defence of nationalist and republican communities has been raised with us.

There is a responsibility on society to ensure that there is no re-occurrence of the pogroms of 1969 and the early 1970s.

There is also a universal responsibility to tackle sectarianism in all its forms.

The IRA is fully committed to the goals of Irish unity and independence and to building the Republic outlined in the 1916 Proclamation.

We call for maximum unity and effort by Irish republicans everywhere. We are confident that by working together Irish republicans can achieve our objectives.

Every Volunteer is aware of the import of the decisions we have taken and all Oglaigh are compelled to fully comply with these orders.

There is now an unprecedented opportunity to utilize the considerable energy and goodwill which there is for the peace process.

This comprehensive series of unparalleled initiatives is our contribution to this and to the continued endeavours to bring about independence and unity for the people of Ireland."

P. O'Neill, Irish Republican Publicity Bureau, Dublin

Notes

Preface to the second edition

1. *The Clonard Priest*, BBC Radio Four, November 29, 2006.

Prologue

1. This account of the last days of the *Eksund* has been derived from a number of conversations with serving and former IRA members in 1998.
2. *Hibernia*, Dec. 20–27, 1979.
3. This account of the IRA's early relationship has been derived from interviews and conversations with former IRA members in 1979 and 1998.
4. U.S. Department of State Libya/PIRA Background Paper, P860082-0954, July 10, 1986.
5. From notes of conversation with former IRA activist, Jan. 19, 1999.
6. Interviews and conversations with former IRA members, 1979 and 1998.
7. Interview with former IRA member, 1998.
8. Interview with senior IRA figure, 1998.
9. Bob Woodward, *Veil: The Secret Wars of the CIA, 1981–1987* (New York: Simon & Schuster, 1987), 506.
10. Ibid., 448.
11. *In Dublin*, Feb. 18, 1987.
12. Interviews with former IRA members, 1998 and 1999.
13. Interview with senior IRA member, 1998.
14. See Jack Holland, *The American Connection: US Guns, Money and Influence in Northern Ireland* (Swords, Co. Dublin: Poolbeg Press, 1993), chap. 3, for a full account of Harrison's IRA career.
15. Interview with IRA member, 1999.
16. Ibid.

17. Interview with IRA member, 1998.
18. Brendan O'Brien, *A Pocket History of the IRA* (Dublin: O'Brien Press, 2000), 108.
19. Interview with IRA source, 1998.
20. Interview with senior IRA source, 1998.
21. Interview with senior IRA member, 1998.
22. "Libya 'Planning to Resume Aid to IRA,'" *Irish Times*, June 18, 1986.
23. "Gaddafi: I'm Stepping up IRA Aid," *Observer*, March 1, 1987.
24. "Libya 'Will Open Centre for IRA,'" *Irish Times*, April 16, 1987.
25. U.S. Department of State Libya/PIRA Background Paper, P860082-0954, July 10, 1986.
26. Interview with IRA source, 1999.
27. Interview with IRA source, 1998.
28. O'Brien, *Pocket History of the IRA*.
29. Interview with senior IRA member 1998.
30. Interview with senior IRA source, 1998.
31. Ibid.
32. Interview with senior IRA source, 1999.
33. Notes of conversation with IRA member, 1999.
34. Interview with senior IRA source, 1998.
35. Interview with former IRA activist, 1999.

One: Roots

1. Interview with a former IRA member, Sept. 2000.
2. Gerry Adams, *Before the Dawn: An Autobiography* (London: Heinemann, 1996), 3.
3. Michael Farrell, *Northern Ireland: The Orange State* (London: Pluto Press, 1976), 93–94.
4. David Sharrock and Mark Devenport, *Man of War, Man of Peace? The Unauthorized Biography of Gerry Adams* (London: Macmillan, 1997), 9.
5. The father of the civil rights leader Bernadette Devlin discovered that the term "politically suspect" had been stamped on his insurance card. He lost his job and was forced to go to England to seek work. His was not an unusual experience.
6. Kevin Kelley, *The Longest War: Northern Ireland and the IRA* (Dingle, Co. Kerry: Brandon Books, 1983), 63.
7. Ibid., 64.
8. Sharrock and Devenport, *Man of War*, 34–35.

9. Ibid., 37.

10. Brendan O'Brien, *A Pocket History of the IRA* (Dublin: O'Brien Press, 2000).

11. Farrell, *Northern Ireland*, 256.

12. J. Bowyer Bell, *The Secret Army: The IRA, 1916–1979* (Dublin: Academy Press, 1979), 344.

13. Kelley, *Longest War*, 85.

14. Ibid., 86.

15. Mike Milotte, *Communism in Modern Ireland: The Pursuit of the Workers' Republic since 1916* (Dublin: Gill and Macmillan, 1984), 265.

16. Kelley, *Longest War*, 87.

17. Unpublished interview with Gerry Adams, Feb. 1984, p. 2, author's copy.

18. Adams, *Before the Dawn*, 124.

19. Unpublished interview with Adams, 5.

20. Adams, *Before the Dawn*, 123.

21. Ciaran de Baroid, *Ballymurphy and the Irish War* (Belfast: Aisling Publishers, 1989), 50.

22. Adams, *Before the Dawn*, 94.

23. Ibid., 110.

24. Interview with Provisional IRA founding member, May 17, 1999.

25. Adams, *Before the Dawn*, 129.

26. *Irish News*, letters page, Nov. 14, 1986.

27. Interview with Ruairi O Bradaigh, Oct. 5, 2000.

28. Adams, *Before the Dawn*, 129.

29. De Baroid, *Ballymurphy and the Irish War*, 57.

Two: The Defenders

1. Sean MacStiofain, *Memoirs of a Revolutionary* (London: Gordon Cremonesi, 1975), 93.

2. Ibid., 135.

3. P. O'Neill, *Freedom Struggle* (Dublin: Provisional IRA, Irish Republican Publicity Bureau, 1973), 64.

4. Kevin Kelley, *The Longest War: Northern Ireland and the IRA* (Dingle, Co. Kerry: Brandon Books, 1983), 129.

5. Ibid.

6. Kevin Bean and Mark Hayes, eds., *Republican Voices* (Monaghan: Seesyu Press, 2001), 50.

7. Ibid., 76.

8. MacStiofain, *Memoirs of a Revolutionary,* 84.

9. O'Neill, *Freedom Struggle,* 19.

10. Interview with former Sinn Fein and IRA member, March 8, 1999, with former Sinn Fein member, Dec. 28, 1998.

11. Interview with former Sinn Fein member, Dec. 28, 1998.

12. Robert W. White, *Provisional Irish Republicans: An Oral and Interpretative History* (London and Westport, Conn.: Greenwood Press, 1993), 55.

13. *Irish News,* Nov. 24, 1998.

14. Undated interview with Brendan Hughes, author's copy.

15. Bean and Hayes, eds., *Republican Voices,* 31.

16. Wolfe Tone, *An Argument on Behalf of the Catholics of Ireland* (1791).

17. Robert Kee, *The Most Distressful Country,* vol. 1 of *The Green Flag* (London, Melbourne, and New York: Quartet Books, 1976), 72.

18. Bean and Hayes, eds., *Republican Voices,* 34.

19. Gerry Adams, *Before the Dawn: An Autobiography* (London: Heinemann, 1996), 118.

20. Ciaran de Baroid, *Ballymurphy and the Irish War* (Belfast: Aisling Publishers, 1989), 59.

21. MacStiofain, *Memoirs of a Revolutionary,* 145–47.

22. Interview with former IRA member, June 14, 1999.

23. Interview with former IRA member, May 9, 2000.

24. Interview with former Belfast IRA member (A), Dr. Anthony McIntyre, Linenhall Library (embargoed collection).

25. De Baroid, *Ballymurphy and the Irish War,* 71.

Three: "The Big Lad"

1. Interview with former Belfast IRA member (B), Dr. Anthony McIntyre, Linen Hall Library (embargoed collection).

2. Ciaran de Baroid, *Ballymurphy and the Irish War* (Belfast: Aisling Publishers, 1989), 79.

3. David McKittrick, Seamus Kelters, Brian Feeney, and Chris Thornton, *Lost Lives* (Edinburgh: Mainstream Publishing, 1999), 1477.

4. Sean MacStiofain, *Memoirs of a Revolutionary* (London: Gordon Cremonesi, 1975), 163.

5. Ibid., 160.

6. P. O'Neill, *Freedom Struggle* (Dublin: Provisional IRA, Irish Republican Publicity Bureau, 1973), 1973.

7. Confidential information, IRA source, Nov. 2000.

8. Interview with former Belfast IRA member, Nov. 2000.

9. Interview with former Belfast IRA member, Nov. 2000.

10. McIntyre interview with former Belfast IRA member (B).

11. O'Neill, *Freedom Struggle,* 39.

12. McIntyre interview with former Belfast IRA member (B).

13. O'Neill, *Freedom Struggle,* 48.

14. MacStiofain, *Memoirs of a Revolutionary,* 219.

15. David McKittrick, Seamus Kelters, Brian Feeney, and Chris Thornton, *Lost Lives* (Edinburgh: Mainstream Publishing, 1999), 1473–93.

16. Notes of conversation with former British military intelligence officer, Sept. 2000.

17. Interview with former IRA member, June 1999.

18. Ibid.

19. Interview with former IRA member, Nov. 2000.

20. McKittrick et al., *Lost Lives,* 390.

21. Notes of conversation with former IRA member, June 1999.

22. Notes of conversation with former IRA member, Nov. 2000.

23. Interview with former IRA member, May 2000.

24. Ibid.

25. Ibid.

26. Interview with former IRA member, June 1999.

27. Ibid.

28. Gerry Adams, *Before the Dawn: An Autobiography* (London: Heinemann, 1996), 189.

29. Conor O'Clery, *Ireland in Quotes* (Dublin: O'Brien Press, 2000), 142.

30. O'Neill, *Freedom Struggle,* 62.

31. Kevin Kelley, *The Longest War: Northern Ireland and the IRA* (Dingle, Co. Kerry: Brandon Books, 1983), 153.

32. Ibid., 172.

33. McIntyre interview with former Belfast IRA member (B).

34. Confidential interview, IRA source, April 2000.

35. Ibid.

36. Ibid.

37. Ibid.

38. Interview with former IRA member, June 1999.

39. McIntyre interview with former Belfast IRA member (B).

40. Confidential interview, republican source, May 2000.

41. Ibid.

42. Ibid.

43. Interview with former IRA member, June 1999.
44. Ibid.
45. Adams, *Before the Dawn,* 213.
46. Confidential information, IRA source, Nov. 2000.
47. Ibid.
48. Ibid.
49. Confidential information, IRA source, May 2000.
50. Ibid.
51. Ibid.
52. Confidential information, IRA source, June 1999.
53. *Sunday Times,* Nov. 26, 2000.
54. Confidential information, IRA source, June 1999.
55. Ibid.
56. Ibid.
57. Richard Deutsch and Vivien Magowan, *Northern Ireland 1972–73: A Chronology of Events* (Belfast: Blackstaff Press, 1974), 316.
58. Ibid., 317.

Four: Cage 11

1. Interview with former IRA member, May 2000.
2. Interview with former Belfast IRA member (B), Dr. Anthony McIntyre, Linen Hall Library (embargoed collection).
3. Interview with former IRA member, May 2000.
4. Ibid.
5. Martin Dillon, *The Dirty War* (London: Hutchinson, 1988), 84.
6. Interview with former Belfast IRA member (A), Dr Anthony McIntyre, Linen Hall Library (embargoed collection).
7. Unpublished interview with a Feakle cleric, June 1994, author's copy.
8. McIntyre interview with former Belfast IRA member (A).
9. Ruairi O Bradaigh, letter to *Irish Times,* April 30, 1992.
10. David McKittrick, Seamus Kelters, Brian Feeney, and Chris Thornton, *Lost Lives* (Edinburgh: Mainstream Publishing, 1999), 1473–75.
11. McIntyre inteview with former Belfast IRA member (A).
12. Interview with former IRA member, April 2000.
13. Gerry Adams, *Before the Dawn: An Autobiography* (London: Heinemann, 1996), 257.
14. Author's note of a conversation with an IRA Army Council member, May 18, 1990.

15. Interview with an IRA member, April 2000.

16. Author's note of a conversation with an Army Council member, May 18, 1990.

17. Ibid.

18. David McKittrick and David McVea, *Making Sense of the Troubles* (Belfast: Blackstaff Press, 2000), 130.

19. Interview with former IRA member, April 2000.

20. Ibid.

21. *Republican News*, Aug. 14, 1976.

22. *Republican News*, June 15, 1977.

23. Ibid.

24. Muammar Qaddafi, "The Green Book, Part One": www.geocities/Athens/8744/zgb1-6htm.

25. *Republican News*, Oct. 28, 1975.

26. Interview with former IRA member, April 2000.

27. Brendan O'Brien, *The Long War* (Dublin: O'Brien Press, 1995), 350.

28. Brendan O'Brien, *A Pocket History of the IRA* (Dublin: O'Brien Press, 2000), 101.

29. Interview with former IRA member, April 2000.

30. Confidential information, republican source, Dec. 2000.

31. McKittrick, Kelters, Feeney, and Thornton, *Lost Lives,* 790.

32. Confidential information, republican source, Dec. 2000

33. Interview with former IRA member, April 2000.

34. Ibid.

35. Ibid.

36. Ibid.

37. Ibid.

38. Confidential information, republican source, Jan. 2001.

Five: "Our Dreyfus"

1. Unpublished interview with a Feakle cleric, June 1994, author's copy.

2. Ibid.

3. Interview with former IRA member, April 2000.

4. Ibid.

5. Interview with former IRA member, April 2000.

6. Interview with former GHQ member, April 2000.

7. Ibid.

8. Interview with former IRA member, April 2000.

9. *Republican News*, May 8, 1976.

10. "There Will Be No More Ceasefires until the End," *Magill*, Aug. 1978.

11. Kevin Kelley, *The Longest War: Northern Ireland and the IRA* (Dingle, Co. Kerry: Brandon Books, 1983), 243–44.

12. *Hansard,* July 7, 1979.

13. Ministry of Defence, "Northern Ireland Future Terrorist Trends," Nov. 2, 1978, author's copy.

14. Interview with former IRA member, April 2000.

15. Dorothy McArdle, *The Irish Republic* (Dublin: Wolfhound Press, 1999), 384, puts the toll at seventeen auxiliaries and three IRA dead, but J. Bowyer Bell puts the British dead at eighteen.

16. *An Phoblacht–Republican News*, Jan. 5, 1980.

17. Interview with former IRA member, April 2000.

18. Interview with former Belfast IRA member (C), Dr. Anthony McIntyre, Linen Hall Library (embargoed collection).

19. Author's note of a conversation with former Army Council and Sinn Fein Ard Comhairle member, April 2000.

20. Interview with former IRA Army Council and Sinn Fein Ard Comhairle member, May 1999.

21. *An Phoblacht–Republican News,* Jan. 27, 1979.

22. Interview with former IRA Army Council and Sinn Fein Ard Comhairle member, Nov. 1999.

23. *Peace with Justice*, publication of the republican movement, reprinted July 1975.

24. Interview with former Sinn Fein Ard Comhairle member, Feb. 2001.

25. "The IRA," *Magill*, Sept. 1980.

26. Interview with former Sinn Fein Ard Comhairle member, Feb. 2001.

27. *An Phoblacht–Republican News,* April 12, 1980.

28. Interview with former IRA GHQ officer, April 2000.

29. David McKittrick, Seamus Kelters, Brian Feeney, and Chris Thornton, *Lost Lives* (Edinburgh: Mainstream Publishing, 1999), 702, lists a total of ten businessmen killed by the IRA between Feb. and May 1977.

30. *An Phoblacht–Republican News*, Feb. 19, 1977.

31. *An Phoblacht–Republican News*, June 18, 1977.

32. For an example of internal tensions over the left-wing moves, see the minutes of the special Sinn Fein Ard Comhairle meeting, April 12, 1980, in appendix 1.

33. "*Eire Nua*: The Social, Economic and Political Dimensions," author's copy.

34. "The IRA," ·*Magill*, Sept. 1980.

35. *Hibernia*, Oct. 19, 1979.

36. "*Eire Nua:* The Social Dimension," Sinn Fein Ard Comhairle, Dec. 8, 1979.

37. *An Phoblacht–Republican News*, Jan. 26, 1980.

38. Interview with the author, Dublin, Feb. 2001.

39. Interview with former Sinn Fein Ard Comhairle member, March 1999.

40. Interview with former Sinn Fein Ard Comhairle member, Feb. 1999.

41. Interview with former Sinn Fein Ard Comhairle member, March 1999.

42. Ibid.

43. Interview with former Sinn Fein Ard Comhairle member, Feb. 1999.

44. Interview with former Sinn Fein Ard Comhairle member, March 1999.

45. Interview with former Sinn Fein Ard Comhairle member, May 1999.

46. Interview with former member of IRA Executive, June 1999.

47. Ibid.; interview with former member of IRA Army Council, May 1999.

48. Interview with former member of IRA Army Council, May 1999.

49. Interview with former Sinn Fein Ard Comhairle member, Feb. 2001.

50. Interview with former member of IRA Executive, June 1999.

51. *Irish Times*, Sept. 9, 1982.

52. Interview with former Sinn Fein Ard Comhairle member, March 1999.

Six: A Long, Hot Summer

1. Note of author's conversation with former Cage 11 inmate, undated, 1997.

2. Interview with former IRA leader (D), Dr. Anthony McIntyre, Linen Hall Library (embargoed collection).

3. Interview with former Sinn Fein Ard Comhairle member, March 1999.

4. Ibid.

5. Ibid.

6. *An Phoblacht–Republican News*, June 9, 1979.

7. Gerry Adams, *Before the Dawn: An Autobiography* (London: Heinemann, 1996), 253.

8. *Fortnight* magazine, July 1981.

9. Patrick Bishop and Eamonn Mallie, *The Provisional IRA* (London: Heinemann, 1987), 301.

10. *An Phoblacht–Republican News*, Nov. 8, 1980.

11. Interview with former Sinn Fein Ard Comhairle member, March 1999.

12. Interview with National H Blocks Committee member, April 2000.

13. *Irish Times*, Oct. 21, 1981.

14. *An Phoblacht–Republican News*, March 1, 1984.

15. Notes of author's conversation with Adams think tank member, Aug. 1980.

16. Interview with former Sinn Fein Ard Comhairle member, Dec. 1998.

17. Interview with National H Blocks Committee member, April, 2000

18. For accounts of this episode see David Beresford, *Ten Men Dead: The Story of the 1981 Irish Hunger Strike* (London: Grafton Books, 1987), 344–47, and Brian Campbell, Laurence McKeown, and Felim O'Hagan, eds., *Nor Meekly Serve My Time: The H-Block Struggle, 1976–1981* (Belfast: Beyond the Pale Publications, 1998), 234–36.

19. Interview with former IRA Army Council member, Feb. 2001.

20. Ibid.

21. *An Phoblacht–Republican News,* June 3, 1982.

22. *An Phoblacht–Republican News,* Oct. 2, 1982.

Seven: "Behind the Scenes"

1. David McKittrick, Seamus Kelters, Brian Feeney, and Chris Thornton, *Lost Lives* (Edinburgh: Mainstream Publishing, 1999), 917.

2. Confidential information from peace process participant, 2000.

3. McKittrick et al., *Lost Lives,* 922.

4. Martin Dillon, *The Shankill Butchers: A Case Study in Mass Murder* (London: Hutchinson, 1989), 240–53.

5. Chris Ryder, *The Ulster Defence Regiment: An Instrument of Peace?* (London: Methuen, 1991), 209.

6. *Irish News,* Oct. 26, 1982.

7. *Irish News,* Oct. 27, 1982.

8. "Collusion," Ulster Defence Association intelligence report, undated but ca. 1988, author's copy.

9. McKittrick et al., *Lost Lives,* 921.

10. Confidential information from peace process participant, 2000.

11. Notes of author's conversation with British official, Aug. 2000.

12. Notes of author's conversation with Belfast INLA member, undated, summer of 1998.

13. Correspondence with author, March 3, 1989.

14. "Haughey and the Priest," *Sunday Tribune,* Sept. 25, 1994.

15. Interview with former IRA prisoner, April 2000.

16. David Beresford, *Ten Men Dead: The Story of the 1981 Irish Hunger Strike* (London: Grafton Books, 1987), 56 .

17. Interview with former IRA prisoner, April 2000.

18. Ibid.

19. Ibid.

20. Interview with Brendan Hughes, June 2000.

21. Unpublished interview in article prepared for *Sunday Tribune*, Sept. 25, 1994.

22. See Clonard website: www.clonard.com/chouse.htm.

23. Gerry Adams, *Before the Dawn: An Autobiography* (London: Heinemann, 1996), 33.

24. *Andersonstown News*, April 15, 2000.

25. Conor O'Clery, *The Greening of the White House* (Dublin: Gill and Macmillan, 1997), 47.

26. Confidential information from peace process participant, 2000.

27. Ibid.

28. Ibid.

29. Brian Campbell, Laurence McKeown, and Felim O'Hagan, eds., *Nor Meekly Serve My Time: The H-Block Struggle, 1976–1981* (Belfast: Beyond the Pale Publications, 1998), 262–63.

30. Confidential information from peace process participant, 2000.

31. *Irish Press*, Jan. 16, 1978.

32. Paul Bew and Gordon Gillespie, *Northern Ireland: A Chronology of the Troubles, 1968–1999* (Dublin: Gill and Macmillan, 1999), 127.

33. *Irish Times*, Nov. 5, 1982.

34. *Sunday Times*, May 29, 1988.

35. Note of author's conversation with senior Catholic cleric, March 2001.

36. Notes of author's conversation with Adams adviser, Nov. 1992.

37. Note of author's conversation with senior Catholic cleric, March 2001.

38. *An Phoblacht–Republican News*, April 19, 1984.

39. Ibid.

40. Ibid.

41. Note of author's conversation with senior Catholic cleric, March 2001.

42. Notes of conversation with peace process participant, 2000.

43. Ibid.

44. Note of author's conversation with senior Catholic cleric, March 2001.

45. *An Phoblacht–Republican News*, Nov. 8, 1984.

46. *Irish Times*, Feb. 24, 1985.

47. *Irish Independent*, March 11, 1985.

48. *Irish Times*, Jan. 3, 1984.

49. *Irish Times*, July 22, 1985.

50. Campbell et al., eds., *Nor Meekly Serve My Time*, 263–64.

51. Interview with former IRA member, 1999.

52. Interview with senior Protestant cleric, Sept. 2000.

53. Note of author's conversation with senior republican, Dec. 1983.

54. McKittrick et al., *Lost Lives,* 981.

55. Interview with former Belfast IRA member, Nov. 2000.

56. Interview with former IRA member, June 1999.

Eight: Dealing with the Brits

1. Sinn Fein, "Setting the Record Straight": A record of communications between Sinn Fein and the British government, Oct. 1990–Nov. 1993 (July 1994).

2. Eamonn Mallie and David McKittrick, *The Fight for Peace: The Secret Story behind the Irish Peace Process* (London: Heinemann, 1996), 99.

3. Interview with the author, Westminster, June 22, 2000.

4. Ibid.

5. Sydney Elliott and W. D. Flackes, *Northern Ireland: A Political Directory, 1968–1999* (Belfast: Blackstaff Press, 1999), 308.

6. Interview with the author, Westminster, Nov. 13, 2000.

7. Ibid.

8. Ibid.

9. Ibid.

10. Confidential interview with peace process participant, Aug. 2000.

11. Secret British message to Gerry Adams, author's copy.

12. Ibid.

13. Interview with the author, Westminster, June 21, 2000.

14. Ibid.

15. Confidential interview with peace process participant, Aug. 2000.

16. Ibid.

17. "What's on the Agenda Now Is an End to Partion," *Irish Times,* Dec. 10, 1986.

18. "Pact Won't Stop War, Warns Adams," *Irish Press,* March 5, 1987.

19. Confidential interview with peace process participant, Aug. 2000.

20. Ibid.

21. Tom King, interview with the author, Westminster, Nov. 13, 2000.

22. Interview with former British official, Nov. 2000.

23. Ibid.

24. Notes of conversation with author, Westminster, Nov. 2000.

25. Interview with the author, Westminster, June 22, 2000.

26. Peter Taylor, *Provos: The IRA and Sinn Fein* (London: Bloomsbury, 1998), 233–34.

27. David Beresford, *Ten Men Dead: The Story of the 1981 Irish Hunger Strike* (London: Grafton Books, 1987), 9–12.

Nine: "Stepping Stones"

1. John Waters, "The Fat Chief's Belly Was to Reassure His Tribe," *Irish Times,* July 15, 1997.

2. Dick Walsh, "Lynch's Rivals Were the State's Biggest Threat," *Irish Times,* Jan. 6, 2001.

3. "Whitaker Advised Lynch to Pursue Unity Peacefully," *Irish Times,* Jan. 2, 2001.

4. "Letter Tells of Haughey Role in Breaking IRA," *Irish Times,* Jan. 2, 2001.

5. Martin Mansergh, ed., *The Spirit of the Nation: The Speeches of Charles J. Haughey* (Cork and Dublin: Mercier Press, 1987), 8.

6. Justin O'Brien, *The Arms Trial* (Dublin: Gill and Macmillan, 2000), 110.

7. Mansergh, ed., *Spirit of the Nation*, 335.

8. Ibid., 334–36.

9. *Irish Press*, Dec. 11, 1986.

10. Brian Campbell, Laurence McKeown, and Felim O'Hagan, eds., *Nor Meekly Serve My Time: The H-Block Struggle, 1976–1981* (Belfast: Beyond the Pale Publications, 1998), 263–64.

11. Confidential information, peace process source, 2000.

12. See Daltun O Ceallaigh, *Irish Republicanism: Good Friday and After* (Dublin: Leirmheas, 2000).

13. The details of the Reid message to Haughey were provided confidentially by two peace process sources, 2000.

14. Martin Mansergh, "The Background to the Peace Process," *Irish Studies in International Affairs* 6 (1995): 155.

15. Ed Moloney, "Haughey and the Priest," *Sunday Tribune,* Sept. 25, 1994.

16. Confidential information, peace process source, 1999.

17. Confidential information, peace process source, 2000.

18. Ibid.

19. Confidential information, peace process source, 1999.

20. Ed Moloney, "There Will Be No Ceasefire," *Sunday Tribune*, Jan. 17, 1988.

21. Ed Moloney, "Impasse over IRA Campaign Threatens SF-SDLP Talks," *Sunday Tribune*, April 3, 1988.

22. See *Irish Times*, Sept. 6, 12, 13, 19, and 26, 1988.

23. Eamonn Mallie and David McKittrick, *The Fight for Peace: The Secret Story behind the Irish Peace Process* (London: Heinemann, 1996), 171.

24. Mansergh, "Background," 153.

25. Confidential account of Duisburg conference, Oct. 14–15, 1988, author's copy.

26. *Irish Times*, Feb. 27, 1989.

27. *Sunday Tribune*, Nov. 5, 1989.

28. *Irish Times*, Nov. 10, 1989.

29. Draft 2, Oct. 1991, author's copy.

30. Confidential information, peace process source, 1999.

31. For a comprehensive account of the intergovernment negotiations, see Mallie and McKittrick, *Fight for Peace*.

32. Text of Downing Street Declaration, Dec. 15, 1993.

33. *Irish Times*, June 16, 2006.

Ten: "No Idle Boast"

1. Confidential information from peace process participant, 2000.

2. IRA Easter message, *An Phoblacht–Republican News*, April 15, 1982.

3. Interview with former IRA member, Nov. 2000.

4. Notes of author's conversation with former IRA Convention delegate, Oct. 1993.

5. "Jailed IRA Men Back Provos Drive for Dail," *Times* (London), Sept. 1, 1986.

6. Interview with former IRA member, Nov. 2000.

7. Interview with former IRA member, Nov. 1998.

8. Interview with former Sinn Fein member, Feb. 1999.

9. Sinn Fein, *The Politics of Revolution* (Dublin: Sinn Fein, 1982), 11.

10. Ibid., 7.

11. Ibid., 20.

12. Ibid., 22.

13. Ibid., 26.

14. Ibid., 27.

15. Interview with former Sinn Fein official, 1999.

16. "Sinn Fein in Search for a New Strategy," *Irish News*, June 21, 1988.

17. "Report of a Wing Discussion: H Block," *Iris Bheag*, Aug. 1988.

18. Ibid.

19. Ibid.

20. "A Pan-Nationalist Alliance?" *Iris Bheag*, June 1988.

21. "The SDLP: An Enemy in Our Midst?" *Iris Bheag*, Sept. 1990.

22. Sinn Fein Ard Comhairle, "Towards a Mass Movement," Jan. 1989.

23. "Delegates Vote to Seek 'Anti-imperialist' Alliances," *Independent*, Jan. 30, 1989.

24. Sinn Fein Ard Comhairle, "Towards a Mass Movement."

25. David McKittrick, Seamus Kelters, Brian Feeney, and Chris Thornton, *Lost Lives* (Edinburgh: Mainstream Publishing, 1999), 1068.

26. The Weasel, "Bodenstown: A Twenty Six County Day Out," *Iris Bheag*, Sept. 1987.

27. Ibid.

28. Ibid.

29. See Bullitt, "Attitudes to the Garda Siochana," *Iris Bheag*, March 1988.

Eleven: Death in Tyrone

1. Interview with former IRA member, April 2000.

2. Peter Taylor, *Families at War: Voices from the Troubles* (London: BBC Books, 1989), 156.

3. Notes of telephone conversation with Tyrone republican source, April 2001.

4. Michael Farrell, *Northern Ireland: The Orange State* (London: Pluto Press, 1976), 205.

5. Notes of telephone conversation with former Army Council member, April 2001.

6. Interview with former Tyrone republican activist, April 2000.

7. Ibid.

8. Interview with former Tyrone IRA member, May 2000.

9. Ibid.

10. Interview with former Tyrone IRA member, April 2000.

11. Interview with former Tyrone IRA member, May 2000.

12. Confidential information, IRA source, Oct. 1998.

13. Notes of author's conversation with former British military intelligence officer, Oct. 2000.

14. Interview with former Tyrone republican activist, April 2000.

15. Notes of conversation with former Northern Command staff officer, Nov. 1990.

16. *An Phoblacht–Republican News*, Nov. 17, 1983.

17. *An Phoblacht–Republican News*, June 21, 1984.

18. Confidential information, IRA source, Dec. 1999.

19. Confidential information, IRA source, Oct. 1998.

20. Interview with former Tyrone IRA member, April 2000.

21. Ibid.

22. Interview with former Tyrone republican activist, April 2000.

23. Confidential information, IRA source, April 2000.

24. Analysis of IRA "War News" column in *An Phoblacht–Republican News* by the author.

25. Interview with former Tyrone IRA member, April 2000.

26. Confidential information, IRA source, Jan. 1999.

27. Interview with former Tyrone republican activist, April 2000.

28. "Triple Murder by IRA Brings Sinn Fein Reprimand," *Daily Telegraph*, March 9, 1989.

29. Interview with former Tyrone republican activist, April 2000.

30. Interview with former Tyrone IRA member, April 2000.

31. Interview with Tyrone IRA member, April 2000.

32. Ibid.

33. Interview with former Tyrone Republican activist, April 2000.

34. Notes of conversation with Tyrone Sinn Fein member, Nov. 1990.

35. Interview with Tyrone IRA member, April 2000.

36. Notes of conversation with former Northern Command member, March 1991.

37. Confidential information, IRA source, Jan. 1999.

38. Notes of conversation with former Northern Command member, March 1991.

39. "Heroic Freedom Fighter," *An Phoblacht–Republican News*, May 14, 1987.

Twelve: "The War of the Twilight"

1. Interview with former IRA member, April 2000.

2. IRA Easter message, *An Phoblacht–Republican News*, April 23, 1987.

3. Interview with former IRA member, Nov. 1999.

4. Ibid.

5. Interview with former IRA member, Oct. 1998.

6. Interview with former IRA member, Jan. 1999.

7. Confidential information, IRA source, Jan. 1999.

8. Ibid.

9. Author's note of conversation with republican source, March 1988.

10. Jack Holland, *Hope against History: The Ulster Conflict* (London: Hodder and Stoughton, 1999), 220.

11. Interview with former IRA member, Oct. 1998.

12. Interview with former IRA member, Jan. 1999.
13. Ibid.
14. "IRA Killers Set to Focus on British," *Observer,* June 1988.
15. "IRA Will Target British Army in Bid to Broaden Support," *Sunday Tribune,* July 17, 1988.
16. Notes of conversation with Tyrone republican, Nov. 1990.
17. Interview with former IRA member, Jan. 1999.
18. Interview with former IRA member, Oct. 1998.
19. *Fortnight,* Sept. 1992.
20. *Andersonstown News,* Nov. 22, 1986.
21. David McKittrick, Seamus Kelters, Brian Feeney, and Chris Thornton, *Lost Lives* (Edinburgh: Mainstream Publishing, 1999), 1096.
22. "SF Leader Refuses to Support Bomb Attack," *Irish News,* June 30, 1988.
23. "Provos Must Get Organised, Says Adams," *Irish News,* July 7, 1988.
24. "Adams 'Shocked' by IRA Killing of Family," *Irish Times,* Aug. 1, 1988.
25. "Killing of Civilians Alienates Voters, Adams Warns IRA," *Independent,* Jan. 30, 1989.
26. "SF's Position One of Critical Support, Says Adams," *Irish Times,* June 9, 1990.
27. Interview with former IRA member, Jan. 1999.
28. Ibid.
29. "Sinn Fein Changes Tactics to Let IRA Speak for Itself," *Irish Times,* Jan. 26, 1991.
30. David Sharrock and Mark Devenport, *Man of War, Man of Peace? The Unauthorised Biography of Gerry Adams* (London: Macmillan, 1997), 284.
31. Ibid., 284–85.
32. Interview with former IRA member, Nov. 1999.
33. Brendan O'Brien, *The Long War* (Dublin: O'Brien Press, 1995), 151.
34. Notes of conversation with Adams aide, Dec. 3, 1990.
35. Peter Taylor, *Provos: The IRA and Sinn Fein* (London: Bloomsbury, 1998), 317.

Thirteen: The Derry Experiment

1. *Derry Journal,* Oct. 26, 1990.
2. Ibid.
3. Andy Pollak, ed., *A Citizens' Inquiry: The Opsahl Report on Northern Ireland* (Dublin: Lilliput Press, 1993), 267.

4. Dr. Ronny Swain, Psychology Department, University of Cork, quoted ibid.
5. Niall O Dochartaigh, *From Civil Rights to Armalites: Derry and the Birth of the Irish Troubles* (Cork: Cork University Press, 1997), xiv.
6. Eamonn McCann, *War and an Irish Town* (London: Pluto Press, 1980), 40.
7. Unpublished interview with Martin McGuinness Aug. 1989, p. 2, author's copy.
8. Ibid.
9. Ibid.
10. Ibid.
11. Ibid.
12. O Dochartaigh, *From Civil Rights to Armalites,* 155.
13. Ibid., 158.
14. Ibid., 160.
15. McCann, *War and an Irish Town,* 87.
16. O Dochartaigh, *From Civil Rights to Armalites,* 237.
17. Unpublished interview with McGuinness, 8.
18. Ibid., 10.
19. "McGuinness Reign Marked by 29 Security Killings," *Irish Independent,* May 3, 2001.
20. McCann, *War and an Irish Town,* 106.
21. O Dochartaigh, *From Civil Rights to Armalites,* 281.
22. Ibid., 279.
23. McCann, *War and an Irish Town,* 102.
24. Unpublished interview with McGuinness, 10.
25. O Dochartaigh, *From Civil Rights to Armalites,* 285.
26. Interview with British government source, Aug. 2000.
27. Interview with confidential Derry source, Nov. 1998.
28. Interview with senior British army source, June 2000.
29. Interview with confidential Derry source, Nov. 1998.
30. Interview with senior British army source, June 2000.
31. Ibid.
32. Ibid.
33. Based on interviews with senior British army source, June 2000, and confidential Derry source, Nov. 1998.
34. Confidential Derry source, Sept. 2000.
35. Interview with confidential Derry source, Nov. 1998.
36. Author's analysis of "War News" column, *An Phoblacht–Republican News,* 1986–94.
37. Interview with senior British army source, June 2000.

38. Confidential Derry source, Sept. 2000.
39. Information from confidential IRA source, Sept. 2000.
40. "The Men of War Promise Third Violent Decade," *Independent*, Sept. 29, 1990.

Fourteen: Seven Men in a Room

1. Constitution of Oglaigh na hEireann, 1986 version, section 8 (b) 1, author's copy.
2. Interview with IRA source, Jan. 1999.
3. Interview with IRA source, Oct. 1998.
4. Author's note of conversation with former IRA Army Council member, Oct. 1993.
5. Interview with IRA source, April 2000.
6. Ibid.
7. Ibid.
8. Ibid.
9. Interview with IRA source, Nov. 1999.
10. Interview with IRA source, Jan. 1999.
11. Ibid.
12. Ibid.
13. Ibid.
14. Author's note of conversation with republican source, Sept. 7, 1995.

Fifteen: Cease-Fire

1. Peter Taylor, *Provos: The IRA and Sinn Fein* (London: Bloomsbury, 1998), 142.
2. "'No Ceasefire' in Northern Ireland Likely Say Provos," *Sunday Tribune*, Feb. 25, 1990.
3. "IRA Could Call Off Campaign—Adams," *Belfast Telegraph*, April 10, 1990.
4. "Provos Call a Ceasefire," *Irish News*, Dec. 24, 1990.
5. Gerry Adams, interview with the author, Jan. 31, 1991.
6. "Adams Dismisses Ceasefire 'propaganda,'" *Irish Times*, Feb. 4, 1991.
7. Sinn Fein, "Towards a Lasting Peace in Ireland" (Dublin), Feb. 1992, p. 12.
8. Jim Gibney, "It Is Our Job to Develop the Struggle for Freedom," June 21, 1992, Sinn Fein press office fax to author.
9. "SF Speech Is Seen as Significant," *Irish Times*, June 23, 1992.

10. Gerry Adams, *A Pathway to Peace* (Cork and Dublin: Mercier Press, 1988).

11. Notes of conversation with republican source, Dec. 2000.

12. Interview with republican source, Nov. 2000.

13. Interview with republican source, Nov. 1999.

14. Sinn Fein, "Setting the Record Straight": A record of communications between Sinn Fein and the British government, Oct. 1990–Nov. 1993 (July 1994), pp. 11–12.

15. Ibid., 27

16. Brendan O'Brien, *The Long War* (Dublin: O'Brien Press, 1995), 271.

17. Eamonn Mallie and David McKittrick, *The Fight for Peace: The Secret Story behind the Irish Peace Process* (London: Heinemann, 1996), 375–77.

18. Ibid., 174.

19. Notes of conversation with think tank member, March 24, 1995.

20. Mallie and McKittrick, *Fight for Peace,* 177.

21. Downing Street Declaration, Dec. 15, 1993.

22. "Adams on IRA Peace Process." *Sunday Tribune,* Dec. 12, 1993.

23. Interview with Belfast republican, Dec. 20, 1993.

24. *Guardian,* Oct. 25, 1993.

25. Notes of conversation with think tank member, March 24, 1995.

26. "McGuinness: Nothing Less Than Withdrawal Acceptable," *Sunday Business Post,* Jan. 2, 1994.

27. Transcript of telephone conversation with West Belfast republican, Feb. 1, 1994.

28. Notes of interview with republican source, April 2000.

29. *Irish Times,* May 26, 1994.

30. Sean Duignan, *One Spin on the Merry-Go-Round* (Dublin: Blackwater Press, 1995), 136.

31. Conor O'Clery, *The Greening of the White House* (Dublin: Gill and Macmillan, 1997), 112.

32. Ibid., 115.

33. O'Clery, *Greening of the White House,* 138.

34. Irish government source, Feb. 2000.

Sixteen: The *Sos*

1. *An Phoblacht–Republican News,* Sept. 2, 1994.

2. Notes of conversation with republican source, Sept. 8, 1994.

3. Duties and powers of the Army Council, IRA constitution, 1986 version.

4. Notes of conversation with British government source, April 24, 1995.

5. Interview with IRA source, Nov. 1999.

6. "Gerry Adams Confirms Meeting with US Delegation to Take Place," SF news release, Aug. 22, 1994.

7. Interview with IRA source, March 1999.

8. "Radical Agendas," *Common Ground*, The Pat Finucane Centre, 1, no. 3 (Winter 1994).

9. Interview with IRA source, Nov. 1999.

10. Paul Bew and Gordon Gillespie, *Northern Ireland: A Chronology of the Troubles, 1968–1999* (Dublin: Gill and Macmillan, 1999), 300.

11. *Irish Times*, Aug. 31, 1995.

12. Interview with IRA source, Dec. 1999.

13. David McKittrick, Seamus Kelters, Brian Feeney, and Chris Thornton, *Lost Lives* (Edinburgh: Mainstream Publishing, 1999), 1401.

14. Interview with Convention delegate, Feb. 2000.

15. Duties and powers of the Army Council, IRA constitution, 1986 version.

16. Clause 5, paragraph 5, Army Control, IRA constitution, 1986 version.

17. Ibid.

18. Duties and powers of the Executive, IRA constitution, 1996 version.

19. Duties and powers of the Army Council, IRA constitution, 1996 version.

20. Ibid.

21. Interview with Convention delegate, March 2000.

Seventeen: The Point of No Return

1. "Any New Ceasefire Would Be Clear Cut—Adams," *Irish Times*, Feb. 22, 1997.

2. Jack Holland, *Hope against History: The Ulster Conflict* (London: Hodder and Stoughton, 1999), 277.

3. *Sunday Tribune*, April 8, 1995.

4. Interview with IRA source, Feb. 2000.

5. Irish government source, Feb. 2000.

6. Ibid.

7. *Irish Times*, July 9, 1997.

8. Notes of conversation with republican source, May 2001.

9. Ibid.

10. Interview with IRA source, April 2000.

Eighteen: The End Begins

1. Sinn Fein press release, May 11, 1998.
2. "Poll of SF Delegates Dislike Good Friday Agreement," *Sunday Tribune*, April 19, 1998.
3. David McKittrick, Seamus Kelters, Brian Feeney, and Chris Thornton, *Lost Lives* (Edinburgh: Mainstream Publishing, 1999), 1431.
4. Paul Bew and Gordon Gillespie, *Northern Ireland: A Chronology of the Troubles, 1968–1999* (Dublin: Gill and Macmillan, 1999), 349.
5. "IRA Blunder in the Jungle Sparks US Rage," *Observer*, Aug. 19, 2001.
6. Ibid.
7. "N Ireland Closer to Weapons Compromise," *Financial Times*, Oct. 13, 1998.
8. Confidential information from IRA source, 1999.
9. Notes of conversation with Irish government source, Sept. 2000.
10. BBC NI webpage: <http//:www.news.bbc.co.uk/hi/english/uk/northern_ireland/ default.stm>, Sept. 24, 2001.
11. *Irish Times*, Oct. 29, 2001.
12. "Hope in Ireland," *Washington Post*, Oct. 26, 2001.
13. "Burying the Guns of Northern Ireland," *New York Times*, Oct. 24, 2001.
14. "Securing the Peace," *Irish Times*, Oct. 24, 2001.
15. "Hand of History," *The Times* (London), Oct. 24, 2001.

Nineteen: The Midas Touch

1. Notes of conversation with Gerry Adams, autumn 1994.
2. Speech by Tony Blair, British prime minister, in Belfast, Oct. 17, 2002.
3. Speech by Tony Blair, British prime minister, in London, March 21, 2006.
4. Notes of conversation with U.S. Department of State official, Oct. 2004.
5. Confidential information, Dec. 2000.
6. Northern Ireland Office, *The Belfast Agreement*, Chapter 7, April 10, 1998.
7. Dean Godson, *Himself Alone—David Trimble and the Ordeal of Unionism* (London: HarperCollins, 2004), 347.
8. Northern Ireland Office, *The Way Forward*, July 2, 1999.
9. Notes of conversation with Department of Foreign Affairs official, Nov. 1998.
10. Notes of conversations with republican dissidents, summer 2000.
11. Channel Four, *The Big Heist*, Sept. 22, 2005.

12. Godson, *Himself Alone—David Trimble and the Ordeal of Unionism*, 686.
13. Ibid.
14. Confidential information.
15. *Daily Telegraph*, Oct. 10, 2002. Confirmed by security force source, Nov. 2005.
16. Confidential information.
17. *Irish Times*, Jan. 23, 2006.
18. House International Relations Committee, *International Global Terrorism: its links with illicit drugs as illustrated by the IRA and other groups in Colombia*. Hearing on April 24, 2002.
19. Ibid.
20. Confidential information.
21. *Daily Telegraph*, May 15, 2002.
22. *Sunday Herald*, Aug. 29, 1999.
23. *Irish Times*, Jan. 9, 1999.
24. Ibid.
25. *Sunday Tribune*, Jan. 31, 1999.
26. Notes of conversation with Irish Department of Foreign Affairs official, March 1999.
27. Michael Benson, *Failed Entity*, The Blanket, <http://lark.phoblacht.net>, Dec. 6, 2004.
28. *Sunday Tribune*, Jan. 17, 1999.
29. Godson, *Himself Alone—David Trimble and the Ordeal of Unionism*, 592.
30. Ibid., 586.
31. Ibid., 556.
32. Interview with former republican activist, autumn 2006.
33. Interview with senior Irish political source, Sept. 2006.
34. Godson, *Himself Alone—David Trimble and the Ordeal of Unionism*, 556.
35. Interview with General John de Chastelain, Sept. 2006.
36. Millward Brown *Ulster, The Good Friday Agreement—Latest Public Opinion*, Oct. 25/26, 2000.
37. *Irish Times*, March 25, 2002.
38. Interview with security source, Nov. 2005.
39. BBC NI webpage, Jan. 13, 2003.
40. Interview with security source, Nov. 2005.
41. Interview with Irish political source, Sept. 2006.
42. *Irish Times*, Oct. 2, 2003.
43. Interview with General de Chastelain, Sept. 2006.
44. *Irish Times*, Oct. 21, 2003.

Twenty: The Last Kalashnikov

1. Chris Ward was charged in connection with the robbery in December 2005. At the time of writing his trial has not been held.
2. Richard O'Rawe, *Blanketmen—An Untold Story of the H-Block Hunger Strike* (Dublin: New Island, 2005), 236.
3. *Irish Independent*, June 10, 1999.
4. Conversation with DUP figure, Aug. 2005.
5. Fourth Report of the Independent Monitoring Commission, Feb. 10, 2005.
6. RTE radio, *This Week*, Jan. 9, 2005.
7. *Irish Times*, Feb. 21, 2005.
8. IRA statement, Feb. 3, 2005.
9. Channel 4 Television, *The Big Heist*, Sept. 22, 2005.
10. Interview with Irish security source, Sept. 2006.
11. Interview with Northern Bank spokesman, Oct. 18, 2006.
12. Confidential information.
13. Fifth Report of the Independent Monitoring Commission, May 24, 2005.
14. Interview with Irish political source, Sept. 2006.
15. Confidential information.
16. *Irish Times*, Feb. 12, 2005.
17. *Irish Times*, Jan. 11, 2005.
18. BBC NI webpage, Jan. 16, 2005.
19. *Daily Telegraph*, July 5, 2006.
20. *Irish Times*, July 4, 2005.
21. Ibid.
22. Confidential information.
23. Ibid.
24. *Irish Times*, Feb. 15, 2005.
25. Anthony McIntyre, *Burdens Unbearable*, The Blanket, <http://lark.phoblacht.net>, Feb. 4, 2005.
26. *Irish Times*, July 4, 2005.
27. Interview with Catherine McCartney, Sept. 2005.
28. *Irish Times*, July 4, 2005.
29. Interview with Catherine McCartney, Sept. 2005.
30. *Irish Times*, March 17, 2005.
31. *Irish Times*, March 16, 2005.
32. BBC NI webpage, March 14, 2005.
33. *Irish Times*, March 18, 2005.

34. Interview with U.S. Department of State official, Nov. 2006.
35. *Sunday Telegraph*, March 20, 2005.
36. *Irish Times*, March 18, 2005.
37. Interview with Catherine McCartney, Sept. 2005.
38. Council on Foreign Relations, <http://www.cfr.org/publication/7935/conversation_with_gerry_adams.html?breadcrumb=default> March 14, 2005.
39. Ibid.
40. Ibid.
41. *Irish Times*, April 7, 2005.
42. *Irish Times*, Oct. 1, 2005.
43. *Irish Times*, Oct. 16, 2006.
44. *Irish Times*, Sept. 27, 2005.
45. *Irish Times*, Oct. 1, 2005.
46. Interview with security source, Nov. 2005.
47. *Irish Times*, Sept. 27, 2005.
48. *Irish News*, Oct. 14, 2005.
49. *Irish Times*, Oct. 8, 2004.
50. *Guardian*, Feb. 22, 2005.
51. *Sunday Independent*, Feb. 27, 2005.
52. *Irish Times*, March 4, 2005.
53. *Irish Times*, May 19, 2006.
54. BBC News website, <http://news.bbc.co.uk/2/hi/uk_news/magazine/3715205.stm>
55. *Sunday Times*, Oct. 2, 2005.
56. *Sunday Times*, May 7, 2006.
57. O'Rawe, *Blanketmen*.
58. The Blanket website, < http://www.phoblacht.net/AMROR1605068g.html>
59. O'Rawe, *Blanketmen*, 257.
60. The Blanketmen website, < http://www.phoblacht.net/AMROR1605068g.html>
61. *Irish News*, March 12, 2005.
62. *Daily Ireland*, June 7, 2006.
63. *Hunger Strike*, DoubleBand Films, RTE, May 9, 2006.
64. *Democratic Dialogue*, April 5, 2006, reproduced on www.openDemocracy.net.
65. *Independent*, Dec. 7, 1997.
66. *Sunday Times*, Oct. 31, 1999.
67. *Belfast Telegraph*, Dec. 21, 2005.
68. *Sinn Fein* website, <http://www.sinnfein.ie/news/detail/8041>

69. *Irish News*, Jan. 8, 2005.

70. Confidential information.

71. A Ministry of Defence gagging writ preventing "Ingram" from referring to "Steaknife" obliged the ex-FRU soldier to coin the name "Stakeknife" instead, a fiction that facilitated continuing media coverage of the story.

72. Confidential information.

73. *Daily Telegraph*, March 29, 1998.

74. Ibid.

75. *Irish News*, Dec. 1, 2001.

76. Mark Urban, *Big Boys' Rules—The Secret Struggle Against the IRA* (London: Faber and Faber, 1992), 181–82.

77. *Sunday Tribune*, Jan. 31, 1992.

78. *Daily Telegraph*, March 29, 1998.

79. *Irish Times*, Dec. 17, 2005.

80. Interview with Irish security source, Sept. 2006.

81. Interview with security source, Nov. 2005.

82. Ibid.

83. Radio Free Eireann interview, Dec. 29, 2005.

84. Interview with former Noraid official, Aug. 2006.

85. *Irish Times*, Dec. 24, 2005.

86. Interview with former Noraid official, Aug. 2006.

87. Confidential information.

88. See website, <http://www.birw.org/Stakeknife.html>

89. *Sunday Times*, Oct. 31, 1999.

90. *The Times*, March 20, 2006.

91. Interview with former republican activist, autumn 2006.

92. Confidential information.

93. *Sunday Independent*, Sept. 17, 2006.

94. Interview with Irish security source, Sept. 2006.

Epilogue: "Turning the *Titanic* in a Bathtub"

1. Confidential conversation with Presbyterian cleric, spring 2001.

2. The Report of the Independent Commission on Policing for Northern Ireland, Sept. 1999, para 12. 18.

3. Confidential source, July 2006.

4. Email to author, February 2007.

Chronology of Events

1170	First English invasion of Ireland led by Strongbow
1541	English Tudor monarch, Henry VII declares himself King of Ireland
1558–1603	Six of Ulster's nine counties "planted" with English and Scots settlers
1690	King William of Orange defeats Stuart King James II at Battle of the Boyne
1795	Orange Order founded after battle between Catholic Defenders and Protestant "Peep O'Day Boys"
1798	United Irishmen rebellion put down.
1801	Act of Union unites Ireland and England creating United Kingdom
1867	Fenian rising defeated
1916	Easter Rising put down
1919	Sinn Fein wins 75 of 105 Irish seats at Westminster and forms First Dail in Dublin
1921–23	IRA wages armed campaign to force British withdrawal and Irish independence
	Anglo-Irish Treaty negotiated
	Irish civil war begins
	Michael Collins killed
	IRA defeated
	Northern Ireland state and the new Free State consolidated
1926	Eamon de Valera forms Fianna Fail
1932	De Valera forms first Fianna Fail government
1938	Anti-treaty remnants of Second Dail elected in 1921 pass on their powers to the IRA Army Council

1939	IRA declares war on Britain with bombing campaign in English cities
1942	Belfast IRA leader Tom Williams hanged Gerry Adams Snr. jailed
1948	Gerry Adams Jnr. born
	IRA General Army Order No 8 promulgated; forbids military action against Southern security forces
1956	IRA begins Border Campaign in Northern Ireland
1959	Eamon de Valera retires as taoiseach; succeeded by Sean Lemass
1962	Border Campaign abandoned in failure
	Cathal Goulding becomes IRA chief of staff
1963	Terence O'Neill becomes prime minister of Northern Ireland
	Roy Johnston and Tony Coughlan join republican movement
1964	Divis Street riots in Belfast over display of Irish flag
1965	O'Neill and Lemass meet in Belfast
	Gerry Adams joins D Coy of Belfast Brigade IRA
1966	UVF re-formed in Belfast and kills Catholics
	Death toll is 3
1967	NICRA formed
	Unionist prime minister Terence O'Neill meets Irish taoiseach Jack Lynch at Stormont; loyalist demonstrators marshalled by Ian Paisley throw snowballs at his car
1968	First civil rights marches in Northern Ireland
1969	Riots in Derry and deaths in Belfast
	British army sent to Northern Ireland
	IRA splits into Official and Provisional wings
	Provisional IRA Convention held; Sean MacStiofain becomes first chief of staff
	Death toll for year is 18, cumulative toll is 21
1970	Sinn Fein splits after majority vote to drop abstentionism, dissidents walk out and give their allegiance to new "Provisional" IRA
	Siege of St. Matthew's and Falls Curfew boost Provisionals
	IRA commercial bombing campaign begins
	Billy McKee is Belfast commander
	Adams heads IRA in Ballymurphy and choreographs Ballymurphy riots, defying McKee

Ian Paisley elected to Westminster parliament

Death toll for year is 28, cumulative toll is 49

1971 IRA campaign intensifies

First British soldier shot dead, and Provo commercial bombing campaign begins in Belfast

Adams on Second Belfast Battalion staff and then commander

Adams on Belfast Brigade staff

Internment without trial introduced

IRA campaign mushrooms

Death toll for year is 180, cumulative toll is 229

1972 Bloody Sunday in Derry

Stormont parliament prorogued and direct rule from London imposed

Adams interned but released to take part in cease-fire talks with British

Adams becomes adjutant of Belfast Brigade

Special category status granted to IRA prisoners

Cease-fire breaks down at Belfast Brigade urging

Adams introduces Armalite rifle to IRA

Car bomb weapon accidentally discovered by Belfast Brigade

IRA kills seven in Bloody Friday bombings

Operation Motorman puts IRA under pressure

Adams becomes Belfast Brigade commander

Four Square Laundry operation

"Unknowns" cell formed by Adams

Belfast Brigade begins to "disappear" double agents including Jean McConville

Breton nationalists introduce IRA to Libyans

IRA establishes "embassy" in Libyan capital, Tripoli

Death toll for year is 496, cumulative toll is 725

1973 London bombings carried out by Belfast Brigade

Adams arrested and interned, later imprisoned for trying to escape

Claudia intercepted en route to Ireland from Libya with weapons

Brian Keenan appointed IRA QMG

Northern IRA leaders stop Sinn Fein contesting elections to Northern Ireland Assembly

Death toll for year is 263, cumulative toll is 988

1974   Power-sharing Sunningdale deal brought down by Ulster
Workers' Council general strike assisted by UDA and UVF
and mainstream loyalist politicians

Libya grows cool on IRA

Death toll for year is 303, cumulative toll is 1291

1975   IRA cease-fire called, IRA leadership believes British wish to
disengage

Lengthy talks with British

Adams and Ivor Bell lead Long Kesh dissidents against Billy
McKee leadership and oppose cease-fire

Loyalist killings of Catholics surge

Sectarian killings by IRA and feuding with Officials intensify

IRA cease-fire peters out

Death toll for year is 267, cumulative toll is 1558

1976   New British security policy introduced

RUC put in charge of security operations, internment phased
out, juryless courts set up, IRA to be treated as criminals in jail

Prison protest by IRA inmates in new H Blocks begins

Loyalist assassination campaign peaks

Peace People movement emerges after two children killed in
IRA-British Army clash

Death toll for year is 308, cumulative toll is 1866

1977   Police interrogation centers begin to process scores of IRA
suspects

Adams released from jail and eventually reappointed as
Belfast Brigade commander

Father Reid mediates in feud between Official and Provisional
IRAs

Adams becomes adjutant-general and joins Army Council

"Long war" speech at Bodenstown in June

Northern Command set up and Revolutionary Council established

IRA campaign of assassination against Northern businessmen
starts

Cellular restructuring of IRA starts

Adams forms "think tank" group of advisers

Adams becomes IRA chief of staff in succession to Seamus
Twomey

Martin McGuinness and Brian Keenan join Army Council

McKee censured by Revolutionary Council over handling of feud with Official IRA

Gerry O'Hare deposed as editor of Dublin IRA paper *An Phoblacht*

Death toll for year is 116, cumulative toll is 1982

1978 Adams loses his rank as chief of staff when he is arrested in the wake of La Mon bombing

Martin McGuinness becomes IRA chief of staff

Adams cleared and released; he becomes adjutant-general, second-in-command to McGuinness

IRA introduces Green Book for recruits

IRA sets up internal security unit to hunt informers

IRA says next cease-fire will happen only when British quit Ireland

An Phoblacht merged with Belfast IRA paper *Republican News* in Adams takeover

British Army document, *Northern Ireland – Future Terrorist Trends* leaked to IRA; names Adams and Bell as architects of IRA restructuring O Bradaigh proposal to contest Euro elections opposed by Adams

Death toll for year is 88, cumulative toll is 2070

1979 Margaret Thatcher becomes British prime minister

Lord Mountbatten killed in IRA bombing

18 British soldiers killed in ambush on Border

Move to left advertised in Bodenstown speech

Army Council rejects Eire Nua policy of O Bradaigh–O Conaill leadership as Adams camps bids for supremacy

Adams denies Marxist influence

Northern IRA leaders oppose Bernadette Devlin's bid for Euro seat on H Blocks issue

Death toll for year is 125, cumulative toll is 2195

1980 First IRA prison hunger strike begins

Northern IRA leaders negotiate secret deal to end fast with Britain's MI6

Hunger strike ends with no significant concessions; IRA leadership tries to disguise defeat

Northern Sinn Fein leaders win ban on standing in council elections

Father Reid suffers a nervous breakdown

Death toll for year is 86, cumulative toll is 2281

1981   Second jail hunger strike starts

IRA prison leader Bobby Sands elected MP for Fermanagh–South Tyrone

When Sands dies Owen Carron is elected in his place

Two IRA prisoners elected to the Dail in Dublin

Qaddafi resumes cash payments to IRA

Hunger strike ends with ten deaths

IRA prisoners condemn behavior of Catholic Church, SDLP and Irish government during the prison protest

Hunger strike support committees become new Sinn Fein branches

Sinn Fein adopts "Armalite and ballot box" strategy and agrees to contest elections

Army Council endorses the decision

Christin ni Elias escapes possible IRA assassination along with British diplomat

Death toll for year is 117, cumulative toll is 2398

1982   Army Council allows Adams and McGuinness to stand in elections to new NI Assembly but McGuinness forced to quit as chief of staff while Adams stands down as adjutant-general, the last time he holds rank in the IRA

Ivor Bell becomes new chief of staff

Christin ni Elias forced out of Sinn Fein

Sinn Fein wins ten percent of the vote in Assembly elections, causing political sensation

UDR Sergeant Cochrane kidnapped and killed by IRA in South Armagh; Father Reid intercedes for him with Adams and begins discussions that lead to the peace process

Sinn Fein rejects Eire Nua policy in major defeat for O Bradaigh–O Conaill faction; Army Council had already ditched it

New Sinn Fein leadership dominated by Adams camp

Death toll for year is 112, cumulative toll is 2510

1983   Gerry Adams elected MP for West Belfast, Sinn Fein tops 100,000 votes in British general election

Adams succeeds Ruairi O Bradaigh as president of Sinn Fein as old guard is vanquished

Ivor Bell forced to quit as chief of staff after arrest

Kevin McKenna succeeds him

Cardinal O Fiach and Bishop Edward Daly of Derry write Father Reid letters of comfort supporting his talks with Adams

Bishop Cahal Daly of Down and Connor rejects offer of participation in talks with Adams-Reid group

Major IRA jail escape: 38 inmates break out of Maze, formerly Long Kesh

Fall of Kevin Mallon over botched IRA kidnappings

Death toll for year is 87, cumulative toll is 2597

1984 Adams makes his correspondence with Cahal Daly public

Libyan embassy in London closed after policewoman shot dead

Libyan intelligence service negotiates arms and cash deal with IRA Army Council

Sinn Fein vote falls in Euro election

Rebellion against Adams leadership by Ivor Bell and Belfast Brigade staff over resources devoted to elections fails

Army Council plans Irish "Tet offensive"

Through intermediaries Adams floats possibility of IRA ceasefire

Adams calls for a pan-nationalist political initiative

IRA bomb Grand Hotel, Brighton, killing five people attending Conservative annual conference; Margaret Thatcher narrowly escapes death

Death toll for year is 72, cumulative toll is 2669

1985 Anglo-Irish Agreement signed; gives Dublin a consultative say in NI's affairs.

Michael McKevitt appointed QMG and Slab Murphy made director of operations to oversee Libyan operation

Martin McGuinness made Northern Commander

Sinn Fein vote drops again in local council elections

Casamara makes two trips from Libya carrying seventeen tons of weapons

Adams publicly seeks talks with SDLP leader John Hume; he also calls for a united nationalist approach to North

Death toll for year is 58, cumulative toll is 2727

1986 Father Reid first approaches Charles Haughey on behalf of Gerry Adams

Contact may also have been opened at this point with Tory NI secretary of state, Tom King

Correspondence between Adams and King leads to secret British offer of talks with Sinn Fein and on terms for IRA cease-fire

Secret British letter tells Adams that London has no interests in NI and offers new definition of British withdrawal

IRA lift ban on taking seats in the Dail at first General Army Convention held since 1970; Sinn Fein follow suit at Ard Fheis—number of delegates nearly doubles for this one meeting

Qaddafi's daughter killed in U.S. air raid launched from Britain

Kula ships 14 tons of guns from Libya

Villa ships 105 tons including Semtex explosives

Vetting of IRA operations by Northern Command intensifies

McGuinness secures authority to appoint Brigade and ASU OCs in North

McGuinness briefs IRA Executive and IRA field commanders about large arms shipments, saying more is on the way

Adams calls for public British declaration of no interests in NI

Death toll for year is 66, cumulative toll is 2793

1987   Charles Haughey becomes taoiseach after Fianna Fail returns to power

East Tyrone Brigade dissidents meet to discuss breaking away from IRA

Eksund trip is postponed when IRA learns Irish Army is expecting its arrival on east coast of country

Sinn Fein publish "Scenario for Peace," calling for all-Ireland constitutional conference in line with Reid–Adams proposal and replaces "Brits Out" with demand for national self-determination

Jim Lynagh, East Tyrone commander, disputes with IRA chief of staff over Northern Command knowledge of planned Loughgall ambush

East Tyrone IRA unit wiped out in SAS ambush at Loughgall

Within days Father Reid sends detailed IRA cease-fire offer from Adams to Haughey outlining proposal for pan-nationalist alliance and acceptance of principle of consent to Irish unity

Later Reid formulates the "concrete proposals" and "stepping stones" documents outlining pan-nationalist political alliance as alternative to IRA violence and a constitutional convention to discuss settlement

On urging of Adams and McGuinness, Army Council orders *Eksund* to set sail; other members advised sending a smaller shipment to test for informers—*Eksund* is intercepted off Brittany coast, betrayed by IRA informer

IRA's "Tet offensive" is drastically scaled down

Libyans cut off supplies of cash to IRA

MI6's Michael Oatley approaches IRA leadership

Enniskillen cenotaph bomb, approved by Northern Command, kills eleven Protestants

Haughey arranges for Hume to represent Irish government in talks with Adams

IRA color party at Bodenstown commemoration demilitarized

IRA ends practice of firing shots over members' coffins at IRA funerals

Death toll for year is 106, cumulative toll is 2899

1988   Army Council secretly softens terms for British withdrawal, saying it can take up to twenty years to happen

Adams tells Army Council of approach from Reid for talks with Haughey

Hume–Adams talk begin

SDLP–SF delegations meet and conclude with no agreement

Secret contacts between Hume and Adams resume immediately afterwards

IRA attempt to kill British Foreign Secretary Sir Geoffrey Howe in Brussels apparently betrayed

Gibraltar bombing ends with three IRA deaths amidst suspicion of betrayal

Republican leaders deny IRA cease-fire on the agenda of SDLP talks

Tom King suspends Reid–Adams dialogue in angry response to upsurge in IRA violence

Secret unionist–nationalist conference in Duisburg, Germany, attended by Father Reid

IRA adopt policy of targeting British military personnel as more acceptable to putative nationalist allies in Republic

Civilian deaths in IRA operations rise

IRA grassroots react badly to Sinn Fein leadership suggestions of alliance with SDLP

For first time police permission sought for Easter IRA parade in Belfast Sinn Fein use NI courts to complain of discriminatory treatment in councils

Sinn Fein members allowed to cooperate with Irish police over McAnespie Border killing by British army

Army Council lays down strict conditions for retaliations against loyalist groups

Death toll for year is 105, cumulative toll is 3004

1989   Sinn Fein criticism of botched IRA operations intensifies

Major IRA informer Joe Fenton killed before he can be fully interrogated

Peter Brooke succeeds Tom King as secretary of state and inherits Father Reid conduit to Adams

Brooke raises possibility of talks with Sinn Fein

IRA flying column attack at Derryard betrayed by informer

Grassroots IRA unease at Northern Command control increases

Death toll for year is 81, cumulative is 3085

1990   Adams threatens to quit IRA over civilian deaths and seeks separation of Sinn Fein and IRA

Revolutionary Council revived to curb IRA

Adams raises possibility of unannounced cease-fire

IRA dismisses speculation of an end to IRA violence

Brooke says Britain had "no selfish strategic or economic interest" in staying in NI

Northern Command secures Army Council permission to use "human bomb" tactic

MI5 officer John Deverill tells Brooke of new British linkman in secret talks with IRA

Danny Morrison arrested in Belfast

Martin McGuinness proposes formal Christmas cease-fire, the first official cessation since 1975

Army Council debates cease-fire amid claims it would need Convention approval

MI6 representative Michael Oatley holds talks with Army Council chairman, McGuinness

Death toll for year is 84, cumulative toll is 3169

1991 Massive criticism of "human bomb" attack in Derry intensifies secret contact between Martin McGuinness, Peace & Reconciliation Group and British aimed at de-escalating conflict in the city

Thatcher resigns as British prime minister

Sinn Fein says it will no longer speak for IRA

Haughey relaunches peace initiative with new British leader, John Major

First versions of joint government declaration on NI, otherwise known as Hume–Adams document, drafted

Death toll for year is 102, cumulative toll is 3271

1992 Adams loses West Belfast seat to SDLP after string of poor election performances by Sinn Fein

Haughey ousted, succeeded by Albert Reynolds, who backs process and keeps on Martin Mansergh as NI adviser

Sinn Fein publishes "Towards a Lasting Peace"

Hume–Adams document agreed but omits time period for British withdrawal

Death toll for year is 91, cumulative toll is 3362

1993 Hume–Adams contacts publicly revealed for first time

Sinn Fein's vote rises for first time in a decade

British send Army Council "Nine Pointer" insisting on "agreed accommodation"

Army Council reject "Nine Pointer"

Adams persuades Army Council not to end talks with British

Army Council replies to British with demand for withdrawal

Army Council begins to vet operations and bans commercial bombing

New drafts of Hume–Adams fail to bridge gap over Army Council demand for timescale for British withdrawal

Irish prime minister, Albert Reynolds, negotiates separate document with British, called Downing Street Declaration (DDS)

Shankill bomb kills nine Protestants and one IRA man

Adams carries coffin of Shankill bomber

Loyalist violence claims sixteen lives

Death toll for year is 90, cumulative toll is 3452

1994   Army Council rejects DSD

Adams persuades Council to hide decision and seek clarification

McGuinness says DSD worthless unless it has a hidden meaning

IRA and Sinn Fein grassroots assured of no cease-fire

IRA mini-Convention opposes cease-fire

Reynolds lifts Irish broadcasting ban on Sinn Fein

Bill Clinton grants Adams 48-hour visa for trip to New York

Think tank develops TUAS strategy offering cease-fire in return for pan-nationalist alliance

Reynolds send 14-point cease-fire proposal to Army Council

Army Council votes five to one with one abstention for four-month cease-fire

British make working assumption cease-fire is permanent; Border roads reopened, broadcasting ban lifted

Army Council disowns South Armagh post office robbery

British raise IRA decommissioning demand and NI Secretary Sir Patrick Mayhew outlines, "Washington Three" demands

McGuinness says he would accept less than Irish unity if this was will of Irish people

Army Council extends cease-fire until April 1995

Death toll for year is 69, cumulative toll is 3521

1995   Adams would accept Stormont Assembly if "transitional" to Irish unity

"Frameworks" document foresees power-sharing government and North–South bodies

West Belfast Westminster seat redrawn to favor Adams re-election chances

Republican grassroots assured cease-fire is temporary

British harden demand for IRA decommissioning before Sinn Fein gets into talks

Clinton gives Adams visa to raise funds in United States

Reynolds government falls, replaced by anti-Sinn Fein Rainbow Coalition

British propose political talks and decommissioning body in tandem

Fifty percent remission restored to IRA prisoners

IRA statement says "no possibility of disarmament except as part of a negotiated settlement"

First British troop withdrawals

Adams tells republican demonstration that IRA hasn't gone away

Senator George Mitchell to head decommissioning body

DAAD killings a cover for IRA

Sinn Fein make submission to Mitchell body

McGuinness suggests voluntary self-decommissioning

IRA calls decommissioning issue "a deliberate and stalling tactic" by British, saying demand is "ludicrous" and adding that it would not happen "either through the front or back doors"

Friends of Sinn Fein set up in United States as Noraid is downgraded

IRA calls demand for decommissioning "untenable and unattainable demand for an IRA surrender"

Death toll for year is 9, cumulative toll is 3530

1996   IRA Executive calls for extraordinary IRA Convention to discuss peace process

Army Council votes seven to nil to end cease-fire

Senator Mitchell publishes six principles of non-violence to govern political talks

Huge truck bomb kills two and causes 100 million damage at Canary Wharf, London

IRA campaign confined to England

Election to negotiating body see Sinn Fein win highest vote ever as nationalists try to strengthen Adams's hand

On eve of delayed Convention car bombs exploded inside British army's NI HQ, killing one

Adams survives Convention when dissidents fail to capture Army Council but suffers setbacks

Power to decommission taken away from Army Council and given to Convention

McGuinness tells Convention there will be no second cease-fire

Brian Keenan deserts dissidents at Convention and backs Adams

Death toll for year is 22, cumulative toll is 3552

1997   McGuinness steps down as Northern Commander but retains Army Council chairmanship

IRA ordered to concentrate on British military targets, commercial bombings again banned

Adams writes letter of condolence to mother of British soldier killed by South Armagh IRA sniper squad

South Armagh sniper squad arrested

British general election called

Army Council authorizes "tactical period of quiet" for election but doesn't tell Executive

Tony Blair wins huge majority as New Labour forms new British government

McGuinness wins Mid-Ulster seat

British *aide-mémoire* sets out terms for new IRA cease-fire

Political talks and IRA decommissioning to happen in parallel

IRA mini-Convention rejects *aide-mémoire*

McGuinness tells Executive there will be no second cease-fire

Fianna Fail wins election in Republic; Bertie Ahern becomes taoiseach

Ahern government sets out terms for new cease-fire

Four days before controversial Garvaghy Orange march Army Council votes seven to nil for second cease-fire; decision kept secret for several weeks

March forced through Catholic area

IRA Executive and Army Council clash over cease-fire decision

In a row over the Mitchell principles the Executive suggests Adams et al. should quit IRA to enable Sinn Fein participation political talks

Dissidents defeated at Convention

Belfast Brigade commander Brian Gillen switches sides to back Adams and wins Army Council seat

Kevin McKenna loses job as chief of staff, Slab Murphy takes over

Executive members, led by QMG Micky McKevitt, quit IRA

Real IRA formed

All-party talks start at Stormont; Sinn Fein attend and subscribe to Mitchell principles

Death toll for year is 21, cumulative toll 3573

1998   Good Friday Agreement negotiated

Pope welcomes agreement

IRA Convention lifts abstentionist ban on taking seats in Stormont Assembly

After two attempts, Sinn Fein Ard-Fheis endorses Good Friday Agreement and lifts abstentionist ban on taking seats at Stormont

IRA prison OC floats idea of voluntary self-decommissioning once Good Friday Agreement is implemented

Botched dissident republican bomb kills 29 at Omagh; bombing is a joint

Real IRA, Continuity IRA and INLA operation but Real IRA gets blame

Death toll for year is 57, cumulative toll is 3630

1999   Second IRA Convention in twelve months restores Army Council's power to decommission

Army Council agrees to locate the bodies of "disappeared"

Eamon Molloy's body returned but not Jean McConville's

IRA appoints a representative, believed to be Brian Keenan, to discuss decommissioning with de Chastelain international body

Power-sharing government set up; Martin McGuinness and Bairbre de Brun are the two Sinn Fein ministers

Death toll for year is 6, cumulative toll is 3636*

2000   IRA says that any move on decommissioning dependent on British military reductions

Peter Mandelson, NI Secretary, suspends Assembly and Army Council executive agrees in principle to initiate a process to put all its weapons "beyond use" and in the interim to international inspection of two arms dumps

British lift suspension of Assembly and Executive

Last IRA and loyalist paramilitary prisoners released

Revd William McCrea of the DUP wins the East Antrim by-election, normally a safe Ulster Unionist seat

Death toll for year is 19, cumulative toll is 3655

---

* Fatality figures up to this date are taken from David McKittrick et al., *Lost Lives* (Edinburgh, Mainstream Publishing, 1999).

2001
  Sinn Fein win two more Westminster seats, Michelle Gildemew in Fermanagh–South Tyrone and Pat Doherty in West Tyrone, giving it four seats to the SDLP's three

  Unionist leader David Trimble resigns as first minister

  Weston Park Conference reaches agreement on decommissioning deal and British demilitarization

  IRA agrees with IICD on method to decommission IRA weapons

  British begin rolling suspension of Assembly

  Three republicans, including GHQ director of engineering, his deputy and Sinn Fein representative to Cuba arrested in Colombia

  IRA withdraws decommissioning proposals

  September 11 attacks in New York and Washington kill nearly 3,000; Bush administration declares war on terrorism

  President George Bush's ambassador to the Irish peace process, Richard Haass, tells Adams and McGuinness that IRA needs to decommission

  IRA decommissions unspecified amount of weaponry

  Police Service of Northern Ireland (PSNI) replaces RUC

  Assembly and Executive restored; Trimble is first minister, Mark Durkan of the SDLP is his deputy

  Sinn Fein accepts office facilities and financial expenses at House of Commons

  Death toll for year is 16, cumulative toll is 3671

2002
  Sinn Fein's four MPs occupy their offices at Westminster but still refuse to take their seats

  Adams tells World Economic Forum in New York that he does not wish to force unionists into a united Ireland against their wishes

  Adams states that he recognizes the Irish Defence Forces as the only legitimate army in the Irish Republic

  Offices of PSNI Special Branch at Castlereagh in East Belfast broken into and files removed; IRA is suspected

  Second act of decommissioning by IRA

  Sinn Fein win five seats to Irish parliament

  Trimble threatens to quit if IRA does not show it has left violence behind for good

IRA spy ring at government offices in Stormont complex uncovered; Sinn Fein Assembly office raided and three charged, including Denis Donaldson, the party's head of administration

Assembly and Executive suspended by NI Secretary John Reid

Death toll for year is 10, cumulative toll is 3681

2003 Blair and Ahern announce delay in holding scheduled May Assembly election

On eve of U.S. occupation of Baghdad, Blair and Bush address parties at Hillsborough Castle on need for peace

Assembly election postponed until autumn over failure to clarify peace deal

IRA says full implementation of Good Friday Agreement could allow for completion of decommissioning

Freddie Scappaticci, former head of IRA's internal security unit, exposed as a British agent

Real IRA leader Michael McKevitt sentenced to twenty-year jail term

Remains of Jean McConville discovered on County Down beach

Independent Monitoring Commission (IMC) begins job of overseeing paramilitary cease-fires

Deal to restore Assembly and Executive collapses over lack of transparency in third act of IRA decommissioning

Postponed Assembly election takes place with Sinn Fein and DUP emerging as largest parties

Death toll for year is 11, cumulative toll is 3692

2004 DUP leader Ian Paisley meets Irish taoiseach in London

Republican dissident Bobby Tohill kidnapped by IRA but rescued by PSNI

Adams denies on Irish TV that he was ever an IRA member

Irish justice minister Michael McDowell alleges Sinn Fein funded by IRA

IMC says senior Sinn Fein members also in IRA

Sinn Fein's Bairbre de Brun wins John Hume's seat in European parliament

Joe Cahill dies

Talks aimed at reaching a settlement begin at Leeds Castle, Kent

Political talks founder over demand for photographs of IRA

decommissioning; Paisley says IRA must wear "sackcloth and ashes"

£26.5 million stolen from Northern Bank cash center in Belfast

Death toll for year is 3, cumulative toll is 3695

2005   Irish taoiseach Bertie Ahern says Sinn Fein leaders knew of planned Northern Bank robbery while they were in peace talks with him

IRA denies involvement in robbery

Belfast man Robert McCartney beaten and stabbed to death by IRA gang

IMC says leading Sinn Fein figures also serve in key IRA leadership positions

McCartney sisters accuse Sinn Fein and IRA members of involvement in brother's murder and subsequent cover-up

Seven people arrested in Republic in hunt for Northern Bank cash

Former IRA prison public relations officer, Richard O'Rawe, publishes account of hunger strike, alleging IRA leadership sabotaged deal to ensure election of Owen Carron

White House decides not to invite NI politicians to St. Patrick's Day celebrations, in snub of Sinn Fein leader Gerry Adams

Leading Irish-American politicians call for IRA disbandment as McCartney sisters meet President Bush

Adams calls on IRA to pursue goal through only political means

Sinn Fein win extra seat at Westminster election but fail to capture John Hume's Foyle seat

Gerry Adams and Martin McGuinness, along with North Kerry TD

Martin Ferris, officially quit Army Council

IRA statement announces end to armed campaign against Britain; IRA ex-prisoner Seanna Walsh reads statement on DVD

IRA completes weapons decommissioning, witnessed by two clerics

Anti-racketeering agencies raid Manchester businesses linked to IRA chief of staff "Slab" Murphy

After charges in Stormont spy ring are dropped, Denis Donaldson admits he has been a long-term British agent

Death toll for year is 8, cumulative toll is 3703

2006 Anti-racketeering agencies raid Slab Murphy's farm on Louth–Armagh border and confiscate cash

Denis Donaldson shot dead at isolated County Donegal cottage

IMC says no IRA activity in last three months

British and Irish governments restore Assembly and set November 24 deadline for final deal

Adams and McGuinness urge alleged kidnappers of Bobby Tohill to surrender to police

One of three new Army Council members quits in protest at fact that Adams and McGuinness still directing IRA policy

Adams nominates Paisley as first minister; he refuses

Conference at St. Andrews, Scotland, agrees outline deal for restoration of Assembly and Executive—Sinn Fein to recognize PSNI

Special Sinn Fein Ard Fheis called to approve St. Andrews deal and recognition of PSNI

Death toll (to October 12) is 6, cumulative toll is 3709*

* Fatality figures from 2000 to 2006 are taken or extrapolated from CAIN web service, <http://cain.ulst.ac.uk/index.html>

Dramatis Personae

Adams, Annie   Mother of Gerry Adams. A former member of the IRA's women's branch, the Cumann na mBan.

Adams, Gerry   Leader of the IRA's political wing Sinn Fein, a member of the IRA's Army Council since 1977, a former chief of staff, adjutant-general and Northern commander. He constructed the peace process in great secrecy.

Adams Sr., Gerry   Gerry Adams' father. He was shot by the RUC and imprisoned in 1942 while on an IRA operation.

Ahern, Bertie   Fianna Fail prime minister from 1997 onward. His election ensured Adams a sympathetic hearing in Dublin and he helped to negotiate the terms for the second cease-fire.

Ashour, Nasser   Senior officer in the Libyan Intelligence Service. He traveled to Ireland secretly to negotiate Quaddaffi arms deal with the IRA Army Council.

Bell, Ivor   A former Belfast commander and chief of staff of the IRA he was once Adams's closest political ally but fell out bitterly over the strategy of fighting elections in the mid-1980s.

Blair, Tony   New Labour prime minister in Britain. After his election in May 1997 he quickly recognized the direction being taken by Adams and softened terms for a second cease-fire. Helped negotiate the Good Friday Agreement but unionists saw him as soft on IRA disarming.

Brooke, Peter Inheritor of the Reid pipeline from Tom King. He made public part of the secret offer to the IRA by pledging British neutrality on the terms of a final settlement.

Bruton, John Garret FitzGerald's successor as leader of Fine Gael and bitterly anti-Provisional IRA, he succeeded Albert Reynolds as taoiseach. His hardline attitude to IRA disarming contributed significantly to the breakdown of the cease-fire in 1996.

Bryson, Jim Along with fellow Ballymurphy men, Gerry Adams's brother-in-law, Paddy Mulvenna and Tommy "Toddler" Tolan, Bryson made up the fearsome trio which helped make the Second Batallion in Belfast, which Adams commanded, one of the toughest IRA units in the city.

Burns, Harry Related by marriage to Gerry Adams. His friendship with Joe Fenton gave the British an invaluable insight into the movement of IRA weapons.

Burns, Ian Northern Ireland Office deputy under-secretary of State. Second most important British official during the 1980s, he transmitted Father Reid's messages to the politicians.

Bush, George W. Succeeded Bill Clinton as U.S. president in 2001 and immediately downgraded the Irish peace process, returning responsibility first to the state department and then outside it; took a tougher line on IRA intentions than Clinton.

Cahill, Joe IRA veteran from the 1940s, a former Belfast commander and IRA chief of staff whose vote swung the 1994 cease-fire decision. Strong Adams supporter. Died in 2004.

Carron, Owen Sands' election agent and his succeedor as Fermanagh–South Tyrone MP. His election was crucial in Adams's bid to win Sinn Fein to an electoral strategy.

Chichester-Clark, James	Successor to Terence O'Neill, his cousin, as unionist prime minister in 1969. He was in office during the early years of the rise of the Provisional IRA.
Cleary, Gabriel	The IRA's director of engineering—was on board the *Eksund* loaded with Libyan weapons in 1987 and discovered that the expedition had been betrayed by an informer.
Clinton, Bill	U.S. president from 1992 to 2000; his decision to give Adams a visa to visit New York in early 1994 enraged the British but obliged Adams to deliver the cease-fire later that year.
Cochrane, Thomas	Protestant member of the Ulster Defence Regiment. His kidnapping and killing in 1982 persuaded Father Alec Reid to open contacts with Gerry Adams and marks the start of the Irish peace process.
Collins, Michael	The IRA's director of organisation and head of intelligence during the Anglo-Irish war of 1919–21, he led the Irish team that agreed the Treaty which gave Ireland partial independence. Gerry Adams compared his own counter-intelligence operations in the early 1970s to those devised by Collins.
Connolly, James	Socialist republican leader of the 1916 Rising. He inspired left-wing republicans but was initially disowned by the Provisionals until Adams invoked his memory during his own move to the left.
Connolly, Niall	Sinn Fein's representative in Cuba. Arrested in Colombia in August 2001 and later named as the contact man with FARC guerillas in a cocaine cash-for-arms training deal with the IRA.
Coogan, Tim Pat	Former editor of the newspaper *Irish Press*. He delivered Father Reid's secret offer of an IRA cease-fire to Charles Haughey in May 1987.

Daly, Cahal	Bishop of Down and Connor, and later cardinal. He rejected efforts by Adams and Reid to back the infant peace process in 1984.
Daly, Edward	Catholic Bishop of Derry. Strongly anti-IRA he nevertheless gave Father Reid a letter of support for his diplomacy with Adams.
Davison, Gerard Jock	Leader of IRA gang accused of knifing Robert McCartney to death.
de Chastelain, General John	Canadian-born chairman of the international decommissioning body that oversaw the destruction of IRA weapons from October 2001 to September 2005.
de Valera, Eamon	A leader of the 1916 Easter Rising in Dublin. He broke with Collins over the 1921 Treaty but after defeat in civil war accepted it and entered constitutional politics. He founded Fianna Fail from the remnants of the beaten IRA and later became president of Ireland.
Deverill, John	The point man for Britain's internal intelligence agency, MI5, in Northern Ireland during many of the peace process years.
Devlin-McAliskey, Bernadette	An early student civil rights leader and Westminster MP. Her strategy of contesting elections was at first bitterly opposed but then enthusiastically imitated by Gerry Adams.
Doherty, Pat	Sinn Fein MP for West Tyrone. A longtime Adams ally, his job was to organize IRA Conventions and other secret meetings.
Donaldson, Denis	Sinn Fein head of administration and member of GHQ IRA intelligence unit. Arrested after the discovery of a spy ring at Stormont. In 2005 he admitted being a long-time British agent. Shot dead in County Donegal in April 2006.
Drumm, Jimmy	IRA veteran who backed anti-Adams elements in the mid-1970s but switched sides when Adams emerged victorious following arguments over the 1975 cease-fire.

Durkan, Mark

Former assistant to John Hume, who took over as SDLP leader in 2001.

Elliott, Mark

British Foreign Office official who headed the London side of the Anglo-Irish secretariat after 1985. His diplomacy in Derry was so secret that his reports to his political masters were written in his own hand.

Faulkner, Brian

Successor to Chichester-Clark. He is remembered for two things: for introducing internment in 1971, which boosted the IRA's fortunes, and for negotiating the 1974 power-sharing Sunningdale deal of 1974, which set the precedent for the Good Friday Agreement.

Fenton, Joe

From West Belfast, possibly the most important informers ever to work for the British. His speedy execution by the IRA in Belfast led many to suspect a high level cover-up.

Finucane, Pat

Belfast lawyer assassinated by UDA in 1989. British security forces knew of the plot to kill him but did nothing.

Fitt, Gerry

A founder member and, for ten years, the leader of the SDLP. He preceded Adams as West Belfast MP. The 1981 hunger strikes effectively ended his political career and paved the way for Adams.

Fitzgerald, Garret

Fiercely anti-Provisional IRA prime minister, or taoiseach in the Irish Republic in the mid-1980s. The leader of Michael Collins's political successors, Fine Gael, he negotiated the 1985 Anglo-Irish Agreement, which threatened to isolate Sinn Fein.

Flynn, Bill

New York-based insurance mogul who eased the way for Gerry Adams in the U.S., especially with the Clinton White House.

Gibney, Jim

East Belfast IRA officer who rose to be a key think tank member. He also floated controversial ideas on behalf of Adams.

Gillen, Brian

Belfast commander of the IRA until 1997. He initially supported the IRA dissidents but unexpectedly backed Adams at the 1997 Convention; he was rewarded with a seat on the Army Council.

Gillespie, Patsy
Derry-based Catholic who was forced to deliver the first IRA "human bomb" to a British army base in October 1990. His death facilitated secret talks aimed at securing an experimental IRA de-escalation in Derry.

Good, Reverend Harold
Methodist minister and witness, along with Father Alec Reid, of September 2005 final IRA decommissioning.

Goulding, Cathal
IRA chief of staff at the time of the split with the Provisionals in 1969. His left-wing politics were much admired by the young Gerry Adams.

Haass, Richard
President Bush's ambassador to the Irish peace process.

Hannaway, Alfie
An uncle of Gerry Adams. He ran the IRAs youth wing, the Fianna na hEireann, and was a close friend of the Redemptorist priests of Clonard.

Hannaway, Kevin
Gerry Adams's cousin. He was IRA quartermaster general when the Libyan arms deal was struck.

Hannaway, Liam
Gerry Adams's uncle and an early Provisional IRA leader.

Hartley, Tom
An important member of Adams's think tank who kited controversial ideas on behalf of the Sinn Fein leader.

Haughey, Charles
Leader of Fianna Fail and Irish prime minister from 1987 to 1992. He was the figure to whom Adams communicated a secret offer of an IRA cease-fire. His decision to talk to Adams via Father Reid made the peace process possible. He died in 2006.

Hegarty, Frank
Member of the IRA quartermaster's department. He betrayed a consignment of Libyan-supplied weapons. His treachery prompted a bitter dispute between Martin McGuinness and

Kevin McKenna over who had allowed Hegarty into the IRA.

Hopkins, Adrian   Captain of the *Eksund*. Wrongly of betraying the 1987 operation, he had successfully smuggled many tons of Libyan arms to the IRA in the previous two years.

Howell, Ted   Highly secretive chairman of Adams's think tank, which effectively controlled and directed the negotiations leading to the 1994 and 1997 IRA cease-fires.

Hughes, Brendan   Former Belfast commander of the IRA. He led the first unsuccessful hunger strike of 1980. A close friend and ally of Adams, he broke with him over the peace process.

Hume, John   The brooding leader of the Social Democratic and Labour Party, the Provisionals' principal opponents. He acted as Charles Haughey's surrogate in secret talks with Adams, which eventually helped create the 1994 IRA cease-fire. He retired as SDLP leader in 2001.

Johnston, Roy   A computer scientist and left-wing activist. He worked along with, Trinity College, Dublin lecturer, Anthony Coughlan, and Cathal Goulding to move the IRA to the left in the 1960s

Keenan, Brian   Known in the IRA as "the Dog," he had a hawkish image belied by his constant and unquestioning support for Adams. His duplicity assisted Adams in defeating a challenge from IRA dissidents after the 1994 cease-fire

Kelly, Gerry   From Ballymurphy, a participant in the first IRA bombing mission to London, organized by Belfast Brigade. After many years in jail in Britain and Ireland, he became IRA adjutant-general during the formative years of the peace process. His hard-line reputation helped win skeptics over to the Adams strategy

Kennedy-Smith, Jean   Sister of Senator Ted Kennedy. Her role in the Irish peace process reached a climax when in August 1994 she persuaded Clinton to give Joe

Mansergh, Martin   Haughey's Northern Ireland adviser. Trusted by Reid and Adams, he was kept on by Reynolds and then by Bertie Ahern because of his unrivalled knowledge of the peace process's secrets.

Mason, Roy   Tough and abrasive British secretary of state in the late 1970s. He very nearly defeated the IRA with a combination of tough interrogation methods and the criminalizing of IRA prisoners.

Mayhew, Sir Patrick   British secretary of state at the time of the first IRA cease-fire of 1994.

McArdle, Colette   Gerry Adams's wife. She came from an active republican background but her activism ceased after her marriage.

McAteer, Aidan   Son of a former IRA chief of staff and longtime Adams aide-de-campe. He often represented Adams' interests in negotiations with the Irish government and loyalists.

McCartney, Robert   East Belfast man stabbed to death by IRA gang after a row in a bar. His sisters accused Sinn Fein and the IRA of covering up his murder and led campaign to have his killers charged. Invited to the White House in March 2005.

McConville, Jean   A low level British army agent who was also shot dead and secretly disappeared by "the unknowns" on the orders of the Belfast Brigade in December 1972. A Protestant who had married a Falls Road Catholic, she was a mother of ten small children when she was abducted from her apartment in the Divis Flats complex in December 1972. Her body was recovered in 2003.

McDowell, Michael   Irish justice minister, deputy prime minister (tanaiste) and Progressive Democrats leader. An acerbic critic of the Provisionals, he named Adams and McGuinness as IRA Army Council members after the Northern Bank robbery.

McFarlane, Brendan "Bik"   Commander of IRA prisoners during the 1981 hunger strikes.

McGrane, Seamus   County Louth-based Chairman of the IRA

Executive that tried but failed to overthrow Adams in 1997.

McGuinness, Frank

IRA director of engineering and Executive member. A dissident leader, his absence from the 1996 Convention ensured Adams's survival.

McGuinness, Martin

A former chief of staff from Derry he was chairman of the Army Council and the IRA's Northern commander during many of the peace process years. A close colleague of Adams, he had a hard-line record that persuaded many IRA doubters to back the peace strategy.

McKee, Billy

The Provisional IRA's first Belfast commander. He and Adams were bitter enemies.

McKenna Kevin

The longest serving IRA chief of staff, from 1982 until 1997. His credibility was undermined after the 1994 cease-fire, and eventually he lost the confidence of the rank and file and was replaced by "Slab" Murphy.

McKevitt Micky

IRA quartermaster general who masterminded the Libyan arms-smuggling operation. He led the revolt against the Adams strategy and when he lost went on to help form the Real IRA. He was sentenced to 20 years in jail in 2003.

McLaughlin, Mitchel

A key member of the Adams think tank and an avid supporter of the peace process strategy, McLaughlin was despised by IRA members for his criticism of botched military operations.

Mitchell, George

Former U.S. Senate Democrat leader. He formulated the rules for IRA decommissioning and set out the six principles of nonviolence that precipitated a split in the IRA.

Molloy, Eamon

The IRA's Belfast quartermaster in 1974. His treachery paved the way for the 1975 cease-fire which catapulted Adams into the republican leadership. He was shot dead and "disappeared."

Molyneaux, James

Leader of the Ulster Unionist Party during the crucial years of the peace process.

Monaghan, James

IRA director of engineering, arrested in

Colombia in August 2001 along with his deputy, Martin McAuley.

Morley, David

Newry-born IRA commander in the Long Kesh prison camp in the mid-1970s. He became the main target for Adams's supporters in the camp's Cage 11 who were opposed to the 1975 cease-fire.

Morrison, Danny

Key member of Adams's think tank. An early editor of *Republican News*, Morrison became IRA publicity director and is famous for first using the "Armalite and ballot box" slogan.

Mountbatten, Lord Louis

The most celebrated of IRA victims, killed in an IRA bomb attack on his vacation boat in County Sligo in August 1979. His death, followed by the killing of 18 British soldiers in an expert ambush on the Border near Carlingford Lough later the same day, was viewed by IRA members as a vindication of Adams' plan to revitalize the IRA.

Mowlam, Mo

Tony Blair's secretary of state. She helped negotiate the 1997 cease-fire and the 1998 Good Friday Agreement. She died in 2005.

Murphy, Tom "Slab"

IRA chief of staff from 1997 on. A former Northern commander and director of IRA operations from South Armagh border, he helped organize the Libyan shipments. He was a wealthy cross-border businessman who had no time for politics, but his support for Adams proved to be crucial.

Nelson, Brian

Ulster Defence Association intelligence chief and British army agent. Information from him saved Adams from UDA assassination in 1998.

ni Elias, Christin

Mysterious supporter of the O Bradaigh–O Conaill faction and bitter adversary of Adams. She may have been targeted for assasination by the IRA in a sting operation.

Oatley, Michael

Senior officer in the British secret intelligence service (MI6). He dealt indirectly and directly with Army Council figures from the mid-1970s on.

O Bradaigh, Ruairi	Chief of staff of the IRA at the end of the 1956–62 campaign and later president of Sinn Fein. His political defeat at the hands of Adams cleared the way for the peace process.
O Conaill, Daithi	An IRA veteran from County Cork who had fought in the Border Campaign of 1956–62 and became one of Adams's chief political opponents. He died in 1991.
O Fiaich, Tomas	The Crossmaglen-born primate of all Ireland was the first to give support to Alec Reid and secured approval for the enterprise in the Vatican.
O'Hare, Gerry	A native from West Belfast, whose removal as editor of the Dublin IRA paper *An Phoblacht* signaled the start of Adams's campaign to capture the Provisional leadership.
O'Neill, Terence	Reforming but patrician unionist prime minister in Northern Ireland when the Troubles broke out in 1968–69.
O'Rawe, Richard	IRA prison public relations officer during 1981 hunger strike. His 2005 account of the protest alleged that a deal to end the protest was sabotaged so as to advance Sinn Fein's electoral strategy.
Paisley, Ian	Protestant leader whose agitation paved the way for the birth and growth of the Provisional IRA. After the fall of David Trimble, he led unionist negotiations with the Provisionals about power-sharing.
Pearse, Patrick	A leader of the secret Irish Republican Brotherhood (IRB) whose poetic oratory inspired the 1916 Rising.
Powell, Jonathan	Tony Blair's chief of staff. He handled most of the minutiae of negotiations with Sinn Fein and the IRA.
Price, Marion	Along with her sister Dolours, she formed the core of the 1973 bombing team sent to London by the Belfast Brigade. Adams ignored evidence that an informer had betrayed the operation. Like Brendan Hughes, the two Price sisters

eventually accused Adams of betraying the IRA's struggle.

Qaddafi, Muammar

Libyan leader who supplied the IRA with weapons and cash from 1972 on.

Reid, Alec

The County Tipperary-born, West Belfast-based Redemptorist priest is the unsung hero of the Irish peace process. His secret diplomacy with Adams and the British and Irish governments laid the theological basis for the peace process.

Reiss, Mitchell

Bush admistration ambassador to the peace process after 2003. He took a touch line with the Provos over decommissioning and recognition of policing.

Reynolds, Albert

Haughey's successor as taoiseach. He enthusiastically backed the peace process when he learned of Haughey's diplomacy with Adams.

Sands, Bernadette

Sister of the dead IRA hunger striker Bobby Sands and wife of the dissident leader Micky McKevitt.

Sands, Bobby

Leader of IRA prisoners in the Long Kesh/Maze prison. He was the first to die during the 1981 hunger strikes. An IRA icon, his election as MP for Fermanagh–South Tyrone paved the way, indirectly, for the peace process.

Scappaticci, Freddie

Former head of IRA's internal "spycatcher" unit. Outed as a British army agent, codename "Steaknife", in 2003.

Spring, Dick

Irish deputy prime minister, or tanaiste, during the Reynolds and John Bruton governments.

Storey, Bobby

IRA director of intelligence. Organized the 2004 Northern Bank raid and a spy ring inside British government offices in 2002. Close ally of Adams.

Thatcher, Margaret

An avowed and bitter enemy of the IRA, the former British prime minister nevertheless sanctioned secret talks with Adams in 1986–87.

Tone, Wolfe

The founder of modern Irish republicanism. He inspired the 1798 United Irishmen rebellion composed of Protestant radicals roused by the writings of Tom Paine and the French

Revolution and the anti-Orange, Catholic Defender Movement, from which the Provisionals trace their origin.

Trimble, David
Ulster unionist leader who backed the Good Friday Agreement, gambling that Adams was making a huge compromise. His failure to secure transparent IRA decommissioning led to his political downfall. He quit as unionist leader in 2005 after losing his Westminster seat to a DUP candidate.

Twomey, Seamus
A former Belfast commander and chief of staff who was dominated by Adams.

Walsh, Seanna
Former IRA prisoner. Read out IRA Army Council statement of July 2005 announcing end to the armed campaign against Britain.

Ward, Chris
Northern Bank official kidnapped along with a colleague, Kevin McMullan. Forced to assist IRA robbery of the bank's cash centre.

Whitelaw, William
The first British secretary of state for Northern Ireland after the imposition of direct rule from London. He met the IRA leadership, including Adams, during secret cease-fire talks in 1972.

William of Orange
A Protestant member of the Dutch royal family who came to Britain at the invitation of the London parliament to oppose the ambitions of Catholic King James II. His victory over the Stuart pretender in the siege of Derry and then at the Battle of the Boyne in 1690 led Irish Protestants to establish the Orange Order to perpetuate their ascendancy.

Wright, Seamus
An IRA double agent who worked for a secret arm of British military intelligence known as the MRF. His confession to the IRA made Adams's name as a counterintelligence expert. Along with another IRA traitor, Kevin McKee, he was killed and secretly buried by "the unknowns."

Glossary of Terms and Abbreviations

Abstentionism   Traditional republican refusal to take seats in or recognize the legitimacy of the Dublin, London, and Belfast parliaments.

AG   Adjutant-general; deputy chief of staff of the IRA; in charge of internal discipline.

AK-47   Romanian-made version of the Kalashnikov automatic rifle smuggled in large numbers to the IRA from Libya in mid and late 1980s.

Alliance Party   Cross-community political party, middle-of-the-road and mostly middle-class.

Apprentice Boys of Derry   Protestant society dedicated to celebrating the Williamite victory over James II at the siege of Derry in 1688.

AP-RN   *An Phoblacht–Republican News*. Weekly newspaper of the Provisional republican movement. Result of a merger of Southern and Northern papers which signaled Adams takeover. Editorial policy effectively decided by IRA leadership.

Ard Comhairle (*ard corlya*)   Ruling Executive of Sinn Fein, the IRA's political wing.

Ard Fheis (*ard esh*)   Annual conference of Sinn Fein. Plural is Ard-Fheiseanna.

Armalite   U.S. automatic and semiautomatic rifle first used by the IRA in early 1970s.

Army Council   Seven-person committee which decides IRA policy.

articles 2 and 3   Constitutional embodiment of the Republic of Ireland's claim to Northern Ireland. Significantly softend under terms of the 1998 Good Friday Agreement.

ASU	IRA Active Service Unit.
Ballymurphy	Sprawling Catholic housing estate in West Belfast where Gerry Adams grew up.
Barrett Light 50	U.S.-made sniping rifle, highly accurate and deadly. Fired a .50 inch slug. Favored by the IRA in South Armagh.
BB	Belfast Brigade of the IRA.
BBC	British Broadcasting Corporation.
black stuff	IRA nickname for home-made explosives.
Bloody Friday	Name given to July 21, 1972, when twenty IRA car bombs exploded in Belfast, killing seven people.
Bloody Sunday	Name given to January 30, 1972 when British para-troopers shot dead fourteen civil rights marchers in Derry.
Bodenstown	The cemetery in County Kildare, west of Dublin, where Wolfe Tone, the eighteenth century founder of Irish republicanism is buried. The annual commemoration in June is the occasion for the IRA leadership to promulgate policy.
Bogside	Catholic ghetto of Derry where the Provisional IRA leader Martin McGuinness was born.
Brit	IRA term for member of the British Army or Government.
Brownie	Pen-name used by Gerry Adams for articles he wrote in Cage 11 AP-RN.
Cage 11	The prison hut in the internment camp outside Belfast where Adams and his allies were held in the mid-1970s. Became shorthand for Adams supporters and their plan to revitalize and take over the IRA.
chairman of the Army Council	Member of the Army Council chosen to represent the IRA in negotiations.
chief of staff	The IRA's military commander.
CIA	Central Intelligence Agency.
Clonard	Nationalist section of mid-Falls Road area in west Belfast, home of the Redemptorist Monastery. Loyalist efforts to burn the area in 1969 led to the birth of the Provisional IRA.
"concrete proposal"	Adams–Reid strategy of pan-nationalism proposed to Irish government in 1986–87.

Connolly Association	British-based Marxist and Irish republican discussion group in 1960s.
cumann/cumainn	Irish word for "group" or "branch", usually in politics.
Cumann na mBan (*cuman naman*)	The IRA's women's wing, now scrapped and integrated into the main organization.
DAAD	Direct Action Against Drugs. Front for IRA, especially during 1994–96 cease-fire.
Dail Eireann (*doyle eran*)	The Irish parliament in Dublin, known to hard-line republicans as Leinster House.
D Coy	Legendary IRA company of the Second Belfast Battalion, formed in the lower Falls Road area. Known in IRA slang as "the Dogs."
Defenders	Catholic defence organization established in late eighteenth century in response to violence of Protestant groups like the Peep O'Day Boys.
DSD	Downing Street Declaration, of December 1993.
DUP	Democratic Unionist Party, founded and led by the Reverend Ian Paisley. Opposes the Good Friday Agreement but takes ministerial posts nevertheless.
Dushkie	Soviet-made DHSK heavy machine gun supplied to the IRA by Libya. It proved far too heavy for the IRA to use, and its gunbelt was too small.
Easter Proclamation	Declaration of Irish independence signed by the leader of the Easter Rising.
Easter Rising	Mostly Dublin-based rebellion of the Irish Volunteers in 1916. Secretly planned and fomented by the IRB leadership.
EGAC	Extraordinary IRA Convention, which only delegates from previous Convention can attend.
Eire Nua (*erah nua*)	New Ireland programme for a federal Ireland proposed by early Provisional IRA leaders.
electoralism	Policy of standing regularly in elections.
EO	Explosives officer.
Executive	Thirteen-person body, elected at Convention which chooses the Army Council.
FBI	Federal Bureau of Investigation, charged with monitoring IRA activities in the United States.
na Fianna Eireann (*na feena eran*)	The IRA's boy scouts, disbanded in late 1970s.

Fianna Fail (*feena foyle*)	The party set up by Eamon de Valera after he broke with the IRA in 1926.
Fine Gael (*finner gail*)	Political descendants of Michael Collins and the Sinn Fein members who supported the 1921 Treaty.
First Dail	Name given to Irish MPs elected in 1919 who refused to sit at Westminster and set up a rival and rebel parliament in Dublin.
flying column	Name given to large, fast-moving IRA force operating mostly in the countryside.
FoSF	Friends of Sinn Fein. Set up during the peace process to raise money for Sinn Fein in the United States.
Free State	Contemptuous term given by republicans to the Southern, twenty-six county state. Taken from its official name in 1922, the Irish Free State.
FRU	Force Research Unit. Agent running section of British military intelligence.
Garda Siochana (*garda sheehonah*)	Police force in the Republic of Ireland.
Gear	IRA slang for weaponry.
General Army Convention (GAC)	Delegate meeting of the IRA membership which is the body's supreme authority. Only the Convention can change the IRA's constitution.
General Army Orders (GAO)	IRA rules and regulations covering, e.g., arrangements for courts-martial and punishments.
GHQ	General headquarters staff. The departmental heads who organize the IRA's structures and military campaign.
Good Friday Agreement	Political deal agreed in Belfast in April 1998 by the pro-peace process parties including Sinn Fein.
Government of Ireland Act	British legislation in 1920 that partitioned Ireland and established authority over Northern Ireland.
Green Book	IRA tutorial cum regulation book, required reading for all IRA members. It also contains the IRA constitution.
GRIT	Graduated and Reciprocated Initiatives in Tension Reduction. Concept behind the secret diplomacy between the British and the IRA in Derry from 1990 on.

H Blocks	Cell blocks in the Maze prison used to house paramilitary prisoners. They replaced the internment compounds and became the focus of a campaign for political status that led to the 1981 hunger strikes.
Hillsborough agreement	Agreement of 1985 between Margaret Thatcher and Garret FitzGerald that gave the Republic a consultative say in Northern Ireland's affairs.
Home Rule	Demand for self-government made by Irish nationalists prior to the 1916 Rising.
human bomb	IRA tactic of early 1990s.
IICD	Independent International Commission on Decommissioning. Body that oversees paramilitary disarmament.
IMC	Independent Monitoring Commission. Monitors and reports of state of IRA and loyalist cease-fires.
IO	Intelligence officer.
INLA	Irish National Liberation Army. Small left-wing republican splinter group known for its extreme violence and vicious feuds. Its political wing is the Irish Republican Socialist Party (IRSP).
IRA	Irish Republican Army. At the last count there were four bodies calling themselves the IRA, each one claiming sole right to the title. The largest of these and the one most identified in the public mind as the IRA is the Provisional IRA, which fought a quarter-century-long campaign against the British presence in Northern Ireland. Also known as the 'RA or as the Army.
IRB	Irish Republican Brotherhood. Secret wing and precursor of the IRA led by Patrick Pearse but later controlled by Michael Collins. Had its roots in the American Fenian movement. Faded away after the Treaty was signed.
LIS	Libyan Intelligence Service.
Long Kesh	Name given to the compounds and cages used to house IRA internees in the early 1970s.
Long War	Concept of a lengthy political and military struggle developed by Adams in Cage 11.
loyalist	An extreme unionist. The term also denotes a readiness to use violence and a hatred for Catholics.

Maidstone	British prison ship used briefly to house IRA interness, including Gerry Adams.
Maze prison	Name given to Long Kesh by the British after the IRA was criminalized in the mid-1970s.
MI5	The British internal security service. Has been in charge of intelligence operations against the IRA since the mid-1980s.
MI6	The British Secret Intelligence Service. Unionists suspect MI6 of pro-Irish nationalist sympathies.
Motorman	Name of British army operation to occupy IRA areas of Belfast and Derry.
Mountain Climber	Name given to MI6 officer Michael Oatley, who secretly negotiated with the IRA.
the movement	Name given by republicans to combined force of the IRA and Sinn Fein and associated bodies.
MP	Member of the British House of Commons at Westminster.
MRF	British undercover unit of the early 1970s. Believed to stand for Military Reconnaissance Force.
NICRA	Northern Ireland Civil Rights Association.
NIO	Northern Ireland Office. British department which governs Northern Ireland.
NLF	National Liberation Front. Broad front of left-wing groups proposed by Cathal Goulding in 1960s.
NSD	National self-determination.
nationalist	Someone sympathetic to the peaceful reunification of Ireland. Also shorthand for Catholic..
Noraid	New York-based IRA support group known officially as Irish Northern Aid.
Northern Command	Separate IRA structure for the "war zone" set up in mid-1970s as part of the Adams reforms. A crucial vehicle for his takeover.
OC	Officer commanding an IRA unit.
Official IRA	The section of the IRA that stayed loyal to Cathal Goulding after the 1969 split.
ONH	Oglaigh na hEireann (ogly na herran). The Irish for IRA, literally the army of Ireland.
OO	Operations officer, "Double O" in IRA usage.

Operation Harvest   Name given to start of IRA's 1956–62 Border Campaign.

Orangeman   Member of the exclusively Protestant and unionist Orange Order.

partition   The division of Ireland into two states by the 1920 Government of Ireland Act.

PD   People's Democracy. Student-based civil rights movement of late 1960s.

Planters   Protestants from Northern England and lowland Scotland settled by Tudor and Stuart monarchs in Ireland, mostly in northeast.

PRG   Derry-based Peace and Reconciliation Group.

Provo/Provie   Slang for Provisional IRA member or supporter.

QMG   Quarter-master general. GHQ officer responsible for acquiring, hiding and supplying the IRA's arms.

Republican Clubs   Name given to Sinn Fein in Northern Ireland in 1960s. Idea borrowed from *Revolutionary Councils* Colonel Gaddafi by Adams and his allies in mid-1970s. It functioned as a mini-Convention and was used to press changes on the Army Council.

RPG-7   Rocket Propelled Grenade, a favorite IRA weapon from the early 1970s on.

RSF   Republican Sinn Fein. Breakaway from Provisional Sinn Fein led by Ruairi O Bradaigh. Objected to dropping of abstentionism in the Dail and has a military wing called the Continuity IRA.

RTE   Radio Telefis Eireann. The state radio and television company in the Irish Republic.

RUC   Royal Ulster Constabulary. Northern Ireland's mostly Protestant police force, renamed the Police Service of Northern Ireland under the terms of the Good Friday Agreement.

SAM-7   Surface-to-air missiles supplied to the IRA by Libya. Their batteries could not be replaced and the weapon was never used in anger.

SAS   Special Air Services. Covert wing of the British army that carried out ambushes against the IRA like that at Loughgall.

SDLP	Social Democratic and Labour Party. Until the peace process it was the largest nationalist party in Northern Ireland.
Second Dail	Parliament elected in 1921 in the last all-Ireland poll. Revered by traditional republicans because of that.
Semtex	Powerful Czech-made plastic explosive supplied to the IRA in large quantities by Colonel Gaddafi.
Sinn Fein (*shin fain*)	Irish for "Ourselves Alone." The political wing of the republican movement.
Sos (*Suss*)	Irish word that means a short pause. Was used by IRA members to describe the 1994 cease-fire.
SPA	Special Powers Act. Unionist anti-IRA law.
Special Branch	RUC's intelligence wing.
Stick	Republican term for IRA members who stayed with the Goulding wing after the 1969 split.
Stormont	The Northern Ireland parliament or Assembly.
Tan War	Another name for the Anglo-Irish conflict of 1919–21, so-named after the British militia "the Black and Tans".
tanaiste (*tonashta*)	Irish deputy prime minister.
taoiseach (*teeshuk*)	Irish prime minister.
Tartan gang	Teenage loyalist gangs in Belfast set up in 1971 after the IRA abducted and killed three young Scottish soldiers.
TD	Member of the Irish parliament.
Tet offensive	Based on the Vietnamese offensive of the same name, the Irish equivalent was supposed to start in 1987.
think tank	Small group of advisers gathered around Adams. It ran the negotiations leading to the 1994 and 1997 cease-fires.
Thirty-two-County Sovereignty Movement	Political wing of the Real IRA which broke with the Provisionals in 1997.
Tory	Alternative name for a member of the British Conservative Party.
Thompson submachine gun	IRA's traditional weapon of choice until the Armalite arrived.
The Twelfth	Annual Orange celebration of King William's victory at the Battle of the Boyne. Held on July 12 each year.

the unknowns	Secret intelligence cell set up by Gerry Adams in early 1970s
TPU	Timer power unit. Bomb-detonating mechanism devised by IRA engineers.
TUAS	Ambiguously titled strategy devised to justify the 1994 IRA cease-fire. Known in the IRA as the Tactical Use of Armed Struggle but to Sinn Fein's mainstream political allies as the Totally UnArmed Strategy.
Ulster custom	Privilege of security of tenancy and compensation for land improvement granted to Protestant farmers.
unionist	Someone who favors retaining Northern Ireland's constitutional link to Britain.
United Irishmen	Fusion of Catholic Defenders and Presbyterian radicals which rose unsuccessfully against English rule in 1798.
UDA	Ulster Defence Association. Once the largest Protestant paramilitary group. Conducted a campaign of terror against Catholics and IRA members. Oppose the Good Friday Agreement.
UDR	Ulster Defence Regiment. Mostly Protestant militia.
UVF	Ulster Volunteer Force. Led mainstream unionist rebellion against Home Rule Bill in 1912. Its modern version was known for vicious torture-murders of Catholics. Supported the Good Friday Agreement.
UUP	Largest unionist political party led during the key years of the peace process by David Trimble. Supported the Good Friday Agreement.
Volunteer	Official name for a rank-and-file IRA member.
WBHAC	West Belfast Housing Action Committee. Founded by Adams in 1960s.

IRA Structure

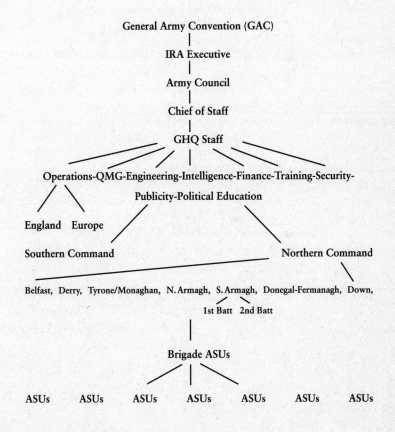

General Army Convention (GAC)

IRA Executive

Army Council

Chief of Staff

GHQ Staff

Operations-QMG-Engineering-Intelligence-Finance-Training-Security-
Publicity-Political Education

England   Europe

Southern Command   Northern Command

Belfast, Derry, Tyrone/Monaghan, N. Armagh, S. Armagh, Donegal-Fermanagh, Down,

1st Batt   2nd Batt

Brigade ASUs

ASUs   ASUs   ASUs   ASUs   ASUs   ASUs   ASUs

Bibliography

BOOKS

Adams, Gerry. *A Pathway to Peace*. Cork and Dublin: Mercier Press, 1988.

———. *Before the Dawn: An Autobiography*. London: Heinemann, 1996.

———. *An Irish Voice: The Quest for Peace*. Niwot, Colo.: Roberts Rinehart, 1997.

Barton, Brian. *A Pocket History of Ulster*. Dublin: O'Brien Press, 1996.

Bean, Kevin, and Mark Hayes, eds. *Republican Voices*. Monaghan: Seesyu Press, 2001.

Beckett, J. C. *The Making of Modern Ireland, 1603–1923*. London: Faber and Faber, 1982.

Bell, J. Bowyer, *The Secret Army: The IRA, 1916–1979*. Dublin: Academy Press, 1979.

———. *The IRA, 1968–2000: Analysis of a Secret Army*. London and Portland, Ore.: Frank Cass, 2000.

Beresford, David. *Ten Men Dead: The Story of the 1981 Irish Hunger Strike*. London: Grafton Books, 1987.

Bew, Paul, and Gordon Gillespie. *The Northern Ireland Peace Process, 1993–1996: A Chronology*. London: Serif, 1996.

———. *Northern Ireland: A Chronology of the Troubles, 1968–1999*. Dublin: Gill and Macmillan, 1999.

Bishop, Patrick, and Eamonn Mallie. *The Provisional IRA*. London: Heinemann, 1987.

Campbell, Brian, Laurence McKeown, and Felim O'Hagan, eds. *Nor Meekly Serve My Time: The H-Block Struggle, 1976–1981*. Belfast: Beyond the Pale Publications, 1998.

Collins, Eamon, with Mick McGovern. *Killing Rage*. London: Granta Books, 1998.

Collins, Tom. *The Irish Hunger Strike*. Dublin and Belfast: White Island, 1986.

Coogan, Tim Pat. *The IRA*. London: Fontana, 1980.

———. *De Valera: Long Fellow, Long Shadow*. London: Hutchinson, 1993.

———. *The Troubles: Ireland's Ordeal 1966–1996 and the Search for Peace*. London: Arrow, 1996.

Cox, Michael, Adrian Guelke, and Fiona Stephen, eds. *A Farewell to Arms? From "Long War" to Long Peace in Northern Ireland*. Manchester: Manchester University Press, 2000.

de Baroid, Ciaran. *Ballymurphy and the Irish War*. Belfast: Aisling Publishers, 1989.

Deutsch, Richard, and Vivien Magowan. *Northern Ireland, 1968–71: A Chronology of Events*. Belfast: Blackstaff Press, 1973.

———. *Northern Ireland, 1972–73: A Chronology of Events*. Belfast: Blackstaff Press, 1974.

———. *Northern Ireland, 1974: A Chronology of Events*. Belfast: Blackstaff Press, 1975.

Dillon, Martin. *The Dirty War*. London: Hutchinson, 1988.

———. *The Shankill Butchers: A Case Study in Mass Murder*. London: Hutchinson, 1989.

Duignan, Sean. *One Spin on the Merry-go-Round*. Dublin: Blackwater Press, 1995.

Eckert, Nicholas. *Fatal Encounter: The Story of the Gibraltar Killings*. Swords, Co. Dublin: Poolbeg Press, 1999.

Elliott, Sydney, and W. D. Flackes. *Northern Ireland: A Political Directory, 1968–1999*. Belfast: Blackstaff Press, 1999.

Farrell, Michael. *Northern Ireland: The Orange State*. London: Pluto Press, 1976.

———, ed. *Twenty Years On*. Dingle, Co. Kerry: Brandon, 1988.

Finlay, Fergus. *Snakes and Ladders*. Dublin: New Island Books, 1998.

FitzGerald, Garret. *All in a Life: An Autobiography*. London and Dublin: Gill and Macmillan, 1992.

Godson, Dean. *Himself Alone—David Trimble and the Ordeal of Unionism*. London: HarperCollins, 2004.

Gove, Michael. *The Price of Peace: An Analysis of British Policy in Northern Ireland*. London: Centre for Policy Studies, 2000.

Harnden, Toby. *Bandit Country: The IRA and South Armagh*. London: Hodder and Stoughton, 1999.

Holland, Jack. *The American Connection: US Guns, Money and Influence in Northern Ireland*. Swords, Co. Dublin: Poolbeg Press, 1989.

———. *Hope against History: The Ulster Conflict*. London: Hodder and Stoughton, 1999.

Holland, Jack, and Susan Phoenix. *Phoenix: Policing the Shadows*. London: Hodder and Stoughton, 1996.

Horgan, John. *Sean Lemass: The Enigmatic Patriot*. Dublin: Gill and Macmillan, 1997.

Kee, Robert. *The Most Distressful Country*. Volume 1 of *The Green Flag*. London, Melbourne, and New York: Quartet Books, 1976.

Keena, Colm. *Gerry Adams: A Biography*. Cork: Mercier Press, 1990.

Kelley, Kevin. *The Longest War: Northern Ireland and the IRA*. Dingle, Co. Kerry: Brandon Books, 1983.

Keogh, Dermot. *Jews in Twentieth Century Ireland: Refugees, Anti-Semitism and the Holocaust*. Cork: Cork University Press, 1998.

Kleinrichert, Denise. *Republican Internment and the Prison Ship Argenta, 1922*. Dublin: Irish Academic Press, 2001.

MacEoin, Uinseann. *The IRA in the Twilight Years, 1923–1948*. Dublin: Argenta Publications, 1997.

MacStiofain, Sean. *Memoirs of a Revolutionary*. London: Gordon Cremonesi, 1975.

Maguire, Maria. *To Take Arms: A Year in the Provisional IRA*. London: Macmillan, 1973.

Major, John. *John Major: The Autobiography*. London: HarperCollins, 2000.

Mallie, Eamonn, and David McKittrick. *The Fight for Peace: The Secret Story behind the Irish Peace Process*. London: Heinemann, 1996.

Mansergh, Martin. "No Selfish Strategic or Economic Interest? The Path to an All-Island Economy." 3rd Annual Frank Cahill Memorial Lecture, August 1995. Regency Press.

———. "The Background to the Peace Process." *Irish Studies in International Affairs* 6 (1995).

———. "The Peace Process in Historical Perspective." *Etudes Irlandes*, no. 20-1 (1996).

———. "Creating a New Era of Understanding and Trust." Gazette inaugural lecture, October 1997.

———, ed. *The Spirit of the Nation: The Speeches of Charles J Haughey*. Cork and Dublin: Mercier Press, 1987.

McArdle, Dorothy. *The Irish Republic*. Dublin: Wolfhound Press, 1999.

McCann, Eamonn. *War and an Irish Town*. London: Pluto Press, 1980.

McKendry, Seamus. *Disappeared: The Search for Jean McConville*. Dublin: Blackwater Press, 2000.

McKittrick, David, Seamus Kelters, Brian Feeney, and Chris Thornton. *Lost Lives*. Edinburgh: Mainstream Publishing, 1999.

McKittrick, David, and David McVea. *Making Sense of the Troubles*. Belfast: Blackstaff Press, 2000.

Milotte, Mike. *Communism in Modern Ireland: The Pursuit of the Workers' Republic since 1916*. Dublin: Gill and Macmillan, 1984.

Moloney, Ed, and Andy Pollak. *Paisley*. Swords, Co. Dublin: Poolbeg Press, 1994.

Murphy, Brian P. *Patrick Pearse and the Lost Republican Ideal*. Dublin: James Duffy, 1991.

National Graves Association. *The Last Post: Details and Stories of Irish Republican Dead, 1916–1985*. Dublin, 1985.

Needham, Richard. *Battling for Peace*. Belfast: Blackstaff Press, 1999.

O Ceallaigh, Daltun. *Irish Republicanism: Good Friday and After*. Dublin: Leirmheas, 2000.

O Dochartaigh, Niall. *From Civil Rights to Armalites: Derry and the Birth of the Irish Troubles*. Cork: Cork University Press, 1997.

O'Brien, Brendan. *The Long War*. Dublin: O'Brien Press, 1995.

———. *A Pocket History of the IRA*. Dublin: O'Brien Press, 2000.

O'Brien, Justin. *The Arms Trial*. Dublin: Gill and Macmillan, 2000.

O'Callaghan, Sean. *The Informer*. London: BCA, 1998.

O'Clery, Conor. *The Greening of the White House*. Dublin: Gill and Macmillan, 1997.

O'Connor, Ulick. *Michael Collins and the Troubles: The Struggle for Irish Freedom, 1912–1922*. New York and London: W. W. Norton, 1996.

O'Malley, Ernie. *The Singing Flame*. Dublin: Anvil Books, 1979.

O'Malley, Padraig. *The Uncivil Wars: Ireland Today*. Belfast: Blackstaff Press, 1983.

O'Neill, P. *Freedom Struggle*. Dublin: Provisional IRA, Irish Republican Publicity Bureau, June 1973.

O'Rawe, Richard. *Blanketmen—An Untold Story of the H-Block Hunger Strike*. Dublin: New Island, 2005.

O'Sullivan, Michael P. *Patriot Graves: Resistance in Ireland*. Chicago: Follett Publishing, 1972.

Pollak, Andy, ed. *A Citizens' Inquiry: The Opsahl Report on Northern Ireland*. Dublin: Lilliput Press, 1993.

Regan, John M. *The Irish Counter-Revolution, 1921–1936.* Dublin: Gill and Macmillan, 1999.

Routledge, Paul. *John Hume.* London: HarperCollins, 1998.

Ryder, Chris. *The Ulster Defence Regiment: An Instrument of Peace?* London: Methuen, 1991.

Sharrock, David, and Mark Devenport. *Man of War, Man of Peace? The Unauthorized Biography of Gerry Adams.* London: Macmillan, 1997.

Taylor, Peter. *Families at War: Voices from the Troubles.* London: BBC Books, 1989.

———. *Provos: The IRA and Sinn Fein.* London: Bloomsbury, 1998.

Toolis, Kevin. *Rebel Hearts: Journeys within the IRA's Soul.* London: Picador, 1995.

Urban, Mark. *Big Boys' Rules: The Secret Struggle against the IRA.* London: Faber and Faber, 1992.

White, Robert, W. *Provisional Irish Republicans: An Oral and Interpretative History.* London and Westport, Conn.: Greenwood Press, 1993.

Woodward, Bob. *Veil: The Secret Wars of the CIA, 1981–1987.* New York: Simon and Schuster, 1987.

IRISH NEWSPAPERS AND MAGAZINES

Hibernia
In Dublin
Magill
Belfast Telegraph
Derry Journal
Irish Independent
Irish News
Irish Press
Irish Times
Sunday Business Post
Sunday News
Sunday Tribune

BRITISH NEWSPAPERS AND MAGAZINES

Hansard
NI Brief, Parliamentary Brief
Daily Telegraph
Guardian

Independent
Observer
Sunday Times
Times
Financial Times

AMERICAN NEWSPAPERS

New York Times
Washington Post

POLITICAL PUBLICATIONS

An Glor Gafa (The Captive Voice)
An Phoblacht
An Phoblacht–Republican News
Fianna Fail: The IRA Connection, Official IRA
IRIS: The Republican Magazine
Irish Bheag
Republican News
Starry Plough
United Irishman

Index

About the Author

Ed Moloney has been a reporter covering the Northern Ireland situation since 1978 and has been Northern Editor of the *Irish Times* (1981–5) and Northern Editor of the *Sunday Tribune* in Dublin (1987–2001). He co-authored a celebrated biography of the Reverend Ian Paisley in 1986 and has contributed to several other books, including a study of media coverage of the Northern Ireland violence. He has written for a wide range of newspapers and magazines in the United States and Britain, including the *Washington Post,* the *NY Daily News,* the *New York Post, The Economist,* the *Independent,* the *Guardian,* the *New Statesman, New Society*, and a variety of Irish publications. He has been a frequent commentator on BBC, CNN and commercial radio and television in Britain and Ireland, and has helped to produce a number of documentaries on the Irish Troubles. In 1999 he successfully defeated an attempt by London's Scotland Yard Commissioner, Sir John Stevens, to force him to hand over notes of an interview with a loyalist paramilitary who alleged a police cover-up of the notorious murder of the Belfast attorney, Pat Finucane. In that year he was elected Irish Journalist of the Year. He is fifty-six, married with one son, and is currently living and working as a freelance journalist in New York.

He just wanted a decent book to read ...

Not too much to ask, is it? It was in 1935 when Allen Lane, Managing Director of Bodley Head Publishers, stood on a platform at Exeter railway station looking for something good to read on his journey back to London. His choice was limited to popular magazines and poor-quality paperbacks – the same choice faced every day by the vast majority of readers, few of whom could afford hardbacks. Lane's disappointment and subsequent anger at the range of books generally available led him to found a company – and change the world.

'We believed in the existence in this country of a vast reading public for intelligent books at a low price, and staked everything on it'
Sir Allen Lane, 1902–1970, founder of Penguin Books

The quality paperback had arrived – and not just in bookshops. Lane was adamant that his Penguins should appear in chain stores and tobacconists, and should cost no more than a packet of cigarettes.

Reading habits (and cigarette prices) have changed since 1935, but Penguin still believes in publishing the best books for everybody to enjoy. We still believe that good design costs no more than bad design, and we still believe that quality books published passionately and responsibly make the world a better place.

So wherever you see the little bird – whether it's on a piece of prize-winning literary fiction or a celebrity autobiography, political tour de force or historical masterpiece, a serial-killer thriller, reference book, world classic or a piece of pure escapism – you can bet that it represents the very best that the genre has to offer.

Whatever you like to read – trust Penguin.

read more
www.penguin.co.uk